Fourth Edition

Foods

Experimental Perspectives

Margaret McWilliams
Ph.D., R.D., Professor Emeritus
California State University, Los Angeles

Prentice Hall
Upper Saddle River, New Jersey 04758

Library of Congress Cataloging-in-Publication Data

McWilliams, Margaret.

Foods : experimental perspectives / Margaret McWilliams.—4th ed.

p. cm.

ISBN 0-13-021282-2

1. Food—Composition. 2. Food—Analysis. 3. Cookery. I. Title

TX531.M38 2000

644—dc21   00-021914

Publisher: Dave Garza
Acquisitions Editor: Neil Marquardt
Associate Editor: Marion Gottlieb
Production Editor: Patty Donovan
Production Liaison: Barbara Cappuccio
Director of Manufacturing
   and Production: Bruce Johnson
Managing Editor: Mary Carnis
Manufacturing Manager: Ed O'Dougherty
Art Director: Marianne Frasco
Cover Design Coordinator: Miguel Ortiz
Cover Designer: Jayne Kelly
Marketing Manager: Ryan DeGrote
Editorial Assistant: Susan Kegler
Interior Design and Composition: Pine Tree Composition
Printing and Binding: Courier Westford

Cover Art: COMPLIMENTS OF CERESTAR U.S.A., INC.
Computer graphic of alpha, beta, and gama cyclodextrins. Beta-cyclodextrin (marketed under Cerestar's self-affirmation as GRAS) is capable of encapsulating flavor molecules, a function of interest in such food products as processed cheese products, snack foods, breakfast cereals, baking mixes, and chewing gum. This family of cyclodextrins is produced by the action of cyclodextrin glucosyl transferases on starch hydrolysates. Alpha-cyclodextrin consists of six glucose units, beta-cyclodextrin contains seven glucose units, and gamma-cyclodextrin has eight. (Poudrier, J. K. 1995, "Corn meets nanotechnology. *Today's Chemist at Work 4* (2): 25.; Pszczola, D. E. 1998. Encapsulated ingredients: providing the right fit. *Food Technol. 52* (12): 70.)

Prentice-Hall International (UK) Limited, *London*
Prentice-Hall of Australia Pty. Limited, *Sydney*
Prentice-Hall Canada Inc., *Toronto*
Prentice-Hall Hispanoamericana, S.A., *Mexico*
Prentice-Hall of India Private Limited, *New Delhi*
Prentice-Hall of Japan, Inc., *Tokyo*
Prentice-Hall Singapore Pte. Ltd.
Editora Prentice-Hall do Brasil, Ltda., *Rio de Janeiro*

10 9 8 7 6 5 4 3 2 1

ISBN 0-13-021282-2

*To my many food science and dietetic students
who made my teaching career
such a pleasure and intellectual challenge!*

Contents

Preface

Food has always been a wonderful subject to study, but today's technological and social changes increasingly are adding to the excitement and challenges involved in feeding the world's people. Biotechnology is at the forefront of research that is directed toward modifying various foods to enhance health and/or improve quality. Food safety increasingly is leaping into the media as food marketing and preparation are modified by shifts in lifestyles and as microorganisms adapt to create seemingly ever more virulent strains invading foods.

The careers evolving from the study of food are extremely varied; they range from the agricultural realm into the technology of producing products for wholesale and retail markets, and the preparation of food in many types of commercial and institutional venues as well as in the home. The discoveries that are emerging from research into cancer and other prominent health risks have been stimulating interest in functional foods. This interest is spawning research by food technologists to develop foods consistent with health needs. Alternatives to the traditional sugars and fats are at the center of a flurry of research and product development in the food industry. Microbiologists are prominent participants in the food industry as concerns with food safety increase.

While I have been working on this revision, arguments and counter-arguments regarding genetically modified foods have been raging and are far from being resolved. Environmental concerns seem to be central to many of the debates regarding food production and the challenges of feeding a mushrooming world population healthfully. An educated and thoughtful public capable of separating emotion from scientific truths with a sound science base is essential if progress is to be made toward producing the optimum food supply to meet the needs of the entire world's people. I have had this situation in the forefront of my mind throughout the writing of this revision. My hope is that my readers will find this scientific approach interesting, stimulating, and helpful in understanding the highly complex world of food science.

This revision has been written to provide the sound scientific foundation food scientists, technologists, and dietitians need in order to confront the technical and communication problems they must solve as they work to bring commercially viable products to well-informed consumers in the marketplace. To be effective in the highly technical field of food science, professionals need a broad scientific and technical background, which ranges across the sciences. These sciences include chemistry (particularly organic), physics, and microbiology.

The first four chapters in Part I examine food research. Basic steps in the research process, including basic laboratory controls, research design, and the techniques and tools used by food scientists to evaluate products, are discussed. Statistical techniques are introduced to facilitate analysis of data and interpretation of significance.

Part II considers some of the physical perspectives underlying food science. Water, its various physical states and its activity are examined in Chapter 5. Energy applied to food preparation and the various states of matter, as well as types of dispersion are explored in the next chapter.

In Part III, the dynamic field of carbohydrates is discussed, with the focus on three types of carbohydrates: sugars and sweeteners, starch, and fiber (notably gums and pectic substances). Emphasis is given to the application of these diverse carbohydrate clusters to food products today. Particular attention is directed toward alternative sweeteners, to fiber types, and their uses.

The two chapters in Part IV examine fats and oils in detail. Chapter 11 presents the chemistry of these compounds and the changes that may take place when they are used in food preparation. A new chapter, Chapter 12, explores the production of fats and oils for various food applications. The selection of particular fats and oils for specific food applications is considered; emphasis is given to the functional roles fats and oils play. In addition, the numerous fat replacements are reviewed.

Part V covers proteins, which play a key role in the structure of such protein-rich foods as milk and milk products, meats and other flesh foods, eggs, and baked products. Because of the unique nature of the various types of protein foods, considerable attention is directed toward the functionality and structure of each of these types of proteins.

The growing concern over food-borne illnesses emphasizes the need for a solid knowledge of microbiology and potential causes of and ways of preventing outbreaks of these illnesses. Chapter 19 provides a broadly based review of the several microbiological contaminants causing problems in this country today. The next chapter discusses ways of keeping food safe through adequate preservation methods, both in the home and commercially. The final chapter examines food additives in our food supply.

And now it is time for you to venture forth into the realm of food science and its applications. I hope you find this field of study as exciting as I do!

EXPERIMENTAL FOODS LABORATORY MANUAL (5th edition) by Margaret McWilliams, the laboratory manual accompanying this text, is available from Plycon Press, 2487 Duraznitos Rd., Ramona, CA 92065 (760) 788-9455 or FAX (760) 788-4627.

ACKNOWLEDGMENTS

My special thanks go to the perceptive and hard-working reviewers who gave me such excellent suggestions and comments regarding preparation of this edition: Kwaku Addo, University of Kentucky; Janice B. Harte, Michigan State University; Manfred Kroger, The Pennsylvania State University; and Frost Steele, Brigham Young University.

1

Research
Perspectives

CHAPTER 1

Dimensions of Food Studies

Today's food marketplace is a complex and ever-changing situation despite the fact that its basic role is to provide the setting for all people to obtain the food they need to maintain their lives. The reality is that many factors are at work in this marketplace to shape it at any given time. The supply of food is the result of the efforts of farmers, fishermen, and agribusinesses around the world, augmented by the transportation industry. Another dimension is added by the food industries that develop and market new products, conduct basic research on food-related topics, and monitor and shape consumer trends in food preferences and dietary concerns. Consumers provide the other part of the food marketplace not only by their current food purchasing patterns, but also by their evolving lifestyles and anticipated changes in food preferences. In short, the dynamics of the food marketplace are truly amazing and often frenetic. The results can provide some wonderful eating opportunities for us all. This multidimensional marketplace also affords a wide variety of career opportunities revolving around the subject of foods. This chapter takes a look at some of the consumer influences on foods in the marketplace and the professional positions that focus on providing food for people.

CONSUMERS: EXPECTATIONS AND CONCERNS

Defining consumers is a daunting task, one that is constantly shifting because of multiple factors and the time frame being considered. At the end of the twentieth century the largest population groups were those less than 35 years of age, and these represented slightly more than half of the total population (Sloan, 1998). However, those below the age of 35 are expected to comprise only about 45 percent of the population by 2030. An increase in the percentage of the population ages 65 and older is also anticipated in 2030. Such age shifts can be expected to alter consumer demands for foods during the next 30 years. Even greater changes in food expectations can be predicted to occur as cultural diversity continues to be altered in the United States, both as a consequence of immigration and differences in birth rates among the various groups comprising the American population in upcoming decades. According to the U.S. Census Bureau, the Hispanic population is increasing 5 times faster than the total population; African Americans and Asian Americans are predicted to have significant increases in population, albeit distinctly less than the Hispanic growth.

In addition to the cultural heritage of consumers, their preferred lifestyles definitely influence the food marketplace. Frequency of meals or even the definition of a meal can evoke very different expectations and behaviors among consumers. Some people, particularly the elderly, still expect to eat three times a day, but for many, eating seems to be appropriate any time of day and any number of times. Perhaps the most noticeable behavior is the lack of agreement on when and how often to eat during the day. Ready availability of prepared foods and snacks for consumption at work, school, home, or anyplace in between has prompted people to eat frequently, if not always wisely.

Among the top interests of Americans is their health and the impact that food has on their health. As environmental concerns have moved to the forefront on the agenda, there has been a strong trend toward buying "natural" foods. Despite the evidence of improved yields and blemish-free fruits and vegetables when farmers apply chemical fertilizers and pesticides to their crops, many consumers insist upon organically-grown food. Their assumption that the food grown using only manure is higher in nutrients than those with chemical fertilizers has been proven to be fallacious in analyses conducted over more than a quarter of a century, but the demand for natural or organically-grown foods continues to grow.

"Natural" and **"organic"** foods are not necessarily synonymous. When used in reference to foods, "natural" means that original food ingredients have been used and that artificial or chemical additives have not been included. An example of a natural coloring agent is use of beet pigments rather than using a red chemical dye to color a food product. The food product could have been made from ingredients that were grown without use of chemical fertilizers and pesticides and thus would be both a natural and an organic food item. Such food products are finding many receptive consumers in the marketplace even though they may cost more.

Cancer and heart disease are two health concerns for many consumers because of the toll these two killer conditions take each year. The ties that are being found between diet and the incidence of these problems have added impetus to the importance of eating plenty of fruits, vegetables, and cereal products, all of which are rich in various minerals, vitamins, and phytochemicals. In fact, phytochemicals are becoming buzz words: lycopene, genestein, catechins, and tocotrienols, for example.

"Phytochemicals" is the term used to designate chemicals in plants which have biological activity that promotes health benefits that are beyond basic nutrition effects. Some examples of phytochemicals include catechins in tea, lycopene in tomatoes and red peppers, and beta glucan in oats (see Table 1.1). Foods rich in chemical compounds identified as promoting health beyond basic nutrition are referred to as **"functional foods."** Plant foods containing significant amounts of phytochemicals are considered to be functional foods, which has fostered considerable product development to bring **"designer foods"** with enhanced levels of phytochemicals to the marketplace in response to consumer interest.

Natural
Term designating that a food product is made without chemical or artificial additives.

Organic
Term designating that no chemical fertilizers or pesticides have been applied when the crops were being grown.

Phytochemicals
Chemical compounds in plants that are important for health to promote various reactions in the body, but that are not classified as nutrients required for life and growth.

Functional Food
Food containing useful amount of chemical compounds that promote health beyond basic nutrition.

Designer Food
Food product formulated to contain enhanced levels of phytochemicals.

Table 1.1 Selected Phytochemicals: Some Sources and Potential and Potential Benefits

Phytochemical	Source	Potential Benefit
Phytoestrogens (e.g., genestein and daidzein)	Soybeans	Compete with or antagonize action of estradiol at estrogenic receptor sites
Catechins	Green tea	Inhibit carcinogenic processes
Beta glucan	Oats	Reduce risk of cardiovascular disease
Lycopene	Tomatoes	Reduce risk of prostate and cervical cancer
Isoflavones	Soy	Lower cholesterol levels

Demand for natural foods and greater consumption of fruits and vegetables is spurring the efforts of biotechnologists to develop plants and even animals that have specific desired characteristics or traits. Genetic engineering is another term to describe biotechnology. A gene is a segment of DNA that encodes enough information to synthesize a protein. By identifying specific genes that provide the codes for making proteins that impart desirable traits, researchers have then been able to transfer the desired genes to other organisms to develop plants or animals that continue to replicate the desired gene(s) in succeeding generations. An example of the use of biotechnology for modifying plants is the development of a vine-ripened tomato that became available in 1994. Other possible applications of plant biotechnology include protection of plants from specific viral or fungal diseases and targeted insect pests, tolerance of environmentally appropriate herbicides, and modifications in the food itself to enhance nutritive value, food quality, and/or processing characteristics.

In many countries in various parts of the world, particularly in Europe, concerns have been raised regarding the growing and marketing of food resulting from **biotechnology.** The European Union (EU) designates such foods as **Genetically Modified Organisms** (GMO) and is raising barriers to the sale of such products. The controversy regarding the safety and also the need for labeling to inform consumers doubtless will rage around the world for an extended period, although plant hybridization has been accepted for many years. If a genetic modification introduces an allergen that may affect some people, the requirement of a label informing consumers of this clearly would be beneficial. However, the need to inform consumers about a modification that does not promote human health problems is a debatable labeling requirement. Such examples illustrate the debate presently about GMO.

Governmental regulatory agencies are involved in approving and regulating the products of biotechnology. The U.S. Food and Drug Administration (FDA) is responsible for food products of plant biotechnology. Agricultural products are under the purview of the U.S. Department of Agriculture (USDA), primarily its Animal and Plant Health Inspection Service (APHIS). Herbicides and pesticides are under the aegis of the U.S. Environmental Protection Agency (EPA). These agencies may all be involved in the regulation and oversight of some products of biotechnology.

The possibilities for improved food products as the result of biotechnology (specifically by techniques of **genetic engineering**) are exciting. Examples that may become commercially viable and earn a permanent spot in the food marketplace include increased essential amino acid content in corn and soybeans, naturally decaffeinated coffee, plant oils with modified fatty acid content, potatoes and

Biotechnology
Development of new products by making a genetic modification in a living organism.

Genetically Modified Organisms
Food and other organisms that are the result of genetic manipulations; commonly referred to as GMO.

Genetic Engineering
Biotechnology in which a genetic modification is achieved by removing, adding, or modifying genes.

tomatoes with higher solids content (to decrease energy needed to remove water during processing), and controlled ripening of fruits and vegetables that are difficult to ship to markets in satisfactory condition.

CAREER OPPORTUNITIES

Because food is absolutely essential to survival, careers centered upon any aspect of food will always exist even though the focus and products may undergo considerable evolution over time. Advances in science and technology, food preferences, lifestyles, economics, and environmental factors combine to alter the food scene and to create the dynamic opportunities for careers based on food. Some careers are oriented toward the interrelationships between food and health, some are based on feeding people in settings away from their homes, and still others are centered on basic food science and the development of marketable products for consumers (and the innumerable steps in bringing food from farms to consumers).

The great emphasis on food and health has spurred the building of bridges between the domain of nutritionists and dietitians and the rest of the food professions. Awareness of the need for healthful dietary habits has created public demand for products that are consistent with good nutrition, but also are appealing to eat. The dialogue that is developing in the various food-related professions is beginning to blur the divisions between the different segments. This change is opening opportunities for individuals to create unique positions that utilize particular strengths they bring to the food industries.

Sound academic preparation is essential for persons planning to become food professionals, and that curriculum must include strong courses in the basic sciences that underlie food—chemistry, microbiology, biology, and physics. This science foundation needs to be incorporated into the study of food and its preparation and evaluation. Appreciation of the role that food plays in influencing the quality of life, because of both its wonderful sensory and nutritional contributions, should be developed so that food professionals will always remember the needs of consumers as real people. Oral and written communication skills are essential for all professionals. Knowledge of research techniques and computer literacy also are part of the tools of the food professional. Basic understanding of business is also a requisite for most careers in this field.

Students wishing to focus on a health-related food career will pursue a degree in nutrition and/or dietetics. For many of these positions, applicants are required to be Registered Dietitians (R.D.). Positions are quite varied in this field and include: clinical dietetics, food service administration, community nutrition, sports nutrition, consulting, nutrition counseling, and industries based on nutrition-related products.

The rapidly expanding realm of hospitality, hotels, and restaurants is the source of many positions requiring extensive knowledge and culinary skills. Preparation for careers in this arena may be obtained through a dietetics curriculum or from programs tailored specifically toward this field. Emphasis is placed on preparation and the applied aspects of food and its service to groups of people. Entrepreneurial-minded students may use this type of preparation to prepare for eventually owning and operating their own restaurants. Others may focus on managerial positions in one of the large corporations that dominate this arena. Still others may wish to enter the field of catering, either on their own or as an employee.

Food businesses provide opportunities that are quite diverse, depending on the interests of students. Product development, quality assurance, food analysis, processing, packaging, microbiology and food safety, sensory evaluation, physical testing, labeling and governmental regulation, and marketing are some of the niches available in the food industry. Depending upon the particular career objective, a student might prepare to enter the food business by obtaining a degree in nutrition and dietetics, food science, food technology, food service, hotel and restaurant (hospitality or culinary) management, or business.

EXPERIMENTING WITH FOOD

A scientific attitude and research orientation are needed to enter the world of the food professional. Basic chemical and physical principles are the foundation of the food science that undergirds the nation's food supply. A thorough understanding of these principles allows the food professional to apply them to achieve the best possible results with the food resources available.

The experimental approach to food study integrates theory and professional research studies with laboratory work. Valuable knowledge of the influence of ingredients and preparation procedures can be gained by performing experiments designed to illustrate key scientific principles involved in food preparation. The characteristics of foods can be identified and measured using subjective evaluation (vision, olfaction, taste, and feel) and objective (mechanical) tests. Frequently, experiments in a class in experimental food science are presented to the class as a group, and individuals conduct a portion of the work so that a suitably broad array of samples will be available to illustrate selected principles. Additional insights into food research are gained when an experiment is planned, conducted, evaluated, and reported individually.

Students of experimental food science quickly find that the emphasis is primarily on the theoretical "why" more than on the "how" approach to food and its preparation. The combination of scientific theory with the laboratory-based illustrations presented in food science courses provides deep understanding of foods—their structure, composition, and behavior. This knowledge provides the cornerstone on which the professional in food science and food service management, including dietetics, functions.

In an experimental foods class, attention is directed to the effects of modifying ratios and types of ingredients in food items and altering methods. One product is prepared correctly to serve as the control, and several variations are made at the same time to illustrate the effects of varying ingredients and/or methods. Careful examination and testing of these samples are of great value in developing a clear understanding of the scientific principles undergirding the field of food science.

At the conclusion of this study of experimental food science, students will be able to evaluate a very broad range of foods accurately, to identify possible errors in their preparation or formulation, and to plan appropriate corrective measures for subsequent preparation of the items. This knowledge is essential for anyone involved in food production, whether it be in supervising production in an institutional food service setting, developing new products, handling production or quality control in a food plant, or working with food in an educational or home context. The dynamic nature of food and its susceptibility to changes during handling, storage, and preparation provide constant challenges to the professional working in the field of food. Solutions for controlling quality can be effected appropriately when the underlying principles are understood and their practical illustrations have been experienced.

Metrics

Metric System
System of measuring length, area, volume, and weight using the decimal system (the system of tens).

Laboratory work in food science is done using the **metric system.** Formulas are based on metric units in classroom experiments as well as in research laboratories. However, consumer information is presented in household measures (teaspoons, tablespoons, cups for recipes, and inches to describe the sizes of baking dishes). Professionals working in a developmental laboratory with the possibility of applying the research to the consumer market need to be able not only to work in the metric system, but also to convert between the language of the consumer kitchen and the research laboratory.

The metric system is a method of expressing length (distance), area, volume, and weight in an orderly fashion in basic units that are quantified by expressing values in decimals, the system of tens. Hence, length is expressed in meters, area in square meters, volume in cubic meters or liters, and weight in grams. Food experimentation utilizes primarily volume and weight.

To achieve reasonable numbers when working in the metric system, prefixes are appended to the unit of measure. A large array of prefixes can be used within this system, as shown in Table 1.2, but food experimentation usually is based on the following: kilo (k), centi (c), and milli (m). By use of a prefix, 1,000 grams can be expressed simply as 1 kilogram; similarly, a hundredth of a meter is 1 centimeter, and a thousandth of a liter is 1 milliliter.

Because household recipes frequently express the quantities of solids in volumetric measures, conversion to weight or volume (if a liquid) in the metric system is necessary if these recipes are to serve as the basis for experimental work. Conversely, metric experimental amounts must be converted to common household measures if recipes are to be made available to the public. These conversions can be done by determining the weight of the required household measure for the various ingredients. Liquids are converted on the basis that a household measuring cup equals 236.6 milliliters (ml) or cubic centimeters (cc). Some of the equivalent

Table 1.2   Prefixes in the Metric System

Prefix	Symbol	Numerical Definition
Tera	T	$1,000,000,000,000 = 10^{12}$
Giga	G	$1,000,000,000 = 10^{9}$
Mega	M	$1,000,000 = 10^{6}$
Kilo	k	$1,000 = 10^{3}$
Hecto	h	$100 = 10^{2}$
Deka	da	$10 = 10^{1}$
Deci	d	$0.1 = 10^{-1}$
Centi	c	$0.01 = 10^{-2}$
Milli	m	$0.001 = 10^{-3}$
Micro	μ	$0.000,001 = 10^{-6}$
Nano	n	$0.000,000,001 = 10^{-9}$
Pico	p	$0.000,000,000,001 = 10^{-12}$

Table 1.3 Equivalent Measures and Conversion Factors Commonly Used to Convert between Household and Metric Measures

Equivalent	Conversion Factor
Weights[a]	
1 kg = 2.2 lb	oz (avdp) × 28.35 = g
454 g = 1 lb	lb (avdp) × 0.454 = kg
28.35 g = 1 oz	g × 0.035 = oz (avdp)
1 g = 0.035 oz	kg × 2.2 = lb (avdp)
Measures[b]	
1 l = 1.06 qt	qt × 0.946 = l
1 gal = 3.79 l	gal × 0.0037 = m³
1 qt = 946.4 ml	l × 1.056 = qt
1 c = 236.6 ml	
1 fl oz = 29.6 ml	
1 tbsp = 14.8 ml	

[a]kg = kilograms, lb = pounds, g = grams, oz = ounces, avdp = avoirdupois (weight).
[b]l = liters; qt = quarts; gal = gallons; ml = milliliters; c = cups; fl oz = fluid ounces (volume); m³ = cubic meters.

measures and conversion factors that may be useful when converting recipes are presented in Table 1.3.

A cup of flour does not weigh the same as a cup of butter or a cup of chopped nuts. The difference in mass of various ingredients that would be measured volumetrically in household recipes requires that the weight of this volume be known if a household recipe is to be used as the basis of an experimental formula. Sometimes it is necessary to determine this weight by weighing the desired volume of the ingredient. Fortunately, tables have been developed by experiment that provide uniform weights for a cup of many of the ingredients commonly used in food preparation. Table 1.4 includes the weights of a few selected ingredients to illustrate the need for determining the weight of various ingredients when recipes are converted for experimental use or back to household measures.

Just as metrics is the language of quantities in the realm of scientific research, so is Celsius the scale used for measuring temperature in the laboratory of the food scientist. This choice is not surprising in view of the fact that the Celsius scale is related to the decimal system, with the freezing point of water being designated as 0 and the boiling point at sea level as 100. To relate Celsius temperatures to the Fahrenheit temperatures commonly used on oven indicators and household thermometers, food professionals need to be able to convert from one of these common temperature scales to the other. Fortunately, this is not difficult to do. In fact, by simply knowing that the boiling point of water is 212°F or 100°C and remembering that the number 32 (the temperature of freezing in Fahrenheit) and either $\frac{5}{9}$ or $\frac{9}{5}$ must be used, you can derive the formulas for conversions quickly (see Figure 1-1). For example, to convert from Celsius to Fahrenheit, derive the formula by converting from 100°C to 212°F:

$$100°C \times \tfrac{9}{5} = 20 \times 9 = 180$$

$$180 + 32 = 212°F$$

Table 1.4 Average Weight of a Measured Cup of Selected Foods

Food	Form	Weight of 1 cup (g)
Almonds	Blanched	
	Whole	157
	Chopped	117
Baking powder	Double-acting	207
Cheese, cheddar	Shredded	98
Cornmeal		
White	Uncooked	140
Yellow	Uncooked	151
Eggs	Whites	255
	Whole	251
	Yolks	240
Flour	Rice, white unsifted	149
	Rye, dark stirred	127
	Soy, full-fat, unsifted	96
	Wheat, all purpose, unsifted	
	Spooned	126
	Dipped	143
	Wheat, all purpose, sifted, spooned	116
	Wheat, cake, sifted, spooned	99
	Gluten, sifted, spooned	136
	Self-rising, sifted, spooned	106
Gelatin	Flavored	187
Margarine	Regular	225
	Soft	208
Rice	White, raw	
	Long-grain	192
	Short-grain	200
	Parboiled	181
Sugar	Brown, packed	211
	Confectioner's sifted	95
	Granulated	196
Yeast	Active dry	142

Adapted from Fulton, L., E. Matthews, and C. Davis. *Average Weight of a Measured Cup of Various Foods,* Home Economics Research Report No. 41, Agricultural Research Service, U.S. Department of Agriculture: Washington, DC, 1977.

Thus the formula is

$$(\underline{\hspace{1cm}}°C \times \tfrac{9}{5}) + 32 = \underline{\hspace{1cm}}°F$$

The formula for converting from 212°F to 100°C is

$$212°F - 32 = 180$$

$$180 \times \tfrac{5}{9} = 20 \times 5 = 100°C$$

This formula then is

$$(\underline{\hspace{1cm}}°F - 32) \times \tfrac{5}{9} = \underline{\hspace{1cm}}°C$$

Table 1.5 provides some corresponding temperatures in Fahrenheit and Celsius.

Taking Control

Meaningful information can be derived from experiments only when controls are established and maintained to eliminate (as much as possible) unintentional variables.

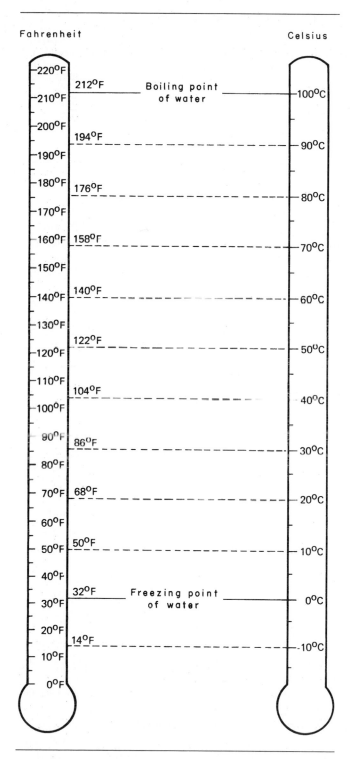

Figure 1.1   Comparison of the Celsius and Fahrenheit temperature scales. (Courtesy of Plycon Press.)

Table 1.5 Selected Examples of Comparable Temperatures in the Fahrenheit and Celsius Scales

Celsius (°)	Fahrenheit (°)	Celsius (°)	Fahrenheit (°)
–10	14	150	300
0	32	163	325
10	50	176	350
20	68	191	375
30	86	204	400
40	104	218	425
80	176		

All aspects of the experiments, from the ingredients and their preparation to the evaluation process, need to be considered carefully to identify potential experimental errors that can lead to invalid results. Researchers conducting experiments intended ultimately for publication spend considerable time developing their methods to eliminate uncontrolled variables and then replicating their experiment numerous times to ensure accurate results. Carefully documented techniques are repeated each time by the same laboratory personnel to eliminate the variability that would occur if others were to do the same task. Such measures enable researchers to obtain results that can be replicated again and again.

Unfortunately, it is not practical for individual students to prepare in class all of the variations needed to illustrate the impact of altering ingredients and/or methods used in food preparation. However, considerable information can be provided in a class laboratory situation if various class members prepare some of the samples required to demonstrate the scientific principles underlying the day's experiment. This broad involvement of class members in sample preparation obviously introduces the possibility of considerable experimental error. To keep this error to an absolute minimum, individual members of the class need to become personally responsible for thoughtfully and carefully preparing the variations assigned to them.

Control of the quantity of ingredients used in preparing samples is essential if results from objective and subjective testing are to be meaningful. In the laboratory, solids are weighed very carefully, and liquids are measured volumetrically in graduated cylinders, pipettes, or burettes. Far greater accuracy is possible with these procedures than with standard household techniques. The diameter of household measuring cups is so great that precise measurements cannot be obtained, whereas the very narrow diameter of a graduated cylinder or other laboratory volumetric equipment reduces the potential for imprecise measurements of liquids. Other errors in household measurements occur as the result of packing of ingredients when they are transferred into the measuring cup. By weighing solid ingredients, the researcher can eliminate this source of potential errors.

Liquid ingredients should be measured in the smallest volumetric device capable of holding the entire measurement at one time. This practice minimizes the use of devices with a larger diameter than is absolutely necessary. For example, 80 milliliters of oil can be measured more accurately in a graduated cylinder with a capacity of 100 milliliters than in one that holds 500 milliliters. On the other hand, if this same 80-milliliter measurement were made by filling a 10-milliliter graduated cylinder eight times, error would be introduced because some oil would cling to the graduated cylinder each time it was emptied. Each liquid measurement should be made at eye level by reading the bottom of the **meniscus,** the usually concave surface of the liquid. Pipettes and burettes provide greater accuracy than graduated cylinders.

Dry ingredients and solids such as fats are weighed on balances, using careful and accurate laboratory techniques. **Trip balances** are available in some instructional laboratories. Ingredients can be weighed to an accuracy of 0.1 percent if 100 grams of food is being weighed. This degree of accuracy requires that the container holding the food on the left pan be counterbalanced precisely with a similar, lighter container on the right pan to which shot or water has been added to zero the balance. The trip balance is an inexpensive, suitable choice because of its durability and satisfactory sensitivity for most laboratory experiments conducted by a class. It is preferred over the spring-type **dietetic** scale because of its greater sensitivity. The error of a dietetic scale is approximately 0.5 gram when 100 grams of food is weighed, whereas the trip balance error for this quantity is about 0.1 gram.

Some **torsion balances** are used for weighing quantities greater than 2 kilograms, for this quantity cannot be weighted satisfactorily on a trip balance. They also are needed for weighing very small amounts, as might be the case for spices. The sensitivity of torsion balances really makes them the preferred balance for all weighing, but cost and possible need for repairs limit their availability in instructional laboratories. Direct-reading, top-loading automatic balances with a sensitivity of 0.01 gram are yet another, but definitely costly, alternative for weighing spices or other foods needed in very small quantities.

Top-loading electronic balances are desirable because of their convenience and accuracy. Unfortunately, their cost limits their availability in student laboratories. These balances save time by making it possible to weigh the container for the food and then use the tare mechanism to offset that weight so that only the weight of the actual food is indicated. Top-loading electronic balances are of particular merit when small amounts of ingredients need to be weighed because they are very sensitive and accurate, even when tiny quantities are required.

Conducting and Evaluating Classroom Experiments

When experiments are conducted by the entire class, more samples can be prepared to demonstrate the effects of selected variables than can be produced by an individual researcher. This advantage is countered by the fact that individual techniques of the class members introduce uncontrolled variables into the experiment. By mixing with electric mixers operating at a specified speed for a defined period of time, some control of mixing techniques can be obtained. In preparations requiring other mixing techniques, the class members should be sure to use the same design of beater, spoon, or other mixing tool; the total amount of mixing and the rate also need to be defined and heeded.

In some experiments, it is possible to set up an assembly line to prepare the samples for the class. When this is done, the same part of the preparation is done on each sample by the same person. The mixture is passed in sequence along the assembly line. The obvious advantage of preparing samples for the class in this manner is that variations in preparation are kept to a minimum.

The completed products should be evaluated very carefully according to the standards of quality appropriate for the type of food being tested. To distinguish

Meniscus
Curved upper surface of a liquid column that is concave when the containing walls are wetted by the liquid and convex when not.

Trip Balance
Balance with two pans: the one on the left is used to hold the food being weighed and the one on the right is used to hold the weights needed to counterbalance the left pan. Riders also are available for counterbalancing.

Dietetic Balance
Single-pan, spring balance suitable for portion control, but not sufficiently accurate for food experimentation.

Torsion Balance
A very sensitive (within 0.02 gram) laboratory balance particularly useful for weighing very small quantities or quantities greater than 2 kilograms.

Top-loading Electronic Balance
Very accurate, electrically operated balance.

the unique qualities of each of the variations available, you will need to examine each sample very carefully under good light and in a quiet place. Avoid biases from other class members by refraining from any comments while evaluation is being done.

Record your comments clearly as you evaluate each sample. A chart listing the variations and the characteristics to be evaluated will make evaluation proceed smoothly and accurately. If the samples are arranged on the display table in the same order as the chart and each sample is clearly labeled, the possibility of confusing the samples when recording results will be kept to a minimum.

SUMMARY

Consumers are constantly reshaping the food marketplace as they increase in cultural diversity and modify their lifestyles and concerns. Among current key concerns are food safety (including environmental and microbiological) and health. Phytochemicals, functional foods, designer foods, genetically modified organisms, and biotechnology are fairly recent additions to consumer vocabularies.

Careers related to food may be in relation to the role of food and health, the feeding of people away from home, or in the broad food industry (from basic food research to all aspects of bringing food products to the consumer, including governmental roles).

Food research, which had its origins primarily in the search for answers to problems observed in the home, is now shifting the emphasis increasingly toward the technological challenges presented as a considerable portion of the food consumed is prepared in factories and processing plants. Whether the food under study is intended for preparation in the home or on a vast commercial basis, the scientific principles underlying the properties and behavior of the various components are the same. A course in experimental foods considers the chemical and physical principles underlying the preparation of the diverse foods commonly served in America. Evaluation and the correlation of cause and effect in preparing many foods are useful means of highlighting the concepts illustrated by laboratory experiments.

The language of experimental foods, like that of other sciences, is metrics. Food professionals need to be able to use the metric system and also to convert between the conventional system and the metrics so that recipes can be converted as needed. Conversions between the Celsius and Fahrenheit scales frequently are necessary in research.

Accuracy of measurements is a key aspect of control in food experimentation. Volumetric devices (pipettes, burettes, and graduated cylinders) are used for measuring liquids, with the bottom of the meniscus being the location for determining the exact volume. Trip balances usually are the main type of balance used to weigh solid ingredients in classroom laboratories. Direct-reading, top-loading electronic balances are desirable for weighing very small quantities, but less expensive and slightly less precise torsion balances may be used satisfactorily for weighing ingredients needed in very small amounts or in quantities exceeding 2 kilograms.

For best results in classroom experiments, all aspects of sample preparation should be controlled as much as possible. Electric mixers are recommended whenever feasible to regulate the speed and duration of mixing. Evaluating class samples needs to be done in an accurate and organized manner.

STUDY QUESTIONS

1. Identify 3 aspects that help define consumers and explain briefly how each influences the food marketplace.

2. Define "organic" and "natural" (in the context of food) and clarify any distinction between the 2 terms.

3. Define: (a) phytochemical, (b) functional food, (c) biotechnology, (d) GMO, (e) genetic engineering.

4. Identify the career that you wish to enter and describe the academic preparation you will need.

5. Why is it important for food researchers to weigh all ingredients carefully or measure them in a calibrated volumetric pipette, burette, or graduated cylinder?

6. Explain how to weigh 225 grams of flour on your laboratory balance.

7. Convert the following measures:
   a. 40°F = _____ °C
   b. 150°C = _____ °F
   c. 375°F = _____ °C
   d. 55°C = _____ °F
   e. 14 tbsp = _____ ml
   f. 472 ml = _____ c
   g. $1\frac{1}{3}$ c = _____ ml
   h. 7 fl oz = _____ ml
   i. 1236 g = _____ kg
   j. 236 ml = _____ l
   k. 1 tsp = _____ ml
   l. 4 tsp margarine = _____ g

BIBLIOGRAPHY

American Dietetic Association. 1995. Position of the American Dietetic Association: phytochemicals and functional foods. *J. Am. Diet. Assoc. 95* (4): 493.

Anonymous. 1994. Food biotechnology: Focus on consumer choices. *Food Insight:* 1.

Anonymous. 1995. *Plant Biotechnology.* The American Dietetic Association and Monsanto Co., St. Louis, MO.

Becker, C. C. and Kyle, D. J. 1998. Developing functional foods containing algal docosahexaenoic acid. *Food Technol. 52* (7): 68.

Bidlack, W. R. 1998. Phytochemicals: Potential new health paradigm. *Food Technol. 52* (9): 168.

Chung, K. T. and Wei, C. I. 1997. Food tannins and human health: Double-edged sword? *Food Technol. 51* (9): 124.

Hoban, T. J. 1999. Consumer acceptance of biotechnology in the United States and Japan. *Food Technol. 53* (5): 50.

Hollingsworth, P. 1997. Beverages: Redefining New Age. *Food Technol. 51* (8): 44.

Institute of Food Technologists. 1999. Classified guide to food industry services. IFT Membership Directory. Chicago, IL. P. 377.

International Food Information Council. 1995. Pesticides and food safety. International Food Information Council Foundation. Washington, D.C. P. 1.

Katz, F. 1996. Biotechnology—new tools in food technology's toolbox. *Food Technol. 50* (11): 63.

Katz, F. 1998. That's using the old bean. *Food Technol. 52* (6): 42.

Liu, K. 1999. Biotech crops: products, properties, and prospects. *Food Technol. 53* (5): 42.

Nguyen, M. L. and Schwartz, S. J. 1999. Lycopene: Chemical and biological properties. *Food Technol. 53* (2): 38.

Ozdemir, M., Yurteri, C. U., and Sadikoglu, H. 1999. *Food Technol. 53* (4): 54.

Sloan, A. E. 1996. Consumer product trends beyond the traditional. *Food Technol. 50* (8): 65.

Sloan, A. E. 1998. Food industry forecast: consumer trends to 2020 and beyond. *Food Technol. 52* (1): 37.

Witwer, R. S. 1999. Marketing bioactive ingredients in food products. *Food Technol. 53* (4): 50.

CHAPTER 2

The Research Process

PLANNING EXPERIMENTS

Although the classroom laboratory often is a structured situation designed to demonstrate scientific principles in an efficient manner, you can also learn much by planning, conducting, and reporting an individual experiment in which you define the purpose and justification. By identifying the problem and actually proceeding through the several steps involved in bringing the research project to fruition, you can begin to appreciate the realm of food research and the many factors involved in conducting, evaluating, and reporting such research. The following sections provide an overview of this process. They are intended to introduce the process of food research and to serve as a guide for students who have an opportunity to do some independent food research.

Defining the Purpose

Drafting a clearly stated purpose is the first step in designing a research study. Initially, it may be helpful to write down the general subject to be studied. This could be a subject as vaguely defined as "various sweeteners in cakes." From this beginning, a specific statement can be developed. The following statement of purpose for an individual project is an example:

> The purpose of this experiment is to determine the effect of substituting fructose for sucrose at two levels in shortened cake.

This statement indicates that two levels of substitution will be used, that the control will be sucrose and the substitute will be fructose, and that the product being tested is shortened cake. The specific characteristics to be evaluated are not indicated in this particular statement. Instead, the general term *effect* is used, which leaves the evaluation methods to be identified when the method is developed. If desired, it is appropriate to define effect more specifically. If this were done, the statement of purpose might read as follows:

> The purpose of this experiment is to determine the effect on volume, texture, flavor, tenderness, and moisture when fructose is substituted for sucrose at two levels in short-ened cake.

Although somewhat cumbersome, this type of statement clearly stipulates the scope of the experiment and aids in development of the methods, particularly the method of evaluation.

Statements of the problem are appropriate for descriptive research studies. However, researchers wishing to apply statistical analysis to their results need to develop a **hypothesis** and a **null hypothesis.** This permits statistical testing to determine the probability that the variable being tested caused the results obtained in the study. A hypothesis is a stated assumption of a consequence that is made re-garding the outcome of application of a variable in a research project. Researchers also state a null hypothesis, which is a statement that there will be no significant difference resulting from application of the variable in the experiment.

An example of a hypothesis is:

> There will be a significant difference in the volume of a shortened cake made with sucrose and one made with fructose.

An example of a null hypothesis is:

> There will be no significant difference in the volume of a shortened cake made with sucrose and one made with fructose.

Because research is often costly in both time and money, experimentalists should consider the justification for conducting the intended experiment. This justi-fication should be developed concomitantly with the statement of purpose. In the case of the research topic just suggested, the justification may be based on the fact that fructose in solution is known to be sweeter than sucrose and that its use in cakes might be useful in reducing the caloric content of cakes. If this experiment demonstrated that fructose could replace sucrose satisfactorily at reduced levels in shortened cakes, reduced-calorie cakes could be developed and marketed to meet consumer demand for desserts with fewer calories.

Justification frequently is based on consumer needs. In some instances, special diet requirements for such physical conditions as a high serum cholesterol level may provide the justification for an experiment using egg substitutes or various other special ingredients related to the condition. Sometimes the cost of similar in-gredients may be the basis of a study determining the feasibility of substituting the less costly ingredient for the more costly one, or even of reducing the amount of the costly item. Other experiments may be based on the need for a longer shelf life for products to maintain their acceptability during the marketing process. These are but a few of the factors that may provide justification for conducting food research.

Hypothesis
Tentative assumption to test logical or empirical consequences of applying a variable in a research project.

Null Hypothesis
Statement that applying a research variable will not make a significant differ-ence in a research project.

Reviewing the Literature

Research projects are most meaningful when they are planned after a thorough search of the literature on the topic being studied. Previous work published on the research topic can provide considerable insight into anticipated problems, appropriate methods, theories, and facts related to the topic, and evaluation techniques. Considerable time can be saved, and the quality of the research can be enhanced by thorough review of the pertinent literature.

The search of the literature can be eased considerably with the help of the librarian who can do a computer search of the literature relating to certain key words. For the preceding example, appropriate key words for the preliminary computer search would include *fructose, cakes, shortened cakes, sucrose,* and *sugar.* If references are desired regarding test methods, these also can be searched via computer.

There are many journals that may have appropriate articles relating to specific research topics. A list of some of the pertinent journals that may be helpful is presented in Table 2.1.

If a computer search is not a possibility or the results of the search are delayed, alternative approaches to finding appropriate research articles may prove helpful. Check the *Biological and Agricultural Index,* an index issued monthly,

Table 2.1   Some Research Journals Pertinent to Food Research Problems

Journal	Types of Topics Covered
Advances in Food Research	Wide range of topics in different years
Agricultural and Biological Chemistry	Chemistry of basic products
American Potato Journal	All aspects of potatoes
Bakers Digest	Applied research in the baking industry
Cereal Chemistry	Some food science applications and scientific research on such topics as starch
Cereal Science Today	Various cereals
Chemistry and Industry	Some industrial applications of food and its chemistry
Critical Reviews in Food Science and Nutrition	Excellent review articles on various food topics
Cryobiology	Effects of freezing
Research Abstracts	
Food Technology	Food industry and problems related to product evaluation, control, and development
Journal of Agricultural and Food Chemistry	Chemical research on food
Journal of American Dietetic Association	A few articles on nutrient content and food ingredients
Journal of Dairy Science	Milk and dairy products
Journal of Food Protection	Food microbiology
Journal of Food Quality	Some review articles on quality
Journal of Food Science	Very wide range of applied and basic food research articles
Journal of Poultry Science	Many aspects of poultry
Journal of Texture Studies	Textural properties and characteristics
Microscopy	Theory and applications

with a quarterly cumulative issue. Another index is the *Applied Science and Technological Index.* As the name suggests, articles indexed focus on applications and technology, rather than on food science. Consequently, this index does not include articles from the *Journal of Food Science,* which is an especially important technical journal in the field. *Current Contents: Agriculture, Biology, and Environmental Sciences,* which weekly publishes the tables of contents from journals pertinent to food research, affords yet another entry to the literature in food research. All of these publications provide the bibliographic information needed to locate articles for study to help you gather the research information available related to your research topic. You will need to obtain the articles themselves to gain the information needed in your literature review.

Abstracts can also be of help in gathering background information for your research topic. Whenever possible, you should read the actual article, rather than relying solely on the abstract. However, articles written in foreign languages or appearing in foreign journals may only be available to you in the form of the abstract. Several sources of abstracts may be available in the library. These include *Food Science and Technology Abstracts, Chemical Abstracts (Section 17),* and *Biological Abstracts.* You will need to survey their subheadings to help you identify the sections of the abstracts that might contain appropriate entries for your topic.

Computers can provide access to still other sources of information regarding pertinent articles. Two data bases available by computer, but not through print, are *Agricola* and *Foods Adlibra. World Wide Web* is an emerging computer index.

You may find that books can provide valuable insights to your topic, too. For some topics, excellent basic scientific information can be found in current books. The subject card catalog in the library is a quick means of locating appropriate books and their call numbers. In addition to the actual information that can be gleaned from these books, you may find some useful bibliographic entries for you to pursue in the journals. Of particular interest in the realm of books are two yearly publications: *Advances in Food Research* and *CRC Critical Reviews in Food Science and Nutrition.* Although these books do not cover all aspects of food science, the review articles they contain provide excellent information on specific topics and also extensive bibliographies.

Be sure to examine the table of contents in the most recent issues of the journals that may be most appropriate for your research topic. You may find that a useful article has just been published. The bibliography in the article will also prove to be helpful. Many of the journals provide an annual index of articles. A quick examination of the index can give you a review of possible articles in that publication. The abstracts of articles in other journals that are a monthly feature of the *Journal of the American Dietetic Association* are yet another possible source of information.

After the articles have been gathered, careful reading and thought are necessary to interpret the findings in relation to the project being undertaken. Ideas for the statement of hypotheses and for the development of method can often be gleaned from the literature. Previous research can help to validate the results obtained in the new experiment. Accepted analytical methods can be learned from the literature, thus enhancing comparison of the new results with previous research.

When studying each article, be sure to record the complete citation in an accepted bibliographic style. This style should be that required either at the university or in the specific class; usually the style selected is based on the format used in an appropriate professional journal. In all forms the basic information needed will include the authors' names (usually with initials), the title of the article, the volume (and issue, if necessary), the page number (either initial page or inclusive pages), and the year. Methodical notation of these pertinent data for each article will avoid the need to relocate the article later to complete the citation. Bibliographic styles differ from journal to journal, as can be seen from the following citations (*Food Technology* and *Journal of the American Dietetic Association,* respectively):

Giese, J. 1996. Fats, oils, and fat replacers. *Food Technol. 50* (4): 79–83.

Reinli K, Block G. Phytoestrogen content of foods—a compendium of literature values. *Nutr Cancer.* 1996; 26:123–148.

Designing the Experiment

When you have stated the purpose of the experiment clearly, you can develop a design to achieve your desired goal. Individual student experiments in an experimental food course can be conducted meaningfully if only one variable is tested. In the example used in the preceding section, the variable is the substitution of fructose for sucrose; the levels of substitution need to be determined. The design of this experiment might be based on preparation of three cakes for each run: a control containing 100 percent sucrose and 0 percent fructose, an experimental cake containing 50 percent sucrose and 50 percent fructose, and a second experimental cake containing 0 percent sucrose and 100 percent fructose.

Variables are any quantity or symbol that has no fixed value. In designing a research project, it is important to identify all aspects of the research that might vary. **Extraneous variables** are those that might add variations into the experiment that are not truly a part of the experiment and that are not useful, e.g., using two different brands of baking powder when that is not the focus of the experiment. Recognition of these undesirable extraneous variables is important so that they can be prevented prior to the conduct of the experiment.

Two types of variables of particular interest in designing an experiment are **independent** and **dependent variables.** An independent variable (also referred to sometimes as the manipulated variable) is defined by the researcher and is not measured. The dependent variable is the variable that will have measured results or data as outcomes of the experiment. In the research above comparing cakes made with sucrose and fructose, the independent variable is the type of sugar and the dependent variable is the volume of the cakes.

Ordinarily, the appropriateness of the planned variations might be tested in some preliminary runs to obtain insight into possible results and to develop the controls necessary for preparing and evaluating the samples; however, the time restrictions of an experimental food course may dictate that this mini-research project be designed with only two runs, with no preliminary runs to develop the optimal formulas and method.

Publishable research requires extensive testing during the planning stage to establish the controls needed to eliminate errors resulting from variation in sample preparation. Actual data collection should begin only after repeatable results are obtained and the problems involved in the evaluation process have been solved. Once data collection begins, it is necessary to include sufficient repetition to ensure that the results are due to the variables and not to chance (Figure 2.1).

Variable
Quantity or symbol that has no fixed value.

Extraneous Variable
Variable that is not intended to be part of the experiment and needs to be eliminated from or controlled prior to the conduct of the experiment.

Independent Variable
Manipulated variable defined by the researcher.

Dependent Variable
The measured variable of an experiment.

Method.   Plans for sample preparation require careful consideration of the entire process. The first step is to identify a formula for the ideal control product so that the experimental samples can be measured in relation to an excellent standard. Then every action involved in preparing that product must be identified and included in the written statement of the method.

All mixing techniques need to be described so clearly that some other person would be able to prepare the same product and obtain the same results following the stated method. Specifically, the type of mixing utensil to be used, the number of strokes (revolutions, or other appropriate control), and the rate (strokes per minute) are examples of the detail necessary in writing the statement of the

Figure 2.1   Products undergo extensive laboratory testing during development. (Courtesy of Provesta Corporation.)

method. The usual statements in recipes (for example, stir until blended) are too vague to ensure the controls necessary for precise laboratory investigations. Similarly, temperatures and times for heating must be very specific.

Even potential variations resulting from the ingredients themselves need to be eliminated as much as possible. For example, all of the eggs to be used in the control and variations for one run can be broken out of the shell and blended together gently for a designated amount of mixing, and then the amount needed for each sample can be weighed from this common source. The flour and other staple ingredients needed for the whole experiment should come from the same packages. If more than one package of an ingredient is needed for the entire experiment, the total amount should be mixed together thoroughly before starting and then stored appropriately for use throughout all of the runs. Of course, perishable ingredients will need to be procured throughout the experiment. Even though there will be some variation in ingredients of this type from one run to another, variation between the samples within a single run should be eliminated.

Evaluation.   Evaluation devices to be used are a key part of the planning process. Careful thought should be given to ensure that all pertinent characteristics are tested appropriately. This means that the necessary objective measurements— volume, tenderness, viscosity, pH, and chemical and physical attributes—are identified and that plans for conducting each measurement are specified. Sensory evaluation requires that a taste panel be designated and that a suitable scorecard be developed. If the panel is to be trained in the use of the scorecard, the training process also needs to be planned. Evaluations by objective and subjective methods are discussed in the next two chapters.

Plans for evaluation, both objective and subjective, need to be formulated so that the quantities of sample needed can be determined. Preparation of the samples for the evaluation also requires a thoughtfully developed written plan. For such objective testing as use of a shortometer, the thickness of the samples to be tested must be controlled, a control usually achieved by rolling the dough on a board specially equipped with parallel guides that dictate the thickness of the dough prior to baking (see Figure 2.2). In other cases, it may be necessary to de-

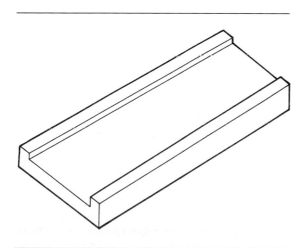

Figure 2.2 Sketch of a board designed to control the thickness of pastry for samples to be tested in a shortometer.

Figure 2.3 Template for preparing samples of a cake to be tested by four judges (samples 1, 2, 3, and 4) and by the penetrometer (P).

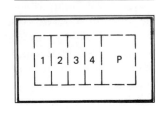

Template
Pattern guide to ensure accurate cutting of samples from a large sample, such as a cake.

velop a **template** to guide the cutting of specific samples for judges and for certain objective tests (see Figure 2.3).

Not only must sample size be determined, but the timing and temperature of samples for testing must also be considered. Significant changes in textural characteristics occur in many foods as they cool after being heated. The notable increase in viscosity of a white sauce as it cools illustrates the need to plan testing circumstances. Baked products become firmer as they cool, making it necessary to specify the time for determining tenderness after removal from the oven. The gel structure of a starch-thickened pudding gradually tightens and becomes less fragile as it is allowed to cool without any agitation. These are but a few examples of the changes that necessitate careful planning of the conditions for evaluation.

Record Keeping.   All information regarding a research project should be entered in a bound laboratory notebook. This information should include the statement of purpose, justification for the project, and the design. The formula and its variations, along with specific directions for preparing the sample, instructions for each phase of the evaluation, and samples of any forms to be used in evaluation should all be recorded in this bound notebook. This notebook also is dated each day, and the day's experimental results and any pertinent notes are written in before leaving the laboratory. Of course, the researcher's name and telephone number should be written clearly in the front of the book. These precautions are important to help assure success with the project.

CONDUCTING THE EXPERIMENT

Each day the experiment is conducted, a new page should be started in the bound laboratory notebook. The date and any pertinent notes on unusual environmental conditions or ingredients should be recorded. Then the samples should be prepared, being certain that the exact procedures specified in the method are being followed. This requires very careful attention on the part of the researcher, for it is all too easy to do portions of the preparation by habit rather than by experimental design. Continuous attention to possible experimental errors is essential to a controlled experiment. Thorough labeling of the variations throughout the preparation period and during evaluation will eliminate that potential for errors. The specific random numbers or symbols used in labeling samples each day must be recorded in the laboratory notebook for convenient reference. The same symbols can be used throughout the experiment, but the sample designated by each symbol should be changed each day according to the plan devised prior to the first run. In this manner, each sample bearing a particular symbol can be presented to the judges an equal number of times. This prevents the judges from expecting that the sample identified by a specific symbol has certain characteristics.

The results of both objective and subjective evaluations should be recorded directly into the laboratory notebook at the time the run is conducted. Accuracy is aided by always reporting the results of the various samples in the same order in the notebook. By recording the results with the designation of the sample specifically in words, the possibility of erroneous interpretation of symbols is reduced. For example, samples might be recorded as "control," "50 percent fructose," and "25 percent fructose," or other suitable names; results then can be posted following each of these. Usually, recording results in a tabular form provides the structure needed to ensure that all data are recorded at the completion of a run.

INTERPRETING AND REPORTING RESULTS

Before results can be seen from a clear perspective, tables of the results of each of the factors being evaluated need to be prepared. Initially, each table should show the measurement for each factor for each run, along with the calculated mean for the control and the mean for each of the variables prepared and evaluated. In the case of tables for the evaluation of subjective factors, each table should show the rating given by each judge on each run, the mean of the judges' scores for each run, and the overall mean for that factor for the total experiment. This type of display permits easy tracking of the consistency of each of the judges for each specific factor. It also permits comparison between judges. If isolated examples of a variance from the usual evaluation are noted, the researcher can then look in the laboratory notebook for notes that might aid in explaining this variance.

When inconsistency from run to run is the pattern noted, there is real reason to question the validity of the results. By probing for an explanation, the researcher may be able to identify flaws in the research method; perhaps the research can be conducted in the future to obtain reliable data for analysis. Obviously, researchers prefer to identify experimental problems early in the experiment so that loss of valuable research time and resources is minimized.

A Look at Statistics

The data collected during the research can be analyzed statistically by the use of **descriptive** or **inferential statistics.** For class experiments with very few runs, descriptive statistical measures used might include one or more of the following: frequency counts and distributions, measures of central tendency (mode, median, and mean), and measures of dispersion (range, mean deviation, standard deviation, variance, and standard error of the mean or difference between means).

Helpful insights into research results can be gained from simple calculations that provide a descriptive look at the collective data. Frequency counts and distributions determine the number of responses that fall into each of the various group's categories. These various totals can then be calculated as percentages of the entire population being studied. To illustrate, if 50 subjects were being interviewed and 5 of them fell in a specific group, this can be expressed as 10 percent of the subjects belonging to a specific group. When this calculation is done for all of the groups, a clear picture of the population in the study can be seen (see Table 2.2).

Descriptive Statistics
Analysis of data by describing results in terms of such calculations as frequency, measures of central tendency, percentages, or various measures of dispersion.

Inferential Statistics
Probability of predicting an occurrence by use of such statistical tests as chi-square, analysis of variance (ANOVA), Student's "t" distribution, or other statistical tools.

Table 2.2   Brand of Orange Juice Preferred
by Consumers in Newtonville

	Responses	
Brand	**Number**	**%**
Esmerelda	5	10
Valley Pride	15	30
Nature's Premium	22	44
Superior	3	6
Naringenita	5	10
	50	

Mode
Score or group receiving the most responses or data points.

When numerous data points are collected, measures of central tendency often are used to permit some comparisons. Determination of the **mode** is one possible measure of central tendency. This is done by plotting every data point on a chart and then finding which score or group contained the largest number of data points. In other words, the mode is the most common score or group. In the example presented by the data in Table 2.2, the mode is 22 (Nature's Premium).

Determining the median also needs to be done by first making a sequential array of the data collected. The middle score in this organized array is the median. In other words, there are as many scores on one side of the median as on the other side. This is simple to identify if there is an odd number of data. When the number of data is even, the value calculated to be halfway between the two middle points is the median score. Note that the median value does not necessarily define a numerical value halfway between the largest and smallest possible scores.

An example of determination of the median in an array with an odd number of data is:

32

68

95 (median)

101

110

When an even number comprises the array, the midpoint between the two middle scores is the **median:**

Median
The score at the midpoint of data arranged in a sequential array.

11

12

16 (median = 17.5)

19

29

32

Mean
The arithmetic average of scores.

Calculation of the **mean** is done by totaling the data and dividing by the number of scores. Despite the fact that the mean is influenced greatly when some data are far from most of the other scores, it is used frequently because it is the most reliable measure of central tendency. The mean is a value that is used in some statistical calculations. The calculation of the mean for the preceding examples is:

$$\frac{32 + 68 + 95 + 101 + 100}{5} = \frac{406}{5} = 81.2 = \text{mean}$$

$$\frac{11 + 12 + 16 + 19 + 29 + 32}{6} = \frac{119}{6} = 19.83 = \text{mean}$$

Each of these three measures of central tendency may be used in working to interpret data. The median is used when scores are skewed markedly. The mode is useful in making a quick rough estimation of the midpoint of data, but it is not suitable for use alone in analyzing data. The mean is well suited to represent the values obtained in the research study when statistical analysis is being done.

Percentages sometimes are calculated to characterize the results of a study. An example of the use of percentages might be to indicate the percentage of people who preferred one sample over two others in a preference test. **Percentile ranks** require that all scores be arranged in sequence so that the position of a specific score can be characterized, for example, the fifth score in an array of ten is in the fiftieth percentile.

Measures of dispersion are used to indicate the conformity of the data points. **Variance** and **standard deviation** are two useful ways of assessing dispersion of values. These two measures are closely related, for standard deviation is the square root of the variance. Either of these may be used in determining tests of significance of the data obtained in a study.

Statistics may be applied to make predictions about populations that meet the same criteria as those used for establishing the population of a study. These types of calculations are designated as **inferential statistics.** Studies in which inferential statistics are to be applied are based on carefully stated hypotheses—a working or alternate hypothesis and a null (negatively stated) hypothesis. The specific statistics to be used for analysis will be determined by the design of the study.

Statistical analyses are conducted to determine the probability that the observed results are caused by the variable applied and not simply chance. Calculations are made appropriate to the type of statistical analysis selected for the experiment and its design. The results of these calculations are compared with the appropriate statistical table(s) to determine whether or not the null hypothesis that was developed for the experiment should be accepted or rejected. These tables are designed with two **levels of significance:** 0.05 and 0.01. The level of significance is a proportion or decimal value at or below which results of the research will be considered significant, and the null hypothesis can be rejected. At 0.05, there are only 5 chances in 100 that that result will occur by chance, and at 0.01 only 1 chance in 100 is the probability of the result occurring by chance.

If a variable is determined to have a significant effect at the 0.05 level but not at the 0.01 level, this is significant. However, this level clearly is not quite as significant as is a result that is at the 0.01 level of significance.

Another way of presenting statistical significance is by **level of confidence,** which is the percent of certainty that the variable caused the result. A statement of a 95 percent level of confidence is equivalent to a level of significance of 0.05. Similarly, a 99 percent level of confidence is comparable to a level of significance of 0.01.

Percent
Portion of a hundred.

Percentile Rank
Relative position of a score within the total array of scores; expressed on the

Variance
Measure of the dispersion of data; the sum of the squares of the deviation of each value from the mean.

Standard Deviation
Square root of the variance.

Inferential Statistics
Statistical analyses conducted to determine the probability of the occurrence of the measured response.

Level of Significance
The decimal value below which the results of research will be considered significant, and the null hypothesis can be rejected.

Level of Confidence
Percentage expression of certainty that the results of a variable are statistically significant.

Chi-square is an appropriate inferential test for a research study with one variable and two categories. It also can be used if there are two or more independent variables, but the calculations become increasingly complex as the number of variables increases.

When data are ordered sequentially or in rank order, other inferential tests can be used to determine the probability of occurrence. Such tests include the sign test, Wilcoxon matched pairs test, the Mann-Whitney U test, the Kruskal-Wallis test, and the rank sums test. Selection of the appropriate statistics to be used is based on the design of the research project.

Interrelationships or the effect of a variable on various components often are of interest in food research. The goal is to determine the correlation between the variable and its effect on the various characteristics of the system. This is called correlational research; statistical analyses of **correlational research** are called **regression.**

Several different tests can be used for regression statistical calculations. Among these are Pearson's Product Moment Correlation Coefficient (fortunately shortened to Pearson's r), Spearman rho, C statistic, and Kendall's tau. The appropriate one to use depends on the form of the data.

Statistical significance can be established for the means of two groups (the experimental and the control groups) by using the **Student's "t" test.** In the event that there is more than one experimental group in the research study, the mean of each of the experimental groups can be compared separately against the mean of the control using the Student's "t" test to determine the significance of each of the group treatments.

Analysis of variance (ANOVA) is widely used to determine the statistical significance between many sets of data. To use ANOVA, the sample should be selected randomly or on the basis of probability. However, ANOVA sometimes is used even when the sampling was not done in these ways. A table of F values is needed to determine the significance. An F value equal to or greater than the value of the criterion F is required if the difference between treatments is to be considered significant. There are several different ways by which ANOVA can be calculated. However, the results all require comparison with the F table to determine significance.

Correlational Research
Research that determines interrelationships between variables.

Regression
Statistical methods applicable to correlational research.

Student's "t" Test
Statistical test to determine the significance of the mean of the experimental group versus the mean of the control group.

Analysis of Variance (ANOVA)
Statistical approach to determining differences between many sets of data.

Overview of the Report

Preparing the research report is the final step. The format will vary, depending on the intended use. When the reports are being written as articles for a selected scientific journal, the style guide for the journal dictates the entire format. Similarly,

Table 2.3   Tenderness and Volume of Angel Cakes Prepared with Three Different Sweeteners (Sucrose, Fructose, and Aspartame)[a]

	Tenderness		
Sweetener	Shear (lb)	Number of Chews	Volume (ml)
Sucrose	.002	5	175
Fructose	.001	3	190
Aspartame	.007	16	105

[a]Information in this table is fictitious and is presented simply to show the format of a table.

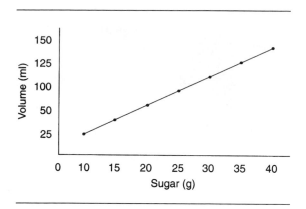

Figure 2.4   Effect of sugar content on volume of plain cake.

research reports prepared as part of an experimental food course usually need to conform to the guidelines established by the professor. Ordinarily, the sections included are Introduction (stating the purpose and the justification for conducting the research); Review of Literature; Method (sample preparation and evaluation techniques, both subjective and objective); Results and Discussion; Conclusions (or Summary and Conclusions); and Bibliography. Appendices are optional, depending on the need for presentation of supporting information that cannot be placed appropriately in the text of the report. Tables and other illustrative materials should be developed and included in the report at the appropriate points to help clarify the research findings to the reader. All illustrative materials should be referenced in the text and should have clearly stated number designations and captions or titles. In tables, each column needs to have a meaningful heading, and units can be indicated if the same designation is appropriate for all entries in a column. Solid lines above and below the area for the headings and also at the conclusion of the table are valuable guides to enable readers to grasp the content readily. If two or more subheads appear below a major column heading, the relationship can be shown by using a line under the major heading that extends over all of the pertinent subheads, as shown in Table 2.3.

   Graphs provide a clear picture of data from experiments if they are constructed carefully. Both axes need to be labeled, and the units of measure must be identified. Accurate plotting of the data points will result in an effective presentation of results from an experiment. Figure 2.4 is an example of a graph format suitable for reporting data. Figure 2.5 presents data in the form of a bar graph. A pie chart (Figure 2.6) can be used when percentages or portions of the whole are to be depicted.

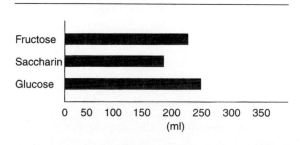

Figure 2.5   Volumes of chocolate cakes made with different sweeteners.

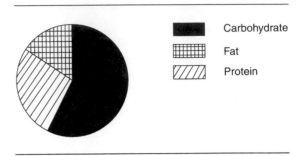

Figure 2.6 Composition of rye bread.

SUMMARY

Although much of the laboratory work in an introductory experimental food science class is done cooperatively by the entire group, a great deal can be learned through small individual experiments conducted during at least a couple of laboratory periods. Ideally, this individual experiment will include identification of the problem, statement of the problem, review of related scientific literature, and design of the experiment. This design should include detailed procedures for preparing the sample and objective and subjective means of evaluating the products.

By keeping a careful log in a bound laboratory notebook, the researcher can efficiently work with the data obtained. Preparation of tables showing all of the results will facilitate analysis of the results. For much food research, descriptive or inferential statistical analyses are needed to determine the comparative significance of the findings.

Measures of central tendency that may be used in analyzing data include the mode, median, and mean. Percent and percentile rank are other ways of expressing information gained in the study. Variance and standard deviation (square root of the variance) describe the dispersion of data obtained in the study. Chi-square is an inferential statistical test that can be applied in a study with one variable and two categories or with two or more independent variables. Several types of inferential statistical tests are available to meet specific research designs. Regression can be used to determine statistical significance in correlational research. Statistical testing of the significance of differences of the means of the experimental and control groups can be done using the Student's "t" test. ANOVA (analysis of variance) is of great use when analyzing many sets of data for statistical significance in a study. Levels of significance commonly identified are .05 and .01, meaning that there is a confidence level of 95 percent and 99 percent, respectively, that the results are not due to chance. Upon completion of the laboratory work and analysis, the entire project can then be written, either in the form required by a specific research journal to which it will be submitted or in the form specified by the professor.

STUDY QUESTIONS

1. Write a statement of purpose that could be used for conducting an individual research experiment.
2. Compare the types of articles and other information that appear in three different professional research journals.

3. Select a research article on food in a professional journal; write a one-sentence statement of the purpose of the research.

4. Write the bibliographic citation for the article selected for study in the preceding question.

5. Find examples of a table, a bar graph, and a pie chart in professional journals. Present the data from each one in a different format (for example, plot a graph of the data provided in the table).

BIBLIOGRAPHY

Adams, G. R. and Schvanveldt, J. D. 1985. *Understanding Research Methods*. Longmans: New York.

Bender, F. E., Douglass, L. W., and Kramer, A. 1982. *Statistical Methods for Food and Agriculture*. AVI Publishing: Westport, CT.

Caragay, A. B. 1992. "Cancer-preventive foods and ingredients." *Food Technol*. 46 (4): 65.

Dowdy, S. and Wearden, D. 1983. *Statistics for Research*. Wiley: New York.

Freund, J. E. 1981. *Statistics: First Course*. Prentice-Hall: Englewood Cliffs, NJ.

Jenkins, M. L. Y. 1993. "Research issues in evaluating 'Functional Foods.'" *Food Technol*. 47 (4): 76.

Joseph, M. I. and Joseph, W. D. 1986. *Research Fundamentals in Home Economics*. 3rd ed. Plycon: Redondo Beach, CA.

Kurzer, M. S. 1993. "Planning and interpreting 'Designer Food' feeding studies." *Food Technol*. 47 (4): 80.

Labuza, T. P. 1994. "Shifting food research paradigms for the 21st century." *Food Technol*, 48 (12): 50.

Leedy, P. D. 1985. *Practical Research Planning and Design*. 3rd ed. Macmillan: New York.

Martens, M. and Martens, H. 1986. "Partial least squares regression." In *Statistical Procedures in Food Research*. Piggott, J. R., ed., p. 293. Elsevier Applied Science Publishers Ltd.: England.

McDonald, P. 1995. "Science libraries of the future: research in the Electronic Age." *Food Technol*. 49 (4): 92.

Piggott, J. R., ed. 1986. *Statistical Methods in Food Research*. Elsevier Science Publishers Ltd.: England.

Puri, S. C. and Mullin, K. 1980. *Applied Statistics for Food and Agricultural Scientists*. G. K. Hall Medical Publ: Boston.

Rupnow, J. and King, J. W. 1995. "Primer on preparing posters for technical presentations." *Food Technol*. 49 (11): 93.

CHAPTER 3

Sensory Evaluation

THE IMPORTANCE OF EVALUATION

Food quality is evaluated by all people, either consciously or unconsciously. Food choices in the marketplace are made by consumers on the basis of their previous experiences with specific brands and various foods. Their at-home evaluations probably were not conducted scientifically; nevertheless, their general reactions to products determine whether or not they buy a particular item again. Their selections serve as an endorsement or proof of consumer acceptance, which then tells the food manufacturer that this quality level is preferred over that of similar products in the marketplace. Thus, the individual consumer's evaluation of food, combined with the decisions of countless other individual consumers, dictates the quality of food to be produced in this nation.

The testing of food quality in the marketplace is too costly for food producers to undertake on a broad basis without considerable preliminary research. **In-house testing** and evaluation are done on a scientific basis, with food scientists planning and supervising experiments. Very careful and thorough tests are conducted to ascertain the product formulations or processing techniques that are anticipated to be successful in the marketplace. Trained sensory panelists evaluate the samples and provide guidance in improvement of the product. This type of testing is termed *sensory evaluation* or *subjective evaluation* because the scores are determined by individual decisions based on the use of the senses and do not rely on mechanical devices. However, mechanical testing usually is done too, to provide additional information about the food being tested. This type of testing is designated *objective evaluation.*

The testing that is done in-house is a measure of the acceptability of the product to the personnel involved in the evaluation, but it cannot be assumed that the general public has the same assessment. Therefore, products can be tested further

In-House Testing
Evaluations conducted within a food company prior to field testing and test marketing.

Sensory Evaluation
A synonym for subjective evaluation; measurements determined by using the senses of sight, smell, taste, and sometimes touch.

Subjective Evaluation
Evaluation by individuals on a panel with a scoring system based on various characteristics that can be judged by using the senses.

Objective Evaluation
Measurement of physical properties of a food by the use of mechanical devices.

by focus groups of 4 to 12 typical consumers who fit the specific demographic characteristics of interest to the food company. Larger scale (200 to 500 consumers) testing can be conducted by use of testing at a central location or in-home testing of the product. These consumer tests provide valuable sensory information related to potential consumer acceptance of the product.

Then products often are market tested on a small scale to obtain information from a selected sampling of the potential market. The results of the test marketing determine whether the product is released into the general market, discontinued, or modified prior to general marketing.

Clearly, the food industry relies very heavily on evaluation in developing new products and in maintaining quality control in existing food items. Persons working within the food industry utilize evaluation techniques as basic tools. Sensory evaluation and objective evaluation are both vital sources of information to the researcher and to the person responsible for quality control.

Persons involved in supervision of institutional food service also have to be able to evaluate food and to identify changes that would enhance the acceptability of the food to the clientele. The professional person can evaluate food precisely and relate this evaluation to the food preferences of consumers. Studies of plate waste provide valuable information regarding food acceptability.

Professional evaluation of food requires careful analysis of the ways of assessing food, the properties of food, and the techniques for measuring these characteristics. Practice in evaluation also is essential. This chapter presents the background needed for conducting meaningful sensory evaluation of food products.

PHYSIOLOGICAL BASES OF SENSORY EVALUATION

Olfactory Receptors

Olfactory Receptors
Nasal organs capable of detecting aromas.

Flavor
The blend of taste and smell perceptions noted when food is in the mouth.

Odors are important preliminary cues to the acceptability of a food before that food enters the mouth. These odors are volatile chemical compounds that interact with the approximately ten million **olfactory receptors** in the nose. Additional information about food is contributed by the olfactory receptors when food is in the mouth, because volatile compounds travel to the nasal cavity where they are detected. Ultimately, these odor messages are blended with the taste messages from the tongue to provide the overall impression termed **_flavor._** The receptor sites for odors are organs housed in the upper area of the nasal cavity in the olfactory epithelium, which is a yellow, mucus-coated area (Farbman, 1967).

The olfactory sense is very keen. Teranishi et al. (1971) noted that the sense of smell is so sensitive that the nose can detect the presence of some odorous compounds at a concentration as low as 10^{-19} M. Individual variation in sensitivity exists as a consequence of possible nasal obstructions or sinus complications. Thus, some individuals are physiologically better suited to be sensory panel members than are others even though they might be less well informed in the technical aspects of food science.

Odor perceptions require that the aromatic compounds migrate to the region in the nose where the olfactory receptors are located. This means that they must be directed toward the superior (upper) region on both sides of the nasal septum. By sniffing a food or its headspace, by swallowing food (which creates a partial vacuum in the nasal cavity and subsequently draws air up into the nose from the oral cavity), and by deliberately exhaling sharply after food has been swallowed, it is possible to force volatile compounds to contact the olfactory receptors. The third technique of exhaling vigorously through the nose immediately after swallowing is particularly important in determination of **aftertaste.**

Taste Receptors

Approximately 10,000 taste buds, most of which are found in the tongue, are the avenue by which the taste of food is perceived. There are four basic tastes: salty, bitter, sweet, and sour. Nagodawithana (1994) suggested umami (L-glutamate and monosodium glutamate, amino acid-based substances [flavor enhancers]) is a fifth basic taste. These tastes are found in many foods in varying ratios and amounts, which ultimately are noted via the taste buds when food is eaten.

The individual taste buds are capable of noting more than one basic taste, although the greatest ability to detect sweetness is in the taste buds on the tip of the tongue; saltiness also is noted particularly clearly by the taste buds on the tip of the tongue. Sour is detected most readily on the sides of the tongue and bitterness at the back of the tongue (see Figure 3.1).

Taste buds are found in the papillae of the tongue. Two types of **papillae** contain taste buds. The mushroomlike **fungiform papillae** on the sides and tip of

Aftertaste
The aromatic message of the flavor impression that lingers after food has been swallowed.

Taste Buds
Tight clusters of gustatory and supportive cells encircling a pore, usually in the upper surface of the tongue; organs capable of detecting sweet, sour, salt, and/or bitter.

Papillae
Rough bulges or protuberances in the surface of the tongue, some of which contain taste buds.

Fungiform Papillae
Mushroomlike protuberances often containing taste buds and located on the sides and tip of the tongue.

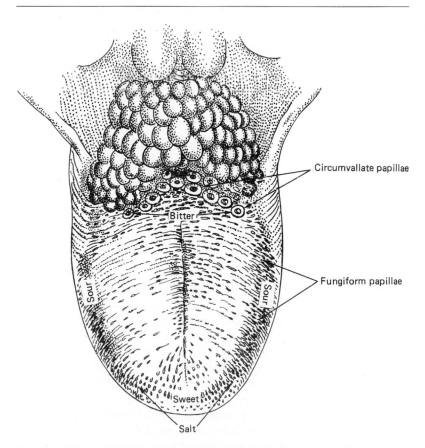

Figure 3.1   Diagram of the taste receptor region of the tongue.

Circumvallate papillae

Bitter

Fungiform papillae

Sour

Sour

Sweet

Salt

Circumvallate Papillae
Large, obvious protuberances always containing taste buds and distinguished easily because they form a "V" near the back of the tongue.

the tongue generally contain taste buds, and the **circumvallate papillae** (elevated, large papillae in the form of a "V" toward the back of the tongue) always contain taste buds. The taste buds on the tongue are of primary importance to adults in perceiving taste, but children have increased perceptions because of the additional taste buds they have in their cheeks, as well as in the hard and soft palates. These taste buds atrophy as children grow older.

Quick examination of the tongue shows that much of the tongue is smoother than the regions containing the fungiform and circumvallate papillae. Fine-structured filiform papillae predominate over much of the tongue, and this type of papilla does not contain taste buds. This lack of taste buds in the comparatively smooth area of the tongue makes it necessary to shift food around in the mouth so that all of the taste buds can be stimulated by the various compounds in the food. No stimulation can occur where the filiform papillae are found.

The taste message is initiated when a substance is dissolved on the tongue and comes into contact with the taste cell. The external shape of the receptor changes slightly with this contact. Potassium ions then escape from the cell, generating an electrical impulse to the brain. If many molecules are impinging on taste cells, the message will be relatively intense.

The ability to detect phenylthiourea is found in approximately 75 percent of the population, but the remaining quarter cannot detect this bitter compound. The ability is genetic in origin, providing evidence that some people are limited in their ability to serve as tasters. The bitter quality of phenylthiourea is attributed to the $-C = S$ moiety. This configuration also is found in cabbage and turnips.

$$| \\ N$$

The perception of a salty taste is deemed to be caused by ionization of inorganic salts, such as sodium, chloride. It is important to note that dry salt cannot be tasted, but when it is moistened by water or saliva, the taste is perceived. The other three tastes—sweet, sour, and bitter—also require solution of the compounds for perception.

Hydroxyl (−OH) groups are credited with contributing to the taste described as sweet. The various sugars, when dissolved in water, have different apparent levels of sweetness. In pure solutions, fructose is the sweetest of the sugars, followed in descending order by sucrose, glucose, and finally lactose. Some amino acids, alcohols, and aldehydes also are perceived as sweet.

Sour is the taste impression created by the presence of the hydrogen ions (H⁺). In the case of organic acids, the presence of the hydroxyl (−OH) group may modify the apparent sourness of a compound.

Threshold Level
Concentration of a taste compound at a barely detectable level.

Subthreshold Level
Concentration of a taste compound at a level that is not detectable, but is capable of influencing other taste perceptions.

The level at which a taste can be noted is designated as the **threshold level.** This level varies somewhat from individual to individual. Below threshold levels, however, various taste compounds still can have an influence on the overall perception of taste. This effect of **subthreshold levels** enables salt to increase the apparent sweetness of a sugar solution or to reduce the apparent sourness of an acid, with the effect on citric and acetic acids being less pronounced than that on tartaric and malic acids. Acid at subthreshold levels increases the apparent saltiness of sodium chloride. Sugar at subthreshold levels reduces saltiness, sourness, and bitterness.

Flavors in foods are extremely important in determining acceptability and quality. Perception of flavor in a specific food is determined by the combined action of the taste buds and the olfactory receptors of the diner. The importance of the use of

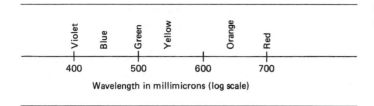

Figure 3.2   Wavelengths of colors in the visible spectrum.

the nose as well as the mouth in detecting flavors is evident when nasal passages are congested by a cold.

Visual Receptors

Some of the first cues a person receives about a food are about shape, texture, and color, messages that are received through the eyes. These pieces of information are possible because of the remarkable design of the eyes. For vision to occur, light must be refracted and the rays focused to give a sharp image. Actually, the image formed is an inverted one, but the brain enables the visual message to be inverted to the true physical orientation of the object. This is possible because of memory of objects gained from experience so that the inversion seemingly is automatic.

The **rods** contribute to the formation of visual messages by breaking down rhodopsin into its two components (retinene and scotopsin) when light impacts the rods. This breakdown sends an electrical message that is conducted by the rods to the bipolar neurons, then to the ganglion neurons, and finally to the optic nerve.

A similar situation is found in the **cones,** but the red, green, and blue pigments in the three types of cones require a much stronger light for the generation of an electrical charge than is necessary in the rods. Because of this difference, color can be seen only when the light is considerably brighter than moonlight. Fortunately, the three colors that are available in the three types of cones provide messages that become mixed to give the rainbow of color that is seen in foods (see Figure 3.2)

Rods
Elongated dendrites of photoreceptor neurons that transmit visual images in dim light, revealing movement and varying intensities of black and white.

Cones
Cone-shaped dendrites of photoreceptor neurons that enhance the sharpness of visual images and add the dimension of color to vision.

SENSORY CHARACTERISTICS OF FOOD

Foods have several characteristics that require evaluation by sensory methods in order to gain knowledge of the human perception of these foods. These attributes include flavor, texture, aroma, and appearance. The following sections introduce the various characteristics and probe the qualities to consider when judging them as a part of sensory evaluation.

Appearance

The appearance of a food can be evaluated on the basis of several subcategories. Perhaps the aspect of appearance that is often deemed the most critical in foods is color. Extensive use of food-coloring agents in commercial food products attests to the value placed on color appeal in foods.

In fact, color often triggers the mind to expect particular flavors. Commonly, people will expect a red-colored food to have a flavor of strawberries or other red fruit and will identify such a food as being strawberry even when it is something quite different in flavor. Because the color of food establishes expectations of the actual product, evaluation and control of color are important aspects of product development and production. Uniform, golden brown crusts generally are desired in baked products. The fact that microwaving fails to produce this color triggered the development of browning units in microwave ovens to offset this negative characteristic. Browning also is an important aspect of cooked meats. Expectations of richness in vanilla puddings are generated by a creamy color.

Although color can be measured objectively, this attribute is so important from the human standpoint that it should usually be included on scorecards for sensory evaluation. The reason for evaluating color by sensory methods is to obtain information on the desirability or acceptability of the food color in human terms, that is, the psychological importance of the color of the food.

Surface characteristics of food products also contribute to the appearance. A baked custard with a very wrinkled surface does not meet accepted standards for the product. Scrambled eggs with a very dry surface also would be rated as less acceptable than those with a suggestion of moistness. Fudge with a glossy surface is rated high, whereas a batch with a coarse, gritty appearance would be scored considerably lower. These are but a few examples of the surface characteristics of foods. Each food can be evaluated on the basis of the desirable surface features commonly understood to be signs of quality in the particular food item. In some products, the volume of the item will influence the evaluation of appearance. This clearly is true in the evaluation of a soufflé or cake.

In addition to exterior appearance, many products need to be evaluated on the basis of their interior appearance. Lumps in a pudding or gravy are visible to the eye, as well as obvious on the tongue. Cell size, uniformity of cells, and thickness of cell walls are all of interest in assessment of cake quality, and these are judged by appearance of the interior of the cake. The presence of layering in foam cakes and soufflés also is noted easily by checking the interior appearance. Often, interior appearance is judged most conveniently and accurately by cutting a clean slice with a sharp knife from the top to the bottom of the product.

Aroma

The odor or aroma of foods frequently is of considerable importance, particularly if the food ordinarily is served hot or warm. The acceptability of the aroma is important to the overall acceptability of the food. A pleasing aroma beckons people to sample the food, whereas a strong, irritating aroma discourages diners. Aroma, of course, is able to penetrate even beyond the visual range when comparatively volatile compounds are abundant, as is true in boiling cabbage, for example. The aroma of boiling cabbage often is quite identifiable in another room, even when the cabbage cannot be seen.

The volatility (and therefore the detectability) of aromas is related to the temperature of the food. High temperatures tend to volatilize aromatic compounds, making them quite apparent for judging; cool or cold temperatures inhibit volatilization. This latter observation is illustrated by considering the evaluation of the aroma of ice cream, a test that clearly would provide only limited information. Because aroma is so temperature related, it is important that aroma of foods be judged when they are at the temperature at which they ordinarily would be served and consumed.

Aroma can be evaluated by sniffing the food. It may be helpful to the judge to fan the air above the sample to direct the aromatic compounds toward the nose with the hand. In planning experiments, it is important to avoid competing aromas from different samples. The nose quickly becomes saturated with odors. Tasting booths or other areas where aroma is to be evaluated should be free of extraneous, competing aromas. Ordinarily, when evaluating aroma judges concentrate on acceptability, but in some experiments the relative strengths of aroma of the various samples may need to be determined.

Flavor

Flavor represents the composite assessment of taste and the blend of odor in the mouth. This is a very important attribute of a food and yet is difficult to communicate. Often the mechanism for evaluating flavor subjectively is simply the level of acceptability of the total flavor. Occasionally, the presence of an aftertaste may be of concern, as often is the case with saccharin-sweetened items. This aspect of flavor should be assessed as a separate entry on the scorecard rather than being encompassed within the single rating for flavor.

The apparent hotness or burning sensation from a highly seasoned food may be another characteristic related to flavor that is best assessed as a separate category on the scorecard. Some other products may require assessment of a particular component of the flavor, such as the comparative sweetness of samples.

The term *hot* is used in two ways in food evaluation. One definition refers to the physical temperature; the other refers to the burning sensation present in the mouth after a very spicy food, such as hot peppers, is eaten. Hot (spicy) foods may effectively mask subtle taste and odor evaluations.

The temperature at which a food is served may have a very important influence on the ability to detect taste and to evaluate flavor. The extremes, whether very hot or very cold, limit the ability of people to judge food accurately. The best temperature range for flavor evaluation is 20 to 30°C (68 to 86°F). However, this range may be inappropriate for evaluation if the food being judged is served at a temperature either above or below this range. Ice cream provides a clear example of the importance of evaluating a food at its serving temperature rather than at the temperature range ideal for detecting taste and flavor.

Intensity of flavors can be enhanced or diminished under certain circumstances. **Flavor potentiators** can be added to foods to enhance the flavor beyond the flavor of the potentiator itself. These potentiators, unlike typical spices, exert their action by enhancing the quality of other flavoring substances already present rather than adding their own distinctive flavor. **Monosodium glutamate** is a familiar example of a flavor potentiator. Some 5'-nucleotides (such as monophosphates of inosinic and guanylic acids) are used in meat and poultry products as flavor potentiators.

Flavor
Sensory message resulting from the combination of taste and aroma.

Flavor Potentiator
Compound that enhances the flavor of other compounds without adding its own unique flavor.

Monosodium Glutamate
Flavor potentiator; sodium salt of glutamic acid.

Inosine 5'-monophosphate

Monosodium glutamate

Flavor Inhibitor
Substance that blocks perception of a taste.

Flavor inhibitors are substances that appear to block the taste sites, thus preventing the normal taste response to a particular food. An example is the miracle fruit of Nigeria, a fruit capable of blocking the perception of sour. When sour perception is blocked in a fruit such as a lemon, the remaining taste is sweet.

Texture

Texture is an expansive term requiring careful definition to persons serving on a sensory panel and thoughtful inclusion in the scorecard. The textural qualities of a food have a relationship to the appearance of a product, as described previously, and to its evaluation in the mouth as well. Texture evaluation in the mouth relies on the **mouthfeel** of the food. The specific aspects that are to be evaluated sometimes need to be listed in separate categories on the scorecard, but often the item listed on the scorecard simply is mouthfeel. This is quite a general term and may lead to confusion unless each judge is informed of the specific aspect of mouthfeel that is to be evaluated. For instance, on a corn chip one judge might be evaluating crispness to obtain the score for mouthfeel while another judge may be reporting on tenderness unless a specific term is used.

Mouthfeel
Textural qualities of a food perceived in the mouth.

The various aspects of mouthfeel that can be noted in different types of foods include grittiness, slickness, stickiness, hardness, crispness, toughness, brittleness, pastiness, lightness, crunchiness, smoothness, viscosity, moistness, burning, cooling, astringency, spiciness, and tingling. Not all of these are appropriate for any single food, but they suggest characteristics to be considered when evaluating texture. Acceptable mouthfeel is vital to repeated consumption of food products and must be developed optimally for a product to be successful in today's competitive marketplace.

The tenderness of a number of items can be evaluated meaningfully by querying the judges regarding this textural feature. In baked products, tenderness may range from products so tender that they readily become nothing but crumbs to products so tough that they are extremely difficult to bite or chew. The researcher ordinarily seeks a product with optimal tenderness, neither too tender nor too tough. This information can be conveyed by using a guide provided on the scorecard. An alternative means of reporting tenderness is to ask the judges to report the **"number of chews."** The technique for this test is controlled by the individual judge. The judge is instructed to use a bite of controlled size for the "number of chews" test and to chew the sample in the same location in the mouth to exactly the same endpoint for each sample being tested. This number is recorded as the number of chews. Although different judges will have different numbers of chews because of differences in their tooth surface area for chewing, the relative scores of the various judges for the same samples should be consistent in their rank order. This test is done by judges, and hence suitably is viewed as a sensory evaluation device, but the mechanical nature of the chewing also makes it possible to view this as a somewhat objective testing method.

Number of Chews
Subjective test in which a judge chews similar bites of food to the same endpoint and records the actual number of chews required to reach that point for each sample.

SENSORY PANELS

Classes in experimental foods will usually employ two very different formats for sensory evaluation. The laboratory experiments conducted by the entire class offer each student the opportunity to evaluate all of the products prepared by the class so that the study of scientific principles in food is reinforced by the laboratory examples. The second type of evaluation is that done by a sensory panel to evaluate the products prepared in individual research projects, which often are conducted as part of a course in experimental foods. This latter type of evaluation is similar in nature to that done by the food industry in research and product development.

Selecting Panel Members

Panel member selection should be based on the factors identified as important for the specific study. Laboratory research frequently requires careful discrimination in evaluation of products. The ability to detect the differences is essential if a panel member is to make meaningful contributions to the project. Preliminary testing to ascertain that potential panel members can discriminate on key aspects of the testing permits selection of a panel that is physically qualified to serve. This is important for tests requiring sharp discrimination about characteristics of samples.

Laboratory testing often extends over a period of weeks or months, which dictates that the personnel ordinarily will be regular employees of the company so that they will be available for the tests when needed. From this potential pool, the actual panelists are chosen. Interest in participation on the panel is necessary to ensure that panelists meet their obligations as panel members. The health of the potential panelist is important because of the need to have the panelist available on a regular and continuing basis for tests. Clarity of the nasal passages also is necessary for flavor and aroma assessment. Persons with chronic sinus conditions or colds may be poor panelists because of their physical inability to perceive flavors. These physical qualifications are more important for serving on a panel than is depth of education in food science, although such knowledge is an asset.

Quite the opposite situation exists when a food company wishes to obtain information about consumer acceptance of a product that is about ready to enter test marketing. Consumers who happen to be available at the testing site and who are willing to answer a few questions about the samples on the day of the testing usually constitute the panel for this type of testing.

Panelists can be screened based on a company's criteria, e.g., demographics or potential use of product. Typically, **consumer panels** may range from 200 to 500 people, which is far larger than the panels used in research laboratories. The types of questions asked of consumer panels (acceptability or preference) can be answered by untrained panelists.

Consumer Panel
Sensory evaluation panel selected from people who happen to be available at a test site and are willing to participate.

Training Panelists

Panels may be of two types: **untrained** and **trained.** The untrained panel is one in which the participants have had no preparation regarding evaluation of the product. Consumer panels often are untrained panels.

The training of panelists for laboratory testing varies with the complexity of the testing. As an absolute minimum, each judge should be briefed prior to the actual collection of data; the researcher should review the scorecard with the judge, clarify any questions, and ask the judge to explain orally to the researcher what is being represented by the score the judge assigns for each response. This verbalization regarding the meanings of the scorecard enables the researcher to identify differences in the interpretation of terms between the various judges. When differ-

Untrained Panel
Sensory evaluation panel that has not been trained specifically regarding the product evaluation being undertaken in the study.

Trained Panel
Sensory evaluation panel that has been given thorough training regarding the use of the scorecard and the evaluation of the various characteristics included in the evaluation.

ences exist, the scorecard may require modification, but sometimes additional explanation to the judges may be sufficient.

Another technique that sometimes is effective is to have the entire panel discuss the product and the scorecard together the first time they evaluate the samples. The goal of this aspect of training is to ensure that all judges use the scorecard according to the same word definitions. Unless adequate work is done with the panel at this stage, experimental error often is introduced because of the differences in interpretation of the meaning of terms on the scorecard, differences that are caused by the judges at some times and at others by the researcher, whose familiarity with the project may cause interpretations of the scorecard that were not intended by the judges.

Another aspect of panel training is instructing members regarding sampling techniques. A common technique is for panel members to rinse their mouths with the room-temperature water provided before they taste the samples. Samples can be spit out into a disposable cup when this seems advisable and appropriate. Samples should be tested in the sequence in which they are presented to the panelist. Ordinarily, judges are not informed of the variable(s) being tested. Every attempt should be made to avoid biasing the judges by giving them information regarding the purpose of the experiment. Such an explanation is not appropriately part of the panel training process.

Descriptive Flavor Analysis Panel (DFAP)
Thoroughly trained panel that works as a team to precisely describe in words the flavor of a sample.

Some food companies form a **Descriptive Flavor Analysis Panel (DFAP)** which is trained to analyze flavor in extremely great detail (see Figure 3.3). This type of panel evolved from the original work, the flavor profile method, developed

Figure 3.3 Descriptive flavor analysis panel tastes a variety of commercial and formulated spaghetti sauces. Before conducting a sensory analysis on sauce enhanced with Provesta Flavor Enhancers, the panel must be fully oriented to the flavors found in typical spaghetti sauces. (Courtesy of Provesta Corporation.)

by Arthur D. Little Company in 1950. These panelists need to be selected on the basis of their communication skills, as well as their knowledge of food and food processing. Flavor profile panelists should be neither extremely weak nor overly powerful individuals. A forceful or retiring personality modifies the interactions of the group. Profiling requires honest and straightforward comments throughout the evaluation process. Unlike other types of panels (where communication between judges does not occur after the training period), profile panelists continually interact to assess and verify their determinations of quality. The great amount of time involved in training flavor profile panelists and in their evaluation sessions underlines the importance of having committed and permanent employees as panelists. Training of panelists for a DFAP requires at least 9 weeks of intensive work to develop the consistency of ratings required to score products accurately and consistently. As much as $4\frac{1}{2}$ months may be involved in training for certain panels.

Quantitative descriptive analysis (QDA) is yet another method in which a highly trained panel interacts under the leadership of one person to very precisely describe the many characteristics of a product and then to quantify (usually using a linear scale) the intensity of the various characteristics being assessed. Such analysis requires a great deal of work over an extended period, yet it is useful during product development of commercial products.

Quantitative Descriptive Analysis
Development of a thorough description of characteristics of a product and a quantification of their intensity.

ENVIRONMENT FOR SENSORY EVALUATION

With the exception of the profile panels, trained judges ideally will not have an opportunity to interact with each other. This situation is optimized by using individual booths (see Figure 3.4). These are fairly compact compartments with a space for the samples to be placed and for the scoring to be done. Suitable side partitions

(a)

(b)

Figure 3.4   Sensory evaluation booths for in-house taste panels: (a) researcher's view, (b) panelist's booth. (Courtesy of Plycon Press.)

prevent eye contact or exchange between judges. The temperature should be comfortable and the air free of odors other than those from the samples. Smoking should not be permitted in the area. The booths will have small sinks for spitting out samples, and the light will be appropriate for the samples being tested. Appropriate light may mean a colored light, usually red, to obscure food color if the color is anticipated to bias the judges—for example, the evaluation of meats cooked to varying degrees of doneness. The varying colors of the samples would bias the judges' decisions unless red light were used to mask the color differences between samples.

When individual booths are not available, judges can be seated in quiet surroundings and preferably in different parts of the room to ensure no interaction. If at all possible, the judges should conduct their evaluations away from all other people. Concentration is necessary for a quality performance in food evaluation.

The American Society for Testing and Materials issued guidelines for the physical requirements of a laboratory designed for sensory evaluation of food (ASTM, 1986). Positive air pressure, filtered air, and controlled temperature and lighting are some of the key aspects of the guidelines. Samples for evaluation should be prepared far enough away from the testing area to avoid any possible cooking aromas in the tasting area.

SAMPLE PREPARATION AND PRESENTATION

An important aspect of planning an experiment is developing the evaluation devices. Included in this planning is the need to know how the sampling of the products will be done, both for sensory and for objective testing. Careful thought needs to be directed toward anticipating all factors that could modify judgment of the samples. For instance, it is necessary not only to decide on the size of the piece of cake to be given to a judge, but also to identify the specific location from which each individual judge's piece will be removed. Reliable data cannot be collected for sensory evaluation if the edge of a cake is used one time and the center is used another time. Consistency from day to day is vital to the successful conduct of experiments. For many products, a template should be developed to serve as a guide in the preparation and distribution of the samples for the judges and also for the objective tests. Using templates reduces the likelihood of variability in the samples used for evaluating each run. Sample size need not be large. A liquid sample of 15 milliliters or a solid of about 30 grams often is enough for panelists.

Plans for sampling must include directions for heating or chilling samples that require this type of control. In a busy laboratory, chilling may prove to be a particular problem because of the frequent opening of refrigerators.

Judges should be given samples that are carefully marked with a symbol that does not connote ratings or quality, for example, a random number lacking meaning (667) or a letter in the middle or end of the alphabet. Use of A, B, C or 1, 2, 3 is not recommended because of the possible influence on judges. Symbols are rotated among samples at each session to eliminate bias. A wax pencil can be used to mark the sample plates with the appropriate identifying symbol. The necessary silverware, a glass of water at room temperature, and a scorecard with a pencil should be placed, along with the appropriately labeled samples, in the scoring area.

TYPES OF TESTS

Overall types of sensory evaluation include (1) **descriptive,** (2) **preference,** and (3) **difference testing.** Descriptive tests enable researchers to characterize their products through selective, critical scoring of specific attributes of each sample. Preference testing is valuable in developing new food products and in evaluating quality. Difference testing can be used to test the sensitivity of judges, as well as to perform such a practical function as determining whether or not a food company should buy an inexpensive ingredient to replace a more expensive one in formulating a food product. Researchers need to define the information desired before deciding on the type of test(s) to be conducted.

Single Sample

Particularly in the early stages of product development, presenting a **single sample** can be valuable in helping to define the direction in which the project should move. This type of test can be designed to test acceptability. The advantage of this method is the ease of conducting the test.

Difference Testing

Paired Comparison. The **paired comparison** is a test of difference in which a specific characteristic is designated. The judge is asked to test the two samples presented to identify the sample with the greater amount of the characteristic being measured. The judge has a 50 percent chance of being right by chance alone in paired comparison testing (see Figure 3.5).

Duo–Trio Test. The duo–trio test is another test of difference. In this test, the control sample is presented first; it is followed by two other samples, one of which is the same as the control. The judge is requested to identify which of the last two samples is different from the control. Again, there is a 50 percent chance of being right by chance alone in a duo–trio test (see Figure 3.6).

Triangle Test. As in the duo–trio test, three samples are given, but in the triangle test all three samples are presented simultaneously. The judge must identify the odd sample. Note that in the triangle test also, two samples are alike; however, the difference in the method of presentation reduces the chance of guessing the right answer to 33.3 percent. The triangle test is designed to determine difference (see Figure 3.7).

Descriptive Testing
Sensory testing designed to provide information on selected characteristics of food samples.

Preference Testing
Sensory testing to determine acceptability or preference between products.

Difference Testing
Sensory testing designed to determine whether detectable differences exist between products.

Single Sample
Presenting one sample early in an experimental project to determine acceptability and to aid in the decision on future development of the product.

Paired Comparison
Difference test in which a specific characteristic is to be evaluated in two samples, and the sample with the greater level of that characteristic is to be identified.

Duo–Trio Test
Difference test in which two samples are judged against a control to determine which of the two samples is different from the control.

Triangle Test
Difference test in which three samples (two of which are the same) are presented, and the odd sample is to be identified.

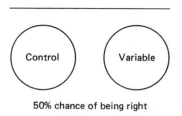

50% chance of being right

Figure 3.5   Diagram for presentation of a paired comparison test.

Figure 3.6 Diagrams for two possible presentations of a duo-trio test.

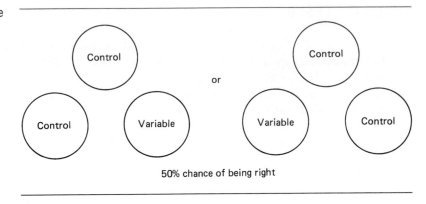

50% chance of being right

Figure 3.7 Diagrams for possible presentations of a triangle test.

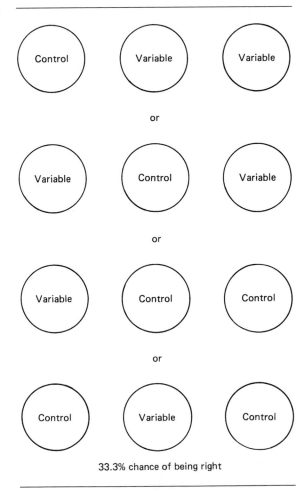

33.3% chance of being right

Figure 3.8 Sensory panelist conducts a preference test on three experimental food products. This preference test is used to determine the rank order of preference. (Courtesy of Provesta Corporation.)

Rank Order. This test is valuable when several samples need to be evaluated for a single characteristic. In this type of difference or preference testing, the samples are simply ranked in the order of intensity of the characteristic being measured (see Figure 3.8).

Descriptive Testing

Although difference testing detects deviations between samples and preference testing provides information about acceptability of samples, descriptive information is a dimension of food samples that is not available with the other two forms of testing. Words describing the various sensory attributes of food samples are essential to the success of this type of evaluation (Civille and Lawless, 1986), and yet the precise vocabulary to convey sensory perceptions is difficult to identify. For example, even such a familiar food as an onion is frustratingly hard to characterize in words that accurately convey such sensory characteristics as aroma, flavor, and texture.

Descriptive testing usually is conducted by using a scorecard containing very careful word descriptions that structure the form of responses by judges. Each of

Rank Order
Preference or difference test in which all samples are ranked in order of intensity of a specific characteristic.

Descriptive Testing
Using descriptive words in sensory evaluation to characterize food samples.

the characteristics of a sample to be evaluated by the judges is described over a range, and the judge selects the specific description matching the sample for each item on the scorecard. The responsibility for selecting the appropriate vocabulary to elicit an accurate picture of the samples rests with the researcher who developed the scorecard, but a well-constructed scorecard will give the desired information.

In another approach to descriptive testing, a group of highly trained panelists work together to develop the vocabulary needed to describe food samples specifically. Unlike the first method in which judges evaluate individually, the whole panel arrives at a single description in this second method, called profiling.

Profiling

Profiling
Very detailed word description (usually of flavor) developed by a highly trained panel against which subsequent production is evaluated to maintain quality of production; other research objectives also can be served by the use of profiling.

Descriptive Flavor Analysis Panel (DFAP) work is done through a cooperative, detailed analysis of the flavor of each of the samples. Very careful selection and training of the panel members is essential to assure a panel that consistently develops accurate word profiles of the specific products that are being studied. Together, they work to describe, in character and intensity, the varied components of the flavors. The outcome is a word portrait of the flavor of the food being tested (Rutledge and Hudson, 1990). This type of testing is used as one means of maintaining exact flavor quality over long production periods so that one year's product will have the same flavor as the subsequent year's output.

Several food researchers have developed techniques and language for evaluating texture by **profiling** (Bourne, 1978; Muñoz, 1986; Szczesniak, Loew, and Skinner, 1975). The great diversity in textual properties makes this aspect of sensory evaluation quite complex. Among the qualities that a texture profiling panel might consider are chewiness, cohesiveness, adhesiveness (to the palate, hands, and lips), moistness or wetness, denseness, gumminess, fracturability, hardness, mouth coating, flakiness, fibrousness, and viscosity. Texture profiling can be done in considerable detail by a trained panel (Rutledge, 1992), just as is true for flavor profiling.

PREFERENCE AND ACCEPTABILITY

The preferences and attitudes of consumers toward food products are vital to success in the marketplace. Therefore, consumer panels often are used to indicate preference of one sample over another. A specific quality (sweetness, for example) can be identified on the scorecard, and the judge then rates preference for one of the samples. Hedonic rating scales can be used to measure the degree of pleasure experienced with each sample. Sometimes the motivation regarding frequency that a judge might desire to eat the sample is measured as an approach to determining the acceptability of the various samples.

SCORECARDS

Designing scorecards for sensory evaluation is challenging and difficult because the key characteristics of the product need to be evaluated on paper in a way that permits the judges to transmit their assessments of the samples accurately to the re-

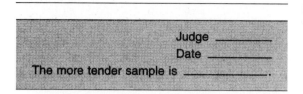

Figure 3.9 Scorecard for paired comparison test.

searcher. A scorecard with too much detail and clutter may discourage careful judgment; too brief a form may fail to obtain some important information.

No single scorecard fits all experiments. Instead, the scorecard needs to be developed for the specific experiment. All scorecards should contain the date and the name of the judge. The researcher should write this information on the sheets before the judging. This avoids the possible problem of a judge forgetting to identify the sheet. It is important to be able to identify the sheets in both of these ways. Sometimes a data point from a sheet may be relatively remote from the other comparable data points, and the identification of the sheets permits the researcher to check back into the laboratory notebook and the notes taken that day to see whether some unusual circumstance might explain that particular rating and add some insight into the validity of the data point in question.

Scorecards for difference testing are the simplest to construct. Figure 3.9 is an example appropriate for use in a paired comparison. The scorecards for the duo–trio test and the triangle test are similar, because they both involve three samples, but the mode of presentation leads to use of slightly different scorecards (Figures 3.10 and 3.11).

It is in the **descriptive scale** that development of the scorecard becomes a critical part of the planning for an experiment. These scorecards occasionally are designed to include careful descriptions of each characteristic to be evaluated (Figure 3.12). These word descriptions are quite cumbersome to place in a scorecard, but they do serve as useful guides to the scoring of the product.

Descriptive scorecards can be structured so that numerical scores can be derived, which enables statistical analysis to be applied to the data. Figure 3.13 is an example of a scorecard that provides descriptive words in a logical progression for some characteristic that is to be evaluated by the judge. The characteristics included in Figure 3.13 are only some of those that probably should be incorporated in a comprehensive evaluation of a muffin. However, the ones listed illustrate the way in which a sequence of descriptive words can be developed. Note that the researcher could easily assign numbers in sequence to each of the scales (e.g., very pale = 1; slightly pale = 2; golden brown = 3; slightly too dark = 4; and burned

Descriptive Scale
Array of words describing a range of intensity of a single characteristic, with each step on the scale representing a subtle degree of intensity.

Figure 3.10 Scorecard for duo–trio test.

Figure 3.11 Scorecard for triangle test.

Judge _____
Date _____

Two of these samples are the same, and one is different. The different sample is

_____.

What was different about this sample?

= 5). Thus, the judges' scores would be recorded as the appropriate numbers, rather than words. The numbers can then be used for analysis, and ultimately the words on the scorecard that appropriately describe the numerical results can be added to the discussion of results.

Rating scales are ordinarily designed with an odd number of points, usually 5 or 9. A 5-point scale is convenient, but some judges feel that such a limited scale restricts their ability to communicate fine levels of difference to the researcher. In contrast, the smaller range represented by each score on a 9-point scale permits finer distinctions to be noted.

A common problem in the construction of a scorecard is illustrated in Figure 3.14. Note that in the categories of crust color, interior color, contour of surface, thickness of cell walls, cell size, and flavor the optimal score is 3; however, in the scoring of aftertaste, the optimal score is 1. This arrangement can be used, but

Name _____			
Date _____			
Characteristic	Descriptive Rating (circle the term that best applies to each characteristic)		
Color of surface	Pale	Slightly brown	Pleasing golden brown	Very dark brown
Tenderness	Extremely crumbly	Somewhat crumbly	Easily broken, slightly crumbly	Tough, little tendency to crumble
Texture	Heavy, thick cell walls	Slightly heavy, medium-thick cell walls	Somewhat coarse cell size, but relatively uniform	Tunneling toward top, fine cells be-tween tunnels
Flavor	Aftertaste	Very slight aftertaste	Pleasing, no aftertaste	Burned

Figure 3.12 Descriptive scorecard for rating muffins.

Characteristics of muffins
(Circle your choice for each)

Judge _____
Date _____
Sample _____

Crust color

| Very pale | Slightly pale | Golden brown | Slightly too dark | Burned |

Contour of surface

| Sunken | Flat | Gently rounded | Somewhat pointed | Pointed |

Interior color

| Stark white | White | Creamy | Somewhat yellow | Yellow |

Figure 3.13 Descriptive scorecard illustrating logical progressions suitable for numerical interpretation of data.

Scorecard	Judge _____ Date _____		
	Sample		
Characteristic	517	727	464
Crust color 1 = pale; 3 = golden brown; 5 = burned			
Contour of surface 1 = flat; 3 = rounded; 5 = pointed			
Interior color 1 = white; 3 = creamy; 5 = yellow			
Thickness of cell walls 1 = very thick; 3 = normal; 5 = too thin			
Cell size 1 = small; 3 = moderate; 5 = large			
Flavor 1 = unsweet; 3 = pleasing; 5 = too sweet			
Aftertaste 1 = none; 3 = slight; 5 = distinct			

Figure 3.14 Detailed scorecard for evaluating muffins with various sweeteners.

judges should be cautioned to note carefully that the scoring to be used in the last category deviates from the established pattern. The researcher, in handling the data and writing the project report, will need to keep the difference in the meaning of the numbers in this category firmly in mind and will need to reinforce this for the reader of the report.

When the goal of an experiment is to identify significant changes resulting from such variations as use of different ratios of an ingredient or different ingredients, specific information may be needed from the judges. These scorecards require considerable thought regarding the characteristics that may be important in the testing and the way in which these characteristics will be recorded. Many variations of such scorecards can be made. The scorecard presented in Figure 3.14 is but one suggested approach to this evaluation problem.

Preferably, the items included for evaluation on a scorecard should be arranged in the same sequence in which they logically will be evaluated. Noninvasive tests (aroma, exterior color, and other external characteristics that may be included in the scoring) should be placed at the beginning of the list, as has been illustrated in Figure 3.14. This ensures that the judge will have the sample intact so that these characteristics can be evaluated. On the interior of the sample, physical characteristics that can be assessed visually (color of crumb and other characteristics that can be evaluated without eating) are the next items listed. The last items are such characteristics as mouthfeel, which can be evaluated only by placing a bite of the sample in the mouth. This arrangement permits an orderly evaluation of the sample as the judge simply works straight down the scorecard. Without this organization of the card, judges need to skip around the card to test the various items and may discover that they do not have an appropriate sample left to score certain items.

Each item on a scorecard needs to be worded specifically so that only one quality is to be scored. For instance, cell size and uniformity could not be listed as a single entry on a scorecard. Two separate entries would be needed if both cell size and cell uniformity were to be evaluated.

The design of the scorecard in Figure 3.13 makes it necessary to give separate scorecards for each sample; each card must have the random number or symbol of the sample clearly marked, and the appropriate scorecard should be placed with its corresponding sample. Figure 3.14 provides information similar to that obtained using the format of Figure 3.13, but judges can mark their scores for the three samples in the columns provided. In this case, judges will need to be instructed that a score of 2 may be assigned for a product that falls between 1 and 3 (or 4 for one between 3 and 5).

The scorecard in Figure 3.14 can be strengthened considerably by modifying the scale to move the optimum score to 5 on a 9-point scale, as shown in Figure 3.15. The expansion of the scale provides the opportunity for finer distinctions between items such as crust color in which the optimum score is 3 when the scale is restricted to only 5 possible scores, as the case in Figure 3.14. Note that one of the scales in Figure 3.15 ends at 5, rather than continuing to 9. This is the case for the category of "aftertaste," because the scale cannot be extended beyond the ultimate, which needs to be the optimum value of 5. For scorecards dealing with different products, other categories may need to be handled in this same fashion.

When constructing the rating scale for a consumer scorecard, it is important to decide whether (1) a specific description of the characteristics or (2) acceptability is the information needed. For instance, judges might be asked to rate the sweetness

Muffin scorecard[a]	Sample		
Characteristic	517	727	464
Crust color 1 = much too pale; 3 = somewhat too pale; 5 = pleasing golden brown; 7 = somewhat too brown; 9 = much too brown			
Contour of surface 1 = absolutely flat; 3 = somewhat rounded; 5 = pleasingly rounded; 7 = somewhat pointed; 9 = very pointed			
Interior color 1 = much too white; 3 = somewhat white; 5 = pleasingly creamy; 7 = somewhat too yellow; 9 = much too yellow			
Thickness of cell walls 1 = extremely thick; 3 = somewhat too thick; 5 = normal thickness; 7 = somewhat too thin; 9 = much too thin			
Cell size 1 = much too small; 3 = somewhat too small; 5 = moderate; 7 = somewhat too large; 9 = much too large			
Flavor 1 = absolutely not sweet enough; 3 = not nearly sweet enough; 5 = pleasingly sweet; 7 = somewhat too sweet; 9 = much too sweet			
Aftertaste 1 = extremely distinct; 3 = somewhat distinct; 5 = none			

Judge _____ Date _____

[a] You may also use numbers 2, 4, 6, and 8. These values are considered to be midway between the preceding and subsequent descriptions.

Figure 3.15 Modified form of Figure 3.14.

of samples; even if they all agree that the same sample is the sweetest, the researcher has no way of knowing whether the sweetest sample pleased the judges the most. Since satisfaction with a food product is important to maintaining repeat sales over time, researchers developing new products must be concerned with the hedonic ratings, not just the descriptive scores.

Name _____
Date _____

Characteristic	Sample		
	517	727	464
Color of surface			
Tenderness			
Texture			
Flavor			

Scale: 1 = Like extremely
      2 = Like very much
      3 = Like moderately
      4 = Like slightly
      5 = Neither like nor dislike
      6 = Dislike slightly
      7 = Dislike moderately
      8 = Dislike very much
      9 = Dislike extremely

Figure 3.16 Scorecard for muffins utilizing hedonic ratings.

Hedonic Scale
Pleasure scale for rating food characteristics.

A table utilizing the **hedonic ratings** ranging from unacceptable to very acceptable is relatively easy to construct and is effective when the desirable and undesirable characteristics of a few samples are sought in an experiment. Figure 3.16 is an example of this type of table; note the use of numerical ratings.

In some testing situations, a picture on the scorecard may prove to be worth quite a few, if not a thousand, words. If the researcher is working with young children, with people who cannot read well, or with people who have very limited use of the English language, a picture scale can prove invaluable in communicating the level of pleasure the food brings to the panelist. Such a scorecard will have simple drawings of a face, with the expression being altered very slightly from one picture to the next to create a picture rating scale. On such a scorecard, the pictures range from a very smiling face to a very deeply frowning face, preferably with a total of nine drawings. The center part of the scale has a face with the

Judge _____ Date _____
Age _____ Sex __ F __ M Food item _____
Directions: Put an x in the box ☐ to show how much you like this food.

Figure 3.17 Scorecard using the "Smiley" scale.

mouth in a straight line, which depicts neither pleasure nor displeasure. Because of the smiling faces, this type of scale is dubbed the **"Smiley" scale** (Figure 3.17).

SUMMARY

Sensory evaluation is a critical part of food experimentation because it is the means of determining how people, the consumers, will react to a food. Such information is needed in basic research and in the food industry. Sensory evaluation encompasses use of all of the senses as they come into contact with the food being evaluated. Visual evaluation includes judgments on color, as well as on contour and texture. The olfactory sense is utilized in evaluating the aroma of the food, and it also contributes to the overall perception of flavor. The taste buds are a significant aspect of flavor evaluation because of their ability to identify sour, sweet, salt, and bitter taste components of flavor. Tactile evaluation is of importance and generally is identified as mouthfeel. Even auditory cues may be a part of food evaluation. Crispness is a textural characteristic with both tactile and auditory stimuli.

Sensory evaluation may be conducted to determine differences between food items. Familiar examples of difference testing are duo- trio and triangle tests. Often it is desirable to determine preference and also to obtain specific information about food samples. Preference and descriptive testing can be done by scoring utilizing a prepared scorecard. Examples of scorecards are presented in this chapter, but each experiment should be evaluated by developing a scorecard specifically designed to procure the evaluation information needed. Ranking of food samples is yet another type of evaluation that may be of considerable help in the food industry. The most sophisticated type of sensory evaluation is the profiling method, a technique that is used in flavor identification and that relies on the services of a very highly trained panel.

STUDY QUESTIONS

1. Why is sensory evaluation of importance in the food industry?
2. Describe the structures involved in (a) color perception, (b) taste perception, and (c) odor detection.
3. Explain the interaction between taste and odor in the perception of flavor.
4. What is the difference between a duo–trio test and a triangle test? How is each conducted?
5. Describe the environment for conducting sensory evaluation in the laboratory.
6. Outline the process by which you would select and train a taste panel.
7. Design a scorecard for an experiment you might conduct in the laboratory.

BIBLIOGRAPHY

Amerine, M. A., Pangborn, R. M., and Roessler, E. B. 1965. *Principles of Sensory Evaluation of Food.* Academic Press: New York.

Amoore, J. E. 1967. "Stereochemical theory of olfaction." In *Chemistry and Physiology of Flavors.* Schultz, H. W., ed. AVI Publishing: Westport, CT. p. 119.

"Smiley" Scale
Sequential series of very happy and continuing through to very unhappy faces used in evaluating food products when respondents are unable to use the language easily.

ASTM. 1979. "Manual on consumer sensory evaluation." ASTM Spec. Tech. Publ. 682. Amer. Soc. Testing Materials: Philadelphia.

ASTM. 1981. "Guidelines for selection and training of panelists." ASTM Spec. Tech. Publ. 758. Amer. Soc. Testing Materials: Philadelphia.

ASTM. 1986. "Physical Requirement guidelines for sensory evaluation laboratories." STP 913, eds. J. Eggert and K. Zook. Comm E-18. Amer. Soc. Testing Materials: Philadelphia.

ASTM. 1988. "Standard practice for establishing conditions for laboratory sensory evaluation of foods and beverages. E480-84. In *ASTM Standards on Sensory Evaluation of Materials and Products,* Comm E-18. Amer. Soc. Testing Materials: Philadelphia.

Beauchamp, G. K. 1990. "Research in chemosensation related to flavor and fragrance perception." *Food Technol. 44* (1): 98.

Bett, K. L. 1993. "Measuring sensory properties of meat in the laboratory." *Food Technol. 47* (11): 121.

Billmeyer, B. A. and Wyman, G. 1991. "Computerized sensory evaluation system." *Food Technol. 45* (7): 100.

Boudreau, J. C. 1986. Neurophysiology and human taste sensations." *Food Technol. 40* (11): 66.

Bourne, M. C. 1978. "Texture profile analysis." *Food Technol. 32* (7): 62.

Chambers, E. 1990. "Sensory analysis—dynamic research for today's products." *Food Technol. 44* (1): 92.

Chambers, E. and Bowers, J. R. 1993. "Consumer perception of sensory qualities in muscle foods." *Food Technol. 47* (11): 116.

Civille, G. V. and Lawless, H. T. 1986. "Importance of language in describing perceptions." *Food Technol. 40* (11): 67.

Dravnieks, A. 1967. "Theories of olfaction." In *Chemistry and Physiology of Flavors,* Shultz, H. W., ed. AVI Publishing: Westport, CT. p. 95.

Dravnieks, A. Compilers. 1985. *Atlas of Odor Character Profiles.* American Society for Testing and Materials: Philadelphia.

Ennis, D. M. 1990. "Relative power of difference testing methods in sensory evaluation." *Food Technol. 44* (4): 114.

Ennis, D. M. 1998. Foundations of sensory science and a vision for the future. *Food Technol. 52* (7). 78.

Farbman, A. I. 1967. "Structure of chemoreceptors." In *Chemistry and Physiology of Flavors,* Schultz, H. W., ed. AVI Publishing: Westport, CT, p. 25.

Galvin, J. R. and Waldrop, H. L., Jr. 1990. "Future of sensory evaluation in the food industry." *Food Technol. 44* (1): 95.

Goldman, A. 1994. "Predicting product performance in the marketplace by immediate- and extended-use sensory testing." *Food Technol. 48* (10): 103.

Jellinek, G. 1985. *Sensory Evaluation of Food: Theory and Practice.* VCH Publishers: Deerfield Beach, FL.

Karahadian, C. 1995. "Impact of global markets on sensory testing programs." *Food Technol. 49* (2): 77.

Kimmel, S. A., Sigman-Grant, M., and Guinard, J. X. 1994. "Sensory testing with young children." *Food Technol. 48* (3): 92.

Kroll, B. J. 1990. "Evaluating rating scales for sensory testing with children." *Food Technol. 44* (11): 78.

Lawless, H. T. 1986. "Sensory interactions in mixtures." *Food Technol. 40* (11): 69.

Lee, W. E. III and Pangborn, R. M. 1986. "Time-intensity: temporal aspects of sensory perception." *Food Technol. 40* (11): 71.

Mega, J. A. 1983. "Flavor potentiators," *CRC Crit. Rev. Food Sci. Nutr. 18:* 231.

Meilgaard, M. M., Civille, G. V., and Carr, B. T. 1987a. *Sensory Evaluation Techniques,* Vol. I. CRC Press: Boca Raton, FL.

Meilgaard, M. M., Civille, G. V., and Carr, B. T. 1987b. *Sensory Evaluation Techniques,* Vol. II. CRC Press: Boca Raton, FL.

Muñoz, A. M., 1986. "Development and application of texture reference scales." *J. Sensory Studies 1:* 55.

Nagodawithana, T. 1994. "Flavor enhancers: their probable mode of action." *Food Technol. 48* (4): 79.

Newsome, R. L., ed. 1986. "Food colors." *Food Technol. 40* (7): 49.

Noble, A. C., et al. 1991. Factors affecting the time-intensity parameters of sweeteners. *Food Technol. 45* (11): 121.

O'Mahony, M. 1986. "Fatigue and adaptation effects." *Food Technol. 40* (11): 67.

O'Mahony, M. 1995. "Sensory measurement in food science: fitting methods to goals." *Food Technol. 49* (4): 72.

Rainey, B. 1986. "Importance of reference standards in training panelists." *J. Sensory Studies 1:* 149.

Riskey, D. R. 1986. "Uses and abuses of category scales in sensory measurement." *Food Technol. 40* (11): 68.

Rutledge, K. P. 1992. "Accelerated training of sensory descriptive flavor analysis panelists." *Food Technol. 46* (11): 114.

Rutledge, K. P. and Hudson, J. M. 1990. "Sensory evaluation: method for establishing and training a descriptive flavor analysis panel." *Food Technol. 44* (12): 78.

Shallenberger, R. S. 1998. Sweetness theory and its application in the food industry. *Food Technol. 52* (7): 72.

Stone, H., et al. 1974. Sensory evaluation by quantitative descriptive analysis. *Food Technol. 28* (1): 24.

Stone, H., McDermott, B. J., and Sidel, J. L. 1991. "Importance of sensory analysis for evaluation of quality." *Food Technol. 45* (6): 88.

Stone, H. and Sidel, J. L. 1985. *Sensory Evaluation Practices.* Academic Press: Orlando, FL.

Szczesniak, A. S. 1990. "Texture: is it still an overlooked food attribute?" *Food Technol. 44* (9): 86.

Szczesniak, A. S., Loew, B. J., and Skinner, E. Z. 1975. "Consumer texture profile technique." *J. Food Sci. 40:* 1253.

Teranishi, R., Issenberg, P., Hornstein, I. and Wick, E. L. 1971. *Flavor Research.* Marcel Dekker: New York.

CHAPTER 4

Objective Evaluation

Sensory evaluation, because of its reliance on human panelists, gives important but sometimes variable results during the course of the experiment. Variability of sensory evaluation is reduced by careful screening prior to training and use of large numbers of participants for consumer panels, both of which are costly. The objective data that can be obtained in the laboratory can be correlated with sensory data as a cost-effective and rapid means of obtaining the needed information and reliability important for research and development.

Objective testing is conducted utilizing equipment of varying degrees of sophistication. The goal of this type of testing is to obtain highly reliable data on the food characteristics that are amenable to physical testing. Quantifiable results are of great significance in food research. Such attributes of a food as rheological properties, tenderness, and volume frequently are measured by objective means. These data supplement and, in some instances, reinforce the data obtained subjectively though sensory evaluation. By utilizing the information obtained from sensory and objective testing, the maximum knowledge can be derived from the experiment.

GENERAL GUIDELINES

Objective testing provides data that have the potential to give researchers a false feeling of security. When numerical values can be read from a testing device, these numbers assume an authenticity that may or may not be warranted. Once the figures are recorded in a laboratory notebook, reasons for questioning their validity may vanish. The good researcher is always on guard against the acquisition of false data. Constant vigilance regarding maintenance and operation of the machines and the preparation of samples for testing must be maintained.

Some of the basic guidelines for objective testing are reviewed below:

1. *Conduct all objective tests appropriate to the experiment for which equipment is available.*
   Even when a sensory measurement is being made on an attribute such as tenderness, an objective test is important to corroborate or challenge the panelists' ratings. Also, consider the possibility of checking the pH of mixtures prior to and after heating. This information often is valuable in explaining results. Flow properties of batters or certain other mixtures prior to heat treatment can be measured and that information used in interpreting and explaining results.

2. *Obtain necessary testing devices.*
   In the preliminary testing phase of an experiment, analyze all steps in the preparation of the product and study the final product to determine whether there are specific characteristics that might be tested objectively if additional testing equipment could be procured or developed for the experiment. Other laboratories and departments within the university or local food companies may be able to provide access to the necessary equipment. Technicians or personnel in the campus machine shop or maintenance area often are able to construct useful devices when these are described and interpreted to them.

3. *Be meticulous about maintenance of objective equipment.*
   In any laboratory, there always is the possibility that somebody may have adjusted, moved, or used the equipment employed in a study. This increases the chance of malfunction of the equipment and the need for readjustments in calibration. Normal usage can contribute to mechanical failures, too. Routine lubrication and checking of equipment to be certain that moving parts are operating normally are responsibilities that need to be assumed by the researcher. Before using any equipment, the good researcher will check to be certain the machine is operating correctly in all aspects. In other words, always be suspicious of equipment and institute appropriate controls to be sure that the objective measurements will be made as accurately as possible.

4. *Carefully define the samples to be used for objective testing.*
   A template of the item being tested often is an essential tool in obtaining comparable samples for objective tests. For example, strips of meat from bottom round must be exactly the same dimensions and from the precise location on the muscle if they are to give comparable data regarding tenderness, as measured by use of the shear apparatus. Similarly, the dimensions of pastry or cookie samples being tested for tenderness on the shortometer must be identical. To obtain these samples, the thickness of the mixture prior to baking must be controlled precisely. Decisions need to be made regarding possible removal of surface skin on a custard to be tested on the penetrometer.

5. *Establish operating conditions for objective testing.*
   For consistency in obtaining results, there must be no variation in the collection of objective data. For example, the temperature of a starch paste being utilized for a line-spread test must be specified and controlled so that the effect of temperature on viscosity of starch pastes is not an uncontrolled variable in the measurement. Gelatin mixtures need to be tested at the temperature specified by the researcher and at the time a specified storage period has elapsed so that the effects of age and temperature are not uncontrolled vari-

ables in the experiment. These are but a few examples of the need to control samples in size, storage and temperature. Each experiment needs to be designed to eliminate uncontrolled variables in objective testing.

PHYSICAL METHODS

Volume

Seed Displacement.   Volume of firm food products can be determined by displacement, usually by seed displacement. Samples for determining volume of baked products are prepared by weighing comparable amounts of dough or batter of each product to be baked for the test. A convenient machine for measuring volume is the **volumeter.** In the volumeter, the volume of seeds (ordinarily rapeseeds) in a closed system is determined with and without the sample; the actual volume of the sample is the difference between the two measurements (see Figure 4.1).

If a volumeter is not available, a box somewhat larger than the sample can be used to measure the seeds required to fill the box level with and without the

Volumeter
Device for measuring volume of baked products; consists of a reservoir for storing the seeds, a transparent column for measuring volume, and a lower compartment in which the sample is placed.

Figure 4.1   Volumeter for measuring volume of cakes, breads, and other baked products that are suited to seed-displacement measurement. (Courtesy of Plycon Press.)

sample. Similarly, cakes may be measured in their pans if the sides of the pan extend well above the cake itself.

Index to Volume
Indirect means of comparing volume by measuring the circumference of a cross section of the product.

Ink Blot
In food research, an impression made on paper after first pressing a cross section of the sample onto an ink pad.

Planimeter
Engineering tool designed to measure distance as its pointer is traced around a pattern.

Specific Gravity
Ratio of the density of a food (or other substance) to that of water.

Index to Volume.   Another approach to the comparison of volumes is the **index to volume,** a measurement made by first tracing a detailed outline of a cross section of the food. In this method, it is essential that the slice be taken from exactly the same location on each sample. This tracing can be done with a sharply pointed pencil or a pen or by making a clear **ink blot** of the cross section. The ink blot is made simply by pressing the cross section of the sample lightly onto an inked stamp pad and then making the imprint of the inked sample on paper. Another way of obtaining the precise outline of the sample is by photocopying a cross section of each sample. A **planimeter** is then used to trace the entire outline of the sample, being careful to follow all indentations and protrusions so that the final measure recorded on the planimeter represents the exact circumference of the slice (see Figure 4.2).

Specific Gravity

Specific gravity is a measure of the relative density of a substance (in this instance, a food) in relation to that of water. The measurement is obtained by weighing a given volume of the sample and then dividing that weight by the same vol-

Figure 4.2   A planimeter can be used to trace the area encompassed by a sample (shown in this ink blot) or in a photocopy. (Courtesy of Plycon Press.)

ume of water (1 milliliter of water weighs 1 gram at 4°C). This technique is used for comparing the lightness of products physically unsuited to the volume measurements previously described. For example, egg white foams can be compared by using specific gravity. Another application of specific gravity was provided by Mackey (1967) when she demonstrated that potatoes with low specific gravity (waxy-type potatoes) had cooking characteristics different from those of potatoes with a comparatively higher specific gravity (see Figure 4.3).

(a)

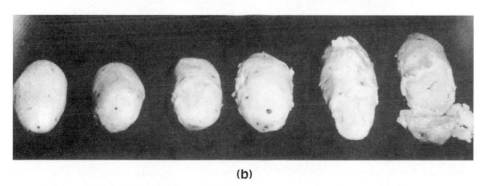

(b)

Figure 4.3 (a) Specific gravity of potatoes in a brine solution (1 part salt to 11 parts water by volume) is an objective test for differentiating non-waxy potatoes for baking (at bottom of brine) from waxy potatoes for boiling (floating). (b) Waxy potato (left) has a low specific gravity (1.070) and retains shape well, while non-waxy potato (right) has high specific gravity (1.115) and sloughs readily. (Photos by Andrea Mackey and courtesy of the Oregon Agricultural Experiment Station.)

Moisture

Press Fluids
Juices forced from meat or other food under pressure.

Press Fluids. Although juiciness or moisture content can be judged subjectively, there are instances where it is desirable also to obtain an objective measure of this characteristic. The juiciness of meats, poultry, and fish can be measured by use of a succulometer, a machine that applies controlled pressure to a sample. The juices, called **press fluids,** are expressed from a weighed sample. After the appropriate pressure has been applied for a controlled length of time, the sample is again weighed. The difference between the two weights represents the amount of juice contained in the original sample. The greater the weight loss, the greater the juiciness of the sample. Press fluids can be measured by similar devices, such as a pressometer or Carver press.

Wettability
Ability of a cake or other food to absorb moisture during a controlled period of time; high moisture retention means a cake is sufficiently moist.

Wettability. Baked products can be tested for moisture level by conducting a test for **wettability.** For this test, the sample is weighed before being placed for 5 seconds in a dish of water. Immediately at the end of the elapsed time, the sample is removed from the water and weighed again to determine the weight gain. High moisture retention is synonymous with good wettability, a sign that a cake probably will be considered to be appropriately moist when judged subjectively.

Moisture Content
(Initial − dried weight/ initial weight) × 100 = % moisture

Drying Oven. A slow method that sometimes is used to determine **moisture content** of a sample is a drying oven. The weight of the original sample is determined, and then the food is dried until the dried weight remains constant. The difference between initial and final weight is calculated, and that value is divided by the original weight and multiplied by 100 to calculate the percentage moisture in the original food.

Karl Fischer Titrator. A much faster way of analyzing moisture content became available in 1990 when the Karl Fischer titrator analyzed water content of various food samples in 10 minutes or less, depending on the type of food. Food to be analyzed by this method is homogenized in a high-speed blender at speeds up to 7,500 rpm to release the water. Following complete homogenization, the water is titrated with Karl Fischer reagent until all the water has reacted with the reagent. The calculation for water content is handled by a microprocessor, which is built into the machine. This costly approach to moisture analysis is well suited to production facilities where a quick response is important.

Texture

Warner–Bratzler Shear
Objective testing device for measuring the force required to shear a sample of meat or other food with measurable tensile strength.

Warner–Bratzler Shear. A **Warner–Bratzler shear** is a device commonly used to measure the tenderness of meat. Meat samples of carefully controlled dimensions are placed through an opening in a thin metal plate, and the force required for two parallel bars to shear the meat as they pass down opposite sides of the plate holding the sample is recorded (see Figure 4.4). Core samples must be cut from exactly the same position from each meat sample using a coring tool. The standing time and temperature of the samples also must be the same at the time of coring and also at testing on the shear.

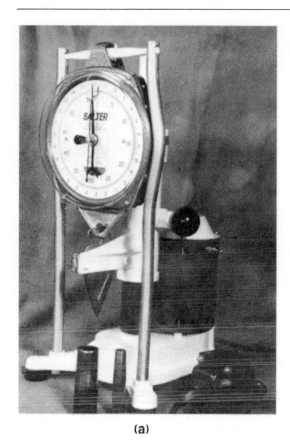

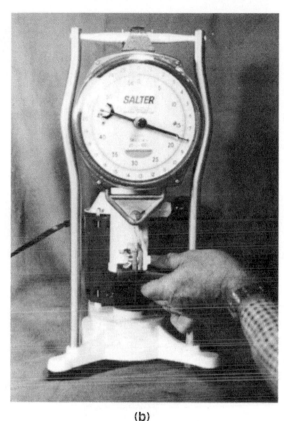

(a)   (b)

Figure 4.4 (a) Warner–Bratzler shear for measuring tenderness of meats and other foods with sufficient resistance for measuring the force required to shear. (Note the coring tools for obtaining controlled sample size). (b) Shear in operation. (Courtesy of G–R Elec. Mfg. Co.)

Shear Press. The **shear press,** a related device, is a machine that compresses, extrudes, and shears the sample at the same time. This is a suitable method for measuring textural characteristics of some fruits and vegetables.

Compressimeter. This **compressimeter** (Figure 4.5) is related to the shear press, but it measures only compressibility, not shear strength. The firmness or compressibility of rather porous baked products can be determined by using the compressimeter. The usual technique for operating the compressimeter is to apply pressure until the sample has been deformed a specific amount and then to measure the force that was required to accomplish this amount of deformation. The greater the force required, the firmer the product. The texture test system (Figure 4.6) is a similar device.

Penetrometer. A **penetrometer** also may be used to measure tenderness of some foods (see Figure 4.7). This device consists of a plunger equipped with a

Shear Press
Objective testing machine that measures compressibility, extrusion, and shear of food samples.

Compressimeter
Objective equipment that measures the force required to compress a food sample a predetermined amount.

Penetrometer
Machine to measure tenderness by determining the distance a cone or other device penetrates the food during a defined period of time and using only gravitational force.

Figure 4.5 Compressimeter measuring compressibility of bread. (Courtesy of C. W. Brabender Instruments, Inc., So. Hackensack, N.J. and Brabender OHG, Dvisberg, Germany.)

Bloom Gelometer
Modification of a penetrometer designed especially for measuring the tenderness of gels.

needle or cone that is allowed to penetrate the sample by gravitational force for a selected period of time. The distance the test device penetrates into the sample is measured to determine the comparative tenderness of samples. The larger the reading, the more tender is the product. Gels and many baked products are particularly well suited to tenderness measurements using the penetrometer. The **Bloom gelometer** is a special type of penetrometer in which lead shot drops into a cup which forces a plunger into the sample. When sufficient weight has been added to the cup to move the plunger a set distance, the test is completed, and the amount of shot required is determined as the measure of the test.

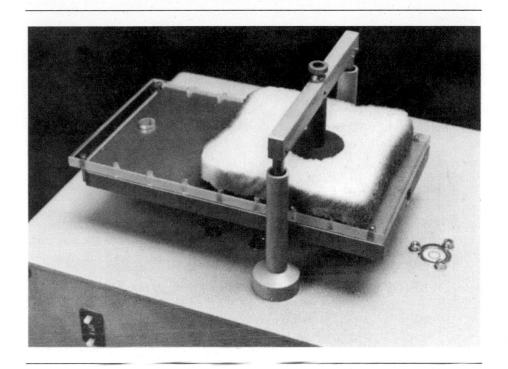

Figure 4.6 Texture test system. (Courtesy of General Kinetics, Inc.)

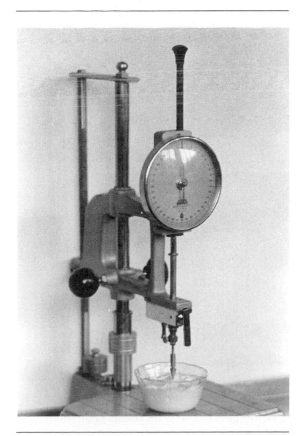

Figure 4.7 Penetrometer for measuring tenderness of gels and other foods which permit gradual passage of a cone or other testing device. (Courtesy of Plycon Press.)

Percent Sag
(Depth in container −
depth on plate/depth in
container) × 100 = %

Percent Sag.   Another test of the comparative tenderness of a gel is the test for **percent sag.** For this test, the depth of a sample such as jelly is measured in its container by using a probe. The product then is unmolded onto a flat plate. Once again the depth of the product is measured with the probe. This second measurement is subtracted from the original measurement; this figure is divided by the original depth of the sample and multiplied by 100 to obtain the percent sag of the sample. The greater the percent sag, the more tender is the gel.

Shortometer
Device designed to measure the tenderness of
fairly tender, crisp foods.

Shortometer.   Pastry, comparatively tender and crisp cookies, and crackers are well suited for tenderness measurements on the **shortometer.** This device consists of a platform containing two parallel, dull blades on which the sample rests. A third dull blade is actuated by a motor to press down on the sample until the sample snaps. The force required to break the sample is the measure of the tenderness of the product (see Figure 4.8).

Universal Testing Machine
Multipurpose, complex machine capable of measuring
various textural properties
of food samples.

Universal Testing Machine.   Instron's **universal testing machine** is a unit with several different testing devices that can be used to measure different aspects of texture in foods. Applications include assessment of food quality on production lines (see Figure 4.9).

The Instron universal testing machine was so named because of its ability to test various facets of food textures. In some foods, hardness might be an important characteristic to measure, while cohesiveness might be of more interest in caramels or similar foods. Actually, the universal testing machine can provide a record showing seven aspects of texture from various foods samples. These are cohesiveness,

Figure 4.8 Shortometer for measuring tenderness of pastry and other crisp foods. (Photo courtesy of Magnuson Corporation.)

Figure 4.9 Food testing being performed on Instron Model 1011 Test Instrument. This is a puncture test for food testing. (Courtesy of Instron Corporation.)

adhesiveness, hardness, springiness, gumminess, chewiness, and fracturability. The versatility of this machine to provide information regarding quality control during food processing has made this an important testing device in the food industry.

Farinograph.   The farinograph (Figure 4.10) measures and depicts gluten development during mixing of batters and doughs.

Texturometer
Simulation device that measures such physical textural properties as hardness, cohesiveness, and crushability of foods.

Texturometer.   The General Foods **texturometer** tests textural properties similar to those tested by the universal testing machine. Surprisingly, adjustments can be made in the General Food texturometer to simulate various chewing actions in the mouth, including biting with the front teeth and chewing with molars.

Masticometer
Machine that measures comparative tenderness of meat and other foods by simulating chewing action.

Masticometer.   **Masticometers** of various designs have been developed to approximate the chewing action of the jaw. The measurements obtained from the masticometer are comparative measures of tenderness of meat or other food.

Rheology

Rheology
Study of deformation and flow qualities of matter.

Rheology is the study of the flow of matter and the deformations that result from flow. The viscosity of fluids is the ability of a fluid to develop and maintain a shearing stress and offer resistance to flow. This is a bit easier to visualize if you think of a liquid as having a top plate that is being forced sideways on the liquid

Figure 4.10 Farinograph is used to measure and record the development of gluten in batters and doughs. (Courtesy of C. W. Brabender Instruments, Inc., So. Hackensack, N.J. and Brabender OHG, Dvisberg, Germany.)

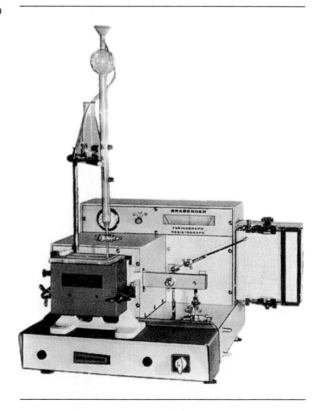

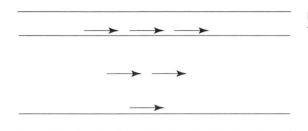

Figure 4.11   Diagram illustrating the shear rate of a liquid.

(Figure 4.11) while the bottom plate of the liquid is moving sideways much less rapidly, and the fluid in the middle is moving at a rate between the top and bottom plates. This movement is the shear rate. Viscosity generally decreases with an increase in temperature of the fluid (see Figure 4.12).

Fluids are categorized as either **Newtonian** or **non-Newtonian,** a distinction based on work by Sir Isaac Newton. Water, sugar syrups, and wine are examples of Newtonian liquids. Newtonian fluids have viscosities that are independent of the shear rate. This means that the viscosity of a Newtonian fluid will be the same even when a rotational viscometer is operated at different speeds.

Newtonian
Classification of materials having a flow rate that is not affected by shear rate, for example, water and sugar syrups.

Non-Newtonian
Classification of materials having a flow rate that is influenced by shear rate, for example, chocolate and emulsions.

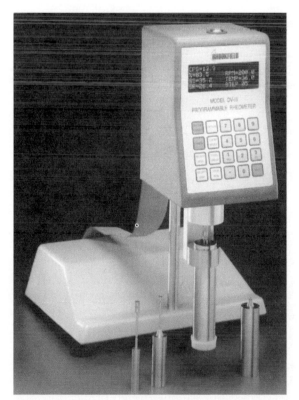

(a)

Figure 4.12   (a) Brookfield DV-III Rheometer. (Courtesy of Brookfield Engineering Laboratories.)

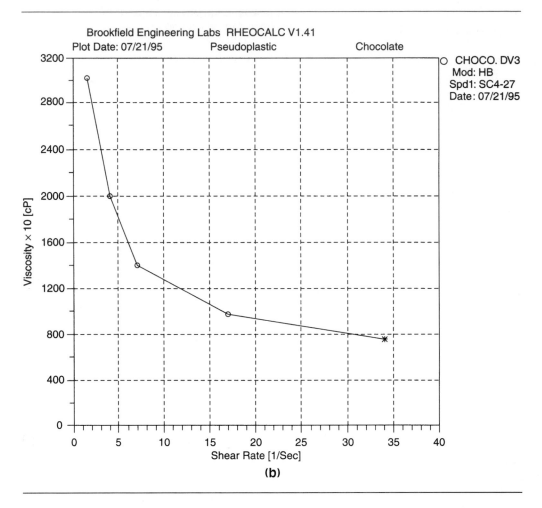

Figure 4.12 (b) Graph depicting the rheology of chocolate. *(Continued)*

Non-Newtonian fluids, such as emulsions and tomato paste, will flow at an altered rate when subjected to shear stress. Mayonnaise and catsup are examples of fluids that thin with increasing shear, but they gradually return to their original viscosity after shearing ceases. Chocolate also responds in this manner, a characteristic that is very useful to commercial candy makers. Shear causes the chocolate to become soft enough to be spread as a coating over the center, and yet this soft chocolate will become firm rather quickly after the shearing action stops. This behavior characterizes **thixotropic** fluids.

Thixotropic
Ability of a gel to become more fluid with increasing shear and then to regain previous viscosity after shear rate is slowed.

Consistometer
Device for measuring the spread or flow of semisolid foods in a specified length of time.

Consistometer.   The Bostwick **consistometer** and the Adams consistometer are used to measure the consistency (viscosity) or spread of semisolid foods. If a measured amount of semisolid food is placed on the slanting trough of the Bostwick consistometer, the distance of flow in a given period of time can then be measured to determine the relative consistency of foods that flow at atmospheric pressure.

The Adams consistometer measures the spread of the sample (the area covered) in a specified length of time.

Line-Spread Test.   The **line-spread test** is a simple variation of the measurement of viscosity by consistometers. A measured amount of sample is placed in a column centered on measured, concentric rings and is allowed to flow for a measured length of time (up to 2 minutes), after which the spread at each 90° increment of the circles is read; the line-spread value is the mean of the four values obtained (see Figure 4.13).

Amylograph.   The Brabender **amylograph** is another piece of objective equipment for measuring consistency. It is used to determine the viscosity of starch pastes at controlled, selective temperatures (see Figure 4.14).

Viscometers.   **Viscometers** (also sometimes called viscosimeters) are functionally very similar to the Brabender amylograph. As their name implies, these objective testing devices measure viscosity of a variety of foods with flow properties. Measurement of viscosity by viscometers is based on either rotational operation (a measure of torsional force) or capillary action. The Brookfield viscometer (Figure 4.15) illustrates measurement based on rotational operation, for it measures the drag the test sample places on a spindle that is rotated mechanically through the sample. A **jelmeter** (a special viscometer similar to a pipette) often is used to test the viscosity of pectin-containing juices to determine the amount of added pectin needed for gelling fruit juices to make jams and jellies.

Line-Spread Test
Measure of flow of a viscous liquid or semisolid food by determining the spread of a measured amount of sample in a specified length of time at 90° intervals on the template of concentric rings.

Amylograph
Device designed to control the temperature of a starch paste and to measure its viscosity.

Viscometer
Objective testing device for measuring viscosity of liquids that flow; measures on the basis of rotational resistance or capillary action.

Jelmeter
Pipettclike viscometer designed to measure the adequacy of the pectin content of fruit juices to make jams and jellies.

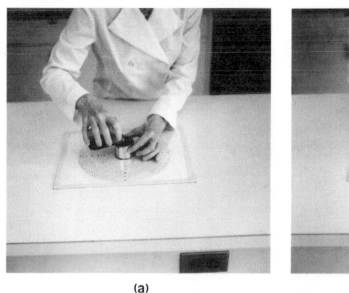   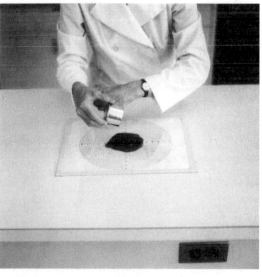

(a)   **(b)**

Figure 4.13   Line-spread test for measuring rheological properties of sauces and other foods that flow: (a) pouring the sample; (b) timing the test. (Courtesy of Plycon Press.)

Figure 4.14   Visco/Angiograph is the objective equipment used to measure the viscosity of starch pastes under various heating/cooling conditions. (Courtesy of C. W. Brabender Instruments, Inc., So. Hackensack, N.J. and Brabender OHG, Dvisberg, Germany.)

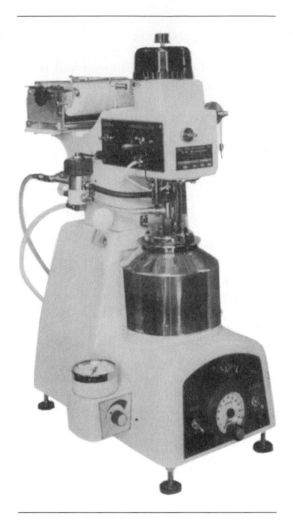

Color

CIE
Commission Internationale de L'Eclairage; group that established a system of measuring color based on spectral color, degree of saturation, and brightness.

Munsell System
System of identifying colors on the basis of hue, value, and chroma, using a numerical scale.

Color is measured according to either the **CIE** (Commission Internationale de L'Eclairage) or the **Munsell system.** These systems consider the spectral color, degree of saturation, and brightness. A spectrophotometer can be used to save considerable time in defining colors under the CIE system. In the Munsell system, hue, value, and chroma are identified on a numerical scale. Hue is measured numerically. Red is expressed numerically as $+a$, green as $-a$, yellow as $+b$, and blue as $-b$. Using these measured numerical values, hue is then calculated using the formula:

$$\text{hue angle } \theta_s = \tan^{-1} a/b.$$

Chroma is determined by using these values in the following formula:

$$(a^2 + b^2)^{\frac{1}{2}} = \text{chroma}.$$

Value is determined based on a range of 100, with 0 representing black and 100 being white.

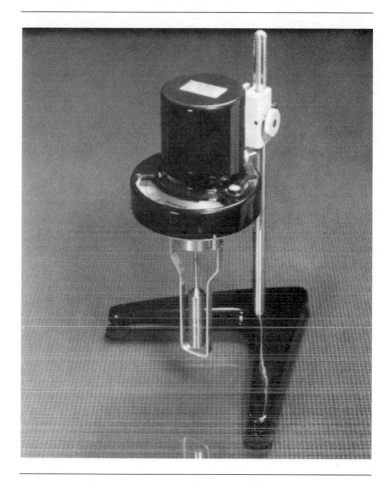

Color samples are available to match with the color of the food being identified. The Hunter **color-difference meter** is a device commonly used to identify food colors. For an overview of color and its measurement, see Setser (1984).

Cell Structure

Cell structure of baked products is an important characteristic to measure, and yet it is difficult to obtain meaningful results using objective testing equipment. Judges on sensory panels provide crucial information on cell structure when their scorecards are designed properly. However, an objective approach is also valuable. One key technique for compiling information about cell structure (including uniformity, size, and thickness of cell walls) is by making photocopies of cross-sectional slices (see Figure 4.16). This simple technique successfully reveals the third-dimensional view into the cells on the cut surface of the sample. Another benefit of this technique is that the actual size is represented clearly, which permits use of the planimeter to determine the circumference, as noted previously in the discussion of index to volume.

Photographs are another valuable tool in depicting information about cell texture. These photographs may be in color or in black and white, but black-and-white photographs are recommended if publication of the research is anticipated.

Color-Difference Meter
Objective machine, such as the Hunter color-difference meter or Gardner color-difference meter, capable of measuring color differences between samples by utilizing the CIE or Munsell color system.

Figure 4.16 Photocopying provides a convenient, detailed record of the appearance of bread (or other suitable baked products).

Because photographs do not ordinarily represent the samples in their exact dimensions, placing a clearly marked ruler adjacent to the sample is a simple and effective way of adding some concept of size to the photographs.

CHEMICAL METHODS

Nutrient Analysis

Particularly since the advent of nutrition labeling, considerable attention has been devoted to analysis of the nutrient content of food (DeVries and Nelson, 1994). The accepted methods for conducting these analyses are contained in a publication by the Association of Official Analytical Chemists (AOAC, 1990).

pH

Measurement of the pH of food mixtures often is essential to determine acidity or alkalinity. Although pH papers are available, a pH meter is a more precise way of obtaining accurate information on this facet of food. The pH meter utilizes a glass indicating electrode and a reference electrode to complete an electrical circuit and measure the effective hydrogen ion concentration (pH) of the food being tested (Figure 4.17).

Most foods have a pH of 7 or less, which means that they are acidic in reaction: the lower the pH number, the more acidic is the food. Bicarbonate of soda is a food ingredient that is alkaline, and egg whites are quite alkaline; that is, their pH is high. Although the general pH value is known for many foods, the pH of a spe-

Figure 4.17   pH meter. (Courtesy of Beckman Instruments, Inc.)

cific food sample may vary slightly from the expected value. In fact, the pH of foods varies with not only the type of food, but also with its freshness and the environmental conditions (temperature, moisture level, and surrounding air or gases). The ingredients which are included in food products also influence the pH of food mixtures. For these reasons, measurement of the pH of food samples can provide important information in food research.

Various models of pH meters are available to meet specific needs in the laboratory or in the field. In some instances, a pH meter which adjusts to changes in temperature during the course of an experimental run can be useful. Basic models usually are appropriate for classroom use.

Sugar Concentration

Refractometers can be used to determine the concentration of a sugar solution. Light is refracted as it passes through sugar solutions, with the specific values being calibrated in degrees **Brix,** an indication of the percent of sucrose in the solution.

Saltiness

Flame photometry is used to analyze the sodium content of foods. Actually, the salts of interest include not only sodium, but also potassium, magnesium, calcium, ammonium, and lithium.

Brix Scale
Hydrometer scale designed to indicate the percentage concentration of sugar in sugar solutions.

Flavor

Flavor analysis is presently a very active research area. The ultimate goal is to identify the numerous volatile and nonvolatile substances that combine to produce the overall flavor impression of a specific food. The key to this type of research has been the utilization of the gas–liquid **chromatograph** (GLC) and the high-pressure liquid chromatograph (HPLC). These instruments can be used to separate the complex mixtures of chemical compounds in foods that constitute the aroma and flavor characteristics of the sample. The various components that are separated by either of these (or other) chromatographs are then collected and identified. Identification of these compounds may involve the use of infrared spectrophotometry or mass spectrometry. The ultimate goal of this sophisticated basic research is to be able to synthesize flavors in the laboratory and then to produce them for industrial use so that nature's flavors can be replicated accurately.

Proximate Analysis

The carbohydrate, lipid (fat), and protein content of a specific food is of interest, in part because these are the energy-yielding nutrients. Proximate analysis of a food is done to determine the amount of each of these nutrients in a known quantity of food. Results can be expressed in grams of carbohydrates, fats, and proteins in a specified serving portion or in percentages. Determination of proximate analysis can be done using the official methods specified by the Association of Official Analytical Chemists (AOAC). These methods are modified frequently and published by the AOAC (1990). Analytical methods also are developed and published by the American Association of Cereal Chemists (AACC, 1983) and the American Oil Chemists' Society (AOCS, 1981).

SUMMARY

Research and development of food products, as well as quality control in food production, require careful and accurate evaluation techniques. Evaluation is of two types: (1) sensory or subjective and (2) objective. Objective testing can provide extremely valuable data if the sampling techniques are well controlled and if the equipment is functioning properly.

Physical measurements can be made by use of a wide range of devices varying in their level of engineering sophistication. Volume can be measured by use of a volumeter, which is a seed displacement method. Index to volume is a related measure of volume. A planimeter is used to trace the detailed circumference of the sample to obtain the index to volume.

Specific gravity, a comparison of the density of the sample relative to water, is a measurement useful in assessing light products such as foams, which are not suited to testing in a volumeter.

Moisture or juiciness in meats and related foods can be tested by placing the sample under pressure in a succulometer to express the press fluids. Wettability of baked products, determined by weighing a sample before and after a 5-second dip in water, is helpful in determining moisture levels in cakes. Use of a drying oven is another good technique for determining moisture content.

Texture of foods has several parameters, and various instruments have been designed to measure different aspects of texture. The Warner–Bratzler shear is used widely for measuring the tenderness of meats. A shear press measures compressibility, extrusion, and shear at the same time. The compressimeter is used to determine the firmness of bread and related baked products. Penetrometers of various design provide another means of measuring tenderness. Percent sag is an unsophisticated but useful technique for measuring gel tenderness when a penetrometer is not available. Other items for testing texture include the masticometer, universal testing machine (Instron), and the texturometer (General Foods). Photocopying and photography afford effective means of providing permanent evidence of cell structure, including cell size, uniformity, and thickness of cell walls.

Rheology, the study of the flow of matter and deformation resulting from flow, is of interest in many Newtonian and non-Newtonian food products, including chocolate. The flow properties of semisolid foods can be tested by a simple line-spread test if the Bostwick or the Adams consistometer is not available. Viscosity of starch pastes can be measured by using the Brabender amylograph. Viscometers, operating by rotation or capillary action, are used to measure flow properties.

Color can be measured and reported very precisely using either the CIE or the Munsell system for color identification. A spectrophotometer is a useful measuring device. The Hunter color-difference meter is used frequently in color measurements.

Chemical measurements used in food evaluation include nutrient analysis, a particularly timely subject of evaluation. The pH meter is an important piece of equipment for checking acidity or alkalinity at various points during the preparation and evaluation of products. Refractometers enable researchers to ascertain the concentration of sugar in solutions, and flame photometry is used to identify selected elements, particularly sodium.

Sophisticated flavor research utilizes the gas–liquid chromatograph (GLC) or high-pressure liquid chromatograph (HPLC) to separate volatile flavoring compounds from the total flavor sample. Purified compounds from the mixture are then identified using infrared spectrophotometry and sometimes mass spectrometry. The ultimate goal is to identify all key components of natural flavors and then to formulate synthetic flavors identical to the flavors found in the natural foods.

Proximate analysis of the carbohydrate, lipid (fat), and protein content of food samples can be done chemically, according to methods developed by recognized professional groups (AOAC, AACC, and AOCS).

STUDY QUESTIONS

1. Outline the exact way in which you would prepare a sample of round steak for use in the shear. Be sure to identify all aspects requiring control to ensure uniform samples.
2. Does the volumeter result in a more accurate volume measurement than is obtained by use of the planimeter to determine the index to volume? Explain your answer.
3. Identify the technique you would select for measuring the tenderness of each of the following and explain your rationale for the choice:
   - baked custard
   - grape jelly
   - round steak
   - pastry
   - bread
4. Outline the method for conducting a line-spread test.

5. Explain the contribution of the following machines when used in flavor research:
- GLC
- HPLC
- infrared spectrophotometer
- mass spectrometer

BIBLIOGRAPHY

AACC. 1983. *Approved Methods of the American Association of Cereal Chemists.* 8th ed. AACC: St. Paul, MN.

AOAC. 1990. *Official Methods of Analysis.* 15th ed. Association of Official Analytical Chemists: Arlington, VA.

AOAC. 1985. *Changes in Official Methods of Analysis—1st Supplement.* 14th ed. Association of Official Analytical Chemists: Washington, DC.

AOCS. 1981. *Official and Tentative Methods.* 3rd ed. American Oil Chemists' Society: Champaign, IL.

Baker, A. E., Walker, C. E., and Kemp, K. 1988. "Optimum compression depth for measuring bread crumb firmness." *Cereal Chem. 65:* 302.

Barfod, N. M. and Pedersen, K. S. 1990. "Determining the setting temperature of high-methoxyl pectin gels." *Food Technol. 44* (4): 139.

Barnes, K. W. 1995. "Introduction to food analysis techniques." *Food Technol. 49* (6): 48.

Bourne, M. C. 1982. *Food Texture and Viscosity.* Academic Press: New York.

Carpenter, D. E. and Sullivan, D. M. 1993. *Methods of Analysis for Nutrition Labeling.* AOAC International. Arlington, VA.

Clark, R. 1997. Evaluating syrups using extensional viscosity. *Food Technol. 51* (1): 49.

Clydesdale, F. M. 1976. "Instrumental techniques for color measurement of foods." *Food Technol. 30* (10): 52, 58.

Clydesdale, F. M. 1984. "Color Measurement." In *Food Analysis: Principles and Techniques. I. Physical Characterization.* Gruenwedel, D. W. and Whitaker, J., eds. Marcel Dekker: New York.

Clydesdale, F. M. 1972. "Measuring color of foods." *Food Technol. 26* (7): 45.

DeVries, J. W. and Nelson, A. L. 1994. "Meeting analytical needs for nutrition labeling." *Food Technol. 48* (7): 73.

Dziezak, J. 1990. "New Karl Fischer titrator eliminates need for sample preparation." *Food Technol. 44* (9): 115.

Francis, F. J. and Clydesdale, F. M. 1975. *Food Colorimetry: Theory and Applications.* AVI Publishing: Westport, CT.

Giese, J. 1995. Measuring physical properties of foods. *Food Technol. 49* (2): 54.

Hamann, D. D., and Diehl, K. C. 1978. "Rheology of soft fleshy fruit." *Food Technol. 32* (7): 57.

Horwitz, W., ed. 1980. *Official Methods of Analysis of Association of Official Analytical Chemists.* 13th ed. Association of Official Analytical Chemists: Washington, DC.

Howard, D. W. 1991. "A look at viscometry." *Food Technol. 45* (7): 82.

Kamel, B. 1987. "Bread firmness measurement with emphasis on Baker compressimeter." *Cereal Foods World 32:* 472.

Kapsalis, J. G. 1987. *Objective Methods in Food Quality Assessment.* CRC Press: Boca Raton, FL.

Konstance, R. P. and Holsinger, V. H. 1992. "Development of rheological test methods for cheese." *Food Technol. 46* (1): 105.

Mackey, A. 1967. "Recent research with potatoes." *Proceedings, 6th Annual Washington State Potato Conference.*

MacNeil, J. H. and Mast, M. G. 1989. "Resistance to tear: instrumental measure of cohesive properties of muscle food products." *J. Food Sci. 54:* 750.

Nagy, S. and Klim, M. 1986. "Gas chromatography—mass spectral techniques in citrus essence research." *Food Technol. 40* (11): 95.

Peppard, T. L. 1999. How chemical analysis supports flavor creation. *Food Technol. 53 (3):* 46.

Pomeranz, Y. and Meloan, C. E. 1978. *Food Analysis: Theory and Practice.* 2nd ed. AVI Publishing: Westport, CT.

Prosky, L., et al. 1984. "Determination of total dietary fiber in foods, food products, and total diets: interlaboratory study." *J. Assoc. Off. Anal. Chem. 67:* 1044.

Rha, C. 1978. "Rheology of fluid foods." *Food Technol. 32* (7): 77.

Schenz, T. W. 1997. Using rheology of weak gels to improve fluid foods. *Food Technol. 51 (3):* 83.

Schneeman, B. O. 1986. "Dietary fiber: physical and chemical properties, methods of analysis, and physiological effects." *Food Technol. 40* (2): 104.

Setser, C. S. 1984. "Color: reflection and transmission." *J. Food Qual 6:* 183.

Shoemaker, C. F., Nantz, J., Bonnans, S., and Noble, A. C. 1992. "Rheological characterization of dairy products." *Food Technol 46* (1): 98.

Stanley, D. W. 1986. "Chemical and structural determinants of texture of fabricated foods." *Food Technol. 40* (3): 65.

Szczesniak, A. S. 1987. "Correlating sensory with instrumental texture measurements—an overview of recent developments." *J. Texture Studies 18.* 1.

Walker, C. E., West, D. I., Pierce, M. M., and Buck, J. S. 1987. "Cake firmness measurements by the universal testing machine." *Cereal Foods World 32:* 477.

Wayne, J. E. B. and Shoemaker, C. F. 1988. "Rheological characteristics of commercially processed fluid milks." *J. Texture Studies 19:* 143.

2

Physical
Perspectives

CHAPTER 5

Water

Water is such a common constituent of foods and is used so frequently in food preparation that it is easy to take it for granted. However, the universality of its occurrence and its unique characteristics make water a subject worthy of close examination.

The behavior of water molecules is influenced strongly by the polarity of the molecule. The two hydrogen atoms are joined to the oxygen atom by two bonds that form an angle of almost 105° (see Figure 5.1). This orientation concentrates the electrons of the oxygen atom toward one side of the molecule (away from the hydrogen atoms). The electrons contribute a negative charge to this portion of the water molecule, whereas the hydrogen atoms provide a positive component, thus making water a **dipole.** This situation promotes the formation of hydrogen bonds between water molecules, the oxygen of one molecule hydrogen-bonding with the hydrogen of another molecule. The formation of hydrogen bonds between water molecules results in innumerable clusters of water molecules when water is in the liquid state. The propensity of water to form hydrogen bonds enables water to be in liquid form over a temperature range that is physically somewhat surprising. Although hydrogen bonds are comparatively weak bonds (being secondary rather than primary bonds), they are sufficiently strong to hold water molecules in close proximity unless a considerable amount of energy is introduced into the system.

Dipole
Molecule that is electrically asymmetrical, i.e., a portion is slightly negative and another part is slightly positive.

STATES OF WATER

Water can be found in solid, gaseous, or liquid form in foods. Consider water at atmospheric pressure. The state in which it is found reflects varying energy states: the crystalline, solid form (ice) represents the lowest energy state, and steam the high-energy, gaseous stage. Energy is lost from the system as water cools. Concomitantly,

Figure 5.1 Diagram of a water molecule showing the bond angle of approximately 105° between the two hydrogen atoms.

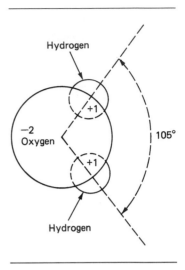

Heat of Fusion
Heat released when a liquid is transformed into a solid (80 calories per gram of water); also called heat of solidification.

the molecules move slower and slower, until at 4°C an organized bonding pattern between molecules begins to appear. As the water continues cooling, the water molecules separate just a bit, causing a small increase in volume. At 0°C, the actual phenomenon of freezing (the change from a liquid to a solid) occurs, but only after almost 80 calories of heat for each gram of water have been removed from the system. The removal of this heat (called the **heat of fusion**) results in a change in state without a change in temperature. The bonding in ice leaves hexagonal openings in the immobilized, somewhat expanded lattice. As a result of the expansion (about 9 percent), ice is less dense than water and floats to the surface (see Figure 5.2).

The reverse situation, that is, the change from a solid to a liquid, occurs when ice melts. For this transformation, just under 80 calories (actually, 79.7) need to be absorbed into the system for each gram of ice to provide the energy needed to break the bonds that formed during the formation of the solid ice. After the ice has melted, the very cold water contracts in volume until it reaches 4°C, the point at which water is the most dense. The warming of the water requires only one calorie per degree Celsius per gram of water, a sharp contrast with the high energy required to transform ice into water.

As water is heated, hydrogen bonds constantly break and form again, and the individual molecules move increasingly rapidly. Finally, some of the molecules move so rapidly that they overcome their attraction to other molecules of water and escape into the air as vapor or steam. For a gram of water to change into gas,

Figure 5.2 At the change of state from water to ice, 80 calories per gram are lost as the result of the heat of fusion, and the volume increases by 9 percent.

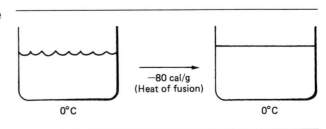

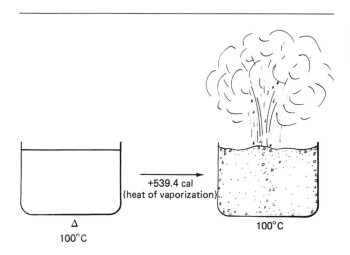

Figure 5.3   When water is changed to steam, almost 540 calories are required as the result of the heat of vaporization.

+539.4 cal
(heat of vaporization)

Δ
100°C

100°C

540 calories (actually, 539.4) is required (see Figure 5.3). This energy requirement is called the **heat of vaporization.** The temperature of water ceases to rise when this point, the boiling point, is reached because any energy introduced thereafter is used to meet the high energy required for the change of physical state from liquid to gas. Table 5.1 summarizes the energy required for transforming ice into steam (Figure 5.4).

Heat of Vaporization
Heat energy absorbed in the conversion of water into steam (540 calories per gram of water).

Factors Influencing Freezing Point

Introduction of a soluble substance, such as sugar, or a substance that ionizes (salt), lowers the temperature at which freezing takes place. This variation is important in preparing, storing, and serving frozen foods, notably frozen desserts. At the freezing point, water in its liquid state is in equilibrium with the solid state, ice. For pure water, this equilibrium is reached at 0°C (32°F), but the freezing point of solutions is reduced somewhat as a consequence of the reduction in vapor pressure effected by the solute.

Sugar is soluble in water, the actual solubility being influenced by the temperature. Very low temperatures decrease the amount of sugar capable of dissolving in water, but even at freezing temperatures some sugar can be dissolved. The dissolved sugar modifies the freezing point of the solution and reduces the vapor pressure. If a gram molecular weight (342 grams) of sucrose is dissolved in a liter of water, the freezing point of the solution drops 1.86°C. In practical terms, a solution of 1¾ cups of sugar in a liter of water freezes at about −1.8°C (28.6°F). The ad-

Table 5.1   Energy Required to Transform 1 Gram of Ice to Steam

Aqueous State	Change Occurring	Energy Involved
Ice (0°C)	Water (0°C)	79.7 cal
Water	0°C to 100°C	100.0 cal
Steam	100°C water to steam	539.4 cal
Total energy required		719.1 cal

Figure 5.4 Calories required to (a) change 1 gram of ice to water at 0°C, (b) heat 1 gram of water from 0 to 100°C, and (c) convert 1 gram of water at 100°C to steam (a total of 719.1 calories).

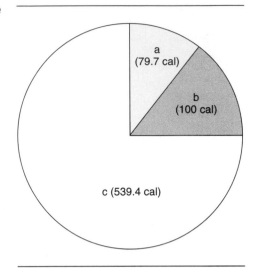

a (79.7 cal)

b (100 cal)

c (539.4 cal)

dition of more sugar (Table 5.2) would continue to depress the freezing point at this rate until no more sugar could dissolve at these depressed temperatures. The effect of sugar on the freezing point extends the length of time required for freezing frozen desserts because of the need to remove more heat from the mixture. It also means that frozen desserts with high sugar content will melt more quickly than will those with little sugar.

Salt, because it ionizes, has twice as great an effect per gram molecular weight as does sugar. A gram molecular weight of salt (58 grams or about 3¼ tablespoons) in a liter of water depresses the freezing point of the solution 3.72°C. The solubility of salt, like that of sugar, is reduced as the temperature drops. The practical limit on the freezing point of a salt solution is about −21°C (−6°F; about 328 grams or 1⅛ cups of salt per liter). Rock salt is added to the ice used to surround the container in crank-type ice cream freezers because of the ability of salt solutions to produce cold temperatures (Chapter 14).

Table 5.2 Depression of Freezing Point of 1 Liter of Water with Varying Amounts of Sugar

Sugar		Depression of Freezing Point[a] (°C)	Actual Freezing Temperature (°C)
Measure (c)	Weight (g)		
1	200	1.09	−1.09
2	400	2.18	−2.18
3	600	3.26	−3.26
4[b]	800	4.35	−4.35

[a] $\dfrac{\text{sugar wt}}{342} \times 1.86 = $ depression of freezing point in °C.

[b] Typical concentration of sugar in ice cream.

Factors Influencing Boiling Point

The **boiling point** is the temperature at which vapor pressure just exceeds atmospheric pressure. At sea level, water boils at a temperature of 100°C (212°F). However, both the atmospheric pressure and the vapor pressure can be modified by various means to change the temperature at which boiling occurs. Both commercially and in the home, examples of these techniques can be cited.

Atmospheric pressure is one of the parameters influencing the temperature at which boiling occurs. Atmospheric pressure decreases with an increase in altitude because of the reduced amount of air above the surface of the earth at high elevations. Atmospheric pressure at sea level is approximately 14.7 pounds per square inch, compared with 12.3 pounds per square inch at 5,000 feet and 10.2 pounds per square inch at 10,000 feet. The vapor pressure required to overcome these levels of atmospheric pressure drops as altitude increases. This drop in the vapor pressure parallels the drop in atmospheric pressure with increasing elevations. For every 500-foot rise in elevation, the temperature of boiling water drops 1°F; an increase of 960 feet in elevation decreases the boiling point of water by 1°C. The effect of elevation on the temperature of boiling water is presented in Table 5.3. In view of the comparatively low temperature of boiling water at very high elevations, a longer cooking time is required for boiling foods in the mountains than is recommended at sea level (Figure 5.5).

In commercial food processing plants, it is feasible to employ a partial vacuum to simulate the effect of altitude on boiling points. By controlling the pressure appropriately within a partial vacuum, liquids can be brought to a boil at such low temperatures that cooked flavors and color changes do not develop. This technique has been used with considerable success in producing fruit juice concentrates.

The reduction in the temperature of boiling can be an inconvenience when food is prepared in the mountains. Fortunately, the pressure saucepan can be used to increase atmospheric pressure artificially. This device forms a tight seal, which traps vapors in the pan. As energy is conducted into the pan's interior, the pressure above the liquid increases, causing the temperature of the boiling water to be hot-

Boiling Point
Temperature at which the vapor pressure just exceeds atmospheric pressure.

Table 5.3   Temperature of Boiling Water at Selected Elevations

Elevation (ft)	Temperature of Boiling Water	
	°C	°F
Sea level	100	212
1000	98.9	210
2000	97.8	208
3000	96.7	206
4000	95.6	204
5000	94.4	202
6000	93.3	200
7000	92.2	198
8000	91.1	196
9000	90.0	194
10,000	88.9	192

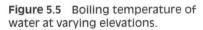

Figure 5.5 Boiling temperature of water at varying elevations.

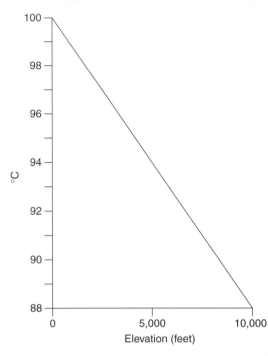

ter. The pressure is increased to the desired level, and the heat source is controlled to maintain this pressure for the appropriate length of time. Careful cooling is required before the seal is released. This is necessary to reduce the pressure in the system to the normal pressure of the surrounding atmosphere.

Using a pressure saucepan saves cooking time because the food is cooked at a higher temperature than can be achieved in a regular saucepan, even when the lid is on the regular pan. The pressure saucepan or pressure canner is of particular merit in the canning of low-acid foods, such as vegetables and meats. These foods may harbor harmful microorganisms, notably *Clostridium botulinum,* which are extremely resistant to heat during processing. Adequate temperatures for processing can be reached only by using pressure.

A pressure of 5 pounds at sea level provides a temperature in the pressurized pan of 109°C (228°F). By increasing the thermal energy in the pan, a pressure of 10 pounds can be produced, resulting in a temperature of 115.6°C (240°F); at 15 pounds pressure at sea level, the temperature reached is 121°C (250°F). Consistent with the previous discussion of the effect of altitude on temperatures of boiling water, the pressure must be increased by 5 pounds if the same temperature is desired at 10,000 feet as is sought at sea level. To illustrate, 20 pounds of pressure need to be developed in the pressure cooker to reach a temperature of 121°C at 10,000 feet, whereas 15 pounds is required at sea level to achieve 121°C in the cooker.

Vapor pressure is the other factor influencing the temperature at which boiling of a liquid occurs. In true solutions, vapor pressure can be modified by dissolving ionizing substances in a liquid. Both sugar and salt are of potential interest in food systems, and sugar is particularly useful because of its palatability. These substances reduce the vapor pressure of a solution, which means that more heat energy must be supplied if the solution is to develop sufficient vapor pressure to overcome the pressure of the atmosphere and boil. In fact, the boiling temperature of a sugar solution increases 0.52°C per gram molecular weight dissolved in the water. This relationship is illustrated by the data in Table 5.4.

Although a gram molecular weight of salt has twice as great an effect on the boiling point of a salt solution as does a gram molecular weight of sugar, salt is of little practical use in this regard. The taste becomes unpalatable, and the health risks are unacceptable at the levels of salt that would be needed if the temperature of the boiling solution were to be elevated sufficiently to reduce cooking times perceptibly. The fact that salt ionizes into one ion of sodium and one ion of chloride explains why a gram molecular weight of salt elevates the boiling point of a salt solution 1.04°C (twice as great an effect as that of a nonionizing compound).

Larger substances, that is, those forming colloidal dispersions or coarse suspensions, have so little effect on vapor pressure that their influence is imperceptible. This means that proteins and coarse, insoluble particles have no measurable influence on boiling points.

Bound Water

Typically, flow properties are associated with water. Water also is expected to be able to dissolve and dilute many substances. However, some water is not able to function in these typical ways because it is held tightly to other molecules and hence is called **bound water.** This bound water fails to exhibit flow properties, and it does not serve as a solvent. Other changes in characteristics are also apparent, including high density, inability to be expressed from tissues, apparent lack of vapor pressure, and inability to enter the frozen state. Fennema (1985) suggests that water can be classified into four types, depending on the degree of binding between the water molecules and the molecules of the material with which they are binding. He classifies pure (free) water as type IV and the water in tissue membranes as typical of type III. The water categorized as type II is hydrogen-bonded in microcapillaries and shows behavior sharply different from that of free water. The bound water classified by Fennema as type I is adsorbed in monolayers on many proteins and other electrically attractive components of foods. There are no sharp divisions separating one type from another, however.

Bound Water
Water that is bound to other substances and no longer exhibits the flow properties and solvent capability commonly associated with water.

Table 5.4   Boiling Temperatures of Varying Concentrations of Sugar Solutions

Sucrose (%)	Boiling Point	
	°C	°F
0	100	212
10	100.4	212.7
20	100.6	213.1
30	101.0	213.8
40	101.5	214.7
50	102.0	215.6
60	103.0	217.4
70	106.5	223.7
80	112.0	233.6
90	130.0	266.0
100 (molten sugar)	160.0	320.0

Bound water, because it lacks flow properties, can contribute significantly to the textural characteristics of foods. A particularly graphic example of the change in flow properties effected when water is transformed from free water (type IV) to tightly bound water (type I) is provided by hydrating gelatin. A quarter of a cup of freely flowing water loses its ability to flow when a tablespoon of dry gelatin is sprinkled into it and allowed to stand briefly to allow time for water to be bound. The bound water is not completely static, for there is some shifting between the bound and free water, but the water can no longer flow. The binding of water in gelatinizing starch mixtures and in denaturing proteins explains some of the textural changes observed when various food products are cooked.

WATER ACTIVITY

Water Activity
Ratio of the vapor pressure of a food sample to the vapor pressure of pure water.

Water activity is a comparison of the vapor pressure of water in a food sample with vapor pressure of pure water. Since vapor pressure is influenced by temperature, the food sample must be at the same temperature as the pure water that serves as the basis for comparison. This relationship can be seen in the following equation, assuming a common temperature:

$$\text{Water activity} = \frac{\text{vapor pressure of water in sample}}{\text{vapor pressure of pure water}}$$

Water activity in all foods is always below a value of 1.0; this is due to the reduction in vapor pressure that is found to varying degrees in all foods. Many familiar foods, including meats and produce, have a water activity of just under 1.0—actually between 0.95 and 1.00 (Table 5.5). The levels of salt and sugar in these foods are comparatively limited, which means that the vapor pressure of water in the food sample will be very close to that of water itself. However, cheeses, salted hams, and dried foods have increased levels of salt and/or sugar, and the vapor pressure of water in the sample will decrease significantly. The result is that water activity in aged cheeses, jams, dried fruits, and similar items usually will be in the range of 0.80 to 0.90 (compared with a value of 1.0 for pure water).

A brief look at Table 5.5 highlights the fact that total water content and water activity are quite different perspectives of water in relation to food. Butterhead let-

Table 5.5   Water Activity (a_w) and Approximate Water Content of Selected Foods

Food	a_w	Approx. water content (%)
Beef chuck, raw	0.95–0.99	50
Watermelon	0.95–0.99	93
Butterhead lettuce	0.95–0.99	96
Pound cake	0.90–0.95	18
White bread	0.90–0.95	38
Aged cheddar cheese	0.80–0.90	41
Corn syrup	0.60–0.70	26

[a]Adapted from Troller, J. A. and Christian, J. H. B. 1978. *Water Activity and Food*. Academic Press. New York and Pennington, J. A. T. and Church, H. N. 1980. *Bowes and Church's Food Values of Portions Commonly Used*. 13th ed. J.B. Lippincott. Philadelphia, PA.

tuce and watermelon have a much greater proportion of water than does beef chuck, and yet lettuce and watermelon cannot be poured despite the abundance of water. The ways in which their water is held or distributed throughout their structures effectively prevent the water from flowing freely. Conversely, corn syrup has such a comparatively low amount of water that you might predict that it could not be poured, but clearly it does flow, if sluggishly. This behavior can be traced to its low level of water activity, which is due to the very high level of sucrose, a compound capable of forming extensive hydrogen bonding with the water molecules that are present.

Related to water activity is the uptake or loss of water by a food at varying levels of relative humidity at a constant temperature. The plotting of the uptake (termed resorption) or the loss of water (desorption) provides a record of a_w (water activity) of a particular food at a particular temperature over varying levels of humidity in the environment. Such a plot is called an isotherm. Surprisingly, the plot for resorption is not identical with the plot for desorption. The a_w values for resorption in the mid-moisture range tend to be higher than those for desorption, i.e., food undergoing desorption will have a higher moisture content at a_w 0.6 than will the same food if it is undergoing resorption (Figure 5.6).

One of the reasons that a_w is so important in foods is that it is an important factor in food spoilage and safety. Among the microorganisms that are inhibited by a level of a_w at 0.95 or just slightly higher are *Pseudomonas, Escherichia,* and *Clostridium perfringens.* Many fresh foods, including meats, milk, and vegetables, have a_w levels in the range of 0.95 to 1.0, which tends to make them unfortunately attractive to many bacteria (Table 5.6). In the a_w range of 0.91–0.95, other bacteria (*Salmonella, Vibrio parahaemolyticus,* and *Clostridium botulinum* are quite capable of surviving and reproducing. Between a_w 0.87–0.91 is a range where yeasts can flourish, and at the still lower a_w range 0.80–0.87 molds are active. A few microorganisms can live at a_w levels below 0.80, but none can reproduce at a_w 0.5 or lower. This explains why dried foods that are at moisture levels of 12 percent or less are not susceptible to microbiological spoilage.

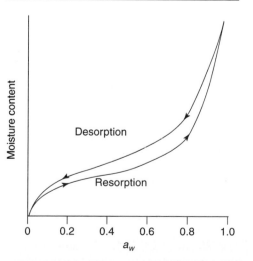

Figure 5.6 Isotherm illustrating the influence of desorption or resorption on water activity (a_w). (Fennema, O. R., *Food Chemistry.* 2nd ed., Marcel Dekker, Inc. New York. p. 55. By permission of Marcel Dekker, Inc.)

Table 5.6 Approximate a_w Range Favorable to Microorganisms[a]

a_w Range of Food	Type of Microorganism
0.85–1.0	Bacteria
0.87–0.91; 0.60–0.65	Yeasts
0.80–0.87; 0.60–0.75	Molds

[a]Adapted from Beauchat, L. R. 1981. Microbial stability as affected by water activity. *Cereal Foods World 26* (7): 345.

Sometimes it may be desirable to alter the a_w of a food. This can be done by different techniques. Drying is a method of preserving food (and concomitantly reducing a_w) that has been practiced for many centuries. Freezing is another preservation technique that reduces a_w in this case by forming ice crystals and therefore removing water from solution in the food. The addition of salt and/or sugar introduces solutes into a food system and lowers a_w. Both of these solutes have been utilized for many years in such preservation products as ham and jams.

WATER IN FOOD PREPARATION

For health reasons, the water consumed should be free of harmful chemicals, microorganisms, and any other materials that can be detrimental to health, and it also needs to have fluoride at a level of approximately 1 part per million to promote sound teeth. Usually chlorine and filtration are used to assure the quality of the water is appropriate for human consumption. Despite the excellent work of many communities in providing safe water, bottled water companies are enjoying huge sales of their products.

In food preparation, the importance of having a safe water supply is recognized, and the water is monitored constantly in cities and towns. However, people relying on their own wells or other private sources of water need to be sure to have the safety of the water checked regularly.

When cooking with water, the softness or hardness of the water is important because hard water (water containing salts of calcium and magnesium carbonate and/or calcium and magnesium sulfate) can influence the quality of such products as tea, coffee, and dried legumes. Boiling water containing calcium or magnesium bicarbonates will cause precipitation of at least some of these salts, which is evidenced by a powdery, metallic precipitate that builds up if a pan is used for this purpose frequently. The fact that these bicarbonate salts can be precipitated from the water means that the water is classified as temporarily hard water. Unlike the bicarbonate salts, the sulfate salts of calcium and magnesium do not precipitate out of water while it is boiling. Water containing calcium and magnesium sulfates is classified as permanently hard water. Hard water of either type causes cloudiness in tea (especially in iced tea) and coffee because of interactions between these salts and the tannins in the beverages. Soft water (either naturally soft or chemically softened) will yield more sparkling versions of these beverages than can be obtained when hard water is used.

Softening of dried legumes is impeded significantly when hard water is used for rehydrating and cooking them. The problem occurs because of interactions between the pectic substances present in the dried legumes and the salts contained in the hard water. The hardness of the water is a significant factor, with extremely hard water making it virtually impossible to soften legumes to the desired extent.

SUMMARY

Water is a common, yet vital, ingredient in food and food preparation. The temperature of boiling water at sea level is 100°C and that of freezing water is 0°C. By addition of a substance capable of forming a true solution or of ionizing, the vapor pressure of the solution is reduced, and the temperature of the boiling liquid is raised. An increase in elevation reduces the temperature of boiling because of the reduction in atmospheric pressure. A similar situation can be created commercially by using a partial vacuum. Conversely, elevated cooking temperatures can be obtained by using a pressure cooker or pressure saucepan to artificially increase atmospheric pressure.

Some water in foods is free water and has flow properties and the ability to act as a solvent. However, water may be hydrogen-bonded within a food system and lose these important characteristics. Even bound water has an influence on the physical properties of food. Water activity is the ratio of the vapor pressure of water in a food and the vapor pressure of pure water. In many foods, this value is between 0.95 and just less than 1.00. Highly salted foods and those with a very high sugar content have values of between 0.80 and 0.90.

Water activity (a_w) values when a food has been resorbing moisture differ from the desorption isotherm in the intermediate moisture content levels. Bacteria are viable when a_w is between 0.85 and 1.0 in a food, with the specific bacteria flourishing only in a somewhat narrower range. Yeasts are active at lower a_w (0.87–0.91 and 0.60–0.65), while molds of various types can live at a_w ranges of 0.80–0.87 and 0.60–0.75. Water activity in a food can be influenced by drying, freezing, and adding solutes (e.g., salt or sugar).

Hard water may be temporarily hard because calcium and magnesium bicarbonates are present or permanently hard because calcium and magnesium sulfates are present. Coffee and tea will be cloudy when made with hard water. Softening of legumes is greatly delayed or even prevented by the salts in hard water when they interact with pectic substances during cooking.

STUDY QUESTIONS

1. Explain why ice floats on water.
2. Compare the amounts of energy involved when water is changed to ice and when water is transformed to steam.
3. Explain why the boiling temperature of water can be altered by use of a (a) vacuum and (b) pressure saucepan.
4. Why does gelatin seem to change when cold water is added and the mixture is allowed to stand briefly?
5. What is water activity? How can it be modified in a food?
6. Why is soft water important when making tea or coffee?

BIBLIOGRAPHY

Fennema, O. R. 1985. *Principles of Food Science. I. Food Chemistry.* 2nd ed. Marcel Dekker: New York.

Hollingsworth, P. 1995. "Pouring it on." *Food Technol. 49* (6): 42.

Knorr, D., et al. 1998. Impact of hydrostatic pressure on phase transitions of food. *Food Technol. 52* (9): 42.

Roos, Y. H. 1986. "Phase transitions and unfreezable water content of carrots, reindeer meat, and white bread studied using differential scanning calorimetry." *J. Food Sci. 51* (3): 684.

Roos, Y. H., et al. 1996. Glass transitions in low moisture and frozen foods: effect on shelf life and quality. *Food Technol. 50* (11): 95.

Simatos, D. and Multon, J. L., eds. 1985. *Properties of Water in Foods.* Martinus Nijhoff Publishers: Dordrecht, Netherlands.

Singh, R. P. 1995. "Heat and mass transfer in foods during frying." *Food Technol. 49* (4): 134.

CHAPTER 6

Physical Aspects of Food Preparation

Food and food products are influenced very significantly by physical principles that are applied throughout harvesting, preparation, and storage. Awareness, appreciation, and understanding of the physical principles that are pertinent to the production of successful food products are keys to the education of food scientists. The following sections highlight some of the topics that illustrate the close relationship between physics and food.

ENERGY AND FOOD

Mechanical Energy

Energy transfer and/or conversion is involved in the preparation of many food products, either as a means of making the foods more palatable or of preserving them. The forms of energy available include mechanical, microwave, ionizing, and heat energy. **Mechanical energy,** such as is available from creaming and mixing, is transformed into a modest amount of heat energy and also can provide enough energy to accomplish a bit of denaturation of egg white and other proteins when they are beaten.

Mechanical Energy
Energy transferred to food through physical movements, such as beating.

Radiation

Radiation is a direct method of transmitting heat energy. Quanta of energy are transmitted from the heat source as electromagnetic waves or rays to the food. Broiling is the familiar example of the use of radiation in food preparation. Radiation heats only the surface of the food in a broiler. For this reason, broiling uses a continuous energy source, with nothing intervening between the food surface and the energy source. In many models of ranges, the oven door needs to be left ajar

Radiation
Direct transfer of heat energy from its source to the surface of the food.

during broiling so that the energy source is on continuously. Failure to do this causes heat to build up rapidly in the oven or broiler unit, and the thermostat will cycle the heat source off and on. When the heat source is off, the food is simply heated by conduction and not radiation. Infrared lamps to keep foods hot in restaurant food service afford another example of radiant heat.

Radiation Energy
Energy traveling as electro-magnetic waves.

Radiant energy is energy traveling as electromagnetic waves. Gamma rays and beta rays are ionizing electromagnetic waves emitted from such radioactive material as ^{60}Co (cobalt-60) or produced by special electron machines.

As the waves and particles pass through food, they collide with molecules in the food and in microorganisms that may be present. These collisions result in chemical alterations of some of the molecules, producing some ion pairs and free radicals, which then undergo additional changes and alter the food by killing micro-

Figure 6.1 Interior of food irradiation chamber. Source (^{60}Co) is immersed in a 20-foot diameter and 20-foot deep pool of highly purified water directly below the floor and is raised by cables (center) when irradiation is being done. (Courtesy of C. J. Dorthalina, International Nutronics, Inc.)

Table 6.1   Terms Designating Amounts of Radiant Energy

Term	Definition
Rad	Basic unit; 10^{-5} joule/gram absorbing material
Gray	100 rads
Kilorad	1000 rads
Kilogray	1000 grays or 100 kilorads or 100,000 rads
Megarad	1000 kilorad or 1,000,000 rads

organisms, inactivating enzymes, and forming some different chemical compounds. Among the compounds that can form from water as a consequence of **irradiation** of food is hydrogen peroxide, a very reactive compound that is toxic to microorganisms (see Figure 6.1). These changes enable irradiated food to be stored for very long periods of time at room temperature without significant changes in other characteristics of the food.

The energy involved in irradiation is expressed as **rads** or multiples of rads (Table 6.1). A rad is an amount of ionizing energy comparable to 10^{-5} joule per gram of absorbing material. The rads impacting a food are determined by the length of time of irradiation and the composition of the food. **Gamma** and **beta rays** and particles are used for irradiating food because these waves are able to penetrate throughout a food. Alpha particles are not used because they lack the ability to penetrate the interior of the food and, therefore, are effective only on the surface (see Figure 6.2).

Irradiation
Exposure to the gamma and beta rays emanating from a radioactive material or source.

Rad
Ionizing energy equal to 10^{-5} joule per gram of absorbing material.

Gamma Ray
Radiant energy of very short wavelength capable of penetrating food, but not lead.

Beta Ray
Radiant energy that is only slightly longer than gamma rays and can penetrate food, but not aluminum.

Figure 6.2   Exterior of the chamber in which food is irradiated. Note the humped ceiling and the extremely thick concrete walls that separate the irradiation chamber from the rest of the food processing facility. (Courtesy of C. J. Dorthalina, International Nutronics, Inc.)

Microwave
Comparatively short (1 to 100 centimeters) electro-magnetic wave.

Microwaves are yet another form of energy used in preparing foods. The heating that occurs when food is subjected to microwaves is caused by the rapid vibration of water, fat, or sugar molecules in the food. Vibration occurs because these types of molecules are dipoles (see Chapter 5), that is, they contain both positive and negative electrical charges that are separated by a very short distance. When the microwaves hit the dipoles, the molecules begin to vibrate against each other, creating friction which is translated to heat within the food rather than over only the surface, as is true in the use of radiation in broiling.

Magnetron Tube
Tube in a microwave oven that generates microwaves at a frequency of 915 or 2450 megahertz.

Megahertz
Measure of frequency defined as one million cycles per second.

Microwave ovens are common appliances in kitchens today. These ovens utilize radiation in a unique way to heat foods. A **magnetron tube** generates microwaves at either 915 or 2450 **megahertz.** The electrical charge in these ovens cycles extremely rapidly, a fact readily apparent when it is recognized that one megahertz is defined as one million cycles per second. The frequency of these cycles causes excitation of water, fat, and sugar molecules as these energy waves penetrate as far as $1\frac{1}{2}$ inches into the food.

Standing Time
Length of time that food is allowed to stand in a microwave oven without operation of the magnetron tube so the residual heat in the food can be transferred by conduction.

The heating that results from the microwaves is augmented by subsequent conduction of this heat energy through the food. Directions for microwave cookery recognize the potential for distributing this heat subsequently by conduction. **Standing times** often are stipulated as a part of the total cookery procedure in microwaving of various foods, particularly bulky and dense foods (meat, for example). The various settings available in microwave ovens automatically cycle the magnetron tube on and off to regulate the duration of energy input in relation to standing time, thus eliminating the need for manual regulation of standing time. In other words, the reduced power settings that are available on microwave ovens are actually timed periods for cycling the microwave energy on and off.

One of the advantages of microwaves as a source of energy for heating foods is speed. When the magnetron is turned on, the microwaves are generated immediately, and heating of the food begins. The actual rate of heating is determined by the amount of energy entering the food and causing the molecules to vibrate. The amount of energy entering the cavity of the microwave oven is constant, regardless of the amount of food in the compartment. When a small amount of food is present, the total energy is absorbed within the food. This same amount of energy is available if a large amount of food is placed in the microwave oven. However, this energy will be dispersed throughout the food, with the result that there actually will be less energy available per unit of food when the oven load is large than when only a little food is present. Therefore, a large load requires a longer microwaving period than a small load to achieve the same temperature in the food. The speed advantage of a microwave oven for small families is apparent.

Not only does microwave cookery modify the way in which foods are heated, it also alters the appearance of the crusts of baked products and of meats. The rapid rate of heating and the lack of intense heat on the exterior of foods in a microwave oven cause the foods to be very pale on the surface. The usual browning reactions do not have an opportunity to occur. The surface of microwaved foods is too cool to cause browning because the energy from the microwaves is being transformed into heat within the food, and the heat then is conducted to the surface. At the surface, the heat quickly is lost to the surrounding air because the chamber of the microwave oven itself is not warmed by the microwave, hence is considerably cooler then the food being microwaved.

In addition to heating by use of microwaves, food may be heated by conduction, convection, and radiation (including microwaves). The mode of energy trans-

fer is different in each type, and the total impact on a food also is different. Consequently, the heating method may be dictated not only by the availability of a particular method, but also by the desired end result.

Conduction

Conduction is a particularly important energy transfer method. In conduction,
thermal energy in transmitted directly from the heat source when it contacts the
pan being used to cook the food. The molecules of metal constituting the outer
surface of the pan transfer the energy to the next metal molecules, which transfer
the energy to the next molecules, and so on until the molecules of metal at the interior of the pan transfer the energy into the molecules of the food that are in contact with the pan. In turn, the molecules in the food pass the energy on to the
other molecules that they contact. The final result is that the food in the pan is hot
and so is the pan.

Conduction is a convenient means of transmitting heat energy, although some
aspects may be disadvantages. For example, time is required for the energy to pass
from molecule to molecule, and some energy is wasted in heating the pan and the
air near the pan of food. Because food is heated from the outside to the inside by
conduction, the food in direct contact with the pan becomes hot much more
rapidly than the food in the interior (see Figure 6.3).

Not all pans conduct heat uniformly well. Heavy cast iron and aluminum are
popular pan materials with excellent heat-conducting properties; however, thin
pans of these metals tend to scorch some foods because some spots in the bottom
of the pan may become too hot before the heat can be conducted uniformly across
the bottom surface. Even inexperienced cooks can use heavy aluminum and cast
iron pans with a minimum risk of burning or scorching the food being heated. In
contrast, stainless steel pans develop hot spots readily as the heat energy tends to
concentrate in one or more small areas of the bottom of the pans. These hot spots
often are responsible for burning or scorching, but the problem can be minimized
by using a moderate or slow rate of heating and by stirring the food constantly (see
Figure 6.4). If the food is heated in a large amount of water, the material of the pan

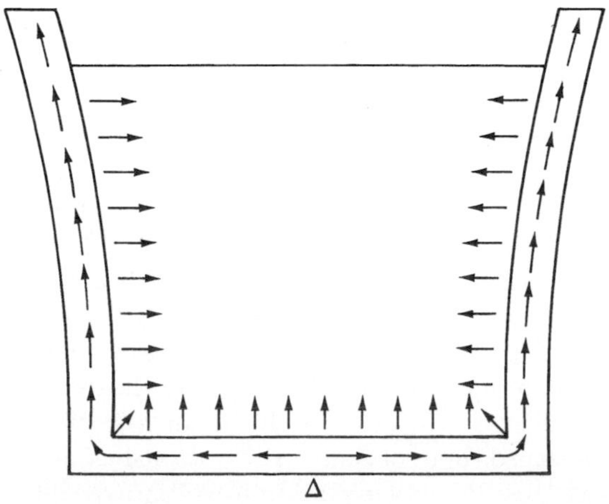

Conduction
Transfer of energy from
one molecule to the adja-
cent molecule in a continuing and progressive fashion
so that heat can pass from
its source, through a pan,
and ultimately throughout
the food being cooked.

Figure 6.3 Conduction of heat
occurs throughout the metal in
the pan to the water.

Figure 6.4   Stainless steel develops hot spots due to uneven conduction of heat by the metal. (Courtesy of Plycon Press.)

is of limited significance. However, if milk and milk-containing foods are being heated and sauces are being thickened, using a heavy aluminum or cast iron pan is very important if scorching is to be avoided and uniform heating is to be assured.

Often water is the medium in which a food is cooked. The temperature of the water rises as the heat is conducted to the water via the pan. In turn, water conducts the heat to the food being cooked in the water. The fat used in deep-fat frying also is an effective conductor and is, in fact, able to transfer far greater thermal energy than can be transmitted via water because of the limitation imposed when water boils; that is, fat can be heated to much higher temperatures than water. Air also can conduct heat, but it does so much less efficiently than either water or fat.

Convection

Convection
Transfer of heat by the circulation of currents of hot air or liquid resulting from the change in density when heated.

When air or liquid is heated, currents are developed. These currents of hot air or hot liquid help to spread heat energy through the container more quickly than can be done by the process of conduction. The circulation or **convection** of the heated material is the natural result of its reduced density. This lighter, heated air or liquid rises through the cooler material in a pan or through the air toward the upper portion of the oven. As the less dense, hot substance rises, it pushes aside the more dense, cooler material. This causes the cooler portion to sink toward the bottom, where it comes into contact with the metal of the pan or the heating ele-

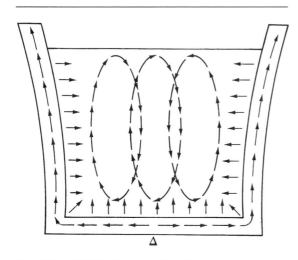

Figure 6.5   Water is heated in a pan by a combination of conduction and convection energy transfer methods.

ment of the oven. This material is heated by conduction, which reduces its density and causes it to begin to rise. As this hot material rises, the cooler portions sink toward the bottom and perpetuate the convection currents (see Figures 6.5 and 6.6).

Convection also contributes to the heating of foods that are being heated by conduction. The two actions complement each other and facilitate the preparation

Figure 6.6   Whether in a standard oven or a convection oven, pans must be arranged so that heat can circulate by convection to bake products uniformly. (Courtesy of Plycon Press.)

Convection Oven
Oven designed with enhanced circulation of heated air to increase heating by convection, reduce baking time, and promote optimal crust browning.

of quality products when used appropriately. The efficiency of convection heating saves time and energy. Commercial bakeries have used convection ovens for many years with excellent success. Accelerated movement of the air throughout the **convection oven** chamber shortens baking time by as much as half and promotes browning to achieve baked products with outstanding crust color. The commercial success of convection ovens has stimulated appliance manufacturers to develop a unit for use in homes. Convection ovens for the home, like their commercial ancestors, augment the natural convection currents with the aid of a fan. Even the home convection ovens do save some baking time over the standard home oven where conduction is the principal mechanism for heating.

Mass Transfer

Mass Transfer
Movement of a food component into or out of a food that is being heated.

Movement of a food component into or out of a food that is being heated is referred to as *mass transfer.* For example, potatoes being fried in deep fat lose some moisture from the outer surfaces into the cooking oil, and that moisture is replaced at the surface by water that has migrated from the interior of the french fry. The net result is that there is not only a reduction in the total amount of water in the center of the french fry, but some of the water-soluble components also are transferred, along with the water. The entry of oil into the french fry during deep fat frying is another example of mass transfer.

Endothermic Reaction
Reaction in which heat is absorbed.

Water that is on the surface of a french fry (or other food being fried) is transformed into steam rather quickly. Formation of steam represents a heat loss from the surface of 540 kilocalories per gram of water vaporized. The result of this **endothermic reaction** is that the surface of the french fry stays cool enough during frying to prevent rapid burning on the surfaces (Blumenthal, 1991). The temperature for frying french fries needs to be controlled because too high a temperature will cause mass transfer of a significant amount of water from the potato into the oil. The problem will be evidenced by the shrunken outline of the fries.

THE STATE OF MATTER

Solids

Solids are defined as substances that do not flow under moderate stress. A solid is in a comparatively low energy state, its molecules moving slowly within a defined space. Very close examination reveals that some solids are organized, crystalline structures, whereas others are amorphous, that is, lacking in organization.

Crystalline solids are organized aggregates of molecules, which are called crystals. Although crystalline solids appear to be inert substances, actually considerable activity occurs within some of these systems. Crystalline candies, such as fudge, are familiar examples of crystalline solids. Crystalline solids that contain water or other liquids are in a dynamic state, one in which some crystals constantly are dissolving and new crystals are forming. The overall result is an equilibrium; the relative proportions of liquid and crystals remain constant, but new crystals form as old crystals dissolve in the liquid.

Because small sugar crystals dissolve more readily than large aggregates of crystals, the smaller crystals dissolve fairly quickly and are replaced by increasingly larger aggregates of crystals. The large aggregates form as some of the dissolved sugar recrystallizes to the solid state on existing crystals. This phenomenon occurs because crystal formation on an existing aggregate results in a lower energy state than would be the case if numerous, very small crystals were formed. Over a period of time, a crystalline candy will exhibit the tendency to become detectably grainy, the result of formation of many large aggregates at the expense of the original small crystals. This phenomenon occurs despite the fact that the crystalline candy is considered to be a solid throughout this ripening or aging process.

The random or disorganized structure of an amorphous solid is exemplified by hard candies, such as toffee. The sugar molecules in amorphous candies are virtually imprisoned within the solid and lack the freedom of movement necessary for them to reorient themselves in an orderly fashion. The very high concentration of sugar molecules within **amorphous** candies serves as a serious deterrent to the freedom of movement that would be required for gross rearrangement of the molecules.

Amorphous solids actually may be fairly dynamic in their nature, depending on their moisture content, temperature, and other storage conditions. Under appropriate conditions [usually very cold and low water activity (a_w) in the solid], the solid will be in a physical state termed a **glassy state.** When the temperature and/or the proportion of a a_w is increased, the material may begin to be somewhat more elastic or rubbery and exhibit reduced stiffness and viscosity. This change, termed the glass transition, occurs over a range of low temperatures despite the fact that a **glass transition temperature (T_g)** exists for specific food solids.

The somewhat dynamic nature of some food solids, e.g., dried milk solids, can create quality and storage concerns for food companies. Clumping of dried milk solids is attributed to **glass transition** problems in which moisture is resorbed on the surface of the dry milk particles, with the result that the temperature for the glass transition can rise to the ambient temperature of the atmosphere in which the milk is being held. This increases plasticity of the dried milk and facilitates bonding between dried milk particles, which is observed as very hard clumps. If the problem of glass transition is to be avoided in the manufacturing of dried milk solids and related protein products, the dehydration process and packaging problems need to be geared toward achieving and maintaining a practical glass transition temperature (T_g). Related problems involving glass state transitions are found in the production of some high starch products, breads, and frozen foods (Roos, et al. 1996).

Liquids

When energy is added to a food, the molecules within begin to move at an ever-increasing rate as the energy level increases. If sufficient energy (usually in the form of heat) is introduced, the molecules move so rapidly that some solid foods begin to change state and become liquids.

A liquid exhibits flow properties. Attractive forces operating between molecules in a liquid give some degree of cohesion despite their transitory status. This transitory bonding in liquids is of far shorter duration than the attractive forces that exist in solids. The energy in liquids is sufficient to maintain a high level of cleavage, but subsequently to reform van der Waal's forces, hydrogen bonds, and other **secondary bonds,** thus resulting in the flow properties observed in various liquids.

The temperature of a liquid is important in determining the fluidity of the material. With an increase in temperature, molecules move more rapidly, which

Amorphous
Form of solid lacking an organized, crystalline structure.

Glassy State
Solid, inflexible physical state formed at an extremely cold temperature and with limited moisture in an amorphous solid; capable of changing to a rubbery or somewhat elastic physical state.

Glass Transition Temperature T_g
Temperature at which an amorphous solid in the glassy state begins to transform to a less rigid state.

Glass Transition
Change of the state of a material from a solid glass to a supercooled rubbery or viscous liquid.

Secondary Bonds
Attractive forces between atoms and functional groups that are less strong than the bonding that occurs when electrons are shared; examples are van der Waal's forces and hydrogen bonding.

increases the tendency of molecules to escape from the liquid and become a vapor. This effort or pressure to be in the gaseous rather than the liquid state is termed ***vapor pressure.*** Vapor pressure increases as temperature rises.

Vapor Pressure
Pressure exerted as molecules of a compound attempt to be in the gaseous rather than the liquid state.

A molecule in the interior of a liquid interacts equally with other molecules of the liquid in all directions. However, a different situation exists in the boundary layer of a liquid; here at the interface between liquid and air (or other gas), interaction with other molecules occurs only on the portion of the molecule that touches other liquid molecules. The outer or upper portion of the molecule has no other molecules of the liquid with which to crosslink. As a result, the molecule may have sufficient energy to break the attractive forces formed with other molecules of the liquid and move away from the liquid into the adjoining gaseous phase. This loss of molecules from a liquid that occurs at the surface as a result of vapor pressure is termed ***evaporation*** (see Figure 6.7).

Evaporation
Escape of liquid molecules into the surrounding atmosphere.

Surface Tension
Attraction between molecules at the surface of a liquid.

Surface tension, a phenomenon related to vapor pressure, may be defined as the attraction between molecules at the surface of a liquid. This phenomenon is important because it controls the loss of molecules from a liquid. For evaporation to occur, vapor pressure needs to be greater than the forces represented by the surface tension.

The effect of surface tension can be observed by carefully examining a drop of water on a flat, clean surface or by placing a sewing needle absolutely flat on the surface of a bowl of water. Note that the drop of water fails to spread infinitely to a uniform thickness, but instead shows some tendency to round into a flattened, ball-like shape. The needle will float on the surface of the water, causing a shallow deformation of the water's contour. Unless the needle is placed so that its entire length is in contact with the water at the same time, it will sink because its density is greater than that of water. However, the surface tension of water is strong enough to buoy the needle if the weight of the needle is distributed over the entire length of the metal shaft. Mercury provides an even more dramatic illustration of surface tension. The surface tension of mercury is extremely high, which causes mercury to form spherelike drops when the liquid is poured or spilled.

Interfacial Tension
The tendency for molecules at the surface of a liquid to remain with the liquid rather than intersperse with molecules of a second adjacent liquid.

The surface tension of liquids varies with the liquid and with the temperature. When two disparate liquids are in contact with each other, their surface phenomena are different. The tendency for molecules at the surface of a liquid to remain within this liquid rather than to intersperse with molecules in an adjoining liquid is referred to as ***interfacial tension.*** Interfacial tension of liquids is of particular interest in relation to food emulsions and is discussed in that context later in this chapter under Emulsions.

Figure 6.7 Interactions on molecules of water and in the boundary layer.

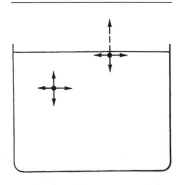

Gases

When a substance is in the gaseous state, the distance between molecules is extremely great when contrasted with the comparatively short distances in liquids and the even shorter distances in solids. Molecules dispersed in the gaseous state move constantly and relatively faster than molecules in liquids. Steam and carbon dioxide are two of the gases of considerable importance in some food products. Swiss cheese is a good example of a product in which the gas formed by microorganisms causes development of a porous texture. The texture characteristics and volume of baked products afford other illustrations of the importance of utilizing gases in making food products.

A particularly important property of gases is their ability to increase in volume and/or to develop pressure as heat is applied to them. This behavior is utilized in the preparation of baked goods, with temperature and time being controlled to produce the desired textural characteristics (see Chapter 17).

Various leavening agents are utilized as sources of gases in batters and doughs to achieve the desired volume and somewhat open texture considered appropriate for specific products. The underlying principle in the action of a leavening agent is that heat causes gases to expand, and this expansion creates sufficient pressure to increase cell size in batters and doughs until their proteins coagulate. This action generally improves texture and increases tenderness by stretching the cell walls thinner and thinner during baking.

DISPERSIONS

Foods represent mixtures or dispersions of two or more types of substances. These substances can be combined together in several different ways. Of particular importance in determining the type of dispersion involved in a food mixture is the size of the molecules or particles to be dispersed. The three basic categories established or defined by particle or molecular size are true solutions, colloidal dispersions, and coarse suspensions.

True Solutions

True solutions have the smallest particle size of the three types of dispersions, for molecules or ions of comparatively small dimensions are the units to be dispersed. Actually, only molecules less than one **millimicron** (1mμ) in diameter can be dispersed in a liquid to form a true solution, and this is true of such simple molecules as sugar. Starch and protein molecules are too large to form **true solutions.**

True solutions are characterized as being the most stable of the three types of dispersions despite the fact that some solutions are made up of electrically charged ions distributed in the liquid. In food preparation, salt (as sodium and chloride ions) or sugar can be dispersed in water to form a true solution. The ions of salt or sugar molecules are designated as the **solute,** the water as the **solvent.**

True solutions can contain varying amounts of ions or molecules of dissolved substances, depending on the solute and the temperature of the solvent. If a true solution contains less solute than the solvent can dissolve at the temperature, it is classified as an **unsaturated solution.** If the true solution contains as much solute as can be dissolved at that temperature, it is classified as a **saturated solution.** If a

Millimicron
A billionth of a meter.

True Solution
Dispersion in which ions or molecules no larger than one millimicron are dissolved in a liquid (usually water).

Solute
Substance dissolved in a liquid to form a true solution.

Solvent
Liquid in which the solute is dissolved to form a true solution.

Unsaturated Solution
True solution capable of dissolving additional solute at the temperature of the solution.

Saturated Solution
True solution containing as much solute in solution as is possible to dissolve at that temperature.

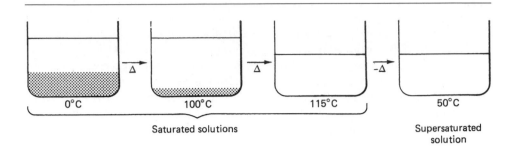

Figure 6.8   The solvent in saturated solutions can dissolve increasing proportions of the solute as the temperature rises, and careful cooling permits the dissolved solute to remain in solution, creating a supersaturated solution with excess solute.

Supersaturated Solution
True solution containing more solute than theoretically can be dissolved at that temperature, a situation created by cooling a heated saturated solution very carefully.

heated saturated solution is cooled a bit under very carefully controlled conditions, more solute can be kept in solution than theoretically can be dissolved by the solvent at this cooler temperature. This seemingly impossible system is designated as a **supersaturated solution** (see Figure 6.8).

As the temperature of a solvent increases, the amount of solute that can be dissolved in it to form a saturated solution increases. This relationship is illustrated in Table 6.2, which gives the amounts of sucrose soluble in water at different temperatures.

Table 6.2 clarifies that a sucrose solution saturated at 20°C is an unsaturated solution at 40°C. Conversely, a sugar solution boiled to a temperature higher than 100°C has the potential to become supersaturated on cooling because the cooler solution cannot dissolve the amount of sugar already dissolved at the higher temperature. Sugar cookery is based on the interrelationships between concentration of sugar, temperatures, and solutions. The key concepts related to sugar cookery are discussed in Chapter 8.

Colloidal Dispersions

Colloidal Dispersion
Two-phase system containing at least one colloid (substance measuring between 0.001 and 1 millimicron in one dimension).

Colloidal dispersions contain molecules intermediate in size between the tiny substances capable of forming true solutions and the gross particles found in coarse suspensions. Specifically, only substances between 0.001 and 1 millimicron can be dispersed in systems classified as colloids. All colloidal systems contain a substance of colloidal dimensions dispersed in a different material. The two com-

Table 6.2   Solubility of Sucrose in Water at Various Temperatures

Temperature of Solution (°C)	Maximum Weight of Sucrose Soluble in 100 ml of Water (g)
0	179.2
20	203.9
40	238.1
50	260.4
100	487.2
115	669.0

Table 6.3 Colloidal Systems in Foods

Name of Colloidal System	Dispersed Phase	Continuous Phase	Example in Food
Emulsion	Liquid	Liquid	Salad dressing
Sol	Solid	Liquid	Gravy
Gel	Liquid	Solid	Baked custard
Foam	Gas	Liquid	Egg white foam
Suspensoid	Gas	Solid	Congealed whipped gelatin

ponents of a colloidal system are found in any of the three states of matter—solid, liquid, or gas—and the system is categorized on the basis of the states involved.

All colloidal systems have two phases: a **continuous phase** and a **discontinuous or dispersed phase.** The continuous phase extends throughout the system, surrounding all parts of the other phase of the system. The dispersed phase or the discontinuous phase is, as the name implies, distributed in isolated or disconnected fashion throughout the entire colloidal system. Technically, colloidal systems may be any combination of solid, liquid, or gas as the continuous or discontinuous phase, as long as the particle size of one phase is within the dimensions of colloids. For example, a colloid might consist of a solid dispersed in a liquid. The colloidal systems of particular importance in foods are categorized as described in Table 6.3. Colloidal systems often are designated on the basis of the state(s) of matter constituting the two phases. To illustrate, a **gel** can be categorized as a liquid in a solid. Similarly, a **sol** is described as a solid in a liquid, and a **foam** is a gas in a liquid.

The behavior of colloids and the systems in which they are found is influenced by various physical characteristics. Some colloids are **hydrophilic** (water-loving) and are hydrated readily. Other colloids exhibit the opposite behavior and are termed **hydrophobic** (water-hating). Hydrophobic colloids do not readily attract water, which makes it possible for such substances to be precipitated with the addition of only a little salt.

The chemical composition of a compound is significant in determining whether the substance is hydrophilic or hydrophobic. In practice, many substances in foods have some parts of their structures that are hydrophilic and other portions that are hydrophobic. The functional groups in molecules that are attracted to water are polar groups. These polar groups include the functional groups in the following organic compounds:

$$\text{organic acid} \left(-C\overset{O}{\underset{OH}{\big\langle}}\right), \text{aldehyde} \left(-C\overset{O}{\underset{H}{\big\langle}}\right), \text{ketone} \left(-\overset{O}{\overset{\|}{C}}-\right)$$

and others, as shown in Table 6.4. Nonpolar structures include cyclic structures and carbon chains. Organic compounds with polar and nonpolar groups tend to collect at the interface between two liquids and thus serve as stabilizing agents in **emulsions** because parts of their molecules are drawn toward the dispersed phase and parts toward the continuous phase.

Continuous Phase
Medium surrounding all parts of the dispersed phase so that it is possible to pass throughout the system in the continuous phase without ever traversing any portion of the dispersed phase.

Discontinuous (Dispersed) Phase
Phase distributed in a discontinuous fashion, making it necessary to pass through at least some of the continuous phase to reach another particle of the dispersed phase.

Emulsion
Colloidal dispersion of a liquid in another liquid with which it is immiscible (not mixable).

Sol
Colloidal dispersion of a solid dispersed in a liquid.

Gel
Colloidal dispersion of a liquid dispersed in a solid.

Foam
Colloidal dispersion of a gas dispersed in a liquid.

Suspensoid
Colloidal dispersion of a gas dispersed in a solid.

Hydrophilic
Attracted to water.

Hydrophobic
Repelling water.

Table 6.4   Polar and Nonpolar Groups

Polar Group (Hydrophilic)	Nonpolar Group (Hydrophobic)

Emulsions. An emulsion is a colloidal system in which a liquid is dispersed in droplets in another liquid (the continuous phase) with which it is immiscible. The old familiar saying "oil and water don't mix" is a colloquial way of recognizing the instability of emulsions. Emulsions can be formed by shaking the two liquids together until they appear to be well mixed. Shaking provides the energy needed to enable the liquid with the higher surface tension to form many small droplets or spheres which then are surrounded by the other liquid. Formation of these numerous small spheres creates a far larger surface area for the dispersed liquid than was the case when the two liquids were in contact as two layers.

Formation of an emulsion requires energy to permit the continuous phase to stretch out and surround the droplets being formed. The overall process is rather complex, for the continuous phase needs to be extended and more surface area needs to be available to surround the droplets that are to be the dispersed phase. The discontinuous or dispersed phase must be split into droplets, and the surfaces of these droplets must be coated with the emulsifying agent. The physical spreading needed for the formation of the emulsion is done by beating, stirring, or shaking. Some resting time can be useful in the formation of emulsions, for the rest provides time for the emulsifying agent to orient its molecules along the newly formed interfaces between the droplets and the continuous phase. Some warming of the ingredients may ease the formation of an emulsion by increasing the fluidity of both phases, a situation that facilitates spreading of the continuous phase and splitting of the other phase into the desired small droplets.

Figure 6.9 An oil-in-water emulsion.

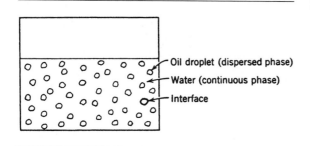

Oil droplet (dispersed phase)
Water (continuous phase)
Interface

The droplets of the dispersed phase tend to coalesce when they bump into each other as they move through the emulsion because the one large droplet (created from two small droplets) represents a lower energy state than the two droplets. Because the one large droplet has less surface area than the two small droplets have cumulatively, the droplets in an emulsion continue to coalesce into larger droplets until ultimately the emulsion breaks or separates into two distinct phases.

Emulsions often are classified on the basis of the type of liquid constituting each of the phases. Thus, an emulsion may be classified as an **oil-in-water emulsion** (o/w) or a **water-in-oil emulsion** (w/o). These categories express clearly that oil is dispersed as droplets suspended in water or that water is dispersed as droplets in oil, respectively (see Figures 6.9 and 6.10).

The stability of emulsions is important in food products, for the behavioral characteristics of the two liquids are quite different in an emulsion than they are in the nonemulsified state. One of the most obvious effects of an emulsion is that the viscosity of the emulsified state is increased over the viscosity of either of the liquids. This is illustrated clearly by mayonnaise. It is possible to add so much oil to a mayonnaise emulsion that the product actually can be sliced. This truly is remarkable when compared with the very fluid state of the vinegar and the only slightly more viscous state of the oil used in preparing mayonnaise. However, if the mayonnaise is frozen or subjected to some other stress that breaks the emulsion, the two liquids separate into discrete phases and resume their fluid natures. The broken emulsion cannot be used satisfactorily to coat salad ingredients or to spread in a sandwich. Clearly, the stability of the emulsion is essential to its use in food preparation (see Figure 6.11).

The stability of an emulsion is determined by the viscosity of the continuous phase, the presence and the concentration of an **emulsifying agent,** the size of the droplets, and the ratio of the dispersed phase to the continuous phase. A key

Oil-in-Water Emulsion
Colloidal dispersion in which droplets of oil are dispersed in water, for example, mayonnaise.

Water-in-Oil Emulsion
Colloidal dispersion in which droplets of water are dispersed in oil, for example, butter.

Emulsifying Agent
Compound that contains both polar and nonpolar groups and thus is drawn to the interface between the two phases of an emulsion to coat the surface of the droplets.

Figure 6.10 A water-in-oil emulsion.

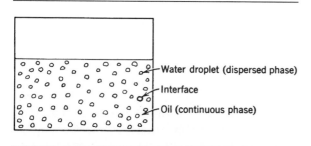

Water droplet (dispersed phase)
Interface
Oil (continuous phase)

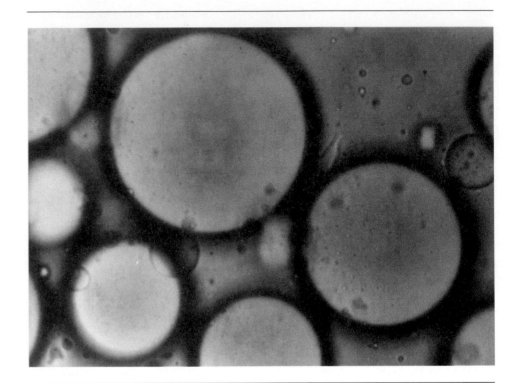

Figure 6.11   Photomicrograph of a 40% oil-in-water dressing after 1 month of storage. Gum tragacanth is the stabilizer (X200). (Courtesy of K. A. Coia, Miles, Inc., Biotechnology Products Division. Reprinted from *Journal of Food Science*. 1987. Vol. 52(1): 167. Copyright (c) by Institute of Food Technologists.)

factor in the formation and stability of emulsions is the presence of an emulsifying agent. An emulsifying agent is a substance that consists of both polar and nonpolar groups and thus has some attraction toward both phases of the emulsion. The polar groups orient the emulsifying agent toward the aqueous phase, and the nonpolar groups pull the molecule toward the oil. The net result of this tug-of-war is that the emulsifying agent is held at the interface of the two phases. The emulsifier forms a monomolecular layer that effectively coats the interfaces to impede the contact between oil droplets in an oil-in-water emulsion (or, conversely, water droplets in a water-in-oil emulsion). Because the emulsifying agent collects around the surface of the dispersed spheres, the droplets cannot touch each other directly and coalesce.

The nature of the emulsifying agent influences the type of emulsion that is formed. If the agent is attracted more strongly to water than to oil, the surface tension of the water is reduced more than that of the oil. The result is formation of an oil-in-water emulsion.

The balance between hydrophilic and lipophilic (or hydrophobic) characteristics in various emulsifying agents can be expressed on a 20-point scale referred to as the **hydrophilic/lipophilic balance (HLB).** On this HLB scale, emulsifying agents with an HLB between 8 and 18 are especially attracted to water and are considered to be suited for forming oil-in-water emulsions, which are the type

Hydrophilic/Lipophilic Balance (HLB)
Scale (20-point) indicating the affinity of an emulsifying agent for oil versus water.

found in most food emulsions. Butter and margarine, both of which are water-in-oil emulsions, can be stabilized (if desired) with an emulsifying agent in the range of 3 to 6 HLB. Such agents are attracted more to oil than water.

The best emulsifier available for forming emulsions in the home is egg yolk, which derives its unique abilities from its **lecithin** and protein content (Chapter 16). Lecithin is a phospholipid that has two largely lipophilic fatty acid chains and a hydrophilic phosphoric acid component. The combination of these features promotes formation of an oil-in-water emulsion because of the way that lecithin is oriented toward both the oil and water. The proteins in the egg yolk also are attracted to the region of the interface between oil droplets and water, further stabilizing the emulsion.

The amount of emulsifying agent present significantly influences the stability of the emulsion. If enough agent is present to form a complete monomolecular layer around each droplet, the emulsion will be stable; any unprotected surfaces, however, will allow the droplets to coalesce when they contact each other. No benefit is obtained from having more emulsifying agent than is necessary to provide total coverage of the interfaces. Up to the point of total coverage, an increase in the amount of emulsifying agent will increase stability. Thorough coverage with an emulsifying agent results in a **permanent emulsion.** Although it is possible to break permanent emulsions, usual conditions of handling and use do not damage these emulsions. Mayonnaise is a familiar example of a permanent emulsion.

Some stability in emulsions is imparted simply by the viscous nature of the emulsion. Sweet salad dressings for fruit may be stabilized by the use of a cooked, viscous sugar syrup or by honey. Although these ingredients are not very effective as emulsifying agents at the interface, their viscous nature produces a fairly thick dressing, one in which the dispersed droplets move rather slowly. Collisions between droplets occur with decreasing frequency as the viscosity of an emulsion is increased. The reduction in contacts between droplets aids in retarding the separation of the emulsion into the two distinct phases, thus imparting fairly good stability. Emulsions stabilized by this technique are termed **semipermanent emulsions.**

Temporary emulsions are quite fluid systems with very little emulsifier present. An oil-and-vinegar dressing is a familiar example of a temporary emulsion. The insoluble seasonings, such as ground pepper, provide very slight protection of the emulsion by orienting themselves at the interface when the oil and vinegar are shaken together. However, simply far too little of these substances is present to provide the protective coating needed to keep the oil droplets from coalescing, and they frequently bump into each other in the fluid emulsion. The finer the particle size of these powders, the more effective is their action as emulsifiers.

Emulsions, even permanent emulsions, separate under certain conditions. Temporary emulsions always separate quite rapidly because their droplets are able to move together freely in the fluid condition typical of these emulsions. However, the more stable emulsions (such as a viscous honeylike dressing or even mayonnaise) also separate if their temperature is changed drastically. Heating increases fluidity and encourages the emulsion to break. Freezing breaks emulsions because the water expands as ice crystals form. Jarring or shaking also can cause permanent emulsions to break, as a result of the different densities of the two phases.

Sols.   Sols are colloidal systems in which a solid of colloidal dimensions is dispersed throughout a liquid. This type of system has flow properties, which may range from rather fluid to extremely viscous, barely flowing. Regardless of the vis-

Lecithin
Phospholipid in egg yolk that is a very effective emulsifying agent; its formula is

Permanent Emulsion
Emulsion containing an amount of emulsifying agent sufficient to enable it to remain intact during ordinary handling and use.

Semipermanent Emulsion
Emulsion with rather good stability because of the viscous nature of the liquid constituting the continuous phase.

Temporary Emulsion
Emulsion that has very little emulsifying agent and that is too fluid to restrict movement of droplets; such instability requires that the ingredients be shaken to form a temporary emulsion immediately before use.

cosity, the dispersed (discontinuous) solid is always distributed throughout the sol; it does not precipitate to the bottom (as can happen in coarse suspensions). Proteins in sols often are aided in remaining dispersed by the electrical charges on their external surfaces. Protein molecules of similar electrical charge repel each other, thereby making it very improbable that they will be able to join together and become too large a unit to remain in the colloidal sol.

Pectin, a complex carbohydrate, provides a useful example of a second way in which solids are able to be dispersed to form a sol. Pectin (Chapter 7) like other carbohydrates and many proteins, is hydrophilic and attracts a layer of water that is bound tightly to the molecules by hydrogen bonds. Water thus forms an insulating shield for the pectin or other hydrophilic colloid, providing a layer that inhibits bonding between the molecules of the colloidal substances (see Figure 6.12).

Sols are characterized as being pourable, or at least able to flow slightly. This property is to be expected, because liquid is the continuous phase. Even when the concentration of solid colloidal material is very high, some liquid still separates each of the solid particles, which ensures that at least some flow is possible. The actual ability of a sol to flow is determined by several factors, among which the temperature of the sol and the concentration of solid in the liquid are particularly important. Sols flow more readily at a high temperature than they do at a low one, a characteristic that must be considered in evaluating the viscosity of sols. The higher the concentration of the solid in a sol, the more viscous is the sol.

Frequently, a sol can be transformed into a second type of colloidal system—a gel. This transition occurs subtly as the energy level of the system drops during the cooling of a sol. The solids in the discontinuous phase move with increasing difficulty through the continuous liquid phase and eventually start to associate with each other.

Several sols commonly are served. These include white sauces, gravy, stirred custard, and other thickened sauces. These sols need to be prepared with the proper ratio of ingredients to achieve the desired viscosity or flow properties at the temperature anticipated for serving. If they begin to thicken too much and to exhibit poor flow properties, they can be reheated to reduce viscosity, or more liquid may be added.

Other sols may be formed as a preliminary step in making a gel, but will not actually be served as a sol. Gelatin is a familiar example in which a sol is formed

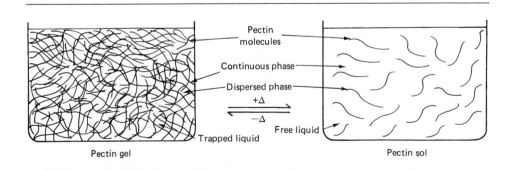

Figure 6.12 In a pectin gel the pectin molecules are the continuous phase and the liquid is the dispersed phase; the sol is the reverse situation, i.e., the pectin molecules are the dispersed phase, and the liquid is the continuous phase.

first by hydrating and dispersing the gelatin molecules in very hot liquid. Jams and jellies made with pectin and starch-thickened puddings are other illustrations of the need to form a sol prior to the desired gel structure.

Gels.   A gel also is a colloidal system, but it is the reverse of a sol. A gel comprises a solid matrix (the continuous phase) and a liquid (the discontinuous or dispersed phase). The solid in the gel is sufficiently concentrated to provide the structure needed to prevent the flow of the colloidal system. Some of the liquid in a gel is adsorbed to the molecules of the solid and is bound water. This binding of some of the liquid accounts, in part, for the loss of flow properties when a gel is formed. The remaining water is free, but is trapped between the solid, interlocking molecules or strands of the solid component of the gel.

Some of the free liquid may be released if the gel structure is cut. Drainage of free liquid from a gel is termed **syneresis.** Syneresis is exhibited in varying degrees by various gels. The type of solid in the gel and its concentration are of particular importance in determining the amount of syneresis. A cranberry jelly provides a clear example of extensive syneresis when it is cut and allowed to stand for a period of time. Although syneresis is undesirable in cranberry jelly, this phenomenon is useful in cheese production. In fact, the production of cheese requires extensive cutting of the curd (a gel structure) to aid in removal of the liquid whey.

Syneresis
Weeping or drainage of liquid from a gel.

Because sols and gels are similar, but reverse types of colloidal dispersions, it is not surprising that many of them can be changed from one form to the other, depending on the conditions. Gelatin dispersions provide a familiar illustration of the reversibility of some sols and gels. When a gelatin dispersion is warm, it is a sol and exhibits obvious flow properties. On adequate cooling, the gelatin molecules form secondary bonds as they pass near each other. Gradually, so much energy is lost from the system as it cools that some "permanent" bonds form between the gelatin molecules, establishing a solid network that is capable of entrapping the water in the system. The result is an apparent solid, the molded gelatin, which is capable of holding its shape when served.

Foams.   **Foams** are dispersions of gases in a dispersing medium. In food foams, the dispersing medium usually is liquid, sometimes strengthened by a solid or modified into a solid by heating. The foams utilized most commonly in food preparation are those made with heavy cream, egg whites, egg yolks, gelatin, and concentrated milk products (see Figure 6.13).

Foam
Colloidal dispersion in which gas is the dispersed phase, and liquid (which may convert to a solid) is the continuous phase.

Formation of a foam is accomplished by providing energy to counteract the surface tension of the liquid and stretch the fluid into thin films encompassing bubbles of gas. Liquids capable of forming foams have low surface tension and thus can spread or stretch easily and so not coalesce readily. They also must have low vapor pressure.

If surface tension is high, the foam will be very difficult to form because of the resistance to spreading and the strong tendency to expose the least possible surface area. High surface tension presents the further problem of limiting the stability of the foam. A foam formed with a liquid of high surface tension collapses very quickly as a result of the tendency to coalesce as the foam stands after beating ceases.

Liquids with high vapor pressure evaporate quickly. When the liquid surrounding a gas bubble evaporates, there is nothing left to retain the gas that had been trapped in the liquid. Clearly, liquids with a low vapor pressure are necessary if useful foams are to be formed.

Figure 6.13 An egg white foam is a colloidal system in which air (gas) is dispersed in a liquid (egg white), and denatured proteins in the egg white add rigidity to the cell walls.

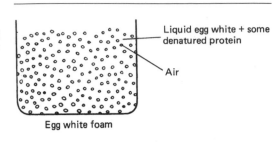

Liquid egg white + some denatured protein

Air

Egg white foam

Additional stability can be provided to foams if some solid matter can be incorporated into the films to increase the rigidity of the walls surrounding the gas. The presence of particles of fat in chilled heavy whipped cream aids in stabilizing foams of this type. In protein foams, the denaturation of the protein provides stability to cell walls (Figure 6.14). This can be noted particularly clearly in the egg foams used so often in baked products, but other protein foams also benefit from the denaturation of the protein.

Foams are important because of their contribution to volume and texture of various food products. The bubbles form a porous texture, which may be quite variable in character, ranging from very fine to extremely coarse cells. These bubbles promote a feeling of lightness in foods containing foams. The volume of foods in increased when foams are formed with some of the ingredients. In baked products, foams contribute very significantly to the volume of the finished product in two ways. The air already trapped in the foam expands in the heat of the oven until the cell walls of the baking food lose their elasticity when the protein denatures. In addition, steam and the carbon dioxide that forms from chemical and/or biological leavening agents during the period in the oven collect in and expand the existing cells of the foam.

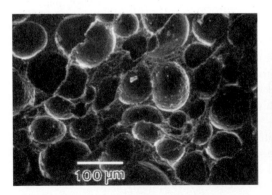
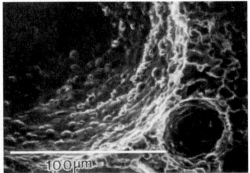

Figure 6.14 The structure of whipped cream as viewed in an electron microscope (left); fat crystals stabilizing an air bubble in whipped cream (right). (Courtesy of Unilever Research, Vlaardingen, The Netherlands.)

Coarse Suspensions

Many dispersions in food preparation consist of mixtures of substances of larger-than-colloidal dimensions (larger than 1 micron). These systems are influenced by gravity and tend to separate as a consequence. An uncooked starch mixture and oatmeal flakes in water are illustrations of a coarse suspension. When the starch or cereal is stirred with water, a coarse suspension results until the suspended food settles by gravity to the bottom of the container, leaving the water on top. When this separation occurs, the coarse suspension no longer exists; however, it can be reformed by stirring.

SUMMARY

Heat in food preparation may be introduced by mechanical energy, conduction, convection, and radiation (including microwave radiation). The various modes of heating may be combined in the preparation of a single food item, with each method providing some specific effects on the character of the final product.

Mass transfer is the term designated to indicate the shifting of a food component into or out of a food during heating. This is illustrated by the loss of water from french fries during frying and the entry of fat.

The behavior of food during harvesting, preparation, and storage follows basic principles of physics. The three forms of matter—gas, liquid, and solid—are found in various foods and food products. Solids, whether crystalline or amorphous, are useful and stable. Amorphous solids can transform to a glassy state that can cause problems in some dried and frozen foods. Ice is an example of a crystalline solid that can be transformed into its liquid state if enough thermal energy is supplied. If still more thermal energy is applied, water can be transformed into its gaseous state.

Liquids exhibit vapor pressure and surface tension. Vapor pressure is the force exerted as the liquid molecules attempt to leave the liquid or evaporate. Surface tension is the energy or attraction between molecules at the surface of the liquid, a force tending to draw the liquid into its smallest possible volume. Vapor pressure and surface tension work in opposition. When two liquids are in contact with each other but are not miscible, their interaction is termed *interfacial tension.*

Gases are important in foods because of the change in volume as the temperature changes. The expansion of gases in batters and doughs during the baking of these products results in a vital expansion that enhances the volume, texture, and general palatability of baked products.

Food dispersions may be categorized as (1) true solutions, (2) colloidal dispersions, or (3) coarse suspensions. True solutions may be unsaturated, saturated, or supersaturated, depending on the amount of solute in relation to solvent and on the temperature and treatment.

Molecules ranging in size from 0.001 to 1 millimicron can be dispersed in a liquid, gas, or solid to form colloidal dispersions of various types. Four types of colloidal dispersions are used frequently in food systems: (1) sols, (2) gels, (3) emulsions, and (4) foams. Sols are composed of a solid of colloidal dimensions dispersed in a liquid. Sols do not precipitate or separate; their common characteristic is that they all exhibit flow properties.

Emulsions are colloidal systems in which one liquid forms the continuous phase and an immiscible liquid is dispersed in it in the form of small droplets. Salad dressings are a familiar example of oil-in-water emulsions, in which oil droplets are dispersed in vinegar (water). Stability of emulsions ranges from temporary to permanent and depends on the viscosity of the emulsion and the presence of emulsifying agents. The hydrophilic/lipophilic balance (HLB) determines whether an emulsifying agent promotes formation of an oil-in-water or a water-in-oil emulsion. Lecithin, a phospholipid in egg yolk, has both polar and nonpolar groups which draw it effectively to both the oil and vinegar components of the emulsion. This concentrates the lecithin at the interface (the surface of the droplets) and provides a protective coating. Ingredients that can coat the surface of droplets and act at the interface between oil and water are called emulsifying or interfering agents.

Sols can be converted into gels, which are colloidal dispersions in which the solid is the continuous phase, and the liquid is the discontinuous phase (just the opposite of sols). Protein and carbohydrate gels are common in the diet. The solid colloidal component crosslinks to other solid particles to form a random yet continuous solid network that traps the liquid to form a gel from a sol. In some cases, gels can be reversed to sols by heating. When gels are cut, some liquid may drain from them, a phenomenon termed syneresis.

Foams in foods ordinarily are air trapped in films of liquid. Frequently, some solid component helps to strengthen the cell walls in foams to give some rigidity and stability to the foam. Proteins often are present to add strength to food foams. Egg white, egg yolk, gelatin, concentrated milk products, and heavy cream foams are familiar foams used in food products. Their formation and stability are influenced greatly by the surface tension of the liquid being whipped and its vapor pressure.

STUDY QUESTIONS

1. Explain why it is possible to float a needle on water.
2. Theoretically a supersaturated solution cannot exist, and yet such solutions can be made. Explain how this is achieved.
3. Define true solution, colloidal dispersion, and coarse suspension.
4. Why is the hydrophilic nature of the solid particles in a sol of importance to the behavior of the sol?
5. Why is the transition temperature of a glassy solid of importance in dried milk solids?
6. Explain the relationship of hydrophilic/lipophilic balance and the type of emulsion formed using various emulsifying agents.
7. Explain how an emulsifying agent is able to enhance the stability of an emulsion.
8. What is the relationship between sols and gels?
9. Why is a foam made with a liquid that has a high vapor pressure a comparatively unstable foam?
10. Compare the mechanisms of heat transfer involved when a meat loaf is baked in a conventional oven with those utilized when meat loaf is baked in a microwave oven equipped with a browning unit.

BIBLIOGRAPHY

Blumenthal, M. M. 1991. "New look at chemistry and physics of deep-fat frying." *Food Technol. 45* (2): 68.

Bruhn, C. M. et al. 1986. "Attitude change toward food irradiation among conventional and alternative consumers." *Food Technol. 40* (1): 86.

Cable, D. W. and Saaski, E. 1990. "Fiberoptic pressure measurement of spontaneous bumping/spattering of foods during microwaving." *Food Technol. 44* (6): 120.

Copson, D. A. 1975. *Microwave Heating*. 2nd ed. AVI Publishing: Westport, CT.

Cunningham, F. E. and Cotterill, O. J. 1974. "Performance of egg white in the presence of yolk proteins." *Poultry Sci. 51:* 712.

DeCareau, R. V. 1985. *Microwaves in Food Processing Industry*. Academic Press: Orlando, FL.

Elias, P. S. and Cohen, A. J. 1983. *Recent Advances in Food Irradiation*. Elsevier: New York.

Fennema, O. R. 1985. *Principles of Food Science. I. Food Chemistry*. 2nd ed. Marcel Dekker: New York.

Friberg, S. E., et al. 1990. In *Food Emulsions*. ed. Larson, K. and Friberg, S. E. Marcel Dekker. New York. 21.

Gerling, J. E. 1986. "Microwaves in food industry: promise and reality." *Food Technol. 40* (6): 82.

Holmes, Z. A. and Woodburn, M. 1981. "Heat transfer and temperature of foods during processing." *CRC Crit. Rev. Food Sci. Nutr. 14* (3): 231.

Hoover, D. G. 1993. "Pressure effects on biological systems." *Food Technol. 47* (6): 150.

Howard, D. 1991. "A look at viscometry." *Food Technol. 45* (7): 82.

Knorr, D. 1993. "Effects on high-hydrostatic-pressure processes on food safety and quality." *Food Technol. 47* (6): 156.

Lauridsen, J. B. 1976. "Food emulsifiers: surface activity, edibility, composition, and application." *Am. Oil Chem. Soc. J. 53:* 400.

Lydersen, A. L. 1983. *Mass Transfer in Engineering Practice*. Wiley: New York.

Mottur, G. P. 1989. "Scientific look at potato chips—original savory snack." *Cereal Foods World 34:* 620.

Mudgett, R. E. 1986. "Microwave properties and heating characteristics of foods." *Food Technol. 40* (6): 84.

Rees, D. A. 1969. "Structure, conformation and mechanism in the formation of polysaccharide gels and networks." *Adv. Carbohydrate Chem. Biochem. 24:* 324.

Rees, D. A. 1972. "Polysaccharide gels." *Chem. Ind.* 630.

Reitz, C. 1986. *Microwave Reference Guide 1986–1987*. International Microwave Power Institute: Clifton, VA.

Roos, Y. H., et al. 1996. "Glass transitions in low moisture and frozen foods: effect on shelf life and quality." *Food Technol. 50* (11): 95.

Sauter, E. A. and Montoure, J. E. 1972. "Relation of lysozyme content of egg white to volume and stability of foam." *J. Food Sci. 37:* 918.

Shoemaker, C. F., Nantz, J., Bonnans, S., and Noble, A. C. 1992. "Rheological characterization of dairy products." *Food Technol. 46* (1): 98.

Singh, R. P. 1995. "Heat and mass transfer in foods during frying." *Food Technol. 49* (4): 134.

3

Carbohydrates

CHAPTER 7

Overview of Carbohydrates

C arbohydrates are, as their name implies, hydrates of carbon. Whether the compound is the smallest (monosaccharide) or the largest (polysaccharide), the ratio of hydrogen to oxygen in the molecule is essentially two to one, just as in water. Chemists categorize carbohydrates on the basis of the number of basic units linked together: monosaccharide, disaccharide, oligosaccharide, and polysaccharide. Nutritionists often refer to the mono- and disaccharides as **simple sugars** and to the polysaccharides as **complex carbohydrates.**

The monosaccharides may contain from three to six carbon atoms, which leads to their generic designations as **trioses, tetroses, pentoses,** and **hexoses.** Note that the common suffix is -ose, which designates that the compound is a carbohydrate. The various monosaccharides are combined to make the other carbohydrates; glucose is the monosaccharide that is found most frequently as the building block of more complex carbohydrates.

The sweet taste of the monosaccharides and disaccharides is of great importance in food products. Other characteristics of value are their ease of solubility, ability to contribute to mouthfeel in candies and syrups, browning at very high temperatures, and their contribution to volume in baked products. Complex carbohydrates exhibit very different characteristics, which vary with the specific type of compound. Starch is valued for its thickening ability. Cellulose and the hemicelluloses modify textures where they are incorporated into food products, contributing a somewhat harsh mouthfeel. Gums and pectin serve as thickening agents that are valued for their very limited calorie contribution.

Simple Sugars
Monosaccharides and disaccharides.

Complex Carbohydrates
Polysaccharides.

Triose
Saccharide with three carbon atoms.

Tetrose
Saccharide with four carbon atoms.

Pentose
Saccharide with five carbon atoms.

Hexose
Saccharide with six carbon atoms, the most common size unit.

MONOSACCHARIDES

Although **monosaccharides** occur in nature to only a limited extent, they nevertheless are of interest to food scientists. Formulas for several of the more common monosaccharides are presented in the sections that follow.

Monosaccharide
Carbohydrate containing only one saccharide unit.

Pentoses

Ribose, arabinose, and xylose are the key pentoses of interest in food products. Their chemical structures, presented as Fischer structures, are presented below:

D-ribose   D-arabinose   D-xylose

Actually, these sugars often occur in nature with a linkage between the oxygen on the first carbon and one of the alcohol (—OH) groups, which results in a ring structure (Haworth structure), as shown:

α-D-ribose   α-D-arabinose   α-D-xylose

Each of these structures is an alpha (α) form of the pentose sugar because of the orientation of the hydroxyl group on the first carbon (C_1). The orientation of the hydroxyl group is reversed in the beta (β) form. Note that the ring structure always involves the first carbon and one of the other carbon atoms (either carbon 4 or carbon 5).

Hexoses

Dextrose
Synonym for glucose, so named because polarized light bends to the right in a glucose solution.

Levulose
Synonym for fructose, so named because polarized light bends to the left in a fructose solution.

Glucose (also called **dextrose** because of its ability to bend polarized light to the right), fructose (sometimes referred to as **levulose** or left-bending), and galactose are especially important hexoses. Others found in foods include mannose, gulose, and sorbose. Hexoses having only one of the carbon atoms external to a 6-membered ring are classified as aldoses; glucose galactose, mannose, and gulose are examples of aldoses. When a hexose has two carbon atoms external to a 5-membered ring, the sugar is identified as a ketose; fructose and sorbose are ketoses.

The Fischer structures of glucose, fructose, and galactose are of particular interest. These are:

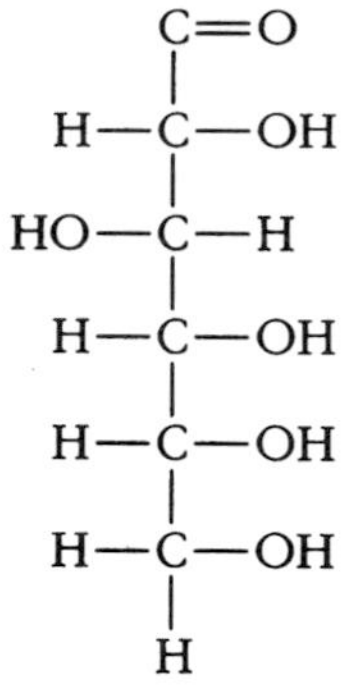

C=O
H—C—OH
HO—C—H
H—C—OH
H—C—OH
H—C—OH
H

D-glucose

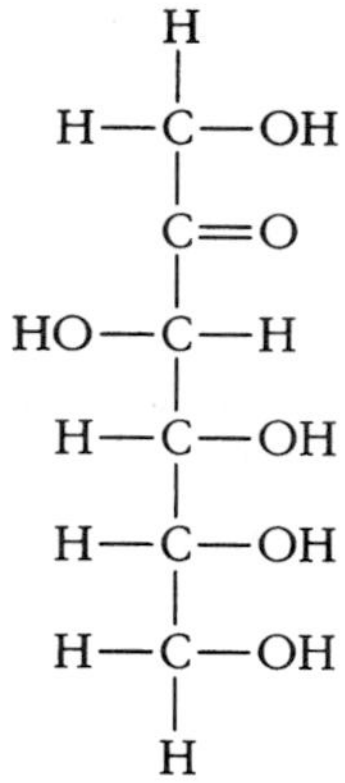

H
H—C—OH
C=O
HO—C—H
H—C—OH
H—C—OH
H—C—OH
H

D-fructose

C=O
H—C—OH
HO—C—H
HO—C—H
H—C—OH
H—C—OH
H

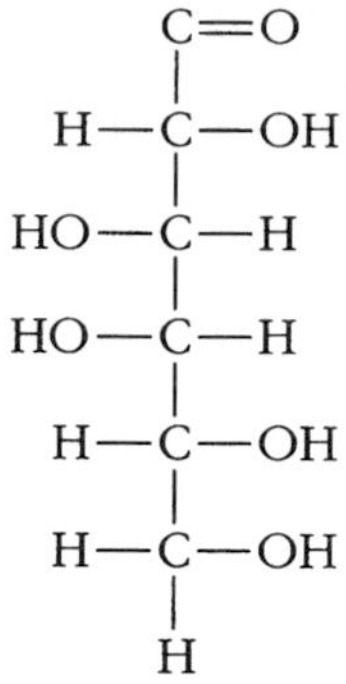

D-galactose

The Haworth or cyclic structures of these three common hexoses are:

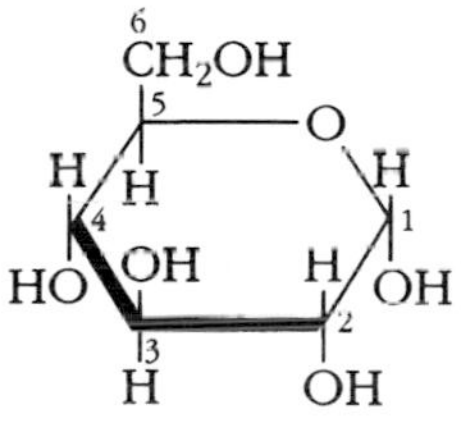

α-D-glucose

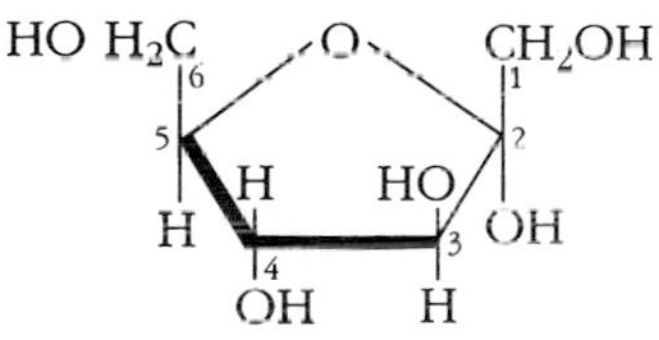

α-D-fructose

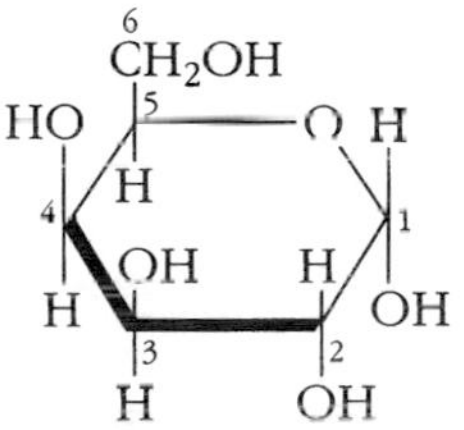

α-D-galactose

Three other hexoses—mannose, gulose, and sorbose—are presented below in their Haworth structures:

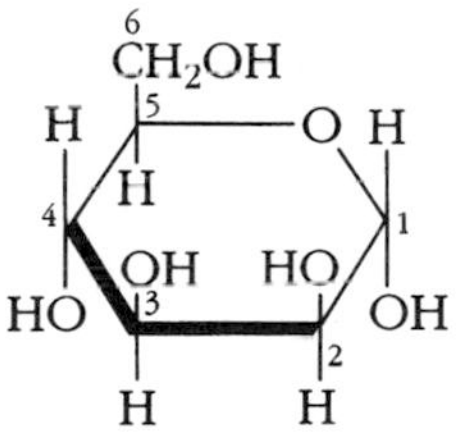

α-D-mannose

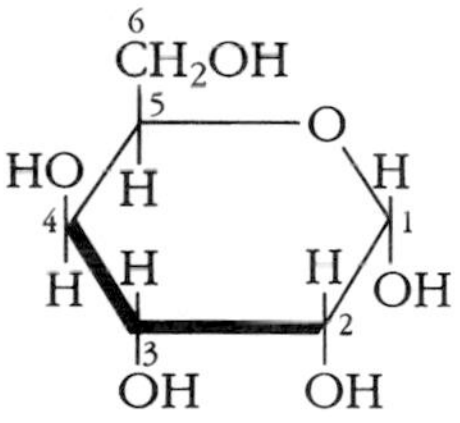

α-D-gulose

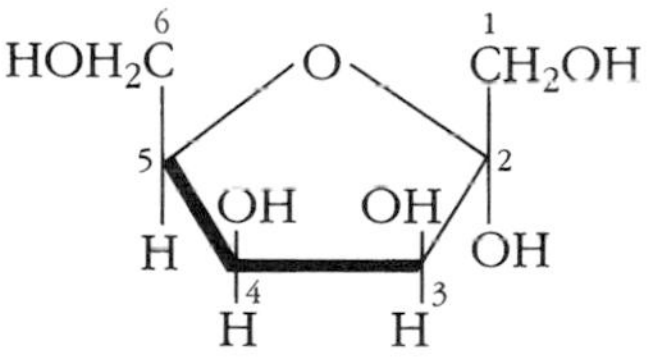

α-D-sorbose

Four of these monosaccharides (glucose, galactose, mannose, and gulose) are **aldoses** and have the sixth carbon atom external to the ring. Note that both fructose and sorbose are **ketoses,** both exhibiting their first and sixth carbon atoms external to the ring.

DISACCHARIDES

Disaccharides are structurally related to monosaccharides. Disaccharides are formed when two monosaccharides join together by a glycolitic linkage, eliminating a molecule of water. In the disaccharides common in foods—sucrose, maltose,

Aldose
Hexose with one carbon atom external to the 6-membered ring.

Ketose
Hexose with two carbon atoms external to the 5-membered ring.

Disaccharide
Carbohydrate formed by union of two monosaccharides with the elimination of a molecule of water.

and lactose—glucose is the monosaccharide common to all three structures. Sucrose forms from glucose and fructose:

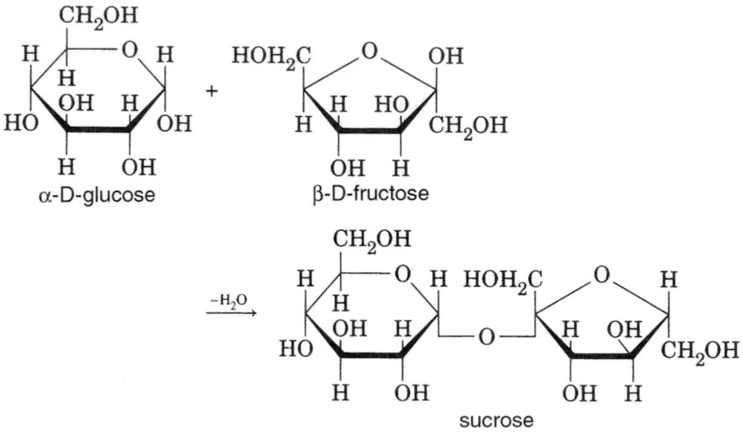

α-D-glucose   β-D-fructose

sucrose

The formation of maltose from two glucose molecules is as follows:

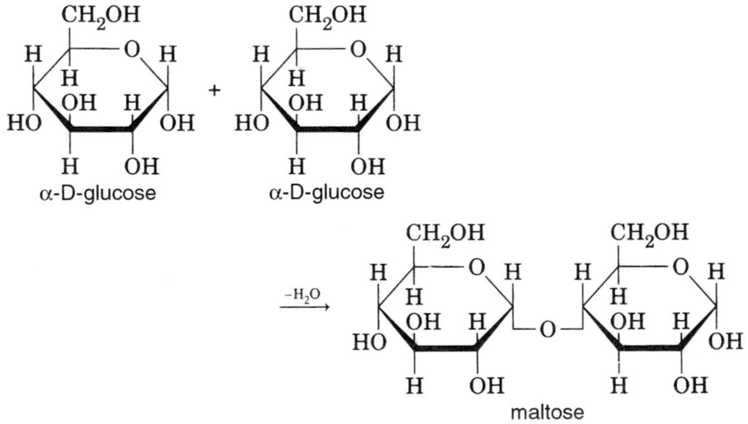

α-D-glucose   α-D-glucose

maltose

The formation of lactose from glucose and galactose is as follows:

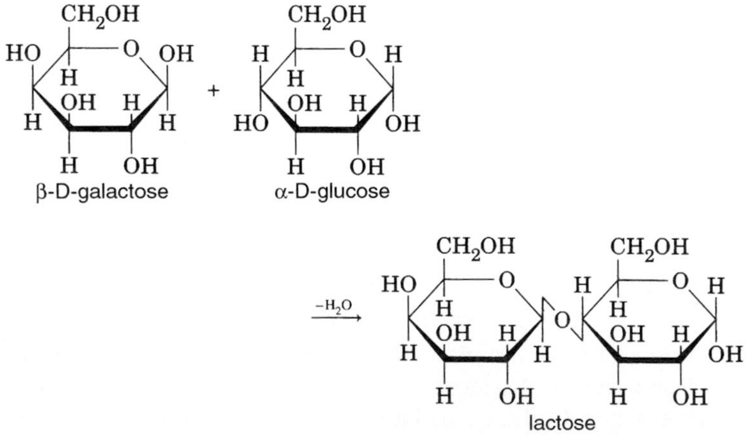

β-D-galactose   α-D-glucose

lactose

OLIGOSACCHARIDES

Many carbohydrates are still more complex than the disaccharides. **Oligosaccharides** are composed of between three and ten monosaccharide units, each joined to the next by the elimination of a molecule of water. These substances are less prominent in foods than either the mono- and disaccharides or the much larger polysaccharides. Oligosaccharides are formed during the transition of complex carbohydrates, such as starch, into simpler di- and monosaccharides.

Two trisaccharides that have been identified in legumes are stachyose and raffinose. Other oligosaccharides identified in foods are maltotriose and manninotriose. The structure of raffinose is

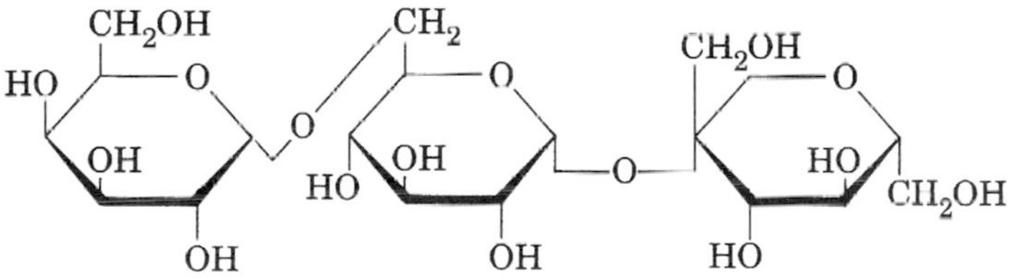

Oligosaccharide
Carbohydrate formed by union of three to ten monosaccharides with the elimination of water.

raffinose

Humans lack the enzyme needed to digest raffinose and stachyose, which causes flatulence. This can be overcome by taking the enzyme orally.

POLYSACCHARIDES

Dextrins

Technically, the oligosaccharides are **polysaccharides,** but generally the term *polysaccharides* indicates much larger molecules. Some of the most important polysaccharides in food are composed only of glucose units linked together by α- or β-glucosidic linkages. The simplest of these substances are the **dextrins.** These molecules range widely in size, but are distinctly shorter in chain length than starch, the related substance. Dextrin molecules are composed entirely of glucose, and these units are linked together by 1,4-α-glucosidic linkages, as was shown previously for maltose under Disaccharides.

Unlike the mono- and disaccharides, which are characterized as sweet in taste and quite soluble, dextrins exhibit rather different properties. Dextrins have slight solubility, a barely sweet taste, and limited thickening ability.

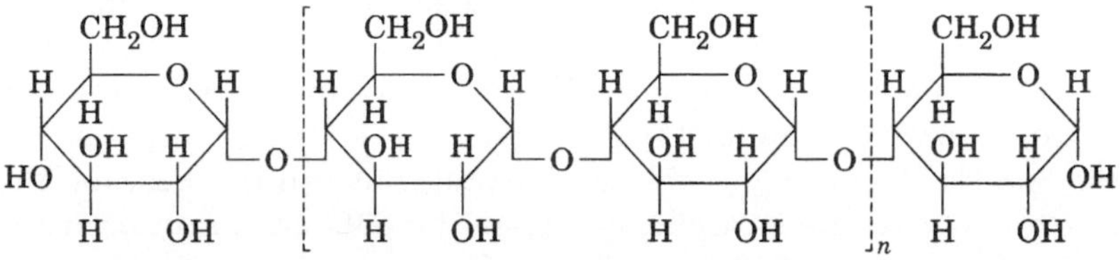

Polysaccharide
Carbohydrate formed by union of many saccharide units, with the elimination of a molecule of water at each point of linkage.

Dextrins
Polysaccharides composed entirely of glucose units linked together and distinguishable from starch because of the distinctly shorter chain length.

dextrins

Dextrans

Dextrans
Complex carbohydrates in bacteria and yeasts characterized by 1,6-α-glucosidic linkages.

Dextrans are yet another type of polysaccharide and are found in bacteria and yeasts. Again, these are composed of glucose, but with a 1,6-α-glucosidic linkage. Branching occurs in dextrans, with the point of branching being unique to a particular species or strain. A portion of a dextran molecule is shown below. Note that dextrins and dextrans differ in their linkages, having 1,4, and 1,6 glucosidic linkages, respectively.

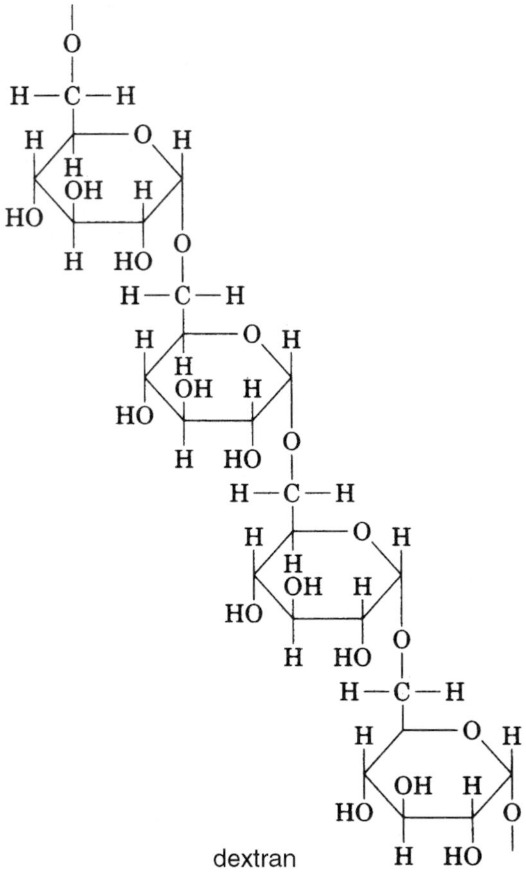
dextran

Starch
Complex carbohydrate consisting of two fractions—amylose and amylopectin—both of which are polymers of glucose joined together by the elimination of water.

Amylose
Straight-chain, slightly soluble starch fraction consisting of glucose units joined together by 1,4-α-glucosidic linkages that were formed with the loss of a molecule of water.

Starch

Amylose. **Starch,** a glucose polymer of very large dimensions, actually comprises two fractions: **amylose** and amylopectin. The simpler of these is amylose, which is a very large molecule consisting of considerably more than 200 glucose units linked by 1,4-α-glucosidic linkages. Amylose molecules are somewhat linear in their spatial configuration, enabling them to hydrogen-bond to each other under certain conditions. Amylose is slightly soluble, but does not have a sweet taste. In the structure of amylose presented below, note that like the disaccharides, the glucose units link by eliminating a molecule of water. As can be seen, the structures of amylose and dextrin are basically the same. The difference is in *n;* that is, amylose has far more glucose units than does dextrin.

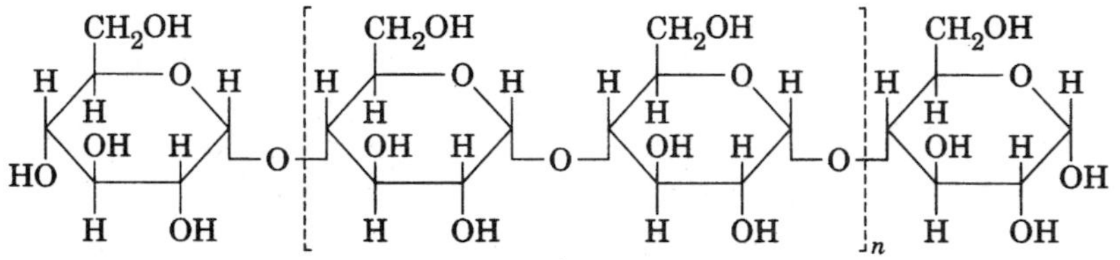

amylose

Amylopectin.   **Amylopectin,** the other starch fraction, is more complicated structurally than is amylose, but it also comprises only glucose units. There are two types of linkages in amylopectin: 1,4-α-glucosidic and 1,6-α-glucosidic. There are far more 1,4 linkages than there are 1,6 linkages. The usual configuration contains between 24 and 30 glucose units linked together consecutively between carbons 1 and 4, at which point a single 1,6 linkage occurs. The 1,6 linkage results in disruption of the linear extension of the molecule wherever it occurs, the result being a branching of the molecule at this linkage. Other glucose units continue to be linked to the unit involved with the 1,6 linkage because the first and fourth carbons are still available for bonding to other units. In nature, this new segment will again have between 24 and 30 glucose units linked by 1,4 linkages before another 1,6 linkage causes additional branching of the molecule.

Amylopectin molecules are extremely large and may have a molecular weight of a million or more. The branching of amylopectin results in a molecule with little solubility; like amylose, it also does not contribute sweetness to food flavors. The structure of amylopectin is presented, in part, below.

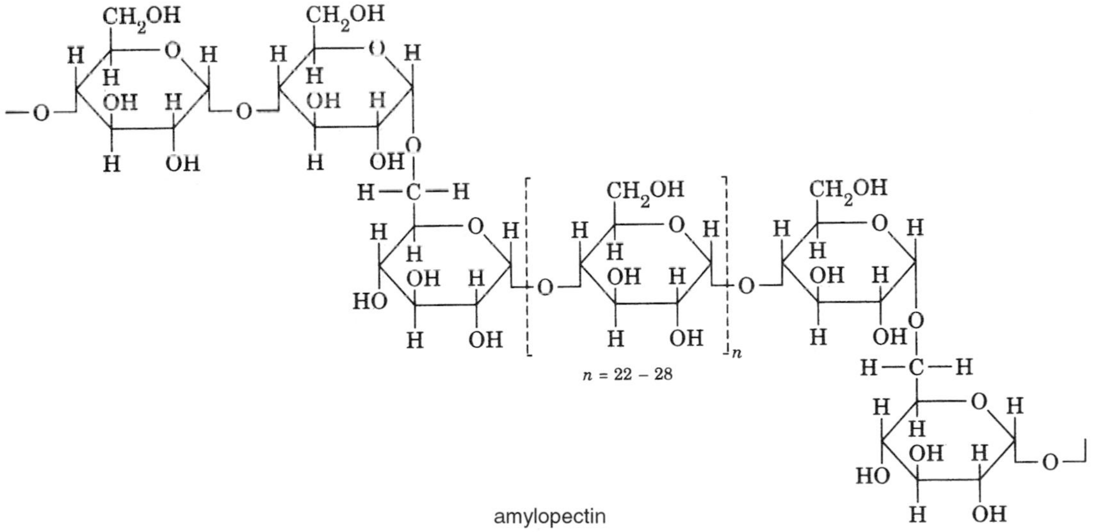

Amylopectin
Branched fraction of starch consisting primarily of glucose units linked with 1,4-α-glucosidic linkages, but interrupted occasionally with a 1,6 linkage resulting in a very large polysaccharide.

amylopectin

$n = 22 - 28$

Glycogen

Glycogen, which is the storage form of carbohydrate in animal tissues, is somewhat comparable to amylopectin in structure. The primary difference between amylopectin and glycogen is that linear segments of the glycogen molecule are generally between 8 and 12 glucose units long, rather than the 24 to 30 found in amylopectin. This gives glycogen a spatial arrangement even more bulky than that of amylopectin. The structure, in part, is presented next.

Glycogen
Complex carbohydrate that serves as the storage form of carbohydrate in animals; glucose polymer with 1,4-α-glucosidic linkages interrupted by 1,6 linkages about every 8 to 12 units, resulting in bulky branching.

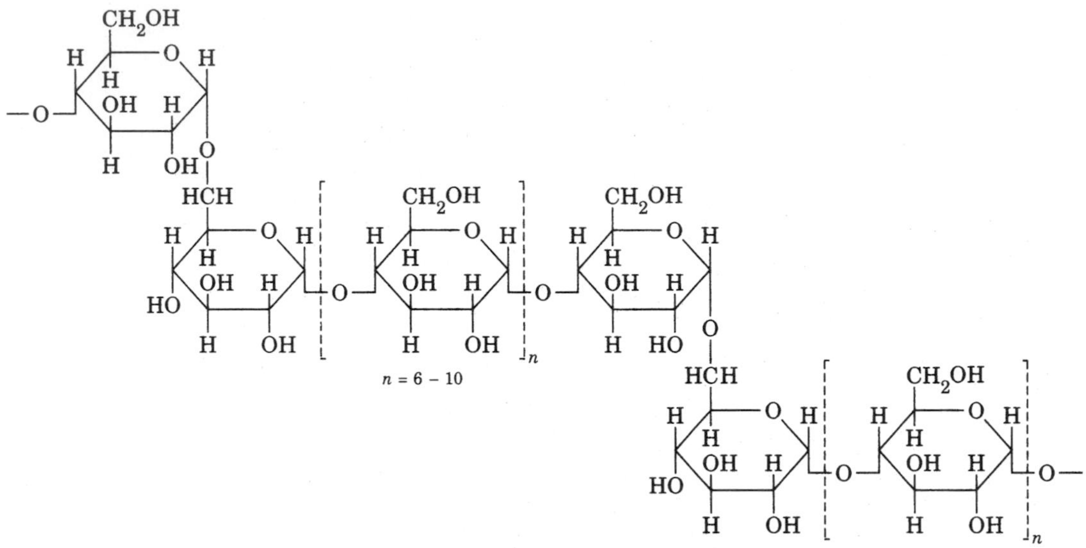

$$CH_2OH$$

glycogen

Cellulose

Cellulose

Complex carbohydrate composed of glucose units joined together by 1,4-β-glucosidic linkages.

The significance of the α versus the β linkage between glucose units is evident if amylose and **cellulose** are compared. Both have a basically linear configuration spatially, as a result of the 1,4 linkage. However, cellulose, which has a 1,4-β-glucosidic linkage throughout, is insoluble and is a key structural component of plants. In contrast, amylose is somewhat soluble. It can be digested by humans to provide ultimately a source of energy to the body, whereas cellulose is not an energy source for people because of their inability to split its 1,4-β-glucosidic linkages.

A portion of the cellulose molecule is shown below. Note that the compound is a polysaccharide composed exclusively of glucose in the 1,4-β-glucosidic linkage.

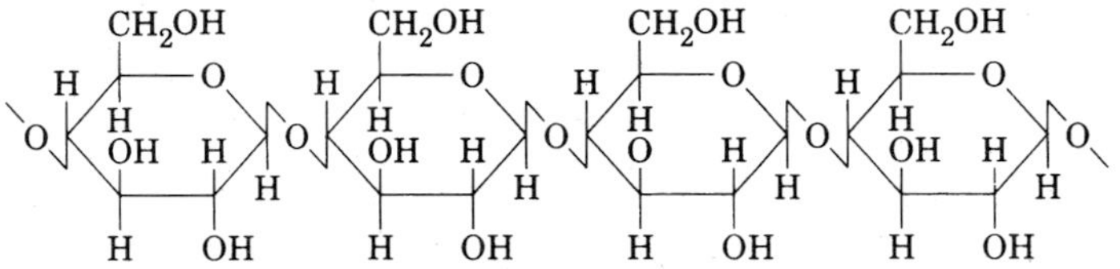

cellulose

Nonglucosidic Polysaccharides

Inulin

Complex carbohydrate that is a polymer of fructose.

Other polysaccharides in which some simple sugar other than glucose is the building block of the molecule are also found in foods. Some are composed of units of fructose, for example, **inulin,** which is found in the Jerusalem artichoke.

Pectic Substances

Group of complex carbohydrates found in fruits; polymers of galacturonic acid linked by 1,4-α-glycosidic linkages and with varying degrees of methylation.

Pectic Substances.   Galactose is the ultimate foundation of the polysaccharides known as **pectic substances.** The actual building block is a derivative of galactose, a uronic acid called galacturonic acid. This acid is polymerized as a long chain of galacturonic acid units linked in a 1,4-α-glycosidic linkage. The acids in the molecule frequently are methylated to form methyl esters when the fruit is barely ripe. This methylated form of the pectic substances is termed pectinic acid or pectin. A portion of this structure is shown below. The significance of pectic substances in making jam and jellies is discussed in chapter 20.

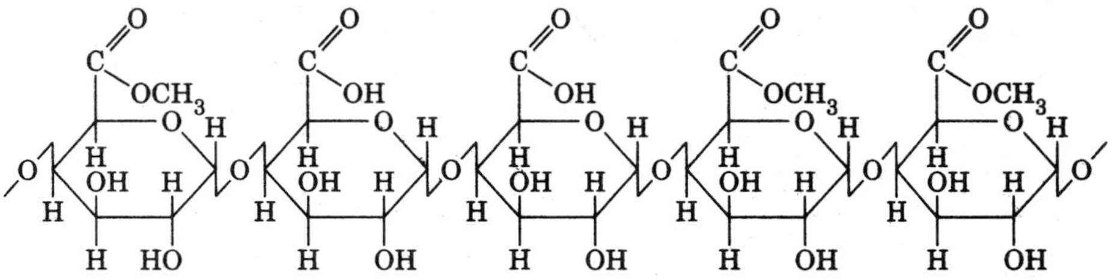

pectin

Gums. Complex polysaccharides based on saccharides other than glucose are found in seeds, plant exudates, and seaweed (see Chapter 10). Depending on the source, these **gums** may contain a variety of sugars in their structures, although most have galactose as a common component. The seed gums also contain mannose. Plant exudates contain a variety of other sugars including two pentoses (arabinose and xylose) and two unusual hexoses (rhamnose and fucose) in which the terminal carbon is a methyl group rather than an alcohol, as shown below.

Gums
Complex carbohydrates of plant origin, usually containing galactose and at least one other sugar or sugar derivative, but excluding glucose.

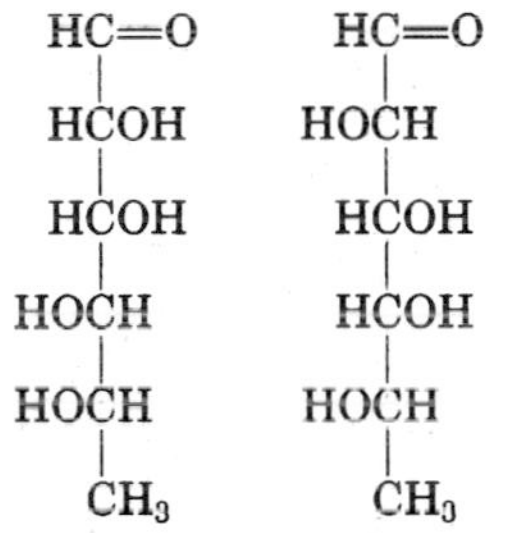

L-rhamnose   L-fucose

SUMMARY

Carbohydrates are composed of carbon, hydrogen, and oxygen; the hydrogen and oxygen are usually present in approximately the 2:1 ratio found in water. The simplest of the carbohydrates are the monosaccharides, which contain between three and six or more carbon atoms. Familiar pentoses are ribose, arabinose, and xylose; common hexoses are glucose, fructose, and galactose, although mannose, gulose, and sorbose also occur occasionally. The common disaccharides—two saccharide units joined together—include sucrose (composed of glucose and fructose), maltose (two units of glucose), and lactose (glucose and galactose).

Oligosaccharides (containing between three and ten glucose units) are not common components of foods, but form as polysaccharides are hydrolyzed into basic components. Polysaccharides are very large polymers of saccharides joined together by 1,4 linkages (which usually are α linkages) and occasionally by 1,6 linkages. Dextrins, cellulose, and the two fractions of starch (amylose and amylopectin) are common polysaccharides in foods. Pectic substances and gums are polysaccharides usually found as polymers of derivatives of galactose; gums sometimes contain other sugar derivatives, as well.

STUDY QUESTIONS

1. Show how maltose is formed from two glucose units.

2. Which monosaccharide is the most common unit in the majority of the carbohydrates? In which complex carbohydrates is this compound absent?

3. How are dextrins distinguished from amylose?

4. Identify the two starch fractions and explain how they differ.

5. Describe the chemistry of pectic substances and compare them with starch.

6. How do gums compare chemically with the pectic substances?

BIBLIOGRAPHY

Baker, C. W. 1993. "Production of sucrose-based carbohydrates for the food industry." *Food Technol. 47* (1): 149.

Bell, J. 1993. "High intensity sweeteners—a regulatory update." *Food Technol. 47* (11): 136.

Birch, G. G. and Green, L. F., eds. 1973. *Molecular Structure and Function of Food Carbohydrates.* Applied Science Publishers, Ltd.: London.

Birch, G. G. and Shallenberger, R. S. 1973. "Configuration, conformation, and properties of food sugars." In *Molecular Structure and Function of Food Carbohydrates.* Birch, G. G. and Green, L. F., eds. Applied Science Publishers, Ltd.: London.

Blankers, I. 1995. "Properties and applications of lactitol." *Food Technol. 49* (1): 66.

Book, S. and Luallen, T. 1996. 25 Years of carbohydrates in IFT. *Food Technol. 50* (12): 51.

Bullens, C., Krawczyk, G., and Geithman, L. 1994. "Reduced-fat cheese products using carrageenan and microcrystalline cellulose." *Food Technol. 48* (1): 79.

Campbell, L. A., Ketelsen, S. M., and Antenucci, R. N. 1994. "Formulating oatmeal cookies with calorie-sparing ingredients." *Food Technol. 48* (5): 98.

Chinachoti, P. 1993. "Water mobility and its relation to functionality of sucrose-containing food systems." *Food Technol. 47* (1): 134.

Davidson, R. L. 1976. *Handbook of Water-Soluble Gums and Resins.* McGraw-Hill: New York.

Dziezak, J. D. 1987. "Crystalline fructose: breakthrough in corn sweetener process technology." *Food Technol. 41* (1): 66.

Giese, J. 1993. "Alternative sweeteners and bulking agents." *Food Technol. 47* (1): 113.

Godshall, M. A. 1997. "How carbohydrates influence food flavor." *Food Technol. 51* (1): 63.

Inglett, G. E. and Grisamore, S. B. 1991. "Maltodextrin fat substitute lowers cholesterol." *Food Technol. 45* (6): 104.

Ink, S. L. and Hurt, H. D. 1987. "Nutritional implications of gums." *Food Technol. 41* (1): 77.

Izzo, M., Stahl, C., and Tuazon, M. 1995. "Using cellulose gel and carrageenan to lower fat and calories in confections." *Food Technol. 49* (7): 1995.

Jeffery, M. S. 1993. "Key functional properties of sucrose in chocolate and sugar confectionery." *Food Technol. 47* (1): 141.

Kulp, K., Lorenz, K., and Stone, M. 1991. "Functionality of carbohydrate ingredients in bakery products." *Food Technol. 45* (3): 136.

Lee, C. K. and Lindley, M. G. 1982. *Developments in Food Carbohydrates.* Applied Science: New York.

Lee, F. A. 1983. *Basic Food Chemistry.* 2nd ed. AVI Publishing: Westport, CT.

Meer, G., et al. 1975. "Water soluble gums—their past, present, and future." *Food Technol.* *29* (11): 22.

Reineccius, G. A. 1991. "Carbohydrates for flavor encapsulation." *Food Technol. 45* (3): 144.

Tomomatsu, H. 1994. "Health effects of oligosaccharides." *Food Technol. 48* (10): 61.

Verdi, R. J. and Hood, L. L. 1993. "Advantages of alternative sweetener blends." *Food Technol. 47* (6): 94.

Whistler, R. L. and Daniel, J. R. 1985. "Carbohydrates." In Fennema, O. W., ed. *Food Chemistry*. Marcel Dekker: New York, p. 69.

Zapsalis, C. and Beck, R. A. 1985. *Food Chemistry and Nutritional Biochemistry*. Wiley: New York, p. 315.

Zhao, J. and Whistler, R. L. 1994. "Spherical aggregates of starch granules as flavor carriers." *Food Technol. 48* (7): 104.

CHAPTER 8

Monosaccharides, Disaccharides, and Sweeteners

S weet, one of the four basic tastes, is provided in foods by a variety of compounds. Although the various mono- and disaccharides numbered among the carbohydrates in nature are the common sweeteners used, such noncarbohydrate compounds as saccharin and aspartame also are being incorporated widely into manufactured foods. The characteristics of each type of sweetener are unique to the specific sugar or sugar substitute, making it important for food scientists to be familiar with the behavior of possible sweeteners and the performance required of sweeteners in various food products. This chapter explores the chemistry and the applications of the common sweeteners available to the food industry today. Particular attention is directed toward the crystalline nature of many candies and the factors that influence crystallinity.

PHYSICAL PROPERTIES OF SUGARS

Sweetness

When dissolved, all sugars are sweet to the tongue, but some are sweeter than others. The relative ability to sweeten a food product is of interest because sugars contribute 4 kilocalories per gram. Theoretically, a sugar that is very sweet can be used in smaller quantities than a sugar that is less sweet, resulting in a reduction in calories without sacrificing sweetness. The relative sweetness of some monosaccharides, disaccharides, and other sweeteners is shown in Table 8.1. Clearly, most of the nonsugar sweeteners that are shown provide far more sweetening than a comparable weight of any of the sugars can contribute. Even though these intense sweetening agents are of merit from the perspectives of taste and calories, sweetness is not the only property of merit in using sugars in foods, as is evident in the section on functional properties of sugars.

The relative sweetness values for sugars are influenced by the temperature of the solution containing the sugar. For example, fructose was judged to be 1.4 times

Table 8.1   Relative Sweetness of Selected Sugar Solutions (5%) and Other sweeteners[a]

Sweetener	Relative Sweetness
Thaumatin[b] (Talin®)	2000–3000
Monellin[b]	1500–2000
Sucrose chloroderivatives[b] (Sucralose®)	5–2000
Stevioside[b]	300
Saccharin[b]	200–300
Acesulfame K[b] (Sunette®)	130–200
Aspartame[b] (Nutrasweet®, Equal®)	100–200
Cyclamates[b]	30–80
Fructose	1.3[c]
Xylitol[b]	1.01
Sucrose	1.0[d]
Invert sugar	0.85–1
Xylose	0.59
Glucose	0.56
Galactose	0.4–0.6
Maltose	0.3–0.5
Lactose	0.2–0.3

[a]Figures compiled from multiple sources including Godshall, M. A. 1997. How carbohydrates influence food flavor. *Food Technol. 51* (1): 63.
[b]Nonsugar sweetener.
[c]Highly variable, depending on temperature. This is a representative value, but measurements may range from 0.8 to 1.7.
[d]Value of sucrose arbitrarily set at 1.0 for reference purposes.

sweeter than sucrose at 5°C, comparable in sweetness when the solution is at 40°C, but only 0.8 times as sweet at 60°C (Doty, 1972). However, maltose sweetness ratings are essentially independent of temperature.

Hygroscopicity

Hygroscopicity
Ability to attract and hold water, which is characteristic of sugars to varying degrees.

Sugars, to varying degrees, are able to attract and hold water. This capability, known as **hygroscopicity,** can be useful in maintaining the freshness of some baked products, but can be a source of potential problems in texture when the relative humidity is high. An elevation in temperature also increases the absorption of moisture from the atmosphere. A comparison of the hygroscopicity of selected sugars under varying temperature and relative humidity is presented in Table 8.2.

Table 8.2   Hygroscopicity of Selected Sugars under Varying Conditions

Sugar	Percentage of Water Absorbed		
	20°C		25°C
	RH[a] = 60%, 1 *hour*	RH = 100%, 25 *days*	RH 90%, *equilibrium*
β-Maltose	5.05		
α-Lactose hydrate, pure	5.05		
D-Fructose	0.28	73.4	41–43
D-Glucose	0.07	14.5	17–18
Invert sugar	0.16	74.0	
Sucrose	0.04	18.4	50–56

[a]RH = relative humidity.

Table 8.3   Solubility of Selected Sugars at 50°C

Sugar	Grams of Sugar Dissolved in 100 ml Water
Fructose	86.9
Sucrose	72.2
Glucose	65.0
Maltose	58.3
Lactose	29.8

Solubility

The amount of sugar that will go into solution in water varies with the type of sugar and also with the temperature of the water. As the temperature of water rises, the amount of sugar capable of being dissolved in a given amount of water also increases. This fact is illustrated by the figures for sucrose solubility, as shown in Table 5.4. The comparative solubility of various sugars is presented in Table 8.3. Solubility is important because of its relationship to food texture. Sugar mixtures, such as candies, containing fructose are softer than those containing other sugars because of the greater solubility of fructose. The very low solubility of lactose (Guy, 1971), the sugar in milk, is a particular problem in the manufacture of ice cream. The low temperature required in ice cream storage promotes the formation of lactose crystals. This is detected on the tongue as a somewhat gritty texture, a characteristic triggered by the low solubility of this particular sugar.

CHEMICAL REACTIONS

Hydrolysis

Disaccharides undergo hydrolysis when heated. An acidic medium favors this degradative reaction, as does the presence of water. However, even if seemingly dry sugars are heated alone, the uptake of a molecule of water and the resultant splitting into the two component monosaccharides occur. The reaction for the hydrolysis of sucrose, the disaccharide particularly susceptible to hydrolysis, is shown below.

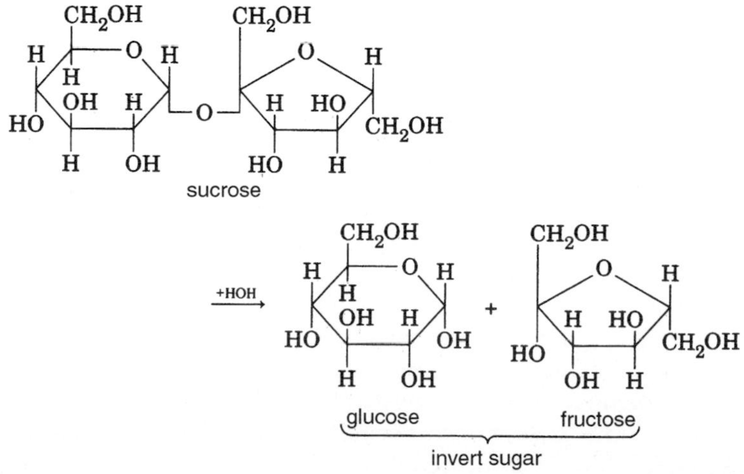

Invert Sugar
Sugar formed by hydrolysis of sucrose; a mixture of equal amounts of fructose and glucose.

The specific reaction forming **invert sugar** from sucrose is called *inversion.*

Hydrolysis occurs during the normal preparation of candies (Hoseney, 1984), the extent being influenced by the rate of cooking and the ingredients used. The effect of this reaction on the texture of candies is discussed later in this chapter.

Degradation

Degradation
Opening of the ring structure as the prelude to the breakdown of sugars.

The first step in the actual heat destruction (Hoseney, 1984) of sugars in cookery is the opening of the ring structure to form an aldehyde or ketone, depending on whether the original sugar was a pyranose or furanose ring, respectively. In the presence of acid, dehydration of the molecule occurs as three molecules of water are eliminated. Organic acids and aldehydes are the result. These reactions occur in an acidic medium, but they take place even more readily in an alkaline medium.

Caramelization

When sugars are heated to such intense temperatures that they melt (170°C for sucrose), a series of chemical reactions begin to take place, which ultimately can lead to a charred or burned product. However, some caramelization of sugar creates pleasing color and flavor changes, with the color ranging from a pale golden brown to a gradually deepening brown before burning actually occurs. Similarly, the flavor begins to assume new and distinctive overtones as the mixture of sugar derivatives undergoes change.

The overall process of caramelization involves a number of steps, beginning with the inversion of sucrose (conversion to invert sugar), described above. After the ring structures in the components of the invert sugar are broken, some condensation of the compounds occurs, which creates some polymers ranging in size from trisaccharides to oligosaccharides (as many as 10 subunits polymerized). Severe chemical changes at the very high temperatures involved also lead to dehydration reactions and the formation of organic acids and some cyclic compounds, as well as many other substances.

Caramelization can be halted abruptly by very rapid cooling of the extremely hot sugar mixture. This is done by adding boiling water, which is much cooler than the caramelizing sugar. Of course, the addition of cool water also will halt the caramelization process; however, this practice is not recommended because of the extreme splattering and potential for burning one's skin that result when the two liquids come into contact and equalize their extreme difference in energy.

Evidence of the creation of acids during caramelization can be seen by stirring some baking soda into the caramelizing sugar, as is done in preparing peanut brittle. The carbon dioxide that forms when the soda neutralizes the acids creates a porous product as the gas expands in the hot, viscous candy solution.

The Maillard Reaction

Reducing Sugar
Sugar having a free carbonyl that can combine with an amine, leading to nonenzymatic browning.

An extremely important browning reaction in the preparation of foods is the Maillard reaction. This reaction, like the series involved in caramelization, is classified as nonenzymatic browning. Actually, the Maillard reaction is a series of reactions involving the condensation of a reducing sugar and an amine. Glucose, fructose, and galactose are reducing monosaccharides; similarly, lactose and maltose are reducing disaccharides. Lactose undergoes nonenzymatic browning the most readily of the **reducing sugars,** followed in descending order by ribose, fructose, and glucose.

These reducing sugars can combine with amines in milk and other protein-containing foods to cause nonenzymatic browning. Sucrose, however, is not a reducing sugar and does not participate in the **Maillard reaction.** It must undergo inversion to glucose and fructose before it can enter into this type of nonenzymatic browning.

The color changes that occur during the series of reactions involved in the Maillard reaction occur rather slowly and with less energy input than is required for caramelization. The progression is from an essentially colorless substance to a golden color and on to a somewhat reddish brown and then a dark brown. This range of colors can be followed as caramels are being boiled to their final temperature or during the baking of a plain or white cake as the crust color develops. Similarly, the reactions can be traced by watching the color development in sweetened condensed milk when it is heated in a water bath. A pH of 6 or higher accelerates the Maillard reaction.

The Maillard reaction proceeds rather quickly at elevated temperatures (Hoseney, 1984), but it also can occur at room temperature during extended periods of storage. In fact, one of the early problems in developing packaged cake mixes was prevention of the Maillard reaction, which sometimes occurred during prolonged marketing operations. The series of reactions appears to consist of many steps, with the first step probably being as follows:

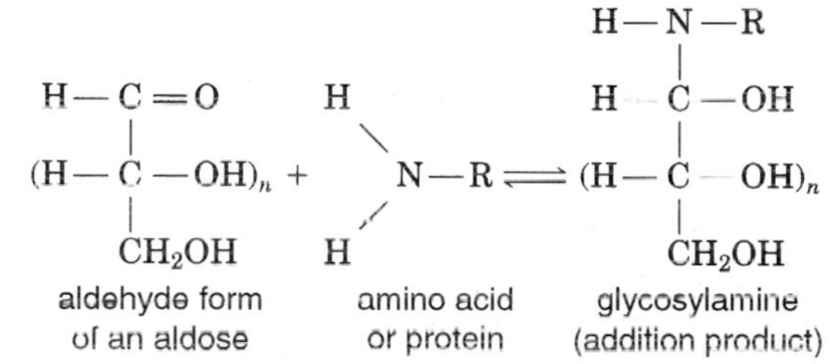

Through **enolization** and dehydration, colored pigments (melanoidins) are formed. The reactions outlined below are possible steps for this transformation.

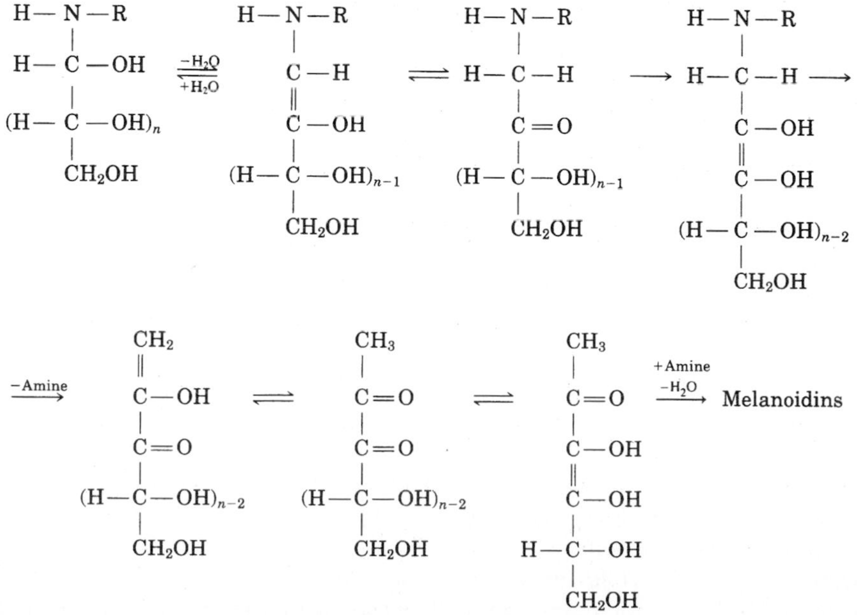

Subsequent steps in the Maillard reaction

Maillard Reaction
Nonenzymatic browning that occurs when a protein and a sugar are heated or stored together for some time.

Enolization
Reversible reaction between an alkene and a ketone.

FUNCTIONAL PROPERTIES OF SUGARS

The sweet taste of sugar is utilized in many food products in amounts ranging from minute to the major ingredient, as in candies. When sugar-containing products are heated to very high temperatures, as occurs in candy making, the degradation products that begin to form contribute additional flavor components.

Sugars contribute color to products that are heated either to a high temperature or for an extended period of time. Part of the color noted on the surface of cakes is due to some chemical breakdown of the sugar, and part is the result of the Maillard reaction (nonenzymatic browning) that also is responsible for much of the color that develops while caramels are boiling; caramelization is the key process responsible for coloring brittles and toffee, which are heated to a much higher temperature than caramels.

Depending on their concentration in a product, sugars can have considerable impact on the texture of various food products. Sugar syrups become increasingly viscous as the sugar content is increased by boiling away ever greater amounts of water. Cakes become more tender as sugar content is increased until a critical maximum is reached. Volume also is increased with some increase in sugar if the sugar level does not become so high that the cake structure falls (see Chapter 17). The effects of sugar content on the mouthfeel of candy are discussed in the next section. Egg white meringues made with sugar as an ingredient are stabilized by the addition of sugar; the sugar also causes the foam to have smaller cells and a finer texture as a result of the need for increased beating. In starch-thickened puddings, sugar serves as a tenderizing ingredient. Protein-containing products with increased sugar levels need to be heated to somewhat higher temperatures to coagulate the protein than is necessary when less sugar is used.

FOOD APPLICATIONS

Crystalline Candies

Crystalline Candies
Candies with organized crystalline areas and some liquid (mother liquor).

Candies that are easy to bite and that have large areas of organized sugar crystals are categorized as **crystalline candies.** These candies can be made merely by boiling sugar and water until the sugar syrup is concentrated sufficiently to form a firm, crystalline structure when cooled. However, most crystalline candy recipes contain other ingredients, too. For example, corn syrup or cream of tartar, butter or margarine, and such flavorings as chocolate or vanilla are found in many candy recipes to improve the quality of the finished product. Even with these additional ingredients, crystalline candies appear deceptively simple to prepare. In fact, they illustrate some key chemical and physical principles of food preparation.

Preparation.   The quantity of sugar relative to the amount of liquid in crystalline candy recipes exceeds the amount of sugar that can be put into solution at room temperature (Table 6.2). Consequently, the mixture feels very gritty when stirred prior to heating. As the candy is heated, the grittiness gradually disappears. By the time the temperature of the boiling candy rises above 100°C, all of the sugar is in solution, and no crystals remain.

Water evaporates while the candy is boiling; therefore, the concentration of sugar in the solution increases gradually. This increase in sugar concentration

Table 8.4   Final Temperatures and Approximate Concentrations of Sugar in Selected Crystalline and Amorphous Candies

Candy	Type	Final Temperature (°C)	Approximate Concentration of Sugar (percent)
Fudge	Crystalline	112	80
Penuche	Crystalline	112	80
Fondant	Crystalline	114	81
Caramels	Amorphous[a]	118	83
Taffy	Amorphous	127	89
Peanut brittle	Amorphous	143	93
Toffee	Amorphous	148	95

[a]The large amount of fat interferes with crystallization.

causes a decrease in vapor pressure, and the boiling temperature rises slowly. The recommended test for determining when a candy is done is to boil the solution to the correct final temperature (Table 8.4). This temperature is correlated with the concentration of sugar, and thus a thermometer is used to indicate when the correct sugar concentration has been reached (Table 8.4). Crystalline candies vary slightly according to the type of candy, but most have a sugar concentration of about 80 percent or very slightly greater. This concentration is achieved when the boiling temperature of the candy is 112°C. A slightly higher temperature means a higher concentration of sugar and a firmer candy; conversely, a lower temperature yields a softer candy.

Acid, usually in the form of cream of tartar, commonly is an ingredient in crystalline candies. During the boiling of the candy, acid effects hydrolysis (inversion) of some of the sucrose molecules. The end products of **inversion** are equal amounts of glucose and fructose, referred to collectively simply as invert sugar. The extent of inversion accomplished by the acid during the boiling period is directly proportional to the rate of heating. A candy that is boiling slowly undergoes more inversion because it requires a longer time to reach the desired concentration of sugar than one boiling so vigorously that a large quantity of steam constantly is escaping from the candy.

This chemical change catalyzed by acid is significant in influencing textural characteristics of the finished product. Extensive inversion causes crystalline candies to be somewhat softer than would be anticipated. Some inversion, however, is helpful in promoting a very smooth texture. The mixture of different types of sugars (sucrose, glucose, and fructose) resulting from some acid hydrolysis makes it somewhat difficult for the crystallizing sugars to form the large crystalline aggregates that give some crystalline candies such a sandy, gritty texture.

Inversion of sucrose by acid hydrolysis is but one of the means used to obtain a mixture of sugars and promote a smooth texture in crystalline candies. Corn syrup actually is a mixture of carbohydrate compounds derived by hydrolyzing cornstarch. All corn syrups contain glucose and maltose plus some larger glucose polymers. The commercial candies made with high-fructose corn syrup also contain fructose. Any of the corn syrups will enhance the texture of crystalline candies in which they are included because of the mixture of sugars they provide. The distinctive shapes of the crystals of different kinds of sugars interfere with ready alignment of crystals into large aggregates.

Inversion
Formation of invert sugar by either boiling a sugar solution (especially with acid added) or adding an enzyme (invertase) to the cool candy.

Fat also interferes somewhat with aggregation of sugar crystals in the finished crystalline candies. When cream is used in preparing candies, the fat is useful in promoting a smooth texture. This is one of the reasons that fudge is more likely to have a smooth texture than is a simple fondant made with water as the liquid and without fat. Not only is fudge commonly made using cream, but it always has a significant amount of fat from the chocolate in the recipe (chocolate is at least 50 percent fat). Traditionally, some butter is added to crystalline candies at the end of the boiling period. This addition has two advantages: it promotes a fine texture by interfering with crystallization and it enhances flavor.

Crystallization.   A key factor in crystalline candy making is control of crystallization (Hartel, 1993). When the boiling candy is removed from the heat, the solution is saturated. No more sugar could be held in solution at that temperature, but all of the sugar that is present is in solution and not in crystals. This is a stable arrangement. As the solution cools, however, the amount of sugar that theoretically can be in solution is reduced. For example, 669 grams of sugar can be dissolved in 100 milliliters of water at 115°C, but only 487.2 grams and 260.4 grams can be dissolved at 100°C and 50°C, respectively (Table 6.2).

Interestingly, it is possible to cool a solution that was saturated at the end of the boiling period without precipitating the crystals immediately. If considerable care is taken to prevent crystal formation, crystalline candies can be cooled to about 45°C while maintaining all of the sugar in solution. At this point, the cooling syrup is quite viscous, and the dissolved sugar greatly exceeds the quantity that theoretically can be in solution. The solution is termed a *supersaturated solution* and is very unstable. Almost twice as much sugar is in solution as can be dissolved at the same temperature. The excess sugar will start to crystallize promptly if any nuclei for crystallization are provided.

The goal in making crystalline candies is to achieve a fine, smooth texture by controlling crystallization. Absolutely no nuclei should be available while the candy is cooling to the desired degree of supersaturation (a temperature of about 45°C). Care should be exercised to avoid the presence of sugar crystals on the sides of the pan in which the candy is cooling. Nothing should touch the surface at any time during the cooling period, and no movement should disturb the candy. Even adjustment of a thermometer in the cooling candy can be sufficient to start crystallization too soon.

When the desired degree of supersaturation has been achieved, beating is initiated to provide constant disruption of the crystals as they attempt to aggregate (see Figure 8.1). The combination of the viscous solution at about 45°C and the agitation results in crystallization of the excess sugar in such small aggregates that the finished product has a smooth, almost velvety feel on the tongue. This is the ideal situation.

If something happens to start crystallization before the candy has achieved the desired degree of supersaturation, it is important to begin beating immediately and to continue until the candy solidifies. This agitation is essential to keep breaking aggregations into as small units as possible so that the texture will be fairly smooth when finished. Even with this effort, the texture will not be as smooth as can be achieved when crystallization is avoided until the candy has become highly supersaturated (see Figure 8.2).

When careful techniques to achieve supersaturation are combined with adequate beating, excellent crystalline candies can be produced. However, the presence of a variety of sugars and other interfering agents enhances quality by promoting a

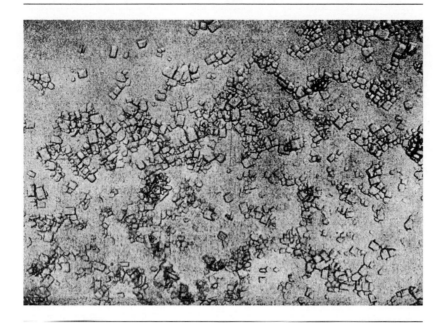

Figure 8.1   Crystals from fondant cooked to 113°C and cooled to 40°C before being beaten until the mass was stiff and kneadable (X200). (Photo by Belle Lowe.)

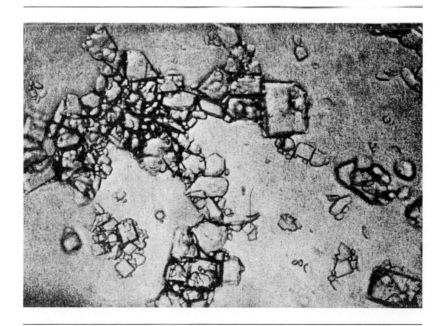

Figure 8.2   Crystals from fondant boiled to 113°C and then beaten immediately and continuously until the mass could be kneaded (X200). (Photo by Belle Lowe.)

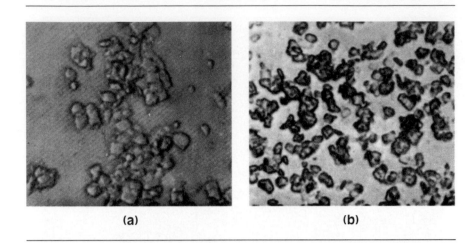

(a) (b)

Figure 8.3 Crystals formed following boiling and cooling of (a) sucrose and water and (b) sucrose, cream of tartar, and water. The finer crystal size evident in (b) is the result of the formation of some invert sugar due to acid hydrolysis effected by the cream of tartar (X200). (From E. G. Halliday and I. T. Noble. *Hows and Whys of Cooking.* University of Chicago Press, Chicago, IL. Reproduced by permission of Isabel Noble and University of Chicago Press.)

smooth texture. By selecting a recipe with interfering agents (cream of tartar and fat-containing ingredients) and by boiling candies containing an acid at a moderate rate to achieve an appropriate amount of inversion, candy makers can help ensure successful crystalline candy products (see Figure 8.3).

Ripening. Although they appear to be in a permanently solid form, crystalline candies actually are quite dynamic in nature. There is continual dissolution and recrystallization of sugar crystals in these products during storage. When viewed under a microscope, the structure is revealed to include some liquid (referred to as mother liquor) as well as many crystals in various-sized aggregations. As crystals dissolve into the mother liquor, other crystals form on existing aggregates. The small, individual crystals are fairly susceptible to going into solution and ultimately being recrystallized. Although this process is rather slow, it is relentless in causing a gradual change in crystalline candies stored for a number of days. The changes are referred to as the ripening of the candy.

Ripening
Changes that occur in crystalline candies when they are stored.

During the first few days of **ripening,** there is a bit of softening and smoothing of the texture as equilibrium is established. However, the texture of ripening candies gradually becomes coarser as the days of storage pass. This increasing grittiness is due to the increasing size of the crystal aggregates. Because there is no agitation while the new crystals are forming, they are attracted to existing crystals rather than forced apart mechanically. This transition is very detectable over several days of storage. An adequate amount of interfering substances in the recipe helps retard undesirable changes caused by ripening (see Figure 8.4).

Chocolates with cream centers are popular commercial candies that require several days of ripening before reaching their optimum texture. The difference between these soft-centered dipped chocolates and homemade candies during the ripening process is due to an ingredient added to the commercial candies. To be

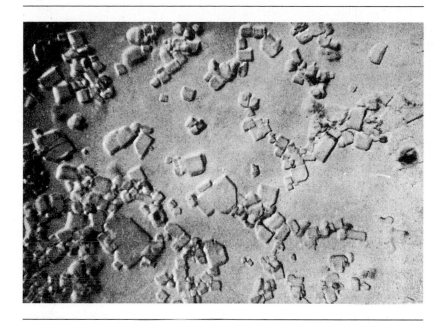

Figure 8.4   Crystals from fondant in Figure 8.1 after 40 days of storage, showing the significant increase in crystal size (X200). (Photo by Belle Lowe.)

dipped easily during commercial production, the chocolates must have firm centers. **Invertase,** an enzyme that catalyzes inversion of sucrose during storage at room temperature, is added to the cooked and crystallized fondant center. The enzyme slowly inverts the sucrose during storage, resulting in a mixture of sucrose, fructose, and glucose in the fondant; this mixture crystallizes less readily than sucrose alone, causing the centers to soften. In this type of candy, the ripening process produces a creamier, smoother texture than is present before ripening.

Invertase
Enzyme that catalyzes the breakdown of sucrose to invert sugar (fructose and glucose).

Evaluation.   Crystalline candies should hold their shape when cut, yet be bitten easily. Their mouthfeel should be velvety smooth. The flavor should be characteristic of the type of candy and pleasing, with no suggestion of scorching.

The firmness of the candy may vary from optimal as a result of certain variables. Commonly, failure to obtain the correct final temperature is the problem, for the thermometer must be read very accurately. Too high a temperature means that the sugar concentration is too great, and the candy will be harder than it should be. Conversely, too low a final boiling temperature results in a candy that has too much water in relation to the sugar, causing the product to be soft and sticky. Either of these problems can be corrected by adding water to the candy and reboiling to the proper temperature, followed by controlled cooling and beating.

The hygroscopic (water-attracting) nature of sugar can cause a candy to be too soft when it is made on a rainy day. When hot candy is cooled on a damp day, the sugar syrup actually takes up moisture from the humid air. This added moisture is sufficient to cause the candy to be less firm than desired. In addition, low atmospheric pressure lowers the boiling point. To compensate for this problem, on stormy days crystalline candies should be boiled to a temperature about one degree higher than the recipe states.

An excessively slow rate of boiling can result in too much hydrolysis when acid is present. Extensive breakdown of sucrose into glucose and fructose can cause an increase in solubility sufficient to result in a very soft candy. This clearly is a case that proves that "more is not always better."

Too little beating of crystalline candies results in a coarse texture, but does not influence the firmness of the candy. Beating is effective in lightening the texture a bit by incorporating some air into the structure. It also causes these candies to become opaque and lighter in color as a result of the disruption of light transmission by the numerous fine-crystal aggregates developed during beating.

A gritty texture may result from addition of too few interfering substances, premature initiation of crystallization, and improper beating (starting too late or quitting too soon). Very rapid boiling allows so little time for inversion that little invert sugar is formed to impede the aggregation of sucrose crystals in the finished product. Omission of acid, corn syrup, or butter (or another source of fat) makes it comparatively easy for the sucrose crystals to aggregate and cause a gritty texture. If crystallization begins while the candy is still very hot, the solution will be rather fluid. Crystals are able to move fairly easily through the hot candy to collect in large aggregates even when the candy is being beaten. When the candy is cooled to about 45°C without any crystal formation, the supersaturated solution is so viscous that the crystals move very slowly through the candy as they form. Beating is sufficient to interfere with the formation of large aggregations of sugar crystals.

Amorphous Candies

Amorphous Candies
Candies that lack an organized, crystalline structure because of their very high concentration of sugar or interfering substances (also called amorphous glasses).

As can be seen in Table 8.4, **amorphous candies** are boiled until they reach an appreciably higher temperature than is used to signal the end of the cooking period for crystalline candies. In essence, this means that the concentration of sugar is far greater in amorphous candies than in crystalline candies, usually above 90 percent (Table 8.4). This high concentration of sugar, often combined with significant quantities of interfering agents, produces an extremely viscous candy even when first taken from the heat. Such viscosity prevents any organization of sugar crystals, hence the term *amorphous candies* or amorphous glasses.

Preparation. The basic ingredients of amorphous candies, like crystalline candies, are sugar and water; often fat is included in the form of cream or butter. The key to preparing amorphous candies is to bring the boiling sugar syrup to the correct final temperature without scorching any portion of the product. Uniform heating is facilitated by the use of a heavy aluminum saucepan or other pan with uniform heating characteristics. Stainless steel pans develop hot spots as a result of nonuniform heat conduction, and the boiling candy may scorch when in contact with the overly hot metal.

Accurate temperature readings are essential, but they may be difficult to obtain, particularly when small quantities of amorphous candies are prepared. Because these candies are extremely viscous, air pockets often form between the candy and the bulb of the thermometer. Readings taken when some air is trapped next to the bulb are lower than the actual temperature of the candy, leading to overheating of the candy and increased risk of burning or scorching.

Extensive chemical changes occur in the sugar during the boiling of amorphous candies (Hoseney, 1984). The very high temperatures involved accelerate chemical breakdowns. The protein in the cream used in making some amorphous candies can combine with the sugars in the Maillard reaction to contribute to the noticeable browning that occurs in the later stages of boiling. The possible mechanism for the Maillard reaction and the formation of the pigmented melanoidins was outlined previously in this chapter.

The intense heat involved in preparing amorphous candies is destructive to sugar molecules. When sugar molecules begin to undergo the extensive changes described earlier in this chapter, the flavor characteristics, as well as the color, change. The extent of change is influenced by the rate of heating and by the final temperature actually reached in the candy. More time is available for the chemical reactions to proceed when the rate of heating is comparatively slow than when it is very rapid. The color begins to become overly dark, changing from a pleasing golden brown to a fairly dark brown, or even black, particularly if the temperature rises too high. Darkening color is a visible signal that flavor changes also are occurring. When the color begins to shift from golden brown to brown, the fragmentation of the original sugar molecules into a jumble of smaller organic compounds results in undesirable flavors. Of course, these breakdown products no longer carry a sweet taste, and the resultant candy tastes less sweet. This difference in sweetness tends to be masked when scorching or burning creates other flavors in the candy.

The extremely viscous nature of amorphous candies when they are removed from the heat prevents sugar crystals from forming in organized aggregates. In fact, caramels can be cut into separate pieces while they are still extremely hot, because they are too thick to flow. This is quite a distinct contrast to the physical properties of any of the crystalline candies. Taffy, with its high concentration of sugar, can still be pulled and twisted when it is cool enough to be held without burning the hands, but it is much too firm to permit easy movement and aggregation of sugar crystals to form a crystalline structure. Toffee has such a high concentration of sugar and is so viscous when poured from the pan onto a sheet that it defies organization of crystals. In fact, it becomes so brittle that it can be shattered easily with a knife handle even while it is still very warm.

Evaluation.   Amorphous candies are evaluated on the basis of their color, flavor, and texture. Each of the amorphous candies is quite unique in the textural characteristics desired, but the color and flavor evaluations are similar for all of them. These candies should have a pleasing, golden brown color that is uniform throughout the candy, with no areas being darker, and the flavor should be pleasing, with no evidence of scorching. The exception in color evaluation is taffy, because pulling of the hot taffy incorporates air into the candy, causing a difference in light refraction and a lighter color.

Caramels may range suitably from very sticky and chewy to somewhat rigid, but still able to be bitten. If a sticky, chewy caramel is desired, the candy should be boiled to a temperature of about 120°C; firmer caramels should be boiled to a temperature of about 125°C. Taffy should be able to be pulled while hot, but not able to be bitten when cold. Brittles and toffees should be able to be bitten with a bit of difficulty, and they should be able to be broken into pieces when hit with a knife handle.

The problems noted in amorphous candies result from errors in the cooking process, not in the handling of the candy during cooling. This is quite different from the crystalline candies, where control of crystallization is the major problem. The primary factors to control when making amorphous candies are use of a heavy saucepan with excellent heat conducting properties, adequate stirring to maintain uniform heating throughout the candy, and accurate endpoint temperature (achieved by avoiding trapping air around the thermometer bulb).

Syrups, Sauces, Jams, and Jellies

Love of a sweet taste has resulted in the production of many different sauces and syrups that are used to top everything from pancakes to elegant desserts. The primary function of sugars in syrups and sauces is to provide sweetness, but the viscosity of these sugar-containing solutions is influenced significantly by the concentration of sugars achieved during the "boiling down" phase in producing these items. Syrups produced in the home can be boiled until the desired flow properties are achieved by the evaporation of excess water. This also can be done commercially, but food additives, such as gums, often are used to achieve the right rheological characteristics quickly.

Sauces for desserts usually are sweetened with sugar, but the sugar concentration often is considerably lower than that in a syrup. This is possible because of the incorporation of another ingredient to aid in thickening the sauce. Frequently, starch serves as the thickening agent (see Chapter 9), but sometimes egg proteins are added to achieve the desired viscosity.

Jams and jellies are very popular because of their sweet, fruity flavors. Sugar is essential for the sweet taste in most jams and jellies, but this ingredient also is vital for preserving the fruit and preventing spoilage. The high concentration of sugar essentially dehydrates microorganisms as a result of the unfavorable osmotic pressure created by the sugar (see Chapter 20).

Baked Products

In yeast-leavened breads, sucrose is split and inverted by yeast invertase to provide glucose and fructose for fermentation. This fermentation is the source of the carbon dioxide that leavens the dough. High-fructose corn syrup (HFCS), corn syrup, and commercial dextrose (glucose) are other possible ingredients that can be used in bread dough for fermentation. Interestingly, the crusts of breads made with sucrose or HFCS brown evenly to a fairly deep color, as contrasted with a lighter, more reddish brown (sometimes referred to as foxy-red) color that is characteristic of breads containing glucose (dextrose) or corn syrup (Kulp, Lorenz, and Stone, 1991). It is apparent from these differences that fructose contributes somewhat different (fairly deep brown) color than that resulting from fermentation of glucose (foxy-red).

Sugar is present in large quantities in most cakes, causing several effects. Shelf life is extended by the presence of sugars. Sucrose interferes with microbiological growth by aiding in reducing water activity in the baked cake; invert sugar (equal amounts of glucose and fructose) is even more effective than sucrose in reducing water activity and inhibiting spoilage. The hygroscopic nature of sugars in a cake also contributes to lengthening shelf life, the result of moisture being drawn into the cake from the air. Large amounts of sugar in cakes dilute the protein structure, which allows increased volume due to delayed setting of the structure (see Chapter 18).

Browning of the crust, the result of the Maillard reaction and some caramelization, occurs most quickly when monosaccharides are contained in a cake. In fact, a cake made with high-fructose corn syrup may brown extremely fast because of the large amount of fructose and glucose. However, sucrose (a nonreducing sugar) needs to be inverted to fructose and glucose for the Maillard reaction to occur. Maltose and lactose are reducing disaccharides and, therefore, can undergo browning, although more slowly than the browning of monosaccharides.

Corn syrup can influence crumb color, as well as crust color of a cake. This is especially true in chocolate cakes; the acidity of corn syrup is sufficient to shift the chocolate color from a reddish overtone to a deep brown lacking any trace of red. High-fructose corn syrup can result in a detectable browning of the interior of white cakes, to the detriment of the cake. This problem can be controlled by reducing the pH of the batter from its probable pH range of between 7.1 and 7.5 to slightly less than 7.0.

Cookies often have slightly less sugar than flour (by weight). Sucrose, the usual type of sugar in cookies, contributes to the spreading of the dough during baking. Dessert sugar causes considerably more spreading in a baking cookie than does granulated sugar. This effect is influenced by the amount of sugar syrup that forms in the cookie. Very small crystals dissolve easily, promoting spreading. After baking, sucrose recrystallizes as the cookies cool, which contributes to a crisp surface. If cookies are made with more than one type of sugar (fructose and glucose, for example), crispness is reduced because of reduced ease of crystal formation.

CHOOSING SWEETENERS

Types

Sugars.   Sucrose is by far the most common sugar available in crystalline form. Granulated sugar (from either sugarcane or sugar beets) is the type used for most applications, but superfine or dessert sugar is desirable for making meringues because of the ease of dissolving the very fine crystals. Confectioners (powdered sugar) is pulverized sucrose crystals blended with cornstarch at a level of 3 percent to prevent caking of the sugar and also to help bind moisture in such products as uncooked icings.

Brown sugars are less refined than white sugars, having had fewer of the impurities removed during processing. The impurities contribute flavors to these sugars; the darker the brown sugar, the more intense are the flavors of the impurities. Brown sugars are more acidic and higher in moisture than granulated sugar. Terminology used in identifying these various brown sugars may include turbinado, light, dark, and raw. Even so-called "raw" sugar has been refined to some extent to remove harmful substances. Selection of a brown sugar should be done on the basis of the flavor desired; none of them has sufficient nutrients other than carbohydrate to make a viable contribution to the diet.

Fructose is available in some consumer markets, as well as in the food industry. The appeal of fructose is its potential for contributing greater sweetening power than sucrose. This is true in some applications, such as sweetening a beverage, but is not so when fructose is used in baked products, apparently because of the presence of other ingredients. However, its comparatively slow rate of assimilation into the body makes this sugar of particular interest to diabetics.

The food industry uses certain other sugars to meet specific requirements. For instance, lactose (because of its relatively low hygroscopicity) sometimes is used as both a source of some sweetness and an anti-caking agent to coat other sugars and restrict their water absorption. Lactose helps to keep candies and icings from becoming sticky on the surface. In contrast, invert sugar and glucose are chosen for their ability to attract moisture and improve shelf life of baked goods.

Corn Syrup
Sweet syrup of glucose and short polymers produced by hydrolysis of cornstarch.

High-Fructose Corn Syrup
Especially sweet corn syrup made by using isomerase to convert some glucose to fructose.

Dextrose Equivalent
Measure of the amount of free dextrose (glucose), which parallels glucose formation by hydrolysis of larger carbohydrate molecules; pure dextrose = 100. D.E.

Molasses
Sweetener produced as a by-product of the refining of sucrose from sugarcane.

Syrups and Liquid Sugars.   **Corn syrup** represents a mixture of carbohydrates, ranging from glucose to oligosaccharides and even dextrins of varying chain lengths. This familiar sweetener is produced by acid hydrolysis or a combination of acid and enzymatic hydrolysis, either of which results in a slightly acidic reaction.

High-fructose corn syrup (HFCS), a particularly popular commercial product, is made by using enzymes to convert some of the glucose in corn syrup into fructose (Fruin and Scallet, 1975; Mermelstein, 1975). Isomerase, an enzyme produced by *Streptomyces,* is the enzyme used to convert as much as 90 percent of glucose to fructose, but usually the level ranges from 45–55 percent depending on the conditions. High-fructose corn syrup has a high **dextrose equivalent** (65 D.E.), which indicates that its sweetness, fermentability, browning reaction potential, and hygroscopicity (ability to attract moisture) are greater than those of regular corn syrup. However, HFCS is less viscous than traditional corn syrup, which usually has a sweetness of 38–49 D.E. High-fructose corn syrup and regular corn syrup differ in composition, with HFCS having approximately twice as high a concentration of mono- and disaccharides.

Molasses, commonly available as the sulfured or unsulfured liquid product, is a by-product of the production of sugar from sugarcane. The boiling of the sugarcane juice first results in the production of light molasses, an acidic liquid containing a maximum of 25 percent water. Subsequent boiling produces molasses darker than that from the first boiling, but still flavorful and palatable. The final boiling yields blackstrap molasses, a product most commonly used in animal feeds. Sulfured and unsulfured molasses may contain as much as 70 percent sugar, the sugars being largely sucrose plus a little glucose and fructose. Unsulfured molasses is reddish brown, in contrast to the sulfured version, which is light to dark brown.

Honey is a popular sweetener because of its distinctive flavor; the specific flavor is influenced significantly by the types of blooms from which the bees gather the nectar. In all types of honey, the fructose content is high; honey actually is the richest source of fructose in natural foods (Doner, 1977). The high fructose content promotes rapid browning when honey is used in baked products. Honey also contains a bit of sucrose and organic acids.

Sorghum
Syrup sweetener produced by boiling the juice of grain sorghum.

Sorghum is made from grain sorghum by boiling down the juice to a syrup containing a maximum of 30 percent water. This syrup, like molasses, can vary from light to dark brown in color, and it has a distinctive flavor.

Polyhydric Alcohols
Alcohols with several hydroxyl groups, enabling them to be used as sweeteners, for example, xylitol and sorbitol.

Alternative Sweeteners.   **Polyhydric alcohols,** although not carbohydrates, have the ability to contribute sweetness to food products and have commercial applications when used in comparatively small amounts (Table 8.5). Xylitol and sorbitol are the alcohol counterparts of the sugars xylose and sorbose, respectively (Heaton et al., 1980). Maltitol is the polyhydric alcohol related to maltose, a disaccharide. Its suitability in sugar-free chocolate products is reported by Rapaille, Gonze, and Van der Schueren (1995).

Table 8.5 Characteristics of Selected Alternative Sweeteners

Sweetener	Type of Compound	Comments
Maltitol	Polyhydric alcohol from maltose	Used in some chocolates
Sorbitol	Polyhydric alcohol from sorbose	Metabolized by fructose-1-phosphate pathway (needs no insulin); baked goods and beverages
Xylitol	Polyhydric alcohol from xylose	Cooling effect; used in chewing gum; does not promote caries
Mannitol	Polyhydric alcohol from mannose	Bulking agent in powdered products; chewing gum (anticariogenic)
Saccharin	Derivative of phthalic anhydride	Bitter aftertaste; not metabolized
Aspartame (NutraSweet®, Equal®)	Dipeptide (L-aspartic acid, phenylalanine)	Not recommended for those with phenylketonuria; used in beverages; heat causes loss of sweetness
Acesulfame-K (Sunette®, Sweet-One®)	Potassium derivative of acetoacetic acid	Use 1 gram to equal 2 teaspoons sucrose; effective with sorbitol
Thaumatin (Talin®)	Protein from Sudan (*Thaumatoccus danielli*) plant	Slow development of sweetness; used in chewing gum only
Cyclamate	Sulfonated cyclohexylamine	Often combined with saccharin or aspartame; banned in U.S.
Sucralose	Sucrose with 3 chlorine atoms	Approved in 1998 for numerous products and baked goods; not absorbed in body
Stevioside	From *Stevia rebaudiana* plant	Menthol, bitter aftertaste; used in a few countries
Isomalt	From sucrose using enzyme	Synergistic sweetener with sorbitol; partially digested (2 kcal/g); browns slowly in baking

$$
\begin{array}{cc}
\text{CH}_2\text{OH} & \text{CH}_2\text{OH} \\
| & | \\
\text{H---C---OH} & \text{H---C---OH} \\
| & | \\
\text{HO---C---H} & \text{HO---C---H} \\
| & | \\
\text{H---C---OH} & \text{H---C---OH} \\
| & | \\
\text{CH}_2\text{OH} & \text{H---C---OH} \\
& | \\
& \text{CH}_2\text{OH} \\
\text{xylitol} & \text{sorbitol}
\end{array}
$$

These alcohols are absorbed much more slowly into the body than are sugars, a quality that has some merit from the standpoint of diabetics. However, the gas produced as a result of the prolonged microbiological action in the intestines causes considerable intestinal discomfort and thus limits the usefulness of polyhydric alcohols as sweeteners for general applications. Once absorbed, sorbitol is converted in the body to fructose and is metabolized via the fructose 1-phosphate pathway, thus circumventing the need for insulin for its metabolism.

Xylitol has been used effectively for sweetening chewing gum without introducing the cariogenic properties associated with sugars as sweeteners. This is a particularly important consideration because of the prolonged contact chewing gum has with teeth. A cooling sensation is noticed in the mouth when xylitol dissolves because solution of this alcoholic sweetener is an endothermic (heat-absorbing) reaction.

Sorbitol is useful as a humectant and bulking agent, as well as a sweetener. Its water-binding capabilities enable sorbitol to help limit mold growth, thus enhancing shelf life. These various attributes have resulted in sorbitol becoming a sugar alcohol that is used in a variety of food products, ranging from baked products to beverages.

Mannitol sometimes can be used as a bulking agent in products where the hygroscopic nature of sorbitol is a detriment. In fact, mannitol is useful in powdered products because water is not attracted to this alcohol. Like xylitol, mannitol is well suited for use in sweetening chewing gums because it is not cariogenic.

Saccharin
Nonnutritive sweetener.

Intense sweeteners have been available for use in foods without adding many, if any, calories, beginning with saccharin in the nineteenth century. Originally, **saccharin** was important as a sweetener in foods for diabetics, but now much of the significance is its use as a noncaloric sweetener. The disadvantage is the distinctive and strong bitter aftertaste that is so evident at comparatively high levels. In some food products, saccharin is combined with another sweetener, such as sorbitol, to yield a synergistic sweetening effect from small amounts of the sweeteners and a greatly reduced problem of aftertaste from saccharin.

saccharin

Aspartame
Very sweet, low-calorie dipeptide composed of phenylalanine and aspartic acid; used as a high-intensity sweetener.

Aspartame is a low-calorie sweetener resulting from the combination of two amino acids—aspartic acid and phenylalanine. Because phenylalanine intake must be controlled very carefully by people who have phenylketonuria, package labels must carry a warning regarding phenylalanine. Aspartame, which is marketed as NutraSweet or Equal by NutraSweet Co. of Skokie, Illinois, provides 4 calories per gram, but so little is needed for sweetening that aspartame affords a practical means of reducing calories in some food products. The fact that aspartame is a dipeptide limits its applications in foods; heat alters the molecule sufficiently to cause a loss of sweetness. An encapsulated form of aspartame may overcome this difficulty. An acidic medium (pH 3 to 5) is especially favorable to aspartame use for sweetening. The soft drink industry has used aspartame enthusiastically in the production of diet drinks.

Acesulfame-K, marketed as Sunette or Sweet-One, is the potassium salt of 6-methyl-1,2,3-oxythiazine-4 (3H)-one-2,2-dioxide and is derived from acetoacetic acid. Its sweetness is similar to that of aspartame (about 200 times that of sucrose), but acesulfame is stable to heat, which makes it suitable for use in baked products,

$$HO-\overset{\overset{\displaystyle O}{\|}}{C}-CH_2-\underset{\underset{\displaystyle NH_2}{|}}{CH}-\overset{\overset{\displaystyle O}{\|}}{C}-NHCH-\overset{\displaystyle O}{\underset{\displaystyle OCH_3}{C}}$$

aspartame

puddings, and various other applications. Acesulfame-K is used widely in Europe, and its use in the United States was approved in 1992 by the Food and Drug Administration. Actually, acesulfame-K provides 4 calories per gram, but its great sweetness makes only a very small amount necessary. Its manufacturer, Hoechst Celanese of Somerville, New Jersey, recommends using 1 gram of Sweet-One as a replacement for 2 teaspoons of sucrose to sweeten beverages, or 12 grams per cup of sucrose in food preparation substitutions. According to Bullock, Handel, Segall, and Wasserman (1992), sorbitol teams well with acesulfame-K to round out the flavor.

$$O=\underset{\underset{\displaystyle K^+}{N^--SO_2}}{\overset{\overset{\displaystyle CH_3}{|}}{\diagup}\diagdown O}$$

acesulfame-K

Thaumatin is a sweetener obtained from a West African plant and is between 2,000 and 3,000 times sweeter than sucrose. Its limitations are the delayed perception of sweetness that it imparts and an aftertaste reminiscent of licorice. Despite these problems, thaumatin is used in Japan and England. Thaumatin is marketed as Talin by Tate and Lyle Specialty Sweeteners of Reading, Berkshire, England.

Cyclamate is used as a sweetener in many parts of the world, but it has been banned from use in the United States since 1970 by the Food and Drug Administration. There has been considerable controversy over the banning of cyclamate because its excellent properties—for example, 30 times as sweet as sucrose, no aftertaste, and no calories—make it desirable to use. More importantly, there has been extensive research conducted to determine its carcinogenicity. Contrary to the claim that spurred the original banning on the basis of cyclamate being a carcinogen, evidence now supports reinstating cyclamate into the food supply.

The tremendous consumer interest in diet foods has stimulated ongoing efforts to develop nonnutritive or low-calorie sweeteners, many of which are either in the developmental or approval stages. Sucralose is one of these products and is of considerable interest because it is 600–800 times sweeter than sucrose, is heat stable, and lacks any unpleasant aftertaste (Barndt and Jackson, 1990). Sucralose, approved by the FDA in 1998, has a sugar-like appearance and can be used in place of sugar in cooking and baking. Stevioside is a sweetener derived from plants and is approximately 300 times sweeter than sucrose. Although used in Japan to sweeten beverages, its use has not been approved by the Food and Drug Administration. Gemsweet, a product being developed by Cumberland Packing Corporation of Brooklyn, New York, is a heat-stable peptide with a sweetness approximately 800 times that of sucrose. The L-sugars (levulorotatory) apparently are not metabolized by people, yet they have the merits of being sweet and useful in preventing spoilage by bacteria. These attributes make them possible sweeteners in the future, but they will require considerable research before they are used as sweeteners in various countries.

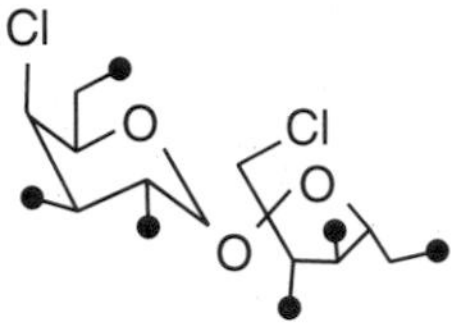

Sucralose

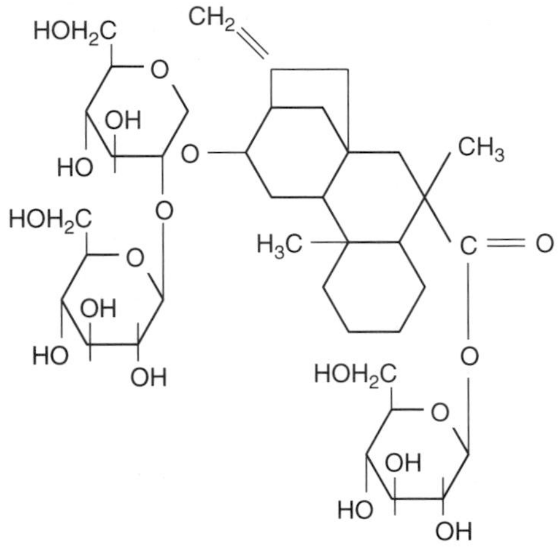

Stevioside

Isomalt is made from sucrose, utilizing an enzyme (sucrose-glucosylfructose-mutase) to make isomaltulose, from which isomalt is formed. Although isomalt has only about 0.45–0.65 percent the sweetening power of sucrose, it acts synergistically as a sweetener when combined with sorbitol or some of the intense sweeteners. Isomalt is very convenient to use because it can be substituted for sucrose on a 1 : 1 basis, and it has the advantage of providing only half as many calories (2 calories per gram) because it is only partially digested and absorbed in the small intestine. It can be substituted for sucrose in a wide array of products, although it does differ from sucrose in that it does not brown quite as readily and it is less hygroscopic. Isomalt is viewed as being an excellent sweetener for use by diabetics in the future.

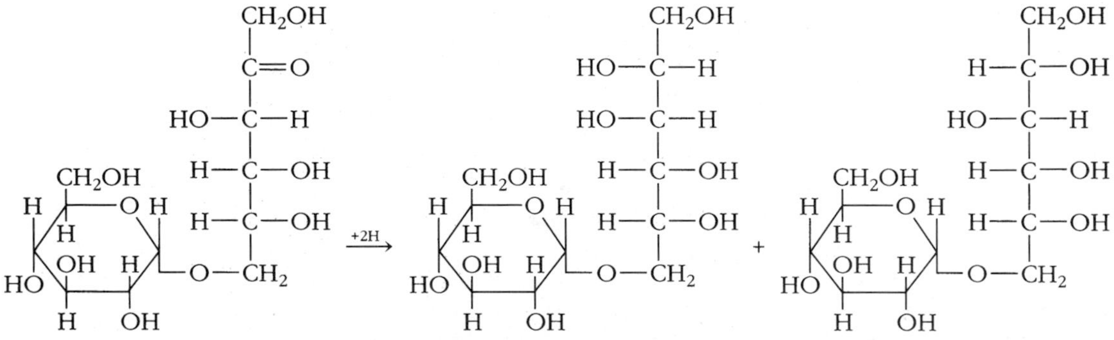

isomaltulose   α-D-glucopyranosyl-1,6-mannitol   α-D-glucopyranosyl-1,6-sorbitol

Isomalt

Some of the future sweeteners may include miraculin, monellin, hernandulcin, and dihydrochalcones. These are under development, but not ready for Food and Drug Administration action yet. Still others are in the early stages of development. This is an area of food research that promises to be dynamic for quite a considerable length of time.

SUBSTITUTING SWEETENERS

Functional and nutritional considerations may determine the choice that will be made in selecting one type of sweetener versus another. When the substitution involves replacing a liquid sweetener with a granular one, or vice versa, the adjustment in formulation of the product must include a change in the liquid as well as the sweetener. Table 8.6 lists feasible substitutions for various household sweeteners. Differences in color and flavor obviously will result in some of the substitutions suggested. Browning may be altered, too. For instance, the fructose in honey causes much more rapid browning than occurs with sucrose. Nevertheless, all of these substitutions will result in acceptable products because the functions of sugar can be provided, at least to a reasonable extent, by the substitutes suggested.

Food manufacturers have many possible sweeteners to consider when formulating their products. Specific nutritional considerations, perhaps for diet foods or for diabetic reasons, may make the choice of a nonnutritive sweetener suitable. However, that selection may trigger the need for other ingredients to perform the other functions sugar would handle. The tremendous difference in quantity that results when aspartame is substituted for sugar in a sweetened gelatin mix is evident if the aspartame-sweetened package contents are placed alongside the comparable sugar-sweetened mix.

Polydextrose is a randomly bonded polymer of glucose, which is used extensively in food products as a bulking agent. The surprising thing is that this carbo-

Table 8.6   Substitutions for One Cup of Selected Household Sweeteners[a]

Ingredient Stated in Recipe	Substitution Equivalent to 1 Cup of the Sweetener in the Recipe
Granulated sugar	1 cup brown sugar, gently but firmly packed
Granulated sugar	1 cup corn syrup, minus $\frac{1}{4}$ cup of liquid specified in recipe[b]
Granulated sugar	$1\frac{1}{3}$ cups unsulfured molasses, minus $\frac{1}{3}$ cup liquid specified in recipe, minus baking powder in the recipe, and plus $\frac{3}{4}$ teaspoon baking soda
Granulated sugar	$\frac{2}{3}$ cup honey, minus $2\frac{2}{3}$ tablespoons liquid in recipe, plus $\frac{1}{16}$ teaspoon baking soda
Granulated sugar	$\frac{2}{3}$ cup honey, plus $2\frac{2}{3}$ tablespoons flour (if no liquid in recipe), plus $\frac{1}{16}$ teaspoon baking soda
Light brown sugar	$\frac{1}{2}$ cup dark brown sugar, plus $\frac{1}{2}$ cup granulated sugar
Turbinado sugar	1 cup granulated sugar
Honey	$1\frac{1}{4}$ cups sugar, plus $\frac{1}{4}$ cup liquid
Corn syrup	1 cup granulated sugar, plus $\frac{1}{4}$ cup liquid (same type of liquid as specified in recipe)

[a]Products resulting from the suggested substitutions will exhibit color and flavor changes, according to the substitution being made.
[b]Substitute for no more than half of the sugar specified in the recipe.

hydrate, which does not have a sweet taste despite its glucose heritage, is the source of only about 1 calorie per gram. This low calorie contribution is the result of incomplete utilization of the compound in the body. Polydextrose is marketed by Pfizer Specialty Chemicals Group, New York, and it is identified by the trademark Litesse®.

r = hydrogen/litesse/glucose/sorbitol/citric acid

Polydextrose (example of a molecule of randomly polymerized dextrose)

SUMMARY

Most of the sugar products on the market are sucrose derived from sugarcane or sugar beets and refined to the desired degree of purity. Fructose is gaining a market for special applications, particularly in commercial food products. Corn syrup (derived by hydrolysis of cornstarch and occasionally altered by isomerase to high-fructose corn syrup), molasses (from sugarcane processing), honey, and sorghum (from grain sorghum) are other sugar-containing products used as sweeteners. Saccharin (a nonnutritive sweetener used for many years) and aspartame (composed of two amino acids, L-aspartic acid and the methyl ester of L-phenylalanine) are sweeteners used when low-calorie products are the goal. Xylitol, sorbitol, and mannitol are sugar alcohols that are useful sweeteners in commercially produced foods. The strong interest in reducing calories in foods has fostered the development and use of several low-calorie and no-calorie sweeteners. Saccharin, aspartame, acesulfame-K, thaumatin, sucralose, and isomalt are examples of sweeteners that are approved for use by the Food and Drug Administration. Cyclamates have been banned in the United States, but they are used in many parts of the world and may be approved for use at some future time in the United States as well.

Disaccharide sugars undergo some hydrolysis during heating in water, particularly when acid is present. With more severe heat treatment, the ring structure of sugar molecules splits, and a variety of acids and aldehydes form as the sugar molecules undergo caramelization. When in contact with proteins, reducing sugars can undergo the Maillard reaction. Caramelization and the Maillard reaction are evidenced by the gradual change in color to a golden brown and even to a deep brown or black if overheating is excessive.

Crystalline candies gain their character from an organized crystalline structure, whereas amorphous candies are so viscous when hot that sugar crystals cannot aggregate in an organized fashion. The physical character of a candy is determined by the concentration of sugar and the presence of interfering substances, lower concentrations (indicated by a final temperature of about 112°C) resulting in crystalline candies and higher concentrations (boiled to as high as 148°C) in amorphous products.

Crystallization in crystalline candies needs to be controlled to achieve a very fine texture, rather than the grainy quality associated with large crystal aggregates. The presence of a variety of sugars and the achievement of a high degree of supersaturation before crystallization is initiated during the cooling period are important to the control of crystal size. Adequate beating from the time the correct point of supersaturation is reached until the crystallizing candy becomes firm is an additional way to keep crystal aggregates very small. During the first day after preparation of crystalline candies, the candy becomes slightly smoother and softer in texture, but ripening beyond this point results in increasingly grainy candy. However, invertase, which often is added to commercial chocolates with fondant centers, acts during storage to hydrolyze sucrose into invert sugar, creating a center smoother and softer than the original center.

Accurate temperature control and uniform heating are essential to the preparation of high-quality amorphous candies. Their very high concentration of sugar is accompanied by extremely high temperatures, and these high temperatures promote very rapid degradation of the sugar. This can lead to scorching and burning. The high concentration of sugar at the end of the boiling period results in an extremely viscous syrup even when it is first removed from the heat. Formation of organized aggregates of sugar crystals is impossible in such a viscous mixture, hence the amorphous nature of these candies.

Sugars can be substituted, but each type of sugar or sugar product has certain unique features. Saccharin is the sweetest of the nonnutritive sweeteners presently in use, being remarkably sweeter than sucrose, but plagued with a bitter aftertaste; aspartame is also much sweeter than sucrose, albeit distinctly less sweet than saccharin or the (banned) cyclamates. Fructose is the sweetest of the sugars and the most soluble, whereas lactose is the least sweet and least soluble of the common sugars. All of the sugars are hygroscopic, with fructose being considerably more hygroscopic than sucrose at room temperature, a characteristic that makes fructose of some interest in minimizing staling in baked products.

STUDY QUESTIONS

1. Compare the recipes for candies from several cookbooks. What is the role of each of the ingredients? Are these same ingredients listed in comparable commercial candies? What additional or different ingredients are listed in the commercial candies?

2. Make a list of all of the sweetening products in a supermarket. What ingredients are included in each of these? How do the prices compare? Can these be used interchangeably?

3. Can fructose be used in place of sucrose in making candies? What differences, if any, might be noted?

4. Can aspartame be substituted for sucrose in making fudge? Explain the reasons for your answer.

5. Compare the applications and results of using saccharin, aspartame, and sucrose in three different products containing sweeteners.

6. What differences would you expect to find when comparing use of regular corn syrup and high-fructose corn syrup in candies? Explain your rationale.

7. Describe the chemical changes that occur during the preparation of toffee.

8. Define saturated solution and supersaturated solution. How is a supersaturated solution prepared? Why is a supersaturated solution essential to the preparation of high-quality crystalline candy?

9. Can a lower-calorie fudge be made by reducing the amount of sugar in the recipe? Explain the rationale for your answer.

BIBLIOGRAPHY

Anonymous. 1991. "Premium-quality polydextrose improves lower-calorie foods." *Food Technol. 45* (5): 102.

Appl, R. C. 1991. "Confectionery ingredients from starch." *Food Technol. 45* (3): 148.

Awad, A. and Chen, A. C. 1993. "New generation of sucrose products made by cocrystallization." *Food Technol. 47* (1): 146.

Bakal, A. I. 1987. "Saccharin functionality and safety," *Food Technol. 41* (1): 117.

Baker, C. W. 1993. "Production of sucrose-based carbohydrates for the food industry." *Food Technol. 47* (1): 149.

Barndt, R. L. and Jackson, G. 1990. "Stability of sucralose in baked goods." *Food Technol. 44* (1): 62.

Bell, J. 1993. "High intensity sweeteners—a regulatory update." *Food Technol. 47* (11): 136.

Blankers, I. 1995. "Properties and applications of lactitol." *Food Technol. 49 (1): 66.*

Book, S. and Luallen, T. 1996. "25 Years of carbohydrates in IFT." *Food Technol. 50* (12): 51.

Bullens, C., Krawczyk, G., and Geithman, L. 1994. "Reduced-fat cheese products using carrageenan and microcrystalline cellulose." *Food Technol. 48* (1): 79.

Bullock, L. M., Handel, A. P., Segall, S., and Wasserman, P. A. 1992. "Replacement of simple sugars in cookie dough." *Food Technol. 46* (1): 82.

Campbell, L. A., Ketelsen, S. M., and Antenucci, R. N. 1994. "Formulating oatmeal cookies with calorie-sparing ingredients." *Food Technol. 48* (5): 98.

Chinachoti, P. 1993. "Water mobility and its relation to functionality of sucrose-containing food systems." *Food Technol. 47* (1): 134.

Cloninger, M. R. and Baldwin, R. E. 1974. L-aspartyl-l-phenylalanine methyl ester (aspartame) as sweetener." *J. Food Sci. 39:* 347.

Doner L. W. 1977. "Sugars of honey—a review." *J. Sci. Food Agr. 28:* 443.

Doty, T. E. 1972. "Fructose sweetness: new dimension." *Cereal Foods World 21:* 62.

Fruin, J. C. and Scallet, B. L. 1975. "Isomerized corn syrups in food products." *Food Technol.* *59* (11): 40.

Giese, J. 1993. "Alternative sweeteners and bulking agents." *Food Technol.* *47* (1): 113.

Godshall, M. A. 1997. How carbohydrates influence food flavor." *Food Technol.* *51* (1): 63.

Guy, E. J. 1971. "Lactose." *Baker's Digest 45* (Apr): 34.

Hartel R. W. 1993. "Controlling sugar crystallization in food products." *Food Technol.* *47* (11): 99.

Heaton, K. C. F. et al. 1980. "Sorbitol." *IFST Proc.* *13* (3): 157.

Higley, N. A. and White, J. S. 1991. "Trends in fructose availability and consumption in the United States." *Food Technol.* *45* (10): 118.

Hoseney, R. C. 1984. "Chemical changes in carbohydrates produced by thermal processing." *J. Chem. Educ. 61:* 308.

Inglett, G. E. and Grisamore, S. B. 1991. "Maltodextrin fat substitute lowers cholesterol." *Food Technol.* *45* (6): 104.

Irwin, W. E. 1990. "Isomalt—sweet, reduced-calorie bulking agent." *Food Technol.* *44* (6): 128.

Izzo, M., Stahl, C., and Tuazon, M. 1995. "Using cellulose gel and carrageenan to lower fat and calories in confections." *Food Technol.* *49* (7): 1995.

Jeffery, M. S. 1993. "Key functional properties of sucrose in chocolate and sugar confectionery." *Food Technol.* *47* (1): 141.

Kulp, K., Lorenz, K., and Stone, M. 1991. "Functionality of carbohydrate ingredients in bakery products." *Food Technol.* *45* (3): 136.

McNutt, K. and Sentko, A. 1996. Sugar replacers: a growing group of sweeteners in the United States. *Nutr. Today 31* (6): 255.

Mermelstein, N. H. 1975. "Immobilized enzymes produce high-fructose corn syrup." *Food Technol. 29* (6): 20.

Miller, W. T. 1987. "Legacy of cyclamate." *Food Technol.* *41* (1): 116.

Nabors, L. O. and Gelardi, R. C. 1986. *Alternative Sweeteners.* Dekker: New York.

Rapaille, A., Gonze, M., and Van der Schueren, F. 1995. "Formulating sugar-free chocolate products with maltitol." *Food Technol.* *49* (7): 51.

Reineccius, G. A. 1991. "Carbohydrates for flavor encapsulation." *Food Technol.* *45* (3): 144.

Shallenberger, R. S. 1998. "Sweetness theory and its application in the food industry." *Food Technol. 52* (7): 72.

Steginik, L. D. 1987. "Aspartame: review of safety issues." *Food Technol.* *41* (1): 119.

Verdi, R. J. and Hood, L. L. 1993. "Advantages of alternative sweetener blends." *Food Technol.* *47* (6): 94.

Zhao, J. and Whistler, R. L. 1994. "Spherical aggregates of starch granules as flavor carriers." *Food Technol.* *48* (7): 104.

CHAPTER 9

Starch

Starch is a complex carbohydrate that has been cursed by dieters in years past, but that now is praised by nutritionists as a particularly healthful source of energy. In food preparation at home, starch is very important as a thickening agent. However, starch is but one of several polysaccharides that are used as thickeners in the food industry. This chapter examines several aspects of starch—its structure, functional properties, applications in food preparation, and selection.

STRUCTURE

Although **starch** is the name used by nutritionists, this complex carbohydrate actually consists of two fractions: amylose and amylopectin. The two fractions occur together in starch from most sources, so the overall behavior of a starch is determined in large measure by the relative amounts of amylose and amylopectin. Each of the fractions has unique properties that contribute to the functionality of starch from various plant sources.

Starch
Complex polysaccharide consisting of two fractions, both of which are polymers of glucose.

Amylose

Amylose, the linear fraction of starch characterized by 1,4-α-glucosidic linkages (see Chapter 7), ranges widely in molecular weight, from a few thousand to as large as 150,000. This large polymer of D-glucose is slightly soluble, a characteristic of importance in starch cookery. The actual length of amylose molecules varies considerably even within a single sample of starch, but generally cereal starches (corn and rice, for example) have shorter, lighter amylose molecules than are found in potato and other starches from roots and tubers.

Although amylose is described as a linear molecule, individual molecules appear to form a loose, rather flexible coil when they are dispersed in a solution. This

Amylose
Linear fraction of starch composed of glucose units linked by 1,4-α-glucosidic linkages.

coiled arrangement allows iodine to be trapped within the helix when it is added to amylose, resulting in a blue color. Each six D-glucose units in the helix can bind one iodine atom. The iodine test is used to determine the presence of amylose in starch dispersions.

Starches from various sources differ in relative content of amylose. Although it is possible to breed plants that produce starch containing essentially no amylose, the more common sources of starch range in amylose content from about 17 percent to around 30 percent. In general, the root and tuber starches contain somewhat less amylose than the cereal starches. Cornstarch typically ranges between 24 and 28 percent amylose; the range for wheat starch is similar but a bit narrower, 25 to 26 percent. The amylose content of potato starch is somewhat lower, usually between 20 and 23 percent. **Tapioca,** which is only about 17 percent amylose, provides the least amylose of the starches commonly used. At the other end of the spectrum, some special species of peas and corn have been bred that have starch with an amylose content as high as 75 percent.

Tapioca
Root starch derived from cassava, a tropical plant.

Amylopectin

Amylopectin
Branched fraction of starch composed of glucose units linked by 1,4- and 1,6-α-glucosidic linkages.

Dendritic
Branching.

The other starch fraction, **amylopectin,** is also a polymer of D-glucose. However, the presence of 1,6-α-glucosidic linkages in addition to 1,4-α-glucosidic linkages (see Chapter 7) results in quite a different spatial arrangement. In contrast to the linearity of amylose, amylopectin molecules are **dendritic** as a result of the shift in direction of the D-glucose chain at each 1,6-α-glucosidic linkage. In essence, amylopectin molecules are linear for a span of about 10 to perhaps 25 or more glucose units, at which point a 1,6-α-glucosidic linkage occurs, causing the molecule to branch. Within a single amylopectin molecule, these branches are found very frequently. Thus, an amylopectin molecule is described spatially as nonlinear, actually rather bushy and dense (see Figure 9.1).

The molecular weight of amylopectin molecules is still a matter of conjecture, although research has revealed that this starch fraction clearly is one of nature's larger polymers. Researchers estimate the molecular weight can be as high as 500 million, with the lower end of the range being about 65 million!

Despite the obviously far greater size of amylopectin compared with amylose molecules, amylopectin still has only one free aldehyde (reducing) group in each molecule. The iodine test commonly used in studying starch results in a purplish-

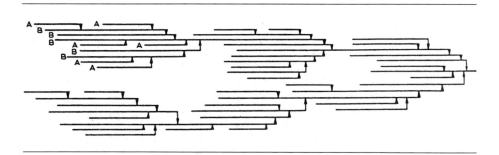

Figure 9.1   Suggested arrangement of amylopectin showing the short lengths (A) and long lengths (B) prior to 1,6-α-glucosidic linkages where branching occurs. (Courtesy of D.R. Lineback and Bakers Digest. 1984. Vol. 58(2): 16. Diagram by D. J. Manners and N. K. Matheson. *Carbohydrate Res.* 1981. 90:99.)

red color when the fraction is amylopectin. This failure to show the blue color that iodine produces with amylose is due to the lack of helical configuration within the amylopectin. The difference in iodine-binding capability of the two starch fractions provides the basis for distinguishing the relative proportions of amylose and amylopectin in starch mixtures.

Typically, amylopectin is far more abundant in starches than is amylose. In root and tuber starches, amylopectin exceeds amylose content by approximately four times; amylopectin ordinarily constitutes about 80 percent of the starch. Cereal starches are composed of around 75 percent amylopectin. However, genetic variations containing starches composed of virtually only amylopectin (e.g., waxy maize) have been developed and are of commercial significance. The relative proportions of amylopectin and amylose in starches are of considerable importance because of the different behaviors of these two starch fractions in cooked starch products.

Starch Granule

In plants, starch is deposited in an orderly fashion in the form of granules (see Figures 9.2, 9.3, 9.4). These granules, composed of amylose and amylopectin molecules, are made in the **leucoplasts** within the cytoplasm of the cells (see Chapter 10). Each granule consists of concentric layers of amylopectin molecules interrupted by some amylose molecules, which often are arranged in a somewhat organized manner within the layers (growth rings). From the very small inner layer, called the **hilum**, layer upon layer of amylose and amylopectin molecules is deposited on the **starch granule** until the mature plant is harvested. Remarkably, the

Leucoplast
Plastid in the cytoplasm of plant cells; the site of starch storage as granules.

Hilum
Innermost layer or the nucleus of a starch granule.

Starch Granule
Concentric layers of amylose and amylopectin molecules formed in the leucoplasts and held together by hydrogen bonding.

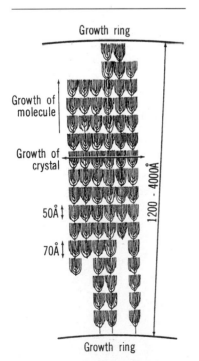

Figure 9.2 Suggested arrangement of amylopectin molecules in a growth ring within a starch granule. (Courtesy of D. R. Lineback and Bakers Digest. 1984. Vol. 58(2): 10. Diagram by D. French. *Starch: Chemistry and Technology.* Academic Press, New York. 2nd ed. 1983.)

Figure 9.3 Diagram of ultrathin sections of starch granule: (a) ordered radial arrangement of amylose; (b) amylose in amorphous region; (c) amylopectin crystalline region. (Courtesy of D. R. Lineback and Bakers Digest. 1984. Vol. 58(2): 16. Diagram of P. Kassenbeck, Stärke 1978. 30: 40.)

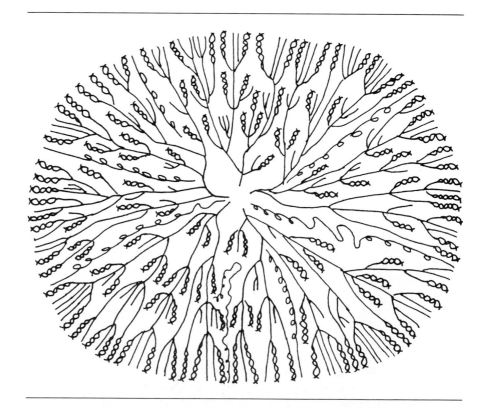

Figure 9.4 Schematic of the organization of a starch granule. (Diagram by D.R. Lineback). (Courtesy of D. R. Lineback and Bakers Digest. 1984. Vol. 58(2): 16.)

molecules within each layer are held together simply by hydrogen bonding, and similarly, the layers are bonded together by the same secondary bonding arrangement.

The physical nature of starch granules has been studied at some length using polarized light and X-ray diffraction. When viewed under polarized filters placed at right angles to each other, starch granules reveal a **birefringence** pattern that looks much like a **Maltese cross** because of the somewhat spherical shape and the crystalline areas. The unique birefringence patterns of starch granules are found only in the raw starch. When starch has been heated with water, the crystalline areas responsible for the original light refraction are altered, and the pattern of the Maltese cross can no longer be seen using polarized light.

FUNCTIONAL PROPERTIES OF STARCH

For starch to be used as a thickening agent in foods, it must be heated with water, a physical change called gelatinization. If it is heated without water, it undergoes a chemical change termed dextrinization. These processes are important in food preparation, for they determine the behavior of starch, its thickening ability in sols, and also its gel-forming properties.

Gelatinization

Gelatinization is a physical process that is unique to starches. The transformation that occurs when starch is heated in water is truly remarkable. The heat energy causes hydrogen bonds in the starch granules to break, which facilitates the entry of water into the granule and the shifting of some amylose molecules into the water surrounding the granules. Water continues to migrate into the granules, causing considerable swelling when the starch mixture is heated to the temperature range required for gelatinization. Because water is not compressible in the starch granule, the volume of the granule increases as more and more water enters and forms hydrogen bonds with the amylopectin and amylose molecules. This bound water not only affects the viscosity of the starch mixture by increasing the physical size of the starch granules, but also reduces the amount of free water external to the granules. The tight organization of the starch granule is disrupted during the gelanization process. Removal of some of the amylose and the physical spreading out or dilution of the remaining amylose and amylopectin molecules in the granule result in loss of birefringence and increased translucence.

Pasting is another term that often is applied to describe the changes that take place in starch as a result of heating starch in the presence of water. This is quite a descriptive word, for gelatinizing starch mixtures do begin to take on the qualities of a paste. Technically, pasting is the word used to describe the changes that occur in the starch granule when heating is continued after gelatinization has taken place. These changes include loss of molecules of starch from the granule and complete loss of the granular organization, which may be described actually as **implosion** of the granule.

Temperatures.   The rate of thickening varies with the type of starch, but there is no single temperature at which gelatinization occurs. Instead, starch pastes gradually thicken as the temperature rises. Loss of birefringence begins for most starches (dispersed in water) at temperatures between 57°C and 65°C, although for rice

Birefringence
Refraction of light in two slightly different directions.

Maltese Cross
A cross consisting of equal-length arms that terminate in a V-shape.

Gelatinization
Swelling of starch granules and migration of some amylose into the cooking water when starch is heated in water to thicken various food products.

Pasting
Changes in gelatinized starch, including considerable loss of amylose and implosion of the granule.

Implosion
Violent compression.

starch it begins at 68°C and for tapioca starch it starts at only 52°C. All evidence of birefringence is lost at about 70°C; the exceptions are wheat and tapioca starches (64°C) and potato starch (66°C).

As heating is continued beyond termination of the loss of birefringence, the granule continues to swell. In fact, most starches can be heated to 100°C with little rupture of starch granules despite their vast increase in size as they imbibe increasing amounts of water. Amylose also leaches out of the granule during the phase of gelatinization; the shorter amylose molecules are the most likely to leave the granule because of their comparatively greater solubility. At temperatures near 100°C, some of the granules begin to implode (compress inward) and fragment, a change that reduces viscosity. However, other granules may still be swelling and offsetting the effect of the few imploding granules. When a starch paste is held at 95°C or higher for several minutes, most of the starch granules reach their maximum volume and begin to implode. This explains the decrease in viscosity of starch pastes that is observed with prolonged heating (see Figures 9.5 and 9.6) It is important to remember that tapioca reaches maximum viscosity at a temperature about 20°C lower than other starches and then begins to thin (Table 9.1).

Type of Starch.   The thickening ability of starches from different sources varies. Potato starch is far more effective than other starches as a thickening agent (Table 9.2). Root starches are somewhat more effective than cereal starches; wheat is the least effective of the starches commonly available. Flour, which is used commonly in the home, is even less effective than pure wheat starch because of the protein

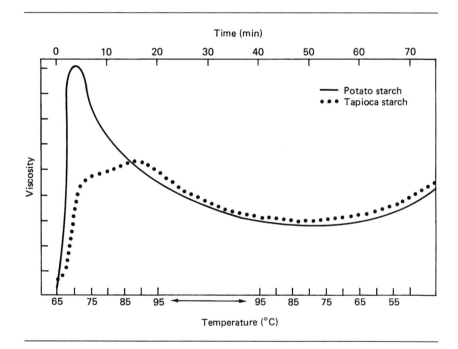

Figure 9.5 Comparison of the viscosity of potato and tapioca starch pastes during heating, holding, and cooling. (Based on data from T. J. Schoch and A. L. Elder. "Starches in the food industry." In *Users of Sugars and Other Carbohydrates in the Food Industry.* Adv. in Chem. Ser. 12, p. 24. 1955. American Chemical Society.)

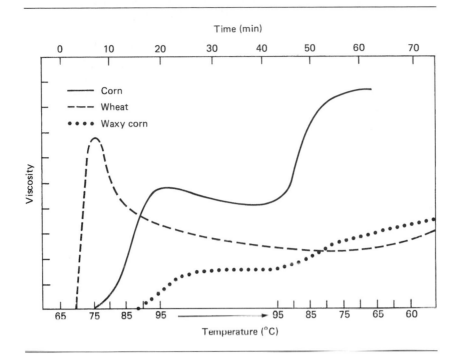

Figure 9.6 Comparison of the viscosity of corn, wheat, and waxy corn starch pastes during heating, holding, and cooling. (Based on data from T. J. Schoch and A. L. Elder. "Starches in the food industry." In *Users of Sugars and Other Carbohydrates in the Food Industry*. Adv. in Chem. Ser. 12, p. 24. 1955. American Chemical Society.)

Table 9.1 Temperature at Which Starch Pastes[a] Reach Maximum Viscosity, Maximum Viscosity, and Temperature and Viscosity 20 Minutes after Reaching Maximum Viscosity

Type of Starch	Temperature, Maximum Viscosity (°C)	Maximum Viscosity (g-cm)	20 Minutes Later	
			Temperature (°C)	Viscosity (g-cm)
Potato	90	105	95	49
Waxy Corn	89	105	95	65
Cross linked waxy corn	93	103	96	115
Waxy rice	87	110	96	106
Waxy rice flour	70	97	92	25
Waxy sorghum	91	108	96	65
Tapioca	71	108	94	59
Arrowroot	80	103	96	85
Sorghum	94	110	97	73
Corn	91	113	95	77
Rice	94	101	97	54
Rice flour	93	100	97	77
Wheat	92	105	94	62
Wheat flour	83	108	95	5

[a]The percentage of starch was varied so that pastes had similar viscosities when they reached maximum viscosity.
Adapted from Osman, E.M. and Mootse, G. 1958. *Food Res. 23*, 554.

Table 9.2   Comparative Thickening Ability of Various Starches

Type of starch	Comparative Amount Needed to Achieve Designated Viscosity of Hot (approx 95°C) Starch Paste
Potato	1.96
Waxy corn	2.98
Waxy rice	3.13
Waxy sorghum	3.42
Tapioca	3.54
Crosslinked waxy corn	4.15
Arrowroot	4.37
Sorghum	4.66
Corn	4.90
Waxy rice flour	5.48
Rice	5.49
Rice flour	5.57
Wheat	6.44
Wheat flour	9.27

Adapted from Osman, E.M. and Mootse, G. 1958. *Food Res. 23,* 554.

content. The waxy starches are more effective thickening agents in starch pastes than are their standard counterparts.

Increased translucence during gelatinization is particularly noticeable in the root starches. Potato starch and tapioca are much more translucent when gelatinized than are the cereal starches. Among the cereal starches, the gelatinized waxy starches are more translucent than their regular counterparts. However, regular cornstarch and, to a lesser extent, rice and wheat starches exhibit a distinct increase in translucence during gelatinization.

The texture of gelatinized starch pastes is of concern because of its influence on palatability. Ideally, a thickened starch paste will be smooth, but unmodified starches (especially root starches) tend to be mucilaginous. Those pastes that are the clearest (potato, for example) are also the most stringy in texture. This is a major disadvantage in the use of potato starch as a thickening agent. Similarly, tapioca-thickened pastes are much too mucilaginous in texture to be competitive with other starches unless the tapioca has been modified. This textural problem is the reason for processing tapioca into pearl tapioca or else modifying the starch chemically. **Pearl tapioca** consists of agglomerates of partially gelatinized starch dried into pellets so hard that they require overnight soaking for practical use in puddings and other products. When the partially gelatinized tapioca is dried in much finer pellets, the extended soaking problem is eliminated without sacrificing the improved texture. Very finely ground minute tapioca is used often because it hydrates quickly.

Cereal starches are much less mucilaginous when made into gelatinized starch pastes than are the root starches. This makes cornstarch an excellent choice as a thickening agent when a starch paste with limited translucence is acceptable. However, waxy cornstarch produces a distinctly stringy, albeit translucent paste. Fortunately, crosslinking during the manufacture of waxy starches alters the textural properties of the gelatinized starch pastes, and the desired smooth paste with excellent translucence can be made using crosslinked waxy cornstarch.

Pearl Tapioca
Large pellets of partially gelatinized tapioca that are dried, resulting in a product that requires a long soaking period before use, but yields a translucent, nonstringy paste.

Effect of Ingredients. When starch-thickened mixtures are incorporated into desserts, sugar usually is a prominent ingredient. The hygroscopic nature of all types of sugars causes the sugar used in the recipe to compete with the starch for the water needed for gelatinization. This competition partially explains the fact that gelatinization is delayed and the final temperature required to achieve gelatinization is raised as the level of sugar in a starch mixture is increased (see Figure 9.7). The other contributing factor appears to be the crosslinking between sugar and starch molecules (Spies and Hoseney, 1982).

Obvious effects of sugar include increased translucence and reduced paste viscosity and gel strength. Monosaccharides have less effect than do most disaccharides; curiously, maltose has less effect (Bean and Osman, 1959) than either lactose or sucrose. The effect of sucrose is of particular interest because of the common use of this sugar in making puddings and pie fillings.

Occasionally, lemon juice or another acid ingredient may be a part of a starch-thickened product. The combination of acid and heat, particularly below pH 4, causes a hydrolytic reaction that begins to break down molecules of starch into slightly smaller molecules. The shorter molecules evolving from starch as a result of acid hydrolysis are able to move somewhat more freely in the thickening paste, resulting in a gelatinized starch paste that is a little thinner than it would be if no acid were present. If starch must be heated in the presence of acid (as is the case when thickening fruit juice for a pie filling), a rapid heating rate will keep the length of time for acid hydrolysis to a minimum and result in a thicker product than is produced when the filling is heated slowly. Whenever possible, the acid should be added after gelatinization is complete so that the thinning caused by

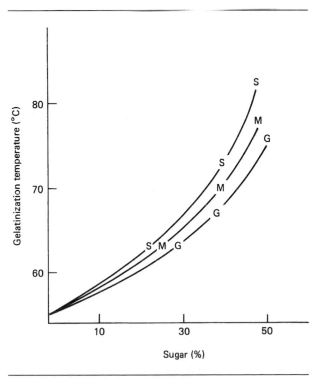

Figure 9.7 Sugar concentration versus gelatinization temperature. S = sucrose, M = maltose, G = glucose. (Adapted from R. D. Spies and R. C. Hoseney. "Effects of sugars on starch gelatinization." *Cereal Chem.* 1982. 59(2): 128. Fig. 1. Courtesy of R. C. Hoseney and the American Association of Cereal Chemists.)

acid hydrolysis will not occur. However, recipes do need to be formulated so that the liquid in lemon juice (or other similar acidic substances) is calculated as a part of the total liquid. This liquid added after gelatinization has occurred is not bound in the starch granules of the paste.

Both sugar and acid are ingredients in some starch-thickened products, such as a lemon pie. In such recipes, the amount of sugar used has a considerable effect on the behavior of the paste. Campbell and Briant (1957) reported that increasing the amount of acid in sugar–starch mixtures causes an increase in the viscosity and a lower gelatinization temperature, but a rapid thinning of the starch paste when heating is continued if the sugar content is fairly low. However, a high sugar content apparently attracts so much of the water needed for gelatinization that the starch granules swell slowly. This delays the molecules from moving out of the starch granules to permit contact with the acid and subsequent acid hydrolysis. When it is necessary to gelatinize starch in the presence of both acid and sugar, sufficient heating is imperative to ensure complete gelatinization and maximum thickening. Careful attention is required so that the point of maximum thickening is recognized and heating is halted before the rather rapid thinning that occurs once hydrolysis becomes the dominant factor. Use of a crosslinked starch is advised when possible for commercial applications; crosslinked starches are more resistant to hydrolysis than are native starches.

Fats are a part of some formulations that are starch-thickened. Their presence results in a reduction in the temperature at which maximum gelatinization and viscosity occur. Milk proteins also lower the temperature required for maximum gelatinization of starch mixtures.

Gelation

Gel
Colloidal dispersion in which the liquid is the discontinuous phase and the solid is the continuous phase.

Gelatinized starch mixtures may exist as sols or **gels** (Chapter 6). Hot starch pastes exhibit flow properties; starch is the dispersed solid phase, and water is the continuous phase. However, many starch pastes (sols) are converted to gels as they cool. Amylose molecules that have left the starch granules during the gelatinization process are free to move about in a paste. The paste loses energy gradually during cooling; the free amylose molecules move more slowly as energy is lost. Occasionally one amylose molecule may happen to move close to another amylose molecule and a hydrogen bond forms between the two molecules. While the paste is still warm, this hydrogen bond may break readily and permit the two molecules to continue their separate journeys through the paste. Increasing opportunity for more stable hydrogen bonding arises as the amylose molecules move sluggishly among the other amylose molecules and swollen starch granules.

The gradual reduction in energy of the system promotes the formation of hydrogen bonds between amylose molecules, with the result that frequently a starch paste is transformed into a gel. When there are enough amylose molecules to establish a continuous network joined by hydrogen bonds, the swollen granules become trapped in the amylose superstructure. This network of solids is the continuous phase of the newly formed starch gel, and the water is now the dispersed or discontinuous phase. This system, termed a gel, no longer has the flow properties associated with a sol. When a gel is formed, the process is called **gelation.**

Gelation
Formation of a gel.

Type and Concentration of Starch. After reading the preceding description of gelation, you should not be surprised to find that starches lacking amylose (i.e., waxy starches) do not form gels in the concentrations normally used in making food products. If the level of starch is raised to 30 percent, the amylopectin molecules from the waxy starches can effect a limited amount of hydrogen bonding and form a soft gel. This is of academic interest, but is not practical in the food industry. When a gel is desired, other starches are used.

Unlike potato and tapioca starches, arrowroot starch is a root starch capable of forming at least a soft gel. In fact, it forms a much stronger gel than does rice starch (Table 9.3). Fortunately, cornstarch forms a pleasingly firm gel, and wheat starch sets to a strong gel. Cereal flours sometimes are used as thickening agents. Although wheat, rice, and even waxy rice flours form starch pastes effectively when gelatinized, they are comparatively poor in their gel-forming ability.

Extent of Heating.   Gelation depends on the availability of free amylose molecules for hydrogen bonding to form the continuous network. These molecules become available when starch has been heated with water sufficiently for some of the hydrogen bonds within the granules to break and release some of the amylose into the surrounding water. For optimal gel strength, starch pastes need to be heated until enough amylose has been released, but not so much that the granules start to split apart into fragments. With a moderate rate of heating, gelatinization is complete and the amylose is available long before the granules are fragmented to any great extent. However, with vigorous stirring and a prolonged heating period, considerable fragmentation does occur. This results in a pasty texture and a weakened gel structure.

Agitation.   For maximum gel strength, starch mixtures should be allowed to cool without disturbance. When hydrogen bonds form between amylose molecules that are in close proximity, they begin to provide the stable network needed for a

Table 9.3   Strnegh of Starch Gels Made from Various Starch Pastes of Approximately Equal Viscosity[a]

Starch	Gel Strength (g-cm)	
	Cooled at Maximum Viscosity	Cooked 20 min beyond Maximum Viscosity before Cooling
Waxy corn	0	0
Waxy rice	0	0
Waxy rice flour	0	0
Potato	0	0
Tapioca	0	0
Crosslinked waxy cornstarch	0	0
Rice flour	11	15
Wheat flour	26	88
Rice	31	30
Arrowroot	87	115
Cornstarch	52	142
Thin-boiling cornstarch	115	210
Wheat	345	440
Thin-boiling wheat	434	1440

[a]See Table 9.2 for the levels of dry starch used.
Adapted from Osman, E.M. and Mootse, G. 1958. *Food Res. 23;* 554

strong gel. Agitation during the gelling period disrupts hydrogen bonds already formed and weakens the ensuing gel. For this reason, butter and flavorings to be added to puddings and pie fillings should be stirred in immediately after these products are removed from the heat, and the mixtures should then be allowed to cool undisturbed.

Effects of Other Ingredients.   Sugar and acid often are added to starch-containing products to alter their flavor, but these ingredients also influence the properties of starch gels. As was noted in the discussion of gelatinization, both sugar and acid have a softening effect on the resulting gel. Sugar not only causes the gel to be more tender, but it also increases its translucence. The extent of softening caused by the acid is determined to a great extent by the presence of sugar as well as by the time at which acid is added, the pH, and the rate of heating if the acid is added prior to gelatinization. When lemon juice or vinegar is added to a gelatinized starch paste prior to gelation, the softening observed is due primarily to the added liquid and not to hydrolysis. If the acid is present during the extended heating period required for gelatinization and the pH is 4 or less, acid hydrolysis will result in a rather tender gel, the consequence of shorter amylose chains.

Fats and proteins may influence gel strength too, in part as a result of the small reduction in the percentage of starch that occurs when other ingredients are added. However, the effect of egg yolk protein in starch mixtures is greater than can be explained by this rationale. When sufficient heat is applied after egg yolk is added to a gelatinized starch mixture to coagulate the yolk proteins (including α-amylase, a starch-digesting enzyme in the yolk), the thickened starch–protein mixture gels on cooling. If the yolk proteins are not coagulated, the cooled thickened mixture does not gel, but instead becomes quite fluid because of α-amylase action, which breaks down starch and yields a product that is far less viscous than the hot starch paste was prior to addition of the yolks. From a practical perspective, careful coagulation of added yolks in a starch-thickened paste is essential to achievement of the desired gel strength.

Syneresis.   Water is trapped within the starch gel. A layer of water is hydrogen bonded all along the individual amylose molecules, as well as being bonded to the surface molecules of the granules. Some water is bound within the starch granules. Additional free water (not actually bound to the starch) is trapped in the interstices within the gel structure. As a gel ages, there is some drawing together of the amylose molecules, and some water is squeezed out of the gel. In a similar fashion, water separates from a starch gel when the surface is cut and the trapped liquid is released from the areas that have been exposed by the cut. This loss of liquid from a gel is termed **syneresis.**

Syneresis
Separation of liquid from a gel.

Retrogradation

Although gels appear to be static after they are formed, some undergo considerable change. This change results from the breaking of some of the hydrogen bonds holding the gel together in a continuous network and the re-formation of other hydrogen bonds as the amylose molecules shift around within the gel. Over a period of time, there is a tendency for the amylose molecules to orient themselves in crystalline regions. This more orderly alignment of amylose (termed ***retrogradation***) is evident on the tongue as a somewhat gritty texture. Amylopectin also partici-

Retrogradation
Gradual increase of crystalline aggregates in starch gels during storage, the result of amylose molecules rearranging in an orderly fashion.

pates in retrogradation, albeit at a slower rate than amylose. The outer branches of the amylopectin molecules also are capable of forming some hydrogen bonds with other molecules in a starch gel. Obviously, retrogradation is undesirable and reduces the quality of the food in which it occurs. A starch-thickened pudding develops this textural quality if held in the refrigerator for a few days. A fairly common example is bread that develops a slightly harsh texture after several days of storage.

The crystalline aggregates of amylose that occur in retrogradation can be eliminated by gently heating the food containing the starch. The heat energy is sufficient to break the hydrogen bonds holding the amylose molecules together and allow them to move in the gel again. This change is detected readily when stale bread is tightly covered and reheated. The heated bread does not exhibit any harshness, but as the bread cools, the amylose molecules reorganize into crystalline aggregates.

Dextrinization

Occasionally, as when browning meat dredged in flour or making certain gravies and sauces, starch is heated without any water being added to the pan. Without water, the temperature rapidly rises beyond the maximum that can be reached when water is present. The high energy causes chemical degradation of starch, via a chemical reaction with the water that is naturally present in the flour to split the starch molecule at one or more of the linkages between the glucose units. The result is formation of shorter molecules of varying lengths called dextrins. The chemical change that occurs, called ***dextrinization,*** is shown below.

Dextrinization
Degradation of starch to dextrins by uptake of one molecule of water wherever cleavage occurs.

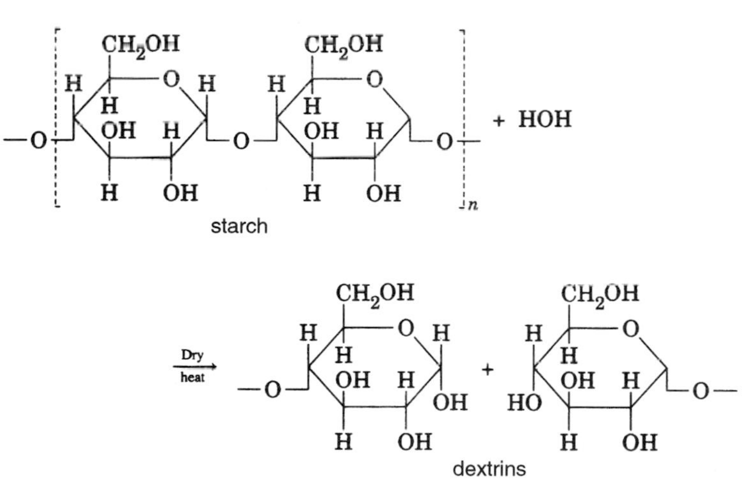

starch

dextrins

EXAMINING STARCHES

Sources

Plants are the source of food starches, with commercially viable sources including cereal, root, and tree starches. The specific cereals that are used as sources of starch include corn, wheat, rice, oat, barley, and rye (Figure 9.8). Although the shape of the various grains or kernels differ from one cereal to another, all grains

Figure 9.8   Cereal sources of starch: (upper left) oats, (upper right) rice, (lower left) wheat, and (lower right) corn.

consist of three components—a bran covering, a small region of germ or embryo, and a major portion called the endosperm. The endosperm is the location of the starch granules within the individual grains of cereal.

The granules of starch in each cereal each have a distinctive shape, depending on the type of cereal (Figure 9.9). Cornstarch typically has polygonal granules ranging in diameter from about 12–25 microns. In contrast, rice starch granules are the smallest of the starches, usually being only 3–8 microns in diameter, but also polygonal in shape. Surprisingly, wheat has two basic forms of granules: small spheres about 10 microns in diameter and larger disks about 35 microns across, significantly larger than the other cereal starch granules.

Root starches are produced commercially from the root of the cassava plant and from the potato (actually a tuber). The starch from the cassava root is marketed as tapioca, which is particularly popular in its cooked form—tapioca pudding. Granules of tapioca starch typically are round, ranging in size from 12–25 microns. In contrast, potato starch granules are shaped much like a very tiny mussel shell. Compared with other starch granules, potato is an amazing 100 microns in diameter.

The sago palm tree, actually the pith from its trunk, is the source of yet another commercial starch. Sago starch granules are somewhat larger than those from potatoes and are elliptical in shape. Arrowroot and milo (also known as grain sorghum) are other sources of commercial starches.

Other plants rich in starch include mature legumes, such as dried beans (Figure 9.10). However, legumes are not processed to obtain starch for use in food

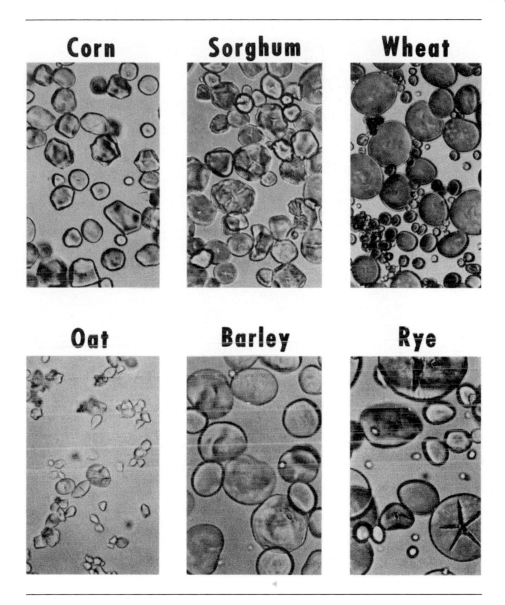

Figure 9.9 Photomicrographs of ungelatinized starch granules (by M. M. MacMasters.) (Courtesy of the Northern Regional Research Center, USDA–ARS. Peoria, Il, and Jerold A. Bietz.)

preparation; instead, they are eaten as the whole seeds because they contain protein, as well as other nutrients.

Unmodified Starches

Numerous choices are available when starch is required as an ingredient. Any of the grain, root, tuber, or tree starches mentioned in the preceding section can be obtained in a comparatively pure state for use in commercial food products. In addition, rice flour and wheat flour are alternatives commonly available commercially

Figure 9.10 Scanning electron microphotograph of Great Northern bean fragment. CS = cell wall; S = starch granule; P = protein matrix; IS = intercellular space. (Reprinted from *Journal of Food Science*. 1984. Vol. 49: 925. Copyright (c) by Institute of Food Technologists. Courtesy of R. T. Tyler, National Research Council of Canada.)

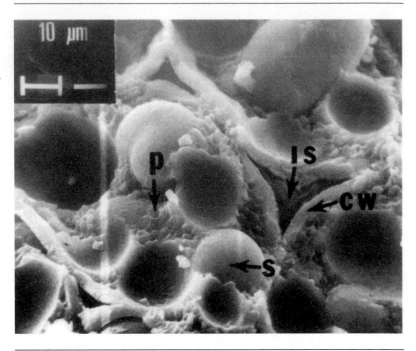

or for home use. These flours provide not only starch, but also some protein and other components of the grains from which they are milled.

Some other starches have unique properties because genetic research has led to new varieties of grains that differ from their cereal ancestors in the composition of the starch they contain. Some have been bred to be approximately 100 percent amylopectin. Such starches are waxy starches. The absence of amylose inhibits the formation of a gel structure when a **waxy starch** is used as a thickening agent; this characteristic makes waxy starches desirable in the preparation of fruit pies and other items in which a thickened but ungelled consistency is desirable. Waxy cornstarch and waxy sorghum starches have unique applications in the food industry because of their chemical composition and consequent properties as thickening agents.

Genetic researchers also have been able to develop starch sources that have an extremely high amylose content, sometimes as high as 75 percent. The remainder of the starch granule is amylopectin. Nevertheless, such high levels of amylose result in unique properties of food products utilizing high-amylose starches. The linear nature of the amylose molecules enables considerable hydrogen bonding to occur; as a result, the high-amylose starches can be made into thin films suitable for wrapping items such as candies. Because these films are made of this special starch, the wrappers are edible, resulting in a unique and definitely marketable item.

Waxy Starch
Starch containing only amylopectin; the result of genetic research and breeding for this composition.

Modified Starches

Modified Starch
Starch that has been altered from its native state by either physical or chemical means.

Today's sophisticated food industry has generated a demand for **modified starches** designed for specific applications. Changes accomplished by physical or chemical means can be very useful in developing a variety of special starches with unique characteristics.

Pregelatinized Starches.   Heavy demands on time have created considerable demand for time-saving products, and it was this priority that prompted the development of **pregelatinized starches.** Pregelatinized starches are starches that have been cooked with water to gelatinize them and then dehydrated after they became swollen. The result is a starch that swells to a desirable thickness when water is added; no heating is necessary. Instant puddings are a popular example of the application of pregelatinized starch as a thickening agent in commercial food products. Pregelatinized starches are examples of products in which a physical change modifies the characteristics of the native starch. **Cold water-swelling (CWS) starch** is a pregelatinized starch well suited for use in microwave cookery.

Thin-Boiling Starches.   Starch is modified chemically to alter its properties for special applications in food products. Treatment of starch with hydrochloric or nitric acid in a controlled reaction results in acid hydrolysis. Depending on the extent of the hydrolytic reaction, the solubility of the starch increases and its thickening power diminishes. **Thin-boiling starches** are formed in this way. These starches contain many debranched molecules of amylopectin, the result of hydrolytic cleavage at the 1,6-α-glucosidic linkage (see Figure 9.11). This reaction facilitated by acid is presented below.

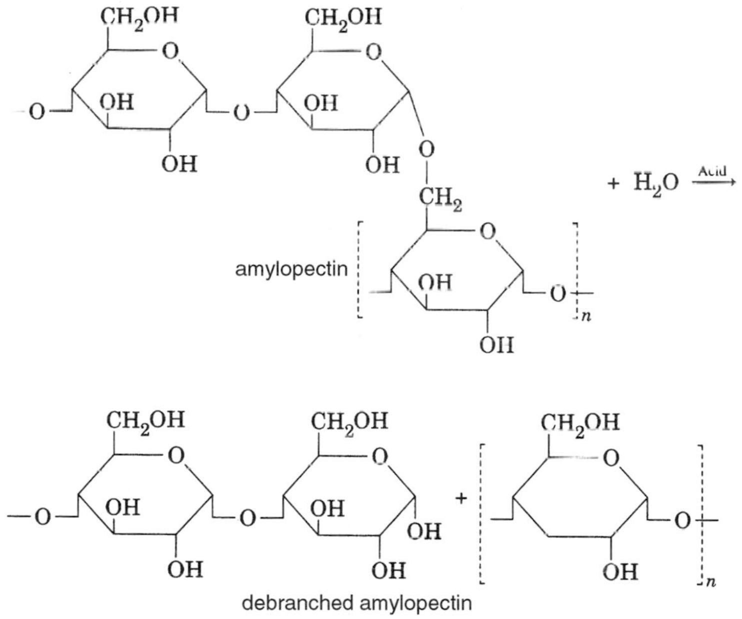

The advantage of thin-boiling starches is exhibited in the production of starch-thickened food items that need to be delivered into packages or molds through pipes. When hot, thin-boiling starches are very fluid and pass easily through the delivery system into containers. Uniquely, these thin liquid starches form strong gels when cooled, apparently because of the greater ease of hydrogen bonding between molecules resulting from the reduced branching of some of the starch.

Oxidized Starches.   A product similar in behavior to acid-hydrolyzed starches results when starch is subjected to reaction with sodium hypochlorite. This is an

Pregelatinized Starch
Starch that has been gelatinized and then dehydrated; addition of water produces a thickened product.

Cold Water-Swelling Starch (CWS)
Newest pregelatinized starch.

Thin-Boiling Starch
Debranched amylopectin, produced by acid hydrolysis of starch, resulting in a starch that forms a thin sol when hot, but a strong gel when cold; useful for making gum drops.

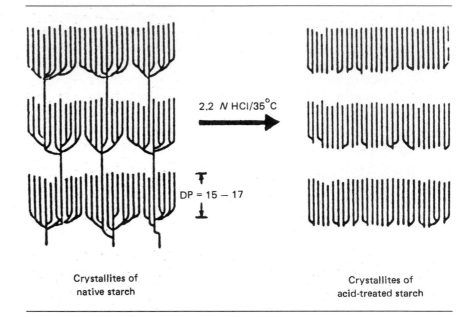

Figure 9.11   Acid hydrolysis of amylopectin molecule in granular starch to form Nageli amylodextrins. (Courtesy of D. R. Lineback and Backers Digest. 1984. Vol. 58(2): 16. Diagram by C. G. Billiardens, D. R. Grant, and J. R. Vose. 1981. *Cereal Chem. 58:* 502.)

Oxidized Starches
Thin-boiling starches produced by alkaline (sodium hypochlorite) treatment, but forming only soft gels.

oxidation reaction and produces **oxidized starches.** These have only limited use in processed foods despite the fact that they also are thin-boiling and are capable of forming gels, albeit softer gels than those from acid treatment of starches.

Cross-linked Starches.   The tendency for starches to undergo retrogradation during storage of starch gels is an undesirable characteristic. However, this tendency can be reduced significantly by altering the hydroxyl groups on the glucose segments, particularly the hydroxyl group on the second carbon (Wurzburg, 1986). Hydroxyalkyl starches are made by reacting starch with ethylene (shown below) which can lead to hydroxyethyl addition at carbons 2, 3, and 6 if the reaction is allowed to proceed for an extended period. The replacement occurs first at carbon 2. Hydroxyethyl starches are used to a limited extent in the food industry as a thickening agent.

Cross-linked Starch
Starch produced under alkaline conditions, usually in combination with acetic or succinic anhydride; notable as a thickener and stabilizing agent that undergoes minimal retrogradation.

Cross-linked starches are effective thickening agents and form gels that undergo very limited retrogradation during storage. Formation of a cross-linked starch requires substitution of the hydroxyl groups on two different molecules within the same granule. Stability during storage is improved considerably by the use of cross-linked starches; temperature, shaking or other agitation, and addition of acids have little effect on the characteristics of stored starch products made using cross-linked starches. Cross-linked starches are formed under alkaline conditions, often by use of either acetic anhydride (to form acetylated products) or succinic anhydride. Both acetate and succinate cross-linked starches are very useful as thickeners and stabilizers in salad dressings and related products.

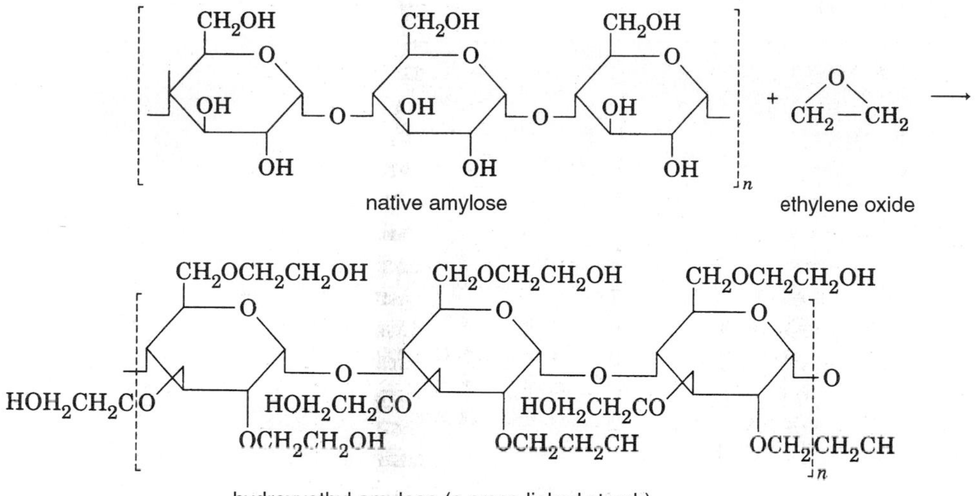

$$\text{[native amylose structure]} + \text{ethylene oxide} \longrightarrow$$

native amylose

ethylene oxide

hydroxyethyl amylose (a cross-linked starch)

Starch Phosphates.   Yet another means of modifying starch chemically is esterification with phosphates, commonly sodium tripolyphosphate. **Starch phosphates** are valuable commercially because they increase the stability and improve the texture of starch pastes thickened with them. This action is accomplished because of the repulsion between molecules containing the electrically charged phosphates. The excellent clarity of starch products thickened with starch phosphates is one of the compelling reasons for their use in commercial food products. Another advantage of stabilized starches such as starch phosphates is their ability to reduce syneresis or weeping. When a starch has been crosslinked and stabilized, its performance is outstanding, being capable of forming smooth, nonstringy pastes and gels with little or no **syneresis.** Waxy starches benefit particularly from both crosslinking and stabilization processing during manufacturing.

Starch Phosphates
Starch derivative made by reaction with sodium tripolyphosphate or other phosphates to achieve a thickener with excellent stability and clarity.

Spherical Aggregates of Starch Granules.   Industrially, small starch granules and a little protein can be spray dried to form edible, spherical aggregates of a somewhat porous nature. This porosity is useful because flavorings can be entrapped in these granular spheres, which then serve as flavor carriers in selected food products. Figure 9.12 illustrates spherical aggregates of amaranth (an herb) starch and of cornstarch. These aggregates can absorb a flavor or essence equal to as much as 60 percent of their weight. Without any protective coating, flavorings will be retained for several months. With a commercial tablet coating, flavors will be trapped for prolonged periods of storage.

Syneresis
Separation of liquid from a gel, the result of contraction when the solid phase of the gel draws together ever tighter, forcing the liquid out.

Uses

Starch is used in a number of different food products because of its ability to thicken sauces and bind fat. White sauces of varying viscosities (depending on their concentration of starch) form the basis for recipes ranging from cream soups to timbales. Thin white sauces are thickened with enough starch to create a soup that is about the same viscosity as cream. Medium white sauces and gravies have moderate flow properties, but are distinctly thicker than a cream soup. Souffles are made using a thick white sauce with only a small amount of flow, enough to be

(a)

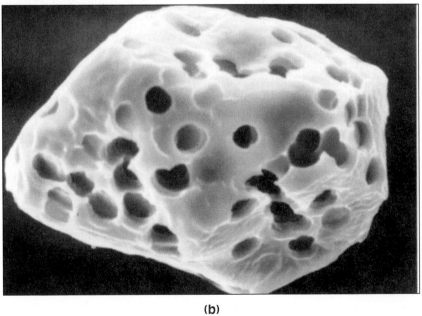

(b)

Figure 9.12   Photomicrographs (X5,000) of spherical aggregates of (a) amaranth starch and (b) microporous cornstarch. (Courtesy of Dr. Roy L. Whistler, Purdue University.)

able to be folded into the egg white foam yet not drain out of the foam before the structure sets during baking. Very thick white sauces are used as binding agents or edible pastes.

There are numerous other starch-thickened sauces. Some are used in the preparation of casseroles or as sauces over vegetables, while others may be served as dessert sauces and even in fruit pie fillings. When these sauces are hot, they will flow, but their viscosity will increase as they cool. In fact, some of them will form gels when they begin to approach room temperature. When formulating starch mixtures, the temperature at which they will be served must be borne in mind so that the correct concentration of starch can be used to achieve the desired flow properties.

Starch-thickened puddings are familiar desserts. Some are made with cornstarch as the thickening agent, while tapioca may be the type of starch selected in others. Cream fillings in such favorite pies as banana cream, coconut cream, lemon, and chocolate are thickened with sufficient starch to form a gel after the filling has cooled.

Cereals of all types contain a considerable amount of starch, which means that part of the changes that occur during boiling of rice or other cereals will be gelatinization of starch. Preparation of oatmeal for breakfast, boiling of pasta, or the making of rice pilaf all require gelatinization of starch.

Criteria for Selecting a Starch

Obviously, many different starches can be considered for inclusion in commercial food formulations. No single starch is ideally suited to the entire array of products in which starches are used. Instead, the starch or starches to be used need to be well suited to the specific requirements of the item being formulated.

If a product is being made for persons seeking a low-calorie option, any starch that might be used would need to have excellent thickening and/or gelling capabilities for the amount of starch used. This enables the product to be thickened adequately with fewer calories than if a greater amount of another starch had to be used.

Mouthfeel may need to be considered. A gummy or stringy feeling in the mouth may be quiet evident in a sauce with very soft ingredients, but would perhaps not be noted if water chestnuts or other distinctive textural components were included in the sauce.

Freeze–thaw stability is the ability of a starch-thickened product to be frozen and thawed without undesirable loss of quality. Syneresis can be a problem when some products have been frozen and thawed. If the item is a stew or other dish that will be reheated and stirred, syneresis presents no problem, even when there has been a considerable amount of drainage. The liquid will all reunite in the sauce during the heating and stirring period. However, if a starch-thickened cream pie filling has been frozen and then exhibits considerable syneresis after thawing, the crust will be soggy, and the quality of the pie will be very poor. In this situation, there is no opportunity to recombine the liquid.

Waxy rice flour is a particularly useful starch for products that are to be frozen and thawed, because this type of starch shows little tendency to form crystalline areas. Apparently the protein in waxy rice flour is partially responsible for its excellent freeze–thaw stability. Purified rice starch is better than many of the other starches for freeze–thaw stability, but is not as good as the waxy rice flour. On the

Freeze–Thaw Stability
Ability of a starch-thickened product to be frozen and thawed without developing a gritty, crystalline texture.

other hand, cornstarch and wheat starch have poor freeze–thaw stability. Unless starch-thickened products are to be frozen and thawed before use, this characteristic of starches is not important in selection of the type of starch. Frozen starch-containing products that are heated and stirred before being served can be made without regard for the freeze–thaw stability of the starch because the crystalline nature of the product is eliminated by the heating.

Retrogradation is a concern in starch-thickened items, such as a pudding that is to be in refrigerator storage. Starches that retrograde easily will quickly develop a rather gritty texture that is very noticeable.

Crosslinked starches are resistant to the formation of crystalline areas in amylose-containing gels. For crosslinked starches to undergo freezing and thawing and still retain a stable gel structure, some of the hydroxyl groups on the amylose molecules must be either acetylated or propionylated. These slightly larger functional groups inhibit the closely ordered alignment of amylose molecules that causes the crystalline areas to form during and after freezing.

Viscosity of starch pastes and the firmness of gels are properties that need to be considered, particularly if special equipment demands need to be met during the production of the item. An example is the need in some operations for a starch sol with little viscosity so that it will flow readily through the pipes involved in the production setup. Marketing stresses may influence the strength of a starch gel that is needed in a pudding or pie filling. Product appeal also is influenced by the flow characteristics of starch-thickened sauces and other sols; rigidity of gels needs to be suited to consumer expectations, too.

These are some factors that need to be considered when a starch is being selected. Specific products may have refinements of these qualities that need to be examined very carefully. In fact there may be many instances when there is a need to consider not only what kind of starch to use, but perhaps whether some other form of thickening is the answer (see Chapter 10 for information on gums, which

Table 9.4   Advantages and Limitations of Selected Starches

Starch	Advantage	Limitation	Use
Potato	Excellent thickening; translucent	Thins with long heating; stringy	Pudding
Corn	Translucent; satisfactory gel	Moderate thickening	Puddings, pie fillings, gravy, sauces
Waxy corn	Will not gel	Stringy	Fruit pie filling
High-amylose	Extrudes in thin films	Will not form traditional gel	Edible films
Pregelatinized	Swells without heat	Reduced thickening	Instant foods
Cold water-swelling	Improved texture, good stability	Reduced thickening	Microwavable sauces and entrees
Thin-boiling	Very fluid sol; strong gel	Gummy texture	Gum drops
Oxidized	Thin-boiling	Soft gel	
Crosslinked	Little retrogradation		Stored starch products
Phosphates	Little syneresis; nonstringy; clear		With waxy starches

increasingly are replacing starches in some food applications). Table 9.4 provides information regarding some of the advantages and limitations of selected starches.

RICE AND ITS STARCH

Rice has been the cereal of choice in many Asian cultures for countless generations, and now its popularity is gaining immensely as an alternative to potatoes as the starch source of choice in American menus, too. The known varieties of rice exceed 40,000 in number! Many of these are not of commercial importance, but about 20 are grown in this country.

Categorization of rice types is based on the length of the grain: long-grain rice measures between 6 and 7 millimeters long, medium-grain is 5 to 5.9 mm, and short-grain is less than 5 mm long. Interestingly, the long-grain rice is higher in amylose than the other two lengths of grains. Since amylose absorbs less water than amylopectin, long grain rice stays more fluffy and distinct than short- or medium-grain rice. These latter two absorb water more readily because of their higher amylopectin, and this water causes them to be more moist and sticky than the long-grain rice.

Specialty rices are gaining a place in American cuisine, having been imported from various countries around the world. Waxy rices (virtually 100 percent amylopectin) are of two types in the United States. Mochigome is a very sticky, pasty rice when cooked. These characteristics are useful in making certain Oriental noodles and confections. Calmochi is the other waxy rice, and its characteristics are very similar to those of mochigome. Either of these waxy rices (also called sweet glutinous rice) is suited for batter coatings used in frying and in making crisp pizza crusts. Arborio is another specialty rice, this one being a particularly absorptive medium-grain rice well suited for preparing risotto and paella. Basmati has a remarkably long grain and a fragrance which carries into the flavor qualities of this rice from India. Jasmine also is an aromatic long-grain specialty rice. Its uniqueness is that it stays soft in the refrigerator rather than undergoing the retrogradation typical of other long-grain rices when they are stored.

SUMMARY

Starch is composed of a linear fraction, amylose, and a highly branched fraction of large molecular weight, amylopectin. These fractions are deposited in granules in the leucoplasts of some cereal grains and roots and some other food sources; about 75 to 80 percent of the granule is amylopectin, and the remainder is amylose (Table 9.5).

Gelatinization is the imbibition of water into the starch granules when the starch is heated in water, and is accompanied by some leaching of amylose molecules into the surrounding water. Different types of starch exhibit slightly different characteristics in their gelatinization, gelation, and retrogradation into crystalline areas during storage. Sugar delays gelatinization and competes with the starch for water, resulting in decreased viscosity, more tender gels, and increased translucence. Acid causes some hydrolysis of starch when it is present during gelatinization, producing some loss in viscosity, especially below pH 4.

Gelation (formation of a gel) occurs when many starch pastes cool. The specific characteristics of starch gels are influenced by the type and concentration of

Table 9.5   Characteristics and Qualities of Selected Starches

Characteristic or Quality	Root and Tuber			Cereal			
	Tapioca	Potato	Arrowroot	Rice	Wheat	Corn	Waxy Corn
% amylose (approx.)	17	20–23			25–26	24–28	0
Granule size (μ)	12–25	100		3–8	10–35	12–25	
Temperature for maximum paste viscosity (°C)	71	90	80	94	92	91	89
Amount for comparable: paste viscosity	3.54	1.96	4.37	5.49	6.44	4.90	2.98
gel strength	0	0	87	31	345	52	0
Translucency	high	high	high	good	good	good	high
Texture	stringy	stringy	stringy	good	good	good	stringy

the starch, the extent of heating, agitation, and the presence of acid and/or sugar. During storage, gels may exhibit syneresis, and some develop a gritty texture when crystalline areas form (retrogradation) as the amylose amylopectin molecules organize themselves more tightly. Retrogradation may be a particular problem when starch gels are frozen and thawed.

Dextrinization is a chemical breakdown (hydrolysis) of starch molecules resulting from intensive dry heat. The shorter molecules have reduced thickening ability.

Unmodified starches used in foods include cornstarch, wheat, rice, potato, tapioca, and waxy cornstarch. Modified starches perform special functions: pregelatinized starches reconstitute quickly to thicken foods without additional cooking; thin-boiling starches (treated with acid to reduce branching of amylopectin) are poured easily and allowed to set to form a strong gel; crosslinked starches form thickened starch gels and sauces that have a pleasing, nongritty texture; and starch phosphates are effective thickening agents that form nonstringy pastes and gels with little, if any, syneresis. The properties of the many varieties of rice are a reflection of the starch composition in them. Long-grain rice has comparatively high amylose content and, therefore, absorbs less water and is less sticky than the medium- and short-grain rices. Waxy (sweet glutinous) rice is extremely sticky because its starch is almost entirely amylopectin.

STUDY QUESTIONS

1. Select five recipes in which starch is used as a thickening agent. Identify the type of starch available to consumers that is best suited to each recipe and explain the reason for the choice. Similarly, select the type of starch available to the food industry that is best suited to a comparable food product and state the rationale for the selection.

2. Sketch a potato starch granule in its native state and then sketch it as it undergoes gelatinization. Write a description of the gelatinization process.

3. What difference can be predicted to exist between a starch-thickened pudding made with lemon juice and a comparable one prepared without lemon juice? Write the chemical reaction involved in the first product.

4. What is the difference between wheat starch and wheat flour? How does this difference influence the use of the two products in cookery?

5. Describe in detail the processes of gelatinization, gelation, and retrogradation.

BIBLIOGRAPHY

Appl, R. C. 1991. "Confectionery ingredients from starch." *Food Technol. 45* (3): 148.

Bean, M. L. and Osman, E. M. 1959. "Behavior of starch during food preparation. II. Effects of different sugars on the viscosity and gel strength of starch pastes." *Food Res. 24:* 665.

Bean, M. M., Esser, C. A., and Nishita, K. D. 1984. "Some physiochemical and food application characteristics of California waxy rice varieties." *Cereal Chem. 61:* 475.

Campbell, A. M. and Briant, A. M. 1957. "Wheat starch pastes and gels containing citric acid and sucrose." *Food Res. 22:* 358.

Dziezak, J. D. 1991. "Romancing the kernel: Salute to rice varieties." *Food Technol. 45* (6): 74.

Evers, A. D. and Stevens D. J. 1985. "Starch damage." In *Advances in Cereal Science and Technology.* Vol. VII. Pomeranz, Y., ed., p. 321. Amer. Assoc. Cereal Chemists: St. Paul, MN.

Filer, L. J., Jr. 1988. "Modified food starch—an update." *J. Amer. Dietet. Assoc. 88:* 342.

Fitt, L. E. and Snyder, E. M. 1984. "Photomicrographs of starches." In *Starch, Chemistry and Technology.* 2nd ed. Whistler, R. L., BeMiller, J. N., and Paschall, E. F., eds., p. 675. Academic Press: Orlando FL.

Freeman T. P. and Shelton, D. R. 1991. "Microstructure of wheat starch: from kernel to bread." *Food Technol. 45* (3): 162.

French, D. 1984. "Organization of starch granules." In *Starch, Chemistry and Technology.* 2nd ed. Whistler, R. L., BeMiller, J. N. and Paschall, E. F., eds., p. 183. Academic Press: Orlando, FL.

Heckman, E. 1977. "Starch and its modifications for the food industry." In *Food Colloids* Graham, H. D., ed. AVI Publishing: Westport, CT.

Holmes, Z. A. and Soeldner, A. 1981. "Effect of heating rate and freezing and reheating of corn and wheat starch–water dispersions." *J. Amer. Dietet. Assoc. 78:* 352.

Hoseney, R. C., Lineback, D. R., and Seib, P. A. 1983. "Role of starch in baked foods." *Bakers Digest 57* (4): 65.

Juliano, B. O. 1984. "Rice starch: production, properties, and uses." In *Starch, Chemistry and Technology.* 2nd ed. Whistler, R. L., BeMiller, J. N., and Paschall, E. F., eds., p. 507. Academic Press: Orlando, FL.

Katzbeck, W. 1972. "Phosphate cross-bonded waxy corn starches solve many food application problems." *Food Technol. 26* (3): 32.

Kulp, K., Lorenz, Kl, and Stone, M. 1991. "Functionality of carbohydrate ingredients in bakery products." *Food Technol. 45* (3): 136.

Luallen, T. E. 1985. "Starch as a functional ingredient." *Food Technol. 39*(1): 59.

Luallen, T. E. 1988. "Structure, characteristics, and uses of some typical carbohydrate food ingredients." *Cereal Foods World 33:* 924.

Pszczola, D. E. 1999. "Starches and gums move beyond fat replacement." *Food Technol. 53* (8): 74.

Reineccius, G. A. 1991. "Carbohydrates for flavor encapsulation." *Food Technol. 45* (3): 144.

Rogols, S. 1986. "Starch modifications: view into the future." *Cereal Foods World 31:* 869.

Rohwer, R. G. and Klem, R. E. 1984. "Acid-modified starch: production and uses." In *Starch, Chemistry and Technology*. 2nd ed. Whistler, R. L., BeMiller, J. N., and Paschall, E. F., eds., p. 529. Academic Press. Orlando, FL.

Spies, R. D. and Hoseney, R. C. 1982. "Effect of sugars on starch gelatinization." *Cereal Chem. 59* (2): 447.

Whistler, R. L. and Daniel, J. R. 1985. "Carbohydrates." In *Food Chemistry*. 2nd ed. Fennema, O. R., ed. Marcel Dekker: New York, p. 69.

Whistler, R. L. and Daniel, J. R. 1984. "Molecular structure of starch." In *Starch: Chemistry and Technology*. 2nd ed. Whistler, R. L., BeMiller, J. N. and Paschall, F. E., eds. Academic Press: Orlando, FL, p. 217.

Wurzburg, O. B. 1986. *Modified Starches: Properties and Uses*. CRC Press. Boca Raton, FL.

Zapsalis, C. and Beck, R. A. 1985. *Food Chemistry and Nutritional Biochemistry*. Wiley: New York.

Zhao, J. and Whistler, R. L. 1994. "Spherical aggregates of starch granules as flavor carriers." *Food Technol. 48* (7): 104.

Zobel, B. F. 1984. "Gelatinization of starch and mechanical properties of starch pastes." In *Starch, Chemistry and Technology*. 2nd ed. Whistler, R. L., BeMiller, J. N., and Paschall, E. F., eds., p. 285. Academic Press: Orlando, FL.

CHAPTER 10

Fiber and Plant Foods

Plants provide considerable variety in the food supply, both in terms of gustatory aspects and nutrition. Fruits and vegetables are found in ever-greater abundance as nutritional research adds increasing evidence of the importance of a variety of both fruits and vegetables in the diet on a daily basis to optimize health. Fresh produce is available in most markets throughout the nation at any time of year. However, there still is a large market for both fruits and vegetables in cans, as frozen items, and even dried. Legumes, while technically vegetables, deserve special recognition because of their uniqueness among vegetables. Cereals are grains and certainly differ from other types of plant foods, but serve as a mainstay of the diet. When thinking of plant food sources, attention needs to be directed to the sea, as well as to the land; seaweed has played a prominent role in Japanese dishes for centuries. Now, gums obtained from seaweed are gaining in importance. Many of the fats and oils used today are derived from various plant sources. This chapter examines these diverse plants and the foods obtained from them. Emphasis is placed on the polysaccharides found in the various plant foods and on the structure and characteristics of the edible parts of plants.

FRUITS AND VEGETABLES

Structure

Fruits and vegetables used as food are composed of tissue systems and various types of cells that altogether comprise the produce in the marketplace. The overall framework or design of fruits and vegetables differs from one specific type to another, yet the tissue systems have certain basic similarities. There obviously are differences between the type of cell found in a pear and that in a mango. Even in the same type of fruit, noticeable differences exist between the underripe and ripe or overripe stages of maturity.

Tissue Systems.   The tissues in fruits and vegetables are designated in three different systems: dermal, vascular, and ground systems. The dermal tissue (skin or rind) is the protective covering of each portion of the plant. Within this dermal tissue is the vascular system, the system responsible for transport of fluids, nutrients, and waste products. The remaining inner portion is the ground system. Details of these systems vary with the specific plant.

The **dermal system** undergoes changes during development and maturation of the plant, yet the protective function remains constant. The layer of **epidermal** cells forms a thin, protective surface coating. Evaporation of moisture from the surface is minimized as a result of a layer of cutin and sometimes various waxes. Potatoes and other tubers develop a somewhat corklike protective coating, the **periderm.** Even more protection is developed in peas, which have strongly supported epidermal cells (supported by hemicellulose) and then a **hypodermal** layer with considerable intercellular spaces.

The **vascular system** is composed of two parts: the **xylem** and the **phloem** (Figure 10–1). The xylem usually is composed of elongated, tubular cells and is the portion of the vascular system that moves water. The phloem tissue is responsible for transporting organic matter in solution.

The remainder of the fruit or vegetable, which constitutes much of the edible portion, is the ground system. The bulk of the **ground system** consists of the parenchyma cells. Supporting tissues may contain collenchyma and sclerenchyma cells.

Parenchyma Cells.   The principal type of cell in fruit and vegetable cookery is the **parenchyma cell,** which is the very abundant type of cell in the ground system. These cells are polyhedral, ranging from 11 to as many as 20 faces. The exact

Dermal System
Outer protective covering on fruits and vegetables, as well as other parts of plants.

Epiderm
Layer of cells providing a continuous outer covering for fruits and vegetables.

Periderm
Layer of corklike cells protecting vegetable tissues underground.

Hypoderm
Layer of cells beneath the epidermal cells.

Vascular System
System in plants that transports water and other essential compounds; composed of the xylem and phloem.

Xylem
The water transport system in plants; the tubular cells that move water.

Phloem
Portion of the vascular system that transports aqueous solutions of substances such as nutrients.

Ground System
Bulk of edible portion of plant foods.

Parenchyma Cells
Predominant type of cell in the fleshy part of fruits and vegetables.

Figure 10.1   Cross section of beet. Note the vascular system (phloem and xylem) in enlarged granules appearing in an orderly arrangement in concentric rings. (Courtesy of Plycon Press.)

number of faces is specific to each species and so is the tightness of the fit between these cells. Intercellular space depends on the fit of the cells. The parenchyma cells of potatoes fit together in a manner resembling the tight fit seen in ancient Incan walls, with the result that only about 1 percent of the volume of potatoes is due to intercellular air spaces. In contrast, apples do not have tightly fitting parenchyma cells. Consequently, apples have a much more open, slightly loose texture; about 25 percent of the volume of apples is intercellular air space, which is why they float.

A look at parenchyma cells begins with the **middle lamella,** the material between adjacent parenchyma cells that serves to hold the cells in a fixed position. The middle lamella is composed primarily of pectic substances, discussed in the following section. The primary cell wall is composed of several complex carbohydrates, including cellulose, hemicelluloses, pectic substances, and noncellulosic polysaccharides. Between the cell wall and the interior of the cell wall is a thin membrane, the **plasmalemma** (see Figure 10–2).

The protoplasm is found immediately within the plasmalemma of the cell. Within this are subcellular structures or organelles of several types: plastids, mitochondria, and the nucleus. The **mitochondria** are of great significance in fresh fruits and vegetables because of their involvement in respiration. Enzymes are associated with them and are responsible for catalyzing numerous biochemical reactions. **Plastids** are of special interest, for it is in these structures that two types of pigments and starch are formed and stored. There are three types of plastids:

Middle Lamella
Region between adjacent cells that cements the cells together; composed mostly of pectic substances.

Plasmalemma
Thin membrane between the cell wall and the interior of the cell.

Mitochondria
Organelles in cells involved in respiration and other biochemical processes.

Plastids
Organelles in the cytoplasm that contain pigments or starch.

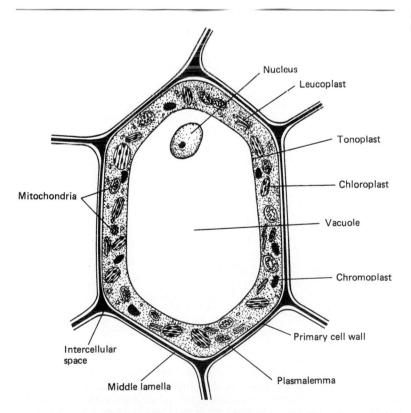

Figure 10.2   Diagram of a parenchyma cell.

Nucleus
Leucoplast
Tonoplast
Chloroplast
Vacuole
Chromoplast
Primary cell wall
Mitochondria
Intercellular space
Middle lamella
Plasmalemma

Chloroplast
Type of plastid containing chlorophyll.

Chromoplast
Type of plastid containing carotenoids.

Leucoplast
Type of plastid in which starch is formed and deposited in granules.

Tonoplast
Membrane separating the protoplasm from the vacuole in a parenchyma cell.

Vacuole
Portion of the cell containing most of the water, the flavoring components, nutrients, and flavonoid pigments.

Collenchyma Tissue
Aggregates of elongated, collenchyma cells providing supportive structure to various plant foods, notably vegetables.

chloroplasts, chromoplasts, and **leucoplasts.** Chloroplasts are the plastids in which chlorophyll is found. Chromoplasts contain the carotenoid pigments. It is in the leucoplasts that starch is made and stored in the form of granules. The relative proportion of the cell occupied by the protoplasm is reduced gradually as the plant matures, but the important functions that take place in the protoplasm continue throughout the lifetime of the cell (see Figures 10–3 to 10–5).

Separating the protoplasm from the remaining interior of the cell is a thin membrane called the **tonoplast.** The **vacuole** inside the tonoplast increases in size during the maturation process and accounts for a large fraction of the cell interior at maturity. A variety of substances is included in the vacuole. This is the portion of the cell where the numerous flavor components, including sugars, acids, and many other organic compounds contributing to the flavor are found. In addition, the flavonoid pigments (notably the anthoxanthins and anthocyanins) are located in the vacuole. The vacuole also is the region where about 90 percent of the cellular water is held and where some of the nutrients, including protein, are found.

Collenchyma Tissue.   Elongated cells such as are found in the fibrous strands of celery are examples of **collenchyma tissue.** These cell walls are chewy and resistant to much softening when cooked. This type of tissue is termed supporting tissue because it contributes to the overall structure of the edible part of fruits and vegetables containing collenchyma cells (see Figure 10–6).

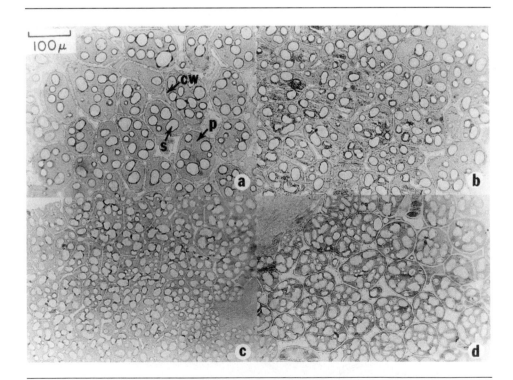

Figure 10.3   Photomicrographs of thin sections from legume seeds (a) Great Northern bean, (b) navy bean, (c) mung bean, (d) field pea. CW = cell wall; S = starch granule, P = protein matrix. (Reprinted from *Journal of Food Science.* 1984. Vol. 49: 925. Copyright (c) by Institute of Food Technologists. Courtesy of R. D. Tyler. National Research Council of Canada.

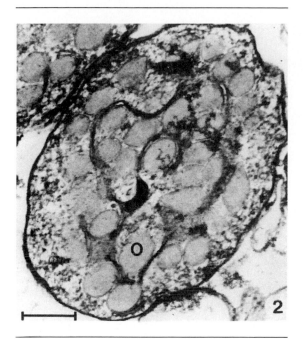

Figure 10.4 Chromoplast of juice from mature Valencia orange. O = oil droplet. Magnification bar = 0.3 μm. (Reprinted from *Journal of Food Science*. 1984. Vol. 49: 1489. Copyright (c) by Institute of Food Technologists. Courtesy of U. Merin. Agricultural Research Laboratory: Bet-Dagan, Israel.)

Sclerenchyma Cells. **Sclerenchyma cells** are woodlike cells that contribute a somewhat gritty texture to some plant foods. The unique texture of pears, for example, is the result of the presence of sclereids, a type of sclerenchyma cell. Both **sclereids** and the other type of sclerenchyma cell, simply called *fibers,* have thick cell walls containing lignin, a woodlike compound. The fibers in asparagus and green beans are examples of the "fiber" type of sclerenchyma cell (see Figure 10–7).

Sclerenchyma Cells
Unique supportive cells with a chewy, fibrous character.
Sclereid
Type of sclerenchyma cell that gives the somewhat gritty texture to pears and certain other fruits.

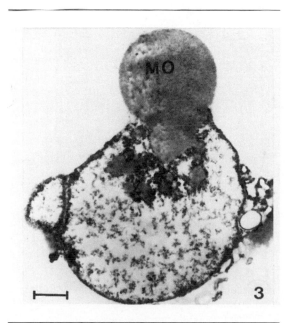

Figure 10.5 Chromoplast with large oil droplet In migration stage throughout chromoplast envelope (MO). Magnification bar = 0.6 μm. (Reprinted from *Journal of Food Science*. 1984. Vol. 49: 1489. Copyright (c) by Institute of Food Technologists. Courtesy of U. Merin. Agricultural Research Organization, Dairy Research Laboratory: Bet-Dagan, Israel.)

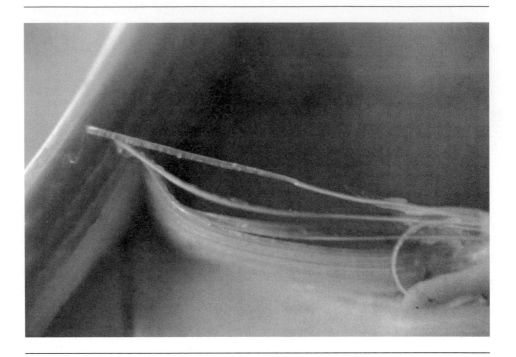

Figure 10.6   Collenchyma tissue in the fibers of celery is comprised of elongated collenchyma cells. (Courtesy of Plycon Press.)

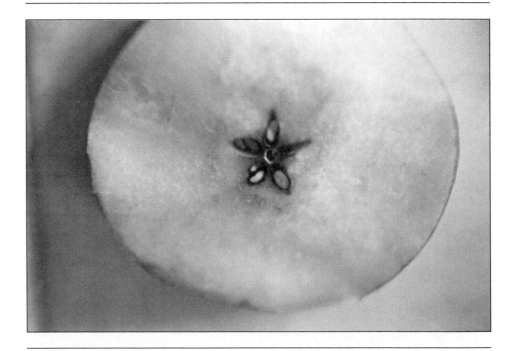

Figure 10.7   Sclereids (unique sclerenchyma cells) contribute the somewhat granular texture noted in pears (Courtesy of Plycon Press.)

Table 10–1   Dietary Fiber—Soluble and Insoluble

Soluble Fiber	Insoluble Fiber
Gums (guar, locust bean, gum arabic, gum tragacanth, gum ghatti, gum karaya, alginates, agar, carrageenan, xanthan, gellan, cellulose gums)	Cellulose Hemicellulose Lignin
Pectic substances	

FIBER

Categories of Fiber

Fiber is the combination of materials in foods that cannot be digested readily. Plant foods are valued in the diet as potentially outstanding sources of fiber. Although the word sounds simple, several different compounds comprise dietary fiber. Nutritionists often categorize fiber as soluble and insoluble fibers. The division of fiber components according to solubility is shown in Table 10–1. Obviously, both soluble and insoluble fibers are found in the same food. However, the relative proportions vary from one plant food to another. Soluble fibers appear to be digested to a limited extent to provide calories to the body, while insoluble fibers are excreted undigested, thus providing stool bulk, but not energy. Soluble fibers may be of some benefit in reducing serum cholesterol levels. Insoluble fibers are possibly beneficial because they speed the transit time, promoting excretion of waste from the body. Citrus fruits, oats, and legumes are some of the foods that are especially good sources of soluble fibers, while wheat, rice, and many of the vegetables are valued for their content of insoluble fibers.

Bran in Food Products

As emphasis on fiber in the diet has increased, the food industry has rallied its efforts to produce numerous products with increased fiber content. A particularly interesting development is a fat replacer made with oat bran, flavorings, and seasonings suitable for incorporation with ground meat. This bran product can be blended with low-fat ground meats to produce a cooked patty containing only 10 percent fat. Because of the water retention effected by the fiber in the bran, the finished patty is juicy, flavorful, and has an acceptable mouthfeel.

Breads and other baked products can be made with bran added up to a level of about 15 percent of the weight of flour. One effect of added bran is a decrease in volume. The rather sharp character of the bran particles cuts some of the gluten strands during mixing, which interferes with maximum stretching of the strands during baking. Bran aids in retaining moisture in bread during storage.

GUMS

Gums, as the word is used in food technology, are complex hydrophilic carbohydrates found in plants. Their hydrophilic nature explains why **gums** are called hydrocolloids. Despite the fact that they are composed of a very large number of monosaccharide units linked together by glycosidic linkages, they undergo little digestion in

Gums
Hydrocolloids composed of large polymers of monosaccharides other than glucose.

Soluble Fiber
Plant gums and pectic substances that undergo some digestion and absorption in the large intestine.

the small intestine. For this reason, they are classified as **soluble fiber.** Their monosaccharide components are more varied than is true for the energy-contributing disaccharides and the glucose polymers (dextrins and starch). Two characteristics of gums are particularly noteworthy: (1) a remarkable ability to attract and bind water, and (2) very limited caloric contribution due to very limited digestion and absorption in the body, notably in the large intestine.

Attention is being focused on gums as possible additives in foods today because of the potential nutritional and health benefits that may accrue when gums are incorporated in food products. The water-holding capacity of gums increases stool bulk until digestion of gums in the large intestine occurs. Even then, the insoluble fibers (cellulose, hemicelluloses, and lignin) still speed transit time of food waste through the remainder of the gastrointestinal tract to excretion. The fact that gums are digested and absorbed quite inefficiently compared with sugars and starch makes them very useful in food products aimed at weight-conscious consumers. Agar, guar gum, gum arabic, and pectin appear to provide somewhere between 1 and 3 calories per gram (Staub and Ali, 1982); carrageenan and xanthan gum probably provide, at the most, 1 calorie per gram. Evidence regarding the anti-carcinogenic nature of gums is not yet definitive, but there is the possibility that gums help protect against cancer.

Functions

Gums are valued as thickening agents; their comparatively lower potential calorie value may be an important reason for a food product to be formulated with a gum rather than with starch to achieve the desired viscosity. Flour and sugar also can be used as thickening agents, but these common ingredients add 4 calories per gram, whereas gums can accomplish essentially comparable thickening with a significant reduction in calories. The most dramatic calorie savings are afforded when gums are used to replace fats and oils, because fats contribute 9 calories per gram. For instance, gums can be used in salad dressings to provide appropriate thickening in place of some of the oil ordinarily included in the formula. Ice creams and baked products, especially cakes, may utilize gums to enhance mouthfeel when fat levels are reduced. In cakes, shelf life is extended, staling is delayed, cell structure is enhanced, and volume is increased by the use of appropriate gums. Large aggregates of ice crystals in ice cream are blocked when gums are added, resulting in a fine texture. Gums even are added in some cases to increase the fiber content of a beverage or food to enhance the nutritional merits of the food.

Sources

Carbohydrate gums are derived from seeds, plant exudates, seaweed extracts, and microorganisms. These, as a group, are hydrophilic polysaccharides. The seed gums of primary commercial significance are obtained from guar and locust bean (carob), both of which are classified as legumes. Gum arabic, tragacanth, karaya, and ghatti are the primary gums from plant fluids (actually the oozing liquid from cuts in tropical trees). Of these, gum arabic is used most commonly. The red and brown algae, familiarly known as Irish moss and giant kelp, provide agar, carrageenan, and algin gums.

Recently, some microorganisms have been used to produce gums. The most successful of these fermentation gums is xanthan gum, a gum that results when *Xanthomonas campestris* ferments glucose in the presence of some trace elements. The potential for developing other gums of commercial value through the use of microorganisms may be great, and work is proceeding in this direction.

Chemical Composition

The various gums have unique structures, but they have in common the fact that they are polysaccharides in which glucose usually is absent. Galactose is common to seed, plant exudate, and seaweed gums (with the exception of algin).

Seed Gums. Both guar and locust bean gums contain only two types of monosaccharides: mannose and galactose.

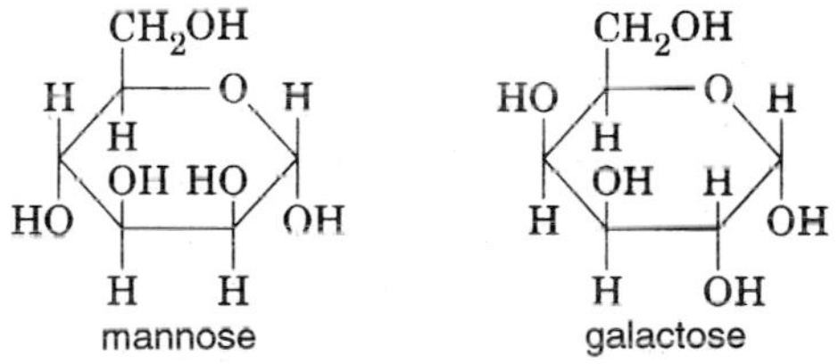

mannose   galactose

Guar and locust bean gums are composed of mannose units linked together by a 1, 4-β linkage, with the galactose being linked by a 1, 6-α linkage at regular intervals. In the structures below, note that guar gum has twice as much galactose as does locust bean gum. Locust bean gum requires heat for maximum hydration, whereas guar gum hydrates in cold water.

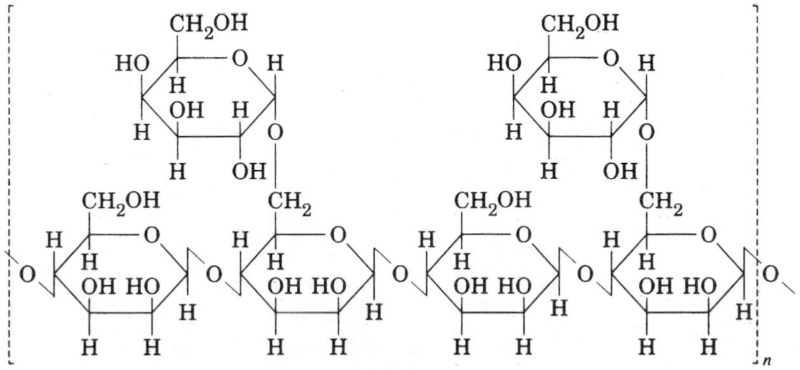

guar gum

locust bean gum

Plant Exudates. The gums from plant exudates (Figure 10–8) are structurally less orderly than the seed gums, and they are likely to have other compounds associated with them, rather than being the pure polysaccharide polymer. Because of this variability, the plant exudates may present problems in food production. Plant exudate gums naturally contain hexuronic acids, most of which are neutralized normally in the gums by the presence of calcium or other ions.

Actual structures of the plant exudate gums cannot be presented because of the great variability of contaminants. However, general observations regarding their primary constituents can be made. The sugars and hexuronic acids found in the plant exudate gums are as follows:

- Gum arabic—galactose, arabinose, rhamnose, galacturonic acid, and the methyl ester of galacturonic acid
- Tragacanth—xylose, arabinose, galactose, fucose, rhamnose, and galacturonic acid
- Karaya—galactose, rhamnose, glucuronic acid, and galacturonic acid

Seaweed Extracts. Seaweed extracts (Figures 10–9 and 10–10) are rich in galactose, often with sulfate esters. Agar comprises two fractions: agarose and agaropectin. Agarose is the linear fraction and is composed of β-D- and α-L-galactose; agaropectin contains sulfate esters and glucuronic acid, as well as the basic components of agarose. Agar is noted for its strong and transparent gels, which are reversible when heated and re-form when chilled once again.

Carrageenan occurs in various fractions, some of which form gels and some of which do not gel. The important quality of carrageenan is its ability to interact with protein to aid in the stabilization of various milk products, notably ice creams, process cheese, and chocolate milks. This gum also works effectively in concert with other gums because of its propensity for crosslinking with them. Carrageenan structurally can be characterized as predominantly sulfate esters of galactose.

Algin is used to form both gels and films. It is a gum with mannose and guluronic acid as its principal components and with numerous salts resulting from the presence of sodium, potassium, and ammonium ions.

Microbial exudates. Fermentation-produced polysaccharides are yet another type of gum. Xanthan gum is such a gum; the microorganism involved is *Xanthomonas campestris*. Glucose and other carbohydrates serve as the substrates for the fermentation. The chemical structure of xanthan gum is based on a chain of glucose units (1, 4-β-glucosidic linkage) with a side chain of two mannose and a glucuronic acid unit attached on every other glucose unit.

Curdlan is another gum produced by microorganism fermentation. *Alicaligenes faecalis* var. *myxogenes* produces curdlan, which is a polysaccharide in which glucose units are joined by 1, 3-β-glucosidic linkages. Curdlan was approved by the FDA in 1996 and is marketed as Pureglucan®. It does not dissolve in water, but it can be suspended in water and heated to 80°C to form a gel that is stable under freezing and retorting. When suspensions of curdlan are heated to 55–60°C and then cooled below 40°C, a gel forms that behaves much like carrageenan.

Figure 10.9   Seaweed forest (kelp) is an abundant source of algin, a food gum. (Courtesy of Kelco Division of Merck and Co., Inc.)

Synthetic gums.   Cellulose serves as the starting material for the production of some synthetic gums. CMC is the best-known of these. Its chemical name is sodium carboxymethylcellulose; sometimes it is designated simply as cellulose gum. The structure is cellulose which has undergone a chemical reaction to add a carboxymethyl group. Another cellulose gum is produced by adding hydroxypropyl groups to cellulose to make hydroxypropyl cellulose. Hydroxypropylmethyl cellulose is another gum developed from cellulose.

Applications

Because of the potential nutritional benefits of adding fiber to various food products, many foods presently are being formulated with gums being added to replace part or all of such traditional functional ingredients as starch or fat. Gum arabic is a soluble fiber that is very well suited to liquid foods, such as soups, because a significant quantity of fiber can be added without causing too much of an increase in

Figure 10.10   Ship harvesting giant kelp. (Courtesy of Kelco Division of Merck and Co., Inc.)

viscosity. Carboxymethylcellulose is another soluble fiber that may be used alone or in tandem with gum arabic to increase fiber content of a food. The high degree of solubility of both gum arabic and CMC makes it possible to use comparatively high levels without developing a gritty texture in liquid foods.

Guar gum and locust bean gum are two seed gums that can be used to replace up to at least half of the starch used for thickening, thus reducing calories in the food. The added advantage is that the fiber has some nutritional benefits. If enhancing fiber content is an objective, a soup that is to be formulated with 4 percent starch can be made by using half as much starch (2 percent) and adding guar gum and CMC at a level of 1 percent each.

Guar gum is useful as a replacement for as much as 10 percent of the flour in some baked products. Andon (1987) reported that replacing 10.35 percent of the flour in biscuits resulted in a satisfactory product with the level of fiber being increased by 9.5 grams per 100 grams. Guar gum replacement for flour in cakes was reported to be satisfactory at 5.5 percent; replacement in bread could be done up to a level of 3.0 percent.

Xanthan gum (a synthetic gum) is used successfully as a thickener in salad dressings. Some type of starch also is included to obtain the desired texture in low-

Table 10–2 Sources, Characteristics, and Applications of Selected Gums

Gum	Source	Characteristics	Applications
		Seed Gums	
Locust bean (carob seed) gum	Seed of evergreen tree (*Ceratonia siliqua*) (Mediterranean)	Insoluble in cold water; viscous at 95°C; nongelling alone; gels with xanthan gum	Stabilize ice cream, bologna, cheese, sauces, processed meats
Guar gum	Endosperm of guar plant (*Cyamopsis tetragonolobus*) (India, Pakistan)	Nongelling; stabilizing; increasing viscosity; water binding; gels with agar and κ-carrageenan	Desserts, baked products, ice cream stabilizer, sauces, soups, salad dressings
		Plant Exudates	
Gum arabic	Sap of *Acacia* tree (Sudan)	Dissolves in hot or cold water; limited viscosity; readily soluble; emulsifying agent	Candies to retard crystallization, flavor fixative, soft drinks; beer (foam stabilizer)
Gum ghatti	Exudate from *Anogeissus latifolia* tree (India)	Nongelling; disperses in hot or cold water; substitute for gum arabic	Butter-containing syrups
Gum karaya	Dried exudate from *Sterculia* tree (India)	Low water solubility; swells greatly in water; boiling reduces viscosity; ropy in alkali; stabilizes foams	French dressing, sherbets and ices, meringues, bologna
Gum tragacanth	Exudate of *Astragalus* (leguminous) bush (Iran, Syria, Turkey)	High viscosity; cold-water soluble; heat stable; water binding; soft gels; emulsifier	Salad dressings, sauces, catsup, relishes, fruit fillings; ice cream, confections
		Seaweed	
Alginates	Brown seaweeds (*Macrocystis pyrifera*, etc.) (U.S., U.K., Japan, Canada)	Irreversible gels with calcium ions in cold water; emulsifier; thickener; binding agent	Salad dressings, lemon pie filling, fruits for baking, meringues, fish coating
Agar	Red seaweeds (*Gelidium cartilagineum*, etc.) (Japan, Mexico, Portugal, Denmark)	Strong gels; insoluble in cold, but very soluble in hot water; gels at 35–40°C; melts at 85°C	Culture medium, stabilizer in puddings, meringues, pie fillings, cheese, icings, sherbets
Carrageenan (Irish moss)	Red seaweeds (*Chondrus crispus*, etc.) (Iberia, North Atlantic, Japan)	Lambda fraction is nongelling; iota and kappa fractions gel (iota with Ca ions, kappa with K ions); heat-reversible gels; protein-binding	Pet food (meats with gravy), low-sugar jams and jellies, low-fat or nonfat salad dressings, chocolate milk, puddings, cheese analogs, bakery fillings and icings
		Microorganism Gums	
Xanthan gum	Culturing of *Xanthomonas campestris* (bacterium associated with rutabagas)	Very soluble in hot or cold water; high viscosity; stable to heat, pH, and enzymes; viscosity unaffected by temperature; thickening; stabilizing; suspending; good freeze–thaw stability	Frozen doughs, meringues, ice cream, tomato sauce, fruit gels

Gum	Source	Characteristics	Applications
Curdlan	Culturing of *Alicaligenes faecalis* var. myxogenes	Water insoluble; stable to freezing, retorting if heated to 80°C; behaves like carrageenan if heated to 60°C and cooled to 40°C	Sausage, ham, and other meat products, Oriental noodles, sponge cake, cheese products, yogurt, low-fat sour cream
Gellan gum	Culturing of *Pseudomonas elodea*	Strong gels; heat to dissolve; gels with cations upon cooling (sets at 20–50°C, melts at 65–120°C; stable to acid and heat	Icings, nonstandardized jams and jellies
Synthetic Gums			
Cellulose gum (sodium carboxy-methyl-cellulose or CMC)	Alkaline conversion of cellulose into ethers	Water soluble; binds water; thins with heat, thickens when cooled; gels	Bulking agent in low-calorie foods, pie fillings, soya protein products
Microcrys-talline cellu-lose (MCC)	Acid hydrolysis of cellulose	Thixotropic gels; stable to acids; stable over temper-ature range; increases film strength; stabilizer	Icings, partial starch re-placement, chocolate drinks, oil replacement in emulsions
Methylcellu-lose (MC)	Chemically derived from cellulose	Soluble at cool tempera-tures; gels at high temp-eratures	Batters for coating fried foods, cream soups, sauces
Hydroxy-propyl-methylcellu-lose (HPMC)	Chemically derived from cellulose	Soluble at cool tempera-tures; gels at high tempe-ratures	Batters for coating fried foods, cream soups, sauces

calorie, low-oil, or no-oil dressings. Carrageenan often is the gum of choice in making smooth ice creams with reduced fat levels. Guar gum, CMC, and locust bean gums may be used to give a firmer body to ice creams. Yet another gum—gum ghatti—is an effective emulsifying agent when used in conjunction with lecithin in the production of butter-containing syrups. The characteristics and appli-cations of these and other gums are summarized in Table 10–2.

CARBOHYDRATE STRUCTURAL CONSTITUENTS

Cellulose

Cellulose contributes to the structure of foods, although the pectic substances and hemicelluloses are also key compounds in determining the specific textural charac-teristics of specific fruits and vegetables. Cellulose is a glucose polymer, but unlike amylose, its glucose units are joined by 1, 4-β-glucosidic linkages. This difference in linkage is responsible for textural differences and also for the inability of people to digest cellulose as a practical source of energy. Cellulose molecules can aggre-gate into fibrils with a somewhat crystalline structure. Parallel clustering of these fibrils occurs in some fibrous vegetables.

Cellulose
Key component of cell walls; a glucose polymer joined by 1, 4-β-glucosidic linkages.

cellulose

Hemicelluloses

Although present in distinctly smaller quantities than cellulose, the **hemicelluloses** still are very important structural components of the cell walls of fruits and vegetables. Their chemical nature is quite heterogeneous. Unlike starch and cellulose, both of which are polymers containing glucose exclusively, the hemicelluloses contain a variety of sugars in their long chains. In fact, they even contain both pentoses and hexoses. Xylose, a five-carbon sugar, combines with glucuronic acid in limited amounts to form a common hemicellulose polymer called **xylan.** Another of the pentoses, arabinose, is the primary constituent of the arabans, which are hemicelluloses that also contribute to the structure of plant foods. Xylan and araban are but two of the hemicelluloses. These are particularly common hemicelluloses, yet they are present in much smaller quantities than cellulose.

Hemicelluloses are matted together somewhat with the pectic substances to serve as a connection between the fibrillar cellulose in cell walls. Hemicelluloses are quite susceptible to an alkaline cooking medium and rapidly become flaccid, even mushy, when heated in cooking water to which soda is added. Even though hemicelluloses are present in much smaller amounts than cellulose in fruits and vegetables, this change resulting from an alkaline medium quickly makes vegetables and fruits unacceptable. Furthermore, the destructive effect of soda on thiamine is sufficient to discourage the use of soda in cooking vegetables, especially legumes, which are good sources of thiamine.

Pectic Substances

The pectic substances constitute a unique group of polysaccharides that are polymers of galacturonic acid, an organic acid in which the carbon external to the ring structure of galactose is combined with oxygen and hydrogen to form the organic acid radical rather than the alcohol radical of galactose.

galactose   galacturonic acid

The middle lamella between cells is made up of pectic substances, the exact form of pectic substance gradually changing during the maturation process. Significant textural changes accompany the transitions from one pectic substance to the next in the middle lamella. Pectic substances also are important in the primary cell wall where they combine with the hemicelluloses to reinforce the structural contribution of cellulose.

Definitions.   Although there is no definite line of demarcation between types of pectic substances, specific terms are used to designate the various pectic substances. The general term for any member of this family of polygalacturonic acid compounds is ***pectic substances.*** This term includes protopectin, pectin, pectinic acid, and pectic acid. Molecular weights range as high as 400,000, a figure indicative of the lengthy polymers involved.

Protopectin is the water-insoluble form of pectic substances occurring in immature fruits and, to a lesser extent, in vegetables. This pectic substance contributes significantly to the firm texture of unripe fruits. Essentially, protopectin is a very long polymer consisting of galacturonic acid units joined by 1, 4-α linkages:

protopectin

As fruit ripens, some demethylation and hydrolysis occur, seemingly randomly, along the protopectin molecules. When only a limited amount of degradation has occurred, the pectic substances are termed ***pectins.*** As additional demethylation occurs and hydrolysis continues, **pectinic acids** form.

If a pectin molecule is esterified completely, that is, all organic acid residues are altered to methyl esters, the pectin will contain a little over 16 percent methoxyl groups. Most pectins contain fewer than 16 percent methoxyl groups. In contrast to this situation are the low-methoxyl pectins (actually **low-methoxyl pectinic acids**) which are valued for their ability to form a gel structure with very little sugar, a characteristic of significance in making dietetic jams and jellies. Low-methoxyl pectinic acids contain methyl esters on no more than every fourth unit, and frequently only about one in eight of the galacturonic acid units has been esterified.

Pectic Substances
Group name for the various derivatives of galacturonic acid polymers contained in the primary cell wall and the middle lamella of fruits and vegetables.

Protopectin
The form of pectic substances found in unripe fruit and some vegetables; a methylated, very long polymer of galacturonic acid.

Pectins
Galacturonic acid polymers in which most, if not all, of the acid radicals have been esterified with methanol; valued for gel-forming properties in making jams and jellies.

Pectinic Acids
Galacturonic acid polymers in which between a fourth and a half of the acid radicals have been esterified with methanol; form of pectic substances formed as fruit begins to soften just a little.

Low-Methoxyl Pectinic Acids (Low-Methoxyl Pectins)
Galacturonic acid polymers in which only between an eighth and a fourth of the acid radicals have been esterified with methanol; form of pectic substances found in fruit that is just beginning to ripen.

The physical properties are modified as protopectin evolves into pectin and then pectinic acid. Of particular importance is the transition from a methylated, water-insoluble polymer (protopectin) to a shorter, methylated compound capable of dispersing easily in water (pectin). Because of this change, it is feasible to heat fruit juices, pectin, and sugar and then let them cool to form pectin gels. Not only are the cooking properties of pectins different from those of protopectin, but pectin's effect on the texture of raw fruits also is remarkable. As demethylation and hydrolysis gradually occur and protopectin is transformed into pectin, the fruits gradually soften from a very hard, green texture to a firm but yielding texture desired in ripened fruits.

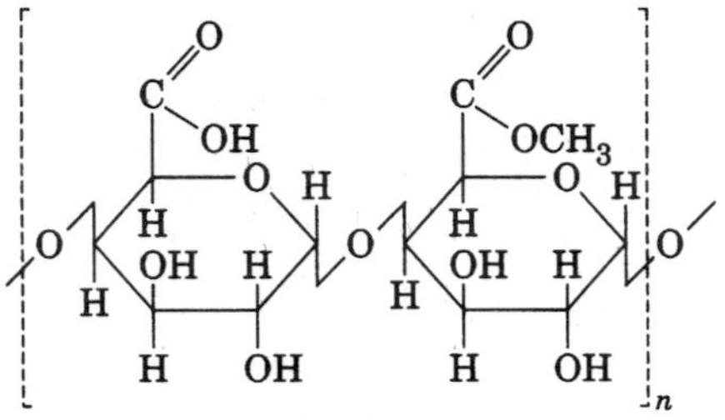

pectinic acid

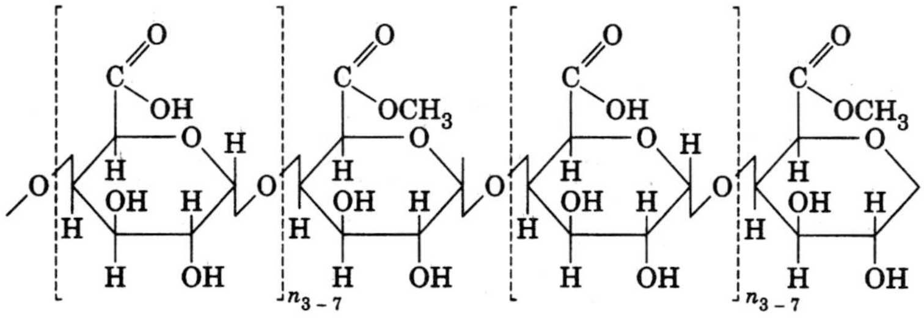

low-methoxyl pectinic acid

Pectinates
Compound resulting from the combination of pectinic acids or pectins with calcium or other ions to form salts and usually enhance gel-forming capability.

Pectic Acid
The smallest of the pectic substances and one lacking methyl esters; occurs in overripe fruits and vegetables.

Pectinic acids form salts with calcium and some other ions. Of particular interest in this regard is the formation of gels utilizing low-methoxyl pectins and calcium ions. The salts formed when ions combine with the organic acid radicals in various pectins and pectinic acids are called **pectinates.** These pectinates are capable of playing an important structural role in forming gels.

As the degradation of **pectinic acids** continues, the molecules gradually become shorter and lose all of their methoxyl groups. These shorter polymers of galacturonic acid are designated as pectic acid. Pectic acid is found in overly ripe, very soft fruits and vegetables. This type of pectic substance has lost the gel-forming ability characteristic of the longer methyl esters of galacturonic acid polymers.

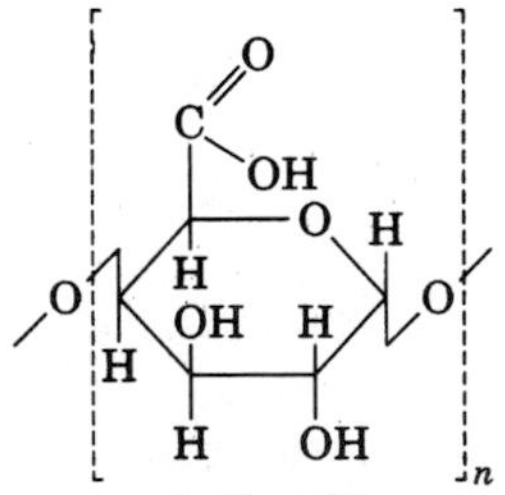

pectic acid

The transition from the very long polymers of protopectin to the somewhat shorter pectins and pectinic acids is a gradual one catalyzed by enzymes and organic acids. **Protopectinases** promote the shortening of the polymeric chains of protopectin to the shorter chains of pectins by the addition of a molecule of water at random locations between galacturonic units. This chain shortening by hydrolysis is essential to the development of the physical properties of pectins.

Yet another change, the demethylation of protopectin, occurs gradually during the ripening of fruits and vegetables. The enzymes responsible for the splitting off of the methyl groups collectively are known as **pectinesterases.** Their action to remove methoxyl groups from the structures of the pectins and pectinic acids causes some loss of the gel-forming properties of the compounds and a distinct softening in the structure of the fresh fruit itself. The pectinesterases are designated by such names as pectin methoxylases, pectases, and pectin demethoxylases.

The reaction for demethylation of the galacturonic acid unit is:

Lignin

Unlike the other constituents of cell walls in plants, **lignin** is a noncarbohydrate polymer of many aromatic structures linked together to form an extremely large, complex molecule that gives a woody quality to plant foods. Although lignin itself does not contain amino groups, one possible genesis of this diverse type of molecular structure is from deamination of two amino acids, tyrosine and phenylalanine. Lignin simply is removed from any portions of fruits and vegetables during their preparation because of its tough and rigid texture.

Changes During Maturation As fruits and vegetables mature, they gradually increase their content of cellulose, hemicelluloses, and even lignin. This increased structural support for cell walls causes fruits and vegetables, particularly the latter, to become less tender as they mature. Vegetables are much more likely than fruits to increase in lignin as they age, resulting in the development of a rather tough, woody texture. Lignin is more likely to be deposited in the xylem of the vascular system than in the phloem region of such root vegetables as parsnips and carrots. This explains the considerable toughening noted in these vegetables when they are quite mature at the time of harvest.

Pectic substances, as described in the previous section, undergo a series of chemical changes during the ripening of fruits. The overall changes are hydrolytic cleavage catalyzed by protopectinase activity to produce shorter polymers and deesterification catalyzed by pectinesterases. These changes are evidenced by the definite softening that occurs as very hard unripe fruits gradually change to the mushy state characteristic of fruits that have been ripened too much.

Protopectinases
Enzymes in fruits and vegetables capable of catalyzing the hydrolytic cleavage of protopectins to shorter chains of pectins.

Pectinesterases
Enzymes that deesterify protopectin and pectin, a change that reduces gel-forming ability.

Lignin
Structural component of some plant foods that is removed to avoid a woody quality in the prepared food.

POSTHARVEST CHANGES AND STORAGE

Senescence
Accumulation of metabolic products, increase in respiration, and some loss of moisture in plant foods after maturation.

Virtually all synthesis of organic compounds halts after harvest, but numerous physiological changes continue in fruits and vegetables during storage. Bulbs, roots, tubers, and seeds become relatively dormant during storage, whereas the fleshy tissues of fruits and vegetables usually undergo ripening after maturation and then continue to **senescence.** Senescence occurs quite rapidly, with an accompanying loss of palatability. Certain types of biochemical activities occur in all fruits and vegetables, including respiration, protein synthesis, and changes in some constituents of cell walls.

The rate of respiration is directly related to the perishable character of fruits and vegetables; that is, those that have a rapid rate of oxygen consumption and carbon dioxide production are the most perishable. Fortunately, the respiration rate of highly perishable fresh produce can be retarded appreciably by refrigeration, a measure that extends shelf life significantly. The rapid rate of respiration in corn results in increased starch deposition at the expense of sugar stores. The sugar in freshly harvested peas also is depleted quite rapidly as a result of the rapid respiration rate typical of the various legumes.

Climacteric
Period of maximum respiratory rate just prior to the full ripening of many fleshy fruits.

Climacteric Fruit
Fruit that continues to ripen after it has been picked; e.g., bananas and peaches.

Nonclimacteric Fruit
Fruit that needs to be harvested when ripe because it will not respire rapidly and ripen after picking; e.g., grapes and oranges.

Respiration rate varies with the stage of maturity and ripening in many fruits, with the rate increasing to a maximum just prior to full ripening, the phase called the **climacteric.** Those fruits that exhibit this increase in respiratory rate just prior to senescence are termed *climacteric fruits.* They are distinguished by their ability to continue to ripen when they are harvested at the time that they are horticulturally mature, but not yet ripe. Peaches and pears are examples of climacteric fruits. Citrus fruits and grapes are familiar examples of fruits that are classified as **nonclimacteric.** Their respiration rate does not accelerate after harvesting. Nonclimacteric fruits are best when ripened before harvesting. Table 10–3 classifies some familiar fruits on the basis of their respiratory pattern.

Vegetables classified as edible stems, roots, or leaves do not exhibit an acceleration in respiration after harvest. Instead, they continue to respire at about the same rate as at harvest or even at a reduced rate. This is in contrast to the tomato, which actually behaves as a climacteric fruit.

Regardless of their classification as climacteric or nonclimacteric, each type of fruit or vegetable has a temperature range over which storage is feasible for at least a short period of time. At the lower end of the range, storage can be done satisfac-

Table 10–3   Selected Examples of Climacteric and Nonclimacteric Fruits

Climacteric Fruits	Nonclimacteric Fruits
Apple	Cherry
Apricot	Citrus fruits
Avocado	Fig
Banana	Grapes
Peach	Melons
Pear	Pineapple
Plum	Strawberry
Tomato	
Tropical fruits, including payaya, mango, and passion fruit	

torily for a much longer time than at the upper end of the range. However, non-freezing temperatures below the range for a particular fruit or vegetable result in chilling injuries that are detrimental to the quality of the produce. For example, potatoes held at a storage temperature of 4°C accumulate sugars at the expense of starch content; apples stored at 3°C gradually develop an internal browning and soft rot.

The atmosphere surrounding fresh produce also influences respiration rate. Lettuce needs at least 1 percent oxygen, and asparagus requires at least 5 percent. Sometimes carbon dioxide is added to retard deterioration of some fruits and vegetables during storage. The maximum level of carbon dioxide tolerated varies with the type of produce, with strawberries being able to tolerate as much as 45 percent and apples being injured by carbon dioxide levels as low as 2 percent.

Enzyme levels frequently undergo change during storage and deterioration of harvested fruits and vegetables because protein synthesis is a normal activity in fresh produce during storage and senescence. Enzymes observed to increase during ripening of fruits include lipase, pectic enzymes, invertase, chlorophyllase, and peroxidase. Research efforts are being directed toward altering gene-directed senescence as a means of extending shelf life and reducing marketing losses in fresh produce.

Ethylene gas is credited with causing accelerated ripening and early senescence of fruits during storage. Because of this action, ethylene gas sometimes is dubbed the "ripening hormone." Formation of ethylene may be the result of oxidative decarboxylation of α-keto acid analogs of methionine. Storage of underripe fruit in an environment containing ethylene gas is a useful technique to speed ripening. In fact, clear plastic, bubble-shaped containers with small holes at the bottom to help regulate gas and moisture levels are available as a means of creating an ethylene enriched environment in which fruits can be ripened quickly.

Cell wall components undergo changes after harvest as a consequence of the action of various enzymes. The pectic substances in cell walls and the middle lamella undergo degradation as a result of the increasing levels of two types of enzymes: pectinesterases and **polygalacturonases.** The action of pectinesterases is valued in making apple and grape juices because the increased solubility of the degraded pectic substances, notably pectic acid, promotes a less cloudy beverage and increases the visual appeal of the juices.

Other enzymes include hemicellulases and cellulase. As a consequence of the reactions catalyzed by these enzymes, some sugars are released from the complex polysaccharides constituting the cell walls. The result is that ripening fruits increase in sweetness despite the fact that they may have little or no starch to serve as a potential source of sugar.

Another possible route for increasing sugar levels in some fruits is by the conversion of starch to sugars. This reaction is catalyzed by amylase. Invertase is the enzyme effective in converting sucrose in fruit into its component sugars, glucose and fructose.

Curiously, the amylase in potatoes held in storage does not appear to be responsible for most of the conversion of starch to sugars that takes place when the storage temperature is below 10°C. Instead, the active enzyme apparently is **phosphorylase** when the temperature is in the range between freezing and 10°C or slightly warmer. Storage of potatoes above the active temperature range for phosphorylase is important if the detrimental effects of a high sugar content in potatoes (excessive browning in frying and too sweet a taste) are to be avoided.

Ethylene
"Plant hormone" produced in vivo; gas that accelerates ripening of fruits.
$H_2C = CH_2$

Polygalacturonases
Pectic enzymes promoting degradation of pectic substances in avocados, pears, tomatoes, and pineapple.

Phosphorylase
Enzyme in potatoes that promotes sugar formation during cold storage.

In starch-containing vegetables such as legumes, potatoes, and carrots, starch synthesis may continue to occur if the storage temperature is approximately normal room temperature or slightly warmer. Although starch is desirable in potatoes, carrots and many other vegetables are considered more palatable when they retain a reasonable level of sugars rather than synthesizing starch. For vegetables in which some sweetness is desired, refrigerator storage is recommended.

TEXTURAL CHANGES DURING PREPARATION

Turgor
Distension of the proto-plasm and cell wall of a plant by its fluid content.

Corn and dried beans are vegetables that achieve part of their change in texture during cooking as a result of the gelatinization of some of their starch content. Spinach and other greens are softened visibly during steaming or other heat treatment because the cell walls become increasingly permeable when they are heated, which causes loss of water and consequently loss of **turgor** in the cells. This change is evidenced by the wilting of the leaves and accumulation of water from the cells in the bottom of the pan, water that is sufficient to cook the greens. Schrumpf and Charley (1975) demonstrated that broccoli and carrots lose more water from their cells when cooked by microwave energy than when boiled conventionally. This difference appears to be at least partially responsible for the somewhat more rigid texture noted in some vegetables prepared in a microwave oven (see Figure 10–11).

Loss of water from cells is but one of the changes taking place in vegetable cookery. The pectic substances undergo some chemical changes to become more soluble than they were in their original form as cementing substances between cells. These changes in some of the pectic substances make it easier to chew and cut cooked vegetables. Hemicelluloses also become softer as vegetables are heated. This contributes to the change in texture noted in cooked vegetables. Acid slows these changes; alkali greatly accelerates softening.

Calcium can influence the texture of cooked vegetables. Considerable delay in softening occurs when calcium ions are able to react with the pectic substances in the middle lamella. The resulting calcium pectinates or pectates precipitate and add rigidity to the structure. This phenomenon is utilized in the preparation of commercially canned whole tomatoes to achieve whole tomatoes rather than shapeless stewed tomatoes.

Preparation of baked beans or other recipes for dried legumes containing molasses unfortunately also has the potential to illustrate the effect of calcium ions on vegetable texture. The recommended procedure is to soften the legumes to the desired extent before molasses is added. If this is not done, the calcium ions from the molasses form insoluble calcium pectinates and pectates in the middle lamella and greatly delay softening.

Dried beans have a hard outer covering that requires some soaking in unsalted water prior to simmering until they are tender. Salt is not used in the soaking water because it makes the outer surface of the beans more resistant to water penetration during cooking. A 2-minute boiling period prior to soaking beans is recommended to inactivate enzymes and avoid possible souring during an overnight soaking in cold water. A quicker alternative (Dawson et al., 1952) is to boil the beans for 2 minutes, soak them in the hot water for an hour, and then simmer until done. These same researchers also found that the addition of 0.5 gram ($\frac{1}{8}$ teaspoon) soda to 623 milliliters ($2\frac{2}{3}$ cups) of water reduced the softening time for cooking beans

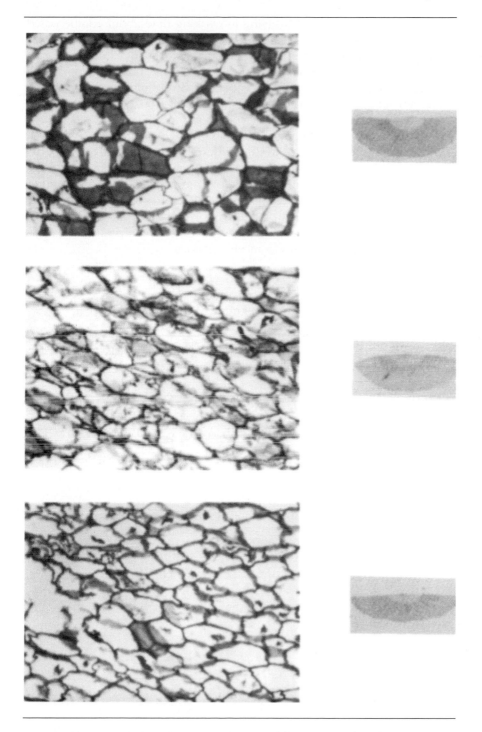

Figure 10.11   Cross section (X2) and parenchyma cells (X41) of the phloem of carrot: (top) raw; (middle) boiled conventionally; (bottom) cooked by microwave energy. (Reprinted from *Journal of Food Science*. 1975. 40: 1025. Copyright (c) by Institute of Food Technologists. Courtesy of H. Charley.)

significantly (by about one-third). This saving in cooking time about compensated for the amount of thiamine lost as a result of the alkaline environment.

Potatoes afford a particularly good example of the changes in texture that occur when a vegetable with high starch content is prepared. Some potatoes slough and seem to become slightly fluffy when they are cooked, whereas other types hold their shape well and remain somewhat more compact after being cooked. The former are classified as mealy (nonwaxy) potatoes; the latter are nonmealy (waxy). Mealy potatoes are characterized by large and numerous starch granules, particularly in the vascular parenchyma cells. These granules swell significantly during cooking; the pectic substances in the middle lamella become more soluble with heating and allow the cells to begin to separate a bit. When waxy potatoes are cooked, their cells tend to remain tightly associated. The exact reason for the difference between these two types of potatoes is not completely clear, but it may be that the waxy potatoes have more calcium ions available to form insoluble precipitates with the pectic substances in the middle lamella than are found in the mealy potatoes.

PIGMENTS

Chlorophyll

The range of green hues available in foods enables the artistic chef to create some exciting monochromatic presentations. On a chemical basis, these variations are the result of rather minor alterations in quite complex molecules. The variations in green noted in green vegetables are possible because of two basic forms of chlorophyll, the varying ratios in which these are found, and the combination of chlorophyll with other pigments at times.

Note: In chlorophyll a, R = CH_3; in chlorophyll b, R = C with O and H

*Pheophytin forms when magnesium (Mg) is replaced by hydrogen (H).

chlorophyll   phytyl group

All chlorophyll-related compounds have the same basic **tetrapyrrole** structure, with connecting methyne bridges:

Chlorophyll molecules actually occur in two different forms, the difference being the functional group (designated as *R* in the structure) attached to one of the pyrroles. **Chlorophyll a,** the more abundant form in nature, has a methyl group at the *R* position. The total resonance of the molecule and the presence of this methyl group result in a pigment color of blue-green. The *R* group in the other form of chlorophyll, chlorophyll b, is an aldehyde group. This difference in the functional group results in the chlorophyll designated as chlorophyll b having a yellowish green color. The ratio of chlorophyll a to chlorophyll b varies, depending on the specific plant. It even varies within the plant, as can be seen by the range of colors within broccoli. In broccoli, chlorophyll a is definitely the dominant form in the blue-green florets, and chlorophyll b is the more dominant form in the yellow-green stalks.

Chlorophyll is a dominant pigment in plants, particularly in unripe fruits. However, other pigments also occur in these foods at the same time, and these pigments contribute to the color seen by the eye. During the ripening of fruits, the amount of chlorophyll present actually diminishes, and the other pigments begin to supersede the chlorophyll to give the characteristic colors of the ripe fruit.

Some vegetables contain **chlorophyllase,** an enzyme that catalyzes the removal of the phytyl group, which is the complex alcohol esterified to the acid radical in the chlorophyll molecule. It is the **phytyl** group that is responsible for the hydrophobic nature of chlorophyll. When chlorophyllase effects the removal of this group, the remainder of the chlorophyll molecule, now termed *chlorophyllide,* becomes water soluble. The action of chlorophyllase prior to the cooking of some fresh green vegetables is responsible for the slightly green appearance of the cooking water, as some chlorophyllide is dissolved in the cooking medium.

When vegetables containing chlorophyll are heated, a gradual color change occurs. First, there is an intensification of the bright green of chlorophyll as air is expelled. This change unfortunately is followed by a slow transformation from bright green to an unattractive olive-drab color, the result of the elimination of the central magnesium ion and replacement with hydrogen to form pheophytin. If the original chlorophyll molecule is the "a" form, the compound formed will be **pheophytin a;** similarly, chlorophyll b converts to **pheophytin b.** This conversion is facilitated by the presence of dilute acids, and these acids are released into the cooking water when vegetables are being cooked. However, some volatile acids can be eliminated from the cooking medium if the vegetables are boiled without a cover. Retention of chlorophyll is also favored by heating the water to boiling before adding the vegetable and by using a slight excess of water to dilute the acids released from the vegetable during cooking. These various precautions are of value when a vegetable is cooked longer than 5 minutes, because the breakdown of chlorophyll to pheophytin begins between 5 and 7 minutes after heating begins. By adding the vegetable to boiling water, the actual time required to tenderize the vegetable adequately is reduced, and chlorophyll retention is improved.

Sometimes chlorophyll loses its magnesium and its phytyl group. This degradation results in a new compound called **pheophorbide** which, like pheophytins, has an olive-drab color. Dill pickles and canned green beans provide examples of this change from chlorophyll to pheophorbide (shown below):

Tetrapyrrole
Complex compound with four unsaturated, five-membered rings (containing one nitrogen and four carbon atoms) linked by methyne bridges, resulting in a very large molecule with a high degree of resonance because of the extensive amount of alternating double bonds.

Chlorophyll a
Blue-green, more abundant form of chlorophyll; the chlorophyll form in which the *R* group is a methyl group.

Chlorophyllase
Plant enzyme that splits off the phytyl group to form chlorophyllide from chlorophyll.

Phytyl
Alcoholic component of chlorophyll responsible for the hydrophobic nature of chlorophyll.

Chlorophyllide
Chlorophyll molecule minus the phytyl group; water-soluble derivative of chlorophyll responsible for the light-green tint of water in which green vegetables have been cooked.

Pheophytin a and b
Compounds formed from chlorophyll a and b in which the magnesium ion is replaced with hydrogen, altering the color to greenish gray for pheophytin a and to an olive-green for pheophytin b.

Pheophorbide
Chlorophyll derivative in which the magnesium and phytyl group have been removed; an olive-drab pigment.

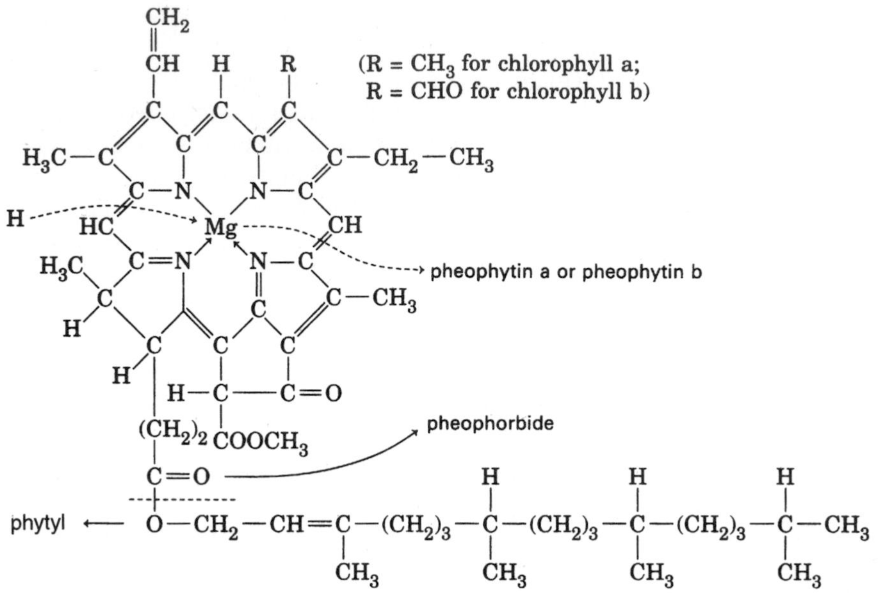

$$(R = CH_3 \text{ for chlorophyll a};$$
$$R = CHO \text{ for chlorophyll b})$$

pheophytin a or pheophytin b

pheophorbide

phytyl

Processing vegetables affects chlorophyll. In the case of green vegetables, the blanching ordinarily done as a part of the preparation for freezing enhances the green because of the expulsion of air from the intercellular spaces. Fortuitously, this bright color is retained very well during freezing and the subsequent boiling prior to serving the vegetables. This excellent retention of chlorophyll is caused by the shortened cooking time and also by the elimination of some of the organic acids during the blanching process, which results in a less acidic medium when the vegetables actually are cooked.

Canning is another means used for preserving green vegetables. In this situation, the extremely long heating period and the high temperatures required for safe processing guarantee that the chlorophyll in the fresh vegetable will no longer be present in the canned product. Instead, pheophytins and, ultimately, pheophorbide are formed, and the color is the typical olive-drab characteristic of green vegetables that have been canned.

The comparatively easy destruction of chlorophyll during cooking and/or processing has generated some interest in finding ways of preserving the desirable green color. Addition of baking soda increases the retention of chlorophyll, but it has an unpleasant effect on texture if the pH rises above 7.0. There also is a pigment change when the pH exceeds 7.0, for the phytyl and methyl groups are eliminated, and a highly water-soluble compound, **chlorophyllin** (shown below), is the result. Chlorophyllin has an unrealistic, bright green color. The undesirable textural change is extreme mushiness caused by breakdown of some of the hemicelluloses in the alkaline medium. By carefully controlling the pH so that there is only enough alkaline material present to neutralize the organic acids in a vegetable, the undesirable formation of chlorophyllin can be avoided. Addition of a small amount of calcium acetate or other calcium salt prevents the mushiness by blocking the breakdown of the hemicelluloses. These additions of alkali and a calcium salt are of interest in the food industry, but are not feasible in home preparation of green vegetables.

Chlorophyllin
Abnormally green pigment formed when the methyl and phytyl groups are removed from chlorophyll in an alkaline medium.

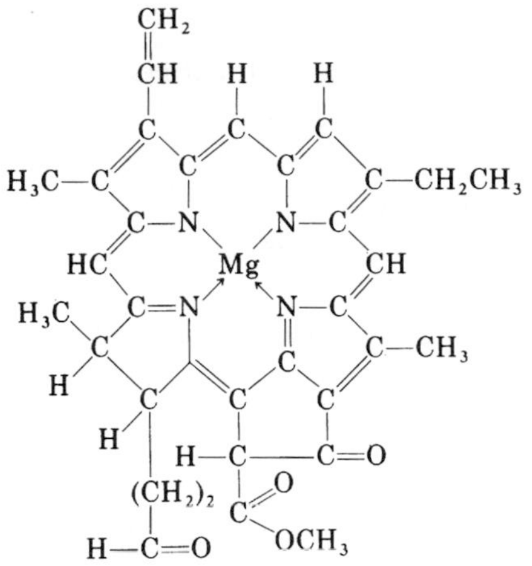

chlorophyllin

Another area of research that is of interest, but not of practical value, is the addition of copper or zinc as a replacement for magnesium in the chlorophyll molecule. Such a replacement makes retention of the desirable green color possible. Unfortunately, these metals cannot be used because of problems with toxicity.

Carotenoids

The pigments constituting the **carotenoids** are especially colorful and important compounds in fruits and vegetables, although their presence may be masked by the intense pigmentation contributed by chlorophyll, particularly in unripe fruits. The colors created by carotenoids range from yellow, through orange, to some reds. With such an array of colors, it is not surprising that many different compounds are included within the carotenoid classification of pigments.

Carotenoids are divided into two groups—the **carotenes** (some of which have potential vitamin A activity) and the **xanthophylls.** Both groups have in common the fact that they are composed of isoprene groups polymerized into larger molecules, usually containing at least 40 carbon atoms and the accompanying hydrogen. The carotenes contain only carbon and hydrogen; the xanthophylls are distinguished from the carotenes by the presence of at least one atom of oxygen.

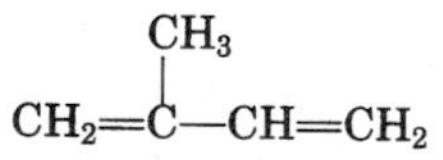

isoprene group

The most prominent of the carotenes is β-carotene, a 40-carbon compound with a closed-ring structure at each end of the isoprenoid polymer chain. A closely related carotene (Table 10–4) is α-carotene, which is identical to β-carotene except that it has a closed ring at only one end of the isoprenoid chain. **Lycopene** is an example of a carotene that is acyclic (i.e., it has no ring structure in the molecule).

Lycopene has been studied extensively because of its possible benefit in protecting against some forms of cancer and coronary heart disease. Its antioxidant

Carotenoids
Class of pigments contributing red, orange, or yellow colors as a result of the resonance provided by the isoprene polymers.

Carotenes
Group of carotenoids containing only hydrogen and carbon in a polymer of isoprene.

Xanthophylls
Group of carotenoids containing some oxygen, as well as hydrogen and carbon, in a polymer of isoprene.

Lycopene
Acyclic carotene responsible for red color in tomatoes, watermelon, and overtones in apricots and other yellow-orange fruits and vegetables; antioxidant that may help prevent some cancers and coronary heart disease.

Table 10–4   Structural Features and Colors of Selected Carotenoids

Pigment	Structural Feature	Color
Carotenes		
α-carotene	One closed ring	Yellow-orange
β-carotene	Two closed rings	Orange
Lycopene	No closed rings	Red
ξ-carotene	No closed rings	Pale yellow
Xanthophylls		
Lutein	One closed ring, 2—OH groups	Yellow
Zeaxanthin	Two closed rings, 2—OH groups	Orange
Cryptoxanthin	Two closed rings, 1—OH groups	Orange

action and seeming interference in formation of low-density lipoproteins (LDLs) are thought to be significant in both diseases (Nguyen and Schwartz, 1999). Actually, lycopene (like other carotenoids) can exist in numerous isomeric forms because of its high degree of unsaturation, but the all-trans form accounts for about 95 percent of the lycopene in foods. All-trans lycopene is quite stable during food preparation. The most common sources of lycopene in the diet are tomatoes and tomato-based products (e.g., spaghetti sauce, catsup, and pizza sauce), but such yellow fruits as apricots, papaya, and grapefruit augment lycopene consumption.

Most carotenoids are in the trans configuration at the double bonds, as can be seen in the structure of β-carotene:

β-carotene

This configuration gives an intensity of color because of the extensive resonance in the molecules resulting from the conjugated double bonds. Although the trans form is quite stable, the heat of cooking can cause some of the carotenoid molecules to be transformed into the cis form at one or two of the double bonds. This modification in the structure results in a molecule with a bend at the double bond in the cis configuration, in contrast to the same molecule with an all-trans configuration, which has a linear character. The hue of carotenoids with a cis configuration is less intense than that of their counterparts with the trans configuration exclusively. The somewhat lighter color of carrots and other carotenoid-containing vegetables that is noted after cooking is an indication that some cis isomers have formed. This change is increased when a pressure saucepan is used because of the high heat.

There is one example of a vegetable that undergoes the reverse transformation during cooking. Rutabagas naturally contain poly-*cis*-lycopene as a dominant pigment; however, some of the cis compound is shifted to form some all *trans*-lycopene, with the result that the orange pigment is intensified in the cooked vegetable.

Oxidation is responsible for some loss of color in fruits and vegetables containing carotenoids. The double bonds are susceptible to oxidation, particularly in dried foods. Blanching prior to dehydration is helpful in reducing the likelihood of oxidation. Apparently, blanching permits the carotenoids to be protected from oxidation by being dissolved in lipids in the cells, a situation that is not possible until the lipids are freed from the protein with which they are complexed as lipoproteins.

Formation of both the xanthophylls and the carotenes occurs in the chromoplasts of the cells in plants. The exact forms of the carotenoids that are formed are determined genetically. Variations in the color of some plant foods, such as the yellow tomato, have been achieved through genetic manipulation. Regardless of the specific form of carotenoid, all carotenoids are naturally fat soluble. In some plants, it appears that the carotenoids do not remain in the chromoplasts, but instead may migrate into the vacuole and dissolve in some of the lipid that is present. Still other molecules of the carotenoids may be found in crystalline form in the vacuole. There are about 300 different carotenoid pigments, and these may occur in varying amounts and in varying locations within the cells; this helps to explain the impressive color array possible in plant foods pigmented with carotenoids. Some examples of the types of carotenoids in fruits and vegetables are presented in Table 10–5.

Flavonoids

The nomenclature for a group of closely related phenolic compounds composed of two phenyl rings and an intermediate five- or six-membered ring is widely varied. One way of categorizing this group of pigmented compounds is to call all of them **flavonoids** and then to subdivide the flavonoids into the anthocyanins and the anthoxanthins. **Anthocyanins** are highly pigmented, water-soluble pigments that range in color from red to purple to blue. The anthoxanthins are colorless or white and may change to yellow. It is in the classification of the anthoxanthins that the confusion over terminology and categorization is found. Sometimes the flavones are classified as one group of the flavonoids, with the other groups being identified as flavonols, flavones, chalcones, aurones, flavonones, isoflavonones, biflavonyls,

Flavonoids
Group of chemically related pigments usually containing two phenyl groups connected by an intermediate five- or six-membered ring.

Anthocyanin
Flavonoid pigment in which the oxygen in the central ring is charged positively.

Table 10–5   Carotenoids in Selected Fruits and Vegetables

Plant Food	Pigment
Fruits	
Pink grapefruit	Lycopene, β-carotene
Watermelon	Lycopene
Peaches	Violaxanthin, cryptoxanthin, persicaxanthin, β-carotene, lycopene
Pineapple	Violaxanthin, β-carotene
Navel oranges	Violaxanthin, β-carotene
Italian prunes	Violaxanthin, β-carotene, lutein, cryptoxanthin
Muskmelons	β-carotene
Vegetables	
Yellow corn	Cryptoxanthin
Tomatoes	Lycopene, β-carotene
Red bell peppers	Capxanthin, capsorubin, β-carotene, violaxanthin, cryptoxanthin
Green bell peppers	Lutein, β-carotene, violaxanthin, neoxanthin
Carrots	β-carotene, α-carotene, γ-carotene, ξ-carotene, lycopene

leucoanthocyanins, and flavonols. For purposes of discussion here, anthoxanthins means any of the flavonoid compounds not classified as anthocyanins.

All of the flavonoid pigments are derived from the following basic structure:

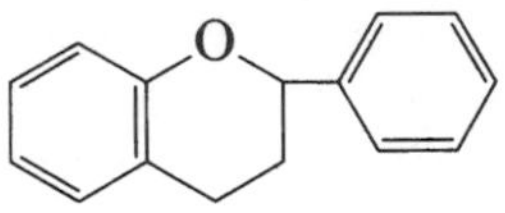

The distinction between the anthocyanins and the anthoxanthins is found in the central ring between the two phenyl rings. The oxygen in the central ring carries a positive charge in the anthocyanins, whereas in the anthoxanthins, the oxygen is uncharged.

Anthocyanins.   Anthocyanins, like the other flavonoids, are contained in the vacuole of plant cells where their solubility in water makes them disperse freely. These compounds are responsible for some of the most exciting colors in plant foods, particularly in fruits. Cherries, red apples, various berries, blue and red grapes, pomegranates, and currants achieve their color appeal because of the predominance of anthocyanins. The red color in the skin of radishes and potatoes and the leaves of red cabbage is caused by anthocyanins, too.

Three of the prominent anthocyanins are pelargonidin, cyanidin, and delphinidin. As can be seen from their structures, these three compounds differ only in the number of hydroxyl groups on the right ring of the formula, yet the result is significant differences in color. Pelargonidin, with its single hydroxyl group, is red, whereas delphinidin is blue because of its three hydroxyl groups. Cyanidin has two hydroxyl groups and is intermediate in color.

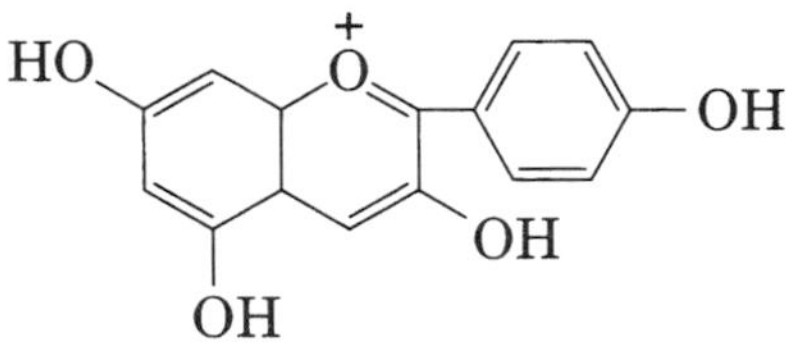

pelargonidin
(red)

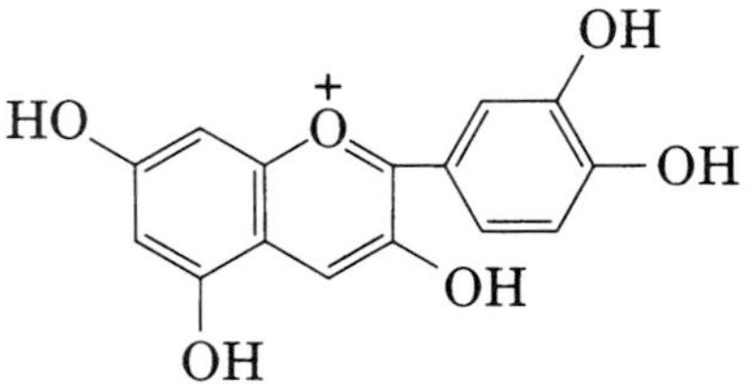

cyanidin
(reddish blue)

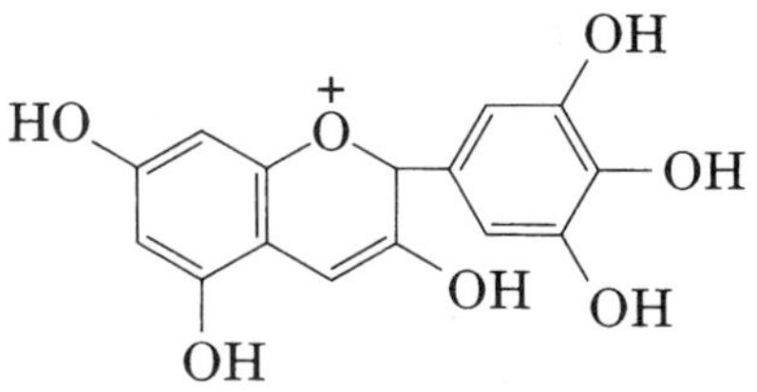

delphinidin
(blue)

Anthocyanidin
Anthocyanin-type pigment that lacks a sugar in its structure.

Technically, pelargonidin, cyanidin, and delphinidin are classified as **anthocyanidins** because they do not have a sugar complexed with them. When a sugar is complexed, the pigment becomes redder than it is as the anthocyanidin. The pigments containing a sugar are designated accurately as anthocyanins; however, this fine distinction commonly is not used, and all of the related compounds are grouped as anthocyanins. Other common anthocyanidins are malvidin, peonidin, and petunidin. In fruits and vegetables, one or more of these compounds may contribute to the overall color impression. Examples of foods colored by anthocyanidins are presented in Table 10–6.

Anthocyanidins often complex with glucose or some other sugar that may be present in the plant to form the anthocyanin. Whether present as an anthocyanidin or an anthocyanin, these compounds are highly sensitive to the pH of the medium in which they are found. The acidity of the cell in which these compounds are formed causes the molecules to have a positive charge on the oxygen atom, as was shown earlier in the structures for pelargonidin, cyanidin, and delphinidin. This form, which is the common form at a pH of 3.0 or less, maintains or shifts the hue toward red. However, the positively charged oxygen form, called an oxonium, is altered to the quinone form as the pH is increased toward a weak acid or even neutral solution. The quinone form has a violet color. In an alkaline medium still another change takes place as a salt of the violet compound, called a color base, is made. The alkaline salt of the color base has a distinctly blue color. These dramatic changes in the color of foods highly pigmented by anthocyanins make it necessary to pay careful attention to pH in working with such foods as red cabbage and several other foods, including those identified in Table 10–6.

The actual susceptibility to gross changes in pigments as a result of shifts in pH varies with the type of pigment. Red cabbage exhibits unusually wild swings in color with a change in pH because of the presence of more than four hydroxyl groups on the anthocyanin molecule. In contrast, strawberries show much less of a color change with a change in pH because their primary pigment has only three hydroxyl groups on the molecule. Considerable care needs to be taken when using Concord grape juice because it is pigmented with delphinidin-3-monoglucoside and cyanidin-3-monoglucoside, which contain six and five hydroxyl groups, respectively, in their pigment structures. This abundance of hydroxyl groups explains the extreme color changes that may occur when Concord grape juice is blended with other juices or with other ingredients that influence the pH of the mixture. Similarly, red cabbage frequently is cooked with the addition of some slices of a tart apple to ensure that the pH is sufficiently acidic to avoid the development of a blue, highly unpalatable pigment color.

Table 10–6   Examples of Anthocyanidins in Selected Foods

Food	Anthocyanidin
Strawberry	Pelargonidin
Raspberry	Cyanidin
Cherry	Cyanidin and peonidin
Cranberries	Cyanidin and peonidin
Apple	Cyanidin
Orange	Cyanidin and delphinidin
Black currant	Cyanidin and delphinidin
Blueberry	Cyanidin, delphinidin, malvidin, peonidin, and petunidin
Grape	Cyanidin and petunidin
Peach	Cyanidin
Plum	Cyanidin and peonidin
Radish	Pelargonidin
Red cabbage	Cyanidin

Heat processing of fruits and vegetables containing anthocyanins also presents significant problems. Strawberry jam affords an example of the potential problems involved in retaining the desirable red color during prolonged shelf storage after the intense boiling required in the production of the jam. A gradual change from the pleasing red to a dull reddish-brown occurs if such factors as a high pH, oxygen in the headspace, and/or a high storage temperature are present. Oxidation of the anthocyanins in the jam is promoted by these conditions and results in a change in the observed color of the pigments.

In addition to heat and oxygen, various metallic ions can cause undesirable color changes in anthocyanins. Special enamel linings in the cans used for heat-processed foods prevent metallic interactions during storage of anthocyanin-containing fruits and vegetables. Iron, aluminum, tin, and copper ions must not contact anthocyanin-containing foods if desirable colors are to be maintained. Unusual colors, ranging from green to slate blue, develop when anthocyanins contact these metals. The presence of ascorbic acid with copper or iron accelerates the oxidation and undesirable color changes of anthocyanin compounds. The disastrous color changes that occur when metallic ions interact with anthocyanins underline the importance of avoiding contact with copper and iron, contact that can occur easily if worn utensils or knives other than stainless steel are used in preparing these foods.

Enzymes also can cause detrimental changes in anthocyanin pigments. Anthocyanase is an enzyme that can catalyze reactions that result in the loss of color of anthocyanins. In a product such as strawberry jam, such a change is undesirable, but in the production of white wines, it can be very helpful. Other enzymes of interest in reactions with anthocyanins include peroxidases, phenolases, and glycosidases. Peroxidases and phenolases naturally present in some fruits and vegetables can catalyze oxidative reactions that are harmful, resulting in less desirable colors.

Glycosidases split the sugar from an anthocyanin to form a very unstable anthocyanidin. Mild heat treatment is sufficient to inactivate these enzymes and eliminate this potential problem of color retention in produce pigmented by anthocyanins.

Betalains

Two groups of pigments that contribute the anthocyanin-like color to beets, but differ chemically from the anthocyanins.

Betacyanins

Group of betalains responsible for the reddish-purple color of beets; not an anthocyanin, but behaving colorwise in the same fashion.

Anthoxanthins

Phenolic compounds contributing white to yellow color and some flavor to plants.

Tannins

Term sometimes used to designate plant phenolic compounds.

Betalains.   Beets contain pigments that are closely related to anthocyanins, but are not actually categorized as such. The two groups of pigments, both of which contain nitrogen, are **betacyanins** and betaxanthins. The distinctive color of beets is derived largely from the presence of the betacyanins; a somewhat yellow pigment is contributed by the betaxanthins. Among the water-soluble pigments within the betacyanin group are betanidin and betanin. Although these pigments are held tightly within cells in the raw vegetable, they diffuse rather rapidly into the cooking water, resulting in the highly pigmented water associated with boiling beets. This problem is aggravated by cutting into beets prior to cooking, a practice that leads to dull coloration in the boiled product. Betacyanins are sensitive to the pH of the medium in which they are located and, in fact, undergo color changes parallel to those noted previously for the anthocyanins. In other words, an acidic medium promotes a reddish color, whereas a neutral or somewhat alkaline pH brings out the blue of the pigment. The betacyanins are the subject of considerable interest as the food industry turns increasingly to natural food colorants.

Anthoxanthins (tannins).   The compounds included in this discussion of anthoxanthins are colorless or white to yellow, depending on the pH of the medium in which they are located. Compared with other pigments in fruits and vegetables, anthoxanthins make only a slight contribution to the beauty of these foods. However, they are responsible not only for some vegetable colors, such as that of cauliflower, but also for some flavor overtones. In white or light-colored vegetables, an acidic pH has a bleaching effect, causing cauliflower to become quite white. At a pH above 7.0, the anthoxanthins change to a distinctly noticeable yellow, although this yellow is much less brilliant than the yellow of the xanthophylls in the carotenoid pigment group.

Flavones and flavonols are especially abundant anthoxanthins in fruits and vegetables. As can be seen in the structures for kaempferol, quercetin, and myricetin (three of the most abundant flavonols), these anthoxanthins are higher in oxygen than are their closely related compounds, the anthocyanidins pelargonidin, cyanidin, and delphinidin. This difference in oxidation appears to account for the significant difference in coloration provided by these similar compounds.

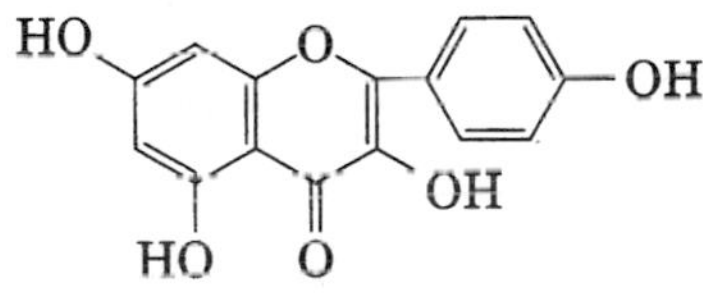

kaempferol

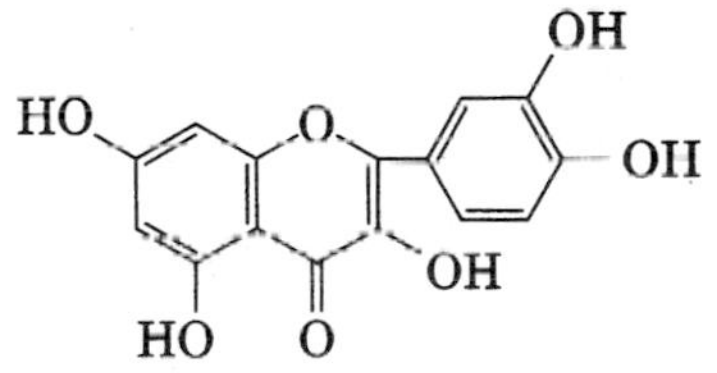

quercetin

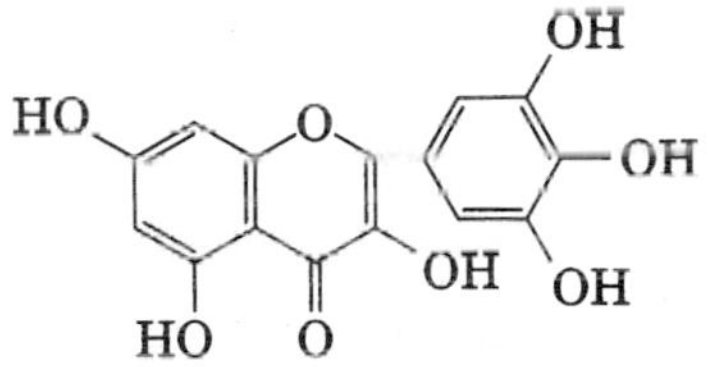

myricetin

Isoflavone is an anthoxanthin in soybeans that is of considerable interest at the present time because of its apparent role in reducing LDL and total scrum lipids when soybeans and various soy products are prominent in the diet (Katz, 1998). The structure of isoflavone (of importance also for the creamy color of soybeans) is:

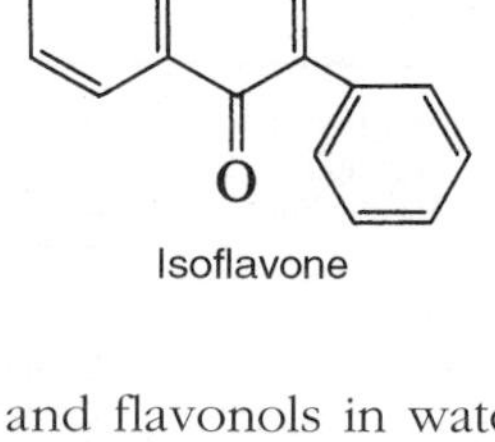

Isoflavone

The solubility of flavones and flavonols in water can be seen; if the water in which the cauliflower or other appropriate plant food is cooked is slightly alkaline, it will have a distinctly yellow color to it. On the acid side of neutral, this coloration is not evident because of the colorless nature of flavones and flavonols in an acidic pH.

One of the confounding problems of flavones and flavonols is their propensity to complex with metal ions. For example, yellow onions and spinach or other leafy vegetables will cause the cooking water to turn a bit yellow when they are cooked in aluminum pans because the flavones scavenge aluminum and form a flavone–aluminum chelate. A similar problem is noted when these compounds come in contact with iron, as occurs when these vegetables are cooked in cast iron pans. Reactions can also occur if canned vegetables interact with metal in the cans. Rutinol, a flavone in asparagus, reacts with iron to form a ferric–rutin complex which produces an unattractive dark color. In fact, the ease with which flavones and flavonones can be oxidized makes them potentially important as antioxidants in processed foods (see Figure 10–12).

Flavonones and flavanols are slightly different in chemical structure from the flavones and flavonols because they do not have the double bond in the middle ring that is found in quercetin and related compounds. This difference in structure is evidenced in the two subgroups of flavanols: catechins and leucoanthocyanins. **Catechin,** gallocatechin, epicatechin, epigallocatechin, catechin gallate, and gallocatechin gallate are included in the flavanols designated as catechins. Of particular interest is gallocatechin gallate. The structures of the **leucoanthocyanins** differ from those of the catechins by only one hydroxyl group, as can be seen by comparing the structures of catechin and leucocyanidin.

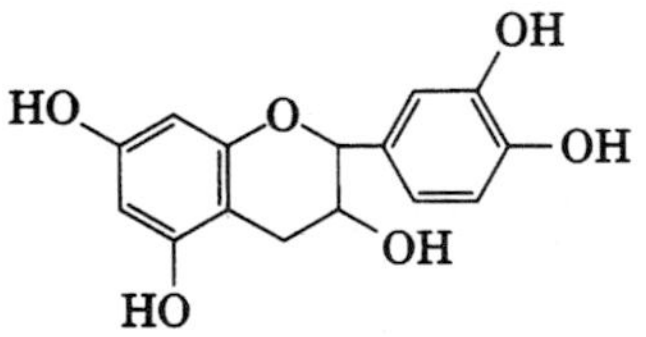

Catechins
Subgroup of flavanols, including catechin, gallocatechin, epicatechin, epigallocatechin, catechin gallate, and gallocatechin gallate; important to color and flavor of tea.

Leucoanthocyanins
Flavonoid pigments that are a subgroup of the flavanols and that are often termed proanthocyanidins.

catechin 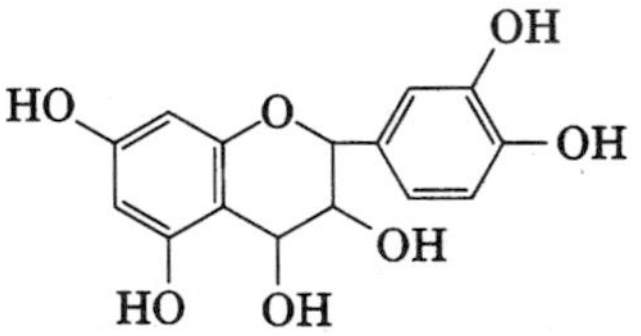   leucocyanidin

Pears and white potatoes sometimes develop a pinkish color in their cut surfaces when they stand for awhile after being peeled or sliced. Apparently this color change is caused by the conversion of the proanthocyanin to the pigmented and closely related compound cyanidin. In canned pears, this color transformation is the result of too much heat processing, that is, too high a temperature or too long a time before the heated product is cooled.

The anthoxanthins, which are all polyphenolic compounds, may undergo browning or blackening reactions when they are bruised, cut, or exposed to air for

ANTHOXANTHINS				
Flavones	**Flavonols**	**Flavonones**	**Flavanols**	
Rutinol	Kaempferol	Naringin	**Catechins**	**Leucoanthocyanins**
	Quercetin	Hesperidin	Catechin	Leucocyanidin
	Myricetin		Gallocatechin	
			Epicatechin	
			Epigallocatechin	
			Catechin gallate	
			Gallocatechin gallate	

Figure 10.12 Subdivisions within the category of anthoxanthin pigments of the flavonoids; specific pigments within the various subdivisions.

a period of time. This darkening is attributed to the action of a group of enzymes, the **polyphenoloxidases.** These enzymes are capable of catalyzing oxidation reactions in such foods as mushrooms, potatoes, bananas, pears, peaches, cherries, apricots, avocados, sweet potatoes, eggplant, and apples. Tyrosine, chlorogenic acid, the various catechins, and several mono- and dihydroxyphenols are among the many compounds that can serve as substrates for oxidation by polyphenoloxidases to cause browning or other discoloration in these foods. The reaction in bananas and white potatoes often leads first to the formation of dihydroindolequinone, a reddish compound sometimes called dopachrome. Subsequently, the chemical transition continues until finally the grayish-black color of melanin is seen. Eliminating oxygen or using an antioxidant blocks undesirable changes in color (Figure 10–13).

Polyphenoloxidase activity can be retarded greatly in fruits and vegetables by cold storage, for low temperatures reduce the effectiveness of these enzymes. When the fruit or vegetable has cut surfaces, it is possible to add an acid to inhibit enzyme action. Citric acid often is used because it is so readily available from lemon juice and other citrus fruits, but ascorbic acid is another useful acid. Sulfur

Polyphenoloxidases
Group of enzymes capable of oxidizing flavonoid (polyphenolic) compounds to cause browning or other discoloration of bruised or cut surfaces in fruits and vegetables containing these compounds after harvest.

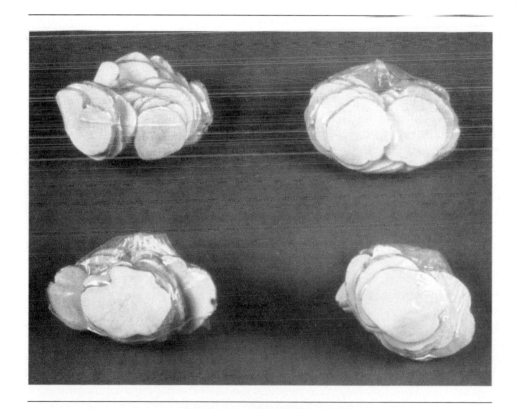

Figure 10.13   Effect of treatment by various antioxidants on discoloration in potatoes stored in Cryovac B-900 bags 14 days at 4°C. Treatment baths prior to vacuum deaeration and packaging are (clockwise): 0.3% citric acid, 0.3% ascorbic acid, 0.2% potassium sorbate; 0.5% citric acid, 0.5% ascorbic acid, 0.2% potassium sorbate; 1.0% citric acid, 1.0% ascorbic acid, 0.2% potassium sorbate; and 0.5% citric acid, 0.3% ascorbic acid, 0.2% potassium sorbate. (Courtesy of Biotechnology Products Division, Miles, Inc.)

in the form of sulfur dioxide gas or in a sulfite, bisulfite, or metabisulfite solution is also used commonly, particularly in the drying of apricots and apples. A sodium chloride solution is effective, but is not used often because of the excessively salty flavor introduced by this procedure.

Ordinarily, the action of polyphenoloxidases is undesirable because of the detrimental darkening of the fruit or vegetable. There is one notable exception to this situation, and that is in the production of oolong and black teas, where the green leaves are deliberately wilted and rolled to bruise the tissues and bring the epigallocatechin gallate and epigallocatechin in contact with the polyphenoloxidases. The resultant reaction forms two orange-pigmented compounds, theaflavin gallate and theaflavin, the two compounds largely responsible for the pleasing, dark orange-yellow color of oolong and black teas when they are brewed. Actually, the final pigmentation is from the **thearubigens** that are oxidized from theaflavin gallate and theaflavin.

Thearubigens
Dark orange-yellow compounds formed when polyphenoloxidases oxidize epigallocatechin gallate and epigallocatechin to theaflavin gallate and theaflavin for ultimate oxidation to thearubigens in oolong and black teas.

FLAVOR

The flavors of fruits and vegetables are extremely important to their acceptance in the diet and have been studied extensively because of their importance. Considerable research in flavors has revealed the highly complex nature of the total combination of chemical compounds that blend together to give the specific flavor impressions that distinguish each type of fruit and vegetable from all others.

The overall flavor impression is the result of the tastes perceived by the taste buds in the mouth and the aromatic compounds detected by the epithelium in the olfactory organ in the nose. Through the combination of these senses, most people can detect distinctive differences from one fruit or vegetable to another. The compounds detected on the tongue are those that have a sweet, sour, salty, or bitter character. In fruits and vegetables, this means that sugars, acids, salts, and bitter quinone-like compounds are tasted while the food is chewed in the mouth.

Several sugars are found in various fruits and vegetables, fruits commonly having a far higher sugar content than vegetables. Sweetness may result from the presence of glucose, galactose, fructose, ribose, arabinose, and xylose, as well as other sugars. Glucose, the most abundant of the sugars, may be found in the free sugar form or may be in phosphate esters or other forms.

Organic acids also contribute significantly to sour perceptions on the tongue and, consequently, to the overall flavor of both fruits and vegetables. The common organic acids in fruits are malic, citric, tartaric, and oxalic; those in vegetables include the ones identified as common in fruits plus isocitric and succinic acids. This is not an exhaustive list, but does include the most abundant organic acids in both fruits and vegetables. Although vegetables contain a somewhat greater array of acids than fruits, the content is not as great. This comparatively low acid content of vegetables explains the distinction between the use of water bath canning for fruits and the requirement for pressure canning of vegetables.

All fruits and vegetables naturally contain at least a small amount of salt, which is detected in the overall taste impressions contributing to flavor.

The flavonones, previously discussed because of their role in pigmentation, also contribute to taste sensations. Hesperidin and naringin, compounds found in the peels of oranges and grapefruit, respectively, have been studied extensively as possible sweetening agents because they become very intensely sweet when their molecules are modified slightly by opening the central ring. However, they are not sweet in their unaltered form. There are several compounds that are quite closely related to hesperidin and naringin and also found in citrus peels; some of these are quite bitter.

Astringency is the feeling of puckering that occurs in the mouth when certain compounds, notably flavanols, are present. Although astringency is not actually a part of the flavor, this puckering sensation in the mouth blends with flavor perceptions in influencing acceptance of the particular fruit or vegetable containing these flavanols. This characteristic astringency is considered to be desirable in limited amounts in many foods, including wines, some fruit juice ciders, and some fruits. When bananas and persimmons ripen, the excessive quantities of flavanols found in the unripe fruit are reduced. Temperature influences the amounts of these flavanols. A warm and clear environment during ripening of peaches results in a lower content of polyphenols than is developed when cooler, cloudy weather is the situation. The lower polyphenolic content imparts a reduced astringency.

Volatile compounds are at least as important as those detected by the taste buds on the tongue. Several organic compounds contribute significantly to the aroma and flavor of fruits and vegetables because of their volatility. Included among these volatile compounds are esters, aldehydes, acids, alcohols, ketones, and ethers. No single type of compound stands out as the key to the aroma and flavor of specific fruits and vegetables. Analysis by gas–liquid chromatography reveals an impressive assortment of organic compounds in the aroma of different fruits and vegetables. A few of the important volatile components of fruits are presented in Table 10–7.

Two types of vegetables have strong flavors resulting from the presence of various sulfur-containing compounds. **Allium** is the genus that includes onions, chives, garlic, and leeks. Brussels sprouts, broccoli, cabbage, rutabagas, turnips, cauliflower, kale, and mustard are members of the family **Cruciferae,** which also contains prominent sulfur compounds.

Alliin is a key compound from which a strong and pungent odorous compound is formed when a garlic clove is crushed. Although the parent compound of a highly aromatic substance, alliin actually is odorless. It is not until **alliinase,** an

Allium
Genus including onions, chives, garlic, shallots, and leeks; unique for its sulfur-containing flavor compounds.

Cruciferae
Family including brussels sprouts, cabbage, rutabagas, turnips, cauliflower, kale, and mustard; a family with sulfur-containing flavor compounds that differ from those found in Allium vegetables.

Alliin
Odorless precursor in garlic that ultimately is converted to diallyl disulfide:

$$CH_2{=}CH{-}CH_2{-}S{-}CH_2{-}CH{-}COOH$$
$$\underset{O}{|} \quad \underset{NH_2}{|}$$

Alliinase
Enzyme in garlic responsible for catalyzing the conversion of alliin to diallyl thiosulfinate, the precursor of diallyl disulfide.

Table 10–7   Some Volatile Flavor Components in Selected Fruits

Fruit	Volatile Flavor Component
Apple	Esters; alcohols; aldehydes; ketone; acids; including hexanal; ethyl 2-methyl butyrate
Banana	Alcohols; esters, including amyl acetate, isoamyl acetate, butyl butyrate, and amyl butyrate
Cranberries	Benzaldehyde; benzyl and benzoate esters
Orange	Acetaldehyde, ethanol, limonene, ethyl esters, linalool; α-terpincol
Peach	Benzaldehyde, benzyl alcohol, γ-caprolactone, γ-decalactone
Pear	Esters of 2, 4-decadienoic acid, especially the esters of ethyl, *n*-propyl, and *n*-butyl
Pineapple	*p*-Allyl phenol; γ-butyrolactone; γ-octalactone; acetoxyacetone; methyl esters of β-hyroxybutyric and β-hydroxyhexanoic acids
Strawberries	Methyl and ethyl acetates, propionates, and butyrates

Table 10–8   Some Flavor Components of Selected Vegetables

Vegetable	Flavor Component
Celery	Phthalides, *cis*-3-hexen-1-yl pyruvate, diacetyl
Cucumber	Nona-2,6-dienal, non-2-enal, hex-2-enal, propanal, ethanal, hexanal
Beans	Methanol, acetone, hydrogen sulfide, methanethiol
Corn	Methanol, acetone, hydrogen sulfide, methanethiol
Parsnips	Dimethyl sulfide, methanol, acetone, hydrogen sulfide
Peas	Methanol, acetone, dimethyl sulfide

Diallyl Disulfide

Key flavor aromatic compound from garlic:

CH₂=CH—CH₂—S
CH₂=CH—CH₂—S

Propenylsulfenic Acid

Compound in onions causing eye irritation and tears:

CH₃—CH=CH—S—H (O)

Sinigrin

Potassium myronate, an isothiocyanate glucoside in cabbage:

CH₂=CH—CH₂—C (S—C₆H₁₁O₅) (N—O—SO₃K)

enzyme found in garlic, comes in contact with alliin that diallyl thiosulfinate is formed. Diallyl thiosulfinate is quite unstable and is quickly converted to **diallyl disulfide,** the compound considered to be the most important one in garlic (and other *Allium* vegetables) aroma. Various other di- and trisulfides, hydrogen sulfide, and propanethiol are among the aromatic compounds identified in onions and other *Allium* vegetables.

The eye-irritating substance in onions is an acid derived specifically from (+)-S-(prop-1-enyl)-L-cysteine sulfoxide as a result of the action of an enzyme. The irritant is **propenylsulfenic acid,** which decomposes rather rapidly. This compound and many of the sulfur compounds contributing flavors to various members of the *Allium* genus are quite volatile and escape during cooking unless the cooking time is short.

Isothiocyanates are among the sulfur-containing compounds found in members of the *Cruciferae* family. **Sinigrin,** an isothiocyanate found in cabbage and some other *Cruciferae,* can be broken down by myrosinase A, an enzyme, to yield a highly pungent compound, allyl isothiocyanate. When vegetables from this family are cooked, hydrogen sulfide is produced, with the production accelerating when cooking extends beyond 5 minutes. Cooked cauliflower yields about twice as much hydrogen sulfide as does cooked cabbage. Broccoli also contributes more hydrogen sulfide than does cabbage. Dimethyl sulfide is a key volatile compound produced when cabbage is boiled. Rutabagas also release hydrogen sulfide and dimethyl sulfide when boiled.

Not all of the flavor of vegetables is caused by sulfur-containing compounds. Studies have shown the importance of short-chain aldehydes, esters, and other volatile organic compounds, a few of which are identified in Table 10–8.

SUMMARY

Fruit and vegetable tissues consist of the dermal, vascular, and ground systems. Parenchyma cells, the predominant type of cell in the fleshy portions of fruits and vegetables, contain several structural features, including the vacuole, chromoplasts, chloroplasts, and leucoplasts where the various pigments and starch are produced. Structural components include cellulose, hemicelluloses, pectic substances (protopectin, pectin, pectinic acid, and pectic acid), and lignin.

Some gums are complex carbohydrates that are used as additives to modify the properties of many manufactured foods today. They may be used as thickening agents, fat replacements, and texturizing agents. The seed gums include guar and locust bean; plant exudates are gum arabic, gum tragacanth, karaya gum, and gum ghatti. Red and brown seaweeds are the source of agar, carrageenan, and alginates. Xanthan and gellan gums are the product of microorganisms. Cellulose is modified to make cellulose gum (CMC), microcrystalline cellulose (MCC), methylcellulose (MC), and hydroxypropylmethylcellulose (HPMC). Bran from cereals is a useful source of fiber, which can be incorporated into reduced-fat ground meat products, as well as into breads and other baked products.

During maturation and following harvest, many changes occur in fresh produce. These changes are the result of enzyme action and respiration.

The pigments in fruits and vegetables include chlorophyll, the carotenoids, and the flavonoids (anthocyanins, betalains, and anthoxanthins). Color changes can occur as the result of heat, changes in pH, oxidation, and enzyme action. Chlorophyll and the flavonoids are more susceptible to change than the carotenoids. Flavors are due to a variety of organic compounds, including aldehydes, ketones, acids, sulfur-containing compounds, esters, alcohols, ethers, and sugars.

STUDY QUESTIONS

1. Describe the tissue systems and the types of cells contained in the edible parts of plants. Name the various structural features.

2. What are the structural constituents of plant foods? Identify their chemical structures.

3. What changes do the pectic substances undergo during maturation, and how do these changes influence their behavior in food products?

4. What changes occur after harvest, and how may the storage environment be controlled to optimize shelf life?

5. What is chlorophyllide, and how is it formed?

6. What is the key difference between the anthoxanthins and the anthocyanins? How does this influence color?

7. What is polyphenoloxidase and what happens when it is present in fresh produce containing anthoxanthins? How can this problem be minimized?

8. Compare the flavoring compounds in fruits with those in onions and with those in cabbage.

9. Find some food product labels that list gums as ingredients. What functions are performed by each of the gums?

10. Why are gums important ingredients in commercial food products, but not in food produced in the home?

BIBLIOGRAPHY

Abers, J. E. and Wrolstad, R. E. 1979. "Causative factors of color deterioration in strawberry preserves during processing and storage." *J. Food Sci. 44:* 75.

Adams, J. B. 1981. "Blanching of vegetables." *Nutr. Food Sci. 73:* 11.

Andon, S. A. 1987. "Applications of soluble dietary fiber." *Food Technol. 41* (1). 74.

Anonymous. 1991. "Oat-bran-based ingredient blend replaces fat in ground beef and pork sausage." *Food Technol. 45* (11): 60.

Baldwin, E. A., et al. 1997. "Use of lipids in coatings for food products." *Food Technol. 51* (6): 56.

Barfod, N. M. and Pederson, K. S. 1990. "Determining the setting temperature of high-methoxyl pectin gels." *Food Technol. 44* (4): 139.

Barrett, D. M. and Theerakulkait, C. 1995. "Quality indicators in blanched, frozen, stored vegetables." *Food Technol. 49* (1): 62.

Bauernfeind, J. C. 1975. "Carotenoids as food colors." *Food Technol. 29* (5): 48.

Borchgrevink, N. C. and Charley, H. 1966. "Color of cooked carrots related to carotene content." *J. Am. Dietet. Assoc. 49:* 116.

Bowman, F., et al. 1971. "Microwaves vs. conventional cooking of vegetables at high altitude." *J. Am. Dietet. Assoc. 68:* 427.

Breidt, F. and Fleming, H. P. 1997. "Using lactic acid to improve safety of minimally processed fruits and vegetables." *Food Technol. 51* (9): 44.

Bressani, R., et al. 1982. "Reduction of digestibility of legume proteins by tannins." *J. Plant Foods 4* (1): 438.

Brouillard, R. 1982. "Chemical structure of anthocyanidins." In *Anthocyanins as Food Colors.* Markakis, P., ed., p. 1. Academic Press: New York.

Clydesdale, F. M. and Francis, F. J. 1976. "Pigments." In *Principles of Food Science. I. Food Chemistry.* Fennema, O. R., ed., p. 385. Dekker: New York.

Crean, D. E. and Haisman, D. R. 1963. "Interaction between phytic acid and divalent cations during cooking of dried peas." *J. Sci. Food Agr. 14:* 824.

Cross, G. A. and Fund, D. Y. C. 1982. "Effect of microwaves on nutrient value of food." *CRC Crit. Rev. Food Sci. Nutr. 16:* 355.

da Silva, J. A. L. and Rao, M. A. 1995. "Rheology of structure development in high-methoxyl pectin/sugar systems." *Food Technol. 49* (10): 70.

Davis, E. A., et al. 1976. "Scanning electron microscope studies on carrots: effects of cooking on the phloem and xylem." *Home Econ. Res. J. 4:* 214.

Dawson, E. H., et al. 1952. *Development of Rapid Methods of Soaking and Cooking Dry Beans.* U.S. Dept. Agr. Bull. No. 1051. Washington, D.C.

Deshpande, F. S. and Cheryas, M. 1983. "Changes in phytic acid, tannins, and trypsin inhibitory activity on soaking of dry beans." *Nutr. Rep. Int. 27* (2): 371.

Dziezak, J. D. 1991. "Focus on gums." *Food Technol. 45* (3): 116.

Emodi, A. 1978. "Carotenoids—properties and applications." *Food Technol. 32* (5): 38.

Fennema, O. 1977. "Loss of vitamins in fresh and frozen foods." *Food Technol. 31* (12): 32.

Glicksman, M. 1991. "Hydrocolloids and the search for the 'oily grail.'" *Food Technol. 45* (10): 94.

Goodwin, T. W. 1976. *Chemistry and Biochemistry of Plant Pigments.* Academic Press: New York.

Gordon, H. T. and Bauernfeind, J. C. 1982. "Carotenoids as colorants." *CRC Crit. Rev. Food Sci. Nutr. 81:* 59.

Gordon, J. and Noble, I. 1964. "Waterless vs. boiling water cooking of vegetables." *J. Am. Dietet. Assoc. 44:* 378.

Haard, N. F. 1976. "Characteristics of edible plant tissues." In *Principles of Food Science. I. Food Chemistry.* Fennema, O. R., ed., p. 677. Dekker: New York.

Haard, N. F. 1984. "Postharvest physiology and biochemistry of fruits and vegetables." *J. Chem. Educ. 61* (4): 277.

Hoover, D. G. 1997. "Minimally processed fruits and vegetables: Reducing microbial load by nonthermal physical treatments." *Food Technol. 51* (6): 66.

Hughes, J. S. 1991. "Potential contribution of dry bean dietary fiber to health." *Food Technol.* *45* (9): 122.

Ink, S. L. and Hurt, H. D. 1987. "Nutritional implications of gums." *Food Technol. 41* (1): 77.

John, M. A. and Dey, P. M. 1986. "Postharvest changes in fruit cell wall." *Adv. Food Res. 30:* 139.

Johnson, A. E., et al. 1971. "Vegetable volatiles: survey of components identified." *Chem. Ind. 1971:* 556 and 1212.

Johnston, D. E. and Oliver, W. T. 1982. "Influence of cooking techniques on dietary fiber of whole boiled potatoes." *J. Food Technol. 17* (1): 99.

Joslyn, M. A. 1962. "Chemistry of protopectin: Critical review of historical data and recent developments." *Adv. Food Res. 11:* 1.

Katz, F. 1998. "That's using the old bean." *Food Technol. 52* (6): 42.

Liu, K. 1997. "Storage proteins and hard-to-cook phenomenon in legume seeds." *Food Technol. 51* (5): 58.

Longe, O. G. 1981. "Effect of boiling on carbohydrate constituents of some non-leafy vegetables." *Food Chem. 7* (1): 1.

Luh, B. S. and Phithakpol, B. 1972. "Characteristics of polyphenoloxidase related to browning in cling peaches." *J. Food Sci. 37:* 264.

Markakis, P., ed. 1982. *Anthocyanins as Food Colors.* Academic Press: New York.

Newsome, R. 1990. "Organically grown foods." *Food Technol. 44* (12): 123.

Nguyen, M. L. and Schwartz, S. J. 1999. "Lycopene: chemical and biological properties." *Food Technol. 53* (2): 38.

Okezie, B. O. 1998. World food security: Role of postharvest technology. *Food Technol. 52* (1): 64.

Olempska-Beer, Z. S., Kuznesof, P. M., DiNovi, M., and Smith, M. J. 1993. "Plant biotechnology and food safety." *Food Technol. 47* (12): 64.

Palmer, J. K. 1984. "Enzyme reactions and acceptability of plant foods." *J. Chem. Educ. 61* (4): 284.

Pressey, R. and Avants, J. K. 1978. "Difference in polygalacturonase composition of clingstone and freestone peaches." *J. Food Sci. 43:* 1415.

Pressey, R., et al. 1971. "Development of polygalacturonase activity and solubilization of pectin in peaches during ripening." *J. Food Sci. 36:* 1070.

Pszczola, D. E. 1997. Curdlan differs from other gelling agents. *Food Technol. 51* (4): 30.

Reineccius, G. A. 1991. "Carbohydrates for flavor encapsulation." *Food Technol. 45* (3): 144.

Sapers, G. M. 1993. "Browning of foods: control by sulfites, antioxidants, and other means." *Food Technol. 47* (10): 75.

Sapers, G. M. and Ziolkowski, M. A. 1987. "Comparison of erythorbic and ascorbic acids as inhibitors of enzymatic browning in apple." *J. Food Sci. 52:* 1732.

Saravacos, G. D. and Kostaropoulos, A. E. 1995. "Transport properties in processing of fruits and vegetables." *Food Technol. 49* (9): 99.

Schrumpf, E. and Charley, H. 1975. "Texture of broccoli and carrots cooked by microwave energy." *J. Food Sci. 40:* 1025.

Shewfelt, R. L. 1990. "Quality of fruits and vegetables." *Food Technol. 44* (6): 99.

Staub, H. W. and Ali, R. 1982. "Nutritional and physiological value of gums." In *Food Hydrocolloids.* Glickman, M., ed., p. 101. CRC Press: Boca Raton, FL.

Szczesniak, A. S. and Ilker, R. 1988. "Meaning of textural characteristics—juiciness in plant foods." *J. Texture Studies 19:* 61.

Taylor, S. L., et al. 1986. "Sulfites in foods: uses, analytical methods, residues, fate, exposure assessment, metabolism, toxicity, and hypersensitivity." *Adv. Food Res. 30:* 2.

Thomas, P. 1986. "Radiation preservation of foods of plant origin. IV. Subtropical fruits: citrus, grapes, and avocadoes." *CRC Crit. Rev. Food Sci. Nutr. 24* (1): 53.

Vandercook, C. E., Tisserat, B., and Berhow, M. A. 1990. "Influence of external factors on quality and composition of citrus." *Food Technol. 44* (4): 142.

Weaver, C. and Charley, H. 1974. "Enzymatic browning of ripening bananas." *J. Food Sci. 39:* 1200.

Wilson, A. M., et al. 1981. "HPLC determination of fructose, glucose, and sucrose in potatoes." *J. Food Sci. 46:* 300.

Zammer, C. M. 1995. "Gun-puffed vegetable snacks: a new way to eat your veggies." *Food Technol. 49* (10): 64.

Zapsalis, C. and Beck, R. A. 1985. *Food Chemistry and Nutritional Biochemistry.* Wiley: New York.

4

Lipids

CHAPTER 11

Overview of Fats and Oils

CHEMISTRY

Lipids, like carbohydrates, are organic compounds composed of carbon, hydrogen, and oxygen. Oxygen, however, is present in a much smaller proportion and hydrogen in a larger proportion in lipids than in carbohydrates. This difference in composition accounts for the large difference in the energy value of lipids (9 kilocalories per gram) and carbohydrates (4 kilocalories per gram).

The two key components of simple fats (the lipid class of greatest significance in food preparation) are glycerol and fatty acids. In these compounds, **glycerol** and a **fatty acid(s)** are linked together to form an ester, as shown below.

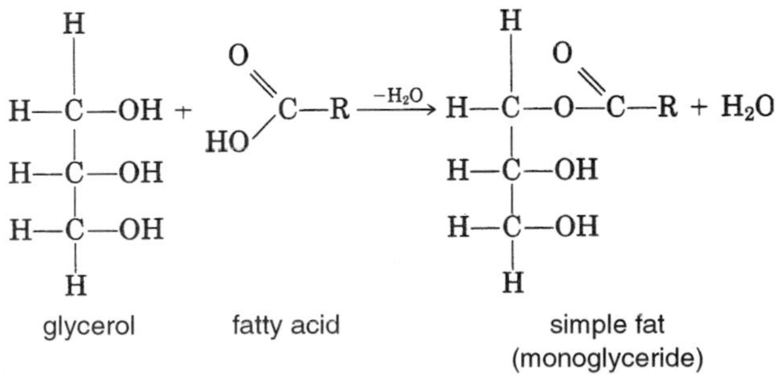

Esterification of glycerol and a fatty acid

Glycerol

As can be seen in the preceding reaction, glycerol actually has three hydroxyl (alcohol or —OH) groups, each of which can be esterified with a fatty acid. The polyhydric nature of glycerol permits formation of a wide range of simple fat mole-

Lipids
Nonpolar, water-insoluble compounds composed of carbon, hydrogen, and a small amount of oxygen.

Glycerol
Polyhydric alcohol containing three carbon atoms, each of which is joined to a hydroxyl group.

Fatty Acid
Organic acid containing usually between 4 and 24 carbon atoms.

cules, because each of the hydroxyl groups can esterify with a different fatty acid. This makes the range of possible molecules of simple fats extremely large. Researchers have found that food fats contain a relatively large and somewhat varying content of the different fatty acids. However, the glycerol molecule remains a constant structural feature.

Fatty Acids

The fatty acids in simple fats are organic compounds with the characteristic carboxyl ($-C\overset{\displaystyle\nearrow O}{\underset{\searrow OH}{}}$) group identifying them as acids. They ordinarily contain an even-number of carbon atoms. The smallest of these compounds possible is acetic acid (two carbon atoms), and the largest occurring with any regularity in foods is arachidonic acid (20 carbon atoms).

The structure of a fatty acid is shown below, using oleic acid as an example:

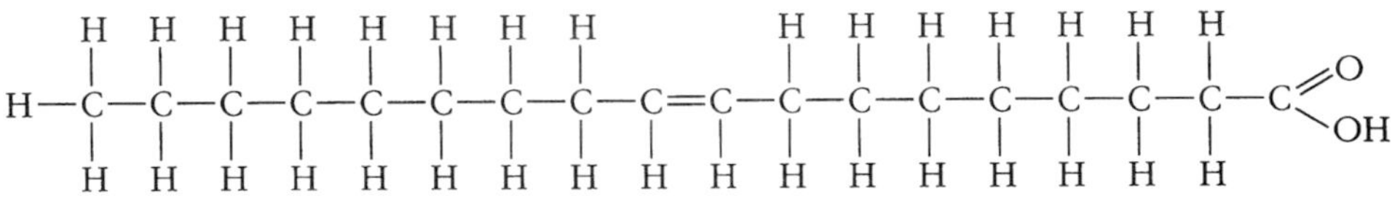

$$H-\underset{\displaystyle H}{\overset{\displaystyle H}{C}}-\underset{\displaystyle H}{\overset{\displaystyle H}{C}}-\underset{\displaystyle H}{\overset{\displaystyle H}{C}}-\underset{\displaystyle H}{\overset{\displaystyle H}{C}}-\underset{\displaystyle H}{\overset{\displaystyle H}{C}}-\underset{\displaystyle H}{\overset{\displaystyle H}{C}}-\underset{\displaystyle H}{\overset{\displaystyle H}{C}}-\underset{\displaystyle H}{\overset{\displaystyle H}{C}}-C=C-\underset{\displaystyle H}{\overset{\displaystyle H}{C}}-\underset{\displaystyle H}{\overset{\displaystyle H}{C}}-\underset{\displaystyle H}{\overset{\displaystyle H}{C}}-\underset{\displaystyle H}{\overset{\displaystyle H}{C}}-\underset{\displaystyle H}{\overset{\displaystyle H}{C}}-\underset{\displaystyle H}{\overset{\displaystyle H}{C}}-\underset{\displaystyle H}{\overset{\displaystyle H}{C}}-C\overset{\displaystyle\nearrow O}{\underset{\searrow OH}{}}$$

To facilitate identification of different carbon atoms in the structure, the carbon in the carboxyl group is considered carbon 1, and the remaining carbons are numbered sequentially. This numbering system would be applied to the carbon atoms in oleic acid as follows:

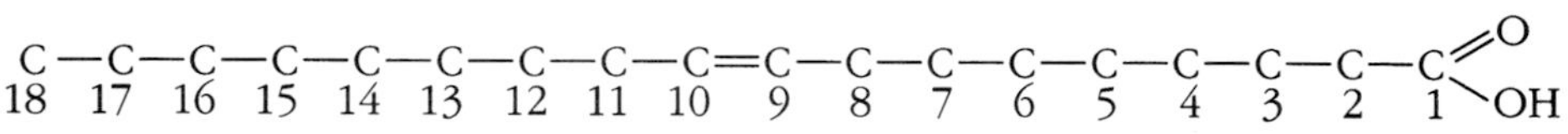

$$\underset{18}{C}-\underset{17}{C}-\underset{16}{C}-\underset{15}{C}-\underset{14}{C}-\underset{13}{C}-\underset{12}{C}-\underset{11}{C}-\underset{10}{C}=\underset{9}{C}-\underset{8}{C}-\underset{7}{C}-\underset{6}{C}-\underset{5}{C}-\underset{4}{C}-\underset{3}{C}-\underset{2}{C}-\underset{1}{C}\overset{\displaystyle\nearrow O}{\underset{\searrow OH}{}}$$

This representation, while accurate, is cumbersome; the total size of the molecule is only known when each of the carbon atoms is counted. A somewhat simpler system retains the accuracy while speeding identification simply by enclosing the CH$_2$ representation in parentheses and indicating the number of carbon atoms by use of a subscript. By this system, oleic acid can be written:

$$CH_3(CH_2)_7CH=CH(CH_2)_7COOH$$

The specific fatty acids in a molecule of fat determine the physical characteristics of the fat. The rheological (flow and deformation) qualities of fats are of particular interest when they are used in food preparation. The fatty acids commonly found in simple fats in foods are presented in Table 11.1. Of special interest in Table 11.1 is the **melting point** of the various fatty acids. The melting point, which is the temperature at which the fatty acid is transformed from a solid to a liquid, is significant in determining specific applications in food preparation.

Melting Point
The temperature at which the crystals of a solid fat melt.

The flow properties and ability to solidify into crystalline form that fatty acids exhibit are related to their chain length and degree of unsaturation. As can be seen in Table 11.1, short-chain fatty acids have lower melting points than do long-chain fatty acids. This means that long-chain fatty acids are more likely to be solid at mixing temperatures than are short-chain fatty acids. When fats are very hard (have high melting points) at room temperature they may be poorly suited for specific preparations, such as creaming a shortened cake mixture.

The other factor that affects melting points of fatty acids is the degree of **unsaturation. Saturated fatty acids** (acids holding all of the hydrogen possible) have higher melting points than do their counterparts containing a **double bond.** The higher the degree of unsaturation (the more double bonds in a fatty acid), the lower is the melting point. This can be seen by comparing the 69.6°C melting point of **stearic acid** (saturated 18-carbon fatty acid), the 14°C melting point of **oleic acid** (18-carbon fatty acid with one double bond), the −5°C melting point of **linoleic acid** (18-carbon fatty acid with two double bonds), and the −11°C melting point of **linolenic acid** (also an 18-carbon fatty acid, but with three double bonds). This is why linoleic and linolenic acids remain fluid in the refrigerator.

At double bonds, the configuration is either **cis** or **trans.** If the double bond is in the **cis** form, the melting point is appreciably lower than when the comparable molecule has a double bond in the **trans** form. Evidence for this is given in Table 11.1 by the melting point data for oleic acid (**cis** form, melting point of 14°C) and elaidic acid (**trans** form, melting point 43.7°C). Because both of these fatty acids contain 18 carbon atoms and one double bond, the difference in melting point is attributable to the difference in configuration at the double bond. The **cis** and **trans** configurations at the double bond are presented below.

Unsaturation
Lack of hydrogen relative to the amount that can be held, a situation characterized by a double bond between two carbon atoms in the fatty acid chain.

Saturated Fatty Acids
Organic acids containing all of the hydrogen they can possibly hold.

Double Bond
Linkage between two carbon atoms that is capable of being broken so that an atom of hydrogen can be added to each of the two carbon atoms.

Stearic Acid
Saturated 18-carbon fatty acid.

Oleic Acid
Monounsaturated 18-carbon fatty acid,

Linoleic Acid
Essential fatty acid (18 carbons) containing two double bonds.

Linolenic Acid
Fatty acid (18 carbons) containing three double bonds.

Trans Configuration
The hydrogens attached to the carbon atoms on either end of the double bond are from opposite directions.

Cis Configuration
The hydrogens attached to the carbon atoms on either end of the double bond are from the same orientation.

Table 11.1   Selected Fatty Acids Occurring in Foods

Common Name	Carbon Atoms	Double Bonds	Melting Pont (°C)	Structure
Butyric	4	0	−7.9	$CH_3(CH_2)_2COOH$
Caproic	6	0	−1	$CH_3(CH_2)_4COOH$
Caprylic	8	0	16	$CH_3(CH_2)_6COOH$
Capric	10	0	31.5	$CH_3(CH_2)_8COOH$
Lauric	12	0	48	$CH_3(CH_2)_{10}COOH$
Myristic	14	0	57–58	$CH_3(CH_2)_{12}COOH$
Palmitic	16	0	64	$CH_3(CH_2)_{14}COOH$
Palmitoleic[a]	16	1		$CH_3(CH_2)_5CH=CH(CH_2)_7COOH$
Stearic	18	0	69.6	$CH_3(CH_2)_{16}COOH$
Oleic[a]	18	1[b]	14	$CH_3(CH_2)_7CH=CH(CH_2)_7COOH$
Elaidic[a]	18	1[c]	43.7	$CH_3(CH_2)_7CH=CH(CH_2)_7COOH$
Linoleic[a]	18	2	−5.0	$CH_3(CH_2)_4CH=CHCH_2CH=CH(CH_2)_7COOH$
Linolenic[a]	18	3	−11.0	$CH_3(CH_2CH=CH)_3(CH_2)_7COOH$
Arachidic	20	0	77	$CH_3(CH_2)_{18}COOH$
Arachidonic[a,d]	20	4	50	$CH_3(CH_2)_4(CH=CHCH_2)_4(CH_2)_2COOH$

[a]Unsaturated fatty acid.
[b]Double bond is cis configuration.
[c]Double bond is trans configuration.
[d]The systematic name is 5,8,11,14-eicosatetraenoic acid.
Source: Adapted from *Van Nostrand's Scientific Encyclopedia.* 5th ed. Considine, D. M., ed. Van Nostrand Reinhold: New York, 1976.

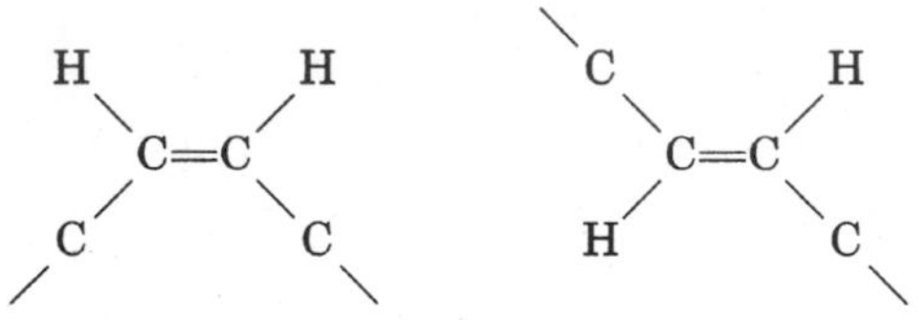

cis
(oleic m.p. = 14°C)

trans
(elaidic m.p. = 43.7°C)

The *trans* form is able to form van der Waals forces fairly easily with other molecules because of its linearity, which permits molecules to approach each other closely. The *cis* form, on the other hand, is somewhat angular because of the bend in the molecule affected by the orientation at the double bond. This makes it slightly difficult for other molecules to align themselves closely enough for van der Waals forces to immobilize the molecules into a crystalline framework. Consequently, crystallization of the *cis* form requires that considerable energy be removed from the system by cooling the mixture to a low temperature so that the molecules move very slowly and van der Waals forces can form.

STRUCTURES OF FATS IN FOODS

Fats in foods can be classified on the basis of the number of fatty acids esterified to the glycerol molecule. If one fatty acid is esterified, the compound is designated as a monoglyceride. The fatty acid may be on one of the terminal carbon atoms or on the center one. The configurations possible are shown below. The *R* group represents the carbon chain of the fatty acid exclusive of the carboxyl group.

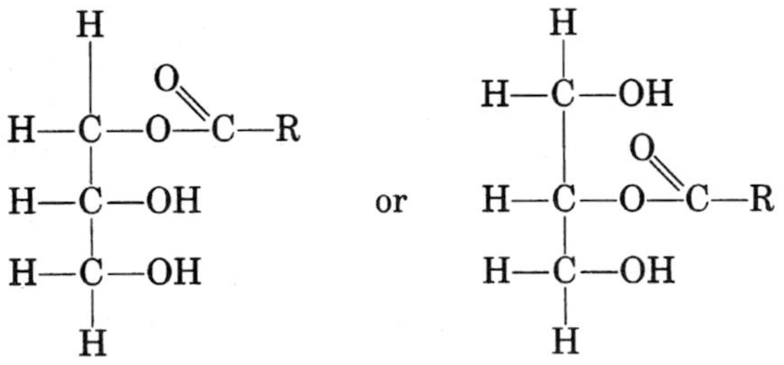

forms of monoglycerides

Diglyceride
Simple fat containing two fatty acids esterified to glycerol.

Diglycerides are formed by esterifying two fatty acids on the glycerol molecule. Esterification of the two fatty acids may be on the two terminal carbon atoms of glycerol or on two adjacent carbon atoms.

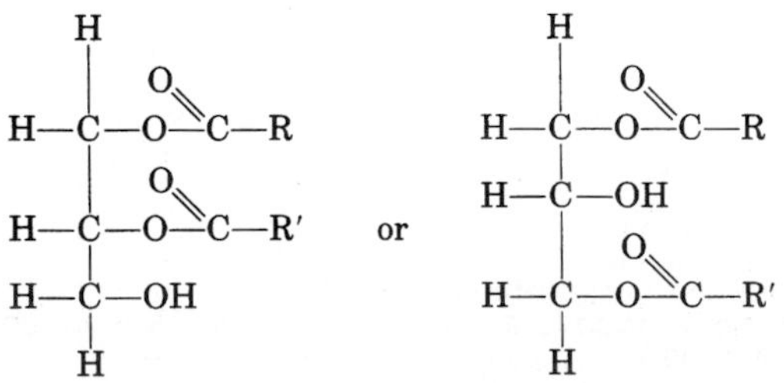

forms of diglycerides

Triglycerides, the most common form of food fats, are composed of three fatty acids esterified to the glycerol molecule. This is the maximum number of fatty acids that can exist in the compound because there are no additional hydroxyl groups where a fatty acid can be esterified. The general formula for this structure is as follows.

Triglyceride
Simple fat containing three fatty acids esterified to glycerol; the most common form of simple fat.

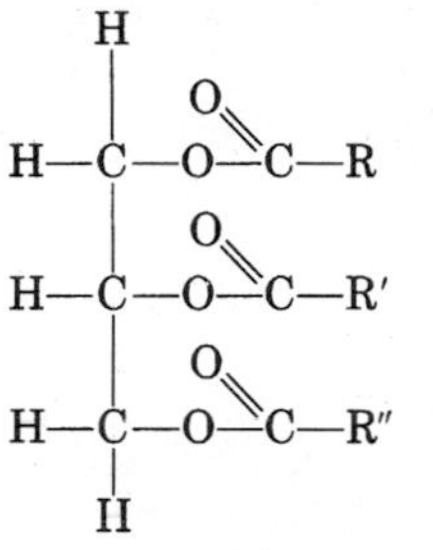

H
|
           O
           ‖
H—C—O—C—R
          O
          ‖
H—C—O—C—R'
          O
          ‖
H—C—O—C—R''
|
H

triglyceride

In the preceding structures, the importance of the fatty acid moiety is minimized by the use of the symbol R to represent any chain length. This is somewhat misleading, for the most common fatty acids found in fats are palmitic (16 carbons, 0 double bonds), palmitoleic (16 carbons, 1 double bond), stearic (18 carbons, 0 double bonds), oleic (18 carbons, 1 double bond), and linoleic (18 carbons, 2 double bonds). These 16- and 18-carbon chains dominate the overall structure of the fat molecules, for they are significantly larger than the 3-carbon chain of glycerol.

Although the structural formula for fat molecules usually is written in the form of a capital letter E, with all three fatty acids seeming to extend in the same direction from the glycerol, steric hindrance precludes this from actually being the case. Instead, the three fatty acids extend spatially in different directions. The tuning fork arrangement is postulated to be one of the feasible configurations. In the diagram below, the glycerol moiety is represented by the vertical line and the three fatty acids by horizontal lines. A chair arrangement also has been suggested as being representative of the actual spatial arrangement.

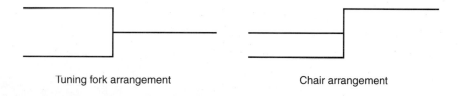

Tuning fork arrangement   Chair arrangement

CRYSTALLINITY OF SOLID FATS

Fats high in polyunsaturated fatty acids are fluid (oils) at room temperature, but many food fats are in solid form at refrigerator and room temperatures. Although these fats appear to be a solid mass, they are actually a mixture of crystals of fat in oil. The nature of the crystals influences the usefulness of these solid fats in food preparation.

When melted fats cool, the molecules gradually move more and more slowly. Occasionally, a molecule links to another by means of van der Waals forces, and crystals begin to form. The tuning fork configuration is well suited to alignment of molecules to form a crystalline matrix (see Figure 11.1).

Figure 11.1   Margarine magnified 500 times (polarized light). The light areas are crystals of fat. Liquid does not show. (Courtesy of J. T. Colburn, Armour and Co. and Bakers Digest.)

Alpha (α) Crystals
Extremely fine and unstable form of fat crystals.

Beta Prime (β′) Crystals
Very fine and reasonably stable fat crystals.

Intermediate Crystals
Slightly coarse fat crystals that form when β′ crystals melt and recrystallize.

Fat crystals may be in any of four forms: alpha (α), beta prime (β′), intermediate, and beta (β). The **α crystals** are very fine and extremely unstable. They very quickly melt and recrystallize into the next larger crystalline form, the β′ form. When fat crystals are in the β′ form, the fat has a very, very smooth surface, as can be noted in a newly opened can of hydrogenated vegetable shortening of high quality. The **β′ crystals** are considerably more stable than the α crystals; in fact, they are stable enough to survive the marketing process unless subjected to high temperatures during storage. For baking purposes utilizing solid fats, β′ crystals are the desirable form. Their presence aids in promoting a fine texture in the finished product (see Figure 11.2).

Intermediate crystals give a somewhat grainy appearance to a fat and are not recommended for use. They may form if a fat is stored at a quite warm temperature. The β′ crystals melt gradually under this condition and then recrystallize into the larger, coarser intermediate form (see Figure 11.3).

Figure 11.2   Photomicrograph of beta prime (β′) fat crystals in polarized light (X200). Grid lines represent 18 microns. (Courtesy of C. W. Hoerr.)

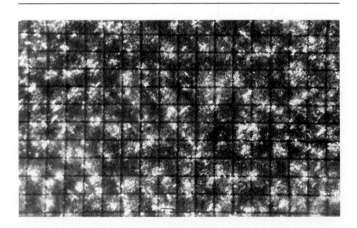

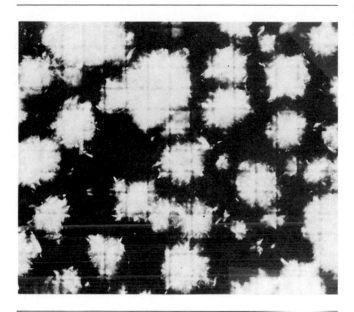

Figure 11.3   Photomicrograph of intermediate fat crystals in polarized light (X200). Grid lines represent 18 microns. (Courtesy of C. W. Hoerr.)

The coarsest crystalline form is the extremely stable β form. **Beta crystals** form when a fat is melted completely and then allowed to recrystallize without being disturbed. This can easily be seen by simply melting a small amount of fat and watching it change in appearance as it cools. One thing that is apparent in this circumstance is the gradual change from the transparent melted fat to the opaque solid fat. This increase in opacity is the consequence of the crystals forming and refracting the light differently (see Figure 11.4).

Controlling crystal size in solid fats is important from the perspective of visual appeal to consumers as well as performance. The β′ crystals, not the intermediate or the β form, are the desired crystals. Agitating the processed fat during cooling is the key to achieving the necessary control of crystal formation in fats. Storage at cool temperatures also is important in the marketing chain if the β′ crystals are to

Beta (β) Crystals
Extremely coarse and undesirable fat crystals.

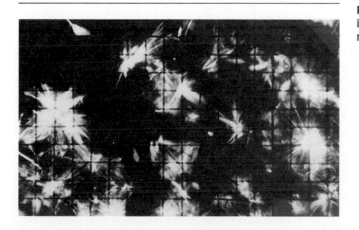

Figure 11.4   Photomicrograph of beta (β) fat crystals in polarized light (X200). Grid lines represent 18 microns. (Courtesy of C. W. Hoerr.)

Figure 11.5 Photomicrograph of beta (β) fat crystals after long aging (using polarized light and x200). Grid lines represent 18 microns. (Courtesy of C. W. Hoerr.)

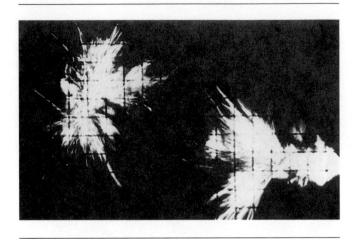

reach consumers. If warehouses or shipping containers are allowed to get extremely warm, the quality of the fats they house begins to be modified as the β′ crystals melt, and the fat recrystallizes in the form of intermediate or even β crystals (see Figures 11.5 and 11.6).

In 1998, Marangoni and Hartel added an in-depth view of a milkfat film crystallized for 24 hours by using their unique application of confocal laser-scanning fluorescence microscopy and multiple photon microscopy. These researchers revealed a delicate crystal network with **spherulites** trapped in it. The liquid oil that normally would be present in a crystallized fat was removed to facilitate the microscopy.

Spherulite
Spherical crystalline body of radiating crystal fibers.

Figure 11.6 Crystal size influences the texture of breads made with lard containing crystals of varying size: (a) control with no lard; (b) beta prime (β′) to intermediate crystals; (c) beta (β) crystals, and (d) beta prime (β′) crystals. Note the increased volume and closed grain when beta prime crystals are present, as compared with the effect of beta crystals. (Courtesy of J. G. Mahdi, Kansas State University and Bakers Digest. In Mahdi, J. G., et al. 1981. "Effect of mixing atmosphere and fat crystal size on dough structure and bread quality." *Bakers Digest 55* (2): 28.)

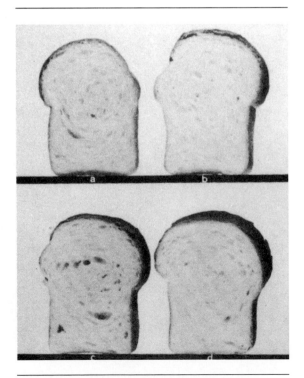

CHEMICAL DEGRADATION

Rancidity

Oxidative rancidity.   **Rancidity** is the chemical deterioration of the quality of a fat by either (1) oxidative or (2) hydrolytic chemical reactions. The overall action of oxidative rancidity involves the uptake of oxygen at a double bond in an unsaturated fatty acid in a fat. When fats are exposed to oxygen, the double bond can be broken so that oxygen can then become a part of the molecule.

Oxidative rancidity begins when a free radical is formed, which often is initiated with a linoleic acid molecule. Its structure is able to form a **free radical** at any of three carbons (9, 11, or 13). The free radical then combines with two oxygen atoms to form a **peroxide.** Subsequently, a hydrogen is removed from another unsaturated fatty acid, and that hydrogen is added to complete the formation of the **hydroperoxide** on the first fatty acid. Unfortunately, a new free radical is formed when that hydrogen atom is removed from the second fatty acid. In turn, two oxygen atoms are added to this second free radical; now yet another fatty acid is stripped of one hydrogen atom to finish formation of the second hydroperoxide, leaving yet another free radical. This process is autocatalytic, that is, it is self-perpetuating.

Oxidative rancidity requires the presence of oxygen, but it is facilitated by the presence of certain metals (iron and copper) and by light and/or warm temperatures. The objectionable flavor changes associated with oxidative rancidity are caused by the formation of a wide range of compounds from the hydroperoxides, including various aldehydes, ketones, and alcohols.

The process of oxidative rancidity can be summarized as:

Rancidity
Chemical deterioration of a fat caused by the uptake of oxygen (oxidation) or water (hydrolysis).

Oxidative Rancidity
Development of off-flavors and odors in fats as a result of the uptake of oxygen and the formation of peroxides, hydroperoxides, and numerous other compounds.

Free Radical
Unstable compound containing an unpaired electron.

Peroxide
Compound with oxygen attached to oxygen.

Hydroperoxide
Compound containing a –O–O–H group.

$$H_3C(CH_2)_4\overset{13}{C}H=CH-\overset{11}{C}H-CH=\overset{9}{C}HCH_2(CH_2)_6C\overset{O}{\diagup}O-$$
$$\underset{OOH}{|}$$

or

$$H_3C(CH_2)_4\overset{13}{C}H-CH=\overset{11}{C}H-CH=\overset{9}{C}HCH_2(CH_2)_6C\overset{O}{\diagup}O-$$
$$\underset{OOH}{|}$$

or

$$H_3C(CH_2)_4\overset{13}{C}H=CH-\overset{11}{C}H=CH-\overset{9}{C}H-CH_2(CH_2)_6C\overset{O}{\diagup}O-$$
$$\underset{OOH}{|}$$

} possible hydroperoxides

(Note the changes at carbons 9, 11, and 13).

Autoxidation
Oxidation reaction capable of continuing easily with little added energy.

The early phase in which this oxygen uptake begins to occur is referred to as the *induction period.* The fact that the oxidation reaction keeps generating additional free radicals to maintain the momentum of the formation of peroxides and hydroperoxides explains why this oxidation is designated **autoxidation.**

Storage in tightly closed containers in a cool, dark place helps slow the onset and continued development of oxidative rancidity. However, some oxygen still remains in the headspace of the closed container, and eventually oxidation will begin. The problems of oxidative rancidity can be delayed considerably by the addition of antioxidants to products high in unsaturated fatty acids, for these fats are particularly susceptible to oxidation.

Antioxidant
Compound that can retard oxidative rancidity by providing hydrogen to block formation of free radicals in fatty acids or by scavenging metal or oxygen.

Antioxidants protect against development of oxidative rancidity by providing a hydrogen atom from their own molecule to react either with a free radical of a fatty acid or with a peroxide that has already been formed. The addition of the hydrogen (from the antioxidant) to the free radical results in return to the original fatty acid. If the hydrogen unites with the peroxide, a stable hydrogen peroxide is formed. In both of these cases, fairly stable compounds are the result, and the autocatalytic continuation of oxidative rancidity is blocked. The free radical that is formed by the donation of the hydrogen atom from the antioxidant is not able to participate in the formation of a free radical in the fatty acid.

Tertiary-Butylhydro-quinone (TBHQ)
Antioxidant often added to animal fats used in baking and frying.

Several synthetic antioxidants are used extensively as additives to help retard oxidative rancidity in fats and oils. **Tertiary-butylhydroquinone (TBHQ)** is particularly effective in both vegetable oils and in most other fats. It is well suited for use not only in the fats and oils themselves, but also retains its antioxidant capability in baking or frying. **Butylated hydroxyanisole (BHA)** is an effective antioxidant in animal fats used for baking. **Butylated hydroxytoluene (BHT)** also is rather effective in animal fats, but not in vegetable oils. **Propyl gallate (PG)** is somewhat useful as an antioxidant in vegetable oils, but its action is enhanced synergistically by combining it with BHA and BHT.

Butylated Hydroxy-anisole (BHA)
Antioxidant effective in animal fats used in baking.

Butylated Hydroxy-toluene (BHT)
Antioxidant used to retard oxidation in animal fats.

Propyl Gallate (PG)
Antioxidant somewhat effective in vegetable oils. Often used in combination with BHA and BHT.

Some other substances act as scavengers to combine directly with copper or iron that might be present, thus blocking the ability of the metal to catalyze the oxidation of the fat or oil. Additives that are effective as sequestrants or scavengers include ethylenediaminetetraacetate (EDTA), ascorbyl palmitate, ascorbic acid, and citric acid. Some compounds (ascorbic acid, for example) can interact to be oxidized themselves before the fatty acids undergo oxidation. Tocopherols are other examples of natural antioxidants, which are effective in retarding oxidative rancidity because of their ease of oxidation.

Hydrolytic Rancidity.   The hydrolytic reaction in which free fatty acids are split from the glycerol in fat molecules, **lipolysis,** is shown below. The uptake of a molecule of water usually is promoted either by the action of **lipase** or by heat. Although some time is required for the complete liberation of a molecule of glycerol from a triglyceride, eventually one triglyceride molecule undergoes lipolysis to yield three free fatty acid molecules and one molecule of glycerol. These free fatty acids may seriously alter the aroma and flavor of a fat or oil in which lipolysis has occurred. This breakdown is termed ***hydrolytic rancidity.***

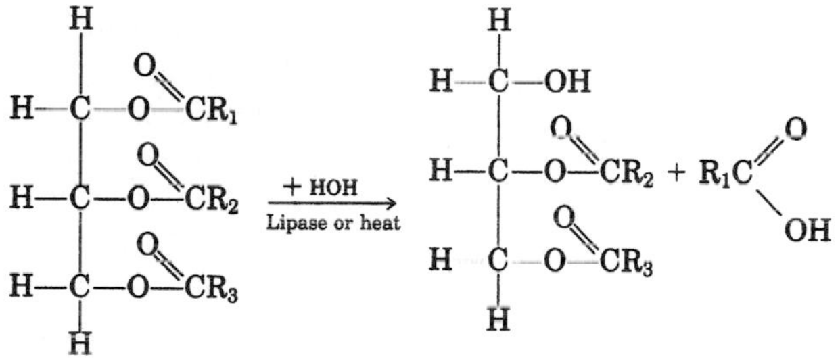

Lipolysis

Reversion

Another deteriorative change in fats occurs with only a small amount of oxygen present and apparently is the result of oxidation of some of the linoleic and linolenic acids (18:2 and 18:3, respectively) in oils. This deteriorative change, which results in development of off-odors and off-flavors, is called ***reversion.*** Flavors developed as a result of reversion are often described as "fishy" or "beany" and are definitely detrimental to quality. The key oil plagued by this problem is soybean oil, but rapeseed oil and various fish oils also are very susceptible to reversion. Some additional flavor problems may be generated by heat reversion, a reaction apparently stemming from changes in glycerol. At the present time, the fact that reversion occurs is recognized as a significant problem when working with products containing the susceptible oils, but research has not yet led to a solution.

Effects of Heat

Smoke Point.   Fats and oils can be heated to extremely high temperatures, but eventually there is so much energy that the molecules begin to degrade. The weakest linkage in their structure is the ester linkage joining the fatty acid(s) to the alcohol (glycerol). With the uptake of a molecule of water, lipolysis occurs, releasing a free fatty acid (shown in the equation for lipolysis). If the molecule is a monoglyceride, glycerol will be the other product of lipolysis. However, diglycerides and triglycerides also undergo lipolysis, with the reaction continuing until the fatty acids have been removed and glycerol is formed. The temperature for such reactions to occur usually is 190°C or higher (temperatures used for frying).

Deteriorative changes do not stop there. Continued heating will cause the removal of two molecules of water from the glycerol, which results in the formation of an unusual aldehyde called acrolein.

Lipolysis
Reacion of a molecule of water with a fat molecule to release a free fatty acid in the presence of lipase or heat.

Lipase
Enzyme catalyzing the hydrolysis of fat to yield free fatty acids and glycerol.

Hydrolytic Rancidity
Lipolysis of lipids to free fatty acids and glycerol, often catalyzed by lipases.

Reversion
Development of an off-flavor (beany or fishy) in soybean, rapeseed, or various fish oils as a result of a reaction involving only very minor amounts of oxygen.

$$\begin{array}{c}
\text{H} \\
| \\
\text{H—C—OH} \\
| \\
\text{H—C—OH} \\
| \\
\text{H—C—OH} \\
| \\
\text{H}
\end{array}
\quad \xrightarrow[\text{Heat}]{-2\text{H}_2\text{O}} \quad
\begin{array}{c}
\text{H—C}{=}\text{O} \\
| \\
\text{H—C} \\
\| \\
\text{H—C—H}
\end{array}
\quad + \; 2\text{H}_2\text{O}$$

glycerol   acrolein

Acrolein
A highly irritating and volatile aldehyde formed when glycerol is heated to the point where two molecules of water split from it.

Acrolein is almost immediately vaporized, causing the fat to smoke. The acrolein-containing smoke is extremely irritating to the eyes and respiratory passages. Fats that have undergone sufficient lipolysis so that the glycerol content is fairly high exhibit a rather serious drop in smoke point and cause considerable discomfort for the chef when they are used for deep-fat frying.

The smoke point of a fat is not a specific temperature. As a fat is being used at very high temperatures over a period of time, the smoke point will gradually drop for that fat until the flavor and appearance of the foods fried in it are unacceptable. Different oils used for frying naturally have somewhat different original smoke points, but the point is sufficiently above 190°C that most oils (with the exception of olive oil) can be used satisfactorily for a reasonable length of time before the smoke point drops to frying temperature or below. Shortenings or other fats that have monoglycerides present quickly are altered so that the smoke point is too low for acceptable fried products. This result is not surprising because only one fatty acid has to be removed before the glycerol is available to begin forming acrolein.

Polymerization
Formation of a variety of polymers, including simple dimers and trimers, when free fatty acids are subjected to intense heat for a long period during frying.

Polymerization.   The free fatty acids formed as a result of lipolysis follow quite a different course from that of glycerol being transformed into acrolein. Instead, these free fatty acids undergo additional chemical modification as the fat in which they are contained continues to be held at the temperatures used in frying, usually at least 190°C. No single route of reaction has been identified as the mechanism in very hot fat. Instead, it appears that several different reactions probably occur, to form polymers or smaller molecules as a result of the coupling of free fatty acids into new compounds. Fatty acids containing at least one double bond are particularly susceptible to **polymerization.** Through formation of new carbon-to-carbon bonds, dimers and trimers of a cyclic nature begin to evolve from the free fatty acids. Oxygen-to-carbon bonds may lead to oxidative polymerization when some hydroperoxides of polyunsaturated fatty acids are found in the fat being used for frying.

Although the specific compounds formed during prolonged heating of fats doubtless are extremely varied, clearly the resulting compounds are appreciably larger than the original free fatty acids. These larger polymers of the free fatty acids increase the viscosity of the hot fat appreciably. In fact, the increased viscosity is very evident to the casual observer and is a sign that the fat is altered significantly in its chemical composition. Darkening of the color of the fat during extended use in frying is yet another indication of loss of quality.

SUMMARY

The physical behavior of fats and oils is determined by the fatty acids that are esterified to glycerol to form monoglycerides, diglycerides, and triglycerides, which are the common forms of fats used in food preparation. Carbon chain length and degree of saturation determine the melting point of fatty acids. These fat molecules are found in foods as oils or as crystalline fats, with the crystal size ranging from alpha to beta prime and then on to intermediate, and finally beta crystals. Beta prime is the preferred size for food applications.

Rancidity in unsaturated fatty acids can develop as a consequence of oxidation, a process which can be hastened by metals and/or warm temperatures. Antioxidants act as deterrents to oxidation of fats. In addition to oxidative rancidity, fats may undergo hydrolytic rancidity, which occurs when fatty acids are split from glycerol by the addition of a molecule of water at the reaction site.

Reversion is the development of beany or fishy aroma and flavor as the result of oxidation of some linoleic (18:2) and linolenic (18:3) acids in an oil.

Fats heated to high temperatures for an extended period will begin to smoke as glycerol and ultimately acrolein are formed. This is possible because of the release of free fatty acids from mono-, di-, and/or triglycerides in intense heat. Fats need to be heated to temperatures below their smoke points to avoid this degradation.

STUDY QUESTIONS

1. Write the chemical reaction for the esterification of glycerol with a molecule of stearic acid, one of oleic acid, and one of butyric acid.

2. Identify three factors that influence the melting point of a fatty acid and describe the effect of each factor.

3. Why is the crystalline form of a fat important in making shortened cakes?

4. Is the crystalline form of a fat of concern when selecting a fat for frying? Explain your answer.

5. Carefully describe the development of oxidative rancidity and of hydrolytic rancidity. Be sure to include chemical formulas and reactions to clarify each of the processes.

6. Describe chemically the degradative changes that an oil undergoes when it is being used for frying over an extended period.

BIBLIOGRAPHY

Allison, D. B., et al. 1999. Estimated intakes of trans fatty and other fatty acids in the US population. *J. Am. Diet. Assoc. 99* (2): 166.

Applewhite, T. H. 1986. *Bailey's Industrial Oil and Fat Products.* Vol. 3. Wiley: New York.

Blumenthal, M. M. 1991. "New look at the chemistry and physics of deep-fat frying." *Food Technol. 45* (2): 68.

Carr, R. A. 1991. "Development of deep-fat frying fats." *Food Technol. 45* (2): 95.

Decker, E. A. and Xu, Z. 1998. Minimizing rancidity in muscle food. *Food Technol. 52* (10): 54.

Dorko, C. 1994. "Antioxidants used in foods." *Food Technol. 48* (4): 33.

Giese, J. 1996. Antioxidants: Tools for preventing lipid oxidation. *Food Technol. 50* (11): 73.

Jacobson, G. A. 1991. "Quality control in deep-fat frying operations." *Food Technol. 45* (2): 72.

Marangoni, A. G. and Hartel, R. W. 1998. Visualization and structural analysis of fat crystal networks. *Food Technol. 52* (9): 46.

Moreira, R. G. and Palau, J. E. 1995. "Deep-fat frying of tortilla chips: an engineering approach." *Food Technol. 49* (4): 146.

Rhee, K. S. 1988. "Enzymic and nonenzymic catalysis of lipid oxidation in muscle foods." *Food Technol. 42* (6): 127.

Saguy, I. S. and Pinthus, E. J. 1995. "Oil uptake during deep-fat frying: factors and mechanism." *Food Technol. 49* (4): 142.

Stevenson, S. G., et al. 1984. "Quality control in use of deep frying oils." *J. Amer. Oil Chem. Soc. 61:* 1102.

Zapsalis, C. and Beck, R. A. 1985. *Food Chemistry and Nutritional Biochemistry.* Wiley: New York.

CHAPTER **12**

Fats and Oils in Food Products

STEPS IN MANUFACTURING FOOD FATS

Extraction

Lipids must first be removed from their natural food sources. In the case of lard and tallow, this means the **rendering** (either wet or dry) of fats from the animal tissues. Dry rendering is done by heating the tissues and collecting the melted fat as it is drained and finally expressed by squeezing the residue. Fats intended primarily for human consumption commonly undergo wet rendering, a process in which tissues are subjected to either very hot water or steam, sometimes under some pressure. The hot, fluids fats are then separated from water, and antioxidants frequently are added to retard the development of rancidity.

Plant lipids are removed by hot pressing or cold pressing. At ambient temperatures, a mechanical or screw-type press can be used to express oils from the seeds, a procedure termed ***cold pressing.*** Cold pressing is considered desirable because of the high quality of the oil that can be extracted in this manner. However, cold pressing does not extract as high a portion of the oil in the seeds as can be obtained by **hot pressing.** In hot pressing, steam is used to warm the tissues to about 70°C and then the hot tissues are pressed to remove the oil. The higher temperatures reached in hot pressing result in a somewhat lower quality product because of the presence of some gums, possible off-flavor overtones, and free fatty acids. Fortunately, a subsequent degumming operation can remove the extraneous gums acquired during hot pressing. Solvent extraction can be conducted on oil seeds after pressing to isolate additional lipids. Another extraction technique involves the application of carbon dioxide at pressures as high as 8000 psi at warm temperatures (at least 31°C).

Rendering
Removing fat from animal tissues by either dry or moist heat.

Cold Pressing
Mechanical pressing of olives to express oil without heat, resulting in an oil of excellent purity.

Hot Pressing
Using steam or hot water to heat plant seeds to about 70°C to facilitate extraction of lipids from the seeds, a process that also extracts some gums, off-flavors, and free fatty acids.

Refining

Undesirable constituents may be found in fats after extraction, particularly if rendering has been the process used. Gums, lipoproteins, lecithins, ketones, and aldehydes are just some of the compounds that may be found in fats at this stage of manufacturing. Several steps may be used in refining these fats to the high level of purity needed to move them through marketing channels and into the kitchen while retaining a high quality. Gums and free fatty acids can be removed by **degumming** and **neutralization** procedures. A hot steam distillation procedure is used to separate the relatively volatile free fatty acids from the fat molecules, one method of neutralizing the fat. Steam can also be used to remove gums that may be present, a process called degumming. Dilute phosphoric acid can be used as an alternative means of degumming.

Bleaching, the refinement process that removes undesirable coloring and flavoring contaminants from fats and oils, can be accomplished by several means, for example, filtering through activated charcoal. A related step is deodorizing, a process that can be accomplished by steam distillation. **Deodorizing** is particularly important to production of high-quality coconut and palm kernel oil. Conversely, olive oil is not deodorized because its natural aroma is considered highly desirable.

Winterizing is a refining technique used to remove lipid fractions with melting points high enough to cause them to become a solid at refrigerator temperatures. If the fat is chilled to crystallize the fractions that would precipitate during storage in the refrigerator and the precipitated fats are filtered to remove the oil, an oil can be produced that is suitable for storage in the refrigerator, yet is able to be poured as soon as it is removed from the cold. Fats that have gone through this process are said to be winterized. Winterizing is a very important step in refining oils that are used in salad dressings or other pourable sauces. The exception is olive oil. This unique oil is not winterized because important flavorful oils would be removed.

Controlling Crystal Size

The final phase in the manufacture of fats is the crystallization of the warm, fluid fat. The comparative stability and fine crystal size of β' crystals make this type of crystal the goal in the final product. Careful control of temperature as the fat is cooling, combined with an appropriate amount of agitation, can be very helpful in achieving a smooth fat, with β' crystals being the predominant crystal size. Without such controls, the very small β' crystals (needle-shaped crystals about 1 μm long) are not able to form readily. Instead, the very large β crystals (usually ranging between 20 and 45 μm) precipitate to give a very coarse texture. Hydrogenated cottonseed oil often is included in the manufacture of fats because of its propensity to form the desired β' crystals. In the manufacture of shortenings, flakes of cottonseed oil and tallow frequently are added because of their effectiveness in promoting the formation of β' crystals.

In the manufacture of special fats for use in the confectionery industry, fats undergo tempering to yield a product with a mixture of crystal shapes (polymorphs). **Tempering** is a process in which temperature is very carefully controlled by removing the heat as it is released when liquid fats crystallize (the heat of crystallization). By this means, the fat can be held at a specified temperature for the time required for the crystals to finish forming and to stabilize in the favored crystal form.

Degumming
Separating natural gums from extracted fats; an important step in refining fats and oils.

Neutralization
Removal of free fatty acids from fats and oils; a step in their refinement.

Bleaching
Refining step in which coloring and flavoring contaminants are removed from fats, often by filtration through active charcoal or other suitable substrate.

Deodorizing
Using steam distillation or other suitable procedure to remove low-molecular-weight aldehydes, ketones, peroxides, hydrocarbons, and free fatty acids that would be detrimental to the aroma and flavor of fats.

Winterizing
Refining step in which oils are chilled carefully to precipitate and remove fractions with high melting points that would interfere with the pourability of salad dressings or other products containing the oils.

Tempering
Removing heat resulting from crystallization of fats and maintaining a selected temperature to promote the formation of stable, desirable crystals.

Fats that have been tempered can be stored with some variations in temperature, sometimes more than 25°C, and still retain their textural qualities.

The fat in chocolate needs to be tempered to help promote the formation of very stable crystals. Otherwise, the smaller crystals in the chocolate melt and then recrystallize in coarse β crystals, which appear as somewhat discolored, granular areas on the surface of chocolate that has been allowed to get a little warm or has been stored a long time. This unique and rather unattractive surface appearance is called **bloom** and definitely is to be avoided.

Bloom
Granular-appearing, discolored areas on the surface of chocolate; the result of melting of less stable crystals and recrystallization as β crystals on the surface.

Quality Determinations

Chromatographic Analyses.   The heterogeneity of lipids makes use of chromatographic analyses to determine the relative amounts of key components of a fat. Both gas–liquid chromatography and high-pressure liquid chromatography are appropriate and practical analytical tools. To volatilize the sample for gas–liquid chromatography, fatty acids commonly are converted to their methyl esters. With high-pressure liquid chromatography, even trace amounts of free fatty acids can be detected.

Iodine Number.   Fatty acids containing double bonds are able to take up iodine at the points of unsaturation. The weight of the iodine that can be held in this way indicates the amount of unsaturation in a fat and is referred to as the iodine number or iodine value.

Peroxide Value.   A related test measures the oxidation of potassium iodide in the presence of a fat to determine the peroxide value of the fat. This value indicates the deterioration of a fat by oxidative rancidity, as measured by the formation of peroxides.

Free Fatty Acid Content.   By titration of a fluid fat sample with a standard sodium hydroxide solution, the free fatty acid content of the fat can be determined. This value rises as hydrolytic rancidity develops in the fat during storage or use.

Standardized Testing.   Methods for testing fats and other lipids have been developed and reviewed extensively by several groups. The groups involved in setting the standards for the testing of lipids include the American Oil Chemists' Society (AOCS), the Association of Official Analytical Chemists (AOAC), the Codex Alimentarius Commission (CAC), and the International Union for Pure and Applied Chemistry (IUPAC).

CHEMICAL MODIFICATIONS

Hydrogenation

Hydrogenation is utilized in the manufacture of a wide range of fat products because this reaction alters the melting points of fatty acids by increasing their saturation with hydrogen. In hydrogenation reactions, a catalyst (commonly nickel) is present in conjunction with hydrogen gas and oil in a heat-controlled environment.

Hydrogenation
Addition of hydrogen to an unsaturated fatty acid in the presence of a catalyst to reduce the unsaturation of the molecule and raise the melting point.

Under these conditions, hydrogen atoms react with unsaturated fatty acids at the points of unsaturation, as shown below.

$$-\underset{\underset{H}{|}}{C}=\underset{\underset{H}{|}}{C}- \quad \xrightarrow[\text{Nickel}]{+H_2} \quad -\underset{\underset{H}{\overset{H}{|}}}{C}-\underset{\underset{H}{\overset{H}{|}}}{C}-$$

Hydrogenation occurs more readily on fatty acids with two or more double bonds than on those with only one. However, hydrogenation does occur on molecules with one double bond when most of the diene and polyene molecules have been modified to the corresponding monoene fatty acid.

Through the use of hydrogenation reactions, vegetable oils can be modified from liquids to solids, a change that makes these former oils very suitable for use as margarines and shortenings. This process also is used to modify peanut butter from its original state (in which it separates to a concentrated solid mass and a layer of oil) to a spread that remains homogeneous even during extended shelf storage.

One undesirable result of the hydrogenation process is that a few unsaturated fatty acids undergo isomerization, resulting in the formation of some double bonds in the *trans* configuration, rather than the *cis* form commonly found in nature. At the present time research is under way to clarify the health implications of isomerization to the *trans* form.

The possibly negative effects of *trans* fatty acids in the diet have spurred efforts to make more healthful spreads with reduced amounts of *trans* fatty acids. Chill fractionation in which the higher-melting *trans* fatty acids are removed is one viable approach. Consumers have been reducing their intake of hydrogenated vegetable oils since 1993 (Allison et al., 1999), which is an effective means of reducing *trans* fatty acid intake, too. Allison et al. (1999) estimated the mean intake of *trans* fatty acids by Americans daily was 5.3 grams, of which between 20 and 25 percent was naturally occurring *trans* fatty acids.

Inter- and Intraesterification

Interesterification
Treatment of a fat, usually lard, with sodium methoxide or another agent to split fatty acids from glycerol and then to reorganize them on glycerol to form different fat molecules with less tendency to form coarse crystals.

Randomized Interesterification
Interesterification accomplished using melted fat.

Directed Interesterification
Process of interesterification in which the fat is kept below its melting temperature.

Fatty acids can be removed from glycerol with the aid of metal salts and/or lipases. When this is done to oils or fats that are composed of quite an array of triglycerides with differing fatty acids, these fatty acids that have been freed can then be joined back onto glycerol to form new triglycerides. The catalyst used for this is usually sodium methoxide; the process is termed **interesterification.** This technique results in the formation of fats with altered characteristics, such as a higher melting point or a difference in crystallization tendencies. It is possible to use interesterification to produce margarines with a higher melting point and with good spreading characteristics while avoiding the *trans* fatty acids that are part of the product when hydrogenation is used to raise the melting point of vegetable oils. If the fat is melted for the interesterification process, all of the fat molecules are able to participate, and the procedure is termed ***randomized interesterification.*** When fat is kept below its melting point, only the lipid molecules that are in the fluid state are altered by the sodium methoxide. This type of reaction is called ***directed interesterification.*** Directed interesterification is useful when the goal of the manufacturer is to raise the melting point of the fat. Either method is very useful for improving the textural characteristics of a fat. In the United States, lard commonly undergoes interesterification in its processing for the market.

Fatty acids that have been removed from glycerol as a consequence of the presence of another substance such as sodium methoxide have the potential to recombine with this glycerol, thus maintaining the same fatty acids of the triglyceride, but in different positions on the glycerol. When this reorganization of the molecule results, the process is called *intraesterification.* Intraesterification, like interesterification, alters the textural characteristics of a fat by modifying the ease of crystallization and crystal aggregation.

FATS AND OILS IN THE MARKETPLACE

Sources

Today's marketplace provides a testimonial to the industriousness of "fat chemists" in recent years, as consumers and food manufacturers are confronted with a most impressive array of fats and oils from which to choose the product best suited to their specific food preparation problems. One choice is between animal fats and plant lipid products. Animal fats are confined primarily to butters and lards, but the additional choices among butters include salted or unsalted and whipped or unwhipped. The options in plant lipids range from fluid oils from various sources to solid fats, the result of chemical modification of the plant oils (see Figure 12.1).

The composition of fats varies with the animal or plant source (Figure 12.2). Generally, animal fats are higher in saturated fatty acids and lower in unsaturated fatty acids than plant lipid sources. In particular, plant sources as a group are higher in the polyunsaturates than are animal sources, although fish oils provide an exception to this generalization. Table 12.1 presents a comparison of the fatty acid composition and cholesterol content of selected animal and plant sources of lipids. Fats in the food supply that are obtained from animal sources include beef tallow and butterfat (milk fat) from cattle and lard from pigs. Plant sources include olives, palm berries and palm kernels, cottonseeds, soybeans, rapeseed (canola oil), corn, sunflower seeds, safflower seeds, coconuts, peanuts, cacao beans, walnuts, macadamia nuts, rice bran, and jojoba seeds (not presently approved for human food use in the United States).

Of nutritional interest is the fact that cholesterol occurs only in animal fats and never in plant lipids. Polyunsaturated fatty acids also are valued because of their potential role in reducing serum cholesterol levels. This is the reason that plant oils have become so prominent in the American diet. However, the high saturated fatty acid content of cocoa butter, coconut oil, and palm kernel oils (as much or even more saturated fatty acids than in animal fats) limits the nutritional merits of these specific plant oils and fats. Monounsaturated fatty acids may be significant in decreasing serum cholesterol. Olive oil is uniquely high in its content of monounsaturated fatty acids, although rapeseed (canola) oil is a very close second. In contrast, safflower oil is particularly rich in polyunsaturates.

Fish oils are gaining prominence as attention is being directed increasingly to the roles that certain foods may play in health beyond their being a source of nutrients. Omega-3 long-chain/polyunsaturated fatty acids (PUFA) include **docosahexanoic acid (DHA)** and **eicosapentanoic acid (EPA),** both of which are found in fish oils. DHA is a fatty acid containing 22 carbon atoms and 6 double bonds,

Intraesterification
Catalyzed reaction in which the fatty acids split from glycerol and rejoin in a different configuration, but with the same fatty acids being retained in the molecule.

Docosahexanoic Acid (DHA)
Omega-3 fatty acid containing 22 carbon atoms and six double bonds.

Eicosapentanoic Acid (EPA)
Omega-3 fatty acid containing 20 carbon atoms and five double bonds.

Figure 12.1   Assorted fats and oils that typify the wide variety of choices available in the retail market. Fats vary in their source, physical properties, and processing for the market. (Courtesy of Plycon Press.)

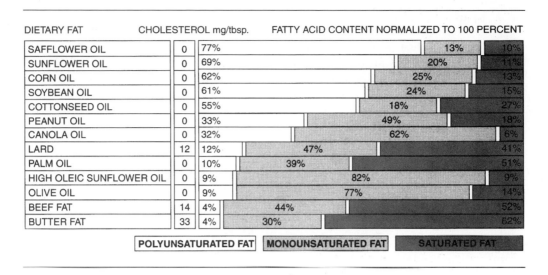

Figure 12.2 Fatty acid profiles of oils.

Table 12.1 Percent Fat, Fatty Acids, and Cholesterol in Selected Fats

Fat Source	Fat (%)	Fatty Acids (%)[a]			Cholesterol (mg/100 g)
		Saturated	Monounsaturated	Polyunsaturated	
Animal sources					
Beef tallow[a]	100	49.8	41.8	4.0	109
Butter	81	50.5	23.4	3.0	219
Lard	100	39.2	45.1	11.2	95
Plant sources					
Cocoa butter	100	59.7	32.9	3.0	0
Coconut oil	100	86.5	5.8	1.8	0
Corn oil	100	12.7	24.2	58.7	0
Cottonseed oil	100	25.9	17.8	51.9	0
Olive oil	100	13.5	73.7	8.4	0
Palm oil	100	49.3	37.0	9.3	0
Palm kernel oil	100	81.4	11.4	1.6	0
Peanut oil	100	16.9	46.2	32.0	0
Rapeseed oil[b]	100	5.0	68.1	22.5	0
Safflower oil	100	9.1	12.1	74.5	0
Sesame oil	100	14.2	39.7	41.7	0
Soybean oil	100	14.4	23.3	57.9	0
Sunflower oil	100	10.1	45.4	40.1	0
Margarine, stick					
Corn oil	80.5	13.2	45.8	18.0	0
Safflower, soybean	80.5	13.8	31.7	31.4	0
Soybean	80.5	16.7	39.3	20.9	0
Sunflower, soybean, cottonseed	80.5	11.9	28.5	36.6	0
Margarine, soft (tub)					
Corn oil	80.4	12.1	31.6	31.2	0
Safflower oil	80.4	9.2	23.2	44.5	0
Soybean oil	80.3	13.5	36.4	26.8	0
Sunflower, peanut oils	80.4	16.1	30.7	30.1	0

[a]For specific information on the content of saturated fatty acids (4–18 carbon atoms), monounsaturated fatty acids (16–22 carbon atoms), and polyunsaturated fatty acids (18–22 carbon atoms), refer to the source for this table.
[b]Erucic acid (22 carbon atoms, one double bond) content is 45% and higher.
Adapted from *Composition of Foods: Fats and Oils Raw, Processed, Prepared:* Consumer and Food Economics Institute. Agriculture Handbook No. 8-4. Science and Education Administration, U.S. Department of Agriculture: Washington, DC, 1979.

Omega-3 Fatty Acid
Polyunsaturated Fatty acid
with the first double bond
on the third carbon from
the methyl end of the molecule.

the first of which occurs at the third carbon from the methyl end (hence the designation as an **omega-3** long-chain polyunsaturated fatty acid). EPA has 20 carbon
atoms and 5 double bonds, beginning at the third carbon from the omega end of
the molecule. Their structures are:

Docosahexanoic Acid (DHA)

Eicosapentanoic Acid (EPA)

Food technologists considering ways of incorporating omega-3 fatty acids into
new products are confronted with a somewhat daunting challenge because of possible fishy flavors associated with the fish oils (Garcia, 1998). One approach with
good potential is the production of DHA by *Crypthecodinium cohnii,* a strain of
marine algae (Becker and Kyle, 1998). This source of DHA produces DHA that is
somewhat more resistant to developing off flavors from oxidation.

Oryzanols
Class of sterols in rice bran
oil of significance for antioxidant properties.

Tocotrienols
Class of sterols related to
vitamin E valued for an-
tioxidant properties; found
in rice bran and palm oils.

Stick Margarines
Spreads made by hydro-
genating plant oils and
adding water, milk solids,
flavoring, and coloring to
achieve a product similar
to butter.

Soft (Tub) Margarines
Spreads with melting
points lower than those of
stick margarines because of
a higher content of polyunsaturated fatty acids.

Diet Margarines
Spreads made from plant
oils that have been partially
hydrogenated and then
blended with more than
twice as much water as is
used in stick margarines.

Whipped Margarines
Stick margarines that have
been whipped mechani-
cally into fat foam; in-
creased volume results in
fewer calories per given
volume.

Products

Oils.   Various oil products are available to consumers and the food industry.
Peanut, corn, cottonseed, safflower, canola, sunflower, olive, and soybean oils are
the ones utilized most commonly, either as a single type of oil or as a blend of two
or more oils. Some special oils also can be found in some markets. These include
various nut oils such as macadamia nut, and also rice bran oil. Rice bran oil is of
some interest because of its content of two types of sterols (**oryzanols** and **tocotrienols**), which are being studied intensively for possible health benefits (Mc-
Caskill and Zhang, 1999). Oryzanols and tocotrienols are of significance for their
antioxidant properties.

Spreads.   Butter, the water-in-oil emulsion formed when milk fat is churned sufficiently to reverse the emulsion, was long the unchallenged fat of choice as a
spread on breads (see Table 14.3). However, technological advances in the ability
to hydrogenate plant oils led to the very successful invasion of margarines into the
former monopoly of butter for a spread. Present margarine products afford a
choice of regular or **stick margarine** (Figure 12.3), which has been engineered to
approximate butter in most characteristics; **soft or tub margarine,** which still can
be spread despite its higher content of polyunsaturates and resulting low melting
point; and **diet margarines,** which contain approximately half as much fat as
other margarines and more than twice as much water. **Whipped butter and margarine** are still other options. These products are made by whipping air into the
original spreads to increase volume and achieve a lighter, more airy texture and
fewer calories per a given volume.

Some margarines are made from a single oil source, such as corn oil margarines. One of the motivations for this is to appeal to consumers seeking margarines high in polyunsaturates as a possible aid in reducing their serum cholesterol. Many margarines are made by blending oil from several sources (Figure

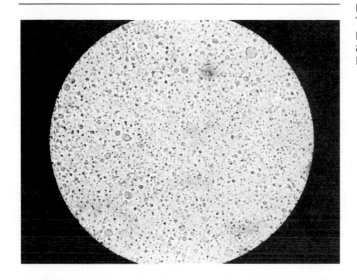

Figure 12.3   Microphotograph of margarine (X500). The droplets of water are seen as the dispersed phase of the emulsion; the crystals of fat and the oil are not clearly defined when seen under ordinary light. (Courtesy of C. W. Hoerr.)

12.4). Package ingredient labels reveal the oil content, at least in a general way. Actually, labels often indicate that one or more of the listed oils is used in the product. This allows manufacturers to change their formulations at various times, depending on the relative cost of the oils identified in the ingredient label.

Peanut butter and the various nut butters are other examples of spreads made utilizing plant oils. However, these differ from butter and margarine in that they contain not only oil, but also some protein and other components of the nuts, which are ground after shelling to make a paste.

Shortenings and Lard.   Shortenings and lard, like oils, are essentially all fat. However, they are solids with considerable plasticity (ability to be spread or whipped to a heavy fat foam). This plasticity is the result of the physical nature of these solid fats, which actually are composed of very large numbers of fat crystals

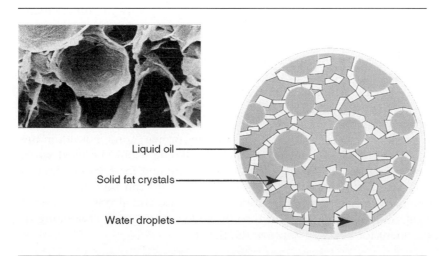

Liquid oil ————————

Solid fat crystals ————————

Water droplets ————————

Figure 12.4   Stabilizing an emulsion (margarine) by means of a network of fat crystals. (Courtesy of Unilever Research, Vlaardingen, The Netherlands.)

with oil interspersed throughout the system. Lard, the fat product rendered from pigs, naturally has a somewhat grainy texture because the fat molecules resulting from the rendering of lard have spatial configurations that associate readily into organized crystalline aggregates. Such a texture is not optimal for preparing fine-grained cakes. This shortcoming of lard has been ameliorated by using the process of interesterification in its manufacture. Other modifications, particularly in fatty acid composition, can be accomplished by altering the diet of the pigs and even by some genetic manipulations.

Shortenings are quite sophisticated products produced through the efforts of technology. The main part of their manufacturing is the hydrogenation of vegetable oils to achieve the desired consistency. In addition, mono- and diglycerides are added to improve the ability of the shortening to form an emulsion in batters and doughs. To simulate the advantages of butter as an ingredient in baked products, shortenings can now be purchased that have β-carotene added to achieve a yellow color and also butterlike flavoring compounds to enhance flavor, too.

Beef tallow is yet another solid fat that has some applications within the food industry. Tallow is rendered from cattle to yield a characteristically hard fat. Small flakes of tallow are added to some shortenings during their manufacturing to help ensure that the shortening will have fine, β' crystals. Tallow generally is not used as a single source of fat in the marketplace.

Substituting One Fat for Another.   Sometimes necessity or health reasons require that a fat or oil in a recipe or formula be replaced with another fat or oil. Any substitution will influence the outcome to some extent even when the quantity has been substituted appropriately. The differences that can be noted are due to the difference in the composition of the fats. Each type of fat has its unique properties as a consequence of the actual fatty acid composition and possibly the amount of water in each fat. Ideally, the type of fat used for a particular product should be the kind that optimizes the desired characteristics. However, that choice is not always possible. Butter may need to be replaced with another type of fat. The problem becomes determining how much of this fat should be used to substitute for the butter. It is important to remember that butter is only about 80 percent fat, and it has a water content of about 16.5 percent. Since stick margarines are similar in composition, an equal amount of margarine can be substituted for butter. However, subtle differences in flavor and texture can be noted by very careful comparison. Tub margarines have the same ratio of fat and water as is found in stick margarines and butter. This suggests that equal amounts of tub margarine could be substituted for either stick margarine or butter. This is true on the basis of tenderness, but the lower melting point of the tub margarines causes cookies to spread far more than is the case when stick margarine or butter is used. Diet margarine, because of its very high water content and reduced amount of fat, presents particular challenges in substitutions.

Shortening and lard can be used in place of butter or margarine, but not in the same quantities. Only about 90 percent as much shortening should be used when shortening is replacing butter. This amount ($\frac{7}{8}$ cup shortening for 1 cup of butter) compensates for the fact that shortening is entirely fat. Lard can be substituted in the same amount as the value given for shortening because lard also is 100 percent fat. A very small amount of salt may need to be added when using shortening or lard as a replacement for butter to improve the flavor.

Oil, like shortening and lard, is 100 percent fat. For an amount of fat that equals that of butter, the same substitution values as are suggested for shortening and lard are appropriate. However, some products can be made with considerably reduced fat levels when oil is substituted for butter. The exact amount to use needs to be determined experimentally for various products because of the difference in mouthfeel and spreading characteristics that oil brings to the different products.

FUNCTIONAL ROLES OF FAT

Color

Butter contributes a yellow to creamy color to products when it is the fat that is used. The importance of this pleasing color is evidenced by the fact that margarines all are colored to simulate the color of butter. Even some vegetable shortenings now have beta-carotene added to provide the desired yellow color.

Flavor

Fats contribute a richness of flavor when used in a variety of food products. In addition, unique flavor qualities are provided by specific fats. Butter, for example, has a complex flavor profile contributed by butyric and other fatty acids, as well as by lactones, aldehydes, and ketones. The flavor of butter is so popular that most margarines and some shortenings have synthetic butter flavoring added to them to simulate the natural flavor of butter. Olive oil and lard are examples of other types of fats that contain distinctive flavor components. Most other fats have a pleasing richness of flavor, yet very limited unique overtones in their flavor profiles.

Texture

Textural characteristics are influenced by fats in several different ways, depending on the type of food being considered. In pastry, the distribution of fat in small pieces contributes flakiness to the baked product. Butter or shortening can be creamed with sugar to obtain a very fine cell structure of great uniformity in a shortened cake. In this case, the fat is carved out by the sharp sugar crystals to create numerous tiny spaces where steam and carbon dioxide collect and expand during baking to produce a fine-textured cake. Fat in a bread dough keeps the crumb and crust soft in comparison with a similar bread made without any fat.

Tenderness

Although tenderness actually is an aspect of textural properties, fat is so vitally important in baked products that it is appropriate to consider this function of fat separately. The unique composition of each type of fat that might be used in preparing a baked product will determine the specific capability that a particular fat may have in tenderizing. Different qualities are desired for particular baked products; selection of the best fat for a specific application requires consideration of several qualities. One of the most important qualities is the ability of a fat to aid in creating a tender baked product. The ability of various fats and oils to tenderize a product is determined by their ability to interfere with the development of gluten, the structural protein complex in wheat flour products. Formation of the gluten complex in a batter or dough requires water, wheat flour, and manipulation of these two key ingredients. When flour proteins become moistened with water and are stirred or beaten, the gluten complex begins to develop, resulting ultimately in a somewhat elastic network which, when placed in the oven and baked, stretches and then is set permanently into the structure of the baked product.

One of the ways that fats and oils interfere with gluten development is by physically preventing or inhibiting contact between water and flour proteins. This obstruction is accomplished by mixing the fat or oil with the flour so that the lipid gradually coats the surface of the gluten complex that is starting to form. Water is unable to penetrate a layer of lipid because lipids are hydrophobic and repel water. A soft fat or an oil can physically be spread over a much larger surface area than can a firm fat. Consequently, such lipids are very effective tenderizing agents.

A closer look at the chemical structures of the fatty acids that may be found in fats helps to clarify the mechanism by which fats are able to cover surface area and partially block water from gluten. The ability of a lipid to accomplish this tenderizing action is called its ***shortening power.*** Much of the fatty acid molecule is a carbon chain to which hydrogen is attached. Saturated carbon chains are hydrophobic and are repelled by water. However, the double bonds in unsaturated fatty acids are hydrophilic and have an attraction for water. Furthermore, the carboxyl group of free fatty acids is attracted to water. In essence, the majority of the molecule does not attract water, but the double bonds and carboxyl group are drawn toward water. This contradictory behavior is theorized to cause unsaturated fatty acid molecules to align themselves along the interface and block the passage of water by the presence of the carbon chains.

The amount of surface area covered by a single molecule is determined by the amount of unsaturation in the fatty acid. A fatty acid with a single double bond is able to cover more surface than can a saturated fatty acid, but is no more effective than a fatty acid with two double bonds. However, a fatty acid with three double bonds is able to cover more surface area than one with only one or two double bonds. Apparently, the chain length between the first and third double bond in a fatty acid with three double bonds is sufficiently long to enable both of these double bonds to reach the interface, as shown in the diagram (see Figure 12.5).

In addition to the ability of fat molecules with unsaturation to collect at the interface and block some of the water from the gluten, unsaturation also influences the physical nature of the fat. As noted earlier, lipids with a high degree of unsaturation are fluid oils at mixing temperatures and, therefore, are able to flow readily throughout any batter or dough in which they are included. In contrast, fats with more saturated fatty acids and less unsaturation are solids, which restricts their movement throughout the mixing process and limits their ability to coat the gluten. Solid fats do vary considerably in their spreadability because of differences in melting points and variations in the extent of saturation. Solid fats that are soft enough to be manipulated and spread quite easily are said to be plastic. Plastic fats have appreciably more shortening ability than do those that are quite hard and difficult to spread. The hard fats are high in saturated fatty acids; consequently, they have high melting points and only a moderate amount of shortening power. This physical nature and the fact that the fatty acid molecules are primarily hydrophobic mean that only a limited amount of surface area is covered by the fat when it is used in mixing batters and doughs. Therefore, such fats have limited shortening power.

Shortening Power
Ability of a fat to cover a large surface area to minimize the contact between water and gluten during the mixing of batters and doughs.

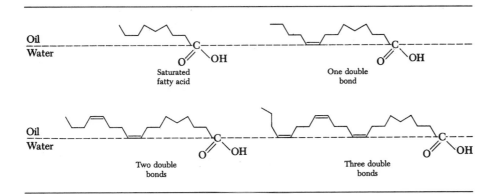

Figure 12.5 Schematics depicting the shortening power of fatty acids according to their composition (number of double bonds). Note that fatty acids with one or two double bonds are more effective in covering surface area than is a saturated fatty acid, but far more area is covered by fatty acids with three double bonds.

Shortened cakes are made with a solid fat as one of the major ingredients. In these cakes, the fat is incorporated as a heavy foam, the result of creaming the fat and sugar together. For creaming to be effective, the fat needs to be able to retain the air pockets that form. Obviously, oils do not meet this criterion. Shortenings have been tailored to meet this requirement, for they have an excellent plastic range. At room temperature, shortenings can be creamed into comparatively light fat–sugar mixtures, entrapping air. Butter and margarines also can be creamed, but with more difficulty than is encountered in creaming shortenings. Butter is quite hard and almost brittle at refrigerator temperatures, yet it can become so soft that it is almost fluid when it is creamed with sugar on a warm day. Margarine has a broader temperature range of plasticity than does butter. This makes it easier to cream margarine than butter without causing the fat to become so fluid that the emulsion in the batter breaks during later mixing. Broken emulsions should be avoided in cake batters; a stable emulsion helps to promote the desired fine cell size desired in shortened cakes. Lard, because of its unique crystallinity, tends to clump as it is being creamed into a batter. This quality is better suited to use in pastries than in cakes.

Chiffon cakes rely on an egg white foam for their cell structure because they are made with oil rather than a solid fat. This emphasizes the need for some form of foam as the basis for the cells and illustrates the inability of oil to perform this role. However, the fluidity of the oil promotes tenderness in the cake. This tenderness is a definite contrast to the textural characteristics of sponge and angel cakes, neither of which contains any fat.

Fat is a major ingredient in pastry, often being included in weights that are about half of the weight of the flour. However, the cutting in of the fat until it is in moderately coarse particles results in very inefficient use as a tenderizing ingredient. All of the fat on the interior of each piece is unavailable to interfere with gluten development. This explains why pastry often is fairly tough despite the large amount of fat it contains.

Flakiness is a highly desirable textural characteristic in pastry. When fat is left in pieces in a pastry dough, it melts during the baking period and flows, leaving a hole where steam collects and pushes upward against the upper surface of the resulting cell. The gluten in the pastry is denatured during baking, and the cell is locked into the extended position. This results in a flaky pastry. Solid fats facilitate formation of a flaky pastry, but the flow properties of oil interfere with formation of the cell pockets needed for flakiness.

Quick breads and most yeast breads contain fat. Biscuits utilize a hard fat so that the fat can be cut into pieces in a fashion similar to the preparation of pastry. This promotes flakiness in biscuits. In muffins and yeast breads, the fat is melted to obtain maximum tenderizing from the fat that is used. Flakiness is not a possibility in breads and muffins when the fat is in the liquid state when incorporated into the mixture. The fat used in breads does contribute some flavor, tenderness, and color, but it is much less important in breads than in cakes, which contain a far higher proportion of fat than is found in breads.

From the preceding discussion, it is evident that oils are particularly effective tenderizing agents and that comparatively soft shortenings and lards are appropriate to use in making tender batter and dough products. Margarines and butters are other possible choices, but it is important to recognize that both of these types of spreadable fats are not pure fat. In fact, they are about 16 percent water and 80 percent fat. Their substitution in a recipe specifying shortening means that too little fat and too much water are being used unless adjustments are made. Unless more butter or margarine and less liquid are incorporated, the baked product will be less tender than anticipated.

Emulsification

Virtually all food systems have an aqueous liquid of some type in their formula, and many also contain fats or oils. The result is that these ingredients may be uniformly dispersed as an emulsion (see Chapter 6) or curdled. For optimal textural qualities, stable emulsions are desired. In most food systems, the type of emulsion formed is an oil-in-water emulsion, in which the oil droplets are dispersed in the aqueous phase. An emulsifying agent of some type is needed to facilitate the formation of stable emulsions.

Shortenings are formulated today with added mono- and diglycerides so that the fat and milk in cake batters are emulsified, resulting in a fine-textured cake. These mono- and diglycerides are effective emulsifiers because they have one or two hydroxyl groups in place of one or two fatty acids, leaving at least one fatty acid carbon chain, which is largely hydrophobic. The hydroxyl groups draw the molecule toward the aqueous phase. The result is that a monomolecular layer of mono- and diglycerides tends to collect around the surface of the fat droplets, serving as a protective coating to keep the fat suspended in the liquid batter (see Figure 12.6).

Emulsifying agents may be provided by other ingredients, too. The best of the emulsifying agents available in the home is the lecithin in egg yolks. Lecithin is a phospholipid that is unusually effective in covering the surfaces of droplets in an emulsion to keep them from coalescing.

Even in the presence of emulsifying agents, some oil-in-water emulsions in foods break because of excessive evaporation of water. This is seen as a particular problem in thick sauces for soufflés, especially in chocolate and cheese soufflés which contain fat from the flavoring ingredients, as well as the fat in the sauce. A similar problem may be found in some gravies. In such instances, the emulsion can

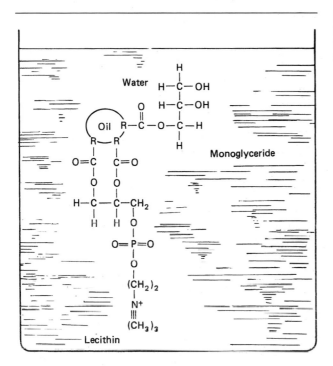

Figure 12.6 Orientation of monoglyceride and lecithin molecules at the interface between water and oil on the droplets to provide a protective layer that stabilizes the emulsion by interfering with the union of oil spheres.

be reestablished by replacing the water lost through evaporation during an extended heating and/or holding period. A broken emulsion vividly reinforces the fact that fats and oils do not evaporate when they are heated in normal cookery procedures.

Cooking Medium

Fats and oils are used as a cooking medium because of their ability to be heated to temperatures well above the boiling temperature of water. Such high temperatures not only cook foods more quickly than can be done in water, but they also cause changes in texture, flavor, and color that are enjoyed by many people. The actual characteristics of foods fried in fats are influenced by the type of fat selected for the frying medium.

Butter and margarines are popular because of their pleasing flavor and color and occasionally are used in shallow frying because of these qualities. Unfortunately, they deteriorate quite rapidly at the high temperatures used in frying. Part of the problem is that the water in these fats causes excessive splattering and increased aeration of the fat during frying. This hastens the development of rancidity if these fats were to be stored for later reuse. To compound the problem, the milk solids they contain begin to brown quickly and soon burn during the frying period.

Shortenings with added mono- and diglycerides are not well suited to frying. These molecules lose their fatty acids rather quickly, leaving free glycerol. In very short order, the glycerol begins to break down to form acrolein, and the smoke point rapidly drops. When the fat is smoking at frying temperatures, the acrolein not only irritates the eyes of the chef, but also begins to be detectable in the flavor of the food.

For these reasons, oils usually are the type of lipid selected for frying foods, although olive oil is not an acceptable choice because of its low smoke point. The smoke points of good-quality oils generally are well above frying temperatures; however, the water from food being fried in oils, the splattering that occurs when foods are introduced into the hot oil, and the extended use of the oil all combine to reduce the smoke point gradually until it drops to the point where the oil is smoking at frying temperatures. The flavor changes and the irritation from the acrolein formed at this stage make continued use of the oil undesirable.

The process of cooking food in deep fat is quite complex when studied from the perspectives of chemistry and physics. Surprisingly, deep-fat frying can be viewed as a dehydrating process, for the intense heat of the fat on the surface of a food such as a french fry evaporates water quickly into the cooking medium. This water loss causes mass transfer to occur in the french fry; this mass transfer of water from the central portion toward the surfaces to replace the lost water is of considerable importance, for soluble materials are carried with the water toward the surface, and some eventually escape into the fat.

Loss of water from the food into the hot frying oil helps to avoid burning on the surface of the food because the water carries thermal energy from the food surface. Blumenthal (1991) reported that the temperature on the surface of a frying food is about 100°C despite the fact that the oil itself may be 180°C. This temperature gradient is due in large measure to the heat of vaporization that is required for converting the escaping water to steam.

Water beneath the surface of a french fry plays a key role in conducting heat into the interior of the piece so that gelatinization of the starch can occur. Enough heat must reach the starch to gelatinize it, but not so much that water is drawn back out of the starch gel. This situation leaves a rather spongy texture in the french fry. If the fat is much too hot, cross linkages cause hardening of the surface of the fry and considerable polymerization of the fatty acids in the oil.

Fat absorption during frying is a matter of interest both from the perspective of food quality and of health. For both of these reasons, as little fat as possible should be absorbed. Maintenance of a frying temperature of at least 175°C and preferably 190–195°C is a very important factor in minimizing fat absorption during frying. The upper part of this range is more effective than 175°C in keeping fat absorption as low as possible. At temperatures above 195°C, foods tend to brown too much before they are heated adequately in the center.

The key to frying is to heat the fat to the correct temperature before adding food and then cooking only a small amount of food at a time. Otherwise, the temperature of the fat drops too much, and the food is fried at a lower temperature than intended. The result is a rather greasy product because of the increased absorption of fat. Use of a fresh oil rather than a frying oil that has begun to deteriorate and become somewhat more viscous from previous use is another means of reducing the amount of oil absorbed (and adsorbed) during frying.

The formulation of a batter or dough being fried has an effect on fat absorption. Increasing levels of sugar and fat in the mixture result in more fat absorption than will occur in less sweet and/or rich batters and doughs. All-purpose and bread flours in batters and doughs absorb less fat during frying than does cake flour.

FAT REPLACEMENTS

One of the most active areas of food research recently has been the development of fat replacements that can mimic the desired qualities contributed by fat without contributing such a large number of calories. Various approaches to developing replacement products have been used. These range from carbohydrate-based products to protein-based replacements and even lipid-based ingredients; caloric contributions differ with the specific replacement. Their suitability in food products differs because of the physical properties inherent in the individual replacement products.

Protein-Based Replacement

Simplesse, a product made by Monsanto Company, has been used as a fat replacement in a frozen dessert. This substitute is made of milk proteins and egg white in very small particulates (0.1–0.3 microns, which is one-tenth the size of powdered sugar) that are able to convey the mouthfeel of fat because of the way the particles move as the product is eaten. Simplesse, because of its protein content, is not suited for use in products requiring heat. Approval by the Food and Drug Administration was comparatively simple because Simplesse is made of proteins from food and water (in a ratio of 1 part protein to 2 parts water), all of which are considered to be safe. The high percentage of water means that Simplesse provides 1.3 calories per gram, which is a dramatic improvement over 9 calories from the fat that would have been needed to provide the smooth texture needed in a quality ice cream.

Carbohydrate-Based Replacements

N-Lite products are fat substitutes based on starch and containing other natural food materials, including gums and nonfat dried milk. National Starch and Chemical Company is the developer and producer of this line of fat substitutes, which includes five different patterns for use in diverse types of foods.

Stellar is another starch-based fat substitute. This product, made by A.E. Staley Manufacturing Company, is a product made from cornstarch. Present applications include use in cheese spreads and frostings. Slendid, a fat substitute made by Hercules, Incorporated, is yet another product based on carbohydrate. However, the carbohydrate utilized for Slendid is pectin.

Oatrim is a fat substitute made from oats by a process patented by the U.S. Department of Agriculture. This fat substitute is made using alpha-amylase to catalyze the formation of maltodextrins from amylose and amylopectin in oat flour. Beta-glucan, also present in oatrim, is the main soluble in oats. When oatrim is heated, the gel it forms provides less than 1 calorie per gram. Probable uses for oatrim include milk-containing beverages, salad dressings, meats, cheese spreads, and high-fiber breads. Rice*Trin 3 Complete is a similar product derived from rice.

Avicel® cellulose gel is a microcrystalline carbohydrate derivative that can be used as a fat substitute in salad dressings. Other fat substitutes are made using cellulose gel in combination with guar gum or with maltodextrins and xanthan gum.

Polydextrose is a starch polymer plus a little sorbitol and citric acid. It is used as a bulking agent, texturizer, and humectant in a range of products including salad dressings, puddings, candies, and other products where it can replace some of the sugar as well as the fat. Although polydextrose is not well utilized in the body, it does provide about 1 kcal per gram. Its somewhat limited digestibility contributes to its laxative effect when consumed at levels above 90 grams per day.

Modified food starches made from various plant sources are other carbohydrate-based fat replacements. The sources for these starches include corn and potato. Paselli SA2 is a potato starch maltodextrin that has many applications in dips, bakery products, dressings, ice creams, and fillings.

Fat-based Replacements

Surprisingly, fat-based products have been developed for use as replacements for the usual fats and oils. Salatrim is an example of this approach. Marketed under the name Benefat®, Salatrim actually is a family of structured triglycerides which result from interesterification of lipids with long chain and medium chain (6 to 12 carbons). The introduction of acids with only two carbon atoms on one or two of the possible binding sites on glycerol impacts how readily the body utilizes Salatrim. The result is that Salatrim contributes 5 kcal/g.

Another structured triglyceride, caprenin, uses capric and caprylic acids (10 and 8 carbon fatty acids, respectively) in combination with behenic acid, a saturated fatty acid with 22 carbon atoms. The source of the capric and caprylic acids in caprenin is coconut and palm kernel oil. Behenin, the saturated very-long-chain fatty acid, is available from peanuts, fish oils, and hydrogenated rapeseed oil, and the hydrogenated rapeseed oil is the chosen source for manufacturing caprenin. Behenic acid is absorbed inefficiently in the small intestine, which means that much of it is excreted. The medium chain acids are metabolized to a limited extent. The net result is that caprenin provides only about 5 calories per gram, rather than the usual 9 calories. This Procter and Gamble product is being used in chocolate coatings for candy and doubtless will find numerous other applications in the future.

The structure of caprenin is:

caprenin

Olestra is a prominent fat replacement that is a bit of a hybrid between a carbohydrate and a fat. It is actually a compound classified as a sucrose polyester. This esterification between the hydroxyl groups on six or eight of the carbon atoms in sucrose and the corresponding number of medium chain (8 to 12 carbon atoms) fatty acids results in quite a bulky molecule that can be used as a fat replacement.

Development by Procter and Gamble and the approval process required 25 years. In 1996, Olestra was finally approved by the FDA. Although sucrose polyester is comprised of digestible carbohydrate and metabolizable fatty acids, this compound cannot be digested and, therefore, cannot be absorbed. Consequently, Olestra does not provide calories to the body. High intakes of sucrose polyester have been shown to cause diarrhea and flatulence, as well as possibly some other symptoms.

SUMMARY

Fats undergo numerous processing steps, including extraction, refining, crystallization, and quality checks before they are ready for the marketplace. Chemical modifications that may be a part of their production include hydrogenation, interesterification, and intraesterification. The large array of fats and oils in the market are derived from animal, marine, and plant sources and are transformed into the diverse products valued in food preparation.

Among the functional roles of fat are contributing color, flavor, texture, tenderness, emulsification, and a cooking medium.

Fat replacements are being used widely in commercial food products to reduce calories and/or enhance health. These replacements may be protein-based, carbohydrate-based, or fat-based.

STUDY QUESTIONS

1. Explain the winterizing of oils. Why is this an important step in processing salad oils?

2. What is the purpose of tempering a fat? How is this accomplished?

3. Describe the processes of (a) hydrogenation and (b) interesterification.

4. Why may interesterification be preferred to hydrogenation in the manufacturing of margarine?

5. Name and write the chemical structures of two Ω-3 fatty acids.

6. Why may oryzanols and tocotrienols be of potential nutritional interest? Identify a food source of these compounds.

7. What is a possible mechanism for a fat or oil in tenderizing a baked product?

8. What can be done to minimize the absorption of fat in frying foods?

9. Identify an example of each of the following types of fat replacements: protein-based, carbohydrate-based, and fat-based.

BIBLIOGRAPHY

Allison, D. B., et al. 1999. "Estimated intakes of trans fatty and other fatty acids in the U.S. population." *J. Am. Diet. Assoc. 99* (2): 166.

American Dietetic Association. 1991. "Position of the American Dietetic Association: Fat replacements." *J. Am. Diet. Assoc. 91* (10): 1285.

Anonymous. 1991. "USDA's Oatrim replaces fat in many food products." *Food Technol. 44* (10): 100.

Anonymous. 1991. "Rice-derived ingredient produces fatty texture and mouthfeel for use in low-fat applications." *Food Technol. 45* (8): 264.

Anonymous. 1990. "Fat substitute update." *Food Technol. 44* (3): 92.

Baldwin, E. A., et al. 1997. "Use of lipids in coatings for food products." *Food Technol. 51* (6): 56.

Becker, C. C. and Kyle, D. J. 1998. "Developing functional foods containing algal docoshexanoic acid." *Food Technol. 52* (7): 68.

Bell, S. J., et al. 1997. "The new dietary fats in health and disease." *J. Am. Diet. Assoc. 97* (3): 280.

Blumenthal, M. M. 1991. "New look at the chemistry and physics of deep-fat frying." *Food Technol. 45* (2): 68.

Boyle, E. 1997. "Monoglycerides in food systems: Current and future uses. *Food Technol. 51* (8): 52.

Clydesdale, F. 1997. "Olestra: The approval process in letter and spirit." *Food Technol. 51* (2): 104.

Coenen, J. W. 1976. "Hydrogenation of edible oils." *J. Amer. Oil Chem. Soc. 53:* 382.

Decker, E. A. and Xu, Z. 1998. "Minimizing rancidity in muscle foods." *Food Technol. 52* (10): 54.

deRoos, K. B. 1997. "How lipids influence food flavor." *Food Technol. 51* (1): 60.

Dreher, M., et al. 1998. "Salatrim: Triglyceride-based fat replacer." *Nutr. Today 33* (4): 164.

Dziezak, J. D. 1989. "Fats, oils, and fat substitutes." *Food Technol. 43* (7): 66.

Eydt, A. J. 1994. "Formulating reduced-fat foods with polyglycerol ester emulsifiers." *Food Technol. 48* (1): 82.

Garcia, D. J. 1998. "Omega-3 long-chain PUFA neutraceuticals." *Food Technol. 52* (6): 44.

Giese, J. 1996. "Fats and fat replacers: Balancing the health benefits." *Food Technol. 50 (9): 76.*

Glicksman, M. 1991. "Hydrocolloids and the search for the 'oily grail.'" *Food Technol. 45* (10): 94.

Haighton, A. J. 1976. "Blending, chilling, and tempering of margarines and shortenings." *J. Amer. Oil Chem. Soc. 53:* 397.

Hamilton, R. J. and Russell, J. B., eds. 1986. *Analysis of Oils and Fats.* Elsevier: New York.

Harrigan, K. A. and Breene, W. M. 1989. "Fat substitutes: sucrose esters and Simplesse." *Cereal Foods World 34:* 261.

Haumann, B. F. 1984. "Canola." *J. Amer. Oil Chem. Soc. 62:* 463.

Haumann, B. F. 1985. "Corn oil." *J. Amer. Oil Chem. Soc. 62:* 1524.

Hernandez, E. and Lucas, E. W. 1997. "Trends in transesterification of cottonseed oil." *Food Technol. 51* (5): 72.

Hippleheuser, A. L., Landberg, L. A., and Turnak, F. L. 1995. "System approach to formulating a low-fat muffin." *Food Technol. 49* (3): 92.

Husted, H. H. 1976. "Interesterification of edible oils." *J. Amer. Oil Chem. Soc. 53:* 390.

Inglett, G. E. and Grissmore, S. B. 1991. "Maltodextrin fat substitute lowers cholesterol." *Food Technol. 45* (6): 104.

Izzo, M., Stahl, C., and Tuazon, M. 1995. "Using cellulose gel and carrageenan to lower fat and calories in confections." *Food Technol. 49* (7): 45.

Kennedy, J. P. 1991. "Structured lipids: fats of the future." *Food Technol. 45* (11): 76.

Kheiri, M. S. 1985. "Present and prospective development in the palm oil processing industry." *J. Amer. Oil Chem. Soc. 62:* 210.

Kilara, A. 1985. "Enzyme-modified lipid food ingredients," *Process Biochem. 20* (27): 35.

Kinsella, J. E. 1986. "Food components with potential therapeutic benefits: n-3 polyunsaturated fatty acids of fish oils." *Food Technol. 40* (2): 89.

Kreulen, H. P. 1976. "Fractionation and winterization of edible fats and oils." *J. Amer. Oil Chem. Soc. 53:* 393.

Liu, K. S. and Brown, E. A. 1996. "Enhancing vegetable oil quality through plant breeding and genetic engineering." *Food Technol. 50* (11): 67.

Marangoni, A. G. and Hartel, R. W. 1998. "Visualization and structural analysis of fat crystal networks." *Food Technol. 52* (9): 46.

Matthews, D. M. and Kennedy, J. P. 1990. "Structured lipids." *Food Technol. 44* (6): 127.

McCaskill, D. R. and Zhang, F. 1999. Use of rice bran oil in foods. *Food Technol. 53* (2): 50.

McGlone, C., et al. 1985. "Coconut oil extraction by a new enzymatic process." *J. Food Sci. 51* (3): 695.

McNutt, K. 1997. What's bothering Olestra opponents? *Nutr. Today 32* (1): 41.

Megremis, C. J. 1991. "Medium-chain triglycerides: nonconventional fat." *Food Technol. 45* (2): 108.

Orthoefer, F. T. 1996. "Rice bran oil: Healthy lipid source." *Food Technol. 50* (12): 62.

Penichter, K. A. and McGinley, E. J. 1991. "Cellulose gel for fat-free food applications." *Food Technol. 45* (6): 105.

Peters, J. C., et al. 1991. "Caprenin 3: absorption and caloric value in adult humans." *J. Am. Coll. Toxicol. 10:* 357.

Prichett, W. 1977. "Margarine." In *Elements of Food Technology.* Desrosier, N. W., ed. AVI Publishing: Westport, CT, p. 229.

Puri, P. S. 1980. "Winterization of oils and fats." *J. Amer. Oil Chem. Soc. 57:* 848A.

Puri, P. S. 1980. "Hydrogenation of oils and fats." *J. Amer. Oil Chem. Soc. 57:* 850A.

Roth, H. and Rock, S. P. 1972. "Chemistry and technology of frying fats. 2. Technology. *Bakers Digest 46* (5): 38.

Saguy, I. S. and Pinthus, E. J. 1995. "Oil uptake during deep-fat frying: factors and mechanism." *Food Technol. 49* (4): 142.

Slover, H. T., et al. 1985. "Lipids in margarines and margarine-like foods." *J. Amer. Oil Chem. Soc. 62:* 775.

Stern, S. and Roth, H. 1959. Properties of frying fat related to fat absorption in doughnut frying. *Cereal Sci. Today 4:* 176.

Stevenson, S. G., et al. 1984. "Quality control in use of deep frying oils." *J. Amer. Oil Chem. Soc. 61:* 1102.

Stillings, B. R. 1994. "Trends in foods." *Nutrition Today 29* (5): 6.

Szuhaj, B. F. and List, G. R. eds. 1985. *Lecithins.* American Oil Chemists' Society: Champaign, IL.

Toma, R. B., Curtis, D. J., and Sobotor, C. 1988. "Sucrose polyester: its metabolic role and possible future applications." *Food Technol. 42* (1): 93.

Waltking, A. E., et al. 1975. "Chemical analysis of polymerization products in abused fats and oils." *J. Amer. Oil Chem. Soc. 52:* 96.

Warner, K., et al. 1986. "Storage stability of soybean oil-based salad dressings." *J. Food Sci. 51* (3): 703.

Young, V. 1980. "Processing of oils and fats." In *Fats and Oils: Chemistry and Technology.* Hamilton, R. J., et al., eds. Applied Science Publishers: London, p. 692.

Zapsalis, C. and Beck, R. A. 1985. *Food Chemistry and Nutritional Biochemistry.* Wiley: New York.

5

Proteins

CHAPTER 13

Overview of Proteins

Proteins are complex in their composition and in their behavior in food products. Careful attention needs to be paid to the preparation of protein-rich foods because the quality of the final product is influenced to a very large degree by the treatment of the protein. The proteins in food are unforgiving of abuse during preparation; heating for too long a total time or heating to too high a temperature can cause some highly detrimental changes in the proteins of a food. The significance of the heat treatment will become apparent as the structure and behavior of proteins are presented. The importance of pH in dealing with protein-rich foods also will become evident in the succeeding chapters.

COMPOSITION

Proteins are molecules composed of many **amino acids** joined together by peptide linkages. A protein may contain several hundred amino acid moieties linked together into a very complex molecule. Amino acids are organic substances containing two characteristic functional groups: the amino ($-NH_2$) group and the carboxyl ($-COOH$) group. The amino and the acid groups and various organic components are attached to a single carbon (the α carbon). These various organic components (designated as R groups) range from the single hydrogen atom of glycine to dual-ring structures such as that in tryptophan. The formulas for the amino acids of importance in foods, all of which are L-amino acids, are provided in Table 13.1.

The **peptide linkage** is a covalent bond formed between the nitrogen of one amino acid and the carbon of the **carboxyl group** of another amino acid; a molecule of water is eliminated in the reaction:

Amino Acids
Organic compounds containing an amino ($-NH_2$) group and an organic acid ($-COOH$) group.

Peptide Linkage
Linkage from the nitrogen of one amino acid to the carbon of the carboxyl group of another amino acid:

Carboxyl Group
Organic acid group:

Table 13.1   Amino Acids in Foods

Name	Formula	Isoelectric Point	Type
Alanine		6.0	Neutral—aliphatic
Glycine		6.0	Neutral—aliphatic
Isoleucine*		6.0	Neutral—aliphatic
Leucine*		6.0	Neutral—aliphatic
Valine*		6.0	Neutral—aliphatic
Serine		5.7	Neutral—hydroxy
Threonine*		6.2	Neutral—hydroxy
Cysteine		5.1	Neutral—sulfur-containing
Cystine		4.6	Neutral—sulfur-containing
Methionine*		5.7	Neutral—sulfur-containing
Asparagine		5.4	Neutral—amide
Glutamine		5.7	Neutral—amide

(continued)

Table 13.1 *(continued)*

Name	Formula	Isoelectric Point	Type
Phenylalanine*		5.5	Neutral—aromatic
Tryptophan*		5.9	Neutral—aromatic
Tyrosine		5.7	Neutral—aromatic
Aspartic acid		2.8	Acidic
Glutamic acid		3.2	Acidic
Arginine		11.2	Basic
Histidine*		7.6	Basic
Lysine*		9.7	Basic
Hydroxyproline		5.8	Imino acid
Proline		6.3	Imino acid

*Essential amino acid.

Peptide linkage

Amino acid + Amino Acid → Dipeptide

Proteins are very large molecules containing 100 or more amino acid residues, which are linked together covalently by peptide bonds. The net result of this arrangement is that a backbone chain with a repeating pattern (–N–C–C–N–C–C–, etc.) is formed, and the *R* group and the = O extend outward from this backbone. This level of protein organization is viewed as the rudimentary molecule and is termed the *primary structure of proteins,* as shown:

primary structure of protein

Primary Structure
Covalently bonded backbone chain of a protein: –C–C–N–C–C–N–C–C–N–.

Secondary Structure
Typically the α-helical configuration of the backbone chain of many proteins and held by secondary bonding forces, notably hydrogen bonds; also may be in other forms (e.g., β-pleated sheet).

Hydrogen Bond
Secondary bond formed between a hydrogen atom (covalently linked to an electronegative atom such as nitrogen) and an electronegative atom (such as oxygen in the carbonyl group of a protein).

Tertiary Structure
Distorted convolutions of the helical configuration of a protein; the form in which many proteins occur in nature and which is held by secondary bonding forces.

The **primary structure** is the foundation of the protein molecule, but the extended linear molecule is stressed somewhat. The energy level required to maintain the extended primary structure of a protein can be reduced if the molecules are coiled, as is the configuration of many protein molecules at the **secondary** level. In this coiled arrangement, called an α-helix, the long chain of the primary structure is formed by **hydrogen bonds** into a right-handed, springlike configuration (Figure 13.1) with a comparatively low energy state. There are 3.7 amino acid residues in each turn of the helix, the turn being determined by the hydrogen bonding between the nitrogen (–NH) and the carbonyl (–C = O) of the residues above or below each other in the helical form.

Although many food proteins exist in the right-handed α-helix at the secondary structural level, some have a highly hydrophobic nature, which can force the molecule into a beta (β) turn that changes direction at every fourth amino acid residue. This can create a spatial arrangement that descriptively is referred to as a β-pleated sheet when such molecules are linked parallel or antiparallel by interchain hydrogen bonds. Secondary structural configurations that also appear in some foods include a random coil, a beta spiral that forms when there is a loosely turned spiral with 13.5 amino acid residues per turn, and a poly-L-proline helix that is an α-helix distorted by the rigidity of the amino acids in it.

The helical secondary structure in native protein is convoluted and folded into various shapes, which are held in their native configurations by secondary bonding forces between the R groups that extend from the backbone chain. The bonding forces involved may be hydrogen bonds, salt bridges, disulfide (covalent bonding force) linkages, and hydrophobic interactions. This shape, characteristic of many native proteins, is the **tertiary structure** [Figure 13.1(b).]

The hydrophobic nature of some parts of the protein molecule is an important aspect of the shape of specific proteins. Some of the amino acid structures are

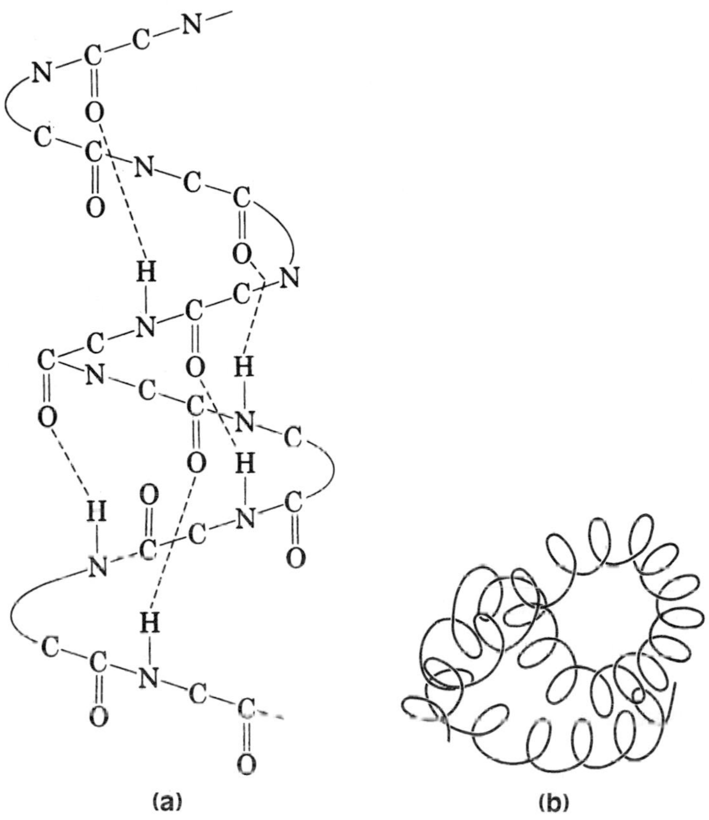

Figure 13.1   (a) α-Helix (secondary structure of a protein) and (b) possible configuration of the tertiary structure of a globular protein.

quite hydrophobic; these include methionine, tyrosine, tryptophan, leucine, isoleucine, valine, and alanine. The hydrophobicity of the R groups causes the protein molecule to be drawn together somewhat tightly in places, thus facilitating the formation of hydrogen bonds in the native protein.

In most proteins, the tertiary structure is the final level of organization for the protein molecule. In some instances (hemoglobin, for example), two or more peptide chains may be held tightly together in a quaternary structure. The quaternary structure represents a close aggregation of protein segments.

TYPES OF PROTEINS

In foods, there are three general categories of proteins: globular, fibrous, and conjugated. Numerous proteins are globular in nature. For example, all enzymes, some hormones, and oxygen-transporting proteins are **globular proteins.** Within the large category of globular proteins, some proteins are termed *albumins*. Albumins are abundant (egg being a noteworthy source), readily coagulated by heat, and soluble in water. Globulins (in meats and legumes) also are coagulated by heat, but their solubility in water is quite limited unless sodium chloride or another neutral salt is added (called *salting in*). Histones and protamines also are globular proteins, but they occur much less commonly than do the albumins and the globulins. His-

Globular Proteins
Native proteins that are rather spherical in the configuration of their tertiary structure.

tones are water-soluble, basic (alkaline-reacting) proteins found in some glandular tissues (such as in the thymus or sweetbread). Protamines are fairly small, very basic globular proteins found in some fish sperm cells.

Fibrous Proteins
Insoluble, elongated protein molecules.

The **fibrous proteins** are noted for their insolubility. Fibrous proteins of particular interest from the standpoint of food are collagen and elastin. These proteins are of structural importance in meats and poultry. One of the unique aspects of the structure and behavior of collagen is the abundance of proline and hydroxyproline and the paucity of the important sulfur-containing amino acids cysteine and cystine.

Conjugated Proteins
Proteins combined with some other type of compound, such as a carbohydrate or lipid.

Various **conjugated proteins** are found in foods. The *mucoproteins* (also called glycoproteins) are composed of a carbohydrate moiety combined with protein. Various sugars occur in mucoproteins. Ovomucoid in egg white is an uncoagulable protein identified as a mucoprotein. Hemagglutinin is a mucoprotein in soybeans. *Lipoproteins* are compounds composed of a protein and a lipid. Among the lipids found in these water-insoluble compounds are cholesterol, triglycerides, and phospholipids. In meats, another type of conjugated protein, *metalloprotein,* is noted. In metalloproteins, the protein is complexed with a metal. Ferritin, a metalloprotein containing iron, is found in the liver. Myoglobin and hemoglobin are other iron-containing metalloproteins. *Nucleoproteins,* proteins combined with nucleic acids, are also of biological importance. *Phosphoproteins* are exemplified by casein in milk. In these conjugated proteins, inorganic phosphates are linked with the protein.

ELECTRICAL CHARGES

Some individual amino acid residues in a protein have the potential to be charged electrically in different ways, depending on the pH of the medium in which the protein is found. The individual protein molecules are said to be **amphoteric**, because they have the potential to function as either an acid or a base, depending on the pH.

Amphoteric
Capable of functioning as either an acid or a base, depending on the pH of the medium in which the compound is found.

A given protein is at its isoelectric point when the number of positive and negative charges on it are equal. At pH values below the isoelectric point (more acidic), protein molecules are drawn toward the cathode, as a consequence of the net positive charge on the molecules. Conversely, a net negative charge develops at pH values above the isoelectric point, and proteins migrate toward the anode (the positive electrode).

Isoelectric Point
The pH at which a protein molecule is electrically neutral; the specific pH differs for various proteins.

The **isoelectric point** of proteins is of considerable importance in food preparation because proteins have their minimum solubility at the isoelectric point. Therefore, when a fluid food containing protein (milk, for example) is brought to its isoelectric point, curdling is very likely to occur. When cheese is the desired end product, the mixture is deliberately brought toward the isoelectric point of casein; however, if a smooth milk product is the goal, the mixture needs to be maintained at a pH well above the isoelectric point (see Figure 13.2).

The ionization states of glycine at different pH values are shown below. This illustrates the effect of pH on the electrical charge carried by the molecule. Note that the isoelectric point of glycine is reached at pH 6.0; isoelectric points of other amino acids are given in Table 13.1.

$$^+H_3NCH_2COOH \underset{H^+}{\overset{OH^-}{\rightleftharpoons}} {}^+H_3NCH_2COO^- \underset{H^+}{\overset{OH^-}{\rightleftharpoons}} H_2NCH_2COO^-$$
pH ~ 1   pH 6   pH ~ 11

Figure 13.2   Scanning electron micrographs of egg white gels show the effect of pH on the aggregation of proteins: A, pH 9 gel; B, pH 6 gel; C, pH 6 gel at higher magnification showing aggregates; D, pH 5 gel; E, aggregates in pH 5 gel; F, pH 5 gel showing larger aggregates. (Courtesy of S. A. Woodward and O. J. Cotterill. Reprinted from *Journal of Food Science 51* (2): 333. 1986. Copyright (c) by Institute of Food Technologists.)

HYDROLYSIS

Protein molecules may undergo hydrolysis to form shorter chains. The reaction usually is the result of enzymatic action by peptidases, but sometimes collagen is cleaved by acid hydrolysis. The result is cleavage of the peptide bond and uptake of a molecule of water, as shown.

The shorter chains resulting from hydrolysis show increased solubility and decreased ability to thicken food products.

DENATURATION AND COAGULATION

Denaturation
Relaxation of the tertiary and the secondary structure of a protein accompanied by decreasing solubility of a protein.

When subjected to stresses, particularly heat, agitation, and ultraviolet light, proteins may undergo such changes as decreased solubility and loss of ability to catalyze reactions (if the protein is an enzyme). These changes are caused by physical alteration of the shape of the protein molecule, called **denaturation.** Different *R* groups appear on the surface of the molecule, causing some changes in behavioral characteristics, such as net charge.

Often, molecules apparently relax from their tertiary state and begin to resemble more closely their secondary helical structure without distortion. As the spherical shape of molecules gradually relaxes into the elongated helical form, it is possible for other elongated protein molecules to align themselves in clumps joined by hydrogen bonding. These coagulated protein aggregates increase the viscosity of the mixture perceptibly, even when the mixture is hot. In fact, in instances in which the concentration of protein is sufficiently high, the fluid mixture may coagulate into a solid, as is true in the cooking of eggs (see Figure 13.3).

Coagulation
Precipitation of protein as molecules aggregate (often as a result of energy input, such as heating or beating).

Denaturation and **coagulation** are physical (not chemical) changes in the protein molecule. They are effected by the introduction of energy into the protein-containing system, energy that is ordinarily provided by heating or beating. The effectiveness of agitation as a means of bringing about denaturation and coagulation can be shown readily by the beating of egg whites. The cell walls of the foam result from denaturation and coagulation of part of the protein in the whites. Heating also, as has been noted in the case of egg cookery, enables permanent physical changes to take place in the protein. Most of the physical changes of denaturation and coagulation are irreversible changes. Therefore, care must be exercised in the preparation of food products to ensure that optimal techniques are used whenever protein-rich foods are the ingredients.

Enzyme
Protein capable of catalyzing a specific chemical reaction.

Related to this discussion on denaturation is the use of **enzymes** in food work. The fact that enzymes are proteins must always be remembered when foods containing enzymes are being prepared. If enzyme action is desired, as is the case when invertase is added to a fondant to aid in liquefication of the center of a chocolate-dipped candy, the enzyme cannot be added until the heating and cool-

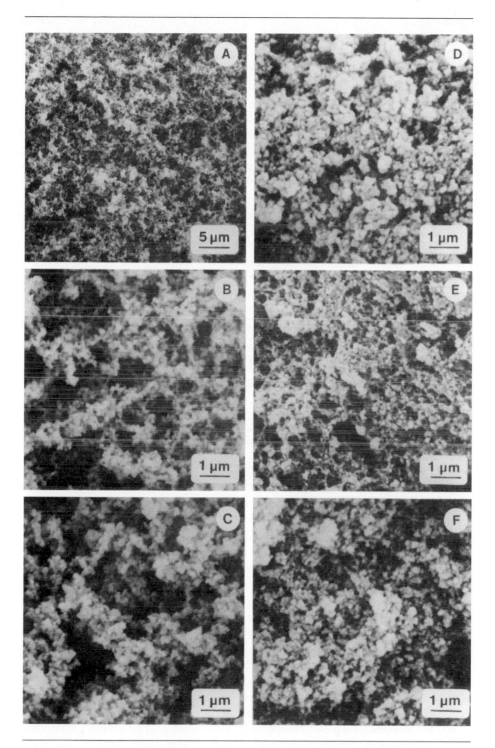

Figure 13.3   Scanning electron micrographs of egg white gels show the effect of temperature and time on the aggregation of proteins: A, heated 10 minutes at 80°C; B, higher magnification of A; C, heated 12 minutes at 80°C; D, heated 15 minutes at 80°C; E, heated 30 minutes at 90°C; F, heated 50 minutes at 90°C. (Courtesy of S. A. Woodward and O. J. Cotterill. Reprinted from *Journal of Food Science 51* (2): 333. 1986. Copyright (c) by Institute of Food Technologists.)

ing of the fondant have been completed. Otherwise, the enzyme may be denatured and its catalytic ability lost. Conversely, there are instances when enzyme activity is to be avoided, as in the preparation of a gelatin salad with pineapple. The bromelin in fresh pineapple is a proteolytic enzyme that hydrolyzes gelatin, resulting in a loss of gel strength. Cooked pineapple can be added to gelatin, however, because heating the pineapple inactivates the enzyme.

Substrate
A general term for the compound that is to be altered by an enzyme.

The action of enzymes occurs at certain active site(s) on the surface of the enzyme molecule. In the native protein, the surface character or shape enables the enzyme to lock temporarily with another compound (the **substrate**) in a food. This intimate arrangement facilities a specific chemical reaction, which results in a change in the food. Subsequently, the enzyme and the resulting compounds disentangle, and the enzyme is free to interact with another substrate molecule.

There are many different enzymes in various foods, and their effects need to be considered when preparing foods. For example, vegetables to be frozen are blanched to inactivate (denature) the enzymes that could continue to cause some deterioration during storage. In other instances, adding an enzyme may enhance the usefulness of a food. An example of this use of an enzyme is the addition of lactase to milk to produce an acceptable milk product for people with lactose intolerance.

Whenever enzymes are being used in food preparation, both the pH and the temperature of the food must be considered if the desired result is to be achieved. Alteration of the pH can greatly retard or even block catalysis by the enzyme because of changes in the electrical profile on its surface. Heat can alter the surface shape of the enzyme, making it impossible for it to lock with the substrate to catalyze a reaction.

FUNCTIONAL ROLES

Among the foods commonly eaten, meats and other flesh foods, eggs, milk and milk products, and legumes are particularly important sources of protein. Cereal grains and gelatin also are very useful sources. Actually, each food source of protein contains many proteins that are unique to that food. The behavioral properties of the proteins specific to each particular food differ, offering a variety of opportunities for using the functions of proteins in food preparation.

An important functional property of gelatin and egg proteins is the ability to form stable foams. These proteins in their native state can be whipped, an action which spreads them into thin foams encasing air. The energy available from the beating action causes denaturation of some of the protein, and it is this denatured protein that gives rigidity to the cell walls, hence some stability to the foam. These stable foams provide a light and airy product with a large volume. Gelatin foam is essential to provide the expected texture of marshmallows, prune whip, chiffon pie fillings, and other whipped desserts. Angel, sponge, and chiffon cakes and also meringues are familiar examples of the foaming power of egg whites and their importance in preparing light products with a large volume. The volume is generated in large measure as a result of the extensibility of the native protein, but rigidity and permanency are imparted by denaturation during baking.

Egg proteins are effective as thickening agents when they are denatured by heat. In baked custards, the denatured egg proteins form a gel structure by cross linking as the proteins gradually unwind into their secondary structure and then form hydrogen and other secondary bonds to establish a continuous network of solid protein molecules. Both egg yolk and egg white proteins denature and coagulate to serve as thickening and emulsifying agents in hollandaise and other sauces. Sometimes they serve this function in salad dressings. Milk proteins undergo denaturation and coagulation to precipitate and form the curd from which cheese is made.

Gluten, the protein complex that forms when wheat flour is manipulated with water, provides the protein network that is responsible for much of the textural characteristics of baked products, including both cell structure and volume. The stretching capability or the elasticity provided by the gluten during mixing defines the potential structure of the product. During baking, the cell walls stretch under the pressure from gases within the cells. When oven heat coagulates the stretched gluten, the walls become rigid enough to maintain the extended cellular structure.

Edible films can be made from wheat and corn proteins using special commercial processing techniques. The wheat films are made with gluten and a heated alkaline alcohol–water mixture (Gennadios and Weller, 1990). Such material can be used as coatings for dry-roasted peanuts and similar coating applications. Zein is the mixture of proteins from corn that is used for making edible films and coatings. Nuts, dried fruits, and jelly beans may be coated with zein films.

SUMMARY

Proteins are composed of amino acids, which are compounds distinguished by the presence of an amino group and an organic acid radical. These amino acids join through peptide linkages between the nitrogen of one amino acid and the carbon of the carboxyl group in the next amino acid to form the primary structure or backbone chain of a protein. Specific R groups distinguish the various amino acids and contribute to the behavioral properties of the protein molecule. This primary structure then is coiled into an α-helical configuration, the secondary structure, which is held by secondary bonding forces in this relaxed shape or other forms. Superimposed on the secondary structure is the distorted or twisted tertiary structure often found in a spherical or globular shape in native food proteins. This tertiary structure also is held by secondary bonding forces. Very rarely are the proteins in food found in a quaternary structure. A few proteins in foods are fibrous, rather than globular, and some are conjugated proteins.

When heat or other energy (beating, for example) is applied to a food containing protein, the protein begins to denature or gradually relax from the tertiary and the secondary, low-energy structure. With continued energy input, molecules may crosslink with each other and precipitate to provide notable thickening and loss of solubility. Coagulation also occurs very readily when proteins are at their isoelectric point, because the reduction in electrical charge on the molecules permits them to clump together rather than repel each other.

Proteins function in important ways in food preparation. A particularly important function is the formation of foams. Egg whites and gelatin are especially useful in forming foams. Egg white foams can be denatured and coagulated to give very stable products. Gelatin foams give stability when cooled. Egg proteins often are used as thickening agents, and milk proteins can be precipitated to form the curd used in making cheese. Gluten provides the structural network for baked products. Both gluten and zein can be the key ingredient in making edible films and coatings.

STUDY QUESTIONS

1. Write the basic structure of an amino acid and then unite it with a peptide linkage to a second amino acid. Be sure to include the actual configuration of the R group for both of the amino acids. Did the amino acids you used seem crowded when the R groups were written out?

2. Select four amino acids and join them with peptide linkages to make one molecule. Now write that molecule in the form of an α-helix according to the information provided in Figure 12–1.

3. When proteins are subjected to heat and undergo denaturation so that the tertiary structure is altered, what happens to the R groups in the interior and on the surface of the molecule? Why is this important?

4. What influence does the clumping together of protein molecules during coagulation have on the solubility of the protein?

5. What effect does heat have on an enzyme's activity? Explain why this is so.

6. Draw structures showing the change in electrical charge on an amino acid as the pH decreases from the isoelectric point to a lower pH.

7. Find a recipe for each of the following and explain the function of any protein-rich ingredients: (a) scrambled egg, (b) mayonnaise, (c) angel cake, (d) bread.

BIBLIOGRAPHY

Andres, C. 1984. "Natural edible coating has excellent moisture and grease barrier properties." *Food Proc. 45* (13): 48.

Crick, F. H. C. and Kendrew, J. C. 1957. "X-ray analysis and protein structure." *Adv. Protein Chem. 12:* 133.

Dutson, T. R. and Orcutt, M. W. 1984. "Chemical changes in protein produced by thermal processing." *J. Chem. Educ. 61* (4): 303.

Dziezak, J. D. 1991. "Enzymes: catalysts for food processes." *Food Technol. 45* (1): 77.

Fennema, O. R., ed. 1985. *Food Chemistry.* 2nd ed. Marcel Dekker, Inc. New York.

Gennadios, A. and Weller, C. L. 1990. "Edible films and coatings from wheat and corn proteins." *Food Technol. 44* (10): 63.

Giese, J. 1994. "Proteins as ingredients: Types, functions, applications." *Food Technol. 48* (10): 49.

Gross, A. 1991. "Enzymatic catalysis in the production of novel food ingredients." *Food Technol. 45* (1): 96.

Haard, N. F. 1998. Specialty enzymes from marine organisms. *Food Technol. 52* (7): 64.

Henley, E. C. and Kuster, J. M. 1994. "Protein quality evaluation by protein digestibility-corrected amino acid scoring." *Food Technol. 48* (4): 74.

Holsinger, V. H. and Kligerman, A. E. 1991. "Applications of lactase in dairy foods and other foods containing lactose." *Food Technol. 45* (1): 92.

Kilara, N. and Sharkase, T. Y. 1986. "Effects of temperature on food proteins and its implications on functional properties." *CRC Crit. Rev. Food Sci. Nutr. 23* (4): 323.

Lahl, W. J. and Braun, S. D. 1994. "Enzymatic production of protein hydrolysates for food use." *Food Technol. 48* (10): 68.

Lee, F. A. 1983. *Basic Food Chemistry.* 2nd ed. AVI Publishing: Westport, CT.

Ma, C. Y. and Holme, J. 1982. "Effect of chemical modification on some physiochemical properties and heat coagulation of egg albumen." *J. Food Sci. 47:* 1454.

Mahmoud, M. I. 1994. "Physicochemical and functional properties of protein hydrolysates in nutritional products." *Food Technol. 48* (10): 89.

Neidleman, S. L. 1991. "Enzymes in the food industry: a backward glance." *Food Technol. 45* (1): 88.

Penet, C. S. 1991. "New applications of industrial food enzymology: economics and processes." *Food Technol. 45* (1): 98.

Powrie, W. D. and Nakai, S. 1985. "Characteristics of edible fluids of animal origin: eggs." In Stadelman, W. J. and Cotterill, O. J., eds. *Egg Science and Technology.* Avi Publishing: Westport, CT.

Pszczola, D. E. 1999. Enzymes: making things happen. *Food Technol. 53* (2): 74.

CHAPTER 14

Milk and Milk Products

COMPONENTS

Milk is a very complex fluid containing a remarkable array of chemical compounds dispersed in an aqueous medium. Whole cow's milk is approximately 88 percent water, 5 percent carbohydrate, 3.5 percent protein, and 3.3 percent fat. Its nutrient content varies from species to species, from breed to breed, seasonally, and even from the beginning of the milking to the end of the process. In the United States, however, cow's milk is used most commonly as a beverage and in food preparation. Therefore, the milk discussed throughout this chapter is cow's milk.

In 1994, recombinant bovine somatotropin (usually abbreviated as bST or BST) was approved for injection in dairy cattle to increase milk production. The process to produce this genetically engineered hormone begins when the gene for bovine somatotropin (a natural bovine hormone) is inserted into a special bacterium and the result is harvested and processed into the recombinant bST that is ready for use. Estimates are that use of bST will increase milk production averages per cow by about 1800 pounds (from approximately 14,841 per cow to 16,641) annually. The milk itself is essentially identical with milk produced without this hormone.

Lipids

Fat content varies considerably. Guernsey and Jersey cows are breeds noted for their comparatively high fat content, actually in excess of 5 percent. In contrast, federal tables of food composition report milk nutrient content on the basis of milk containing only 3.3 to 3.7 percent fat, some of the fat having been removed to achieve this accepted standard.

Although milk contains phospholipids, carotenoid pigments, sterols, and fat-soluble vitamins, it is the milk fat (containing triglycerides in abundance) that generates the primary interest in food products. Milk fat is a notable type of fat because of the array of fatty acids found in its triglyceride molecules. The length of the fatty acid carbon chains ranges from 4 to 26 and these are chains containing primarily an even number of carbon atoms. Altogether, 64 different fatty acids have been identified in milk fat. By far the most common of the saturated fatty acids is palmitic acid (16 carbon atoms); oleic acid (18 carbons) is even more abundant than palmitic acid and is the most plentiful monounsaturated fatty acid in milk fat, as shown in Table 14.1. Linoleic acid is the most abundant of the polyunsaturated fatty acids, but it is found in rather small quantities compared with both palmitic and oleic acids.

The triglycerides containing these diverse fatty acids are dispersed in milk in the form of tiny **fat globules,** each of which is surrounded by a membrane containing phospholipids and proteins, including enzymes and lipoproteins (Figure 14.1). Lipoproteins are effective emulsifying agents because they contain hydrophilic and hydrophobic components, enabling them to form a protective layer around the triglyceride molecules. Even with this protection, the cream separates slowly from the aqueous portion of fresh, unprocessed milk. Before the era of widespread homogenization of milk, people often poured the cream from the top of the milk for use on their cereal and in their coffee.

Fat-Globule Membrane Outer layer of fat globule in milk; phospholipids and protein coating the fat globule to aid in emulsifying the fat.

Carbohydrates

A cup of milk contains 11 to 12 grams of carbohydrate, almost all of which is in the form of lactose. This disaccharide, which is only about a fifth as sweet as sucrose, is quite an uncommon carbohydrate and is not found in significant amounts in foods other than milk and milk-containing products.

Among the familiar sugars found in foods, lactose stands out as being particularly difficult to dissolve and to keep in solution. Instead, it tends to precipitate fairly easily, especially at cool temperatures. These lactose crystals are quite irregular in shape and are very noticeable on the tongue, sometimes creating a significant textural problem because of the gritty quality they can impart to ice cream. The majority of the problem with sandy-textured lactose crystals is the result of precipitation of crystals of α-lactose, which are distinctly less soluble than β-lactose crystals. Unfortunately, as α-lactose crystals precipitate in cool or frozen milk products, the β-lactose in the milk gradually shifts to the less soluble α-lactose. The

Table 14.1 Fatty Acid Composition of Milk Fat

Type of Fatty Acid	Percent of Total Fat	Fatty Acid	Composition[a]	Percent of Total Fat
Saturated	62.3	Butyric	4:0	3.3
		Caproic	6:0	1.7
		Caprylic	8:0	1.2
		Capric	10:0	2.3
		Lauric	12:0	2.6
		Myristic	14:0	10.2
		Palmitic	16:0	26.3
		Stearic	18:0	12.0
Monounsaturated	28.7	Oleic	18:1	25.1
Polyunsaturated	3.6	Linoleic	18:2	2.4

[a]Number of carbon atoms: number of double bonds.
Adapted from "Composition of Foods: Dairy and Egg Products." Agr. Handbook 8–1. ARS, U.S. Dept. Agriculture: Washington, DC, 1976.

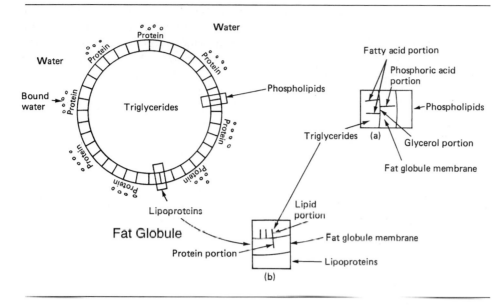

Figure 14.1   Schematic of a fat globule in milk; enlarged areas show (a) arrangement of a phospholipid at the fat globule membrane and (b) lipoprotein also at the fat globule membrane.

process of crystallization, isomerization, and crystallization may continue until the texture becomes quite sandy.

Crystals of **α-lactose** form during the processing of dried milk solids. These highly hygroscopic crystals attract and hold water to form a crystalline hydrate, causing the powdered milk to begin to lump. Lumping is a large problem in powdered milks unless moisture is blocked very effectively from coming into contact with the dried milk.

In addition to the lactose dissolved in milk, there are very small amounts of galactose and glucose, the two component sugars of lactose. Very minor quantities of oligosaccharides also have been noted in milk. These other carbohydrates are present in such small amounts that they have little apparent effect on the characteristics of milk. In contrast, the level of lactose is sufficient to give a distinctly sweet taste to milk and to contribute to the browning of heated milk products.

Proteins

Casein.   The two basic categorizations of milk proteins are casein and the proteins in **whey.** The reason for this distinction is very evident when the pH of milk is adjusted to 4.6, for at this acidity, casein is quite insoluble and precipitates readily to form a soft **curd,** which can be separated from the remaining liquid (whey) by cutting and draining the casein curd. The whey proteins are but a part of the resulting whey, which is a watery mixture that also contains lactose, some minerals, and water-soluble vitamins.

The proteins in the curd are called **casein,** but they actually represent a group of three primary forms of casein and very small amounts of other proteins. The three predominant forms of casein are α_s-casein (actually α_{s1}, and α_{s2}), β-casein,

α-Lactose
Less soluble form of lactose, the disaccharide prominent in milk; form of lactose largely responsible for the sandy texture of some ice creams.

Whey
Liquid that drains from the curd of clotted milk; contains lactose, proteins, water-soluble vitamins, and some minerals.

Curd
Milk precipitate that contains casein and forms readily in an acidic medium.

Casein
Collective name for milk proteins precipitated at pH 4.6.

and κ-casein. A fourth form, γ-casein, is not as abundant as the other forms. The isoelectric point of casein is 4.6, which represents integration of the isoelectric points of the four casein fractions. The most abundant form of casein is α_s, and its isoelectric point is 5.1 (Table 14.2). Countering this figure is the isoelectric point of the κ form, which is lower than 4.6 (actually 3.7–4.2). Together, the caseins are present at levels about four times those of the whey proteins.

The various types of casein molecules are joined into raspberry-like organized aggregates called micelles. These micelles also contain many phosphate groups bridged by calcium. The surface of casein micelles is formed by concentrating κ-casein molecules, which effectively block aggregation of casein micelles because of a particularly hydrophilic portion, which promotes solvation of micelles and reduces interactions. Other forms of casein are shielded within the micelles, with the result that their hydrophobic nature is not of significance. Casein micelles, although they are much smaller than fat globules, effectively block light transmission in milk to cause the characteristic opacity of milk.

Casein precipitates or becomes insoluble under two conditions that often are used in milk processing where curd formation is desired. Acid can be added to milk, which moves the milk closer to the isoelectric point of κ-casein, which is the protein that is preventing the micelles from precipitating. The negative electrical charges that normally are on the surface of **casein micelles** are counteracted by the plus charges of the hydrogen ions from the acid, and the repulsive forces no longer keep the micelles apart.

Rennin, the proteolytic enzyme obtained from the stomach lining of calves, destablizes casein micelles in quite a different way. This enzyme splits off the hydrophilic portion of κ-casein that was primarily responsible for the stabilizing effect of κ-casein on the surface of the casein micelles. In the presence of calcium, this para-κ-casein becomes insoluble. Consequently, the micelles then can aggregate easily to form a gel (Figure 14.2). Clearly, the two mechanisms—the alteration of the pH to approach the isoelectric point of casein and the use of rennin—are quite different, but are both effective in precipitating casein.

Whey Proteins. The various caseins account for a little less than 80 percent of the total protein in milk (Table 14.2); the various whey proteins contribute the re-

Casein Micelle
Casein aggregate that is comparatively stable and remains colloidally dispersed unless a change such as a shift toward the isoelectric point or the use of rennin destabilizes and precipitates casein.

Rennin
Enzyme from the stomach lining of calves that eliminates the protective function of κ-casein in micelles and results in curd formation.

Table 14.2 Approximate Percentage Composition of Major Milk Proteins and Their Isoelectric Points

Protein	Percentage of Total Protein		Isoelectric Point
Caseins	78		4.6
α_{s1}-Casein		42.9	5.1
β-Casein		19.5	5.3
κ-Casein		11.7	3.7–4.2
γ-Casein		3.9	5.8
Whey proteins	17		
β-Lactoglobulin (an albumin)		8.5	5.3
α-Lactalbumin		5.1	5.1
Immunoglobulins		1.7	4.0–6.0
Serum albumin		1.7	4.7

Adapted from Zapsalis, C. and Beck, R. A. *Food Chemistry and Nutritional Biochemistry.* Wiley: New York, 1985, 112.

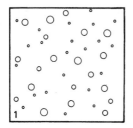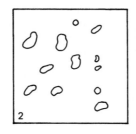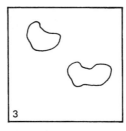

Figure 14.2   Sketch of the gradual clumping of casein micelles to form a soft gel when rennin is present: (1) 1 minute; (2) after 4 minutes; (3) after 8 minutes.

mainder (see page 300). These whey proteins sometimes are categorized as either lactalbumins or lactoglobulins. These designations of the whey proteins are confused a bit by the finding that one of the lactalbumins is called β-lactoglobulin. Whey proteins are of interest because of their sensitivity to heat.

Enzymes

Milk contains many enzymes, including alkaline phosphatase, lipase, protease, and xanthine oxidase. The resistance to denaturation by heat varies with the enzyme. Protease is quite resistant, a fact that can create problems in some milk that has been subjected to high-temperature, short-time heat treatment methods. Conveniently, alkaline phosphatase is inactivated when milk has been heat-treated adequately to destroy potentially harmful microorganisms, indicating that the adequacy of pasteurization can be determined by testing for the presence of active alkaline phosphatase. Lipase is responsible for catalyzing lipolysis of the fats in milk, a chemical change that is avoided by heat denaturation. Xanthine oxidase is considered to be a useful enzyme in milk because of its ability to catalyze the breakdown of flavin-adenine dinucleotide (FAD) to yield riboflavin.

Vitamins and Minerals

Milk naturally is an excellent source of riboflavin, calcium, and phosphorus. It also provides valuable amounts of thiamin, niacin, and vitamin A. In fact, milk is a very outstanding source of nutrients, except iron and vitamin C, which are present in very small amounts. Vitamin D is added to almost all milk that is sold today (which is indicated on the label); milk with vitamin D added is the best source of vitamin D in the foods commonly consumed. Vitamins A and D, being fat soluble, are not found in the whey that is separated from the casein curd in cheesemaking. However, whey is so high in riboflavin that it even has a greenish-yellow color, the result of the riboflavin that is present.

Flavor Components

The compounds that contribute to the overall flavor profile of milk are varied and complex. They include various volatile organic compounds, notably aldehydes, ketones, and acids. The actual compounds in a particular milk sample are determined by previous treatment of the milk, for example, heating, fermentation, and storage. During these processes, chemical changes alter the flavor components. Heat-treated milk often is described as having a "cooked" flavor, which is the result of heat-assisted chemical reactions promoting degradation of the lactose and interaction with proteins.

Fermentation by microorganisms results in the formation of acid from lactose, a change that alters both flavor and texture. Lipase action on lipids, as well as oxidative changes during storage, releases butyric acid and other fatty acids that ultimately have a strong influence on flavor. Sunlight can also alter the flavor of milk by triggering formation of different sulfur-containing compounds, such as hydrogen sulfide. Even the feed the lactating cattle eat influences the flavor of the milk they produce.

PROCESSING

Pasteurization

Milk not only is a remarkably fine food for humans but it also is a medium in which many microorganisms can thrive. As soon as milk is expressed from the cow's udder, contamination can be a problem. For this reason, most dairies are very attentive to maintaining as clean an environment for milking and milk handling as is possible. Cows' udders are washed carefully, handlers are checked to be sure they are not carriers of such diseases as tuberculosis and typhoid fever, and the equipment coming into contact with milk is sanitized. Even with all of these precautions and prompt refrigeration, some microorganisms are present in milk.

Milk as it comes from the animal is designated as raw milk, meaning that no heat treatment has been used on the milk. In a few places in this country, certified raw milk is marketed. This milk is so-named because it has been produced in an environment clean enough to keep the microorganism count sufficiently low to meet the criteria required for identifying raw milk as "certified." Just because milk is marketed as **certified raw milk** does not mean that it is safe to drink, however, because the microorganisms that are in the milk are alive, and some that may be present can cause serious illnesses, such as tuberculosis and undulant fever.

Fortunately, by far the majority of the milk on the market today has been heat-processed and is marketed as pasteurized milk. **Pasteurized** milk (named after Louis Pasteur, the inventor of this important sanitizing process) is milk that has been treated with heat to kill potentially harmful microorganisms. As is true with sanitization of any food, the higher the temperature the shorter the time required to kill the microorganisms. In pasteurizing milk, it is necessary to kill problem microorganisms without seriously reducing the quality of the milk. The **hold method** of pasteurizing requires that milk be heated to only 63°C (145°F) and held there for 30 minutes, followed by a quick cooling to 7°C (45°F). A very common pasteurization method is **HTST** (high-temperature short-time). For this method, the milk is heated to 72°C (161°F) and held for at least 15 seconds before cooling to 10°C (50°F) (see Figure 14.3).

Milk that has been pasteurized by the preceding methods or even slightly more rigorous methods is safe to consume when kept refrigerated, but some deteriorative changes do occur gradually, ultimately making it unsatisfactory for food use. Because refrigeration is minimal or lacking in much of the world, research has

Certified Raw Milk
Milk that has a small microorganism population, but has not been heat-treated and, therefore, may cause serious illnesses.

Pasteurization
Heat treatment of milk adequate to kill microorganisms that can cause illness in people.

Hold Method
Pasteurization in which milk is heated to 63°C and held there 30 minutes before it is cooled to 7°C.

HTST Method
High-temperature short-time pasteurization in which milk is heated to 72°C and held there at least fifteen seconds before it is cooled to 10°C.

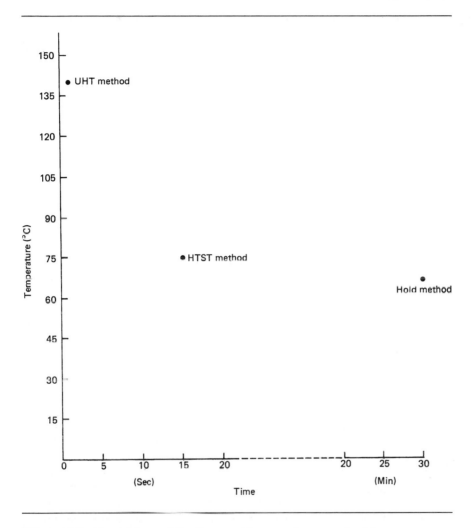

Figure 14.3 Comparison of the time and temperature required for pasteurizing milk by UHT, HTST, and hold methods. Note that the higher the temperature, the shorter the time.

been directed toward developing a technique for making it possible to store milk safely without refrigeration. The present answer is **UHT** (ultrahigh-temperature) **pasteurization.** In this very rigorous process, milk is heated very fast to 138°C (280°F), held there for at least 2 seconds, and then stored in a sterile container. Such a severe treatment kills all of the microorganisms in the milk, which makes it possible to store UHT-treated milk at room temperature until the carton is opened. As soon as it is opened, live microorganisms can enter the milk; after the container is opened refrigeration is necessary, just as it is for any other type of milk. The high temperature used in UHT pasteurization causes the development of a slightly "cooked" flavor, but this product appears to have good potential for finding a market niche in the world.

The importance of pasteurization of milk and milk products springs into the news periodically. Certified raw milk has been the source of salmonellosis outbreaks. *Salmonella dublin,* a particularly hazardous species of *Salmonella,* has

UHT Pasteurization
Extreme pasteurization (138°C for at least 2 seconds) that kills all microorganisms and makes it possible to store milk in a closed, sterile container at room temperature.

been traced to raw milk in the diets of several people in each outbreak in spite of the fact that the milk was certified. The headlines about soft Mexican cheeses manufactured in California drew attention in 1985 to another microorganism, *Listeria monocytogenes,* which also entered the food supply from raw milk and ultimately resulted in the deaths of a number of people. Such examples underline the importance of using only pasteurized milk and milk products.

Homogenization

When allowed to stand, the fat globules in milk tend to aggregate into clusters and rise to the top of the milk. The clustering of fat globules is facilitated by the presence of a protein called agglutinin, which apparently serves as an adhesive to form collections of fat globules of fairly large diameter that rise to the surface. This process of separation of cream from the aqueous portion of the milk is called **creaming.** Although creaming is useful if the cream is to be separated from milk, it is a nuisance to shake milk thoroughly each time it is used just to disperse the fat uniformly throughout. This inconvenience led to the development of the process of homogenization.

Creaming
Separation of fat from the aqueous portion of milk that takes place when fat globules cluster into larger aggregates and rise to the surface of the milk.

Homogenization
Mechanical process in which milk is forced through tiny apertures under a pressure of 2,000 to 2,500 psi, which breaks up the fat globules (3–10 microns in diameter) into smaller units (less than 2 microns in diameter) that do not separate from the milk.

Homogenization is a mechanical process in which milk is forced through tiny apertures under a pressure ranging from 2,000 to 2,500 psi. These apertures through which the milk is forced are so small that the fat globules split into units so small (less than 2 microns in diameter) that they no longer are capable of coalescing and rising to the surface. Instead, these tiny units remain dispersed uniformly throughout the milk, eliminating the formation of a layer of cream on the surface of the milk and thus the need to shake the milk before use.

Homogenization causes milk to lose its ability to cream not only because it yields tiny fat globules but also because these globules now have a reduced ability to bind together, apparently as a result of formation of an adsorbed layer of protein around the individual globules. Increased viscosity and a whiter appearance are other physical changes that can be observed in homogenized milk. Homogenized milk also is less stable to heat, is more sensitive to oxidation caused by light, and foams more readily. In addition, curds formed from homogenized milk are softer than they would be if the milk had not been homogenized. This may result from the binding of many casein molecules to the surface of the numerous tiny fat globules in the homogenized product, leaving less casein free in the plasma phase of the milk.

Milk flavor is less distinctive after homogenization, which is thought to be caused, at least in part, by the casein coating of the fat globules in homogenized milk. It is also possible that the fat, with its increased surface area, may begin to develop a slightly rancid flavor in homogenized milk exposed to light.

Evaporation

The large percentage of water in milk (just under 90 percent) contributes greatly to the bulk of milk that is to be stored. Consequently, various canned milks are produced by evaporation of enough of the water to about double the concentration of protein and fat. The milk is evaporated under a partial vacuum so that water can be removed at a temperature well below that required at normal atmospheric pressure. This decision is of some help in minimizing the flavor and color changes that would occur if the temperature of evaporation were higher.

Homogenization is a key step in the preparation of **evaporated milk** products. Without this vital step, the fat in the milk would separate and cause significant textural difficulties. Fortunately, homogenization results in an emulsified fat that is quite stable during evaporation.

Although milk can be evaporated at moderate temperatures, the canned evaporated milk has to be sterilized at 116°C for 15 minutes to ensure destruction of any microorganisms that might be present. This intense heat causes some of the lactose and milk protein to undergo the Maillard reaction (see Chapter 8). A related product, **sweetened condensed milk,** is particularly susceptible to nonenzymatic browning as a consequence of the large amount of sugar added to evaporated milk (1.8 pounds of sucrose per 10 pounds of milk before evaporation. This level of sugar (42 percent sucrose or glucose, plus about 12 percent lactose) promotes browning during storage and/or heating and also is an effective antimicrobial agent.

Drying

Milk is dried to produce a food that can be stored for an extended period of time without refrigeration and/or to reduce the problems of transporting fluid milks, which are subject both to spoilage and to high shipping costs because of the large amount of water in them. When dried, the milk powder consists of lactose in either an amorphous or a crystalline state, fat in globules or free, and protein in the form of casein micelles and precipitated whey proteins, with air interspersed throughout. These components of dried milk tend to lump together when they are rehydrated with water. This problem has been overcome with various creative solutions. An effective technique is to instantize the dried milk by adding moisture to the dried product to make it sticky and then drying it a second time to obtain rather spongy particles. When water is added to reconstitute the **instantized milk,** the particles absorb water and sink downward, dispersing as they fall.

Lumping is but one of the problems with dehydrated whole milk. Spray-dried milk causes lactose to solidify in an amorphous or glasslike state. The highly hygroscopic nature of **"glassy" lactose** increases the absorption of moisture during storage; very effective, airtight packaging is important to good shelf life.

Fermentation

Various microorganisms are used commercially to ferment lactose in milk and milk products. The goal is the production of lactic acid by one or more types of microorganisms. Frequently, *Streptococcus lactis* initiates the fermentation process, with lactobacilli of various types (e.g., *Lactobacillus casei, L. bulgaricus, L. lactis,* and *L. helveticus*) continuing the fermentation as the pH drops into their effective range. The thickening associated with fermented products is the result of the association of casein micelles, often accompanied by β-lactoglobulin. When a comparatively large amount of β-lactoglobulin is bound to the casein micelles, a fairly stable gel is formed and syneresis is minimal. Buttermilk is somewhat thickened as a result of fermentation, whereas yogurt is acidified to the point where a gel forms as a result of fermentation and controlled heat. Whey can be fermented to produce such comparatively sweet cheeses as Mysost and Gjetost.

Unfortunately, undesirable microorganisms can be grown under essentially the same conditions as are needed to achieve controlled, desirable fermentation. Prod-

Evaporated Milk
Sterilized, canned milk that has been concentrated to about half its original volume by evaporation under a partial vacuum.

Sweetened Condensed Milk
Canned milk to which sugar is added (contains more than 54 percent carbohydrate because of milk sugar and added sugar); evaporation of about half the water and heat treatment to kill harmful microorganisms precede the canning process.

Instantized Dehydrated Milk
Milk that has been dried, moistened until sticky, and then redried into spongy aggregates of solids that rehydrate readily without lumping.

"Glassy" Lactose
Amorphous (noncrystalline) milk sugar.

ucts may become ropy in consistency if a microorganism such as *Bacillus subtilis* happens to be present. *Lactobacillus tardus* can generate unpleasant aromas or flavors by suppressing lactic acid production and promoting citric acid formation. *Pseudomonas putrefaciens* is an example of a microorganism that forms compounds with a putrid odor. Molds may grow in butter fairly easily because of the low water content. *Alcaligenes* and *Aerobacter* are but two of the types of bacteria that can cause a slimy curd to develop. *Pseudomonas nigrificans* can result in the formation of a black color in butter. These are just some examples of undesirable fermentation in dairy products. Clearly, the problem is to control the microorganisms that are present by promoting the growth of those desired and eliminating the undesirable ones through careful sanitation and attention to quality control.

Products

Milks.   Milk and milk products are available to consumers and food manufacturers in several different forms. In the fluid form, milk can be categorized on the basis of fat content [nonfat (fat-free), low-fat, reduced-fat, and whole], as shown in Table 14.3. Shoemaker et al. (1992) found the rheological properties of nonfat milk were quite different from the other three milks. All of these are excellent sources of most nutrients except vitamin C and iron; the lower the fat content of these milks, the higher is the content of the other nutrients.

Kefir
Fermented milk which is about 3 percent alcohol because of fermentation by *Lactobacillus kefir,* which also adds CO_2.

The fermented milks include cultured buttermilk, sweet acidophilus milk, **kefir,** and Lactaid®. Yogurt is clotted milk. These fermented milks are the choice of many people because of the pleasing qualities and the uniqueness of each type. Persons who are lactose intolerant often are able to consume these products without discomfort. Lactase-containing milks, such as Lactaid, are particularly effective for them because lactase digests a considerable portion of lactose into its component monosaccharides (galactose and glucose). (Technically, lactase-containing milk is not fermented; acid is not made.) *Streptococcus thermophilus* and *Lactobacillus bulgaricus* are the microorganisms used to ferment milk to yogurt. Fermentation produces lactic acid, but yogurt is not allowed to continue to ferment once an acidity of pH 5.5 is reached because the taste becomes too acidic (Kroger, 1976).

Butter.   Butter technically is a dairy product, actually being a water-in-oil emulsion containing about 15 percent water and at least 80 percent fat. Its manufacture is accomplished through churning to reverse the colloidal dispersion, transforming the water from the continuous to the dispersed phase by establishing tiny water droplets. The fat is sufficiently warm at churning temperatures to form a continuous network. Subsequent chilling produces fat crystals in the β' form. These crystals give rigidity to the butterlike mixture, which then can be squeezed sufficiently to force out enough water to bring the level to about 15 percent. Usually sweet cream is the milk product from which butter is churned. If the color is not sufficiently yellow at certain times of year, annatto or another coloring agent is added to provide the expected yellow color. Usually salt is added for flavor, although there also is a market for unsalted butter.

Creams.   Creams vary in fat content from 10.5 percent (half-and-half) to 36 percent (heavy whipping cream). They are obtained by the centrifugation of milk to separate varying amounts of the lighter cream from the aqueous portion of the milk,

Table 14.3 Distinguishing Characteristics and Uses of Milk and Milk Products

Name of Product	Fat (%)	Characteristics	Uses
Fluid Milks			
Whole	3.25+	Rich flavor	Beverage, cooking
Reduced-fat	2.0	Some richness	Beverage, cooking
Lowfat (light)	1.0	Slight richness	Beverage, cooking (calorie and cholesterol control)
Fat free (nonfat)	0.1	Not rich flavor, somewhat thin	Beverage, cooking (calorie and cholesterol control)
Cultured butter-milk	0.1	Tangy flavor (lactic acid bacteria), somewhat thick	Beverage, baking
Kefir		3% alcohol, CO_2	Beverage
Sweet acidophilus milk	3.25+	Somewhat sweet (*L. acidophilus*)	Beverage, cooking (for lactose intolerance)
Yogurt	0.1–3.25+	Tangy coagulum (*S. thermophilus, L. bulgaricus*)	Dressing, dessert, frozen dessert (tofutti)
Lactaid	0.1–3.25+	Slightly sweet (lactase)	Beverage, cooking (for lactose intolerance)
Creams			
Sour	18	Tangy	Dips, toppings, baking
Half-and-half	10.5–18.0	Slightly viscous	Added to cereals and beverages
Coffee (light)	18–30	Somewhat thick	Added to coffee, sauces
Light whipping (whipping)	30–35	Whips to fairly stable foam	Whipped topping
Heavy cream (heavy whipping)	36	Whips easily to stable foam	Whipped topping
Butter	80	Yellow water-in-oil emulsion	Spread, baking, flavoring agent
Cheese			
Natural	Varies	Firmness and flavor vary with manufac-turing and ripening; acid and rennet used to form clot	Sliced, grated; eaten alone or as an ingredient
Process	Varies	Emulsifier added to natural cheeses; 41% moisture	Casseroles, sandwiches
Process cheese food	Varies	Process cheese with 45% moisture	Casseroles, warm dip
Process cheese spread	Varies	Process cheese with 50% moisture	Spread
Ice Creams			
Ice cream	10 or more	20% milk solids, sweeeners, gums or other stabilizers	Dessert
Low-fat ice cream	2–7	11% milk solids	Dessert
Sherbet	0	2–5% milk solids	Dessert
Mellorine	10	Butterfat is replaced by less saturated fat	Dessert
Parevine	10	No butterfat or milk solids	Dessert

depending on the type of cream desired. Production of cultured sour cream begins with a 30-minute holding period at 74–82°C to pasteurize the cream and destabilize some of the protein, and is followed by the addition of lactic acid-forming bacteria and controlled incubation to generate the acid needed to form the clot.

Cheeses.   Cheese production requires the formation of a curd and removal of a considerable amount of water (whey). Clotting is facilitated with the addition of *Streptococcus lactis* and *S. cremoris* to generate lactic acid. Acid causes calcium phosphocaseinate in the casein micelles to eliminate calcium. Acid precipitation is used to make cottage cheese and cream cheese. For making most other cheeses, rennin, the active enzyme from the stomach lining (fourth stomach) of calves, traditionally has been used to convert κ-casein into para-κ-casein. Para-κ-casein then participates in curd formation by uniting with calcium, which forms an insoluble material. Alternative sources of enzymes capable of precipitating casein are being sought. Potential microbiological sources include *Escherichia coli* and *Saccharomyces cerevisiae.* The enzymes they produce appear to produce better results than the enzymes that have been obtained from *Mucor milhei, Mucor pusillus,* and *Endothia parasitica.* The curd is cut to release the whey. Gentle heating (35°C for hard cheeses and 32–33°C for soft cheeses) and squeezing cause the curd to draw tighter so that the whey can be drained, leaving the highly concentrated protein and fat-containing curd. The whey contains the lactose, water-soluble vitamins (notably riboflavin), and serum (whey) proteins. Usually the moisture content of cheeses is around 37–40 percent, which is quite a reduction from the 87 percent water content of whole milk (Figures 14.4–14.9).

Natural Cheese
Any cheese made by clotting milk to form a curd and then concentrating the curd by draining the whey; variations are produced by varying the curd concentration and by ripening with or without the addition of selected microorganisms or other ingredients.

Numerous cheese products are available. The **natural cheeses** are categorized according to their firmness or moisture content. Some of these natural cheeses undergo a ripening or aging period in a controlled environment at a cool temperature. Microorganisms that could be harmful to humans are no longer viable after 60 days at a storage temperature of around 1.7°C, which makes it possible to use raw milk in making some well-aged cheeses.

Even when pasteurized milk is used for making cheese, ripening is beneficial because of the numerous chemical changes that occur. These changes result in a variety of end products, ranging from some individual amino acids via some minor degradation of the original proteins, to very large polypeptides. Distinctive flavor and textural changes are associated with these proteolytic reactions. Casein proteolysis is responsible. in part, for the rather soft texture of semisoft and soft cheeses. A textural comparison of green cheddar cheese and a well-ripened cheddar reveals a change from the rubbery, tough green product to a more tender and soft or even crumbly texture as ripening progresses. These proteolytic reactions during ripening result in a cheese that can be incorporated readily into a wide range of hot foods; the green cheese blends with considerable difficulty.

Chemical changes in the fats in cheeses during aging are responsible for some of the distinctive flavors associated with ripened cheeses. Fatty acids and other organic compounds such as lactones, alcohols, methyl ketones, various other ketones, aldehydes, and esters combine to delineate the complex flavors of ripened cheeses. Microorganisms often are added deliberately to cheeses that are to be aged, and it is the work of these microorganisms that causes many of the chemical degradative reactions in the fats. A familiar example is provided by the various blue cheeses. Incorporation of dried spores of the blue mold *Penicillium roqueforti* allows the mold to break the fat-globule membrane so that the lipase present

Figure 14.4   Manipulating the curd during curd formation, the first step in producing cheddar cheese. (Courtesy of Plycon Press.)

Figure 14.5   Following curd formation, the curd is cut in the production of cheddar cheese. (Courtesy of Plycon Press.)

Figure 14.6 Cheese curd is fed into a mill which cuts the curd into smaller pieces for the salting process. (Courtesy of Plycon Press.)

Figure 14.7 Salting of the curd, a step important to the development of the desired cheddar cheese flavor. (Courtesy of Plycon Press.)

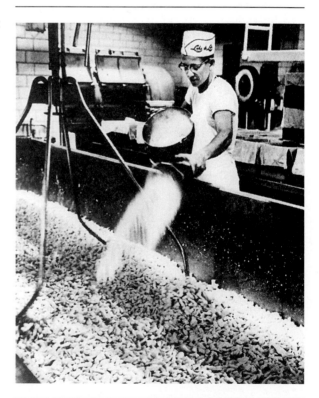

Figure 14.8   The salted cheese curd is placed in steel hoops lined with dampened, clean press cloth. (Courtesy of Plycon Press.)

Figure 14.9   A pressure of 60 pounds per square inch is applied to the filled hoops to remove still more whey and give the desired moisture level and compactness to the cheese. (Courtesy of Plycon Press.)

in the cheese can split the fat molecules into their components and release free fatty acids. It is these free fatty acids that are the key to the distinctive flavor of Roquefort cheese. Part of the flavor of well-aged Swiss cheeses, such as Emmentaler, is the result of lipolytic breakdown to such short-chain fatty acids as butyric (four carbons), caproic (six carbons), caprylic (eight carbons), and capric (ten carbons). However, the sweet flavor detected in Swiss cheeses is due primarily to free amino acids derived from the proteolytic reactions that occur during aging.

The appearance of some cheeses is unique because of the changes during ripening. One readily apparent result of ripening in the blue cheeses is the marbled or streaked appearance where the blue mold has penetrated the product. The distinctive eyes in the various Swiss-type cheeses also are the result of microorganisms that reproduce during the ripening period. The holes or eyes are caused by the formation of carbon dioxide from lactic acid, the product of various *Propionibacterium* species or other lactic acid-producing bacteria, including several *Lactobacillus* species and *Streptococcus thermophilis.* The textural change of Camembert cheese during ripening results from the growth of the mold *Penicillium camemberti* on the surface of the green cheese. This mold is the source of the proteolytic enzymes that migrate slowly into the Camembert during ripening and catalyze proteolysis to produce a very soft to almost fluid cheese. This reaction limits the shelf life of Camembert because the continued action of these enzymes ultimately can produce so much ammonia that the flavor becomes unpleasant. This problem can be reduced by the presence of other bacteria, notably *Candida, Geotrichum,* or *Mucor* strains. Some of the key aspects of the production of the unique flavors and textures of aged cheeses are presented in Table 14.4.

A variation from the natural cheeses is found in the **process cheeses;** these products are manufactured by heating natural cheeses and adding an emulsifying agent, such as disodium hydrogen phosphate or sodium citrate. Both the keeping and the cooking characteristics of the original natural cheeses are altered by these two aspects of process cheese production. Microorganisms are killed by the heating, which reduces the potential for spoilage during storage. Addition of the emulsifying agent is effective in controlling the separation of fat from the cheese during cooking, thus eliminating a significant problem associated with natural cheeses.

The combination of heat (between 65 and 71°C) and citrate and phosphate salts alters the protein molecules by reducing their molecular size somewhat, a change that increases the protein's solubility and water-binding capacity. Using freshly made natural cheeses (less than 7 days old) in the manufacturing of process cheeses contributes a rather rubbery consistency and an innocuous flavor. For these reasons, some ripened or aged cheeses usually are included in the production of process cheeses to enhance the flavor and textural characteristics.

Process cheese food is very similar to process cheese, but the moisture level is usually about 45 percent, around 4 percent higher than the moisture content of process cheeses. When the moisture level is approximately 8 percent above that of process cheeses, the product is designated as **process cheese spread.** The comparatively high moisture level (about 50 percent) of process cheese spreads permits easy spreading on bread and crackers.

Coldpack or club cheeses also are manufactured from natural cheeses with added emulsifiers. They differ from process cheeses because they are not subjected to the heat treatment that causes proteolysis and increased solubility in the process cheeses. Nevertheless, the added emulsifier does enhance the spreadability of coldpack cheeses over that of the natural cheeses used in its manufacture.

Process Cheese
Cheese product made by heating natural cheeses with an emulsifier and then cooling in a brick form; moisture level is about 41 percent.

Process Cheese Food
Process cheese product with a moisture content of about 45 percent, which causes the food to be comparatively soft, yet firm.

Process Cheese Spread
Spreadable process cheese product with a moisture content of about 50 percent.

Coldpack (Club) Cheese
Cheese product made by adding an emulsifier to a mixture of natural cheeses.

Table 14.4 Unique Aspects of Selected Natural Cheeses

Variety	Milk	Approximate Moisture Content (percent)	Description	Aging (months)	Microorganisms Added
Parmesan	Low-fat cow's	30	Very hard, used grated	>12	L. bulgaricus, S. thermophilus
Sapsago	Nonfat cow's	38	Green, pungent due to powdered clover; sour whey is added	5	
Cheddar	Whole cow's	37	White or yellow, firm to crumbly	1 to 12+	S. lactis, S. cremoris; L. casei and L. plantarum appear during aging
Swiss (Emmentaler)	Whole cow's	39	Holes (eyes), white, smooth	3–10	Propionibacterium, L. helveticus. L. bulgaricus, L. lactis, S. thermophilus, S. lactis
Mozzarella	Whole or low-fat cow's	45–55	Mild, soft	0	L. bulgaricus, S. thermophilus
Camembert	Whole cow's	53	Very soft; mold-coated rind	1–2	P. camemberti; Brevibacterium linens, Candida, Geotrichum, and Mucor may develop
Blue or bleu	Whole cow's or ewe's[a]	40	Firm, heavily veined with blue mold	2–6	S. lactis, S. cremoris, P. roqueforti

[a]Roquefort cheese is made from ewe's milk and aged in caves in the southwest of France at the town of Roquefort. Similar cheeses include Stilton, which is made in England from cow's milk, and Gorgonzola, the Italian blue-veined cheese made from cow's and/or goat's milk. European blue-veined cheeses often are designated as bleu cheeses, in contrast to the American spelling—blue cheese.

Reduced-fat cheeses first appeared on the market in 1986 in response to consumer interest in reducing fat and cholesterol in the diet. Various approaches have been taken in an attempt to develop cheeses that are low in fat and high in palatability. The most straightforward way is simply to remove the fat, which can be done comparatively successfully up to a critical level. Olson and Johnson (1990) noted that fat performs several functions in cheese, including contributing significantly to mouthfeel, firmness, and adhesiveness, as well as flavor. Banks et al. (1989) reported satisfactory results if the fat level was not reduced more than 25 percent in a cheddar-type cheese. These workers and also Rank (1985) found that a reduction of 33 percent fat in this type of cheese was acceptable, but 50 percent reduction produced a cheese of definitely inferior quality, albeit fewer calories.

Another approach to making a reduced-fat cheese is to remove all of the butterfat from the milk before beginning manufacturing and then adding some oil. The fluidity of the oil overcomes some of the problems of the reduced-fat cheeses at a lower calorie level than can be achieved with whole milk as the starting point. Some of the reduced-fat cheeses are made with various gums being added to help achieve the desired textural characteristics of the product. Considerable research is still being conducted to develop acceptable reduced-fat cheeses because the market for these cheeses seemingly is a very strong one, both because of health concerns and the problem of overweight and obesity in the United States.

Whey.   Whey protein concentrate is a by-product of cheese manufacturing, which is available in very large quantities as a result of the large amount of cheese manufacturing that is done. Two proteins, α-lactalbumin and β-lactoglobulin, constitute approximately 80 percent of the proteins in whey (about 25 percent and 55 percent, respectively). These proteins contribute to the viscosity and stability of food products to which they are added by food manufacturers. Whey in the form of whey protein concentrate and whey protein isolate can be effective in achieving desirable textural properties. For example, Simplesse® (NutraSweet Co.) utilizes a mixture of whey protein solution and egg white that has been heated and sheared to make extremely tiny spheres (0.1–3.0 μm; Singer, 1990). Surprisingly, this protein product, because of its extremely tiny spheres, provides a mouthfeel similar to that contributed by fat, but with far fewer calories.

Whey protein concentrate is useful in promoting water retention in some meat products; this action is the result of the tendency of this whey product to promote gel formation. Calcium ions may interfere somewhat with gel formation. The abundance of whey in the food industry spurs research efforts to find ever more uses of such a healthful and economical ingredient.

Ice Cream (Also Called Plain Ice Cream)
Frozen dessert containing at least 10 percent milk fat and 20 percent total milk solids and no more than 0.5 percent edible stabilizer; flavoring particles must not show.

Ice Creams and Frozen Desserts.   **Ice cream** is a frozen mixture of cream (which contributes considerable milk fat), milk solids, and flavorings into which some air has been stirred. This is a type of food for which a federal standard of identity has been established: at least 10 percent milk fat, 20 percent total milk solids (which may be reduced as a result of added flavorings), and optional additives (0.5 percent stabilizer and 0.2 percent emulsifier). The comparatively high fat content of ice creams contributes a smoothness of texture and richness of flavor that are prized by consumers. The added milk solids further enhance the texture and flavor. The sweeteners (sugar or various corn sweeteners) lower the melting and freezing points of ice cream, a physical phenomenon that aids in production of a smooth ice cream with a pleasingly light texture. Carboxymethylcellulose, gelatin, or such gums as guar gum, alginates, or carrageenan are useful stabilizers in ice creams because of their ability to bind water and increase the viscosity of the ice cream mixture prior to freezing. Monoglycerides are added to serve as emulsifying agents. Similar to the plain ice cream defined above, **composite ice creams** are very similar high-fat (at least 8 percent milk fat) ice creams with at least 18 percent total milk solids. Actually, the difference between plain and composite ice creams is caused by the bulkiness of the flavoring components in the composite ice creams; these components cannot exceed 5 percent of the volume of ingredients.

Several other related products also are on the market. These products range in composition from **frozen custards** to ices and even imitation ice creams. A frozen custard differs from ice cream in that it is made by cooking added egg (usually yolks) to form a custard before freezing the mixture. Egg is added at the rate of 1.4 percent for regular ice creams and 1.12 percent for bulky ice creams containing visible pieces of flavoring substances.

Lowfat ice cream contains only between 2 and 7 percent milk fat and at least 11 percent total milk solids. It is definitely less rich than ice cream (at least 10 percent milk fat and a minimum of 20 percent total milk solids). This compositional difference results in a reduced level of calories, a distinction of interest to dieters. **Sherbet** may be even lower in fat than some ice milks; it contains between 2 and 5 percent total milk solids and essentially no fat. The acidity level—at least 0.35 percent—is specified in sherbets, but not in ice milk or ice cream.

In some markets, imitation ice cream products are available. One type is called mellorine. **Mellorine** is a frozen dessert with basically the same ingredients as ice cream, except the milk fat is replaced by a different type of fat. This dessert may be of interest to those persons who are trying to eliminate butterfat from their diets and replace that fat with less saturated fats. The other type of imitation ice cream is parevine, a frozen dessert containing no milk fat or milk solids. **Parevine** fits within the guidelines of the Jewish food laws, making this a popular frozen dessert for people of the Jewish faith.

Composite Ice Cream
Frozen dessert containing at least 8 percent milk fat and 18 percent total milk solids and no more than 0.5 percent edible stabilizer; flavoring particles are not to exceed 5 percent by volume.

Frozen Custard
Ice cream-like product that is a frozen, egg yolk-thickened custard.

Low fat Ice Cream
Frozen dairy product containing 2 to 7 percent milk fat and 11 percent total milk solids.

Sherbet
Frozen dessert containing acid, from 2 to 5 percent milk solids, and no milk fat.

Mellorine
Imitation ice cream in which the milk fat has been removed and replaced by a different fat.

Parevine
Imitation ice cream in which both the milk fat and the milk solids have been replaced by nondairy ingredients.

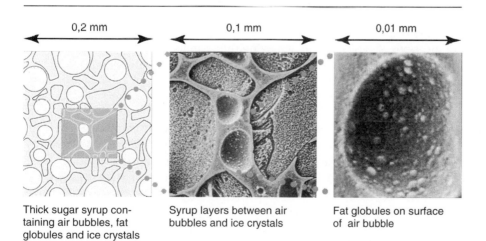

0,2 mm   0,1 mm   0,01 mm

Thick sugar syrup containing air bubbles, fat globules and ice crystals

Syrup layers between air bubbles and ice crystals

Fat globules on surface of air bubble

Figure 14.10 The structure of ice cream, progressively enlarged: (left) thick sugar syrup bubbles containing air bubbles, fat globules, and ice crystals; (middle) syrup layers between air bubbles and ice crystals; (right) fat globules on surface of air bubble. (Courtesy of Unilever Research. Vlaardingen, The Netherlands.)

A frozen ice cream product is a colloidal dispersion classified as a foam, with the ice crystals forming the solid continuous phase and the air incorporated from agitation during freezing being the discontinuous or dispersed phase (Figure 14.10). Preparation of ice cream begins with the blending of ingredients, followed by rapid cooling and freezing, preferably with some agitation. Rapid freezing is required for the formation of very fine ice crystals, which are essential to achieving the desired smooth texture. The necessary fast rate of freezing can be accomplished by surrounding the ice cream container with a mixture of eight parts ice to one part salt (by volume). This ratio of ice to salt is sufficiently cold to enable small ice crystals to form quickly, yet still allows time for adequate agitation to incorporate sufficient air during the freezing process.

The addition of salt to ice to facilitate freezing utilizes the effect of salt on the freezing point of water. Substances that dissolve in water depress the freezing point of the solution by 1.86°C (3.35°F) for each gram molecular weight dissolved in 1,000 grams of water. Because salt ionizes, it depresses the freezing point of water 3.72°C (6.7°F) for each gram molecular weight (58 grams) dissolved in 1,000 grams of water (1 liter). When the salt is sprinkled on the ice, the ice begins to melt, and a salt solution forms. This salt solution has a different vapor pressure than does the ice, a difference that causes the ice to continue to melt in an attempt to establish equilibrium between the two media. Energy is absorbed by the melting ice because this change in physical state is an **endothermic reaction** requiring 80 calories per gram of ice melted. This heat energy is absorbed from the surrounding salt solution. The maximum effect of salt in lowering the freezing point of ice occurs when the ratio of ice to salt is about 3:1. At this high concentration of salt, the freezing point is depressed to about −22°C (Chapter 5).

Endothermic Reaction
Reaction in which heat is absorbed.

When freezing ice cream, it is necessary to reduce the temperature of the ice cream mixture below the freezing point of water because the sugar in the formula depresses the temperature required for freezing to occur. However, the maximum effect of salt is not utilized in making ice cream. Not only is the cost increased by using such a high ratio of salt to ice, but the texture of the resulting ice cream is too solid and compact. Freezing occurs so rapidly that there is little opportunity for the agitation to promote the coalescence of some of the fat globules and the occlusion of air, both of which aid in achieving the optimal texture.

Agitation during freezing of ice cream ordinarily is done to help control various aspects of texture. A key function of agitation is to aid in achieving a comparatively uniform temperature throughout the freezing mixture (Figure 14.11). Without agitation, the mixture touching the edges of the container is much colder than the interior. This lack of uniformity promotes the formation of comparatively large ice crystals because the small crystals that form first quickly melt and then recrystallize to make larger aggregates of ice crystals that feel coarse on the tongue.

Another physical effect of agitation is the coalescence of some of the fat globules. Some clumping is desirable to help present a smooth mouthfeel. However, excessive agitation prior to freezing can cause very rich ice cream mixtures to churn into a reversal of the emulsion to form the water-in-oil emulsion found in butter. The rate of agitation and the time and temperature at which freezing occurs need to be coordinated to avoid breaking the oil-in-water emulsion, and yet allow some melding of fat globules.

When the ice cream mixture is chilled and begins to freeze, agitation results in the incorporation of some air into the system. This air actually becomes incorporated in the foam formed during freezing and causes an increase in the volume of

Figure 14.11 Agitation during freezing of ice cream aids in maintaining some uniformity of temperature throughout the mixture, promotes coalescence of some fat globules, and occlusion of air to promote a smooth, light texture. (Courtesy of Plycon Press.)

the mixture. This increased volume of the frozen mixture beyond that of the initial mixture is termed **overrun.** A desirable level of overrun in commercial ice creams generally is between 70 and 80 percent. At this level, the ice cream texture is pleasingly light, yet neither frothy nor compact. When overrun approaches 100 percent, frothiness is quite detectable. Sherbets usually have only about 30 to 40 percent overrun. In home-cranked ice cream, the overrun level rarely exceeds 50 percent.

Overrun
Increase in volume (%) that occurs when ice cream is frozen with agitation. Calculated as:
(Volume of dispersion − original volume/original volume) × 100

Ice creams frozen in the freezer unit of a refrigerator frequently have poor textural characteristics compared with similar products made in a crank-type home or commercial freezer. The lack of agitation in still-frozen ice creams results in rather coarse ice crystals and extremely limited overrun. Some air can be included if whipped cream, egg white, or evaporated milk foams are components of the mixture. Crystal growth also can be influenced by choice of ingredients. Gelatin, chocolate, egg white, and starch-thickened pastes are effective in stabilizing the textural character of the ice crystals because they interfere with the growth of crystal aggregates somewhat, even when agitation is lacking.

The situation in freshly frozen ice creams is quite dynamic at first. Very small ice crystals that have formed will melt in the sweet, unfrozen portion of the ice cream, and other crystals will form as heat is removed from the freezing mixture. There is a tendency for larger crystal aggregates to form gradually, replacing the labile fine crystals formed initially. As long as agitation is continued in the freezing mixture, the dasher helps to prevent this aggregation. However, the undisturbed hardening that occurs after agitation has ceased does allow some opportunity for aggregation to occur. This is when stabilizing agents are important, for they make it difficult for the ice crystals to clump together into coarse, large crystals. For example, an ice cream made with a large amount of fat tends to be noticeably smoother in texture than one made with only the minimal amount of fat. The fat content of chocolate makes this a useful ingredient in promoting a fine-textured ice cream. The protein provided by egg white or added milk solids also performs a stabilizing function.

Occasionally, an ice cream may have a rather sandy texture which can be detected quite easily on the tongue. The usual cause is the presence of crystals of lactose, the sugar contained in the dairy products used to make ice cream. Lactose has a tendency to crystallize far more readily than some of the other sugars and will influence the texture of ice cream. The interfering substances or stabilizers noted above also are helpful in reducing the aggregation of lactose crystals. The use of corn syrup or another type of sugar in the formula also inhibits the crystallization of lactose into large aggregates; however, excess corn syrup can have a negative impact on flavor.

PHYSICAL AND CHEMICAL EFFECTS ON MILK PRODUCTS

Heat

The whey or serum proteins, notably α-lactalbumins and β-lactoglobulins, precipitate gradually with prolonged heating; the higher the temperature, the faster is the denaturation of the whey proteins. After half an hour of heating at 70°C, a little less than a third of the β-lactoglobulin and α-lactalbumin is denatured, whereas at 80°C more than 80 percent is denatured. This gradual relaxation of these susceptible proteins from their native tertiary state to the secondary state exposes an increased number of sulfhydryl (–SH) groups, a transition that contributes to the typical "cooked" flavor of heated milk. Visual evidence of the denaturation of these whey proteins is seen in the thin layer of precipitated protein that collects on the bottom of the pan in which the milk is being heated. This precipitated protein becomes quite hot because of its concentration on the hot bottom surface of the pan, and scorching soon becomes evident. The color and flavor changes that occur as the precipitated whey proteins interact with the lactose in milk are gradual as nonenzymatic browning (Maillard reaction) proceeds.

The comparative ease with which whey proteins precipitate to the bottom of a pan of milk and begin to interact with lactose to produce undesirable browning and flavor changes makes scorching one of the chief problems in milk cookery. A heavy pan, such as heavy aluminum, distributes heat quite uniformly and reduces scorching. However, stirring still needs to be done thoroughly and very frequently to prevent the denatured whey proteins from collecting on the bottom of the pan and becoming overheated.

Denaturation of the whey proteins also leads to scum formation in milk-containing products heated to and held above 60°C, because the denatured protein molecules gradually join together. Evaporation of water from the surface of milk being heated compounds the problem of scum formation by increasing the concentration of casein and the salts in milk, particularly calcium phosphate. This situation results in decreased solubility of the protein salts, causing them to coalesce gradually as the heating is continued. Even when the scum is removed, newly precipitated milk proteins quickly form a new layer on the surface. Steam pressure builds under the scum, and the milk may boil over easily.

Casein micelles are distinctly resistant to heat treatment when the pH of the medium is essentially neutral, but this stability gradually changes if casein is heated in an acidic environment. A severe heat treatment at a pH of approximately 7.0, however, can cause casein to form a coagulum. This change may be caused, in part, by the splitting of some of the phosphate that had been esterified to the casein and also by some proteolysis of peptide bonds in the casein molecules. The time and temperature usually involved in milk cookery are not ordinarily sufficiently severe to cause denaturation and coagulation of casein within the milk product.

Enzyme Action

Occasionally, rennet is used in making clabbered (clotted) desserts. This is the same process used in the manufacture of cheese when rennet is added to hasten curd formation. Maintenance of the temperature between 15 and 60°C is essential to the action of the enzyme. Outside these extremes, the proteinaceous enzyme is inactivated, and clotting is blocked. The clot that forms is stronger when the pH of the milk is about 5.8 than either more acidic or more neutral.

Milk to be used in making rennet-clabbered desserts should not be heated above 60°C at any time, either before or during the making of the dessert. Although the reason that previous heat treatment influences the rate of clabbering is not clear, there does appear to be an interaction between the casein micelles and the β-lactoglobulin in the whey; α-lactalbumin and β-lactoglobulin complexed with κ-casein are not coagulated by the action of rennet.

Acid

Casein, the most abundant protein in milk, is least soluble and most easily precipitated at a pH of about 4.6, which is its isoelectric point. Although the pH of milk normally is comfortably above the isoelectric point of casein, inclusion of fruits and a few vegetables can reduce the pH of the milk enough to approach the isoelectric point. The result is decreased solubility of casein and increased likelihood of curdling.

Curdled milk-containing products are not aesthetically satisfying and should be avoided. When fruits or quite acidic vegetables, such as tomatoes, are included in a recipe containing milk, the acidic ingredient should be stirred carefully into the milk and heated just as short a time as possible. This technique keeps the likelihood of curdling to an absolute minimum. Curdling is more likely to occur when asparagus, peas, string beans, or carrots are cooked in milk than when cabbage, cauliflower, or spinach is the vegetable used. The different behavior of these various vegetables probably results from the difference in polyphenol (tannin) content, as well as in pH.

Salts

Salts of various types also influence the stability of the proteins in milk-containing recipes. The ability of salt ions to interact with electrical charges on the surface of milk proteins enables the conflicting electrical charges to be reduced to an absolute minimum, which favors the denaturation and coagulation of milk proteins. The valence of the salt ions and the concentration play critical roles in determining the influence of a specific salt on milk proteins in a food product. A concentration of between 0.2 and 0.6 percent calcium chloride causes milk to coagulate if the temperature is maintained between 45 and 65°C .

Salts can complicate the problem of heating meats in milk, as meats naturally contain some salts. Cured meats have a considerable amount of salt added, a situation that is very likely to result in formation of milk curds during cooking. The problem is accentuated if salty meats and acid-containing ingredients are included.

EFFECTS OF HEAT ON CHEESE PRODUCTS

The moisture and fat content of natural cheeses, as well as the pH, influence the ease with which cheeses can be utilized in cooked products. Its high moisture content enables cream cheese to blend readily with other ingredients during heating. In comparison, cheddar cheese, which is lower in moisture, is more difficult to blend; however, cheddar that has been aged for several months blends readily. It appears that the solubility of some of the protein increases as a result of the chemical changes that occur during ripening of cheddar cheeses with a comparatively high fat content. Cheeses with a low fat content, however, do not show significant improvements in cooking characteristics during aging; instead, they are likely to become increasingly stringy and tough as aging proceeds.

Stringiness can be a problem in products containing heated natural cheeses. The stringy nature of these heated cheeses is accentuated at a pH between 5.0 and 5.6, but the textural difficulties are reduced detectably if the pH of the cheese and other ingredients is at least 5.8 or higher. This difference may result from the interaction of calcium with phosphates at the higher pH, a change promoting easier blending of the casein.

Stringiness, toughness, and fat separation are problems that can be noted when products made with natural cheeses are heated excessively. Either an extended period of heating or a high cooking temperature is likely to cause a hot cheese-containing food to develop some or all of these characteristics. The longer the heating period and the higher the temperature, the greater are the detrimental changes. With such high energies in the food, the protein molecules draw ever tighter together, forcing fat and water out of the system and increasing the density of the proteins. Such changes are not reversible and can be controlled best by using moderate temperatures, aged cheese, and keeping heating periods to a minimum. The presence of an emulsifying agent in process cheeses helps to avoid the loss of fat and the consequent increased concentration of protein when these cheeses are used for cooking.

FOAMS

Milk Foams

The proteins and water in milk can be extended into thin films by agitation. These thin films enclose small air bubbles to make a foam in which the protein and water provide the continuous network of the colloidal dispersion, and the air is the discontinuous or dispersed phase. This arrangement is possible because the native proteins in milk have a low surface tension and low vapor pressure. The low surface tension makes it possible to spread the liquid proteins into thin films, and the low vapor pressure reduces the likelihood that evaporation will occur.

In fluid milks, the concentration of protein is too low to permit the production of a foam with any stability. However, evaporated milk can be whipped into a foam with a very large volume. The increased protein and fat concentrations of the undiluted evaporated milk make it possible for the foam to form, and the foam will even have some limited stability. Foam formation and stability are enhanced if the undiluted evaporated milk is chilled until ice crystals start to form in it. This condition causes the fat to be rather firm, which concentrates the protein in the remaining unfrozen water and also helps to give some rigidity to the cell walls in the foam. Still more stability can be achieved by adding lemon juice because the acid promotes precipitation of the milk proteins to give more strength to the cell walls. Although evaporated milk foams can be formed, they are of limited usefulness unless a stabilizer, such as gelatin, is added. Even with the use of gelatin, evaporated milk foams may be unacceptable to consumers unless they are used in a product with sufficiently strong flavors to mask the cooked flavor imparted by the evaporated milk foam.

Nonfat dried milk solids also can be used to make milk foams. To do this, the solids must be combined with water in equal amounts by volume. This dilution results in a concentrated protein mixture that readily forms a foam with large volume and limited stability. As is true with evaporated milk foams, gelatin is needed to provide suitable stability if this type of foam is used. Foams made with nonfat dried milk solids gain their limited stability from the comparatively high concentration of denatured milk proteins. There is essentially no fat present to enhance stability. Although this type of foam has little flavor because of the absence of fat, it does have the advantage of being quite low in calories.

Cream Foams

Whipping cream, with its fat content of at least 30 percent, can be beaten to a foam, but cream with 36 percent fat can be beaten quickly to a more stable foam. At a fat level of at least 30 percent, the foam forms fairly readily if the cream is chilled (but not frozen). The fat is quite firm and contributes considerable rigidity to the cell walls in a whipped cream foam that is kept chilled. Overbeating whipped cream causes reversal to a water-in-oil emulsion; butter results.

As fat is the principal component contributing to the strength of the cell walls, it is essential that whipped cream be stored under refrigeration until the time it is served. If the cream is allowed to begin to warm to room temperature, the fat will start to soften, and the rigid cell walls containing the warming fat will weaken. If warm enough, the whipped cream foam may melt into a liquid system.

Whipping cream ordinarily is pasteurized to ensure the absence of harmful microorganisms. This heat treatment has a slightly detrimental effect on foam formation, but the benefit of safety outweighs this small disadvantage. On the other hand, homogenization is not usually done because the disruption of the fat globules into smaller spheres interferes significantly with foam formation and stability and offers no advantage.

Cream that has aged for about 3 days whips somewhat better than very fresh cream. This effect is thought to result from the slight drop in pH during this period.

Sugar often is added to whipped cream for flavor despite the slight negative effect it has on stiffness. This effect is noted whether sugar is added before, during, or after the cream is whipped.

SUMMARY

Milk contains less than 4 percent fat, more than half of which is saturated and about a third of which is monounsaturated. Lactose is the type of carbohydrate in milk. Casein is the protein complex comprising the curd formed when milk reaches the isoelectric point of casein (pH 4.6) or is treated with rennin, a milk-clotting enzyme. The whey proteins include β-lactoglobulin and α-lactalbumin.

Pasteurization is a heat treatment that kills potentially harmful microorganisms that might be present in milk. Homogenization is done by forcing milk through tiny apertures to modify the size of the fat globules and alter the protein slightly. Evaporation and drying are techniques used to preserve milk for later use. Fermentation is used to alter the physical and chemical properties of some milk products, such as buttermilk.

Numerous products are available in the dairy department, ranging from homogenized, pasteurized fluid milks (whole, reduced fat, low-fat, and nonfat) and chocolate milk, through fermented milks (cultured buttermilk, acidophilus milk, yogurt, and Lactaid), creams of varying fat content, butter, canned milks (evaporated milks of varying fat levels and sweetened condensed milk), and dried milks. Cheese is made from milk by forming a curd (with the use of acid, rennin, or both), draining much of the whey, and then heating and pressing gently to achieve the desired moisture level, usually around 40 percent. These natural cheeses often are aged to modify flavor and texture. Process cheeses are made by heating selected natural cheeses with an emulsifier. Ice cream (either plain or composite), frozen custard, low-fat ice creams, and sherbet are frozen dairy desserts. Mellorine is an imitation ice cream in which the milk fat has been replaced, and parevine is an imitation product in which both the milk fat and milk solids have been substituted.

Ice creams are frozen by agitating them in a container surrounded by a mixture of ice and salt in the ratio of about 8:1. Freezing needs to occur rapidly enough that small ice crystals can be formed while the mixture is agitated. Agitation incorporates some air, producing overrun and a pleasingly light texture with fine crystals. Fat, egg white, various sweeteners, and other interfering substances can be included in an ice cream formula to help prevent the formation of large ice crystals and lactose crystals, thus enhancing texture.

Natural cheeses blend with other foods, depending on moisture content, aging, and pH. High moisture content aids in blending. Aged natural cheeses with a high fat content blend well because of increased solubility of the protein. Stringiness, toughness, and fat separation can be problems when cooking with natural cheeses unless the heating period is short and the temperature comparatively low. Process cheeses are less likely to show these detrimental changes because of the emulsifier they contain. Reduced-fat cheeses are being developed and marketed.

Rennet can be used to make clabbered desserts. The pH should be about 5.8, and the temperature should be within the range 10 to 65°C.

When milk is heated, some of the β-lactoglobulin and α-lactalbumin denature and precipitate to form a thin layer of protein on the bottom. This protein gradually undergoes nonenzymatic browning (the Maillard reaction) with lactose, leading to scorching. In addition, a scum can form when milk is heated. This rough protein scum coats the surface and can easily hold in steam until enough pressure builds up, forcing it to rise, and the milk boils over. Casein is quite resistant to precipitation when heat is applied, but severe heating can cause casein to form a curd at a pH of 7.0.

When preparing products with milk, it is important to be aware of the isoelectric point of casein and the acidity of fruits and some vegetables. If the acid is added to the milk and the heating time is kept short, curdling can be avoided or kept to a minimum. Salts can increase the likelihood of milk protein curdling by providing ions that combine with the electrical charges on the protein molecules to reduce the electrical repulsion between the molecules. This change facilitates the aggregation and precipitation of the milk proteins.

Fluid milks are not able to form stable foams, but undiluted, chilled evaporated milk and nonfat dried milk solids diluted with an equal volume of water can be whipped into foams; these foams need to be stabilized with gelatin or gums if they are to be used in food products. The cooked flavor of an evaporated milk foam is detectable unless it is masked with other strong-flavored ingredients. The foam made with nonfat dried milk solids is very mild in flavor and is low in calories because of the lack of fat. Protein is the stabilizing agent in nonfat dried milk solids foams, and protein and fat help to stabilize the evaporated milk foam. Whipped cream gets its stability primarily from its high fat content (preferably 36 percent); it must be kept chilled so that the fat will be firm.

STUDY QUESTIONS

1. Identify the principal proteins in milk. Describe the form in which casein occurs.
2. How is milk pasteurized? Why is this an important treatment?
3. What changes occur in milk as a result of homogenization?
4. Name three fermented milk products and describe the production of each.

5. Compare the advantages and disadvantages of fluid milks, evaporated milks, sweetened condensed milk, and nonfat dried milk.

6. Describe the production of cheese. How does the production of natural cheese differ from that of process cheese?

7. What are the differences between ice cream, sherbet, frozen custard, mellorine, and parevine?

8. What changes occur in milk when it is heated? How does the addition of acid influence the product?

9. Describe the effect of salts on milk that is being used in a heated cream soup.

10. Identify three ways of achieving a fine texture in ice cream. Explain the action of each.

BIBLIOGRAPHY

Adda, J., et al. 1982. "Chemistry of flavor and texture generation in cheese." *Food Chem. 9:* 115.

Aguilera, J. M. 1995. "Gelation of whey proteins." *Food Technol. 49* (10): 83.

Anonymous. 1994. *Use of Bovine Somatotropin (BST) in the United States: Its Potential Effects.* Executive Summary. Executive Branch of Federal Government. Washington, D.C.

Arbuckle, W. S. 1986. *Ice Cream.* 4th ed. AVI Publishing: Westport CT.

Babayan, V. K. and Rosenau, J. R. 1991. "Medium-chain triglyceride cheese." *Food Technol. 45* (2): 111.

Banks, J. M., Brechany, E. Y., and Cristie, W. W. 1989. "Production of lowfat Cheddar-type cheese." *J. Soc. Dairy Technol. 42:* 6.

Barach, J. T. 1985. "What's new in genetic engineering of dairy starter cultures and dairy enzymes." *Food Technol. 37* (10): 73.

Barr, A. 1990. "Consumer motivational forces affecting sale of light dairy products." *Food Technol. 44* (10): 97.

Bassette, R. and Fung, D. 1986. "Off-flavors in milk." *CRC Crit. Rev. Food Sci. Nutr. 24* (1): 1.

Bernal, V. and Jelen, P. 1985. "Thermal stability of whey proteins." *J. Daily Sci. 68:* 2847.

Blaser, M. J. 1986. "Brainerd diarrhea: Newly recognized raw milk-associated enteropathy." *J. Am. Med. Assoc. 256* (July 4): 510.

Bruhn, C. M. and Schultz, H. G. 1986. "Consumer perceptions of dairy and related-use foods." *Food Technol. 40* (1): 79.

DeKanterewicz, R. J. and Chirife, J. 1986. "Color changes and available lysine during storage of shelf-stable concentrated cheese whey." *J. Food Sci. 51* (3): 826.

Descamps, O., et al. 1986. "Physical effect of starch/carrageenan interactions in water and milk." *Food Technol. 40* (4): 81.

Dutson, T. R. and Orcutt, M. W. 1984. "Chemical changes in proteins produced by thermal processing." *J. Chem. Educ. 61* (4): 303.

Fennema, O. R. 1985. *Food Chemistry.* 2nd ed. Marcel Dekker, Inc.: New York.

German, J. B. and Dillard, C. J. 1998. Fractionated milk fat: Composition, structure, and functional properties. *Food Technol. 52* (2): 33.

Hansen, A. P. 1987. "Effect of ultra-high-temperature processing and storage on dairy flood flavor." *Food Technol. 41* (9): 112.

Jost, R., et al. 1986. "Heat gelation of oil-in-water emulsions stabilized by whey protein." *J. Food Sci. 51* (2): 440.

Kantor, M. A. 1990. "Light dairy products: Need and consequences." *Food Technol. 44* (10): 81.

Kilara, N. and Sharkase, T. Y. 1986. "Effects of temperature on food proteins and its implications on functional properties." *CRC Crit. Rev. Food Sci. Nutr. 23* (4): 323.

Kleyn, D. H. 1992. "Textural aspects of butter." *Food Technol. 46* (1): 118.

Konstance, R. P. and Holsinger, V. H. 1992. "Development of rheological test methods for cheese." *Food Technol. 46* (1): 105.

Kosilkowski. 1986. "New cheese-making procedures utilizing ultrafiltration." *Food Technol. 40* (6): 71.

Kroger, M. 1976. "Quality of yogurt." *J. Dairy Sci. 59:* 344.

Kurtzweil, P. 1998. "Skimming the milk label." *FDA Consumer 32* (1): 22.

Law, B. A. 1981. "Formation of aroma and flavor compounds in fermented dairy products." *Dairy Sci. Abstr. 43:* 154.

Mangino, M. E. 1992. "Gelation of whey protein concentrates." *Food Technol. 46* (1): 114.

Mermelstein, N. H. 1998. Ice cream challenges. *Food Technol. 52* (9): 106.

Morr, C. V. 1992. "Improving texture and functionality of whey protein concentrate." *Food Technol. 46* (1): 110.

Olson, N. F. and Johnson, M. E. 1990. "Light cheese products: characteristics and economics." *Food Technol. 44* (10): 93.

Onwulata, C. I., Smith, P. W., Konstance, R. P., and Holsinger, V. H. 1995. "Baking proper ties of encapsulated milkfat." *Food Technol. 49* (3): 82.

Osterholm, M. T., et al. 1986. "Outbreak of newly recognized chronic diarrhea syndrome associated with raw milk consumption." *J. Am. Med. Assoc. 256* (July 4): 484.

Pitcher, W. H. 1986. "Genetic modification of enzymes used in food processing." *Food Technol 40* (10): 62.

Pszczola, D. E. 1998. "An interview with Elsie." *Food Technol. 52* (2): 63.

Rank, T. C. 1985. "Proteolysis and flavor development in lowfat and whole milk Colby and Chedder-type cheeses." Ph.D. thesis. Univ. Wisconsin: Madison.

Rizvi, S. S. H. and Bhaskar, A. R. 1995. "Supercritical fluid processing of milk fat: fractionation, scale-up, and economics." *Food Technol. 49* (2): 90.

Ropp, K. L. 1994. "New animal drug increases milk production." *FDA Consumer 28* (3): 24.

Salminen, S. J. and Saxelin, M. 1996. "Comparison of successful probiotic strains." *Nutr. Today Suppl. 31* (6): 32S.

Schroder, B. G. and Baer, R. J. 1990. "Utilization of cholesterol-reduced milk fat in fluid milks." *Food Technol. 44* (11): 145.

Shank, F. R. and Carson, K. L. 1990. "Light dairy products: regulatory issues." *Food Technol. 44* (10): 88.

Shoemaker, C. F., Nantz, J., Bonnans, S., and Noble, A. C. 1992. "Rheological characterization of dairy products." *Food Technol. 46* (1): 98.

Singer, N. S. 1990. "Simplesse—The natural fat substitute." Proc. Dairy Products Techn. Conf. Am. Dairy Products Inst. Chicago and Center for Dairy Res., Univ. of Wisconsin: Madison. P. 85.

Tharp, B. W. and Gottemoller, T. V. 1990. "Light frozen dairy desserts: effect of compositional changes on processing and sensory characteristics." *Food Technol. 44* (10): 86.

Thompson, M. S. 1990. "Light dairy products: issues and objectives." *Food Technol. 44* (10): 78.

Wong, N. P., Jenness, R., Kenney, M., and Marth, E. H., eds. 1988. *Fundamentals of Dairy Chemistry.* 3rd ed. Van Nostrand Reinhold: New York.

CHAPTER 15

Meats, Fish, and Poultry

CLASSIFICATION

Flesh foods usually are categorized as either **meat, poultry,** or **fish.** According to this classification, meat is understood to include all red meats from animal sources, although the only ones commonly available are beef, veal, pork, and lamb (or mutton in some countries). Poultry includes turkey, chicken, and duck, as well as pheasants and other less available fowl. Fish, in the broad sense, is the term used to designate aquatic animals, but frequently fish is the more narrow classification that includes only those with fins, gills, a backbone, and a skull. **Shellfish,** the other classification of aquatic animals, is subdivided into **mollusks** and **crustaceans,** the former having a shell and the latter having a horny covering.

STRUCTURE

Muscle Tissue

Components. Muscle has water as its primary constituent; actually it is about 75 percent water. The next most abundant substance, protein, is a distant second, constituting only about 18 percent of the total muscle content. The amount of fat is highly variable, but commonly ranges from 4 to 10 percent of the content of muscle tissue. Carbohydrate, primarily in the form of glycogen plus a small amount of glucose and glucose 6-phosphate, accounts for just over 1 percent of the total. Vitamins, minerals, and trace amounts of various organic compounds complete the picture.

The specific composition of muscle tissue varies from muscle to muscle and even from one spot to another within a muscle. This variation makes the testing of meats a challenging task. Additional complications are found because of the differences existing between carcasses.

Meat
Red meats, including beef, veal, pork, and lamb.

Poultry
Fowl, notably turkey, chicken, and duck.

Fish
Broadly defined as aquatic animals, but more narrowly defined to designate those with fins, gills, a backbone, and a skull.

Shellfish
Subclassification of fish; includes mollusks and crustaceans.

Mollusks
Shellfish with a protective shell.

Crustaceans
Shrimp, lobsters, crabs, and other shellfish with a horny covering.

Myosin
Principal myofibrillar protein.

Actin
Myofibrillar protein existing primarily in two forms (F and G).

Tropomyosin
Least abundant of the three principal myofibrillar proteins.

Actomyosin
Muscle protein formed from the union of actin and myosin during muscle contraction.

Adenosine Triphosphatase (ATPase)
Enzyme in muscle tissue involved in glycolytic reactions leading to lactic acid formation.

Pyrophosphatase
Group of enzymes in muscle tissue influencing the water-holding capacity of meat.

Cathepsins
Group of proteolytic enzymes that can catalyze hydrolytic reactions leading to the passing of rigor mortis.

Calcium-activated Factor (CAF)
Proteolytic enzyme activated by calcium; contributes to tenderizing of aging meat.

Myofilament
Simplest level of organization in muscle; classified as thick or thin myofilaments.

Thick Myofilament
The thicker, longer type of myofilament; composed of myosin molecules joined together to form a screw-like, thick, and elongated filament.

Thin Myofilament
Thin filament formed by the helical twisting of two strands of polymerized actin.

Myofibril
Linear bundle of several myofilaments that contains a number of sarcomeres.

Sarcomere
Portion of a myofibril consisting of the area between two Z lines.

Z Lines
Region in a myofibril where the thin myofilaments of actin adjoin, creating a dark line that defines the end of a sarcomere.

Proteins. Myofibrillar proteins are the proteins often referred to as the muscle proteins. The three most abundant are myosin, actin, and tropomyosin. **Myosin** is a comparatively long, thin protein molecule with a molecular weight of approximately 500,000. **Actin** is found in two forms—G-actin and F-actin. F-Actin is very long, and its molecular weight is extremely great, ranging into the millions. G-Actin is much smaller, with a molecular weight of only 50,000 or slightly greater; it can aggregate to form F-actin. **Tropomyosin** is slightly greater in molecular weight than G-actin and is considerably smaller than myosin, actually only about one fourth as long.

A very important myofibrillar protein is formed by the union of actin and myosin. This protein is called actomyosin. The formation of **actomyosin** actually is a reversible reaction catalyzed by ATP and the presence of calcium and magnesium ions. Five lesser muscle proteins (tropomyosin, troponin, M-protein, α-actinin, and β-actinin) may influence the formation of actomyosin or its degradation to actin and myosin again. The transformation of myosin and actin into actomyosin and the reversal releasing these two protein components are reactions accompanying contraction and relaxation of muscle tissue.

Enzymes contribute to the total protein found in muscle tissue. Some soluble **adenosine triphosphatase (ATPase)** is found in the sarcoplasm, the jellylike protein in muscle fibers. The action of this enzyme postmortem, ultimately leading to the formation of lactic acid and the resulting drop in the pH of the tissue, may be largely responsible for the onset of rigor mortis. Neutral **pyrophosphatases** (PPase) may influence the water-holding capacity of meat. **Cathepsins** and **calcium-activated factor** are other enzymes found in muscle tissue. These are important because of their probable role in proteolytic reactions leading to the softening of tissue that marks the passing of rigor mortis.

Organization. The structure of muscle tissue is quite complex in its organization; it begins with the association of protein molecules (including myosin and actin) into **myofilaments** and continues as these initial structures associate with increasingly larger structures until finally the complete muscle is defined (Figure 15.1). This can be traced most clearly by examining the myofilaments first. Myofilaments are classified as either thick or thin. **Thick myofilaments** are about 100 angstroms (Å) thick and about 1.5 millimicrons long. In thick myofilaments, myosin molecules are arranged in a linear, head-to-foot orientation which then is coiled so that the heads are directed toward the outer portion of the myofilaments. **Thin myofilaments** are composed of spherical actin molecules polymerized into strands, with two of these strands twisted in a helical configuration to form a single, thin myofilament about 50 Å thick and somewhat shorter than the thick myofilaments. The actin of the thin myofilaments is able to associate with other muscle proteins (including troponin, tropomyosin, and α-actinin), which adds to the complexity of the basic organization of muscle.

These myofilaments are arranged in units called **sarcomeres,** and it is these sarcomeres arranged in a linear fashion that together constitute the units called myofibrils. The arrangement of the myofilaments to make a sarcomere is quite orderly and results in distinct patterns that can be seen in electron micrographs (see Figure 15.2).

In an electron micrograph, fairly thin dark lines perpendicular to the axis of the sarcomere can be seen, lines that are referred to as *Z lines.* The Z lines are the

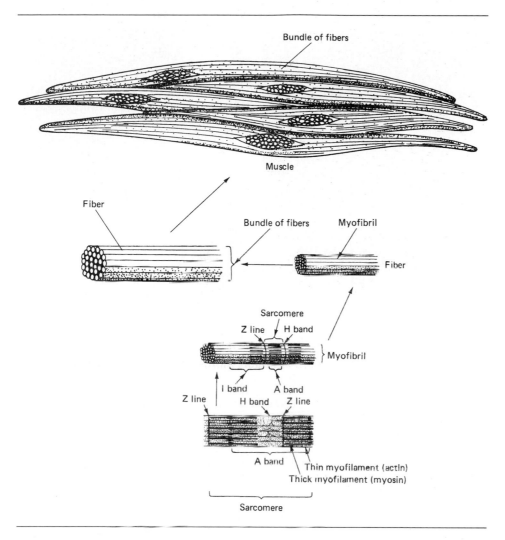

Figure 15.1 Schematic diagrams showing the organization of thin (actin) and thick (myosin) myofilaments into ever higher levels of organization to form a muscle.

points where thin myofilaments of actin come together and overlap, with their filaments extending from both sides of the junction. The area on either side of the Z line is quite light in an electron micrograph and is referred to as the ***I band.*** The I band is the region where only thin myofilaments of actin are found and where they are not adjoining, as is true of the Z line.

A moderately dark, fairly wide region can be noted adjacent to the I band; this is the region where both thin and thick myofilaments occur, but still in a linear, orderly arrangement. The thin myofilaments extend into this region where the thick myofilaments are found. However, the thick myofilaments extend much farther along the length of the sarcomere. This same configuration extends from the Z line at the other end of the sarcomere but, again, because they are shorter, the thin myofilaments do not extend far enough to meet the thin myofilaments extending from

I Band
The light region on either side of the Z line in a sarcomere, consisting of nonoverlapping myofilaments of actin.

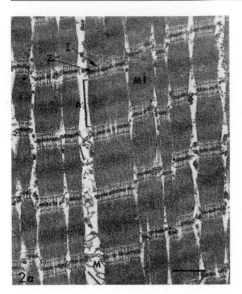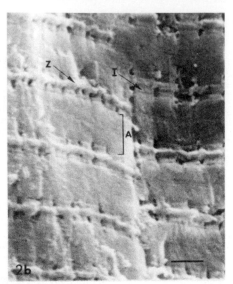

Figure 15.2   Muscle cell structure in aged bovine semitendinosus muscle viewed by (left) transmission electron microscopy and (right) scanning electron microscopy. Myofibrils (Mf) run vertically. Bandings on the sarcomeres are the, Z, I, and A bands. Mitochondria (M) are degraded. Bars = l_u. (Courtesy of S. B. Jones, U.S. Department of Agriculture, Agricultural Research Service, North Atlantic Area Eastern Regional Research Center. Reprinted from *Food Technology*. 1977. Vol. 31(4): 83. Copyright (c) by Institute of Food Technologists.)

H Band
Region in the center of a sarcomere where only thick myofilaments of myosin occur.

A Band
Total portion of the sarcomere in which thick and thin myofilaments overlap; includes the H band.

Fiber
Bundle of myofibrils and sarcoplasm encased in the sarcolemma.

Sarcoplasm
Jellylike protein surrounding the myofibrils in muscle fibers.

Sarcolemma
Thin, transparent membrane surrounding the bundle of myofibrils that constitute a fiber.

the opposite end. The result is a region in the center of the sarcomere where only thick myofilaments of myosin occur. This region of myosin myofilaments in the middle of the sarcomere is designated the **H band.** The length of the sarcomere from one end of the overlapping thin and thick myofilaments to the end of the other region in the same sarcomere is termed the **A band,** which encompasses the H band.

The nature of the organization of the myofilaments of myosin and actin is important to the theory of muscle contraction and relaxation. According to Huxley (1971), contraction occurs when thin actin filaments bond briefly with a portion of the myosin filaments and then slowly migrate toward the middle of the sarcomere, causing the sarcomere to shorten or contract. The complex that forms between myosin and actin myofilaments is called actomyosin. Relaxation and lengthening to the original dimensions of the sarcomere occur when the actomyosin dissociates into the component actin and myosin myofilaments (see Figure 15.3).

Myofibrils are held in long bundles called **fibers.** Each fiber consists of many myofibrils oriented together in a linear fashion and surrounded by a distinctly viscous protein sol, the **sarcoplasm.** This assembly is held together by a thin, transparent membrane called the **sarcolemma.** The diameter and length of these fibers in meat vary considerably with the muscle and the animal. They usually range between 10 and 100 micrometers (millionths of a meter) in diameter, and may be millimeters, or even centimeters, long (see Figure 15.4).

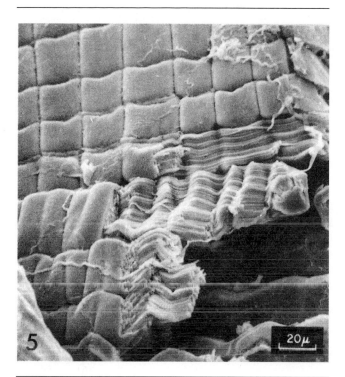

Figure 15.3   Severely contracted fibers of cold-shortened longissimus dorsi muscle (SEM micrograph). (Courtesy of S. B. Jones, U.S. Department of Agriculture, Agricultural Research Service, North Atlantic Area Eastern Regional Research Center. Reprinted from *Food Technology*. 1977. Vol. 31 (4): 83. Copyright (c) by Institute of Food Technologists.)

Figure 15.4   Muscle fibers of bovine semitendinosus muscle imaged at low magnification by scanning electron microscopy. (Courtesy of S. B. Jones, U.S. Department of Agriculture, Agricultural Research Service, North Atlantic Area Eastern Regional Research Center. Reprinted from *Food Technology*. 1977. Vol. 31 (4): 3. Copyright (c) by Institute of Food Technologists.)

Connective Tissue

Proteins.   Four categories of materials are abundant in the connective tissue of meats. All of these are either pure protein or conjugated protein compounds. Of the four, collagen is perhaps the most important. The others are elastin, reticulin, and ground substance.

Collagen is of importance in meats because it is the fibrous protein found in the structural sheaths both within and between muscles. It is a rather complex protein that comprises strands of tropocollagen, which are produced by the cells and then transferred to the ground substance for actual integration into molecules of collagen. **Tropocollagen** is a fibrous, coiled molecule consisting of three strands linked together to make a long, thin unit (see Figure 15.5).

Collagen
Fibrous protein composed of three strands of tropocollagen.

Tropocollagen
Fibrous protein consisting of three strands twisted together and containing large amounts of glycine, proline, and hydroxyproline.

Figure 15.5   Schematic diagram of a collagen molecule.

Collagen

Tropocollagen

The presence of an abundance of hydroxyproline and proline (about 25 percent) accounts for the fibrous nature of tropocollagen because the linkage of this amide through the **pyrrolidine ring** sterically hinders the molecule from assuming the usual helical configuration that leads to a spherical protein. In other words, the nitrogen in either proline or hydroxyproline is involved in the primary structure (the backbone chain) of the strands of tropocollagen, and the planar rigidity of the pyrrolidine ring prevents the bond angles that lead to the usual α-helix and ultimate spherical nature of most food proteins. This rigidity is significant because of the unusually large quantity of the two pyrrolidine-ring amino acids, proline and hydroxyproline, as shown below.

Pyrrolidine Ring
Organic ring structure containing one atom of nitrogen; linkage to another amino acid through this nitrogen favors formation of a linear, fibrous protein molecule.

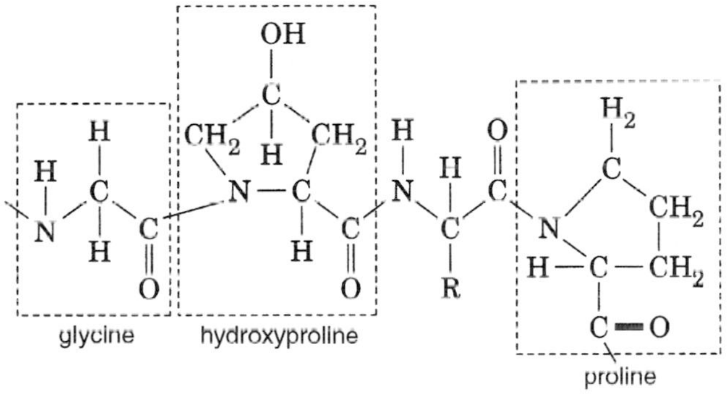

glycine   hydroxyproline   proline

The other unique aspect of the chemical composition of tropocollagen is that it contains a large amount of the extremely simple amino acid glycine. Actually, a third of the molecule is glycine. A variety of amino acids constitute the remaining approximately 42 percent of the amino acids in tropocollagen.

The association between the three strands to form the tropocollagen molecule is caused by the formation of hydrogen bonds. In turn, these molecules are held in the larger collagen molecule as a result of a combination of bonding forces, including hydrogen bonding. The stability of the native collagen molecule is due in large measure to the formation of covalent bonds that crosslink the three strands of tropocollagen to form a molecule of collagen. The number of covalent bonds formed between the three tropocollagen constituents increases gradually over time, which helps explain the increasing toughness of the meat from animals as they grow older.

Elastin, in contrast to the relative abundance of collagen, is found in very limited amounts intramuscularly. The yellow color of elastin makes it quite distinguishable from collagen, which is white. Unlike collagen, which can be converted during cooking to gelatin, elastin is very resistant to chemical change. The rubbery character of elastin accounts for its name. Two unusual amino acids, desmocine and isodesmocine, provide important structural contributions because their tetracarboxylic–tetraamino acid functional groups permit them to crosslink with as many as four chains of amino acid residues. Only a somewhat limited amount (less than 3 percent of the total protein) of hydroxyproline is found in elastin.

Elastin
Yellow connective tissue occurring in limited amounts intramuscularly and in somewhat greater concentrations in deposits outside the muscles.

Ground substance is a protein-containing substance in meat; its main constituents are plasma proteins and glycoprotein. The constituents of the ground substance include amino acids with excess carboxylic acid groups. In contrast to collagen, ground substance proteins are low in glycine and void of proline. Interestingly, it is apparently in the ground substance that the tropocollagen strands are

Ground Substance
Undifferentiated matrix of plasma proteins and glycoproteins in which fibrous molecules of collagen and/or elastin are bound.

crosslinked securely so that collagen molecules, each containing three strands of tropocollagen, are formed. The proteins in the ground substance frequently are bound very tightly to mucopolysaccharides, and these glycoproteins form an amorphous matrix in which collagen and elastin can be held to form connective tissue.

Reticulin is the fourth category of protein in connective tissue. Although it is a fibrous protein similar to collagen, the linkage with myristic acid (a 14-carbon fatty acid) clearly distinguishes this material from collagen.

Reticulin
A type of connective tissue protein associated with a fatty acid (myristic acid).

Endomysium
Very delicate connective tissue found between fibers.

Perimysium
Connective tissue surrounding a bundle of several fibers.

Epimysium
Connective tissue surrounding an entire muscle (many bundles of bundles of fibers).

Muscle
Aggregation of bundles of bundles of fibers surrounded by the epimysium.

Organization.   Connective tissue, consisting primarily of ground substance and collagen, is found between each fiber. This connective tissue is designated the **endomysium** (innermost). The next level of organization in muscle tissue is the bundling together of several fibers to give a thicker fibrous bundle, which then is encased in still more connective tissue; this tissue is referred to as the **perimysium.** Finally, many of these bundles of fibers, each surrounded by its perimysium, are gathered into large collections of fibers and surrounded by yet another layer of connective tissue called the **epimysium** (outer). These structures are the **muscles** contained in meats (see Figures 15.6 and 15.7).

The complexity of muscle organization in red meats can be summarized as follows:

1.   Structural components and organization into muscle
    A.   Myofilaments
        1.   thick (myosin)
        2.   Thin (actin, plus such proteins as troponin, tropomyosin, and α-actin)
    B.   Sarcometes (organized myofilaments) that form
        1.   Z lines
        2.   I band
        3.   H band
        4.   A band

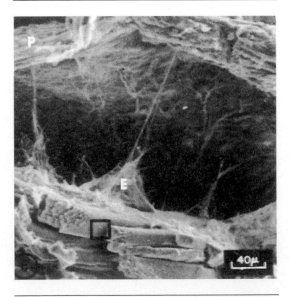

Figure 15.6 Interface of perimysium (P) and endomysium (E) at muscle bundle surface. (Courtesy of S. B. Jones, U.S. Department of Agriculture, Agricultural Research Service, North Atlantic Area Eastern Regional Research Center. Reprinted from *Journal of Food Science.* 1977. Vol. 42: 125. Copyright (c) by Institute of Food Technologists.)

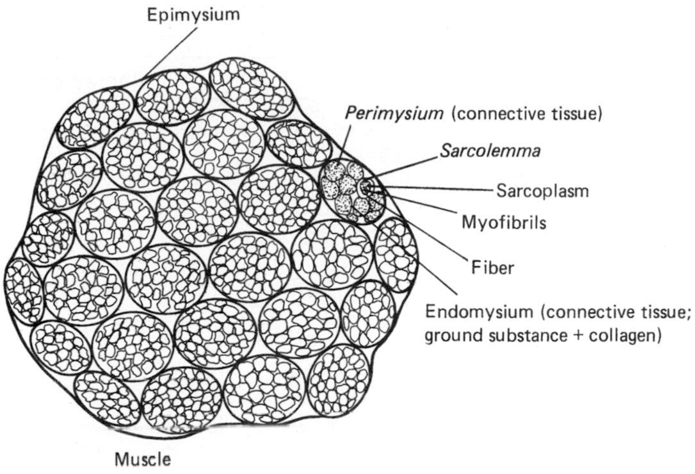

Figure 15.7 Diagram of a cross section of muscle.

Fish flesh is structurally very similar to that of red meats. Myofibrils in fish are much like those found in red meats, except that some (but not all) of the myofibrils in fish muscle are flat, rather than cylindrical. The fibers containing fish myofibrils are only about 3 centimeters long, yet are comparatively thick. The ultimate level of organization in fish tissue is parallel layers of these fibers **(myotomes)**, which then are attached to sheets of the connective tissue **(mycomatta).** The actin and myosin levels (and consequently the actomyosin level, too) are not only higher in fish than in red meats, but the actomyosin and collagen in fish also are more sensitive to heat. These characteristics dictate the need for careful temperature control when preparing fish.

Myotomes
Fibers in fish; these are thick and about 3 centimeters long.

Mycomatta
Sheetlike connective tissue in fish.

Fat

Lipids are found in muscle tissue and also in fatty deposits or fat depots. The fatty acids found most abundantly in the triglycerides in the fat depots are oleic (18 carbon atoms, 1 double bond), palmitic (16 carbon atoms, no double bonds), and stearic (18 carbon atoms, no double bonds). In the cells, the lipid and lipid-related compounds include cholesterol, **glycolipids,** phospholipids, plasmalogens,

Glycolipid
Molecule with a sugar moiety and a lipid portion.

  C. Myofibrils
      1. Sarcomeres
      2. Myofilaments
  D. Fibers
      1. Myofibrils
      2. Sarcoplasm
  E. Bundles of fibers
  F. Muscle (bundles of bundles)
  2. Binding components
    A. Sarcolemma (encases fibers)
    B. Endomysium (between fibers)
    C. Perimysium (surrounds bundles of fibers)
    D. Epimysium (surrounds many bundles of fibers to encase muscle)

Table 15.1   Fat Components of Selected Foods (g/100 g edible portion)[a]

Food	Total Fat	Fatty Acids						Cholesterol (mg)
		Total Saturated	Total Mono-unsaturated	Total Poly-unsaturated	18:3	20:5	22:6	
Beef, chuck, raw	23.6	10.0	10.8	0.9	0.3			73
Lamb, leg, raw	17.6	8.1	7.1	1.0	0.3			71
Chicken, light, no skin, raw	1.7	0.4	0.4	0.4	tr	tr	tr	58
Chicken, dark, no skin, raw	4.3	1.1	1.3	1.0	tr	tr	tr	80
Turkey with skin, raw	9.7	2.8	3.2	2.5	0.1	tr	tr	82
Ocean perch	1.6	0.3	0.6	0.5	tr	0.1	0.1	42
Salmon, sockeye	8.6	1.5	4.1	1.9	0.1	0.5	0.7	—
Crab, Alaska king	0.8	0.1	0.1	0.3	tr	0.2	0.1	—
Scallop, Atlantic	0.8	0.1	0.1	1.1	0.2	0.5	tr	101

[a]Selected from Hepburn, F. N., Exler, J., and Weihrauch, J. L. 1986, "Provisional tables on content of omega-3 fatty acids and other fat components of selected foods." *J. Am. Dietet. Assoc. 86:* 788.

and sphingomyelin. These lipid components are deposited in fat cells in a matrix of connective tissue, primarily collagen. The presence of fat contributes to the juiciness and flavor of meats, and it also is of interest from the perspective of nutrition.

Beef fat, with its comparatively high content of saturated, long-chain fatty acids (Table 15.1) is quite different from pork, lamb, or various types of poultry and fish. Nutritional concern regarding the composition of fats in flesh foods has generated interest in the content of omega-3 fatty acids. Omega-3 fatty acids are particularly abundant in fish oils (Hepburn et al., 1986).

Changes in fats during storage or cooking are important to the quality of flavor and aroma (see Chapter 11). **Phospholipids** are particularly susceptible to chemical changes. Oxidative rancidity may be increased as a result of the presence of phospholipids. Chemical changes may occur as a result of high temperatures in deep-fat frying and broiling, particularly if the time is extended.

Phospholipid
Complex phosphoric ester of a lipid.

PIGMENTS

Myoglobin and Related Compounds

The two key pigments responsible for the color of meats are hemoglobin and myoglobin. Although hemoglobin contributes to the color of meats, much of the coloration is caused by the presence of myoglobin or various forms of myoglobin. Actually, **myoglobin** and hemoglobin are closely related chemically, for they both are iron-containing pigments with heme as the common component. They differ only in their protein component. In contrast to hemoglobin with its four polypeptides, myoglobin has only one strand of protein polymer and has a molecular weight of about 17,000.

Hemoglobin is about four times as large as myoglobin. It consists of four heme–polypeptide polymers joined together. **Heme** comprises four pyrrole rings linked covalently to form a large complex that is joined to a central atom of iron by attachment to the nitrogen atoms in each of the pyrrole rings (Figure 15.8). In turn,

Myoglobin
Purplish-red pigment consisting of heme containing ferrous iron and a polypeptide polymer (globin).

Heme
Compound composed of four adjoining pyrrole rings linked to an atom of iron.

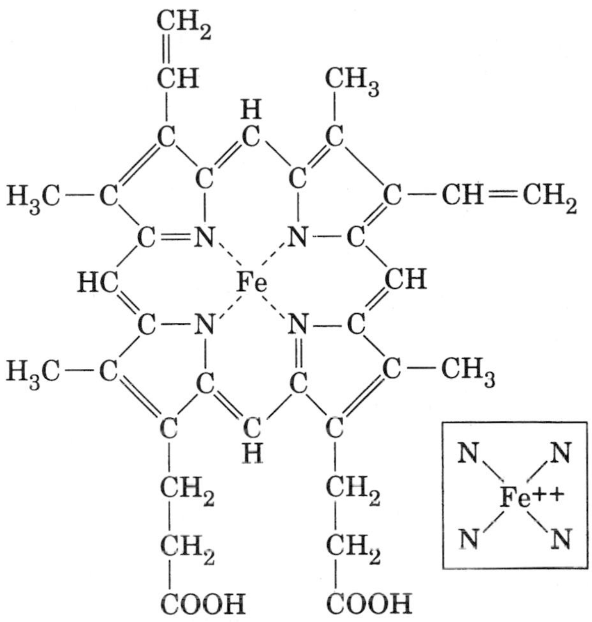

Figure 15.8 Structure of heme (and the abbreviated representation).

four heme–polypeptide polymers also are linked to make the very large molecule designated as **hemoglobin.** Its molecular weight is approximately 68,000.

The iron atom in the center of heme is capable of complexing with other atoms or compounds to form new compounds, resulting in alterations in the color of the meat. Other color changes result from changes in the valence of the iron atom itself.

Myoglobin is of particular interest in the study of meat color because it is the predominant pigment and contributes about three times as much color as hemoglobin does. Myoglobin is a purple red. This color is the result of iron being in the ferrous (2+) state and free of additional atoms or compounds. When meat is fresh and protected from contact with air, it exhibits the purple-red color of myoglobin.

In the presence of air, myoglobin readily adds two atoms of oxygen to form a new compound, **oxymyoglobin.** This new form of myoglobin is responsible for the rather intense red seen on the cut surfaces of meats that have been allowed to stand exposed to air for a while. Availability of an abundance of oxygen favors the formation of oxymyoglobin and ensures that meat will have a pleasingly bright red color. The use of a plastic wrap permeable to oxygen for packaging precut meats helps ensure that the cuts will have the bright red color of oxymyoglobin that appeals to consumers. Tetrasodium pyrophosphate, sodium erythorbate, and citric acid are an effective combination to maintain oxymyoglobin longer when meat is marketed in modified-atmosphere packaging (Manu-Tawiah et al., 1991).

If the oxygen supply available to myoglobin is rather limited or meat is exposed to fluorescent or incandescent light too long, a brownish-red pigment, **metmyoglobin,** forms. This less desirable color results from oxidation of the iron atom to the ferric (3+) state and complexing of a molecule of water. Metmyoglobin can be reduced back to myoglobin. Depending on the environment, myoglobin pigments may be converted between oxymyoglobin, myoglobin, and metmyoglobin according to the following scheme:

Hemoglobin
Very large, iron-containing compound consisting of four heme–polypeptide polymers linked together; contributes to the color of meat.

Oxymyoglobin
Cherry red form of myoglobin formed by the addition of two oxygen atoms.

Metmyoglobin
Brownish-red form of myoglobin formed when the ferrous iron is oxidized to the ferric form and water is complexed to the oxidized iron.

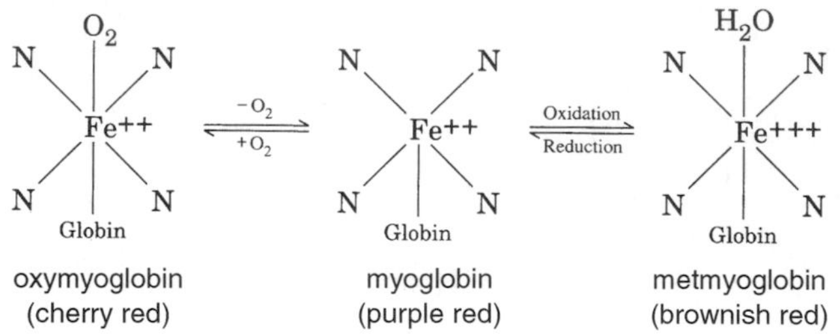

oxymyoglobin
(cherry red)

myoglobin
(purple red)

metmyoglobin
(brownish red)

In contrast to the red color of various animal meats, fish and poultry generally are pigmented quite lightly. Hemoglobin contributes to the light coloration in poultry. Quite a few vertebrate fish have two muscles—a light-colored, large lateral muscle and a less desirable dark muscle deeply pigmented with myoglobin. The lateral muscle in salmon derives its unique color from the presence of **astaxanthin,** which is classified as a carotenoid pigment.

Astaxanthin
Reddish-orange carotenoid pigment in salmon and in cooked crustaceans.

Changes Effected by Heating

While red meat is being cooked, heat changes the pigments. First, the myoglobin present in the interior of muscles is transformed to oxymyoglobin. Continued heating converts the oxymyoglobin into denatured globin hemichrome, the grayish brown associated with well-done meats. Denatured globin hemichrome is the counterpart of metmyoglobin, the difference being that the protein (globin) component has been denatured by the heat. This reaction is illustrated below. All uncured, fresh red meats undergo this change gradually. The heating of beef to various stages of doneness, ranging from rare to well-done, illustrates the gradual nature of the conversion of myoglobin, first to the bright red of oxymyoglobin observed in rare beef and then slowly to the grayish brown of **denatured globin hemichrome** throughout the muscle.

Denatured Globin Hemichrome
Myoglobin derivative formed when heat triggers the oxidation of iron to the ferric (+3) state and denatures the globin portion of the compound while the oxygen of oxymyoglobin is replaced with water complexed to the iron atom, resulting in a gray-brown color.

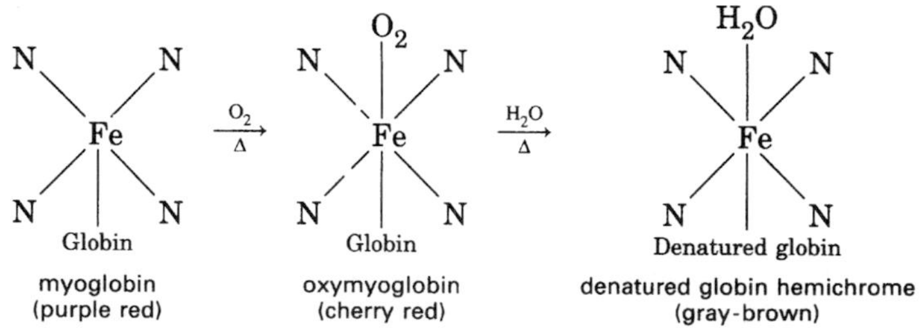

myoglobin
(purple red)

oxymyoglobin
(cherry red)

denatured globin hemichrome
(gray-brown)

Heating enhances the light color of fish by increasing opacity, but this is not a dramatic change. Quite a different situation is found in crustaceans, for the drab, blackish-green characteristic of uncooked crab, lobsters, and shrimp is changed as astaxanthin becomes dominant and the former predominant pigment loses its effect as a result of the denaturation of the protein with which it is complexed.

As is true with fin fish, poultry ordinarily is essentially colorless when cooked. If young poultry has been frozen and some hemoglobin has leaked from the marrow, there may be some hemoglobin in the flesh close to the bones, which becomes dark when cooked. Sometimes poultry that has been subjected to very intense heat during preparation develops a reddish-pink color. This is the result of hemoglobin reacting with carbon monoxide and nitric oxide generated by an electric heating element or flames when barbecuing.

Changes Effected by Curing

Meats sometimes are cured; this process usually involves treatment with either nitrates or nitrites to preserve meats for long-term storage. One of the important functions of nitrite is to prevent botulism in cured meats.

Of particular interest in a discussion of pigments is the effect of nitrites on meat color. The nitric oxide, which forms from the nitrates and nitrites in meat curing, combines with myoglobin to form nitric oxide myoglobin. This compound changes to nitric oxide myochrome when a second nitroso group replaces the globin during the slow heating involved in curing. Nitric oxide myochrome is a key pigment in cured meats and contributes to the stability of their familiar pinkish-red color. Exposure to light and air causes oxidation of the ferrous iron to the ferric (3+) state, which results in development of a brownish color.

Nitrosyl-hemochrome forms during the curing of meats when a nitroso group joins with myoglobin and the globin portion of the molecule is denatured by heat. This compound is also a pink pigment abundant in cured meats. On oxidation of the iron in nitrosyl-hemochrome, the pigment structure is altered to denatured globin nitrosyl-hemochrome, which is brownish.

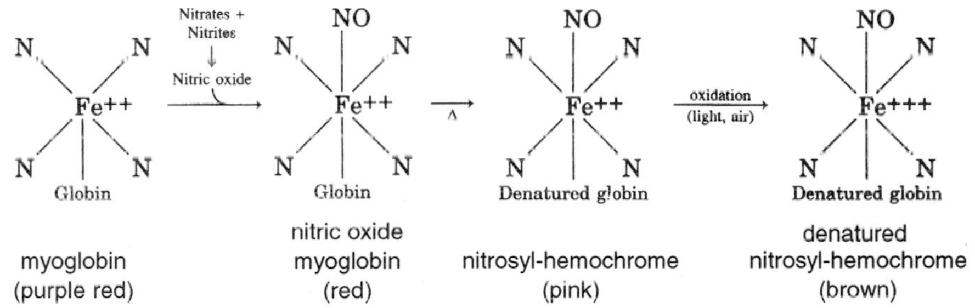

myoglobin
(purple red)

nitric oxide
myoglobin
(red)

nitrosyl-hemochrome
(pink)

denatured
nitrosyl-hemochrome
(brown)

Exposure to light and additional oxygen hastens the breakdown of pigments in cured meats. In particular, light promotes removal of the nitroso group from pigments. This sets the stage for oxidation of ferrous pigments to the ferric state, with the resulting discoloration. Occasionally the porphyrin ring is oxidized, which leads to fading of pigments and sometimes development of a fluorescent green or yellow color. The almost rainbowlike appearance occasionally noted on the surface of packaged cured meats may result from the way light is refracted from the pigments.

FACTORS AFFECTING QUALITY

Maturity

The physical changes that occur from the time an animal is born until it is slaughtered affect the characteristics of the resulting meat. Young animals have a comparatively low ratio of lean to bone. They also have a relatively large amount of connective tissue and little fat. These characteristics can be seen in veal, which is from animals not more than 3 months old. Somewhat greater range is seen in lamb, as animals up to the age of 14 months are marketed as lamb. However, mutton is over 2 years old. Unlike the distinctions made in both cattle and sheep to facilitate marketing at different ages, pork generally is from animals that are 6 months or just slightly older.

The increased fat content of animals raised to a mature state influences the flavor of the meat and contributes to apparent juiciness, an important contribution because moisture content decreases. Connective tissue within the lean tissue increases in total amount as an animal matures, but is present in somewhat smaller percentages than were present when the animal was very young. Despite this small shift, meat from mature animals may be less tender than a comparable cut from a young animal. This decrease in tenderness may result from increased formation of crosslinkages between the fibers of collagen within the lean muscle as the animal matures and grows older.

Beef flavor undergoes change as an animal ages. Fat content influences this, but other changes also may contribute to the stronger, characteristic flavor of mature beef. The color of the uncooked flesh gradually becomes redder and sometimes darker. The pH of muscle also may decrease. Differences from one carcass to another make information regarding changes caused by maturation difficult to verify.

Postmortem Changes

Rigor Mortis
Temporary rigidity of muscles that develops after death of an animal.

Biochemical processes in the body continue several hours after slaughter and considerably influence the quality of meat that is being readied for sale. The level of glycogen stores in the animal at the time of slaughter is paramount in determining onset of **rigor mortis** and key palatability factors in the meat when it is ready to be marketed. The importance of glycogen is tied to the fact that this complex carbohydrate undergoes biochemical degradation to produce lactic acid after slaughter. Desirably, the pH in the flesh of cows and other mammals drops from approximately neutral (commonly pH 7.0 to as high as 7.2) to a pH of about 5.5 (only pH 6.2–6.5 in fish). This postmortem lactic acid production occurs if the animal is in a rested, comparatively calm state at the time of slaughter. However, stress and exercise just prior to slaughter reduce the glycogen levels in the animal, which limits the amount of lactic acid that is formed postmortem.

The chemical changes associated with the onset of rigor mortis begin with the loss of available oxygen from blood when circulation ceases. Anaerobic reactions occur as a result of this change. ATP (adenosine triphosphate) can continue to be formed from ADP (adenosine diphosphate) until there is no more creatine phosphate available. Then the ATP level falls, and lactic acid forms anaerobically from glycogen. The muscles lose extensibility because the lack of ATP blocks the unlocking of actin-myosin links. Accumulation of calcium ions due to lack of ATP causes contraction and rigidity of the muscles. Some fluid also is forced from tissues.

The time of onset of rigor mortis differs between species and even a bit between carcasses of the same species. Fish may begin to develop rigor mortis an hour after being killed (Table 15.2), although onset may be delayed by as much as 7 hours.

Rigor mortis is extended in fish if the fish are iced as soon as they are killed and maintained in a chilled storage environment. This extends the time that fish remain fresh because bacterial spoilage commences only after rigor mortis has

Table 15.2   Usual Elapsed Time between Slaughter and Passage of Rigor Mortis

Species	Elapsed Time from Slaughter to Passage of Rigor Mortis
Fish	1 to 7 hours (unless stored in ice)
Chicken	4 hours or more
Turkey	12 hours or more
Pork	1 day or more
Beef	11 days

passed. However, even careful icing during storage cannot extend the storage time of fresh fish more than about a week from the time of death.

Onset of rigor mortis is usually somewhat slower in poultry than in fish. For chickens, rigor mortis should begin and end after at least 4 hours have elapsed, and for turkeys at least 12 hours after slaughter is normal. Cooking or freezing should not begin until rigor mortis has passed because the flesh will be tough. Very prompt chilling of poultry carcasses by immersion in ice water as soon as possible after slaughter is important in retarding rigor mortis and achieving tenderness.

Animal carcasses require somewhat longer to pass through rigor mortis than do poultry or fish. Pork needs to be aged at least a day for it to pass through rigor. The various muscles in beef exhibit different behavior; some need to be aged 11 days before achieving maximum tenderness. During this aging period, desirable storage conditions include ultraviolet light to control growth of microorganisms, a controlled humidity of 70 percent, and a temperature just above freezing. These measures are important to keep the meat from becoming microbiologcally unsafe or too dry. However, beef may be held at a temperature of 16°C for between 16 and 20 hours after slaughter before being aged at 2°C to promote tenderness.

Electrical stimulation (between 100 and 600 volts) of carcasses for 1 or 2 minutes within 45 minutes of slaughter is a comparatively recent technique used to help promote tenderness in poultry and meats. The electricity stimulates fast muscle contractions, causing both physical and biochemical changes that favor development of tenderness.

When meat is chilled too rapidly after slaughter, the muscles contract drastically, a phenomenon termed ***cold-shortening.*** This shortening of muscle length varies from one muscle to another and also is influenced by whether or not the muscle is attached to a bone, which restricts contraction somewhat. The very tough quality evidenced when a muscle is deeply in rigor mortis is the result of considerable formation of crosslinkages between myosin and actin in the contracted muscle.

Even in carcasses held under optimum temperature controls, rigor mortis does develop. Fortunately, the contraction that occurs during rigor is reversed gradually as the carcass is **aged.** The Z lines (see Figure 15.1) begin to become indistinct; myofibrils begin to break up, and the meat gradually becomes tender. This increased tenderness is theorized to be the result of both some action of cathepsins and calcium-activated factor (proteolytic enzymes) on the muscle proteins to produce simpler proteins and the breaking of linkages between actin and myosin. Clearly, aging promotes the development of tenderness in beef and other types of meat from animals.

Tenderness also is enhanced by carefully hanging carcasses so that the muscles are stretched beyond their normal, resting state prior to the onset of rigor. Ordinar-

Cold-Shortening
Severe contraction of muscles in carcasses that have been chilled too quickly and severely after slaughter.

Aging
Holding of meat while it passes through rigor mortis and sometimes for a period extending several days or even 2 weeks, depending on the quality and type of carcass; storage of meat to enhance tenderness.

ily the carcass is hung from the Achilles tendon, a position that stretches the tenderloin muscle to more than half again its resting length. Another option is to suspend the carcass from the aitchbone (hip bone); this position favorably influences the tenderness of several other muscles.

The color of beef and pork can be influenced by the pH reached in the carcass (a reflection of glycogen stores at the time of slaughter) during the aging period as the carcass passes through rigor mortis. In the case of beef a final pH of about 6.6 (well above the normal value of around 5.5) is accompanied by the presence of a very deep red, almost black color in the flesh and a sticky, rather slimy feeling. Such beef is called **dark-cutting beef.**

The detrimental variation seen in pork as a consequence of reaching an abnormally low pH during rigor mortis is termed *pale, soft, and exudative pork,* usually designated simply as **PSE pork.** PSE pork occurs when the pH drops as low as 5.1, or even 5.4. This excessively acidic condition results in light-colored, mushy pork with considerable drip loss during cooking. Both of these pH problems cause the carcasses to bring a very low market price.

Dark-Cutting Beef
Very dark, sticky beef from carcasses in which the pH dropped to only about 6.6.

PSE Pork
Pale, soft, and exudative pork from carcasses with a very low pH, ranging usually between pH 5.1 and 5.4.

IDENTIFYING MEAT CUTS

Meat cuts used in research reports must be identified as to species, approximate age (if known), presence (or removal) of bone, cut (if a standard retail cut, according to the Uniform Retail Meat Industry Standard), and specific muscles studied. For research purposes, the names of various muscles are used to identify the exact muscle from a cut that is used for testing. This identification is necessary because of the variation in physical properties found in the different muscles within a single cut, as can be seen by comparing the relative tenderness scores (Table 15.3). For example, the psoas major, commonly referred to as the tenderloin, and the longissimus dorsi are two muscles often used in meat research, but the T-bone steak that contains these two muscles also may include the gluteus medius and the internal oblique muscles. The longissimus dorsi is such a long muscle that it also is found as the principal mus-

Table 15.3   Relative Tenderness of Selected Muscles as Measured by Shearing

Muscle	Force Needed to Shear (pounds)
Porterhouse steak	
Psoas major	7.2
Longissimus dorsi	7.9
Gluteus medius	7.5
Internal oblique	12.6
Round steak	
Adductor	10.0
Semimembranosus	12.0
Semitendinosus	11.0
Biceps femoris	10.7
Vastus lateralis	11.4
Rectus femoris	9.0

Source: Ramsbottom, J. M. and Strandine, E. J. 1948. "Comparative tenderness and identification of muscles in wholesale cuts of beef." *Food Res., 13:* 315.

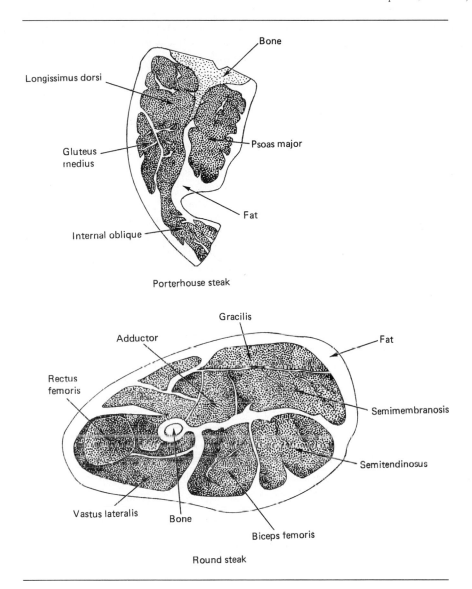

Figure 15.9   Muscles in porterhouse steak and round steak.

cle in standing rib roast. In contrast to the limited number of muscles in cuts from the rib and short loin, round steak has several muscles: rectus femoris, adductor, semi-membranosus, semitendinosus, biceps femoris, and vastus lateralis (see Figure 15.9).

PREPARATION

Changes Effected by Heat

When meats are heated, fat softens and melts and proteins are denatured. The overall effect on palatability depends on the conditions used in heating the meats. While cuts are being heated, water is lost. Initially during heating, there is some

Water-Binding Capacity
Amount of water held by
muscle protein as bound
water; cookery reduces capacity.

conversion of bound water to free water as the **water-binding capacity** of the
meat is reduced. This newly available free water offsets the water lost in the early
period of cookery, and the meat remains juicy. When meat reaches temperatures
between 74 and 80°C (well-done stage), bound water is converted to free water
very rapidly. However, the loss of water exceeds this conversion, resulting in reduced juiciness.

Muscle fibers undergo changes in dimensions as a result of heating. Shrinkage
begins to occur in the width of fibers soon after heating is initiated and is completed at a temperature of 62°C. Fibers begin to shrink lengthwise at about 55°C
and continue until about 80°C. Waterbinding capacity is reduced as the fibers become narrower. The narrowing width of fibers appears to be the result of the un-
winding of the tertiary structure of the proteins, a change that is followed by
crosslinkage of the coagulating proteins, causing shrinkage of the length.

Other changes in muscles ensue. One of the changes noted under magnification is cracking in the I bands (see Figure 15.1). These cracks widen to leave distinct gaps in the actin filaments of the I band. Particularly in the biceps femoris and
semimembranosus of round steak, cracks in the I band lead to a granular or mealy
character because of the large amount of structural disintegration. In contrast is the
behavior of the longissimus dorsi of the rib and short loin; this muscle tends to
form an increasingly solid and less tender muscular mass as the temperature rises
(see Figures 15.10 to 15.12).

Muscle proteins in meat become less tender when heated. This toughening is a
two-step process (Davey and Gilbert, 1974). When meat fibers are heated to between 40 and 50°C, myosin becomes less soluble, and hydration of myosin and
other muscle proteins decreases. The second phase affecting the tenderness of
muscle proteins occurs when they reach temperatures between 65 and 75°C.

Connective tissue in meats also needs to be considered in a discussion of the
tenderness of cooked meats. Elastin is not modified, but collagen molecules slowly
change when subjected to moist heat, because hydrogen bonds begin to break be-

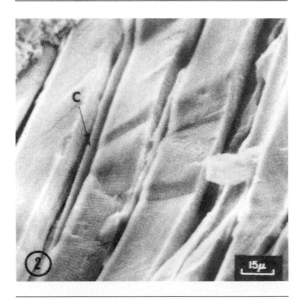

Figure 15.10 Semitendinosus
heated at 50°C for 45 minutes. Fibers
well separated and endomysial
collagen (C) standing free. (Courtesy
of S. B. Jones, U.S. Department of
Agriculture, Agricultural Research
Service, North Atlantic Area Eastern
Regional Research Center. Reprinted
from *Journal of Food Science.* 1977.
Vol. 42: 125. Copyright (c) by Institute
of Food Technologists.)

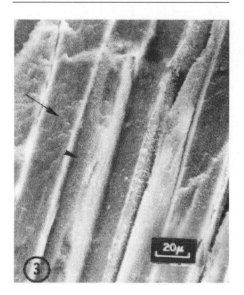

Figure 15.11 Fracture after 60°C cooking has cleaves through (arrow) and around (arrowhead) fibers. (Courtesy of S. B. Jones, U.S. Department of Agriculture, Agricultural Research Service, North Atlantic Area Eastern Regional Research Center. Reprinted from *Journal of Food Science.* 1977. Vol. 42: 125. Copyright (c) by Institute of Food Technologists.)

tween the component tropocollagen strands. This permits some movement within the collagen molecules, and the gelatin components of collagen begin to move away from each other. Evidence for this formation of gelatin can be seen when drippings from a pot roast are refrigerated, causing the gelatin to form a gel (see Figures 15.13 to 15.16).

Conversion of collagen to gelatin has considerable effect on the tenderness of meat cuts that are heated for an extended period, as is done when preparing less tender cuts of meat. The length of time that meat is held above 65°C is important in promoting collagen conversion to gelatin.

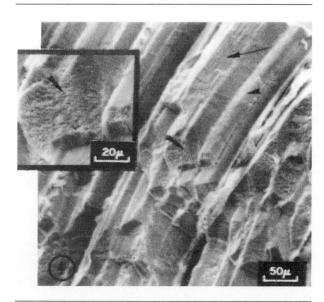

Figure 15.12 Fracture after 90°C cooking through (arrow) and around (arrowhead) fibers, for a stair-step effect both at fiber level and myofibril level (double arrowheads). Inset is enlarged view of area indicated by double arrowhead. (Courtesy of S. B. Jones, U.S. Department of Agriculture, Agricultural Research Service, North Atlantic Area Eastern Regional Research Center. Reprinted from *Journal of Food Science.* 1977. Vol. 42: 125. Copyright (c) by Institute of Food Technologists.)

Figure 15.13 Endomysial collagen between muscle fibers in 50°C cooked muscle shows no change from the raw control. (Courtesy of S. B. Jones, U.S. Department of Agriculture, Agricultural Research Service, North Atlantic Area Eastern Regional Research Center. Reprinted from *Journal of Food Science*. 1977. Vol. 42: 125. Copyright (c) by Institute of Food Technologists.)

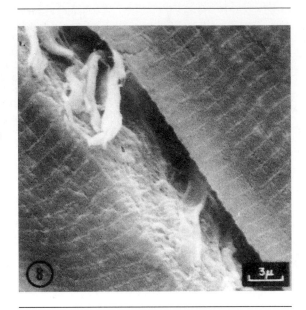

Clearly the tenderizing effect of heating collagen for an extended period is opposed by the toughening effect of heat on muscle proteins. Optimal preparation of a particular cut requires a choice of cookery compatible with the composition of the meat. If collagen content is high, as is true in cuts classified as less tender, extended heating is desirable to permit considerable conversion of collagen to gelatin. This tenderizing action will more than compensate for the toughening of the muscle proteins that is occurring at the same time. However, tender cuts of meat will become less tender with extended heating if the meat reaches temperatures above 60°C. This effect is the result of the toughening of the muscle proteins,

Figure 15.14 Heating at 60°C caused endomysium (C) to congeal and sarcolemma (SL) to become granular. Myofibrils (Mf) remain intact. Other coagulated material is deposited on the endomysium and sarcolemma (arrow). (Courtesy of S. B. Jones, U.S. Department of Agriculture, Agricultural Research Service, North Atlantic Area Eastern Regional Research Center. Reprinted from *Journal of Food Science*. 1977. Vol. 42: 125. Copyright (c) by Institute of Food Technologists.)

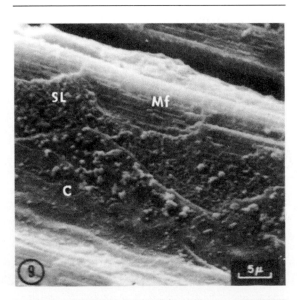

Figure 15.15   Endomysial collagen (C) of 60°C cooked muscle. Collagen is no longer fibrous and may have begun to form gelatin. (Courtesy of S. B. Jones, U.S. Department of Agriculture, Agricultural Research Service, North Atlantic Area Eastern Regional Research Center. Reprinted from *Journal of Food Science.* 1977. Vol. 42: 125. Copyright (c) by Institute of Food Technologists.)

a change that cannot be offset by the conversion of limited amounts of collagen to gelatin.

The importance of the opposing effects of collagen and muscle proteins during heating is seen particularly clearly in the preparation of fish. Only a small amount of collagen occurs in fish, which means that the major effect of heating is change in muscle proteins. By heating fish just until it flakes, some softening of collagen occurs to permit easy separation of fibers while some denaturation of the muscle proteins also occurs. At this point, the fish flesh is still tender. Continued heating beyond this point results in increasing toughness as a result of continuing detri-

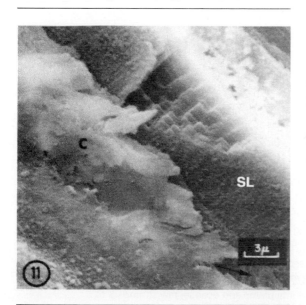

Figure 15.16   Muscle cooked at 90°C. Endomysial collagen (C) is congealed. Sarcolemma (SL) appears to be granular. Certain fibrous areas remain (arrow). (Courtesy of S. B. Jones, U.S. Department of Agriculture, Agricultural Research Service, North Atlantic Area Eastern Regional Research Center. Reprinted from *Journal of Food Science.* 1977. Vol. 42: 125. Copyright (c) by Institute of Food Technologists.)

mental changes in the muscle proteins. Overcooking of fish results in considerable loss of palatability. The temperatures used for cooking fish are quite unimportant in determining the quality and overall palatability of the finished product as long as heating ceases as soon as the fish muscle can be separated into flakes. However, overcooking is more likely to occur when very high temperatures are used because of the rapid rise in temperature of the fish.

Dry Heat. Dry heat methods are designed to maximize the quality of muscle proteins, rather than considering the changes that could be brought about in collagen if heating were extended longer. Tender cuts of meat, because of their relatively high proportion of muscle protein and reduced quantity of collagen, are well suited to dry heat cookery. Only in roasting is there much opportunity to convert collagen to gelatin; cooking times for other dry heat methods are too short for effective conversion to occur. Recommended final interior temperatures are given in Table 15.4.

The usual temperature for roasting is 163°C. This temperature results in the preparation of meats that are pleasingly juicy, tender, and flavorful, and the cooking losses are less than occur when an oven temperature of 218°C or hotter is used (Cline et al., 1930). Bayne et al. (1969) found that less tender roasts could be

Table 15.4 Recommended Interior Temperatures for Selected Meat, Poultry and Fish to Assure Safety[a]

Food	Final Temperature °F
Meats	
Beef, veal, lamb:	
Ground	160
Roasts, steaks	145 (medium rare)
	160 (medium)
	170 (well done)
Pork:	
Ground	160 (medium)
	170 (well done)
Roasts, chops	160 (medium)
	170 (well done)
Ham:	
Fresh	160
Fully cooked (reheat)	140
Poultry	
Chicken, turkey:	
Ground	165
Whole, unstuffed	170 (medium)
Whole, stuffed	180 (well done)[b]
Breasts	170
Thighs, wings	Juices run clear
Fish	
All types[c]	145

[a]Food Safety and Inspection Service. "USDA rule mandates safe handling statements for raw meat and poultry products." *FSIS Backgrounder*, May, 1994: 3; National Fisheries Institute. "News about seafood safety and consumer tips." 1994. Arlington, VA.

[b]Stuffing must be at least 165°F.

[c]Time often must be used because fish is likely to be too thin for accurate thermometry. Suggested times are: baking at 450°F, broiling, steaming, grilling, or poaching—10 min/inch; boiled lobster—4 to 6 min/lb; shucked shellfish—until plump and opaque; raw shrimp—3 to 5 min (until pink); scallops—3 to 4 min.

roasted at 93°C to achieve a very pleasing roast of top round, definitely a less tender cut prior to roasting. The very long roasting period required for the meat to reach an internal temperature of 67°C enabled the collagen to convert effectively into gelatin (Penfield and Meyer, 1975).

Broiling is a direct heat method in which meat is subjected to an intense heat until the desired degree of doneness has been reached. Not surprisingly, the higher the internal temperature reached in the meat, the greater are the cooking losses. Very thick pork chops, when broiled, are less juicy than comparable chops about half as thick (Holmes et al., 1966). In broiled ground beef patties (Kregel et al., 1986), juiciness and tenderness decreased, while flavor improved as the final interior temperature rose. Law et al. (1967) found that cooking losses were greater in broiling than in microwaving, but were least in roasting.

Fast food operations and some institutional settings are utilizing restructured meats, which often are prepared either by frying or grilling. Breading is especially important for palatability if deep-fat frying is the method chosen (Quenzer et al., 1982). Broiling, grilling, or roasting were found by these researchers to produce meats that were more juicy and had a better texture than resulted from deep-fat frying.

Microwave cooking of meat usually results in greater cooking losses and less juiciness than occur in other meat cookery methods (Ream et al., 1974). This may be due to extreme tightening of protein molecules, which could force water from the meat. A possible advantage of microwave cookery of meat may be reduced fat content, possibly the result of comparatively rapid heating of fat in the inner portions, which may facilitate drainage of fat from the cut. Fat, particularly fatty acids with double bonds, is agitated even faster than water when subjected to microwaving. The flavor of the outer areas of meat prepared in a microwave oven is not as appealing as comparable cuts that have been oven roasted (Ream et al., 1974; Korschgen et al., 1976).

Although microwave cookery of meat is essentially a dry heat method, heating of the meat occurs in a somewhat different manner than in other methods of dry heat meat cookery. Microwave heating is accomplished when microwaves cause oscillation of water and fat molecules in the meat (see Chapter 5). This heat is distributed farther into the interior of the cuts by conduction, a process that requires time. Ordinarily, meats heated in a microwave oven are prepared using a moderate setting, which automatically alternates periods of microwaving with standing time to provide the opportunity for conduction and to enhance the equalization of heat in the cuts. Standing time must be provided manually if meats are prepared in a microwave oven that lacks the controls to regulate standing time automatically.

One of the shortcomings of meats prepared in a microwave oven is their unattractive, bland gray surface. Films designed for use in the microwave oven to aid in enhancing the palatability of microwaved meats have been found to be of some merit in improving color, flavor, and general acceptability (Armbruster and Haefele, 1975). These films aid in retaining heat in the cut so that the surface gets hot enough to develop a more pleasing color than is possible without the film. Tenderness is affected adversely when meat is microwaved. Surprisingly microwaved meat cuts usually are less tender than comparable cuts prepared by roasting (Ream et al., 1974) and broiling even though the cooking time is reduced by microwaving.

Bacon can be microwaved very successfully, perhaps because of its high fat content. However the particular benefit of a microwave oven in meat cookery is for reheating meats that have been cooked previously. The flavor of meats reheated in a microwave oven is more appealing than that of meats reheated by traditional methods.

Moist Heat. Moist heat, either braising or stewing, is designed to provide sufficient time for collagen to be converted to gelatin without toughening the muscle proteins unduly. The liquid in which the meat is braised or stewed prevents the surface of the meat from becoming hot enough to dry and brown excessively. Sufficient heat input is needed to maintain the liquid at a simmering temperature or even at a gentle boil, for the meat will be in a hot enough environment for collagen to begin to unwind and separate slowly into molecules of gelatin. However, the likelihood of evaporating all of the cooking liquid with this controlled rate of heating is minimal. As long as water is present, the meat cannot get hot enough to burn and toughen extensively. Less tender cuts of meat, when they have been braised or stewed until they reach an interior temperature of about 98°C for about 25 minutes, will be fork tender. Cuts that are high in connective tissue are well suited to this type of meat preparation because of their comparatively high collagen content. The increased tenderness resulting from the conversion of collagen more than offsets the toughening in the muscle proteins. Tender cuts of meat are not well suited to prolonged moist heat cookery; the comparatively high amount of muscle protein is toughened by the heat and tends to counteract the effect of collagen conversion.

Poaching or steaming can be used to prepare fish, but the preparation time needs to be just long enough to coagulate the muscle proteins. There is so little connective tissue in fish that the muscle proteins clearly are the dominant type of protein to be considered.

Crock pots or slow cookers are small electric appliances designed specifically for moist heat cookery. The temperature reached in different models varies somewhat, but ordinarily is less than 107°C (225°F). Several hours are required for the interior of the meat to be heated sufficiently to tenderize the connective tissue and kill microorganisms that may be present. Sensory evaluation of meats prepared in a slow cooker (Brady and Penfield, 1977) indicated that palatability is very satisfactory, and tenderness scores are better than when a pressure saucepan is used.

In contrast to the crock pot, the pressure saucepan speeds moist heat meat cookery because the pressurization results in a hotter temperature for braising than can be achieved in a regular Dutch oven or other nonpressurized, covered pan. When braising is done in a pressure saucepan, the meat is less juicy (Schock et al., 1970) than when a nonpressurized pan is used. Flavor and overall acceptability are not altered by use of a pressure saucepan for braising.

Sometimes meats are roasted in aluminum foil or in special roasting bags. These devices trap moisture around the meat, changing roasting from a dry heat cookery method to a moist heat one. At the oven temperatures ordinarily used for roasting (150–163°C or 300–325°F), wrapping the meat in aluminum foil increases cooking time significantly. Compared with roasts prepared without foil, foil-wrapped roasts prepared in an oven at 150°C (300°F) are less pleasing in flavor and are also less juicy and tender. Roasting bags produce results similar to those obtained using a foil wrapping.

Cooking Losses
Total losses from meat by evaporation or dripping during cooking.

Drip Losses
Combination of juices and fat that drip from meat during cooking.

Evaporative Losses
Losses of weight from meat during cooking as a result of evaporation.

Cooking Losses. **Cooking losses,** while frequently discussed as a single entity, actually are the combination of evaporative and drip losses. **Drip losses** include both juices and melted fat. **Evaporative losses** are calculated as the difference between the weight of the uncooked meat and the weight of the cooked meat plus drippings.

Because of both the relatively high cost of meats and the reduced juiciness associated with losses during cooking, the effect of the method of meat cookery on cooking losses and the resulting impact on yield are important. Use of aluminum foil or film wrapping when heating meats causes greater cooking losses than occur when the wrapping is omitted. Cooking losses are greater for meats prepared in a slow cooker than when a faster cooking method is used (Sundberg and Carlin, 1976). Predictably, the higher the final temperature of meat, the greater is the cooking loss. Cooking losses for sirloin roasts heated in a convection oven were less when the oven temperature was 93°C (200°F) than when it was 149°C (300°F), and the yield also was greater, as would be anticipated (Davenport and Meyer, 1970). In a conventional oven, cooking losses are lower at 125°C (257°F) than at 163°C (325°F), but the long roasting period required for the lower temperature usually makes the higher oven temperature the one ordinarily used.

Effects of Altering pH

Hydration of meat is important to evaluation of juiciness in the cooked product. If an alkaline ingredient is added, the color of the meat is darkened by the increase in pH, and the influence on hydration is minimal. Increased tenderness does not develop, so the addition of soda is not recommended. Adding an acid is another possibility, and marinating a less tender cut in undiluted vinegar for 2 days can result in increased juiciness and tenderness when the meat is braised (Lind et al., 1971). Possible negative effects on aroma, flavor, and acceptability may offset the improved tenderness and juiciness.

Effect of Salt

The main effect of salt on meats during preparation is enhanced water retention. This ability to hold water in the meat improves juiciness. It may have a minor role in promoting tenderness, but the overall impact of salt on palatability of meat is much too minor to outweigh the health advantage of avoiding use of excess salt.

Meat Tenderizers

Enzymes.   Certain proteolytic enzymes can be used to increase the tenderness of less tender cuts of meat. The most common of these is a commercial blend of enzymes from papaya and salt, a blend that is referred to simply as **papain.** The three enzymes in this substance are chymopapain, papain, and a peptidase. This blend is used by applying it to the surface of the meat and then piercing the meat repeatedly with a fork to help carry the enzymes into the interior. Unless piercing is done, the enzymes will be able to aid in tenderizing the meat only on the surface and for a very short distance (no more than 2 millimeters) into the muscle because of the very limited penetrating capability of the enzymes.

Papain
Term used to designate either a single proteolytic enzyme from papaya or a blend of three enzymes from this fruit.

Papain has little effect at room temperature, but it does become active when the temperature of the meat reaches 55°C and increases in activity with additional heating even as high as 80°C. Activity ceases when the enzyme is denatured by heat; it is definitely inactive at 85°C. Much of the tenderizing effect is the result of the enzyme destroying the sarcolemma surrounding the myofibrils in the fibers, hydrolyzing actomyosin, and then continuing hydrolytic breakdown of various proteins in the fiber. Collagen also may be hydrolyzed to contribute still further to the tenderizing effect. The result of this enzymatic action often is the development of a somewhat mushy texture in regions where the enzyme has acted. This is true whether or not the enzyme has been allowed to stand on the meat for a period before cooking, because the enzyme exhibits its major action in the hot meat.

Although papain is the principal enzyme used for tenderizing meats, other proteolytic enzymes also can be utilized for this purpose. For example, bromealin is an enzyme found in fresh pineapple. Its action sometimes occurs when the fresh fruit is an ingredient in such recipes as kabobs or stir-fried chicken. Ficin, a proteolytic enzyme in figs, is another possible enzyme for tenderizing meat.

Mechanical Tenderization.   Commercially, meat can be run through a tenderizer equipped with needles or blades to cut some of the connective tissue and increase tenderness. This makes it possible for some less tender cuts to be used in the same way as tender cuts. Mechanical tenderization changes the texture somewhat, but it does not produce the mushy character sometimes found in cuts tenderized by enzymes. Another means of mechanical tenderization is pounding to break some of the muscle fibers and connective tissue. Yet another technique, one a bit more rigorous than pounding, is cubing. In cubing, the meat is passed through a machine that cuts through a fair portion of the muscle, a process that may be repeated to increase tenderness still more. The ultimate means of mechanical tenderization is the grinder, which is used to make ground meats. This intensive shearing of the fibers and connective tissue results in very tender meat from cuts that were clearly less tender before being ground.

MODIFIED MEAT PRODUCTS

Reduced Fat Meats

Consumer interest in weight control and cholesterol has created a demand for meats and meat products with reduced fat levels. An early approach toward satisfying this demand was modification of the beef grading criteria to enable beef with a comparatively low fat content to be graded as USDA Select. Now, the meat mixtures themselves are being modified to formulate ground meats with a fat content as low as 10 percent. Oat bran (LeanMaker™) is one product that is being used to replace part of the fat in ground meats. Other suitable replacements include wheat bran, rice bran, barley bran, soy protein and/or fiber, and carrageenan (Pszczola, 1991). These products can add fiber to the diet; they also are important because of their ability to bind water, reduce cooking losses, and maintain satisfactory juiciness. Satisfactory products have been made using a fat level of only 5 percent in turkey and chicken breast. Other formulations range from these lows to 10 percent in beef patties, but all are well below pork sausage with 45 percent fat.

Restructured Meats
Meats made from meat cuts that are somewhat less expensive; made by creating small particles, adding fat and other ingredients, and shaping into uniform portions.

Restructured Meats

Portion control and quality control are two major problems of purchasing meat for institutional use. **Restructured meats** provide the answer to these problems and a challenge to food technologists. Aspects of production that require careful attention include the size of the protein flakes, the amount of fat, and the content of connective tissue. Bernal et al. (1988) found that flakes no larger than 6 millimeters produced a more desirable restructured meat than was possible if flakes were a little more than twice that size. Large pieces of connective tissue are detrimental to the quality of the product. Although the resulting products are not identical to regular meat cuts, restructured meats are sufficiently pleasing to have gained a strong entry into the food service industry and even into the home.

Comminuted Meats

Meats can be chopped into very tiny pieces, mixed with water, and heated to denature the proteins. Phosphate, sodium chloride, and other salts may be added to improve the physical characteristics of the meat mixture and increase such sensory qualities as juiciness and texture (Sofos, 1986). Modifications in fat type and amount are emerging to expand the acceptability of **comminuted meats,** such as hot dogs and sausages.

Comminuted Meats
Products made by almost pulverizing meats and adding the desired fat and salts before heating the resulting mixture.

Structured Seafood Products

Public interest in nutrition in recent years has been reflected by increased consumption of fish, a change that has stimulated efforts to provide new types and products in the marketplace. One of the products of fish processing is minced fish meat. This minced fish is washed thoroughly to eliminate fat, pigments, and other compounds that would present flavor and storage problems during frozen storage. A preservative of some type, commonly sorbitol or sugar, is added before minced fish is frozen in preparation for its use in structured seafood products. This intermediate seafood product is called **surimi.**

Surimi
Purified and frozen minced fish containing a preservative; intermediate seafood product used in making structured seafood products.

Technically, surimi could contain any type of minced fish. However, pollack is the predominant choice; other types of fish (especially the less popular fish that are caught along with more costly types) are included as available. Preparation of surimi requires deboning of either filleted or headed and gutted fish; filleting (Figure 15.17) results in a higher grade surimi with lighter color and better gel-forming ability. Mincing of the deboned fish with a drum that has very small perforations (1 to 2 millimeters) produces a particularly high-quality product. The minced fish requires careful, thorough washing, rinsing, straining, and some dehydration to achieve a moisture level of around 82 percent. The last step prior to freezing is incorporation of the preservative or cryoprotectant.

The principal use of surimi for human food has been in fabricating structured seafood products, notably crab and shrimp analogs. As minced fish alone does not have the textural characteristics associated with crab and shrimp, fiberization and the addition of other ingredients are done to achieve an end product that rather closely approximates the texture of the actual crab meat or shrimp. Both egg white and a starch (the type used depends on the product being made) are added to the surimi to achieve the desired firmness without rubberiness. These two ingredients appear to regulate the influence of the other, with starch promoting rubberiness and egg white interfering with the structural matrix that contributes a rubbery texture to the original surimi. A limited amount of oil (not more than 4 percent) is added to improve the freeze–thaw characteristics of these structured seafood products. This mixture is extruded as a sheet and is heated briefly so that the sheet is elastic and can be folded and molded. After the extruded mixture is in the desired

Figure 15.17   Fish being filleted. Filleted white fish, usually pollack, is used to make surimi. (Courtesy of the U.S. Department of Agriculture.)

final form, it is heated sufficiently to gelatinize the starch and completely denature the protein without causing excessive toughness and rubberiness. The surface is colored to simulate crab and shrimp products.

Considerable research effort is being directed toward the development of surimi-based structured seafood products, and it may be anticipated that these products will become an accepted choice by consumers. The distinct economy of the shrimp and crab analogs and their present level of quality have made these analogs viable frozen fish products.

SOY PROTEIN

Products

Plant proteins have been of continuing research interest for many years as alternatives for animal proteins. So far, soy protein has proven to be by far the most versatile and economically feasible of the plant proteins that have been studied. At the present time, several soy protein products are available to consumers to add variety in flavor and texture to many main dishes and other recipes. Dried soybeans are remarkably high in protein, actually about 34 percent. The blend of essential amino acids is unusually complete for a plant protein, which is an important reason why soy protein is recommended by nutritionists and dietitians as an excellent means of meeting part of the day's protein needs. Methionine is the limiting essential amino acid in soy protein.

Soybeans undergo several steps in their processing to obtain the products seen in the marketplace. After the beans are dehulled, the oil is extracted, and the remaining portion is soy flour, with a protein content of about 50 percent. Additional steps utilizing alkali and acid at various points to alter pH result in a variety of **soy concentrates and isolates,** with protein levels ranging from 70 percent in the concentrates to as high as 95 percent in the isolates.

From the isolates, texturized soy protein products are made by various processes including the extrusion of cooked soy flour and spinning fibers; this is accomplished by forcing the dissolved isolate through a spinnerette and coagulating the resulting product as fibers. The fibers can be fabricated into simulated meat products, sometimes with rather good success. Imitation bacon bits of textured soy protein are a familiar example. **Textured soy protein** may be referred to as TSP, but it also often is called **TVP (textured vegetable protein).**

Although textured vegetable protein is the form of soy used most frequently, soy flour and soy grits also have some specific uses. **Soy grits** are made by grinding defatted flakes of soy to a distinctly coarse particle size. These are incorporated into some commercial food products to alter textural characteristics of some ground meat products and cereals. If grinding is continued so that a fairly fine powder is formed from the soy flakes, the product is **soy flour.** For optimal shelf life, defatted soy flour is suggested. This type of flour is used as an ingredient in some bakery products because of its nutritional merits and favorable influence on tenderness and crust color (see Figure 15.18). However, it needs to be used at levels no greater than 3 percent of the weight of wheat flour in some baked products and certainly no higher than about 10 percent in doughnuts. The lack of the structural protein complex (gluten) limits the usefulness of soy flour in batter and dough mixtures, making it necessary that enough wheat flour be incorporated to ensure adequate strength of structure.

Soymilk is yet another soy product. It is available in grocery stores for people to drink as a beverage (often as a substitute for cow's milk when milk protein creates an allergic response). Soymilk is made by grinding soybeans and then creating a slurry of the desired viscosity by adding water. Often calcium is added to enhance the nutritive value for those who are drinking soymilk in place of cow's milk.

A very different type of soy product is made by forming a curd from soy milk, a process rather similar to making cheese from animal milks. The result is a bland, slightly spongy precipitated soy protein food called **tofu.** Tofu is made in three different forms commonly available to provide the texture needed for easy use in a wide variety of recipes. Firm tofu is the most concentrated, dense form and is well suited to recipes where cubes of tofu are desired. Soft tofu has a high enough moisture content to assure easy blending into soups or sauces. Silken tofu, with its custard-like texture, also blends well or can be served with a simple topping. Nutritionally, silken tofu is interesting because it has a fat content providing only 30 percent of the calories, compared with fat calories of 45 percent from firm tofu or 52 percent from soft tofu. Tofu needs to be kept covered with water during refrigerated storage, with the water being changed every day.

Tofu is a common ingredient in many Oriental recipes and is included to add variety in texture and flavor, as well as to increase the protein content of the dish. This meat alternative may be used effectively as large, distinct cubes in main

Soy Protein Concentrate
Defatted soy product usually containing about 70 percent protein.

Soy Protein Isolate
Defatted, highly concentrated (up to 95 percent) soy protein; used to make many textured soy products.

Textured Soy Protein (TSP)
The end product of a series of steps producing fibers from soybeans.

Textured Vegetable Protein (TVP)
Another means of indicating textured soy protein.

Soy Grits
Coarsely ground soy flakes.

Soy Flour
Finely ground soy flakes.

Soymilk
Milk-like beverage consisting of ground soybeans, water, and calcium (optional additive).

Tofu
Soybean curd.

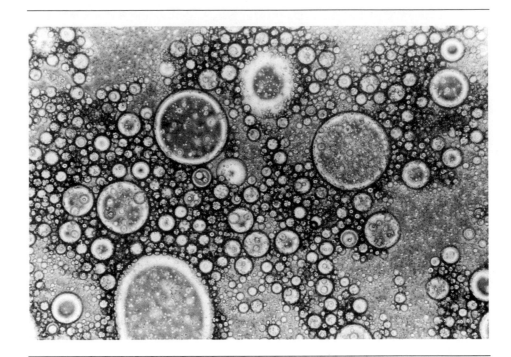

Figure 15.18   Photomicrograph (213X) of an emulsion from water-soaked (60°C) soy flour at 50 ml oil level per 50 ml of dispersion. The emulsifying capability of soy flour enhances its use in baked products. (Courtesy of H. L. Ashraf, Southern Illinois University. 1986. Reprinted from *Journal of Food Science. 51* (1): 193. Copyright (c) by Institute of Food Technologists.)

Tofutti
Frozen dessert made of sweetened and flavored tofu: the soybean counterpart of ice cream.

Tempeh
Fermented cooked soybean product resembling cake.

Natto
Fermented cooked soybean product useful as a spread or in soups.

dishes, soups, and salads. It also may be pureed so that it blends smoothly with other ingredients in sauces or even in desserts such as cheesecake. Yet another illustration of the versatility of tofu in food preparation is in the frozen dessert, **tofutti.**

Fermented soy products are popular in Asian cuisines. **Tempeh** is a chewy, cake-like product made by cooking soybeans and then adding a culture to ferment the beans. **Natto** also is fermented after cooking whole soybeans. Fermentation results in a smelly, very viscous (almost cheeselike) product for use in soups or as a spread.

Use of Textured Soy Protein

Although textured soy protein products can be made into meat analogs, which are consumed in place of meat, a different application as a meat extender has gained reasonable acceptance. By mixing some textured soy protein with ground meats, a given quantity of meat can be used to serve an increased number of people, thus reducing food costs. The amount that can be used has been studied to determine just how much soy can be added successfully. An important contribution made by the added soy protein is improved juiciness in comparison with all-beef patties. However, flavor and texture are influenced negatively when the level of soy protein is close to 20 percent.

The comparatively low cost of soy protein as contrasted with that of beef makes the use of textured soy protein as an extender attractive when beef prices are high. Federal school lunch programs are permitted to extend meat by using up to 25 percent textured soy protein in ground meat mixtures. The binding capability of textured soy protein and other soy products enhances juiciness, in part because of water content. However, fat that may be present in a beef patty or meat loaf made with soy protein being included as an ingredient will be bound by the soy protein and retained in the final product. This retentive characteristic limits the usefulness of TVP as a meat extender; retained fat cannot be removed, which may mean the final product has a higher fat content than it would have had if the fat were carefully removed from the 100 percent beef patty or loaf.

GELATIN

Composition

Gelatin is a stabilizing and gelling agent that has a variety of applications in the food industry as well as at home. Although it must compete with an array of carbohydrate gums in the food industry, this unique protein remains unchallenged in home food preparation. The chemical structure accounts for its ability to form edible gels.

The origin of gelatin is the tropocollagen strands of collagen, a protein in the connective tissue of meat that undergoes a change during heating. Three strands of tropocollagen crosslink to form a fibrous strand, and three of these strands then crosslink to form a molecule of the connective tissue protein called collagen. The proteins at all of these levels of organization are fibrous, elongated molecules because of the abundance of proline and hydroxyproline, two amino acids that restrict the coiling of the protein chain wherever they occur. Much of the behavior of gelatin that is valued in food preparation stems from this elongated structure.

Gelatin
Protein derived from collagen via tropocollagen when heated for an extended period, useful in gel formation.

Properties

Hydration.   When gelatin is used in food preparation, the first step is to convert it from a firm, friable substance to one that is soft and pliable. The elongated gelatin molecules have many polar groups exposed, making it possible for water to be bound by hydrogen bonds at many points along each molecule. As water is bound, the gelatin swells very noticeably. This can be observed easily by placing a packet (tablespoon) of gelatin in one-fourth cup of water. The remarkable ability of gelatin to bind water and also to trap free water in the interstices between molecules enables a small amount of gelatin to hold a far greater amount of water in a very short period. Evidence of this is the swollen volume of the hydrated gelatin and the lack of water that can be poured off.

The swelling of gelatin resulting from the absorption of water is influenced by the pH and the presence of salts. Swelling is bimodal in that it is less at its isoelectric point than it is at either a more acidic or a more alkaline pH. For many gelatins, the pH at which hydration is at a maximum is around pH 3.2 to 3.5 or 9. The effect of different salts on hydration is variable, but salts do favor swelling at the isoelectric point of gelatin. Unfortunately, no specific isoelectric point can be given for gelatin because of its heterogeneous nature and the fact that different production methods influence the pH of the isoelectric point. Usually, the isoelectric point for alkaline-processed gelatins is between 4.75 and 5.2 and that for acid-processed gelatins is between 5.5 and 6.5

Sol Formation.   After hydration of gelatin in cold water, the swollen gelatin can be dispersed readily in hot water or other hot liquid. Apparently this ability to be dispersed as a sol is aided by the physical dissociation of the gelatin molecules in their closely packed, dehydrated state. The distancing that occurs between gelatin molecules weakens intermolecular association and enables hot water to complete the dissociation, allowing the long gelatin molecules to move freely as the discontinuous phase in the sol. The high temperature facilitates the breaking of weak hydrogen bonds that exist in the hydrated gelatin. Unless gelatin has been hydrated first in cold water, a gelatin sol can be derived only with considerable difficulty when the hot liquid is added.

For gelatin to be an acceptable ingredient in any food product, the individual molecules must be dispersed in a very hot liquid. When molecules adhere to each other rather than dispersing, their fibrous and compact nature makes them quite rubbery and tenacious, characteristics that definitely are undesirable in foods. For this reason, hot gelatin sols are stirred until they appear to be absolutely transparent and totally homogeneous. If this state is not reached with a reasonable amount of stirring, it may be necessary to heat the sol longer to provide the energy needed for dissociation of the molecules of gelatin.

Enzymatic Hydrolysis.   Various proteolytic enzymes are able to cleave the long gelatin molecules into shorter polypeptides. This change in molecular length quickly eliminates the usual ability of gelatin to form gels. If ingredients containing enzymes capable of catalyzing this proteolysis are incorporated into gelatin mixtures, a satisfactory gel cannot form. Among the foods containing these enzymes are papaya (which contains **papain**), pineapple (**bromealin**), figs (**ficin**), and kiwi fruit (**actinidin**). These enzymes lose their catalytic capability if they are heated until denatured, which explains why canned pineapple can be used in gelatin salads whereas frozen and fresh pineapple cannot.

Papain
Proteolytic enzyme in papaya capable of cleaving gelatin so that it loses its gel-forming ability.

Bromealin
Proteolytic enzyme in pineapple.

Ficin
Proteolytic enzyme in figs.

Actinidin
Proteolytic enzyme in kiwi fruit.

Gel Formation.   Under appropriate conditions, a gelatin sol can convert to a gel as the sol is cooled. The formation of a gelatin gel is only one familiar example of gel formation. In the case of a gelatin gel, the gelatin molecules crosslink to form a continuous network of solid protein to which some water is bound and in whose interstices additional water is trapped as the discontinuous phase.

The formation of a gelatin gel is endothermic and occurs gradually as the energy of the system dissipates. A surface film forms as some of the gelatin molecules crosslink in a comparatively compact configuration. When the interior begins to gel, the molecules of gelatin are organized quite randomly. However, there is considerable formation and subsequent disruption of secondary bonds and reformation of new bonds with the molecules in slightly different positions as the gel structure ages. Gradually, a somewhat more organized arrangement evolves in a gelatin gel that has been stored many hours. In other words, a gelatin gel actually is a somewhat dynamic colloidal dispersion and is subject to gradual change, which is evidenced by decreasing tenderness during storage.

Conversion from a gelatin sol to a gel depends on several factors. First, enough gelatin molecules must be present to crosslink through the entire system to form the continuous network. If the gelatin concentration is too dilute, the sol will remain in that state. Even when there is enough gelatin to form a gel, the concentration of gelatin influences gel formation. As the concentration of gelatin increases, the rate of gel formation also increases, that is, the gel forms more quickly with an increasing concentration of gelatin. It is necessary to avoid too high a concentration of gelatin, because the concentration influences the texture of the gel formed as well as the rate of its formation. Increasing the concentration of gelatin causes the gelatin gel to become increasingly firm and less tender. Too high a concentration is undesirable because of the rubbery consistency that develops. A satisfactory gel often can be formed with a concentration of only 1.5 percent gelatin by weight, but in some other systems, the level of gelatin may need to be about 3 or even 4 percent. An average figure of about 2 percent is appropriate for many applications.

The temperature to which a gelatin sol must be cooled for gelation to occur is influenced by the rate of cooling. The temperature of gelation will be lower if the sol is cooled rapidly by adding ice to the dispersed gelatin or by packing the bowl containing the sol in ice than if the gel is cooled slowly at refrigerator temperature. Despite the fact that the gel sets at a lower temperature when ice is used, the time required for gelation is less than is necessary when cooling occurs in the refrigerator, because the temperature drops quickly as the ice melts. Similarly, a gelatin sol with a high enough concentration of gelatin can be gelled in about 3 hours by allowing it to cool at room temperature, a rate that is obviously considerably slower than that occurring in the refrigerator. Even when the gelatin concentration is very high, a gelatin sol must be cooled to at least 35°C (95°F) before a gel can form. The energy of the system is too great to permit the necessary bonding between molecules if the sol is above 35°C, and there is inadequate stability to any bonds that might be able to form.

Stability of the gel is influenced by the rate at which the gel forms. Gelatin gels that are set in the refrigerator require considerable patience, because of the long time required for them to set. They do have the advantage that they are much more resistant to melting back to a fluid sol when they are served on a warm day, which makes this method of gel formation particularly appealing if the gelatin gel must be held at room temperature or warmer for a long period, as often is true at buffets or picnics. Fortunately, for people with severe restrictions on their preparation time, addition of ice cubes to the dispersed gelatin or chilling of the gelatin in a bowl placed in ice water makes a gel that remains sufficiently firm for easy service at most meals if the product is made far enough in advance to allow time for the gel to become stronger by crosslinking during storage.

Electrolytes have an influence on the temperature of gelation; several anions depress the gelation temperature. Those of particular interest in food preparation are citrate, tartrate, chloride, and acetate. Of these four, the citrate anion has a limited effect on the gelation temperature of a gelatin mixture, whereas tartrate depresses the gelation temperature somewhat. Acetate depresses the temperature needed for gelation to occur still more, and chloride depresses gelation temperature the most of these four familiar food anions.

Early researchers in the field found that use of milk as the dispersing liquid in place of water produced a stronger gelatin gel than use of a comparable amount of fluid in the form of water. These workers theorized that the increased strength was due to the interactions of the gelatin with the milk proteins and salts. This is of particular interest when gelatin is added as a stabilizing agent in ice cream, and it also has application when cream cheese, cottage cheese, and other dairy products are incorporated into a gelatin salad.

To a limited extent, variations in the pH of the gelatin system influence the strength of the gelatin gel formed. Greatest strength is found in systems between pH 5.0, and 10.0, but the flavor generally is particularly pleasing at pH 3.0 to 3.5, significantly more acidic than the isoelectric point of gelatin. Gel strength is very adequate at this range.

To temper the acidic taste of tart gelatin mixtures, sugar frequently is added. The effect of sugar on gelation time and gel strength depends on the concentration of sugar. In concentrations up to 0.02 to 0.03 *M,* sugar delays gelling. At levels above 0.1 *M,* sugar has the opposite effect and actually speeds gelation. This level is reached by adding 68.4 grams (about ⅜ cup) of sugar to a liter of gelatin mixture. This level is less than half the amount of sugar that frequently is added to sweetened and acidified gelatin sols. Therefore, it is reasonable to anticipate that gelatin sols containing sugar ordinarily set more rapidly than they would without the sugar because of the rather high level of sugar added. However, these large amounts of sugar in gelatin do increase the tenderness of the resulting gel.

Thixotrophic
Capable of undergoing thixotrophy (the transition to a sol from a gel on agitation).

Gelatin gels are **thixotrophic;** that is, they can revert to a sol when agitated. This reversal is due presumably to the breaking of hydrogen bonds between gelatin molecules in the gel. Evidence of this is seen when fruit or another ingredient is stirred into a gelatin mixture that has gelled enough to pile; it softens and becomes quite smooth with the agitation necessary to blend the fruit uniformly into the entire mixture.

Gels also can be reversed to sols if the temperature rises sufficiently. The reversibility of gelatin gels to sols and back to gels can be demonstrated repeatedly, for the hydrogen bonds and other secondary bonds that may be responsible for establishing the gel structure can be broken by providing sufficient energy and reformed by removing energy, specifically by cooling. Interestingly, the temperature required for gelation to occur is somewhat lower than the temperature required for reversal to form a sol. One of the curious aspects of gelatin is that gelation occurs more rapidly the second time the product is gelled.

Gelatin can be beaten into a foam if handled properly. The excellent foaming properties of this protein make it possible for gelatin to increase as much as threefold in volume when beaten. The optimal time at which to beat a gelatin foam is when the dispersed gelatin sol has cooled to the point where viscosity is increasing noticeably and the mixture is the consistency of a very thick syrup. The surface tension is low enough so that the gelatin can be spread into extensive thin films surrounding bubbles of air, and the cooled gelatin will congeal very quickly to add stability to the cell walls in the foam. This capability of gelatin is used in preparing some stabilized foam desserts and whipped gelatin salads. Beating must be done before the gelatin actually congeals because the gelatin will then be so brittle that it will break into pieces and will not be capable of being spread to form the cell walls needed for foam formation. Fortunately, gelatin can be warmed a bit when this happens so that the problem can be rectified.

Gelatin is used in numerous recipes, most frequently as the background matrix for a congealed salad with various other ingredients added to give variety. In some cases, the plain granulated gelatin is used; other recipes utilize pulverized, sweetened gelatin with coloring and flavoring added. The plain gelatin requires hydration with cold water prior to dispersal in very hot liquid. Otherwise it clumps very badly. The finer consistency of the sweetened gelatin product and the dilution of the gelatin by the sugar enable this type of gelatin to be dispersed directly in very hot liquid without preliminary hydration. Yet another gelatin product is another sweet one, but one sweetened with a sugar substitute to reduce the calories. This product also does not require preliminary hydration.

SUMMARY

Flesh foods are categorized as meat, poultry, or fish, the latter being divided into fish and shellfish (mollusks and crustaceans). These contain both muscle and connective tissue. The proteins in muscle consist of enzymes and the myofibrillar proteins, which are abundant. The principal myofibrillar protein is myosin, a long and thin molecule. Actin, another myofibrillar protein, is found as F-actin (very heavy and long) and G-actin (small subunits that can aggregate to make F-actin). The other prominent myofibrillar protein is tropomyosin, a comparatively short and small molecule. In the presence of ATP, calcium, and magnesium ions, actin and myosin unite to form actomyosin in a reaction that is reversible and is accompanied by contraction and relaxation of muscles (when actin and myosin are released from actomyosin).

Connective tissue is also composed of proteins, including elastin, reticulin, ground substance, and collagen, the most important in meat cookery. Tropocollagen, the basic component of collagen, is made of three fibrous strands. Three strands of tropocollagen, in turn, are twisted together to form long and fibrous strands of collagen. Hydroxyproline and proline, amino acids present in unusual abundance in tropocollagen and collagen, account for the fibrous nature of these proteins. Elastin is the yellow, tough connective tissue that is found to a small extent intramuscularly and also in some large deposits intermuscularly. Ground substance provides the protein matrix in which collagen and elastin are deposited to form connective tissue. Reticulin is another fibrous protein associated with a fatty acid in connective tissue.

Triglycerides containing a variety of fatty acids (particularly palmitic, oleic, and stearic) are the predominant form of lipids in meats. Others are cholesterol, glycolipids, phosphoglycerides, plasmalogens, and sphingomyelin. These various components constitute the fat depots in which they are embedded in a matrix of connective tissue.

Organization of muscle tissue is complex, beginning with thick and thin myofilaments consisting of myosin and actin, respectively. Myofibrils are formed by the orderly alignment of myofilaments into sarcomeres, which then are organized into the larger myofibrils. Z, I, H, and A bands can be seen in muscle tissue examined microscopically. These bands are the result of the overlap of thick and thin myofilaments in a rather organized fashion in the sarcomeres. Myofibrils, surrounded by sarcoplasm, are surrounded by a thin membrane (sarcolemma) to form a fiber. Connective tissue, the endomysium, encases the fibers. Several fibers are held together in bundles by more connective tissue, the perimysium. Bundles of these bundles are finally encased in still more connective tissue, the epimysium, to form the completed muscle.

Hemoglobin and myoglobin are the two principal iron-containing pigments in red meats. Myoglobin, in its various forms, is particularly important. In the ferrous (2+) form, it is the purple-red color of fresh meat. Exposure to air adds two atoms of oxygen to make oxymyoglobin, a bright red pigment. Metmyoglobin, a brownish red pigment, forms if the iron is oxidized to the ferric (3+) state. Heating causes gradual changes in pigment to the grayish-brown compound, denatured globin hemichrome. With the addition of nitrites, nitric oxide myoglobin forms during curing of meats and undergoes conversion to nitric oxide myochrome when heated, resulting in the stable reddish color of cured meats. Another pigment found in cured meats is nitrosylhemochrome. Poultry and fish generally have little pigmentation, although poultry may have some reddish color from hemoglobin, and fish may have some dark muscles colored by myoglobin. Salmon red is the result of astaxanthin, a carotenoid pigment.

Prominent among changes after slaughter is development and passage of rigor mortis. The rate of onset and passage of rigor are the result of the species and the physical condition at the time of slaughter. Quality of the various meats is judged on the basis of texture, marbling, and overall palatability; yield is based on the amount of muscle in relation to bone and fatty deposits. Meat cuts can be identified on the basis of the size of the cut, color, muscles present, and bone shape.

When heated, muscle fibers shrink a bit lengthwise and lose some of their water-binding capacity. Concurrently, connective tissue (specifically collagen) begins to be converted slowly to gelatin. An acid marinade is of limited benefit in promoting palatability of less tender cuts of meat. Meat tenderizers are somewhat effective in destroying the sarcolemma surrounding fibers and in hydrolyzing actomyosin, as well as possibly hydrolyzing some of the collagen. The overall effect may be to create a somewhat mushy texture in some areas. This action occurs during the heating of the meat. Mechanical devices can be used to tenderize less tender cuts of meat prior to heating. Less tender cuts may be prepared effectively by braising and stewing; fish may be poached. Dry heat methods for tender cuts include roasting, broiling, pan broiling, pan frying, deep-fat frying, and microwave cookery. Cooking losses vary with various factors, such as temperature and method of heating, as well as final temperature of the meat.

Textured soy protein can be made into such meat analogs as imitation bacon bits and can also be used to extend ground meats. Soy grits and soy flour are used to some extent in the baking industry to enhance the protein content of baked products. However, they can replace only about 3 percent of the wheat flour in most baked products, whereas a substitution of 20–25 percent can be made when textured soy protein is used to extend meat. Tofu is another form of soy protein which is used to a limited extent in a variety of recipes. Other analogs are made using surimi, a minced fish intermediate product that usually contains pollack and other available fish.

Gelatin is the protein derived by extraction from the collagen obtained from animal skins and bones. The molecules are somewhat varied, but are fibrous as a result of the high content of proline and hydroxyproline. Commercial gelatin usually is obtained by alkaline extraction and finally is dried and marketed as granular or pulverized gelatin. Plain gelatin requires hydration so that it can be dispersed by swelling as it binds water and traps water in the interstices between gelatin molecules. When hydrated gelatin is dispersed in hot water, it forms a sol, which on cooling forms a gel. The presence of proteolytic enzymes in a gelatin gel results in liquefaction as the gelatin molecules are cleaved to shorter, more soluble molecules by the enzymes.

A gel forms as the gelatin molecules begin to establish a continuous, solid network by forming hydrogen bonds and other secondary bonds. Water is bound to these molecules and also is trapped within the framework. The strength of the gel depends on the concentration of gelatin, the rate of cooling, the temperature of the gel, the age of the gel, the presence of electrolytes, the pH, and the amount of sugar present. Mechanical agitation causes thixotrophy in gelatin gels. Gelatin gels and sols are reversible, depending on the temperature. When gelatin is just beginning to congeal, it can be beaten into a useful, light foam for use in desserts and salads.

STUDY QUESTIONS

1. What are the two major categories of proteins in muscles? Identify and briefly describe at least three proteins in each category.
2. Name and describe four types of proteins in connective tissue.
3. Describe the chemistry of collagen in some detail, being sure to discuss its unique amino acid composition.
4. Explain the organization of a muscle, beginning with the composition of myofilaments.
5. Describe the chemical changes and the resulting color shifts that occur when myoglobin is subjected to different conditions.
6. Why is cured meat a different color than uncured meat?
7. What changes occur in the carcass after slaughter?
8. Describe the changes that occur in meats when heated.
9. What are the effects of extending ground meats with textured soy protein?
10. What is surimi and how is it used?
11. How does the chemical nature of gelatin influence its physical behavior in food preparation?
12. What factors influence the temperature at which gelatin mixtures form gels?
13. What factors determine the tenderness of a gelatin gel?

BIBLIOGRAPHY

Anderson, R. H. and Lind, K. D. 1975. "Retention of water and fat in cooked patties of beef and of beef extended with textured vegetable protein." *Food Technol. 29* (2): 44.

Armbruster, G. and Haefele, C. 1975. "Quality of foods after cooking in 915 MHz and 2450 MHz microwave appliances using plastic film covers." *J. Food Sci. 40:* 721.

Ashgar, A., Gray, J. I., Buckley, D. J., Pearson, A. M., and Booren, A. M. 1988. "Perspectives on warmed-over flavor." *Food Technol. 42* (6): 123.

Ashgar, A., et al. 1985. "Functionality of muscle proteins in gelation mechanisms of structured meat products." *CRC Crit. Rev. Food Sci. Nutr. 22:* 27.

Ashgar, A. and Henrickson, R. L. 1982. "Post-mortem stimulation of carcasses: Effects on biochem, biophysics, microbiology, and quality of meat." *CRC Crit. Rev. Food Sci. Nutr. 18:* 1.

Baity, M. R., Ellington, A. E., and Woodburn, M. 1969. "Foil wrap in oven cooking." *J. Home Econ. 61:* 174.

Baldwin, R. E., Korschgen, B. M., Vandepopuliere, J. M., and Russell, W. D. 1975. "Palatability of ground turkey and beef containing soy." *Poultry Sci. 54:* 1102.

Batcher, O. M. and Deary, P. A. 1975. "Quality characteristics of broiled and roasted beef steaks." *J. Food Sci. 40:* 745.

Bayne, B. H., Meyer, B., and Cole J. W. 1969. "Response of beef roasts differing in finish, location, and size to two rates of heat application." *J. Animal Sci. 29:* 283.

Bazinet, L., et al. 1997. "Electroacidification of soybean proteins for production of isolate." *Food Technol. 51* (9): 52.

Beilken, S. L., et al. 1986. "Some effects on mechanical properties of meat produced by cooking at temperatures between 50° and 60 °C." *J. Food Sci. 51* (3): 791.

Bernal, W. V. M., Bernal, V. M., Gullett, E. A., and Stanley, D. W. 1988. "Sensory and objective evaluation of a restructured beef product." *J. Texture Studies 19:* 231.

Bernard, D. T. and Scott, V. N. 1999. *"Listeria monocytogenes* in meats: new strategies are needed." *Food Technol. 53* (3): 124.

Berry, B. W. and Leddy, K. 1984. "Beef patty composition: Effects of fat content and cooking method." *J. Amer. Dietet. Assoc. 84:* 870.

Berry, B. W., Marshall, W. H., and Koch, E. J. 1981. "Cooking and chemical properties of raw and precooked flaked and ground beef patties cooked from the frozen state." *J. Food Sci. 46:* 856.

Berry, B. W., Smith, J. J., and Secrist, J. L. 1986. "Effects of connective tissue levels on sensory, Instron, cooking and collagen values of restructured beef steaks." *J. Food Protection 49:* 455.

Bett, K. L. and Dionigi, C. P. 1997. "Detecting seafood off-flavors: limitations of sensory evaluation." *Food Technol. 51* (8): 70.

Blaker, G. G., Newcomer, J. L., and Stafford, W. D. 1959. "Conventional roasting vs. high-temperature foil cookery." *J. Amer. Dietet. Assoc. 35:* 1255.

Bolton, D. J., et al. 1999. "Integrating HACCP and TQM reduces pork carcass contamination." *Food Technol. 53* (4): 40.

Bowers, J. A. and Engler, P. P. 1975. "Freshly cooked and cooked, frozen, reheated beef and beef-soy patties." *J. Food Sci. 40:* 624.

Bowers, J. A. and Goertz, G. E. 1966. "Effect of internal temperature on eating quality of pork chops." *J. Amer. Dietet. Assoc. 48:* 116.

Brady, P. L. and Penfield, M. P. 1977. "Comparison of four methods of heating beef roasts: Conventional oven, slow cooker, microwave oven, and pressure cooker." *Tenn. Farm and Home Sci. Issue 101:* 15.

Bramblett, V. D., Hostetler, R. L., Vail, V. E., and Draudt, H. N. 1959. "Qualities of beef as affected by cooking at very low temperatures for long periods of time." *Food Technol. 13:* 707.

Buchanan, R. L. 1991. "Microbiological criteria for cooked, ready-to-eat shrimp and crabmeat." *Food Technol. 45* (4): 157.

Carlin, F., et al. 1978. "Texturized soy protein in beef loaves: cooking losses, flavor, juiciness and chemical composition." *J. Food Sci. 43:* 830.

Carpenter, Z. L., Abraham H. C., and King, G. T. 1968. "Tenderness and cooking loss of beef and pork. I. Relative effects of microwave cooking, deep-fat frying, and oven broiling." *J. Amer. Dietet. Assoc. 53:* 353.

Cassens, R. G. 1997. Residual nitrite in cured meat. *Food Technol. 51* (2): 53.

Cassens, R. G. 1995. "Use of sodium nitrite in cured meats today." *Food Technol. 49* (7): 72.

Cline, J. A., Trowbridge, E. A., Foster, M. T., and Fry, H. E. 1930. "How certain methods of cooking affect the quality and palatability of beef." *Bull.* 293. Missouri Agric. Exp. Station, Columbia.

Cole, D. J. A. and Lawrie, R. A., eds. 1975. *Meat.* AVI Publishing: Westport, CT.

Costello, C. A., Penfield, M. P., and Riemann, M. J. 1985. "Quality of restructured steaks: Effects of days on feed, fat level, and cooking method." *J. Food Sci. 50:* 685.

Davey, C. L., and Gilbert, K. V. 1974. "Temperature-dependent cooking toughness in beef." *J. Sci. Food Agr. 25:* 931.

Davenport, M. M. and Meyer, B. H. 1970. "Forced convection roasting at 200° and 300°F: yield, cost, and acceptability of beef sirloin." *J. Amer. Dietet. Assoc. 56:* 31.

Decker, E. A. and Xu, Z. 1998. "Minimizing rancidity in muscle foods." *Food Technol. 52* (10): 54.

Deethardt, D., et al. 1973. "Effect of electronic, convection and conventional oven roasting on the acceptability of pork loin roasts." *J. Food Sci. 38:* 1076.

Dunajski, E. 1979. "Texture of fish muscle." *J. Texture Studies 10:* 301.

Ferry, J. D. 1948. "Protein gels." *Adv. Protein Chem. 4:* 1.

Forrest, J. C., et al. 1975. *Principles of Meat Science.* Freeman: San Francisco.

Giese, J. 1992. "Developing low-fat meat products." *Food Technol. 46* (4): 99.

Hall, D. A. 1961. *Chemistry of Connective Tissue.* C. C. Thomas: Springfield, IL.

Harrington, W. F. and VonHippel, P. H. 1961. "Structure of collagen and gelatin." *Adv. Protein Chem. 16:* 1.

Hepburn, F. N., Exler, J., and Weihrauch, J. L. 1986. "Provisional tables on content of omega-3 fatty acids and other fat components of selected foods." *J. Amer. Dietet. Assoc. 86:* 788.

Holmes, Z. A. Bowers, J. A., and Goertz, G. E. 1966. "Effect of internal temperature on eating quality of pork chops." *J. Amer. Dietet. Assoc. 48:* 121.

Holmes, Z. A., and Woodburn, M. 1981. "Heat transfer and temperature of foods during processing." *CRC Crit. Rev. Food Sci. Nutr. 14* (3): 231.

Honikel, K. O. and Reagan, J. O. 1986. "Influence of different chilling conditions on hot-boned pork." *J. Food Sci. 51* (3): 766.

Horan, F. E. 1974. "Meat analogs." In *New Protein Foods:* Altschul, A. M., ed. Academic Press: New York.

Hostetler, R. L. and Landmann, W. A. 1968. "Photomicrographic studies of dynamic changes in muscle fiber fragments. 1. Effect of various heat treatments on length, width and birefringence." *J. Food Sci. 33:* 468.

Hultin, H. O. 1984. "Postmortem biochemistry of meat and fish." *J. Chem. Educ. 61* (4): 289.

Huxley, H. E. 1971. "Structural basis of muscular contraction." *Proc. R. Soc. London Ser. B 178:* 131.

Inglett, G. E. 1975. *Fabricated Foods.* AVI Publishing: Westport, CT.

Jennings, T. G., et al. 1978. "Influence of fat thickness, marbling and length of aging on beef palatability and shelf-life characteristics." *J. Anim. Sci. 46:* 658.

Jones, S. B., et al. 1968. "Ultrastructure of pork liver after freeze-thaw cycling and refrigerated storage." *J. Food Sci. 51* (3): 761.

Kang, C. K. and Rice, E. E. 1970. "Degradation of various meat fractions by tenderizing enzymes." *J. Food Sci. 35:* 563.

Kang, C. K. and Warner, W. D. 1974. "Tenderization of meat with papaya latex proteases." *J. Food Sci. 39:* 812.

Katz, F. 1998. "That's using the old bean." *Food Technol. 52* (6): 42.

Khan, A. W. 1971. "Effect of temperature during post-mortem glycolysis and dephosphorylation of high energy phosphates on poultry and meat tenderness." *J. Food Sci. 36:* 120.

Khan, A. W., et al. 1973. "Post-slaughter pH variation in beef." *J. Food Sci. 38:* 710.

Kilara, A. and Sharkasi, T. Y. 1981. "Effects of temperature on food proteins and implications on functional properties." *CRC Crit. Rev. Food Sci. Nutr. 23* (4): 323.

Korschgen, B. M., Baldwin, R. E., and Snider, S. 1976. "Quality factors in beef, pork, and lamb cooked by microwaves." *J. Amer. Dietet. Assoc. 69:* 635.

Kregel, K. K., Prusa, K. J., and Hughes, K. V. 1986. "Cholesterol content and sensory analysis of ground beef as influenced by fat level, heating, and storage." *J. Food Sci. 51:* 1162.

Laakkonen, E., Wellington, G. H., and Sherbon, J. W. 1970. "Low-temperature, long-time heating of bovine muscle. I. Changes in tenderness, water-binding capacity, pH, and amount of water-soluble components." *J. Food Sci. 35:* 175.

Lamkey, J. W., et al. 1986. "Effect of salt and phosphate on texture and color stability of restructured beef steaks." *J. Food Sci. 51* (4): 873.

Lanier, T. C. 1986. "Functional properties of surimi." *Food Technol. 40* (3): 107.

Law, H. M., Yang, S. P., Mullins, A. M., and Fielder, M. M. 1967. "Effect of storage and cooking on qualities of loin and top round steaks." *J. Food Sci. 32:* 637.

Lawrence, R., et al. 1986. "Formation of structured protein foods by freeze texturization." *Food Technol. 40* (3): 77.

Lawrie, R. 1985. *Developments in Meat Science.* Elsevier: New York, Vol. 3.

Lee, C. M. 1986. "Surimi manufacturing and fabrication of surimi-based products." *Food Technol. 40* (3): 115.

Lillard, H. S. 1994. "Decontamination of poultry skin by sonication." *Food Technol. 48* (12): 72.

Lind, J. M., Griswold, R. M., and Bramblett, V. D. 1971. "Tenderizing effect of wine vinegar marinade on beef round." *J. Amer. Dietet. Assoc. 58:* 133.

Liston, J. 1990. "Microbial hazards of seafood consumption." *Food Technol. 44* (12): 56.

Loffler, A. 1986. "Proteolytic enzymes: sources and applications." *Food Technol. 40* (1): 63.

Lusk, J. L., et al. 1999. "Consumer acceptance of irradiated meat." *Food Technol. 53* (3): 56.

MacDonald, G. A. and Lanier, T. C. 1991. "Carbohydrates as cryoprotectants for meats and surimi." *Food Technol. 45* (3): 150.

MacFarlane, J. J., et al. 1986. "Binding of meat pieces: Influence of some processing factors on binding strength and cooking losses." *J. Food Sci. 51* (3): 736.

MacLeod, G. and Coppock, B. M. 1978. "Sensory properties of the aroma of beef cooked conventionally and by microwave radiation." *J. Food Sci. 43:* 145.

MacLeod, G. and Seyyedain-Ardebili, M. 1981. "Natural and simulated meat flavors." *CRC Crit. Rev. Food Sci. Nutr. 14* (4): 309.

Maga, J. A. 1982. "Pyrazines in foods: an update." *CRC Crit. Rev. Food Sci. Nutr. 16:* 1.

Mandigo, R. W. 1986. "Restructuring of muscle foods." *Food Technol. 40* (3): 77.

Manu-Tawiah, W., Ammann, L. L., Sebranek, J. G., and Molins, R. A. 1991. "Extending color stability and shelf life of fresh meat." *Food Technol. 45* (3): 94.

Marsden, J. and Pesselman, R. 1993. "Nitrosamines in food-contact netting: regulatory and analytical challenges." *Food Technol. 47* (3): 131.

Martin, R. E. 1986. "Developing appropriate nomenclature for structured seafood products." *Food Technol. 40* (3): 127.

Mattison, M. L., et al. 1986. "Effect of low dose irradiation of pork loins on the microflora, sensory characteristics, and fat stability." *J. Food Sci. 51* (2): 284.

Mermelstein, N. H. 1993. "Controlling *E. coli 0157:H7* in meat." *Food Technol. 47* (4): 90.

Miller, M. F., et al. 1986. "Effect of fat source and color of lean on acceptability of beef/pork patties." *J. Food Sci. 51* (3): 832.

Murphy, P. A., et al. 1997. Soybean protein composition and tofu quality. *Food Technol. 51* (3): 86.

Nielsen, L. M. and Carlin, A. F. 1974. "Frozen, precooked beef and beef soy loaves." *J. Amer. Dietet. Assoc. 65:* 35.

Patterson, R. L., ed. 1986. *Biochemical Identification of Meat Species.* Elsevier: New York.

Pearson, A. M. and Dutson, T. R., eds. 1986. *Advances in Meat Research. Vol. 2 Meat and Poultry Microbiology.* AVI Publishing: Westport, CT.

Penfield, M. P. and Meyer, B. H. 1975. "Changes in tenderness and collagen of beef semi-tendinosus muscle heated at two rates. *J. Food Sci. 40:* 150.

Price, J. F. and Schweigert, B. S., eds. 1987. *Science of Meat and Meat Products.* 3rd ed. Food and Nutrition Press: Westport, CT.

Prochaska, J. F., et al. 1998. "Meat fermentation research opportunities." *Food Technol. 52* (9): 52.

Pszczola, D. E. 1999. "Ingredients that get to the meat of the matter." *Food Technol. 53* (4): 62.

Pszczola, D. E. 1997. "20 ways to market the concept of food irradiation." *Food Technol. 51* (2): 46.

Pszczola, D. E. 1991. "Oat-bran-based ingredient blend replaces fat in ground beef and pork sausage." *Food Technol. 45* (11): 60.

Quenzer, N. M., Donnelly, L. S., and Seideman, S. C. 1982. "Institutional cookery of restructured beef steaks." *J. Food Qual. 5:* 301.

Ream, E. E., Wilcox, E. B., Taylor, F. G., and Bennett, J., A. 1974. "Tenderness of beef roasts." *J. Amer. Dietet. Assoc. 65:* 155.

Resurreccion, A. V. A. and Galvez, F. C. F. 1999. "Will consumers buy irradiated beef?" *Food Technol. 53* (3): 52.

Schaller, D. R. and Powrie, W. D. 1972. "Scanning electron microscopy of beef, chicken, and rainbow trout muscle." *Canadian Institute of Food Sci. and Technol. 5:* 184.

Schock, D. R., et al. 1970. "Effect of dry and moist heat treatments on selected beef quality factors." *J. Food Sci. 35:* 195.

Seideman, S. C. 1986. "Methods of expressing collagen characteristics and their relationship to meat tenderness and muscle fiber types." *J. Food Sci. 51* (2): 273.

Shaffer, T. A., et al. 1973. "Effects of end point and oven temperatures on beef roasts cooked in oven film bags and open pans." *J. Food Sci. 38:* 1205.

Shorthose, W. R., et al. 1986. "Influence of electrical stimulation, cooking rates and aging on the shear force values of chilled lamb." *J. Food Sci. 51* (4): 889.

Skrede, G. and Storebakken, T. 1986. "Characteristics of color in raw, baked, and smoked wild and pen-reared Atlantic salmon." *J. Food Sci. 51* (3): 804.

Smith, G. C., et al. 1978. "Postmortem aging of beef carcasses," *J. Food Sci. 43:* 823.

Sofos, J. N. 1986. "Use of phosphates in low-sodium meat products." *Food Technol. 40* (9): 52.

Stiffler, D. M., et al. 1986. "Effects of electrical stimulation on carcass quality and meat palatability traits on Charolais crossbred bulls and steers." *J. Food Sci. 51* (4): 883.

Sundberg, A. D. and Carlin, A. F. 1976. "Survival of *Cl. Perfringens* in rump roasts cooked in an oven at 107° or 177°C or in an electric crockery pot," *J. Food Sci. 41:* 451.

Thayer, D. W., et al. 1986. "Use of irradiation to ensure microbiological safety of processed meats." *Food Technol. 40* (4): 159.

Tompkin, R. B. 1986. "Microbiological safety of processed meat: new products and processes—new problems and solutions." *Food Technol. 40* (4): 172.

Vecchio, A. J. et al. 1986. "N-nitrosamine ingestion from consumer-cooked bacon." *J. Food Sci. 51* (3): 754.

Walter, J. D., et al. 1965. "Effect of marbling and maturity on beef muscle characteristics. I. Objective measurements of tenderness and chemical properties." *Food Technol. 19:* 841.

Weakley, D. F., et al. 1986. "Effects of different chilling methods on hot processed vacuum packaged pork." *J. Food Sci. 51* (3): 757.

Welke, R. A., et al. 1986. "Effect of cooking method on texture of epimysial tissue and rancidity in beef roasts." *J. Food Sci. 51* (4): 1057.

Williams, C. W. and Zabik, M. E. 1975. "Quality characteristics of soy-substituted ground beef, pork and turkey meat loaves." *J. Food Sci. 40:* 502.

Wright-Rudolph, L., et al. 1986. "Survival of *Clostridium perfringens* and aerobic bacteria on ground beef patties during microwave and conventional cooking." *J. Food Protect. 49:* 203.

Yu, L. P. and Lee, Y. B. 1986. "Effects of postmortem pH and temperature on bovine muscle structure and meat tenderness." *J. Food Sci. 51* (3): 774.

CHAPTER 16

Eggs

FORMATION

Egg formation begins in the ovaries of poultry with development of a yolk in which the germ cell (ovum) is located. From the ovaries, the yolk moves into the oviduct where layers of egg white are secreted into the albumen-secreting region to surround the yolk. If sperm pass the oviduct and reach the yolk before it is encased by this coating of egg white proteins, the yolk is fertilized, and the final egg laid is a fertile egg.

Encasement of the yolk and white is accomplished gradually as the developing egg continues its passage down the oviduct. Two membranes—an inner, somewhat fragile membrane and a tough outer membrane—confine the yolk and white. Finally, a shell develops around the outer membrane as the egg moves through the region of the oviduct where minerals are secreted to provide this strong outer protection for the egg. Calcium is the mineral of particular importance in the shell.

During egg formation, various defects may develop. If a blood vessel happens to rupture in the ovary or along the oviduct, blood spots can occur in the yolk or in the white, depending on the location of the lesion in relation to the stage of development of the egg. Although uncommon, chickens may have an infection or even a parasite in the oviduct, which then becomes a part of the developing egg and is enclosed by the shell.

STRUCTURE

The yolk is more complex structurally than may be thought at first glance. At the very center is a light-colored structure called the **white yolk.** Leading from this white yolk to the **germinal disk** or blastoderm is a connecting tube called the

White Yolk
Small sphere of light-colored yolk at the center of the yolk.

Germinal Disk
Blastoderm of the yolk, which is located at the edge of the yolk and is connected to the white yolk.

355

Latebra
Tube connecting the white yolk to the germinal disk in the yolk.

Vitelline Membrane
Sac enclosing the yolk.

Chalazae
Thick ropelike extensions of the chalaziferous layer that aid in centering the yolk in the egg.

Chalaziferous Layer
Membranous layer surrounding the vitelline membrane of the yolk.

Albumen
The white of an egg; consists of three layers.

Thin Albumen
The rather fluid egg white adjacent to the yolk and to the inner membrane.

Thick Albumen
The viscous white forming the middle layer of albumen.

Air Cell
Space between the inner and outer shell membranes at the large end of the egg.

Shell Membranes
An inner membrane encasing the white and an outer membrane adjacent to the shell of the egg.

latebra. These structures, plus concentric rings of light and dark yolk layers, constitute the contents of the yolk. The **vitelline membrane** serves as the enclosure or sac for the yolk. The strength of this membrane is important when yolks and whites need to be separated in cookery. Two important, rather twisted membranous structures extend from opposite sides of the yolk into the white. These projections, called the **chalazae,** are extensions of the **chalaziferous layer** (membranous layer surrounding the yolk) and aid in keeping the yolk centered in the white by impeding movement through the thick white (see Figure 16.1).

The **albumen,** often called the white, surrounds the yolk to provide a protective buffer. Although all of the albumen appears to be transparent and somewhat fluid, the white actually comprises three layers of material. The innermost layer is a fairly fluid material called the inner **thin albumen.** A distinctly viscous layer encompasses the inner thin albumen, a layer called the **thick albumen** or albuminous sac. Another layer of thin albumen, the outer thin albumen, is the final layer of white.

Two membranes enclose the entire contents of the white and yolk of an egg. The inner shell membrane is immediately adjacent to the outer thin albumen and serves to confine this fluid outer layer of white. An outer shell membrane is right next to the shell. At the large end of the egg, an air space or **air cell** is found between the inner and outer **shell membranes.** The final layer is the shell, which surrounds the entire egg and is quite a rigid packaging material for the total egg. Although at first glance the shell appears to be a solid, it actually has many tiny pores which may permit passage of gases or tiny microorganisms into and out of

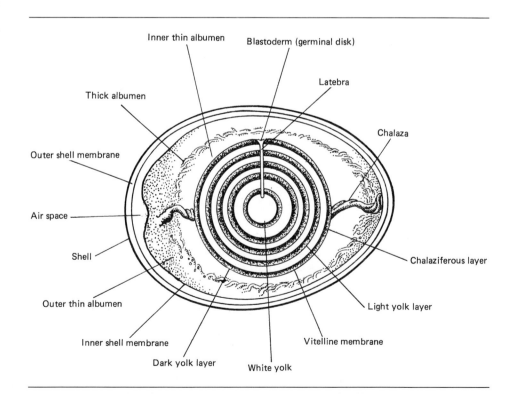

Figure 16.1   Cross-sectional diagram of an egg in the shell.

the shell. The egg's natural protection against such a microorganism invasion is a natural, thin coating called **"bloom,"** which is on the egg when it is laid and effectively seals the pores in the calcium carbonate-rich shell.

COMPOSITION

Gross differences in composition are found between the white and the yolk, differences that are somewhat evident even from casual observation. First, there is considerably more white than yolk. In fact, there is about twice as much white as yolk in an egg on the basis of weight. On the basis of volume, approximately 20 milliliters of yolk and 30 milliliters of white ($1\frac{1}{3}$ tablespoons of yolk and 2 tablespoons of white) equal one egg. This ratio remains fairly constant despite the actual size of the egg.

Pure yolk contains quite a different ratio of fluids than pure white. As can be seen in Table 16.1, the white is fluid because it contains close to 90 percent water and almost no fat. On the other hand, the yolk is not quite half water and almost a third fat. The protein concentration of the yolk is about 1.5 times that of the white.

When the actual content of one egg white is compared with that of one egg yolk (as would be appropriate in thinking about one egg), a somewhat different picture emerges because of the difference in the relative amounts of yolk and white. On this basis, an egg white provides about $1\frac{1}{3}$ times as much protein as the yolk (Table 16.2). One egg white has only a trace of fat, while one yolk contains 4.6 grams. This difference in fat content between the yolk and the white is largely responsible for the fact that one yolk provides about 3.5 times as many calories as one white. Nutritionally of interest is the fact that the yolk contains some iron (0.8 milligram) and a bit of vitamin A, both of which are missing in the white.

Several different lipid compounds are found in the yolk. About half of the lipids in the yolk are triglycerides. Phospholipids, including lecithin and cephalin, account for about a fifth of the egg yolk solids. Lecithin is of special interest because of its remarkable emulsifying ability, the result of the hydrophobic nature of the fatty acids in the molecule and the hydrophilic character of the phosphoric acid component (Chapter 6).

Cholesterol is a sterol of nutritional concern found in the lipid component of egg yolks. The yolk of an egg contains about 213 milligrams of cholesterol, which

Table 16.1   Approximate Percentage Composition of Chicken Egg Yolk and White

| Portion | Percent | Constituents | | | |
		Water	Protein	Fat	Ash
Whole egg	100	65.5	11.8	11.0	11.7
White	58	88.0	11.0	0.2	0.8
Yolk	31	48.0	17.5	32.5	2.0

| | | Carbonates | | Calcium Phosphate | Organic Matter |
		Calcium	Magnesium		
Shell	11	94.0	1.0	1.0	4.0

From U.S. Department of Agriculture.

Table 16.2   Composition of One Chicken Egg Yolk Versus One White

Component	White	Yolk
Weight	29 g	15 g
Calories	15	52
Protein	3.2 g	2.4 g
Fat	Trace	4.6 g
Iron	Trace	0.8 mg
Vitamin A	0 IU	510 IU

Adapted from U.S. Department of Agriculture Handbook No. 456: *Nutritive Value of American Foods in Common Units*. U.S. Department of Agriculture, ARS: Washington, D.C., 1975.

makes egg yolks off limits for people who need to limit their cholesterol intake. As whites do not contain lipids, they are not a potential source of cholesterol and can be used freely in the diet.

Other key lipids are the lipoproteins, the combination of a protein with a lipid. Lecithin, for example, combines with a protein to make a specific type of lipoprotein designated as a lecithoprotein. The protein components of the lipoproteins are discussed under Proteins.

PROTEINS

Albumen

Ovalbumin
By far the most abundant protein in egg albumen; denatured readily by heat.

The albumen proteins, 12 of which have been identified, contribute various characteristics to the behavior of eggs in food preparation. The most abundant of these proteins is **ovalbumin,** which accounts for more than half of the protein in egg white (Table 16.3). Ovalbumin is denatured comparatively easily by heat.

Table 16.3   Proteins in Egg Albumen

Protein	Relative Amount in Albumen (%)	Isoelectric Point	Molecular Weight	Characteristics
Ovalbumin	54	4.6	45,000	Phosphoglycoprotein
Conalbumin	13	6.6	80,000	Binds metals
Ovomucoid	11	3.9–4.3	28,000	Inhibits trypsin
Lysozyme (G_1 globulin)	3.5	10.7	14,600	Lyses some bacteria
G_2 globulin	4.0?	5.5	30,000–40,000	—
G_3 globulin	4.0?	5.8	?	—
Ovomucin	1.5	?	?	Sialoprotein
Flavoprotein	0.8	4.1	35,000	Binds riboflavin
Ovoglycoprotein	0.5?	3.9	24,000	Sialoprotein
Ovomacroglobulin	0.5	4.5–4.7	760,000–900,000	?
Ovoinhibitor	0.1	5.2	44,000	Inhibits some proteases
Avidin	0.05	9.5	53,000	Binds biotin

From Powrie, W. D. "Characteristics of edible fluids of animal origin: Eggs." In *Principles of Food Science I*. Fennema, O. R., ed. Dekker: New York, 1976, p. 665.

Conalbumin is significant because of its ability to bind metals, forming undesirable colors if ions of iron, aluminum, copper, or zinc are present. Complexes of iron and conalbumin cause a red color in egg whites, whereas copper ions (2+) form a yellow complex with conalbumin. Although these metal–conalbumin compounds are stable to heat, conalbumin itself is heat sensitive. As these ions usually are not available to bind the conalbumin, conalbumin is considered to be susceptible to denaturation when heated. However, egg whites to be pasteurized can be treated with metals to give conalbumin heat stability.

Ovomucoid is a glycoprotein which may include a variety of carbohydrates, including mannose, galactose, and deoxyglucose. This protein is quite resistant to denaturation by heating unless it is in an alkaline medium.

Lysozyme is a very unusual albumen protein, because it has a fraction (G_1 globulin) that has an isoelectric point of 10.7. Only avidin, among the other albumen proteins, has an isoelectric point in the alkaline range, and the isoelectric point of avidin is only 9.5. Another characteristic of lysozyme is that it has bactericidal action because of its ability to hydrolyze a polysaccharide in the cell wall of specific bacteria to help prevent bacterial spoilage in eggs.

Two ovoglobulins important for their foaming ability are G_2 globulin and G_3 globulin. These globulins, along with ovomucin and conalbumin, are of great merit in the foaming of egg whites when they are beaten.

Ovomucin has a somewhat fibrous character. This rigidity of structure accounts for the difference in the flow properties of thin versus thick albumen, for ovomucin is four times more abundant in thick albumen than it is in thin albumen. These fibers of ovomucin may be cut by the action of a rapidly moving egg beater during the whipping of whites to shorter lengths that enhance the stability of egg white foams. Although ovomucin contributes to the stability of egg white foams, it is quite resistant to denaturation by heating.

Among the other albumen proteins that have been studied fairly extensively is **avidin.** This protein is of interest nutritionally because of its ability to bind biotin, thereby preventing absorption of this vitamin. This fact was used in structuring an experimental diet to determine the role of biotin in humans. This ability to bind biotin is eliminated when avidin is denatured by heating and hence does not present a realistic dietary problem for people.

Yolk

Egg yolk consists of four types of particles—yolk spheres, granules, low-density lipoproteins, and myelin figures—dispersed in a plasma containing livetin, a globular protein, and low-density lipoproteins. Most of the yolk spheres are found in the white yolk, yet a few are located in the yellow yolk, which constitutes almost all of the yolk. Granules account for almost a fourth of the total solids in yolks, and about 60 percent of the content of these granules is protein (Powrie, 1976).

Livetin, a prominent protein in the plasma of egg yolk, actually can be separated into three fractions: α-, β-, and γ-livetin. These three forms of livetin are thought to have their origin in the blood of the hen developing the egg.

Low-density **lipoproteins (LDLs)** constitute the remainder of the proteins found in yolk plasma. Actually, the LDL fraction consists largely of lipids, with protein representing somewhat over 10 percent (Powrie, 1976).

The granules in egg yolk contain three types of protein—**lipovitellins** (classified as HDLs), phosvitin, and low-density lipoprotein. They also contain phosphorus primarily in the form of phosphatidylcholine.

Conalbumin
Protein in egg albumen capable of complexing with iron (Fe^{3+}) and copper (Cu^{2+}) ions to form red and yellow colors, respectively.

Lysozyme
Albumen protein with an isoelectric point of pH 10.7; notable for its ability to hydrolyze a polysaccharide in the cell wall of some bacteria, thus protecting against contamination by these bacteria.

Ovomucin
Rather fibrous protein occurring in thick white at about four times the concentration in which it occurs in thin white; protein contributing significantly to the viscous, gel-like texture of thick white.

Avidin
Albumen protein that binds biotin when in the native state, but not when it is denatured.

Livetin
Yolk plasma protein found in three forms (α, β, and γ).

Lipoproteins (LDLs)
Combination of lipid and protein: in yolk plasma the protein level is just over 10 percent

Lipovitellin
High-density lipoprotein in the granules in egg yolk; the most abundant granular protein.

Phosvitin
Small protein in the yolk granules that is unique because of its high serine content and its function of binding iron and incorporating it into the yolk.

In addition to the lipovitellins, yolk granules contain about 16 percent phosvitin and somewhat less (about 12 percent) low-density lipoprotein. **Phosvitin** is a comparatively small protein (molecular weight approaching 40,000) with a phosphorus content of about 10 percent and a high content (almost one third of the amino acid residues) of serine. Of particular interest is that phosvitin, with its ability to bind ferric ions in a soluble complex, is the means by which iron is incorporated into the yolk.

EGG QUALITY

The quality of eggs can be graded in or out of the shell; the grade designation assigned to federal standard descriptions of the shell, air cell, white, and yolk is shown for the three federal grades in Table 16.4. Candling, the technique used for grading eggs in the shell, is based on observing the eggs in silhouette while being rotated. A special micrometer (Figure 16.2) is used to measure the height (in **Haugh units**) of the thick albumen in the white in relation to the weight of the egg. Other measures of quality out of the shell are **albumen index** and **yolk index.**

Haugh Unit
Units used to denote quality of albumen: correlates thick albumen height with egg weight.

Albumen Index
Grading measurement of albumen to determine quality on the basis of the amount of thick white.

Yolk Index
Measurement of egg quality based on the ratio of the height of the yolk to its width.

Particularly in shell eggs, the quality indicated by the grade designation may not be what actually is found at the time of use because egg quality declines continuously after laying. The extent of the changes depends on the conditions under which eggs are stored and the length of storage. However, the changes occur in predictable fashion and are clearly visible, whether viewed from above or sideways when they have been broken from the shell (see Figure 16.3).

The air cell at the large end of the intact shell forms between the inner and outer membranes as the warm, freshly laid egg cools to ambient temperature and contracts. This air cell continues to grow as the egg loses both moisture and carbon dioxide through the pores during storage. Loss of carbon dioxide also causes the pH of the white to rise, with the result that egg albumen gradually increases in alkalinity, from its original pH of about 7.6 to as high as 9.4. The alkalinity of the albumen of low-quality eggs is unique among foods, for virtually all other foods become increasingly acidic as they deteriorate.

A gradual transition in the ratio of thick white to thin white is another change that occurs as eggs lose quality. In an egg of high quality, the thick albumen is

Table 16.4 Standards for Grading Eggs in the Shell

Grade	Shell	Air Cell	White	Yolk
AA	Clean, unbroken; practically normal	$\frac{1}{8}$ inch or less in depth	Clear; firm (72 Haugh units or higher)	Outline slightly defined; practically free from defects
A	Clean, unbroken; practically normal	$\frac{3}{16}$ inch or less in depth	Clear; may be reasonably firm (60–72 Haugh units)	Outline may be fairly well defined; practically free from defects
B	Clean to very slightly stained, unbroken; may be slightly abnormal	$\frac{3}{8}$ inch or less in depth	Clear; may be slightly weak (31–60 Haugh units)	Outline may be well defined; may be slightly enlarged and flattened; may show definite but not serious defects

From the U.S. Department of Agriculture, 1968.

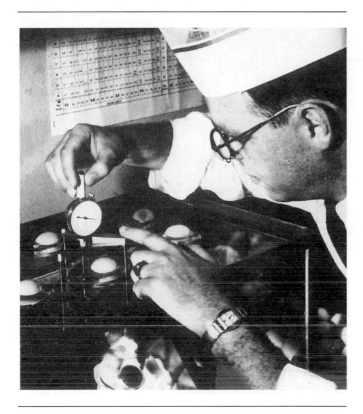

Figure 16.2 Measuring the height of the thick albumen to determine the grade of an unshelled egg. (Courtesy of the U.S. Department of Agriculture.)

held fairly firmly around the yolk and does not spread very far. A gradual change to an increasingly shallow albumen with a wider spread occurs as the ovomucin in the thick albumen undergoes degradation and the thin white increases. The apearance of the egg changes from one that is relatively thick and occupying a comparatively small space to one that spreads thinly over a large area. The thinner albumen allows the yolk to move away from the center and toward the edge of the egg.

The yolk also changes in appearance as the quality of an egg declines. A strong vitelline membrane in an egg of high quality results in a well-rounded yolk. However, the change in the pH of the albumen appears to have an effect on the chalaziferous layer and the vitelline membrane, with the result that the vitelline membrane stretches and becomes weaker. These changes cause the yolk to become increasingly flatter and to spread farther. Weakening of the vitelline membrane also makes it more difficult to separate yolks from the whites without breaking them. The migration of a small amount of water from the white into the yolk contributes to the stretching and weakening of the vitelline membrane.

Although the albumen changes much more in pH than the yolk does during storage, both parts of the egg reflect the loss of carbon dioxide through the pores. Accompanying this increase in pH is a subtle modification of flavor. The brightness of a fresh egg flavor slowly changes to a flavor with increasing overtones of sulfur. Oil-dipping can be done to seal the pores and block loss of water and carbon dioxide from the egg during storage, but this oil traps volatile flavoring compounds that are generated within the egg, which can lead to off-flavors if the egg is held in storage for a prolonged period (Stadelman, 1986).

AA Quality

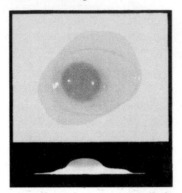

1. Egg covers small area; much thick white surrounds yolk; has small amount of thin white; yolk round and upstanding.
2. White—firm—72 Haugh units minimum.

A Quality

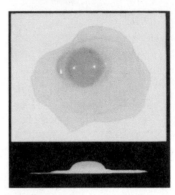

1. Egg covers moderate area; has considerable thick white; medium amount of thin white; yolk round and upstanding.
2. White—reasonably firm—60 Haugh units minimum.

B Quality

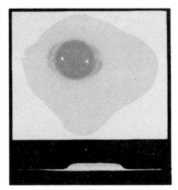

1. Egg covers very wide area; has no thick white; large amount of thin white thinly spread; yolk very flat and enlarged.
2. White—weak and watery—less than 60 Haugh units.

Figure 16.3 Quality guide to eggs broken out of the shell (top and side views). (Courtesy of the U.S. Department of Agriculture.)

Eggs can be held in cold storage or refrigerator storage for 6 months and retain satisfactory quality, but eggs held at room temperature will drop at least a grade level within a week. Storage of eggs in closed containers during refrigerated storage slows the rate of deterioration. Egg cartons are suitable for this purpose.

SAFETY

Eggs can provide an excellent medium for the growth of microorganisms. Therefore, care must be taken to avoid contamination from external sources. Egg producers employ strict sanitation standards to maintain clean facilities and to wash and sanitize eggs. Such measures are effective in eliminating numerous potential hazards, but they do not address the contamination of eggs by ***Salmonella enteritidis*** (Chapter 19). Unfortunately, this bacterium infects the yolk of the egg while the egg is being formed and before the shell is made. Therefore, sanitary handling of the eggs has no effect on the presence and viability of *Salmonella enteritidis*. Control of this potential source of food-borne illness must focus on sanitary procedures at all stages of handling of the laying flock as a means of helping to prevent the hens from being infected with this dangerous form of *Salmonella*. At the present time, there probably is only a chance of about 1 in 10,000 eggs being contaminated with *Salmonella enteritidis,* but even this risk level necessitates careful attention to adequate heat treatment to kill any bacteria that might be present. Pasteurized egg products can be used to avoid this source of infection. Good sanitary measures also are necessary. Refrigeration of shell eggs at 7.2°C (45°F) by warehouses, transport trucks, and retailers is now required (FSIS and FDA regulations) to promote the safety of eggs.

Even if eggs are not contaminated with Salmonellae, they still are a perfect medium for the growth of most microorganisms with which they might become infected during food handling. Prompt refrigeration of eggs and egg-containing dishes or holding of hot egg dishes at or above 60°C should be the rule at all times to help avoid food-borne illnesses that could be caused by improperly managed eggs.

Salmonella enteritidis
Form of bacteria that can be incorporated into the yolk of an egg as the hen is forming the egg; potential source of food-borne illness if egg is not heated sufficiently during preparation.

PRESERVATION

Pasteurization

When food is prepared in institutional quantities, the labor involved in breaking eggs can become quite costly. This has led to a market for eggs sold out of the shell. Unfortunately, eggs can spoil extremely rapidly once they are removed from the protective shell. Therefore, pasteurization of eggs being marketed outside their shells is necessary to ensure the safety of these products. Various methods of pasteurization are suitable; a common technique is to hold liquid whole eggs at 61°C for 3.5 minutes, a temperature sufficient to kill harmful microorganisms without causing undesirable denaturation in the eggs. Yolks can be pasteurized in similar fashion, although those to which sugar or salt is added require a higher temperature to kill salmonella and other potentially harmful microorganisms that may be present. Even though egg whites are more sensitive to pasteurization than either yolks or whole eggs, they still are very satisfactory for producing foams after pasteurization.

Drying

Preservation of eggs by drying or freezing is done for convenience and safety, but these products are available primarily to the food industry for use in manufacturing other food items. Spray drying is the technique commonly utilized to dry eggs. Dried eggs are of interest because of the convenience afforded by the long-term storage that is possible without refrigerated or frozen storage facilities. Among the dried egg products available are whole-egg solids, yolk solids, fortified whole-egg solids with varying proportions of whites and yolks, and whites.

Production of spray-dried egg whites presents a particular challenge because of the potential changes that can impair whipping characteristics, color, and flavor. During a fermentation period by bacteria or yeast, glucose can be eliminated from the whites prior to drying, thus eliminating the negative impact of this sugar on the dried whites. When glucose remains in dried egg whites, browning occurs as the Maillard reaction proceeds during storage. Dried whites that have undergone bacterial fermentation prior to drying can be used effectively in making products containing such foams. Adding a surface-active agent to dried egg whites in angel cake mixes enhances foaming to help overcome the slightly detrimental effect resulting from small amounts of fat that may be incorporated as a contaminant from broken yolks during the initial separation process.

Glucose also complicates the production of dried yolks and dried whole eggs. During storage, glucose can react with cephalin in the yolk to produce an off-flavor. The fat in the yolks makes it necessary to eliminate oxygen from the packaging to prevent oxidation during storage. If the glucose is eliminated by fermentation prior to drying and the adequately dried yolk or whole-egg mixture is packaged tightly with inert gas replacing any oxygen, the storage life and usefulness of these egg products are excellent.

Freezing

In freezing, whites perform very well and do not require special treatment. Unlike the situation when whites are to be dried, glucose does not present a problem when whites are to be frozen. With normal freezer packaging precautions, frozen egg whites can be stored in the freezer and then thawed for use in any way that fresh whites would be used. Foaming power and flavor are excellent after freezing and thawing.

Unfortunately, egg yolks form gels as a consequence of freezing, making thawed yolks or whole eggs very viscous and unsatisfactory to use unless either sugar or salt is added prior to freezing. For commercial purposes, 10 percent salt or sugar (by weight of the yolks) can be added to either whole eggs or yolks before they are frozen. Of course, this alters the flavor of the product, making it necessary to be certain that the appropriate flavor of frozen egg yolk or whole egg is available when needed. Scrambled eggs made using frozen whole eggs to which sugar was added will not meet expectations! If yolks or whole eggs are to be frozen in small quantities, the yolks or whole eggs are mixed to blend them and then either half a teaspoon of salt or two tablespoons of sugar can be added per cup to reduce the problems of yolk gelation.

Unlike many other frozen foods, eggs stored at colder freezing temperatures are not better than those stored at somewhat more moderate freezing temperatures, because of the impact of extreme cold on the gelling properties of protein. Storage at about −17°C causes less problems with gelation than storage at −23°C or −29°C (Palmer et al., 1969).

Frozen "long eggs" can be purchased for commercial uses when sliced egg or chopped egg may be desired for garnishing or for incorporation in prepared food products. Frozen cooked white has an undesirable texture, which is both rubbery and tough. Textural problems are overcome by binding the water in the cooked egg white through blending the cooked white with a gum or starch. This blend is forced into a long tube in which a concentric smaller tube is centered. Yolk is used to fill the center tube, and then the assembly is cooked. Subsequently, the "long eggs" are frozen and marketed (Cotterill, 1986).

As consumers are increasingly demanding pre-prepared products, there is incentive for developing frozen products containing cooked egg. One of the key problems that needs to be overcome is syneresis. Several approaches may be helpful in improving the quality of cooked egg products that ultimately will be frozen, thawed, and reheated. The addition of gums, such as is done in making "long eggs," helps to bind the water within the egg mixture. Citric acid can be added to alter the pH from essentially neutral to a somewhat acidic pH of around 6.0 (Feiser and Cotterill, 1982). Salt may also be added, although the consumer concerns about salt in processed foods may be a factor in promoting other solutions to syneresis.

FUNCTIONAL PROPERTIES

Eggs, either as yolks, whites, or whole eggs, are unique among food ingredients because of their amazing versatility in the functional roles they can fulfill in a variety of products. These functions can be categorized as (1) coloring agent, (2) emulsifier, (3) thickening agent, and (4) texturizing agent. These are contributions above and beyond the excellent nutrient content they provide. Their only negative roles are providing a source of cholesterol (approximately 213 milligrams per yolk) and protein to which a few people have an allergic response.

Coloring

The bright pigments in the yolk add color to light-colored food products in which they are used. Marusich and Bauernfeind (1981) identified four major carotenoid pigments in the yolk. The two pigments contributing the majority of the color are lutein and zeaxanthin, the former being a xanthophyll with a closed ring and two hydroxyl groups and the latter possessing a single hydroxyl group and two closed rings (Chapter 10). Cryptoxanthin, another xanthophyll, and carotene also contribute to the overall color of the yolk. Yolk color varies somewhat with the season of the year in this country, but ranges from a fairly pale yellow through a slightly subtle orange tone. The yolks in Guatemala are an amazing nasturtium-orangish red color! The hen's diet has a strong impact on yolk color.

Emulsification

Egg yolk itself is an example of a naturally occurring oil-in-water emulsion. Lecithin and lysolecithin are key compounds responsible for the remarkable ability of egg yolk to act as an emulsifying agent in food systems in which it is incorporated. An oil-in-water emulsion is the type formed when egg yolk is utilized as an ingredient in food mixtures containing some type of fluid fat and water or other aqueous liquid. Yolk particles (including low-density lipoproteins, myelin figures, and high-density lipoproteins) contribute to the stability of an emulsion by interacting at the surface of the oil droplets to form a layer (Fennema, 1985). Mayonnaise is a classic example of a food emulsion stabilized by egg yolk (Chapter 5). Numerous other examples of the effectiveness of egg yolk as an emulsifying agent can also be cited.

Hollandaise sauce is a classic sauce noted for its capricious behavior. The generous use of butter in this sauce results in a fat content approaching 50 percent, and this large amount of fat needs to be formed into an emulsion, with lemon juice and water serving as the liquid portion. The emulsion is traditionally prepared by gently heating the yolks and liquid to thicken the mixture by partial denaturation, at which time the yolk mixture is removed from the heat and cooled slightly by the addition of some butter to reduce the risk of overheating and curdling the yolk mixture. Then melted butter is added very gradually with agitation to emulsify the fat as it is incorporated into the sauce. Temperature control is essential to the retention of this delicate oil-in-water emulsion, for excess heat will cause the yolk proteins to draw more tightly together, reducing their ability to cover a large amount of surface area at the interface between the oil droplets and the aqueous phase. Loss of too much liquid from evaporation can also be responsible for curdling the sauce. If this is the case, a small amount of liquid must be added to replace the water. The key to success with a hollandaise sauce is formation of a semi-viscous, stable emulsion, and egg yolks provide the essential emulsifying agent, lecithin.

Baked products containing egg yolk also benefit from the emulsifying action of lecithin and lysolecithin. Cake batters sometimes have a tendency to curdle, particularly in very warm weather when the fat becomes quite soft, but egg yolk in the recipe can provide a definite deterrent. Undoubtedly the most dramatic example of egg yolk as an emulsifying agent in baked products is cream puffs. The paste formed for cream puffs is made by melting butter in boiling water and making a very thick paste with added flour. At this point egg yolks are beaten in, one at a time, to form an oil-in-water emulsion. This process alters the texture of the paste to a velvety smoothness and a viscosity capable of being dropped as small balls onto a baking sheet. The remarkable increase in volume that occurs when cream puffs are baked in a very hot oven depends on the formation of a stable oil-in-water emulsion, which is possible because of the generous amount of egg yolk available to serve as the emulsifying agent.

Thickening Agent

Eggs are used as thickening agents in a wide array of food products because of the effect of heat on their proteins, resulting in denaturation and coagulation (Chapter 13). One of the confounding problems of using eggs as thickening agents is that coagulation occurs over a rather wide temperature range, depending on the specific conditions being applied. Unlike the preparation of candies in which security is provided by carefully boiling the candy to the correct final temperature, thickening with eggs requires personal judgment to determine when the product is done. Failure to judge this point correctly can lead to curdled sauces, weeping custards, tough fried eggs, and other culinary embarrassments.

The proteins in egg whites begin to coagulate at about 60°C and lose their ability to flow when the temperature reaches approximately 65°C if no other ingredients are added. Yolk proteins, being somewhat more resistant to the impact of heat, begin coagulation around 65°C and cease to flow when the temperature rises to about 70°C when no liquid or other ingredient dilutes them. Coagulation occurs at a higher temperature when the rate of heating is rapid than when it is slow; the slower rate of heating provides more time for molecules to unwind to the secondary structure and clump as they denature and coagulate before the temperature rises too far into the range within which coagulation occurs.

When liquids or other ingredients (e.g., sugar) are added to eggs, the coagulation temperature of the mixture is raised. Undiluted egg products, such as poached or fried eggs, coagulate at temperatures lower than those needed to coagulate custards or egg-containing dessert sauces. Custards and dessert sauces are examples of egg-thickened products in which liquid (usually milk) and sugar dilute the protein and raise the coagulation temperature.

If a thermometer is inserted in a custard during baking and the temperature is observed carefully as the egg proteins in the custard begin to denature and coagulate, a gradual, slow rise in temperature is seen until coagulation occurs. At this point, the slow rise either stops abruptly or the temperature drops slightly for a short time before it begins to rise again. This plateauing is evidence that coagulation is an **endothermic reaction** requiring additional heat input.

If heating is continued beyond the point where coagulation occurs, undiluted egg proteins draw together tightly and become increasingly tough. Diluted protein mixtures curdle as the proteins tighten and separate from the liquid in the systems. To avoid these problems, eggs and egg-thickened products should be served as soon as they are coagulated or else cooled promptly to eliminate residual heat that can cause internal temperature to rise and curdle the food.

Endothermic Reaction
Reaction in which heat is absorbed without an increase in temperature of the reactants.

Custards. **Baked and stirred custards** are sweetened milk mixtures thickened with egg and usually flavored with salt and vanilla. Although the ingredients and proportions are the same for both (one egg or two yolks per cup of milk), either a sol or a gel (Chapter 6) may form when the mixture is heated, depending on the manipulation during heating. Continuous stirring results in a sol, called a stirred custard or a soft custard. When the mixture is baked in the oven without any agitation, the product gels and is termed a baked custard. In both instances, the proteins of the whole eggs provide almost all of the thickening, with the milk protein contributing only an insignificant increase in viscosity. However, milk provides the mineral salts needed for coagulation of the egg protein. Without salts, precipitation of the proteins to form a gel does not occur, as is evident when a baked custard is made with distilled water in place of milk.

Several factors influence the coagulation temperature of custards. Ordinarily custards are made with whole eggs, but yolks or whites sometimes are substituted for the whole eggs. Not surprisingly, custards made with egg whites coagulate at a lower temperature than those made with whole eggs, whereas use of yolks only results in a still higher temperature of coagulation. The amounts of milk and sugar added to custard recipes also have an effect on coagulation temperature due, at least in part, to the diluting effect they have on protein content. The more milk and the more sugar added, the higher is the coagulation temperature.

The rate of heating is yet another factor influencing coagulation temperature. As noted previously, a faster rate of heating results in a higher temperature of coagulation. However, less time is required even though the custard must be heated to a higher temperature when the rate of heating is fast than is needed for coagulation when the heating rate is slow and the coagulation temperature is somewhat lower. This time factor is of particular concern in heating custards. A moderate to high heat makes removal of either baked or stirred custards from the heat at the right point extremely difficult, and overheating (with its accompanying curdling) likely is the result. In other words, residual heat is of far more concern than the actual temperature required for coagulation when rate of heating is being considered. Stirred custards ordinarily are prepared over a very low heat or in a pan surrounded by simmering water, and baked custards are set in a pan of boiling water and heated in an oven at 177°C (350°F).

Stirred Custard
Sweetened milk and egg mixture that is heated to form a sol; agitation during heating prevents formation of sufficient intermolecular linkages to form a gel.

Baked Custard
Sweetened milk and egg mixture that is baked without agitation until the egg protein coagulates and forms a gel.

Cooked Salad Dressings and Sauces. Occasionally, recipes for salad dressings are based on the use of egg yolk or whole egg as a thickening agent, either as the sole thickener or in concert with starch. The advantage of this type of salad dressing is the low fat content and consequently low caloric contribution. When both starch and egg proteins are included in the same recipe, the egg is withheld until the starch mixture has been thickened and then is added and heated to coagulate the protein. This procedure is based on the fact that optimum thickening from the gelatinization of starch requires a higher temperature than is appropriate for egg yolk proteins. The addition of egg to a hot mixture requires care to avoid creating lumps of coagulated protein. By quickly stirring a spoonful of the hot sol into the egg and repeating this process about three times, the egg protein will be diluted enough to raise the coagulation temperature a bit, making it possible to then stir the diluted mixture into the hot sol without forming lumps. This egg-containing sol now needs to be heated enough to coagulate the egg protein, but not so much that fine lumps of overcoagulated egg develop.

Salad dressings and some egg-thickened sauces contain fruit juice or other acidic liquid which reduces the pH of the system, usually bringing it closer to the isoelectric points of the egg proteins. Denaturation and coagulation occur at a somewhat lower temperature at the isoelectric point than at a pH somewhat remote from it. This increased ease is due to the decreased repulsion between molecules that is present when the electrical charges on the surfaces are at a minimum.

Cream Pies and Puddings.

α-Amylase
Amylose-digesting enzyme present in abundance in egg yolk and to a lesser extent in egg white.

Cream pie fillings and cream puddings are similar to salad dressings and sauces that are thickened by use of both a starch and egg protein. However, they differ in that cream pie fillings need to form a soft gel, rather than a sol, when they are chilled. Recipes for cream pies incorporate sufficient starch and egg yolk to achieve the desired gel when starch gelatinization and egg yolk protein coagulation are accomplished. Unfortunately, inadequate heating of the filling after the yolk has been added can cause a seemingly thick filling to become quite fluid after chilling. This thinning is the result of the action of **α-amylase** from the yolk in digesting some of the starch, which decreases the size of the starch molecules and reduces the amount of amylose available to provide the network needed for gel structure.

Denaturation of α-amylase must occur in the preparation of cream pie fillings if a gelled filling is to be achieved. The factors that influence denaturation and coagulation of egg proteins also are applicable to α-amylase specifically. Of particular concern is that the sugar content of cream pie fillings is quite high, which raises the coagulation temperature of the proteins. The process of stirring spoonsful of the hot starch-thickened filling into the egg yolks before returning the mixture to the rest of the filling cools the total filling a bit. Adequate heating is necessary after the egg yolk is added to ensure that the α-amylase has been inactivated by coagulation. However, this must be achieved without overheating and curdling the yolk proteins. Recipes often direct that the filling be heated over very low heat and stirred frequently for 5 minutes or until the mixture loses its gloss. The underlying explanation of such directions is that this technique causes the temperature to rise to slightly over 85°C, which is hot enough to denature the α-amylase.

Custard-type pie fillings are another example of the use of eggs as thickening agents. Unlike the cream pie fillings which usually use only the yolks (the whites being reserved for the meringue), custard-type pies include the whole egg as the sole source of thickening. Problems with α-amylase are not found in custard-type pies because starch is not included as a thickening agent. The critical aspect of preparing custard-type pies is to ensure sufficient heating to coagulate the egg proteins without overheating them to the point where curdling and syneresis are evident. Basically, preparation principles for these types of pie are the same as for baked custards, the only differences being the insulation effect of the bottom crust and the additional ingredients used to achieve different flavors and textures. Examples include pumpkin and pecan pies.

Hard-cooked Eggs.   Hard-cooked eggs immortalize the quality of an egg; the peeled and sliced egg reveals the size of the air space, the location of the yolk (which indirectly reveals the amount of thin and thick white in the egg), and often even the freshness. A large air space indicates that considerable carbon dioxide and water have been lost through the pores since the egg was laid. A yolk that is well-centered indicates a large amount of thick white, whereas a yolk that has drifted up to the top of the egg while being heated, leaving only a curtain of white at the edge, is proof that there was little thick white and a considerable proportion of thin white. A darkish green ring of ferrous sulfide around the yolk is more likely to form in an egg of low quality than in one that is fresher. This is due to the somewhat higher pH that is found in eggs as they lose carbon dioxide.

The firmness of the coagulated white in a hard-cooked egg is influenced by the final temperature reached in the egg and also by the temperature of the water in which it was cooked. Sheldon and Kimsey (1985) found that boiling eggs for 20 minutes caused the eggs to be less tender than those that were either steamed or simmered for the same length of time. The method preferred by the American Egg Board (1994) is to cover the eggs with water at room temperature, heat the water to boiling, and then let the eggs sit in the water without additional heating for 15 to 17 minutes before cooling under cold, running water. For eggs larger than medium in size, the time in the hot water needs to be extended up to about 3 minutes. However, Irmiter et al. (1970) found that eggs heated by placing them in boiling water and then simmering for 18 minutes were less likely to crack and were easier to peel than were those prepared from a cold water start.

Ferrous sulfide is an undesirable compound that can form on the surface of the yolk. Prolonged heating, whether from too extended a cooking period or too slow a rate of cooling, promotes development of ferrous sulfide. This combination of iron from the yolk with sulfur occurs with increasing ease as the pH of the egg rises. Increased alkalinity is evidence of an egg that is staling. By using only fresh eggs, cooking them just until the yolk is set completely, and then cooling very rapidly under cold, running water, ferrous sulfide formation can be avoided completely.

These same problems are faced in greatly increased quantities by companies that are marketing hard-cooked eggs for commercial uses. The fact that hard-cooked eggs with whites that are at a pH of at least 8.8 are easier to peel than less basic eggs is appealing, and techniques are being tested to attempt to manipulate egg storage to achieve this pH level (Stadelman and Rohrer, 1984). Hard-cooked eggs can be held in a brine or organic acid solution to help preserve them, but the solution used will modify flavor somewhat if the eggs are held more than a day (Sheldon, 1986).

Poached Eggs.   Poached eggs should have the white congealed tenderly surrounding the yolk, which is slightly coagulated and still not set, even at the edges. By gently slipping a high-quality egg into salted water heated to just under boiling and then simmering until the desired endpoint has been achieved, a pleasing poached egg is produced. To assure destruction of *Salmonella enteritidis* that might be present in the yolk, the Food and Drug Administration (Blumenthal, 1990) recommends poaching eggs 5 minutes in boiling water.

Whites of lower-quality eggs spread and give a jagged, rather feathery appearance when they are poached; the yolk also tends to separate or pull away from the white. The yolk also is likely to break when the poached egg is being spooned from the water. This problem of spreading can be alleviated by adding a small amount of acid (vinegar or lemon juice) to the water when low-quality eggs are being poached. Adding salt to the water is helpful in poaching a low-quality egg, because it provides sodium and chloride ions to cancel the electrical charges on protein molecules and thus facilitates the coagulation process slightly. The addition of acid when poaching low-quality eggs speeds the coagulation and minimizes spreading of the whites because the acidified water is closer to the isoelectric point of the albumen proteins, thus favoring hastened coagulation and diminished spreading. The reduced surface ionization of the albumen proteins near the isoelectric point enables the molecules to aggregate fairly quickly, thus reducing the time when the albumen can spread freely in the water.

The problem of a poached egg spreading in the poaching water can be relieved by confining the egg in an egg poacher. The small cups in a poacher eliminate this problem because the egg never has the opportunity to enter the water. Another physical approach to limiting spreading is to swirl the pan containing the simmering water until the water develops a whirlpool-like movement. Then the egg is slipped into the water in harmony with the movement of the water. The water helps to hold the egg together when this motion is accomplished correctly, but it can be detrimental to limiting the spreading if the egg is moving in opposition to the water.

Even when the spreading problem of whites has been limited as much as possible in an egg of low quality, the flavor of such an egg will still be a bit sulfury and strong. The vitelline membrane also is likely to be too weak to withstand the stress of being spooned out of the poaching water or the poaching cup. A broken yolk is considered a clear sign of lack of quality in a poached egg.

Fried Eggs.   Egg quality and controlled heating are the keys to achieving a pleasing fried egg. The excessive amount of thin white and weak vitelline membrane found in eggs of less than AA quality allow a fried egg to cover a large surface area, with the white tending to drain from around the yolk and the yolk flattening and spreading. The risk of breaking the yolk while turning or removing from the frying pan is great when the vitelline membrane is weak.

The Food and Drug Administration (Blumenthal, 1990) recommended that eggs to be fried sunnyside up should be fried for 7 minutes at 121°C (250°F), for 7 minutes uncovered, or for 4 minutes if covered. Over-easy fried eggs should be cooked for 3 minutes at 121°C before they are turned and fried for 2 more minutes. These methods are designed to assure that the yolks are heated sufficiently to kill *Salmonella enteritidis* if they are present.

Scrambled Eggs.   Prior to heating scrambled eggs, the egg mixture is diluted with a liquid, usually milk. Sufficient beating is done to mix the egg albumen, yolk, and milk completely, but without creating a foam. Unless adequate mixing is done at this time, streaks of yellow or white may be seen in the finished product. Liquid (about 20 milliliters per egg) is added to dilute the egg proteins and promote tenderness in the finished product.

To assure that scrambled eggs do not contain viable *Salmonella enteritidis,* they need to be heated at 121°C (250°F) for 1 minute (Blumenthal, 1990). If working in large quantities, no more than 3 quarts of eggs should be scrambled at a time. Eggs being held on a steam table need to be held at 60°C (140°F) or hotter.

Overcooking scrambled eggs with added liquid will cause syneresis as the protein in the eggs draws tighter together and toughens from the heat. Without added liquid, the egg mass can become quite tough with overheating.

If scrambled eggs are held on a steam table for an extended period, they begin to turn an unsightly greenish-grey as ferrous sulfide forms. This is the same compound that forms in hard-cooked eggs with extended heating.

Microwave heating is useful when previously cooked scrambled egg products are being reheated. The flavor is preferred over scrambled eggs that are reheated conventionally (Cremer and Chipley, 1980). French omelets and scrambled eggs which have been prepared and then chilled prior to being reheated and served are finding considerable use in such settings as airline meals and institutional settings because of their ability to be reheated satisfactorily in a microwave oven.

FOAMS

Yolk Foams

Occasionally, yolk foams are utilized in certain baked products, notably sponge cakes and puffy omelets. Egg yolks can be beaten into somewhat heavy foams with considerable effort. However, yolk foams are quite heavy compared with white foams. As the yolks are beaten, a concomitant increase in volume and lightening of foam color can be observed. After several minutes of beating at top speed with an electric mixer, a comparatively stable yolk foam forms, and this yolk foam is ready for use, usually for folding into an egg white foam. Yolk foams are sufficiently stable to permit them to be folded with other ingredients and then baked, thus contributing to the textural characteristics and volume of the baked product. They do not become stiff enough to form peaks, but they do pile when beaten enough. Whole egg also can be beaten to a soft foam.

White Foams

Foams (Chapter 6) need to be stable if they are to have a role in food preparation. Stability is enhanced if the surface tension is low, if vapor pressure is low, and if a substance solidifies on the surface of the bubbles. Egg white meets all of these requirements, making it a particularly useful food when a foam is desired. With agitation, the egg albumen can be spread over a large surface area, and air can be incorporated into the bubbles created by beating the proteins. Some of the proteins are denatured by the beating action and then aggregate to enhance stability of the developing foam (Fennema, 1985).

The two factors of utmost importance in egg white foams are stability and volume. Several factors influence one or both of these characteristics and are of significance regardless of the product into which the foam is ultimately incorporated.

Rate of formation is of interest, although the use of mechanical means to develop the foams makes speed somewhat less important than stability and volume.

Stability.   Stability of a foam can be judged by measuring drainage of liquid from a given quantity of foam over a specified period of time. The conditions for such a measurement need to be specified for a given experiment so that results from variations can be compared, but the specifics may differ from one research project to another, making it impossible to compare specific results from different projects. A convenient technique is to place a weighed amount of foam in a funnel of known capacity and bore and then collect the drainage in a graduated cylinder into which the funnel has been placed. The funnel needs to be covered with plastic wrap to prevent evaporation. The drainage is read after the specified length of time. The more drainage, the less stable is the foam.

The extent of beating is an important factor in stability of an egg white foam. As beating progresses, the foam becomes increasingly stable up to a critical point, after which continued beating decreases stability. Maximum stability is reached when the whites just bend over, but before maximum volume has been reached. If beating continues beyond the point of maximum stability, the surface begins to look slightly dry, and the foam exhibits some brittleness. Foam formation is delayed when the whites are well below room temperature.

The addition of other ingredients also influences stability. Sometimes salt is added to an egg white foam for flavor, but this addition reduces stability slightly. Occasionally recipes include some added liquid in making an egg white foam. This dilutes the proteins in the foam and decreases stability. If yolk happens to contaminate the white at all, as can happen during the separation of yolks and whites, stability of the foam formed from the whites is reduced.

Not all ingredients reduce stability. In fact, the addition of sugar has a very laudatory effect on foam stability. A possible explanation is that the addition of sugar delays foam formation significantly, which means that considerably more beating is necessary to reach the proper stage of foam development. This increased beating results in a foam with a finer texture and more surface area; this foam is stabilized with protein that has been partially denatured by beating.

Acidic ingredients, commonly either cream of tartar or lemon juice, are useful stabilizing agents when making egg white foams, particularly when added early in the formation of the foam. Although stability is promoted by reducing the pH of the egg white foam, formation of the foam is delayed by this addition. Again, the delay in reaching the desired endpoint in whipping the foam results in increased total agitation and a finer, more stable foam. Cream of tartar is particularly effective as the acid ingredient when the pH of the white foam approaches pH 6.0 whereas citric acid and cream of tartar are about comparable in their effect at pH 8.0.

Volume.   The temperature of the whites influences volume, because surface tension is greater in whites just removed from the refrigerator than in whites warmed to room temperature. The quality of the whites plays a significant role in determining volume of the foam. When there is a comparatively large amount of thin white, the foam forms quickly and reaches a large volume, but that volume is reduced when beating is extended. In contrast, thick white requires more beating to reach the desired endpoint, but the foam achieved holds its volume well.

The type of beater used is yet another factor influencing volume. A wire whisk can be used to create a foam with larger volume than is achieved using a rotary hand beater if the whisk is in the hands of an experienced chef, but lack of experience can have a detrimental effect on volume. Electric mixers can be used effectively to achieve foams with high volumes, but they may produce foams that are overbeaten and consequently of low volume, unless sugar or acid is added to delay foam formation. When these ingredients are added, an extended beating time is required to reach the desired endpoint, where the peaks just bend over; this makes use of an electric mixer desirable.

The extent of beating has a definite influence on volume, as well as stability. Volume increases gradually as beating progresses to the foamy stage, the point where the whites are still transparent and fluid, yet are definitely whipped into large bubbles throughout. With further beating beyond the foamy stage, the foam continues to expand, gradually becomes more opaque, and exhibits the ability to be pulled up into peaks. At first these peaks sag quickly; then rounded, soft peaks form that progress to stiff peaks with more beating. At this point, maximum volume is achieved. Additional beating results in a dry, rather brittle foam of smaller volume; foams beaten to the dry stage are not useful in food preparation.

Added ingredients definitely influence volume. Acid ingredients reduce volume a little (but the increased stability helps to offset this negative effect). Sugar has a similar impact on volume. However, sugar has such a positive effect on promoting elasticity and stability that it makes foams very easy to fold with other ingredients, with minimum loss of volume from the egg white foams when they have been beaten sufficiently to attain peaks that just bend over. Contamination of the whites with even a trace of yolk has a negative impact on the volume of an egg white foam. This is due to the presence in the yolk of fat, notably lipovitellenin and lipovitellin, both of which interfere with the foaming of two key foaming proteins in the white, ovomucin and lysozyme. Salt is yet another ingredient with a slightly detrimental effect on volume. In fact, water is the one ingredient that has a positive effect on volume of egg white foams, the effect being rather impressive if viewed quickly. Unfortunately, the dilution of the protein resulting from the addition of water decreases foam stability, which limits the usefulness of water in increasing volume.

Meringues

Meringues are egg white foams containing sugar. The quantity of sugar used in their formulations determines whether or not the meringue is classified as a soft or a hard meringue. **Soft meringues,** the topping often used on cream pies (Figure 16.4), usually contain 25 grams (2 tablespoons) of sugar per egg white, which is a volume approximately equivalent to that of the white. An increase to 32 grams ($2\frac{1}{2}$ tablespoons) per egg white results in a meringue with excellent appearance and superior cutting quality (but with extra calories). In comparison, **hard meringues** contain 50 grams (4 tablespoons) of sugar per white.

Soft meringues are delicate to make, because of their propensity for beading and leaking (drainage of liquid from the meringue to the surface of the pie filling on standing).

Leaking likely is caused by failure to coagulate all the foam proteins, a problem that usually can be eliminated by placing the meringue on the filling while the filling is still hot (60–77°C) and then baking immediately. The heat from the filling helps bring the temperature of the foam toward the bottom of the meringue to a high enough point that the sweetened meringue with its egg white proteins can coagulate. Unless this is done, there is the likelihood that the proteins toward the bot-

Meringue
Egg white foam containing sugar.

Soft Meringue
Egg white foam containing about 25 grams (2 tablespoons) of sugar per egg white; topping on cream pies.

Hard Meringue
Egg white foam containing about 50 grams (4 tablespoons) of sugar per egg white; baked to a dry, brittle cookie or dessert shell.

Leaking
Draining liquid from a soft meringue to the surface of the filling of a cream pie.

Figure 16.4   Soft egg white meringues, made by incorporating 25 grams (2 tablespoons) sugar per egg white while beating the whites, are stable foams in which heat has been used to continue the denaturation of protein that was initiated during beating. (Courtesy of Sunkist Growers.)

tom of the meringue will not be heated to a temperature sufficiently high during the baking period, because the foam itself conducts heat poorly during baking (Hester and Personius, 1949).

Beading, the result of overcoagulation of some of the protein at the surface of a baked meringue, is the formation of droplets of a golden-brown color when the finished pie has had an opportunity to stand for a while. The problem is most likely to be found when the meringue has been placed on a hot pie filling, because the additional heat contained in the meringue may bake the meringue more quickly than anticipated, leading to overbaking of the meringue.

Beading
Collecting small drops of amber-like droplets on the surface of an overbaked soft meringue.

One technique that can be used effectively when the meringue has been placed on a hot filling is to bake it in a hot oven (218°C or 425°F) until a pleasing golden-brown color develops, which takes a little over 4 minutes. This quick heating limits the amount of residual heat accumulated in the interior and reduces the likelihood of overbaking and beading, but leakage may be greater than if the meringue is baked at 163°C, the temperature ordinarily suggested for baking meringues (Hester and Personius, 1949). These researchers also found that meringues baked at 218°C were more tender and less sticky than those baked at 163°C. Regardless of the oven temperature used, any regions of a meringue that are overbaked not only are prone to beading, but also are likely to become sticky and difficult to cut. However, any soft meringue will be sticky and hard to manage within 24 hours of its preparation and baking.

Commercial bakers are confronted with the difficulty of making meringue pies that are still pleasing when the customer is ready to cut and eat the pie. Meringues for commercial use may have carrageenan or some other type of gum or stabilizer added to improve the storage characteristics of the meringue portion of the pie.

Hard meringues are totally different in their characteristics from soft meringues. Instead of being soft and pleasingly browned, hard meringues are considered ideal when they are crisp and dry, with an extremely pale surface. They should cut easily because of their crispness and tenderness. If they are not dried sufficiently, they will be tough and slightly sticky to cut. The extremely large quantity of sugar in hard meringues extends the beating greatly. The time can be kept manageable by beating the whites to the soft peak stage before adding any sugar and then adding the sugar gradually while operating the electric mixer at full speed. Beating should be continued until stiff peaks can be pulled up. Overbeating is virtually an impossibility because of the large amount of sugar.

Puffy or fluffy omelets and soufflés are other egg dishes in which the properties of egg foams are used. The egg white foam in both the omelets and the soufflés can acquire optimum stability if cream of tartar, lemon juice, or other compatible acidic juice is added to reduce the pH of the egg whites. The yolk used in making the sauce for soufflés is important as an emulsifier to help emulsify the comparatively large amount of fat used in making the thick sauce that is to be folded into the beaten egg whites.

Foam Cakes

Egg foams figure prominently in three types of cakes: angel food, sponge, and chiffon. The formation of high-quality egg white foams is critical to the final product in all three cakes. In addition, egg yolk foam is an important component of sponge cakes. Discussion of these cakes is presented in detail in Chapter 17.

EGG SUBSTITUTES

Concern over the cholesterol content of egg yolks has prompted the development of several different commercial products known collectively as egg substitutes. The formulations differ with each product, but the basic goal is to simulate whole egg without any cholesterol. In other words, the product is based on the use of egg white together with a synthesized yolk mixture. Because the yolk is replaced in an egg substitute, the color of the final product depends on the inclusion of a coloring agent in the formulation. Usually, a carotenoid in the form of one of the carotenes is added for this purpose.

Egg substitutes are available in either the frozen form or in a fresh, fluid product requiring refrigeration. They provide an alternative to abstention from eggs for people who must limit their cholesterol intake; however, egg substitutes are not identical to whole eggs in their potential uses. Of course, egg substitutes cannot be separated into whites and yolks, which limits their use in such products as sponge cakes and soufflés. Aroma and flavor are not as good as when fresh whole eggs are used (Childs and Ostrander, 1976). Volume is greater in cakes made with eggs than in those made with egg substitutes (Leutzinger et al., 1977). Fortunately, many whole egg products can be made with egg substitutes to obtain results that are satisfactory even though they are not quite the equal of the same products made with fresh eggs.

SUMMARY

The egg is a complex structure consisting of a multilayered yolk encased in the vitelline membrane and a chalaziferous layer, all of which is surrounded by three layers of albumen (thin, thick, and thin layers). An inner membrane and an outer membrane separate the contents of the egg from the porous shell. The white is largely water, with a useful amount of protein; the yolk contains somewhat less water, a significant amount of lipids, and about half as much protein as the white. Among the lipids in the yolk is lecithin, a very effective emulsifying agent. Cholesterol also is found in the yolk. Egg substitutes have been developed and marketed to enable consumers to avoid cholesterol while eating egg-containing foods.

Twelve egg white proteins have been studied. Ovalbumin, by far the most abundant of the proteins in the white, and lysozyme are especially important because of their foaming ability, although the others also contribute to the unique foaming qualities of egg white. Conalbumin is the protein that binds with ions of copper and iron in complexes that produce undesirable color changes when present. Ovomucin contributes much of the fibrous character to the thick albumen. The prominent yolk proteins in the plasma are livetin (found in three fractions) and the lipoproteins (low-density); the proteins prominent in the granules of egg yolk are lipovitellin (two forms, both of which are high-density lipoproteins), phosvitin, and low-density lipoprotein.

Quality of eggs is determined in the shell by candling and out of the shell by such measurements as yolk index and albumen index or Haugh units. Considerable deterioration of egg quality is likely to occur between the grading and marketing of eggs. The pH, particularly of the white, rises significantly with loss of carbon dioxide through the shell. Some moisture loss contributes to the growth of the air cell at the large end of the egg. The white becomes thinner, and the vitelline membrane weakens.

Because of the easy deterioration of eggs, they need to be stored carefully under refrigeration or else processed for longer storage. Processing may include pasteurizing, drying, or freezing. The glucose in whites must be digested prior to drying to avoid serious problems with discoloration. Either sugar or salt must be added to yolks if they are to be frozen, because of the gummy character that develops during frozen storage.

Eggs are an excellent medium for the growth of microorganisms. To avoid bacterial contamination, egg shells should be uncracked and should be cleaned and sanitized prior to refrigerated storage. *Salmonella enteritidis* sometimes may be present in the yolk of an egg if the hen producing the egg is infected. Adequate heat treatment is needed for all forms of egg preparation to assure safety from this bacterium.

Eggs are important because of their ability to serve as an emulsifier (largely the result of the presence of lecithin in the yolk), as a thickening agent (because of the changes that occur when the proteins in both the white and the yolk undergo denaturation and coagulation when heated), and as a foaming agent (as a consequence of the comparatively low surface tension and vapor pressure and the ability of the proteins to be denatured by beating). Products that illustrate these different roles of eggs include hollandaise sauce, mayonnaise, cake batters, cream puffs, custards, cooked salad dressings and sauces, pie fillings and cream puddings, eggs cooked in the shell (hard- and soft-cooked), eggs out of the shell (poached, fried, scrambled, French omelet), meringues (hard and soft), puffy omelets, soufflés, and foam cakes (angel food, sponge, and chiffon).

STUDY QUESTIONS

1. Sketch the cross section of an egg, naming the parts and describing the changes that take place as egg quality declines.

2. What is the significance of the presence of lecithin in egg yolk? Describe its role in at least five different food products.

3. What occurs when egg white comes into contact with (a) copper ions and (b) iron ions? How can this happen?

4. Identify six important albumen proteins and describe unique features of each.

5. What changes are made when an egg substitute is formulated (in comparison with the natural egg)? Why are these changes made?

6. Identify five factors that influence the coagulation temperature of the proteins in a custard and explain the action of each factor.

7. Compare the use of eggs in custards with the use of eggs in cream puddings and pie fillings. How are the eggs combined with other ingredients in the two types of products?

8. What factors influence the stability of an egg white foam? Explain the effect of each factor.

9. What factors influence the volume achieved in an egg white foam? Explain the effect of each factor.

BIBLIOGRAPHY

Abe, Y., Itoh, T., and Adachi, S. 1982. "Fractionation and characterization of hen's egg yolk phosvitin." *J. Food Sci. 47:* 1903.

American Egg Board. 1994. *Eggcyclopedia.* 3rd ed. American Egg Board. Park Ridge, IL.

Blumenthal, D. 1990. "*Salmonella enteritidis:* From the chicken to the egg." *FDA Consumer 24* (3): 6.

Chang, C. H., et al. 1977. "Microstructure of egg yolk." *J. Food Sci. 42:* 1193.

Childs, M. T. and Ostrander, J. 1976. "Egg substitutes: Chemical and biological evaluations." *J. Am. Dietet. Assoc. 68:* 229.

Cotterill, O. J. 1986. "Freezing egg products." In Stadelman, W. J. and Cotterill, O. J., eds. *Egg Science and Technology.* 3rd ed. AVI Publishing: Westport, CT, p. 262.

Cremer, M. L. and Chipley, J. R. 1980. "Hospital ready-prepared type foodservice system: time and temperature conditions, sensory and microbiological quality of scrambled eggs." *J. Food Sci. 45:* 1422.

Cunningham, F. E. 1976. "Properties of egg white drainage." *Poultry Sci. 55:* 738.

Cunningham, F. E. and Cotterill, O. J. 1972. "Performance of egg white in presence of yolk proteins." *Poultry Sci. 51:* 712.

Elgidaily, D. A., et al. 1969. "Baking temperature and quality of angel cakes." *J. Am. Dietet. Assoc. 54:* 401.

Feiser, G. E. and Cotterill, O. J. 1982. "Composition of serum from cooked-frozen-thawed-reheated scrambled eggs at various pH levels." *J. Food Sci. 47:* 1333.

Fennema, O. R., ed. 1985. *Food Chemistry.* 2nd ed. Marcel Dekker: New York.

Fischer, J. R. and Fletcher, D. L. 1983. "Effect of adding salt (NaCl) to preservation solution on the acceptability of hard cooked eggs." *Poultry Sci. 62:* 1345 (Abstract).

Funk, K., et al. 1971. "Hard meringues prepared with foam-spray-, freeze-, and spray-dried albumen." *Poultry Sci. 50:* 374.

Gillis, J. N. and Fitch, N. K. 1956. "Leakage of baked soft-meringue topping." *J. Home Econ. 48:* 703.

Hale, K. K., Jr. and Britton, W. M. 1974. "Peeling hard cooked eggs by rapid cooling and heating." *Poultry Sci. 53:* 1069.

Heath, J. L. and Owens, S. L. 1978. "Effect of oiling variables on storage of shell eggs at elevated temperatures." *Poultry Sci. 57:* 930.

Hester, E. E. and Personius, C. J. 1949. "Factors affecting the beading and leakage of soft meringues." *Food Technol. 3:* 236.

Irmiter, T. R., Dawson, L. E., and Reagen, J. G. 1970. "Methods for preparing hard cooked eggs." *Poultry Sci. 49:* 1232.

Janky, D. M. 1986. "Variation in pigmentation and interior quality of commercially available table eggs." *Poultry Sci. 65:* 607.

Kim, K. and Setser, C. A. 1982. "Foaming properties of fresh and commercially dried eggs in presence of stabilizers and surfactants." *Poultry Sci. 61:* 2194.

Leutzinger, R. L., Baldwin, R. E., and Cotterill, O. J. 1977. "Sensory attributes of commercial egg substitutes." *J. Food Sci. 42:* 1124.

Lowe, B. 1955. *Experimental Cookery.* 4th ed. Wiley: New York.

Marusich, W. L. and Bauernfeind, J. C. 1981. "Oxycarotenoids in poultry feeds." In Bauernfeind, J. C., ed. *Carotenoids as Colorants and Vitamin A Precursors.* Academic Press: New York, p. 181.

Meehan, et al. 1961. "Relation between internal egg quality stabilization methods and peeling difficulty." *Poultry Sci. 40:* 1430.

Navidi, M. K. and Kummerow, F. A. 1974. "Nutritional value of Egg Beaters® compared with 'farm fresh eggs.'" *Pediatrics 35:* 565.

Palmer, H. H., et al. 1969. "Salted egg yolks. I. Viscosity and performance of pasteurized and frozen samples." *Food Tech. 23:* 1480.

Paul, P. E. and Palmer, H. H., eds. 1972. *Food Theory and Applications*. Wiley: New York.

Powrie, W. D. 1976. "Characteristics of edible fluids of animal origin: eggs." In Fennema, O. R., ed. *Principles of Food Science I:* Marcel Dekker: New York, p. 829.

Powrie, W. D. and Nakai, S. 1985. "Characteristics of edible fluids of animal origin: eggs." In Fennema, O. R., ed. *Food Chemistry*. 2nd ed. Marcel Dekker: New York, p. 829.

Pratt, D. E. 1975. "Lipid analysis of a frozen egg substitute." *J. Am. Dietet. Assoc. 66:* 31.

Richardson, T. and Kester, J. J. 1984. "Chemical modifications that affect nutritional and functional properties of proteins." *J. Chem. Educ. 61*(4): 325.

Sauter, E. A. and Montoure, J. E. "Relation of lysozyme content of egg white to volume and stability of foam." *J. Food Sci. 37:* 918.

Schmidt, R. H. 1981. *Gelation and Coagulation*. ACS Symposium Series 147; American Chemical Society: Washington, DC.

Sheldon, B. W. 1986. "Influence of three organic acids on quality characteristics of hard-cooked eggs." *Poultry Sci., 65:* 294.

Sheldon, B. W. and Kimsey, H. R., Jr. 1985. "Effects of cooking methods on chemical, physical, and sensory properties of hard-cooked eggs." *Poultry Sci. 64:* 84.

Spencer, J. V. and Tryhnew, L. J., 1973. "Effect of storage on peeling quality and flavor of hard-cooked shell eggs." *Poultry Sci. 52:* 654.

Stadelman, W. J. 1986. "Preservation of quality in shell eggs." In Stadelman, W. J. and Cotterill, O. J., eds. *Egg Science and Technology*. 3rd ed. AVI Publishing: Westport, CT, p. 279.

Stadelman, W. J. and Cotterill, O. J., eds. 1973. *Egg Science and Technology*. AVI Publishing: Westport, CT.

Stadelman, W. J. and Rhorer, A. R. 1984. "Quality improvement of hard cooked eggs." *Poultry Sci. 63:* 949.

Wang, A. C., et al. 1974. "Effect of sucrose on quality characteristics of baked custard." *Poultry Sci. 53:* 807.

Whitaker, J. R. and Tannenbaum, S. R., eds. 1977. *Food Proteins*. AVI Publishing: Westport, CT.

Woodward, S. A. and Cotterill, O. J. 1987. "Texture and microstructure of cooked whole egg yolks and heat-formed gels of stirred egg yolk." *J. Food Sci. 52:* 63.

Woodward, S. A. and Cotterill, O. J., 1986. "Texture and microstructure of heatformed egg white gels." *J. Food Sci. 51* (2): 333.

Yang, S. S. and Cotterill, O. J. 1989. "Physical and functional properties of 10% salted egg yolk in mayonnaise." *J. Food Sci. 54:* 210.

CHAPTER 17

Dimensions of Baking

$\mathbf{B}$aked products range in complexity from the simple ingredients of a plain pastry to the numerous components of a shortened cake. Despite the many differences that exist, both in ingredients and in techniques for combining and baking them, baked products are based on the use of certain basic ingredients and on the roles that these ingredients can perform, both in mixing and in baking. This chapter presents these key dimensions of baking to provide the scientific foundation for the study of diverse baked products.

WHEAT FLOUR

Production

Milling. Although the term ***flour*** ordinarily is used to mean wheat flour specifically, technically flour is the product of milling any type of grain. Usually the name of the grain is included (rice flour, for example) if the flour is made from a grain other than wheat to eliminate ambiguity. In this book, flour means wheat flour unless another grain is indicated.

Flour production involves grinding and refining cereal grains by a process called **milling.** The milling process consists of many steps, but the basic objective is to produce a comparatively fine powder consisting of some portion or almost all of the grain, depending on the specific product desired. Milling begins with the whole grains (Figure 17.1) of wheat (or other cereal), which are first subjected to a brief **tempering** treatment with steam to ease removal of the outer bran layers. At this point, more than one variety of wheat (or other grain) may be blended together and any unsound grains removed (Figure 17.2).

Grinding is the process that begins to split the grains in preparation for passage through corrugated rollers that break the grain into coarse particles. This ac-

Flour
The fine particles of wheat (or other grain) produced from milling.

Milling
Grinding and refining of cereal grains.

Tempering
In the context of flour milling, this is the steam treatment preliminary to grinding and is the means of facilitating removal of outer bran layers.

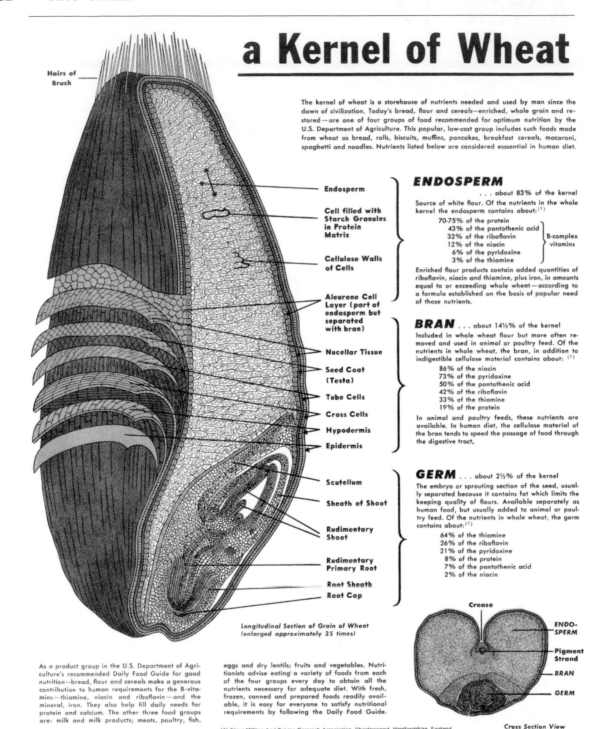

a Kernel of Wheat

The kernel of wheat is a storehouse of nutrients needed and used by man since the dawn of civilization. Today's bread, flour and cereals—enriched, whole grain and restored—are one of four groups of food recommended for optimum nutrition by the U.S. Department of Agriculture. This popular, low-cost group includes such foods made from wheat as bread, rolls, biscuits, muffins, pancakes, breakfast cereals, macaroni, spaghetti and noodles. Nutrients listed below are considered esssential in human diet.

Hairs of Brush

Endosperm

Cell filled with Starch Granules in Protein Matrix

Cellulose Walls of Cells

Aleurone Cell Layer (part of endosperm but separated with bran)

Nucellar Tissue

Seed Coat (Testa)

Tube Cells

Cross Cells

Hypodermis

Epidermis

Scutellum

Sheath of Shoot

Rudimentary Shoot

Rudimentary Primary Root

Root Sheath

Root Cap

*Longitudinal Section of Grain of Wheat
(enlarged approximately 35 times)*

ENDOSPERM
. . . about 83% of the kernel

Source of white flour. Of the nutrients in the whole kernel the endosperm contains about:[1]

70-75% of the protein	
43% of the pantothenic acid	
32% of the riboflavin	B-complex
12% of the niacin	vitamins
6% of the pyridoxine	
3% of the thiamine	

Enriched flour products contain added quantities of riboflavin, niacin and thiamine, plus iron, in amounts equal to or exceeding whole wheat—according to a formula established on the basis of popular need of those nutrients.

BRAN . . . about 14½% of the kernel

Included in whole wheat flour but more often removed and used in animal or poultry feed. Of the nutrients in whole wheat, the bran, in addition to indigestible cellulose material contains about: [1]

86% of the niacin
73% of the pyridoxine
50% of the pantothenic acid
42% of the riboflavin
33% of the thiamine
19% of the protein

In animal and poultry feeds, these nutrients are available. In human diet, the cellulose material of the bran tends to speed the passage of food through the digestive tract.

GERM . . . about 2½% of the kernel

The embryo or sprouting section of the seed, usually separated because it contains fat which limits the keeping quality of flours. Available separately as human food, but usually added to animal or poultry feed. Of the nutrients in whole wheat, the germ contains about:[1]

64% of the thiamine
26% of the riboflavin
21% of the pyridoxine
8% of the protein
7% of the pantothenic acid
2% of the niacin

Crease

ENDO-SPERM

Pigment Strand

BRAN

GERM

Cross Section View

As a product group in the U.S. Department of Agriculture's recommended Daily Food Guide for good nutrition—bread, flour and cereals make a generous contribution to human requirements for the B-vitamins—thiamine, niacin and riboflavin—and the mineral, iron. They also help fill daily needs for protein and calcium. The other three food groups are: milk and milk products; meats, poultry, fish, eggs and dry lentils; fruits and vegetables. Nutritionists advise eating a variety of foods from each of the four groups every day to obtain all the nutrients necessary for adequate diet. With fresh, frozen, canned and prepared foods readily available, it is easy for everyone to satisfy nutritional requirements by following the Daily Food Guide.

(1) Flour Milling And Baking Research Association, Chorleywood, Hertfordshire, England.

Figure 17.1   Diagram of a wheat kernel. (Courtesy of Wheat Flour Institute.)

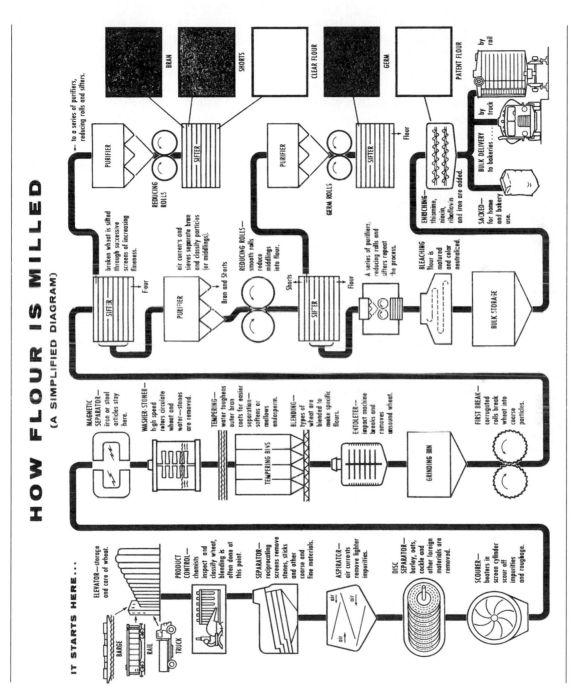

Figure 17.2 Schematic diagram of the milling of flour. (Courtesy of General Mills.)

Bran
Outer layers (fibrous and very high in cellulose) encasing the interior endosperm and germ of cereal grains.

Endosperm
Large inner portion of cereal grains composed largely of starch and some protein.

Germ (Embryo)
Small portion of cereal grain containing fat and a small amount of protein as well as thiamine, riboflavin, and other B vitamins.

Whole Wheat Flour
Wheat flour containing most of the bran and shorts.

Refined Flour
White flour resulting from removal of at least 25 percent of the bran and shorts during milling of flour.

Extraction
Removal of bran and shorts during milling of wheat.

Cake Flour
Soft wheat, short-patent wheat flour (about 7.5 percent protein).

Short-Patent Flour
Wheat flour comparatively high in starch and low in protein because of the use primarily of the streams containing very fine particles of flour from the center of the endosperm, for example, cake flour.

Medium-Patent Flour
Wheat flour using about 90 percent of the flour streams, resulting in a somewhat higher content of protein and relatively less starch, for example, all-purpose flour.

tion results in splitting of the grains into their components, as well as a breaking up of those parts. In other words the outer bran layers, somewhat brittle because of their high fiber content, are shattered by grinding into moderately small, thin, and jagged pieces of **bran.** The major portion of the grain, the **endosperm,** is broken into coarse particles, too. At this point, the small **germ** or **embryo** may still be adhering to the endosperm.

Following grinding, much of the bran and shorts may be left with the endosperm to be made into whole wheat flour. The greater the portion of bran retained, the darker the **whole wheat flour** will be. To make white, **refined flour** from wheat, the bran and shorts are removed, a process called **extraction.** Extraction is accomplished by sifting or by an air classification system that blows the bran up from the heavier endosperm and germ portions, allowing the bran to be directed out of the system for subsequent processing and packaging as bran or shorts.

The remaining endosperm and germ are passed through reducing rollers to press the germ into flakes and to continue breaking the endosperm into very fine particles. This enables the germ and endosperm to be separated by sifting, and the germ is removed which enhances the shelf life of the flour because the fat that would eventually become rancid is removed.

Types of Milled Wheat Flour

As is shown in Figure 17.3, several different refined flours can be obtained by milling wheat. The character of these flours is altered by the amount of the total flour used. The flour made using only a small portion of the total stream of flour is extra-short or fancy-patent flour. **Cake flour** often is made from this type of flour (Table 17.1) or from **short-patent flour,** the result being a flour that is comparatively high in starch and low in protein. **Medium-patent flour** is made using 90 percent of the flour streams, with the result that the protein level is greater than in

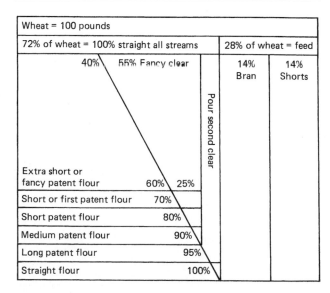

Figure 17.3 Yields of milled fractions obtained from 100 pounds of wheat. (From C.O. Swanson. *Wheat Flour Quality.* 1938. Burgess Publishing Co. Minneapolis, MN.)

Table 17.1   Profile of Milled Wheat Flours

Type of Flour	Patent	Mill Stream (%)	Protein (%)	Type of Wheat
Cake	Fancy and/or short	40–70	7.5	Soft
Pastry	Short and medium	80–90	7.9	Soft
All-purpose	Medium	90	10.5	Hard or hard and soft blend
Bread	Long	95	11.8	Hard

cake flour and the starch content is a bit less. Bread flour may be produced using between 95 and 100 percent of the flour streams, producing a flour with still higher protein content.

The most common wheat flour on the market is **all-purpose flour,** a flour usually containing all or mostly hard wheat. The protein level in all-purpose flour is approximately 10.5 percent, which accounts for the comparatively strong textural properties contributed by this flour to baked products. Home baking of cookies, pastries, and quick breads usually is done using all-purpose flour. Cakes, however, preferably are made with cake flour, the flour made from soft wheat. Usually the protein content of cake flour is only about 7.5 percent.

Commercial bakers have more options in protein levels in flours than are found in retail markets. **Bread flour,** one of these options, is the flour obtained by using almost all of the streams and is designated as a **long-patent flour.** By including such a large proportion of the streams, the edges of the endosperm are incorporated, resulting in greater gluten (protein) content. This type of flour, made entirely from hard wheat, has a protein level of about 11.8 percent. The strength of the protein in bread flour is excellent for the physical properties desired in yeast breads.

Another option available to commercial bakers is **pastry flour.** Its protein level of about 9.7 percent is intermediate between all-purpose and cake flour. Production of pastry flour involves use of 80 to 90 percent of the streams (short- and medium-patent) of milled soft wheat. As the name implies, this flour is tailored specifically to the requirements of making a tender pastry.

Self-rising flour is a unique flour in the retail market that may be considered a "semimix" or shortcut to baking because it is formulated with both leavening and salt ingredients. The acid salts (monocalcium phosphate and sometimes sodium acid pyrophosphate and sodium aluminum phosphate) and baking soda are the leavening ingredients added in amounts sufficient to generate carbon dioxide equivalent to the use of $1\frac{1}{2}$ teaspoons of baking powder per cup of flour. The salt (NaCl) level is equal to $\frac{1}{2}$ teaspoon per cup of flour. Most commonly, self-rising flour is used in making quick breads, particularly sour milk biscuits. Its inherent leavening action makes it an unsuitable choice for pastry and other unleavened products or for yeast breads where yeast provides the leavening needed. If self-rising flour is substituted in a recipe for regular all-purpose flour, the baking powder and salt in the recipe should be altered to compensate for the presence of these ingredients in the self-rising flour. Conversely, all-purpose flour can be substituted for self-rising flour if baking powder and salt are added ($1\frac{1}{2}$ teaspoons of baking powder and $\frac{1}{2}$ teaspoon of salt per cup of flour).

Some specialty stores sell **gluten flour,** and this type of flour also is used occasionally in commercial breads in which a very high protein content is desired.

All-Purpose Flour
Multi-use flour made from hard wheat or a mixture of hard and soft wheat; contains about 10.5 percent protein.

Bread Flour
Hard wheat, long-patent flour with a protein level of about 11.8 percent.

Long-Patent Flour
Wheat flour made from 95 to 100 percent of the flour-streams, yielding flour of rather high protein content, for example, bread flour.

Pastry Flour
Soft wheat, short- and medium-patent flour with a protein level of about 9.7 percent.

Self-Rising Flour
Flour (usually soft wheat) to which baking powder and salt have been added during production.

Gluten Flour
Specialty wheat flour made by adding vital wheat gluten to increase the protein level to about 41 percent.

Vital Wheat Gluten
Dried crude gluten.

Vital wheat gluten (concentrated protein from wheat) is added to flour to bring the protein level to about 41 percent. Bread made with this type of flour is quite chewy and tough, yet very palatable.

Modifying Wheat Flour

Freshly milled flour is not considered ideal for baking, but two procedures commonly are followed to enhance appearance and performance. One of the objections to freshly milled flour is its somewhat yellow color, resulting primarily from the presence of xanthophylls (carotenoid pigments). If flour were allowed to stand exposed to air for several weeks, the xanthophylls would be bleached, and the flour would develop the desired white color. This is not a practical procedure when dealing with large quantities of flour. However, addition of a very small amount of benzoyl peroxide to flour (a practice approved by the U.S. Food and Drug Administration) bleaches the xanthophylls rapidly and at very little cost. Furthermore, **benzoyl peroxide** is an additive that seems to have no effect on the baking quality of the flour to which it is added.

Benzoyl Peroxide
Food additive approved by the U.S. Food and Drug Administration for bleaching the xanthophylls in refined flours.

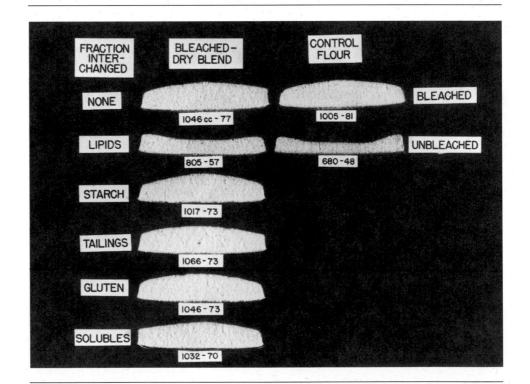

Figure 17.4 Control cake made using bleached flour (top row) has a significantly greater volume than the control cake made with unbleached flour (second row, right). Cakes from dry blends of fractions from hexane-extracted chlorinated (bleached) commercial base flour in which single fractions were substituted with counterparts from untreated (unbleached) flour. Control flours refers to cakes from chlorinated (bleached) and untreated (unbleached) patent flours, respectively. Labels show cake volume and crumb score, respectively. (Courtesy of J. R. Donelson, W. T. Yamazaki, and L. T. Kissell. American Association of Cereal Chemists, Inc. 1984. *Cereal Chem. 61* (2): 88.)

The baking performance of wheat flours improves when they are allowed to **age or mature,** apparently the result of changes in the protein during storage. Such changes can be accelerated greatly by the addition of chemical compounds classified as maturing agents. Among the maturing agents that may be added are chlorine (as gaseous chlorine, chlorine dioxide gas, or a mixture of nitrosyl chloride and chlorine), acetone peroxide, and azodicarbonamide. As flour is aged or matured, some of the sulfhydryl groups (—SH) in the protein are altered, apparently crosslinking to form disulfide (—S—S—) bonds. This change alters the ability of the flour proteins to stretch and makes doughs containing aged flours exhibit reduced extensibility, which improves the adhesive quality needed in baked products. Bread doughs with too many sulfhydryl bonds and too few disulfide bonds are evidenced by their stickiness and inelasticity. Cake flour especially depends on the addition of gaseous chlorine to mature the flour and lower the pH. Particularly rich cakes are quite susceptible to falling during baking if the cake flour has not been treated with gaseous chlorine because of the weak protein in the untreated flour. Lipids also undergo beneficial changes during maturing of (chlorinated) flours (see Figures 17.4 to 17.6).

Refinement of wheat during processing results in some loss of nutrients. In recognition of this loss and, more importantly, the significant consumption of

Aging (Maturing)
Chemical process used to alter the physical behavior of flour proteins by modifying some of the sulfhydryl groups to disulfide linkages; maturing agents include gaseous chlorine, chlorine dioxide gas, a mixture of nitrosyl chloride and chlorine, acetone peroxide, and azodicarbonamide.

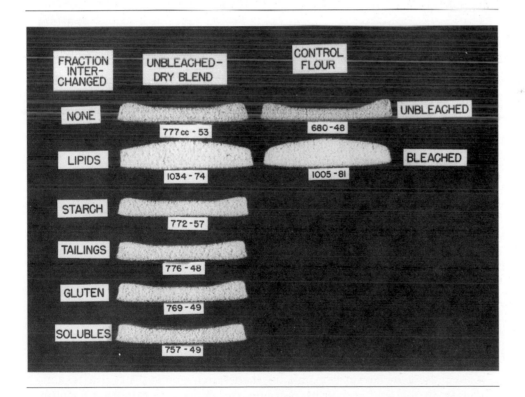

Figure 17.5 Cakes from dry blends of fractions from hexane-extracted unbleached commercial flour in which single fractions were substituted with counterparts from chlorinated (bleached) flour. Control flour refers to cakes from untreated (unbleached) and chlorinated (bleached) patent flours, respectively. Labels show cake volume and crumb score, respectively. (Courtesy of J. R. Donelson, W. T. Yamazaki, and L. T. Kissell. American Association of Cereal Chemists, Inc. 1984. *Cereal Chem. 61* (2): 88.)

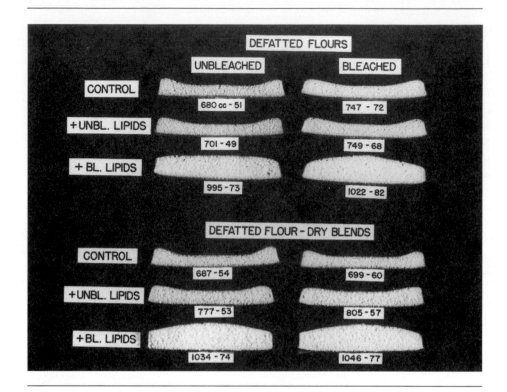

Figure 17.6   Top: Cakes from hexane-extracted commercial base flour without added lipids (control), with added lipids from untreated (unbleached) flour, and with added lipids from chlorinated (bleached) flour. Bottom: Cakes from dry blends of fractions from hexane-extracted commercial base flour without added lipids (control), with added lipids from untreated (unbleached) flour, and with added lipids from chlorinated (bleached) flour. Labels show cake volume and crumb scores, respectively. (Courtesy of J. R. Donelson, W. T. Yamazaki, and L. T. Kissell. American Association of Cereal Chemists, Inc. 1984. *Cereal Chem.* *61* (2): 88.)

wheat-containing products, federal regulations now require the enrichment of wheat products and also other cereal grains with thiamin, riboflavin, niacin, folic acid, and iron. The addition of these B vitamins and iron is important nutritionally, but does not have negative effects on products made from enriched flours.

Composition of Wheat Flours

Although the presence of proteins in various wheat flours was mentioned earlier, proteins are but part of the total composition of these products. Proteins are emphasized because of their key role in providing structure in baked products, yet they are present in far smaller amounts than starch (Table 17.2). Fat content is somewhat variable, but even at its maximum (in whole wheat flour), it contributes only 2 percent of the total components. The moisture level is relatively constant from one type of flour to another; ordinarily about 12 percent of the weight is due to moisture, and it may rise to a maximum of 15 percent.

Several carbohydrates are found in the wheat kernel. Cellulose is found primarily in the bran and is eliminated to a large extent during milling of refined

Table 17.2   Composition of Various Wheat Flours (Average Values)

Type of Flour	Carbohydrate (%)	Protein (%)	Water (%)	Fat (%)	Ash (%)
Whole wheat (hard wheat)	71.0	13.3	12	2.0	1.7
Straight, hard wheat	74.5	11.8	12	1.2	0.46
Straight, soft wheat	76.9	9.7	12	1.0	0.42
All-purpose	76.1	10.5	12	1.0	0.43
Cake	79.4	7.5	12	0.8	0.31

Watt, B. K. and Merrill, A. L. *Composition of Foods,* Agricultural Handbook No. 8; U.S. Department of Agriculture: Washington, DC, 1963.

flours. A small amount of cellulose is present in the endosperm, although at such low levels that its presence is not evident. **Pentosans,** polymers of arabinose and xylose (pentoses), are categorized as hemicelluloses occurring in cell walls in the endosperm. Both water-soluble and water-insoluble pentosans account for about 2 to 3 percent of the weight of refined flour. Although somewhat less than half of the pentosans are classified as water-soluble, the water-soluble pentosans contribute to the development of a cohesive dough during mixing. Dextrins, polymers of glucose just a bit shorter than amylose and amylopectin (Chapter 7), occur in trace amounts (less than 0.2 percent of total flour weight). Maltose and lesser amounts of glucose, fructose, and sucrose contribute somewhat less than 2 percent of total flour weight.

By far the most abundant carbohydrate is starch, which is found in granules embedded in a protein matrix in the endosperm. On a dry weight basis, starch constitutes up to 80 percent of the total weight of flour. Amylopectin content averages 75 percent and amylose, 25 percent. The high concentration of starch in flour has significant implications in the structure of baked products because of the imbibition of water by the granules in an attempt to gelatinize the starch during baking. This uptake of water results in much less free water, the presence of more bound water, and increased rigidity of structure as a consequence of the reduced free water and the swelling of the granules during gelatinization.

Even in whole wheat flour, the lipid content is low; much of the total lipid is found in the germ and, therefore, is removed when refined flours are produced. In the endosperm, about 1 percent or slightly more of the total weight represents the lipid component. Lipids occur in a variety of forms, the most important of which is the free polar lipid fraction. Included among the individual compounds in the free polar lipid fraction are lecithin (phosphatidylcholine), glycolipids (notably monogalactosyl glyceride), and cephalins (see Figure 17.7).

The proteins in flour can be divided into the soluble proteins (subdivided into albumins and globulins), gluten proteins (glutenins and gliadins), and enzymes (Paul and Palmer, 1972). Gluten, because of its singular importance, is discussed in the next section. Albumins contribute to the structure of baked products even though they constitute in the vicinity of only 10 percent of the total protein in flour. The other water-soluble proteins are the globulins, which are present in similar amounts. Their role in developing the structure of baked products appears to be quite minor, certainly less than the role fulfilled by albumins.

The enzymes in wheat probably are soluble protein classified as either albumins or globulins. However, enzymes represent only a small portion of these proteins in flour. Despite their small quantity, enzymes are of interest because of their

Pentosans
Polymers of the pentoses xylose and arabinose.

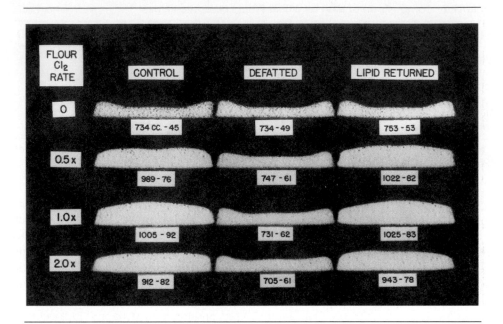

Figure 17.7 Cross sections of cakes made from serially chlorinated patent flours; control (whole), defatted, and with lipids returned (reconstituted by contact wetting). Boxed numbers give cake volume and internal crumb score (100-point scale). (Courtesy of L. T. Kissell, J. R. Donelson, and R. L. Clements. American Association of Cereal Chemists, Inc. 1979. *Cereal Chem 56* (1): 11.)

potential for altering the characteristics of flour as they catalyze chemical changes. Maltose units are split from starch molecules as β-amylase attacks 1,4-α-glucosidic linkages. Action halts at branch points in amylopectin when β-amylase encounters a 1,6-α linkage, leaving smaller amylopectin-type compounds called limit dextrins. Dextrins result when α-amylase cleaves amylose molecules randomly at various 1,4-α-glucosidic linkages to create linear fragments of the former amylose chain. The fact that β-amylase is most active at about 50°C limits the action that can occur during baking, whereas α-amylase has more time to act before being denatured, because its very active temperature range is 60–65°C. In ordinary circumstances, changes resulting from action of wheat amylases are undetectable. In the baking industry, fungal α-amylase may be added to improve dough handling properties, its action occurring well below the warm temperatures needed for wheat amylase activity.

Two types of enzymes in wheat contribute toward the problems of rancidity in flours containing the germ and its fat, notably in whole wheat flour. Free fatty acids are formed during storage as a consequence of the action of lipases on glycerides. Lipoxidase is the most active of the oxidases in wheat flours, causing the development of oxidative rancidity in whole wheat flours and whole grains during storage as it catalyzes formation of peroxides in unsaturated fatty acids.

Gliadin
Protein fraction in wheat gluten that is soluble in alcohol, compact and elliptical in shape, and sticky and fluid.

Gluten

Gliadin and Glutenin.   Gluten, the protein complex formed when wheat flour is manipulated with water, comprises two fractions—gliadin and glutenin—in approximately equal amounts. **Gliadin** is the fraction soluble in 70% alcohol and is characterized as being rather sticky and fluid. The proteins in the gliadin complex are probably elliptical single polypeptide chains, resulting in quite compact molecules that are held in this shape by internal (intramolecular) disulfide bonds (see Figure 17.8)

Glutenin is the fraction consisting of the alcohol-insoluble proteins in gluten. Additional differentiation of the proteins in glutenin is accomplished by the addition of dilute acetic acid, which acts as a solvent for one subfraction and fails to dissolve the other subfraction. The combination of these two subfractions results in glutenin, the gluten fraction that is characterized as very elastic. Glutenin has a fibrous nature, providing a sharp contrast to the elliptical character of gliadin.

The chemical compositions of the gliadin and glutenin fractions are different, thus helping to explain their distinctly different behavior. Gliadin consists of various molecules of differing molecular weight. The majority of the gliadin proteins are single chains of amino acids with a molecular weight around 36,500, although some polypeptide chains may be so small that they have a molecular weight of only about 11,400, and others so complex that they appoach a molecular weight just over 78,000. Of particular importance internally in the gliadin proteins is the presence of disulfide bonds. **Glutamine,** an amino acid particularly prominent in the makeup of gliadin proteins, is thought to be of importance in effecting hydrogen bonding between molecules in developing gluten. **Proline** is another fairly prominent amino acid; its unique structure inhibits the shape that proteins may take wherever a proline residue occurs in the backbone chain, thus contributing to the elliptical shape that predominates in gliadin proteins.

The isoelectric point of the gliadin fraction is reported by different investigators to range from pH 6.1 to 6.7. Solubility of gliadin is least at pH 6.5 and increases with either increasing acidity or increasing alkalinity, solubility being greater at high pH levels than at low levels.

Glutenin
Alcohol-insoluble protein fraction in wheat gluten that is characterized by its fibrous, elongated shape and elastic quality.

Glutamine
Amino acid prominent in gliadin protein molecules and important in intermolecular hydrogen bonding:

$$H_2N-\underset{\underset{O}{\|}}{C}-CH_2-CH_2-\underset{\underset{NH_2}{|}}{CH}-COOH$$

Proline
Amino acid prominent in gliadin with a cyclic ring structure that restricts protein shape:

$$\begin{array}{c} H_2C{-}CH_2 \\ | \quad\;\; HC\;\;\;COOH \\ H_2C{-}NH \end{array}$$

Figure 17.8 When manipulated with water, the proteins in flour form an elastic and cohesive complex, gluten (left); glutenin, one part of the complex, contributes elasticity (center); the remaining protein, gliadin, adds cohesiveness (right). (Courtesy of R. J. Dimler. *Bakers Digest 37* (1): 52. 1963.)

Compared to gliadin, the molecular weights of the various proteins constituting glutenin are much greater, ranging from about 100,000 to as high as 15 million (Huebner, 1977). The very high molecular weights of some of the molecules in glutenin appear to be the result of disulfide bonding between polypeptide subunits. This disulfide linkage is one of the differences between glutenin and gliadin, for in gliadin the disulfide linkages are confined apparently to intramolecular bonding. It should be noted that intramolecular disulfide bonding also occurs in glutenin. The isoelectric point of glutenin is lower than that of gliadin and is reported by Kent-Jones and Amos (1967) to be between pH 5.2 and 5.6. Even as the pH of a batter or dough is shifted away from the isoelectric point, glutenin remains somewhat difficult to dissolve and is far less soluble than gliadin.

Gluten
Complex of gliadin and glutenin that develops in wheat flour mixtures when water is added and the batter or dough is manipulated by stirring, beating, or kneading.

The Gluten Complex.   Only when flour (with its components of gliadin and glutenin) and water are manipulated together does the **gluten** complex begin to form. Formation of this complex is the key to successfully producing baked products; variations in the extent of development of this complex are responsible for much of the difference in textural characteristics observed in baked products containing exactly the same ingredients.

For the gluten complex to develop, the individual proteins must be hydrated by the addition of water or an aqueous liquid. Approximately twice as much water as gliadin and glutenin (by weight) is needed to hydrate the proteins completely (Paul and Palmer, 1972); hard wheat flours bind more water than soft wheat can. On initiation of mixing, the hydrated proteins begin to be altered in their physical relationships to each other. In the dry flour, the proteins are found in aggregates with starch, in endosperm cells, and in wedges of the protein matrix in which starch is embedded in the endosperm. Mixing the hydrated protein disrupts these associations and breaks many intermolecular secondary bonds and forms new bonds, resulting in the development of a cohesive gluten matrix that provides the foundation of the structure of baked products (see Figures 17.9 and 17.10).

The variety of functional groups, for example, the disulfide in cystine and the amide in glutamine, provides ample opportunity for formation of new intra- and intermolecular bonds as the gluten complex develops during mixing. Flours with lower levels of gliadin require more mixing but result in a more stable gluten matrix than is true for flours with more gliadin. Flours with a comparatively high level of gliadin characteristically produce a weaker structure than those produced when less gliadin is contained in the gluten complex.

Various theoretical structures for the gluten complex have been developed over the years, but agreement has yet to be reached regarding the actual structure. One clear fact is that the lipids that naturally occur in flour are necessary for normal gluten development. Pomeranz (1973) theorized that glycolipids (bound carbohydrate–lipids attracted to water) are bound to glutenin by hydrophobic bonds and to gliadin by hydrogen bonds as the hydrated gliadin and glutenin molecules are manipulated together to form the gluten complex. Evidence of the importance of lipids is clear when bread made with defatted flour is compared with a comparable loaf made with regular flour which contains the lipids normally present; the loaf made with defatted flour is significantly smaller in volume. Cakes made with defatted flour also demonstrate the importance of lipids in gluten development (see Figures 17.7 and 17.11).

The appearance of the hydrated mixture of gliadin and glutenin changes with manipulation. At first the surface is quite rough and some sharp points protrude.

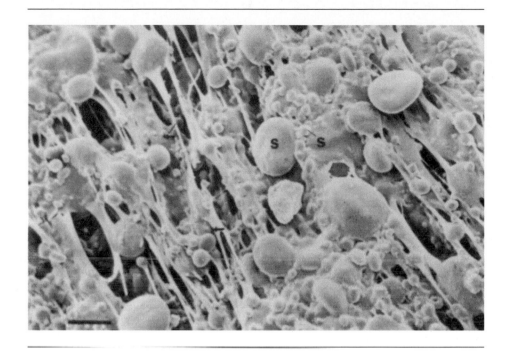

Figure 17.9 Scanning electron micrograph showing incubated optimally mixed flour-water dough after stretching. F = gluten fibrils formed on stretching; s = starch granules. Bar is 20 μm. (Reprinted from *Scanning Electron Microscopy III*: 583. 1981. Courtesy of L. E. Peters and G. M. Pearson.)

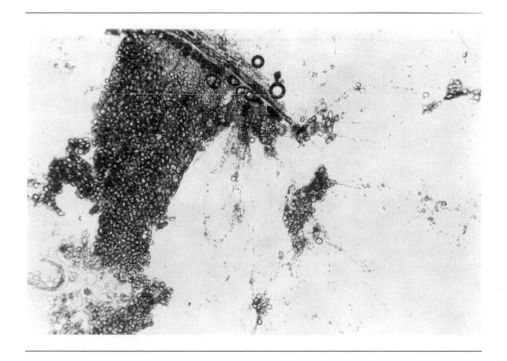

Figure 17.10 Under a microscope, protein fibrils reveal starch grains mixed with them when a particle of flour is wetted with a drop of water. (Reprinted by permission, J. E. Bernardin and D. D. Kasarda. *Cereal Chem. 50:* 531. 1973.)

Figure 17.11 Sketch of lipoprotein model of gluten sheet proposed by J. C. Grosskreutz. *Cereal Chem. 38:* 336. 1961.

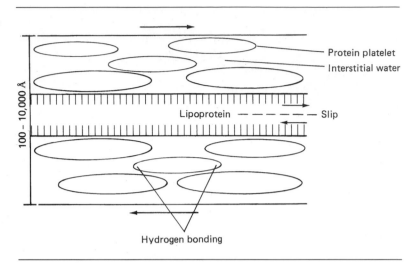

Gradually, strands or stringy filmlike areas can be seen as manipulation is continued. Eventually, the surface becomes quite smooth, and the individual ropelike strands no longer can be seen at all. This transformation occurs (Bernardin and Kasarda, 1973) as the protein-containing, hydrated flour mixture is mixed, causing the protein to develop into thin sheets that break into fibrils that tend to stick to each other and stretch as the glutenin strands touch each other during kneading or other manipulation.

The process of gluten development is perhaps easier to understand if you visualize gliadin as having some flow properties, while also being a bit sticky. In contrast, glutenin is a protein that has regions that are somewhat like string interspersed with coiled or kinky regions that are responsible for the elastic nature of glutenin. The number of functional groups on the surface and available for interaction on a gliadin molecule is far more limited than is true for the very long strands of glutenin molecules. Sulfhydryl groups (—SH) on the surface of the molecules are prominent during early mixing, but they do not provide the strong linkages that are formed later as disulfide (—S—S—) bonds form and begin to lock the network of glutenin and gliadin molecules into the stretchy network called gluten. Because of the presence of gliadin molecules in the network, some movement of the network is still possible, making the dough mixtures containing gluten manipulable, yet comparatively elastic.

The rate at which gluten development takes place depends on several different factors. The gluten complex formed in hard wheat flours develops more slowly and can be manipulated for a longer period without breakage of protein strands than can the gluten in soft wheat flours. This phenomenon can be seen by comparing farinograms recorded when doughs containing hard wheat are manipulated in a **farinograph** operated under the same conditions used to develop a dough made with soft wheat. Gluten from soft wheat develops more rapidly and starts to break down more quickly than does gluten from hard wheat (see Figures 7.12 and 7.13).

Temperature of the dough mixture influences the rate of gluten development. As the temperature is increased, the rate of hydration of the proteins also is accelerated, a change that is accompanied by an increased rate of gluten development.

Farinograph
Objective testing equipment that measures the resistance of stirring rods moving through a batter or dough and records the results graphically.

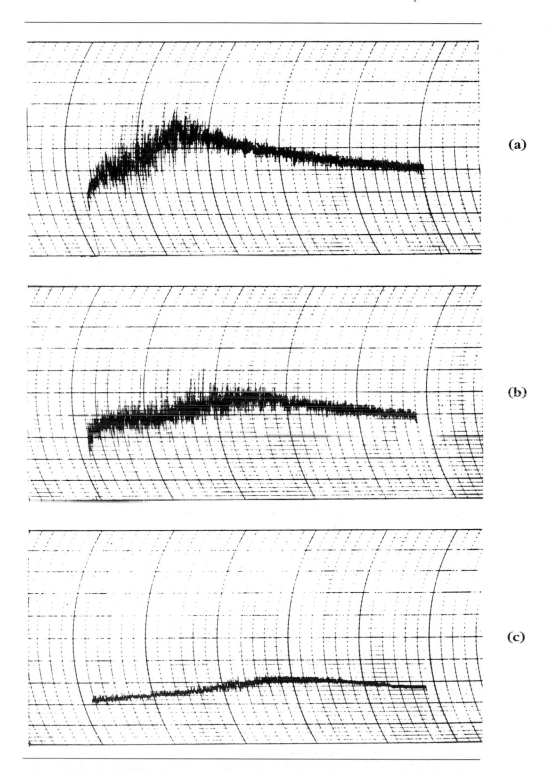

(a)

(b)

(c)

Figure 17.12 Gluten development, as recorded in mixograms. Gluten is developing in the ascending pattern on the left and breaking down as the pattern descends on the right. Mixograms are for baker's hard wheat flour (a), all purpose flour (b), and cake flour (soft wheat) flour (c). (Courtesy of H. Charley.)

Figure 17.13 Cake flour (soft wheat) gluten ball (left) reveals the smaller quantity and weaker nature of its gluten, as contrasted with all-purpose (hard wheat) gluten ball (right).

Sugar added to a batter or dough retards gluten development. This effect is caused by the intense competition between sugar and the flour proteins for water in the mixture. Because of its hygroscopic nature, sugar effectively attracts water, resulting in reduced hydration of flour proteins and, consequently, slower development of gluten.

Increasing the level of fat in a batter or dough also delays gluten development. The inhibiting effect of fat is due to the ability of fat to coat the surface of gluten, thus making hydration of the flour proteins quite difficult. There may be an additional effect, resulting from the ability of the fat to serve as a lubricant, thereby reducing the tendency of the strands to stick to each other during mixing.

The viscosity of a batter, that is, the amount of water in relation to flour, is yet another factor influencing gluten development. When equal amounts of flour and liquid are included in a batter, an excess of fluid is available, resulting in a fluid mixture, such as is seen in popover batter. The protein molecules are diluted so much by the liquid that it is quite difficult for strands to cling to each other even when they happen to touch during mixing. In contrast to the 1:1 ratio of flour to liquid in popovers, muffins have a ratio of approximately twice as much flour as liquid (a 2:1 ratio). This is a very sticky ratio, and the gluten develops very rapidly in muffins as the strands of gluten are stretched on coming into sticky contact with other molecules when the batter is mixed. Gluten develops so quickly when muffins are mixed that overmixing may occur readily, and undesirable textural changes can be noted (Chapter 18).

Other Flours

Instantized Flour.   Wheat flour passed through moist air sticks together (agglomerates). This agglomerated flour can then be dried to give small pellets of flour that neither pack nor contain fine dust of flour particles. The resulting product, called **instantized flour,** blends easily with water and does not require sifting, thus overcoming two inconveniences associated with regular flour. Unfortunately, gluten does not develop readily when instantized flour is used, which limits the usefulness of this type of flour in making batter and dough products, particularly breads.

Instantized Flour
Flour made of sand-like granules produced by adding moisture to agglomerate the flour, then drying to produce the granules.

Rye Flour.   Flours can be milled from any of the cereal grains, but their proteins lack the ability to develop the necessary plasticity and elasticity that are needed for producing the texture desired in baked products and that are available so uniquely in wheat gluten. Even rye, the cereal grain that most closely approaches the characteristics of wheat gluten, cannot approximate the performance of wheat flour in making bread products. The proteins in rye flour include glutenin and gliadin, but they cannot be manipulated into a gluten complex with sufficient elasticity to produce light-textured baked products. Bread made with rye flour is very heavy. Breads made with a combination of rye and wheat flours have a better texture than those made only with rye.

Triticale Flour.   **Triticale** is a unique cereal grain developed by crossing wheat with rye and bears some of the characteristics of each of the parent grains. It has nutritional merit, because its protein content ranges to more than 16 percent, and the lysine content is higher than that of wheat. The yield per acre also is high. Although triticale flour can be used in baking, its texture is not as acceptable as that provided by wheat flour (Haber et al., 1976). There is potential for satisfactory use of this type of flour either by combination with wheat flour or by use of dough conditioners. Actual characteristics of triticale are somewhat variable, because the strains of this hybrid grain vary in the relative contribution of wheat and rye in the cross breeding. The greater the influence of the wheat, the better are the baking characteristics.

Triticale
Hybrid grain produced by crossing wheat and rye.

Rice Flour.   Rice flour is another cereal flour that is available. Its use in baked products (as is true for flour from corn, barley, and oats) is frustrating because the name suggests that it should be possible to make a satisfactory baked product substituting rice or any of these other flours for wheat flour. Unfortunately, all of these grain flours lack the elastic and cohesive qualities needed to provide a framework for baked products. In addition, the somewhat gritty texture of rice flour is quite apparent, seemingly defying hydration. However, some of the wheat flour can be substituted fairly satisfactorily by one of the alternative grain flours (Table 17.3). Commercial baking operations are able to add carboxymethylcellulose to batters and doughs to help complement the bit of structure that can be contributed by the starch in these flours. Baked products made from these other grain flours are particularly important to people who have an allergy to gluten. Satisfactory alternatives for baked products made with wheat flour are being explored, but the ultimate objective of a totally satisfactory replacement has not yet been achieved.

Corn Flour.   Corn flour, like rice flour, is limited in its usefulness by its inability to form a useful protein network to provide the structure required in baked products. Somewhat larger granulation also may be used in the form of cornmeal. Either corn flour or cornmeal can be included to supplement wheat flour in making

Table 17.3   Profile of Selected Alternate Flours

Flour	Protein in Flour (%)	Acceptable Replacement Level (%)	Characteristics Noted in Baked Products
Rye	12.1	20–40	Heavy texture, smaller volume
Triticale	10.7–16.3	40–50+	Limit mixing and fermentation time for optimal result
Oat	17	30	Heavy in bread
Rice	6.5–7	5–30	Satisfactory at 5%; somewhat acceptable at 30%
Corn (maize)	7–8	?	Used as masa[a] to make tortillas

[a]Corn cooked and steeped in lime, then washed and ground.

baked products, such as corn bread, but the texture is likely to be quite crumbly because of the lack of gluten in the cornmeal. Flavor and color are benefits gained from using cornmeal or corn flour, but the texture is compromised a bit.

Potato Flour.   Potatoes are a tuber, not a grain, but they can be used to produce either flour, flakes, or granules which can be used to add some interest and variety in selected baked products, particularly breads. The component that makes some contribution to the texture of baked products is starch. The flavor of baked prod-

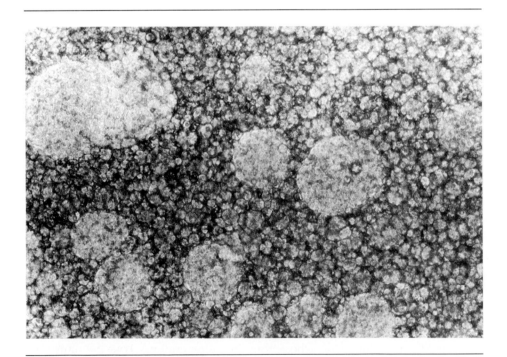

Figure 17.14   The emulsifying properties of soy flour are seen in this photomicrograph (213X) of an emulsion containing 140 ml water-soaked soy flour per 50 ml dispersion. (Courtesy of H. L. Ashraf, Southern Illinois University. Reprinted from *Journal of Food Science*. 1986. Vol. 51(1): 193. Copyright (c) by Institute of Food Technologists.)

ucts is influenced subtly by the use of potato flour or related potato products. No gluten is provided, which makes it important to include sufficient wheat flour as an ingredient in baked products that include potato flour or granules.

Soy Flour.   Soy flour differs from the other flours mentioned in this section because it is produced from a legume, not a grain. However, its common availability and nutritional interest make this an appropriate flour to include here. Nutritionally, soy flour has some importance because its high lysine content provides a ready complement to wheat flour, which is limited in its nutritional benefit by its comparatively low content of lysine, an essential amino acid. Soy flour aids in forming emulsions in batters. Unfortunately, soy flour lacks the cohesive and elastic qualities of gluten, but it does provide both protein and starch to strengthen the structure when it is combined with wheat flour in baked products. Supplementation with soy flour can be done to add to the nutritive value of baked products, although its distinctive flavor becomes objectionable at high levels. The starch added when soy flour is included as an ingredient makes it necessary to increase the amount of liquid in recipes. Gates (1987) recommends that the added liquid equal the weight of the soy flour and that the proofing time for yeast breads be lengthened when soy flour supplementation is a part of the recipe (see Figure 17.14).

ROLES OF INGREDIENTS

Wheat and Other Flours

Wheat flour is the basic structural component of most batter and dough products. It is able to perform this textural function because of the gluten content, which allows expansion of cells and provides rigidity of structure after baking. Starch is another very important compound in not only wheat, but other flours as well. Water is bound by the starch as it gelatinizes during baking, thus contributing significantly to the remarkable change from a somewhat fluid batter or dough to the firm, rather rigid structure of the baked product. Clearly, starch in flour plays an important role in baked products, albeit a somewhat less dramatic one than that of gluten, which was discussed earlier in this chapter.

Other minor roles are performed by flour. Some of the sugar needed by yeast as food during fermentation in making yeast breads is provided by flour. Also, crust browning during baking is dependent on the combination of proteins with sugars, and flour provides the protein needed.

Liquid

Water or other liquid in batters and doughs serves as a solvent, dissolving sugar, baking powder, salt, or other dry ingredients and hydrating yeast when it is present. As mentioned earlier in this chapter, liquid must be present for gluten to develop, because the proteins must be hydrated before they can be manipulated so that they adhere to each other and form the elastic, plastic network needed for structure. Until water or other aqueous liquid is present, no gluten develops. During baking, available liquid is bound in starch granules as they gelatinize. Although batters and doughs usually do not contain enough liquid to permit complete gelatinization of starch, at least partial gelatinization is possible because of the liquid that is a part of the recipe. Furthermore, liquids serve as a source of steam during baking, and steam is important as either an auxiliary or the primary source of leavening in baked products. The significance of this role is discussed under Leavening in this chapter.

When milk is the liquid used, it also contributes to (1) crust browning because of its protein and sugar content and (2) softening of crumb texture because of its fat content (whole and low-fat milk). Fruit juices reduce the pH of batters and doughs when they are the liquid, which alters the flavor and modifies the solubility of the gluten proteins slightly.

Eggs

As discussed in some depth in Chapter 16, eggs contribute to baked products in several ways. In a batter or dough, they contribute liquid during mixing and in baking. Although the quantity of liquid provided by eggs usually is rather small, this aspect of eggs cannot be ignored. Of course, the proteins of eggs are of particular importance when they are used in batters and doughs. Coagulation of the proteins during baking contributes to the structure of the finished product and reduces tenderness. Emulsification is effected by eggs, particularly by the yolks, during mixing of batters and doughs. Formation of an emulsion promotes more uniform dispersion of liquids and fats and favors a fine texture. Yolks also contribute color to light-colored baked products. Texture of cakes and a few quick breads is enhanced by incorporating egg foams, which usually are egg white foams. The abundance of air trapped within the bubbles of egg protein creates many small cells that expand from the heat during baking and then are permanently set in their extended position when the egg (and flour) proteins are denatured and coagulated late in the baking period.

Fats

Depending on the fat used, fats may play various roles in baked products. Butter and margarine contribute a pleasing and rather distinctive flavor, whereas other fats add to the richness of flavor. Lard has a mild, unique flavor which may be appreciated in certain products, such as pastry. Yellow fats (butter, margarine, or colored shortenings) add a creamy color that subtly implies richness. Texture is influenced by fats too. For example, oil in a pastry promotes a mealy texture, whereas particles of fat made by cutting a solid fat into the flour yield a flaky, layered texture. Shortenings with added mono- and diglycerides favor development of a fine texture in cakes because of the emulsifying action of the mono- and diglycerides. Regardless of the type used, fats are very effective in promoting tenderness of baked products. Their hydrophobic action inhibits gluten development, the extent of this inhibition being determined by the type, temperature, and amount of fat used, as well as by the method of incorporation.

Sugar

The obvious role of sugar in baked products is as a sweetener. However, this is but one of its functions. Browning of the crust is due in part to caramelization, as well as to the sugar–amine reaction (Maillard reaction). Sugar serves as a tenderizing agent first by retarding gluten development during mixing and then by elevating the coagulation temperature of the structural proteins so that there is more time for cell walls to stretch and volume to increase before coagulation occurs to define the final volume of baked products.

Salt

Salt is a flavoring agent at the levels used in most baked products. The sole exception to this is found when salt is considered in yeast breads. In yeast doughs, salt limits the growth rate of yeast, which serves as a check against excessive carbon dioxide production resulting from the action of yeast and sugar during fermentation and the early period of baking.

Leavening Agents

Leavening agents contribute significantly to the textural properties of baked products by expanding the batter or dough, sometimes during mixing and always during baking. The physical behavior of gases generated by leavening agents is explained in Chapter 6. The various sources of leavening that can be used in batters and doughs are outlined and discussed in the next section.

LEAVENING

Air

Air is always a leavening agent in baked products because some air always is trapped within the mixture while the ingredients are being blended. This air, which is trapped naturally during mixing, is essential to the formation of the many cells needed to produce light and pleasing baked products with the expected cell size. However, this trapped air is insufficient to achieve the volume usually desired. Sometimes egg white and/or egg yolk foams are prepared and gently folded into a batter to increase the amount of air that is available for leavening the mixture.

Considerable variation in volume is found when air is the principal leavening agent, even when an egg white foam is included as a source of air. To achieve good volume in an angel cake, a cake that relies heavily on air for leavening, a stable egg white foam of high volume must be folded very gently and efficiently with the other ingredients and then baked promptly in a preheated oven.

There are two critical operations where individual technique can make a significant difference in the volume of the batter prior to baking. First, the air must be incorporated into the foam to produce a large foam. This requires knowledge of the appropriate times at which to add stabilizing agents (acid and sugar) and of the appropriate point at which to stop beating. Overbeating or underbeating has a deleterious effect on foam volume. An overbeaten foam is rather rigid and brittle and hence difficult to fold in gently with the other ingredients. Second, careful folding is imperative, for there still is ample opportunity for loss of air during folding. The operator who is rough and very vigorous will break many of the cells and release air from the mixture. A very slow worker will lose air unnecessarily because of some evaporation from the surface of the foam and the collapse of some cells while the batter is folded slowly. Inefficient and excessive folding can result in considerable loss of air and a decreased volume. These losses are compounded if the cake must stand before being baked. In short, air is an essential, but only partially reliable, leavening agent.

Steam

Steam is a far more effective leavening agent than air, because volume is increased 1,600-fold when water is converted to steam. Compare this with air, which expands volume by 1/273 for each degree Celsius that the temperature rises. Popovers usually about triple in volume during baking, and most of this leavening is caused by steam (Figure 17.15). Cream puffs are also leavened mostly with steam. Both of these products have equal amounts of liquid and flour by volume, a ratio that is very favorable to considerable steam leavening. Even when a baked product contains as little water as is found in pastry, steam can effect appreciable leavening.

Two classic studies are useful in determining the significance of air and steam as leavening agents. When use of air as a leavening agent is extremely important, as certainly is true in angel cakes, which are predominantly egg white foams contributing a large volume of air to the batter, steam provides between two and three times as much leavening action as air. Hood and Lowe (1948) studied the relative leavening contributions of air and steam in air- and steam-leavened cakes made with butter, oil, and hydrogenated lard. Air was trapped more effectively in batters containing the solid fats than in those containing oil, and hydrogenated lard re-

Figure 17.15 Popovers illustrate the remarkable leavening action of steam. The very fluid batter and hot oven, combined with a small amount of air whipped into the batter, creates a very large interior cavity and about a threefold increase in volume during baking. (Courtesy of Plycon Press.)

Table 17.4   Relative Leavening Action of Air and Steam in Fat-Containing Cakes

Fat in Cake	Relative Leavening (%)	
	Air	Steam
Butter	19.8	80.2
Oil	11.4	88.6
Hydrogenated lard	25.0	75.0

Adapted from Hood, M. P. and Lowe, B. 1948. "Air, water vapor, and carbon dioxide as leavening gases in cakes made with different types of fat." *Cereal Chem.* *25,* 244.

tained more air for leavening than did butter, as shown in Table 17.4. Of particular significance is the far greater leavening provided by steam than by air regardless of the type of fat used; the actual difference ranged from almost eight times as much action from steam as from air in the oil-containing cakes to about four times as much with butter and three times as much with hydrogenated lard as the fat.

Biological Agents

Yeast.   Carbon dioxide, a gas that provides very effective leavening in baked products, may be from either a biological or chemical source. The usual biological source is the fermentation of sugars by yeast, one-celled plants capable of actively producing carbon dioxide in a dough at room temperature and briefly at oven temperatures during the early phase of baking. The strain normally used in making yeast breads is ***Saccharomyces cerevisiae.*** Because this yeast must be alive for the fermentation to proceed so that carbon dioxide is produced, environmental conditions must be controlled carefully to achieve satisfactory production (see Figure 17.16).

Saccharomyces cerevisiae
Strain of yeast commonly used as the source of carbon dioxide in yeast-leavened products.

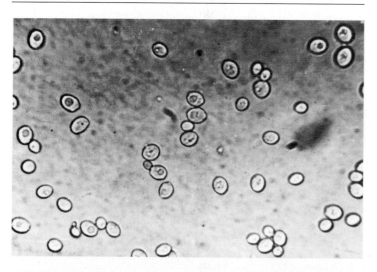

Figure 17.16   *Saccharomyces cerevisiae,* as seen under a microscope.

Even the conditions under which the yeast is added to the dough influence the final product, and the optimal conditions are determined by the form of yeast used. Three forms of *S. cerevisiae* are available: **compressed yeast** cakes, **active dry yeast,** and **quick-rise active dry yeast.** Compressed yeast cakes contain cornstarch and about 72 percent moisture, which limits the refrigerated shelf life to about 5 weeks. Compressed yeast needs to be dispersed in a small amount of lukewarm water (32–38°C) before it is added to a dough. This active form of yeast is convenient to use, but its short shelf life and the need for refrigeration during storage limit its market.

Active dry yeast is a granular form with a very low moisture (8 percent) content, which makes it possible to store this form of yeast in tightly sealed containers at room temperature for at least 6 months or in a freezer for as long as 2 years. Rehydration of this form of *S. cerevisiae* requires a higher temperature than is used for dispersing the compressed cake; the preferred temperature range for rehydration is 40–46°C. This high a temperature is needed to keep glutathione from leaving the yeast cells and subsequently causing breakage of disulfide bonds in the dough, which would reduce the elastic nature of the dough and increase stickiness (Oszlanyi, 1980). For convenience, active dry yeast sometimes is combined with the flour without rehydration of the yeast. The liquid must be at even higher temperature (49–54°C) if this technique is used because the other ingredients in the dough mixture will, on contact, cool the liquid to a safe temperature range for the yeast. Quick-rise active dry yeast is very similar to active dry yeast, but the strain of *S. cerevisiae* used in this product produces carbon dioxide particularly rapidly in doughs and is capable of saving approximately an hour in fermentation time.

Even after yeast has been combined with the other ingredients in a dough, care still must be taken to ensure that the yeast remains viable and actively produces carbon dioxide. Temperature control and time are the factors necessary for adequate leavening to occur when the yeast is used. After it is mixed, the dough is left to rest to allow time for the *S. cerevisiae* to metabolize glucose and release carbon dioxide. The overall reaction is shown below.

Compressed Yeast
Saccharomyces cerevisiae in a cornstarch-containing cake with a moisture level of 72 percent; requires refrigerated storage; dispersion is best at 32–38°C.

Active Dry Yeast
Granular form of dried *Saccharomyces cerevisiae* (8 percent moisture); storage can be at room temperature; rehydration should be at 40–46°C.

Quick-Rise Active Dry Yeast
Special strain of *Saccharomyces cerevisiae* available as the active dry yeast and capable of producing carbon dioxide so rapidly in the dough that fermentation time is reduced by about an hour.

$$\text{glucose} \xrightarrow{\textit{S.cerevisiae}} 2C_2H_5OH + 2CO_2\uparrow$$

glucose · ethyl alcohol · carbon dioxide

Temperature of the dough during the fermentation period has a tremendous influence on the rate of gas production in the dough. Fermentation ideally is accomplished between 25 and 27.7°C (78 and 82°F), but the production of carbon dioxide actually can occur at refrigerator temperatures or as high as 35°C (95°F) or even slightly higher. The rate of fermentation increases rapidly with the temperature, tripling as the temperature rises from 20 to 30°C and doubling between 25 and 35°C (Pomper, 1969). Despite the very rapid fermentation occurring at

35°C, such a warm temperature is not recommended because of the development of a sour, yeasty flavor as other microorganisms also flourish at the elevated temperature. A fermentation temperature of 43°C kills yeast in an hour, thus eliminating production of carbon dioxide.

Glucose is the form of sugar preferred by *S. cerevisiae,* and a small amount of glucose is present in the flour used in the dough. Most yeast bread recipes include sucrose as the significant source of sugar for metabolism by the yeast. The inversion of sucrose to glucose and fructose, which is necessary before the yeast can utilize this source of sugar, is catalyzed by the sucrase present in yeast. Maltose can become available by enzymatic action on starch, and this sugar can be metabolized by yeast if no other source of sugar is available. The principal enzyme effecting the production of maltose from starch to provide food for yeast during fermentation is β-amylase. Some action may also occur as the result of α-amylase. If the weight of the sugar exceeds 10 percent of the weight of the flour, some osmosis will occur, and the yeast will metabolize sugar slowly.

Salt also has a negative effect on metabolism of sugar by yeast because of its influence on osmotic pressure in yeast. On the other hand, salt is beneficial in a yeast dough because its presence enhances the activity of β-amylase and α-amylase in breaking starch to sugars to provide food for the yeast. It also aids in reducing the breakdown of some of the flour proteins by proteases. Too little salt allows so much protease activity that the gluten weakens to the point where many of the cells break as pressure from carbon dioxide is generated, and the resulting bread has an uneven, porous texture. Salt usually should not exceed 2 percent of the weight of flour.

An appropriate balance between sugar and salt levels is needed for good gas production in sweet yeast doughs. The high level of sugar in sweet doughs delays gas production, an effect that can be offset to some extent by reducing the level of salt.

The pH of a yeast dough influences the rate of gas production during the fermentation period. *S. cerevisiae* activity is best between pH 4.0 and 6.0. Fortunately, fermentation produces some organic acids as well as carbon dioxide, which causes the pH of the dough to drop from its initial pH of about 6.0 to between 5.0 and 5.5, a range favorable for good gas production. The activity of *S. cerevisiae* is reduced if the pH of the dough drops below 4.0.

Bacteria and Yeast.   Two other strains of yeast, **Saccharomyces exigus** and **Saccharomyces inusitatus,** are used to produce carbon dioxide in acidic (sour) bread doughs, such as sourdough bread. These two yeasts are active at or below pH 4.5 and function well in conjunction with the use of a lactobacillus, **Lactobacillus sanfrancisco.** *L. sanfrancisco* produces lactic acid, which reduces the pH of the dough to the range where *S. exigus* and *S. inusitatus* can generate carbon dioxide effectively, but where *S. cerevisiae* is not the preferred yeast. A mixture of these microorganisms is contained in sourdough starters. The resulting bread using these microorganisms has a pleasingly sour flavor (the result of the acid produced by the *L. sanfrancisco*) and good volume because of the carbon dioxide produced by the *S. exigus* and *S. inusitatus*. Other starters also can be effective in generating carbon dioxide by the action of assorted microorganisms. Care must be taken to avoid off-flavors and odors resulting from the incubation of undesirable microorganisms in uncontrolled cultures.

Saccharomyces exigus **and** *Saccharomyces inusitatus*
Two yeasts used to produce carbon dioxide in acidic bread doughs.

Lactobacillus sanfrancisco
Bacterium producing lactic acid in some bread doughs.

Chemical Agents

A chemical reaction between an acidic and an alkaline ingredient in a baked product can generate carbon dioxide for leavening. The effectiveness of various ingredients or compounds in gas production depends not only on the total amount of gas generated, but also on the speed of the reaction. When chemical compounds react, no more gas is produced after both reactants are gone. A rapid reaction means that all of the gas is generated very quickly (probably during mixing), and some (or much) of the gas escapes from the batter or dough before baking sets the structure.

Acid Ingredients.   Various acid ingredients may be included in a batter or dough recipe to add flavor variety as well as to serve as a component of a leavening reaction. Soured dairy products, including cultured buttermilk, yogurt, sour milk, and sour cream, are able to react with an alkaline ingredient to release carbon dioxide as soon as the alkaline ingredient is dissolved in the milk or cream. Usually about a cup of the sour milk or cream and a half a teaspoon of baking soda produce enough leavening for a batter or dough containing two cups of flour. Other acidic ingredients that may be used include honey, molasses, fruit juices, and cream of tartar. The acidity of these ingredients is somewhat variable, which makes it difficult to be certain that the amount of carbon dioxide produced will be optimal. All of the aforementioned acidic ingredients react with baking soda quickly, which necessitates prompt mixing and baking once the acid and alkali have had the opportunity to react.

Alkaline Ingredients.   Acidic ingredients alone cannot generate carbon dioxide. They must react with an alkaline ingredient, and the common alkaline ingredient used in food preparation is **bicarbonate of soda** (also called sodium bicarbonate and baking soda). This soluble powder must be dissolved before it is capable of reacting with acids. Solution and reaction occur very quickly when baking soda comes in contact with the liquid ingredients in a recipe. Unless the batter or dough contains an acid, baking soda will produce only a little gas for leavening. If there is insufficient acid to react with all of the bicarbonate of soda, the mixture will be alkaline, causing a soapy flavor due to formation of sodium carbonate (Na_2CO_3) and a yellowish hue in light-colored baked products. The volume also may be poor.

Bicarbonate of Soda
Alkaline food ingredient ($NaHCO_3$) used to react with acids to form carbon dioxide.

Baking Powders

Baking powders contain at least one acid salt in addition to the alkaline baking soda. In short, baking powder is a complete mixture the provides both the acid and the alkali needed for the reaction to produce carbon dioxide for leavening in a batter or dough.

Commercial baking powders prepared for the retail market were actually one of the first convenience items or mixes. The baking powders on the market today are mixtures of acid salts and baking soda carefully formulated to produce between 12 and 14 percent carbon dioxide by weight; the minimum legal level is 12 percent. The leavening results obtained with using baking powder are more reliable and reproducible than those obtained by use of separate acid and alkali in a recipe, because of the precision possible in manufacturing the powder and the delay in the release of carbon dioxide that is possible in formulating baking powders. When baking powder is used to supplement the leavening provided by air

Baking Powder
Mixture of acid and alkaline salts and a standardizing agent to produce at least 12 percent of the carbon dioxide available for leavening.

Table 17.5   Relative Leavening Action of Air, Steam, and Carbon Dioxide in Fat-Containing Cakes

Fat in Cake	Relative Leavening (%)		
	Air	Steam	Carbon Dioxide
Butter	8.0	32.3	59.7
Oil	5.6	44.1	50.3
Hydrogenated lard	6.7	20.7	73.1

Adapted from Hood, M. P. and Lowe, B. 1948. "Air, water vapor, and carbon dioxide as leavening gases in cakes made with different types of fat." *Cereal Chem. 25,* 244.

and steam in fat-containing cakes, the relative amount of leavening provided by the carbon dioxide from the baking powder is far greater than that provided by either air or steam alone and even more than the leavening provided by the combined effect of air and steam (Table 17.5).

The essential ingredients in a baking powder are bicarbonate of soda, an acid salt, and cornstarch. The acid and alkaline salts are required for the chemical reaction that produces carbon dioxide. Cornstarch does not produce gas, but does perform two valuable functions in the powder. It helps to extend the shelf life of the powder by absorbing moisture that may enter the can, thus preventing the moisture from dissolving the acid and soda and blocking reaction of the active ingredients. Another role of cornstarch is that of a standardizing agent. Cornstarch is added at the level needed to dilute the active ingredients so that the correct amount of carbon dioxide is generated by a measured amount of baking powder. This function is important because not all acid salts are required in the same amounts to react with a given amount of baking soda. If a large amount of acid is needed, a small amount of cornstarch is needed to standardize the baking powder, whereas a small amount of an acid salt in a baking powder formulation necessitates an increased amount of cornstarch to serve as a filler.

The acid salts available for commercial applications are much greater in number than are found in baking powders for retail sale. The somewhat limited market for baking powders at the retail level has resulted in a decrease in the variety of products available today. The baking powders in the grocery store today are double-acting baking powders, a name indicating clearly that carbon dioxide is produced at two different times when the powder is used in a batter or dough product. First, some carbon dioxide is produced from one of the acid salts during mixing to help in development of a light-textured product. The acid salt responsible for this aspect of leavening must react at room temperature with dissolved bicarbonate of soda. Monocalcium phosphate monohydrate is the acid salt selected for inclusion as the one to act at room temperature during mixing. It reacts with bicarbonate of soda according to the following reaction:

$$3CaH_4(PO_4)_2 + 8NaHCO_3 \longrightarrow Ca_3(PO_4)_2 + 4Na_2HPO_4 + 8CO_2 + 8H_2O$$

monocalcium phosphate   bicarbonate of soda   tricalcium phosphate   disodium phosphate   carbon dioxide   water

SAS-Phosphate Baking Powder
Leavening with sodium aluminum sulfate and monocalcium phosphate as the acid salts; double-acting baking powder.

For reaction primarily in the oven, sodium aluminum sulfate (SAS) is the second acid salt in double-acting **(SAS-phosphate) baking powders.** A two-step reaction is required for this salt to produce carbon dioxide in the oven during baking. The first reaction produces sulfuric acid, and then this acid reacts with the bicarbonate of soda:

$$Na_2Al_2(SO_4)_4 + 6H_2O \longrightarrow 2Al(OH)_3 + Na_2SO_4 + 3H_2SO_4$$

		aluminum	sodium	sulfuric
SAS	water	hydroxide	sulfate	acid

$$3H_2SO_4 + 6NaHCO_3 \xrightarrow{H_2O} 3Na_2SO_4 + 6H_2CO_3$$

sulfuric	soda	
acid		

$$\downarrow$$

$$6CO_2 + 6H_2O$$

The usual ratio of monocalcium phosphate to sodium aluminum sulfate is one part monocalcium phosphate monohydrate to two parts sodium aluminum sulfate.

Cream of tartar (potassium acid tartrate) is an acid salt that can be used effectively in formulating baking powder for home use to make a tartrate baking powder. Tartrate reacts rather completely in about 2 minutes, making it difficult for slow workers to use effectively. This is one of the primary reasons that tartrate baking powders no longer are available in retail markets. The major advantage of a tartrate baking powder is the lack of an aftertaste from the sodium potassium tartrate residue remaining after baking. The reaction of cream of tartar with sodium bicarbonate is

$$NaHCO_3 + KHC_4H_4O_6 \xrightarrow{H_2O} KNaC_4H_4O_6 + CO_2 + H_2O$$

	potassium	sodium		
sodium	acid	potassium	carbon	
bicarbonate	tartrate	tartrate	dioxide	water

Homemade tartrate baking powder can be prepared easily by mixing cream of tartar and baking soda together in a ratio of two parts (by volume) cream of tartar to one part baking soda. To achieve a standardized mixture so that one teaspoon of this powder provides the equivalent leavening of one teaspoon of double-acting baking powder, one part of cornstarch needs to be added.

The amount of leavening to be provided by baking powder varies with the recipe, for recipes utilizing egg white foams do not need to rely so heavily on carbon dioxide. Between one and two teaspoons of baking powder per cup of flour provides an appropriate leavening action in most breads, whereas slightly less can be used in shortened cakes because of the leavening they gain from the air incorporated in creaming the fat and sugar. Too much baking powder in baked products results in a coarse and slightly harsh texture.

The type of baking powder used in a formula influences the pH of the resulting batter or dough. Of the acids tested by McKim and Moss (1943), tartrate baking powders produce the most acidic biscuit dough, with phosphate producing an intermediate value, and double-acting (SAS-phosphate) being the least acidic. The values obtained by McKim and Moss (1943) for biscuit doughs were pH 6.4 for tartrate, 6.7 for phosphate, and 7.0 for SAS-phosphate baking powders. The more acidic the mixture, the lighter in color and the more tender the final product. A double-acting baking powder leaves residue salts, including aluminum hydroxide. The aluminum hydroxide promotes increased elasticity and viscosity in batters and doughs and contributes to the cracking in the sides of biscuits.

An ideal baking powder would release some carbon dioxide during mixing at room temperature, but provide most of its carbon dioxide at oven temperatures, particularly in the early phase of baking. It also should not have an aftertaste. Ready availability and low cost are other criteria. No ideal baking powder exists. Tartrate powders give off too much carbon dioxide at room temperatures to make them suitable for slow workers or in situations where the mixture may need to stand before baking. SAS-phosphate, because of its double action from the two acid salts, provides leavening in both mixing and baking. Its real disadvantage is the rather metallic aftertaste. Although this aftertaste is not ordinarily a problem in most recipes, it can be unpleasant when increased levels of baking powder are used.

SUMMARY

Cereal grains (comprising bran, endosperm, and germ) can be milled into flour, which may be the whole grain or refined product depending on whether the bran and germ are removed. Among the types of flour available from the milling of wheat are whole wheat, all-purpose, bread, pastry, self-rising, gluten, cake, and instantized flours. Benzoyl peroxide is used to accelerate the bleaching of the xanthophylls to produce a white flour. Maturing agents (chlorine, acetone peroxides, and azodicarbonamide) are added to increase the disulfide bonding and enhance the adhesive, elastic properties of the flour gluten.

Starch is the most abundant component of flours, but it is the protein properties that are of special interest in baking. Fat content is very low, yet it does contribute to the gluten complex that develops in wheat flour when batters and doughs are mixed. Gliadin, the alcohol-soluble protein fraction in gluten, is elliptical in shape, sticky, and fluid. Glutenin, a fibrous and elastic protein complex, constitutes the other fraction of gluten.

The gluten complex formed when wheat flour is mixed with water is unique and is not duplicated in any other cereal flour, although rye has a limited ability to form this type of structure. When the flour proteins are hydrated, intermolecular bonds are broken, and new bonds are formed as the rather sticky glutenin fibers touch each other during mixing. Gliadin also becomes enmeshed and bonded within this network, although it does not provide the strength of structure that is contributed by the glutenin molecules. Hard wheat flours have a stronger gluten and can be mixed longer than soft wheat flours without breaking strands of the gluten. Sugar and fat delay gluten development; the effect of water depends on the amount of water in relation to the flour. Equal parts of liquid and flour delay gluten development, whereas twice as much flour as liquid (2:1) facilitates rapid development of gluten.

Other flours are available for special applications, and they may be used in baked products with a fair degree of success when combined with wheat flour at a sufficient level to provide the gluten structure. These flours include rye, triticale (a cross between wheat and rye), soy, rice, corn, and potato.

In baked products, flour is used to provide the basic structure. Liquid hydrates the gluten, dissolves sugar and other dry ingredients, gelatinizes starch, and provides steam for leavening. Eggs provide liquid, protein for added structure, emulsification, flavor, color, and a lighter texture when added as a foam. Fats have a tenderizing effect, enhance flavor, influence texture, and may contribute to color.

Sugar not only sweetens, but also increases volume, tenderizes, and promotes browning. Salt adds flavor, and it slows carbon dioxide production in yeast doughs. Leavening agents provide expansion to give large volumes and tender cells in baked products.

Leavening occurs in any baked product as the result of the presence of air and steam, although the importance of these two ever-present leavening agents varies with the particular product being prepared. Air increases 1/273rd of its volume for each degree Celsius rise in temperature during the early phase of baking, but steam expands to 1,600 times the volume occupied by the water from which it is formed, making steam a far more effective leavening agent than air, although air is essential.

Carbon dioxide, an extremely effective gas leavening agent, can be introduced into batters and doughs through the metabolism of *Saccharomyces cerevisiae,* the baker's yeast commonly used in yeast breads. Glucose, sucrose (inverted to glucose and fructose), and maltose are converted to ethyl alcohol and carbon dioxide slowly by yeast during the fermentation period. Salt regulates the speed of production of carbon dioxide. *S. cerevisiae* produces carbon dioxide well at the usual pH of doughs (between pH 5.0 and 6.0). If bacteria such as *Lactobacillus sanfrancisco* are added to a dough, lactic acid production drops the pH of the dough below the range where *S. cerevisiae* is a good yeast to use; *S. exigus* and *S. inusitatus* are excellent yeasts to add for carbon dioxide production in sourdough breads.

Chemical reactions can produce carbon dioxide, as a result of the inclusion of either separate acids and alkali or baking powder. Acids and alkali (baking soda) react as soon as the soda is dissolved, limiting their effectiveness as leaveners unless mixing and baking are done very quickly. Baking powders contain at least one acid salt, soda, and a standardizing agent to take up moisture, prevent reaction in the can, and provide at least 12 percent carbon dioxide from a specified measure of the powder. SAS-phosphate, a double-acting baking powder, is the baking powder available in grocery stores today; it has the ability to provide carbon dioxide during both mixing and baking. It has a rather harsh, metallic aftertaste when used in excess. Tartrate baking powders can be made using cream of tartar as the acid salt to produce a leavening agent without distinctive aftertaste, but one that requires fast mixing and baking to avoid excessive loss of carbon dioxide.

STUDY QUESTIONS

1. What are the merits and disadvantages of whole wheat flour in baked products?

2. Describe the milling process and explain how the streams used in making various flours influence the characteristics of the resulting flours.

3. Identify the three overall categories of proteins in flour. What proteins are included in each category? What is the contribution of each category to baked products?

4. Describe both fractions of protein constituting gluten and explain how each contributes to the behavior of gluten in batters and doughs.

5. How may flours from cereals other than wheat be used in baked products? Why might there be an advantage in including triticale flour, cornmeal, rye flour, soy flour, and potato flour?

6. Briefly explain the roles of each of the following in baked products: flour, liquid, eggs, fats, sugar, salt, and leavening agents.

7. Compare the effectiveness of air, steam, and carbon dioxide as leaveners in baked products.

8. Although most yeast breads are made with *Saccharomyces cerevisiae,* a few are made with *Saccharomyces exigus* and *Saccharomyces inusitatus.* Why?

9. Why is *Lactobacillus sanfrancisco* not used alone as a source of leavening?

10. What are the characteristics of an ideal baking powder? Evaluate SAS-phosphate baking powder against the criteria.

BIBLIOGRAPHY

Berglund, P. T. and Hertsgaard, D. M. 1986. "Uses of vegetable oils at reduced levels in cake, pie crust, cookies, and muffins." *J. Food Sci. 51* (3): 640.

Bernardin, J. E. and Kasarda, D. D. 1973. "Hydrated protein fibrils from wheat endosperm." *Cereal Chem. 50:* 529.

Bernardin, J. E. and Kasarda, D. D. 1973. "Microstructure of wheat protein fibrils." *Cereal Chem. 50:* 535.

Bietz, J. A. and Walls, J. S. 1972. "Wheat gluten subunits: molecular weights determined by sodium dodecyl sulfate-polyacrylamide gel electrophoresis." *Cereal Chem. 49.* 416.

Bietz, J. A., et al. 1973. "Glutenin." *Baker's Digest 47* (1): 26.

Birch, G. G. and Lindley, M. G. eds. 1986. *Interactions of Food Components.* Elsevier: New York.

Bloksma, A. H. 1975. "Thiol and disulfide groups in dough rheology." *Cereal Chem. 52.* 170.

Chang, K. C., et al. 1986. "Production and nutritional evaluation of high-protein rice flour." *J. Food Sci. 51* (2): 464.

Chauhan, G. S., Eskin, N. A. M., and Tkachuk, R. 1992. "Nutrients and antinutrients in quinoa seed." *Cereal Chem. 69* (1): 85.

Clark, J. P. 1986. "Texturization processes in cereal foods industry." *Food Technol. 40* (3): 91.

Claus, W. S. and Brooks, E. M. 1965. "Some physical, chemical, and baking characteristics of instantized wheat flours." *Cereal Sci. Today 10:* 41.

Conn, J. 1980. "Chemical leavening systems in food products." *Cereal Foods World 26* (3): 119.

Deman, J. M. 1980. *Principles of Food Chemistry.* AVI Publishing: Westport CT.

de Tonella, M. L. and Yepiz, M. S. 1986. "Effects of lysine and methionine fortification on dough and bread characteristics." *J. Food Sci. 51* (3): 637.

Dutson, T. R. and Orcutt, M. W. 1984. "Chemical changes in proteins produced by thermal processing," *J. Chem. Educ. 61* (4): 303.

Ewart, J. A. D. 1972. "Recent research in dough visco-elasticity." *Baker's Digest 46* (4): 22.

Fretzdorff, B. and Brummer, J. M. 1992. "Reduction of phytic acid during breadmaking of whole-meal breads." (Abstract) *Cereal Foods 37* (2): 228.

Gates, J. C. 1987. *Basic Foods,* 3rd ed. Holt, Rinehart, & Winston: New York.

Haber, J., et al. 1976. "Hard red wheat, rye, and triticale." *Baker's Digest 50* (6): 24.

Hautera, P. and Lovgren, T. 1975. "Fermentation activity of baker's yeast—its variation during storage." *Baker's Digest 49* (3): 36.

He, B. and Hoseney, R. C. 1992a. "Factors controlling gas retention in nonheated doughs." *Cereal Chem. 69* (1): 1.

He, H. and Hoseney, R. C. 1992b. "Effect on quantity of wheat flour protein on bread loaf volume." *Cereal Chem. 69* (1): 17.

Hood, M. P. and Lowe, B. 1948. "Air, water vapor, and carbon dioxide as leavening gases in cakes made with different types of fats." *Cereal Chem. 25:* 244.

Hoseney, R. C. 1979. "Dough forming properties." *J. Am. Oil Chem. Soc. 56:* 78A.

Hoseney, R. C. ed. 1986. *Principles of Cereal Science and Technology.* American Association of Cereal Chemists: St. Paul, MN.

Hoseney, R. C. and Finney, K. F. 1971. "Functional (breadmaking) and biochemical properties of wheat flour components. XI. Review." *Baker's Digest 45* (4): 30.

Hoseney, R. C. and Seib, P. A. 1973. "Structural differences in hard and soft wheat." *Baker's Digest 47* (6): 26.

Hosomi, K., Nishio, K., and Matsumoto, H. 1992. "Studies on frozen dough baking. I. Effects of egg yolk and sugar ester." *Cereal Chem. 69* (1): 89.

Huebner, F. R. 1977. "Wheat flour proteins and their functionality in baking." *Baker's Digest 51* (5): 25.

Kent-Jones, D. W. and Amos, A. J. 1967. "Composition of wheat and products of milling." In *Modern Cereal Chemistry.* Food Trade Press: London, 211.

Kahn, K. and Bushuk, W. 1978. "Glutenin: Structure and functionality in breadmaking." *Baker's Digest 52* (2): 14.

Kichline, T. P. and Conn, J. F. 1970. "Some fundamental aspects of leavening agents." *Baker's Digest 44* (4): 36.

Kline, L. and Sugihara, T. F. 1971. "Microorganisms of San Francisco sour dough bread process." *Appl. Microbiol. 21:* 459.

Krull, L. H. and Wall, J. S. 1969. "Relationship of amino acid composition and wheat protein properties." *Baker's Digest 43* (4): 30.

Lambert, L. L. P., Gordon, J., and Davis, E. A. 1992. "Water loss and structure development in model cake systems heated by microwave and convection methods." (Abstract) *Cereal Foods 37* (2): 229.

Lin, J. C., et al. 1986. "Sensory and nutritional evaluation of wheat bread supplemented with single cell protein from torula yeast." *J. Food Sci. 51* (3): 647.

Lindahl, L. and Eliasson, A. C. 1992. "Comparison of some rheological properties of durum and wheat flour doughs." *Cereal Chem. 69* (1): 30.

Lorenz, K. J. 1975. "Irradiations of cereal grains and cereal grain products." *CRC Crit. Rev. Food Sci. Nutr. 6:* 317.

Lorenz, K. J., et al. 1972. "Comparative mixing and baking properties of wheat and triticale flour." *Cereal Chem. 49:* 187.

Lowe, B. 1955. *Experimental Cookery.* 4th ed. Wiley: New York.

Luh, B. S. and Liu, Y. K. 1980. "Rice flours in baking." In *Rice: Production and Utilization.* Luh, B. S., ed. AVI Publishing: Westport, CT, p. 85.

Maoffin, C. D. and Hoseney, R. C. 1974. "Review of fermentation." *Baker's Digest 48* (6): 22.

McCullough, M. A., et al. 1986. 1943. "High fructose corn syrup replacement for sucrose in shortened cakes." *J. Food Sci. 51* (2): 536.

McKim, E. and Moss H. V. 1943. "Observations on the pH of chemically leavened products." *Cereal Chem. 20:* 250.

Mecham, D. K. 1972. "Flour proteins and their behavior in doughs." *Cereal Sci. Today 17:* 208.

Mecham, D. K. 1973. "Wheat and flour proteins." *Baker's Digest 47* (10): 24.

Morrison, W. R. 1976. "Lipids in flour, dough and bread." *Baker's Digest 50* (1): 29.

Oomah, B. D. 1983. "Baking and related properties of wheat–oat composite flours." *Cereal Chem. 60* (1): 220.

Oszlanyi, A. G. 1980. "Instant yeast." *Baker's Digest 54* (8): 16.

Paul, P. C. and Palmer, H. H. 1972. *Food Theory and Applications.* Wiley: New York.

Pomeranz, Y. 1986. *Advances in Cereal Science and Technology III.* American Association of Cereal Chemists: St. Paul, MN.

Pomeranz, Y. 1973. "From wheat to bread: biochemical study." *Am. Sci. 61:* 683.

Pomeranz, Y. 1985. *Functional Properties of Food Components.* Academic Press: Orlando, FL.

Pomeranz, Y. 1966. "Soy flour in breadmaking." *Baker's Digest 40* (3): 44.

Pomper, S. 1969. "Biochemistry of yeast fermentation." *Baker's Digest 43* (2): 32.

Pyler, E. J. 1988. *Baking Science and Technology.* 3rd ed. Vol. 1. Sosland Publishing: Merriam, KS.

Raidl, M. A. and Klein, B. P. 1983. "Effects of soy or field pea flour substitution on physical and sensory characteristics of chemically leavened quick breads." *Cereal Chem. 60:* 367.

Ranhotra, G. S., Gelroth, J. A., Glaster, B. K., and Posner, E. S. 1992. "Total and soluble fiber content of air-classified white flour from hard and soft wheats." *Cereal Chem. 69* (1): 75.

Reiman, H. M. 1977. "Chemical leavening systems." *Baker's Digest 51* (4): 33.

Trivedi, N. B., et al. 1984. "Development and applications of quick-rising yeast." *Food Technol. 38* (6): 51.

Tsen, C. C. and Hoover, W. J. 1973. "High-protein bread from wheat flour fortified with full-fat soy flour." *Cereal Chem. 50:* 7.

Tsen, C. C., et al. 1973. "Baking quality of triticale flours." *Cereal Chem. 50:* 16.

Webster, F. H. ed. 1986. *Oats: Chemistry and Technology.* American Association of Cereal Chemists: St. Paul, MN.

White, J. W., Jr. 1978. "Honey." *Adv. Food Res. 24:* 304.

Wilson, C. M. 1992. "Zeins in Sweet Corn (Sugary-1)." *Cereal Chem. 69* (1). 113.

CHAPTER 18

Baking Applications

The variations are countless, but the diverse baked goods that can be made and that are popular throughout this country and in many other parts of the world as well can be divided into breads (quick and yeast), pastry (plain and puff), cakes (foam and shortened), and cookies (drop, rolled, and bar). The unique aspects of these categories are explored in this chapter from the context of the ingredients, their functions, the techniques used to make the batter or dough, and changes in baking.

QUICK BREADS

Types

Several different products are classified as quick breads, and many variations of each are familiar. These include muffins, biscuits, popovers, cream puffs, waffles, pancakes, and cake doughnuts. This variety of products is the result of differences in actual ingredients and their ratios, methods of mixing, and ways of baking.

Ingredients

Variations in the ingredients and their proportions are responsible for many of the unique qualities of specific quick breads. Only three ingredients (flour, liquid, and salt) are common to all quick breads, and the ratio of flour to liquid is quite different from one type of quick bread to another (Table 18.1).

    In most instances, the flour used in **quick breads** is all-purpose, but some rich coffee cakes are made using cake flour. A variety of grain flours may be used to supplement wheat flour and modify texture and flavor as well as color. These flours are most likely to be found in muffins, but pancakes and waffles sometimes include them too.

Quick Breads
Breads leavened primarily with a leavening agent other than yeast, ordinarily by either steam or carbon dioxide generated from reaction of an acid and an alkali.

415

Table 18.1   Relative Proportions of Ingredients in Basic Quick Breads on the Basis of Volume

Quick Bread	Flour (c)	Liquid (c)	Fat (tbsp)	Sugar (tbsp)	Eggs	Baking Powder (tsp)	Salt (tsp)
Popovers	1	1	0[a]	0	2	0	0.5
Cream puffs	1	1[b]	8	0	4	0	0.25
Waffles	1	0.9	4.25	0.4	0.8	1.6	0.2
Pancakes	1	0.8	1.66	0.5	0.8	2.4	0.5
Muffins	1	0.5	2	2	0.5	1.5	0.5
Biscuits	1	0.38	2.66	0	0	1.5	0.25
Cake doughnuts	1	0.14	0.09	0.2	0.9	0.9	0.14

[a]Oil is used to grease cups if needed, but is not in the batter.
[b]Liquid is boiling water; all other liquids are milk.
Adapted from McWilliams, M. *Illustrated Guide to Food Preparation*, 8th ed.; Plycon Press: Redondo Beach, CA, 1998.

Most commonly the liquid in quick breads is milk, although fruit juices, water, or even such moisture-laden vegetables as zucchini may be the liquid used in a recipe. Coffee cakes, muffins, and loaves of quick breads are the types of quick breads most likely to incorporate these variations in liquid.

The type of fat used and the way it is incorporated vary considerably from one type of quick bread to another. Butter or margarine frequently is the choice because of the pleasing color and flavor contributions. When the muffin method of mixing is used, this hard fat is melted. As a convenience in making muffins, pancakes, loaves of quick breads, or other types of quick breads where liquid fat is needed, salad oil may be the choice rather than melted butter or margarine. Hydrogenated shortening usually is chosen for making biscuits because of its ability to be cut into pieces. It also is the choice in making some quick bread loaves in which the fat is creamed with sugar.

Mixing Methods

Most recipes for quick breads are made by one of three basic methods: biscuit method, muffin method, or conventional method. The method used is dictated by the manner in which the fat is distributed. In the biscuit method, a solid fat is cut into small pieces. The liquid fat is dispersed with the other liquid ingredients in the muffin method. A plastic, hard fat is creamed with the sugar in the conventional method.

Biscuit Method
Mixing method in which the dry ingredients are combined, the fat is cut into small particles in the flour mixture, all of the liquid is added at once and stirred in just to blend, and the dough is kneaded; a flaky product results.

Biscuit Method.   In the **biscuit method** one begins by sifting the dry ingredients together, and then adding shortening or other solid fat, which is cut with a pastry blender into particles about the size of rice grains (using a light, lifting motion to cut in the fat). Finally, the liquid is added all at once, and the mixture is stirred carefully with a fork to just moisten the dry ingredients. In doughs made by this method, gentle kneading is the final step prior to shaping and baking. The final product has a flaky texture.

Fat is cut in to promote a flaky texture, but much of the tenderizing potential from the fat is not available. All of the fat that is on the interior of each flour-coated piece is unable to come in contact with and lubricate the flour proteins during mixing. The kneading action in making biscuits is basically a folding action, which also promotes the development of flaky layers. In the oven, the fat gradually melts and spreads out, leaving a space where steam and carbon dioxide (from baking powder) can collect and expand.

Muffin Method. Muffins and some other comparatively simple quick breads are made by an extremely quick method—the **muffin method.** In this method, all of the dry ingredients are sifted together into one mixing bowl. The liquid ingredients (which include either oil or melted fat) are blended together thoroughly in a second bowl prior to being added all at once to the dry ingredients. A brief stirring, done efficiently with a wooden spoon, completes the preparation for baking. Baked products prepared by the muffin method have a somewhat coarse, open texture and may be slightly crumbly.

Conventional Method. For a fine texture, tender crumb, and good keeping qualities, the **conventional method** of mixing usually is best. The first step, creaming of the solid fat and sugar, is followed by addition of the beaten egg. The dry ingredients are added, a third at a time, followed by brief mixing and alternated with two additions of milk (half of the liquid at each addition). This method is definitely more labor intensive than the muffin method, but the results are optimal, especially for quick breads containing fairly high proportions of sugar and fat.

Selected Examples of Quick Breads

Popovers. Popovers are a quick bread with a high liquid-to-flour ratio (in fact, equal volumes are used), the result of which is a very fluid batter. In such a dilute flour mixture, gluten does not develop readily with mixing so there is no reason to be concerned about the amount of beating that is required to make a perfectly smooth batter. The large amount of liquid allows gelatinization of the starch in the flour during baking, which is evidenced by the slightly gel-like interior walls in baked popovers. This liquid also is critical to the production of a large quantity of steam to help create the very large cavity expected in the interior of popovers. Although some air is incorporated into the batter during beating, the fluid state of the batter releases most of the air, leaving almost all of the leavening task to steam, which is created rapidly during the early part of the baking period in a preheated, very hot (220°C) oven, or in an oven reaching 220°C within 5 minutes.

The structure of popovers is due largely to the high content of egg proteins and starch from the flour. Expansion is possible because the steam generated in baking presses against the cell walls while the egg proteins are still not coagulated and the small amount of gluten that is present is still extensible. If an inadequate quantity of egg is used, popovers will be quite compact and spongy in the center and will lack the expected large cavity. This problem clearly illustrates the importance of egg proteins in the structure of popovers. Egg white proteins, in particular, are important to the popping action in the center of popovers. A practical rule of thumb is that at least two large or three medium eggs are needed per cup of flour in a popover batter (see Figure 18.1).

The depth of pans is important to successful popping action, too. Popover pans are approximately twice as deep as muffin pans. This depth permits generation of steam to create interior pressure before the egg proteins become rigid and before the starch is gelatinized. In the absence of popover pans, custard cups provide a suitable alternative. The oven should be preheated to ensure rapid generation of steam and popping of the uncoagulated popovers.

Muffin Method
Mixing method in which the dry ingredients are sifted together in one bowl, the liquid ingredients (including fat) are mixed in another bowl and then poured into the dry ingredients, and the mixture is stirred briefly and baked; the result is a rather coarse, slightly crumbly product that stales readily.

Conventional Method
Mixing method in which fat and sugar are creamed, beaten eggs are added, and dry ingredients (a third at a time) and liquid ingredients (half at each addition) are added alternately; fine texture and excellent keeping qualities are advantages of this laborious method.

Popover
Quick bread made with equal volumes of flour and liquid, including at least two large eggs per cup of flour, and baked in deep cups in an oven preheated to 220°C.

Figure 18.1   Eggs, particularly the whites, are essential to the formation of a large cavity in popovers during baking. (Courtesy of Plycon Press.)

Other factors that may interfere with achievement of the desired large interior cavity are related to ingredients. If too much liquid is present in relation to the amount of flour, the protein structure will be too weak and will release the expanding steam without having gotten hot enough to coagulate the protein and maintain the expanded structure. The presence of too much fat in the greased cups can also weaken the structure of popovers and allow the steam to escape prematurely.

When ingredient proportions are right, the batter is beaten until smooth, and the batter is baked in appropriate pans in a preheated oven, the resulting popover should be ideal. It will have a very large volume and a large interior cavity. The interior will be very slightly moist, and the popover will be crisp.

Cream Puff
Quick bread containing a very great quantity of fat and eggs that puffs remarkably as a result of the steam generated during baking at 232°C for 15 minutes and at 163°C for 25 minutes.

Cream Puffs.   **Cream puffs** are classified as a quick bread despite their normal function as an edible container for either an appetizer or a dessert. Although their appearance is somewhat reminiscent of popovers and their liquid-to-flour ratio is the same as that for popovers, there are some very significant differences between these two distinctive quick breads. Cream puffs, unlike popovers with essentially no fat, contain half as much fat as liquid (Table 18.1). To bind this large quantity of fat, a large number of eggs (four per cup of flour) must be included in the recipe to aid in emulsifying the fat and the boiling water. Much of the liquid is bound in the gelatinizing starch during preparation of the paste; the gelatinized starch paste also helps to prevent the oil-in-water emulsion from breaking.

Preparation of cream puffs is begun by adding the flour and salt to the mixture of boiling water and melted fat, stirring vigorously while heating the paste until the starch gelatinizes and a ball of paste forms. Care must be taken to avoid having excessive evaporation of water during this period, for inadequate water will cause the emulsion to break and the fat to separate from the paste. Each egg is beaten into the cooling paste to enhance the emulsion (see Chapter 16) that already exists in the paste and to increase the liquid level very slightly. If the emulsion breaks, it must be reformed by replacing the moisture that has been lost. By adding water slowly and stirring it in until the paste once again assumes its shiny, smooth surface appearance, a broken emulsion can be reformed with no damage to the quality of the finished cream puff.

Baking is done after small mounds of dough have been piped onto a nonstick baking sheet and placed in a preheated over at 232°C (450°F) for 15 minutes, followed by an additional 25 minutes at 163°C (325°F) to allow time for heat to penetrate to the interior and coagulate the protein structure. The large amount of steam generated in the puffs by this intense heat is able to expand the puffs, creating a large interior cavity before the proteins (particularly those in the egg whites) lose their ability to stretch as they are coagulated.

Cream puffs should have a pleasing, golden brown surface, and the volume should be large in proportion to the amount of dough used to form the cream puff; the interior should be only moderately moist, and the cavity should be large. The most likely problem in making cream puffs is failure to puff and create the desired interior cavity. This most commonly is the result of a broken emulsion, a problem evidenced either before or during baking by fat visibly oozing from the dough. The usual reason for a broken emulsion is too much evaporation from the dough, probably during the gelatinization of starch before the eggs are added. It is imperative that the emulsion be reformed by stirring in enough water to reestablish the emulsion prior to baking. If a cream puff dough is too soft, the steam will not be able to be trapped in the baking puff long enough for the expanded structure to set; escape of the steam through broken cell walls deflates the cavity, and a compact puff is the result. Too low an oven temperature also can cause problems because of failure to generate enough pressure from steam before the proteins coagulate and lose their elasticity.

Muffins.   **Muffins** contain a ratio of two parts flour to one part milk (Table 18.1); other ingredients are fat, sugar, egg, baking powder, and salt. These ingredients are mixed by the muffin method described earlier in this chapter. Eggs need to be beaten thoroughly, yet not whipped into a foam. Thorough beating ensures that the eggs blend completely with the other liquid ingredients, thus avoiding areas in the baked muffin where the egg protein is concentrated. Inadequate beating of the egg causes some thick cell walls and a somewhat waxy character where the concentrated egg protein is found. There is no need to beat the eggs to a foam, because adequate leavening is available from the steam and carbon dioxide generated from the baking powder.

The extent of mixing is of paramount importance in determining the characteristics of muffins. The very sticky nature of the batter facilitates rapid gluten development when the ingredients are stirred together. The appearance of the batter changes quickly during mixing. It begins with a very lumpy batter in which big clumps of dry ingredients are encased by the liquid and developing gluten. If the batter containing these large lumps is baked, the volume of the muffins produced will be poor, because not all of the baking powder will have been moistened enough to react completely. They also will be very crumbly as the result of inadequate gluten development to hold the structure together (see Figure 18.2).

Muffin
Small, rounded quick bread baked from a batter containing a 2:1 flour-to-liquid ratio, plus egg, fat, sugar, baking powder, and salt.

Figure 18.2 Effects of the extent of mixing of muffin batter: (left) undermixed; (center) optimum mixing: (right) overmixed. (Courtesy of Plycon Press.)

With only a bit more stirring with a wooden spoon, the batter will still be noticeably lumpy, but there will not be any large aggregates of dry ingredients. After a total usually of 25 strokes, sufficient mixing has been done to achieve this appearance, and the batter is ready to be spooned into greased muffin cups and baked at 218°C (425°F) until the crust is a golden brown (usually about 20 minutes).

If stirring is continued beyond this point, excessive gluten development results. The batter gradually becomes smooth, and development of tenacious gluten strands can be noted if the batter is allowed to flow from the spoon. The volume of the batter begins to be reduced as a result of the loss of some air and the release of a little carbon dioxide from the baking powder at room temperature.

With overmixing, the surface of muffins begins to be increasingly smooth as mixing proceeds until the baked crust looks very much like the crust of yeast rolls. Instead of having a nicely rounded top, overmixed muffins exhibit a peaked or pointed appearance. When these overmixed muffins are cut in half to reveal a vertical cross section that intersects the highest point of the peak, tunnels converging on the peak are evident, and the texture between the tunnels is fairly fine. The tunnels develop as steam and carbon dioxide collect in a few areas and begin to exert pressure against the cell walls. As the batter is heated most quickly near the outer edges and on the bottom, the protein structure coagulates and loses its ability to stretch in these regions first, leaving the center and upper region elastic until somewhat later. This continuing elasticity permits the gluten in the center and upper region to stretch upward with the pressure from the leavening gases; the strength of the gluten strands is sufficient to channel the expansion upward, resulting in the development of tunnels when the gluten is overdeveloped. A deep pan is a bit more likely to promote gluten development than is a regular muffin pan. Sometimes muffins baked at excessively high temperatures have an increased tendency to develop tunnels, but this does not always promote tunnel development. Overmixing is guaranteed to create tunnels. The likelihood of tunnels in muffins is reduced by the use of either whole wheat or some other type of flour to supplement all-purpose flour. The increased cellulose and other fiber from whole wheat and the lack of gluten in the other cereal flours interfere with gluten development a bit, making the formation of tunnels unlikely.

Biscuits.   In **biscuit** doughs, the ratio of flour to liquid varies somewhat with the flour, but is in the vicinity of three parts flour to one part liquid (3:1), making this dough much less sticky than muffin batter. This means that gluten does not develop as readily in biscuits as in muffins. Because of this difference, biscuits ordinarily are stirred about 25 strokes with a table fork and then gently kneaded 10 to 20 times with the fingertips prior to rolling and baking. Unless the dough is stirred adequately and kneaded sufficiently, the desired flaky texture may not be achieved because of a lack of gluten development. This amount of manipulation, though definitely greater than recommended for muffins, is necessary because of the comparatively slow rate of gluten development in biscuit dough. However, too much mixing causes toughness and humping of the crust.

Sour milk and soda are the source of carbon dioxide in some biscuit recipes, more commonly in drop than in rolled biscuits. When these recipes produce a slightly acidic dough, the biscuits are snowy white inside, in contrast to the somewhat yellow color that develops in a slightly alkaline dough. Use of buttermilk fosters the desirable white color. On the other hand, high levels of baking powder promote a somewhat creamy color because of the mildly alkaline residue. Thiamine retention is enhanced by using either buttermilk or sour milk with no excess of soda, or a minimum of baking powder to keep the dough close to a neutral pH.

Biscuit
Quick bread with a ratio of about 3:1 (flour to liquid) and also containing fat cut into small particles, baking powder, and salt; usually kneaded and rolled, but sometimes dropped.

YEAST BREADS

Ingredients

The functions of flour, liquid, salt, sugar, and yeast were discussed in Chapter 17. These are the basic ingredients in yeast breads, yet this rather simple combination forms a type of food so basic that it is referred to as "the staff of life." The proportions of these ingredients can be compared conveniently by expressing them as percentages of the weight of flour, the basic ingredient. On this basis, the range of quantities of the different ingredients can be viewed to gain some perspective on the formulas used for making yeast breads (Table 18.2).

Yeast breads can be made without any fat, but the crust and the crumb will be a bit hard and crisp. This characteristic is sought deliberately in formulating French bread and a few related specialty breads, but some fat is added to most other breads to tenderize the product. Up to a maximum of 3 percent, adding fat increases volume (Pomeranz et al., 1969). Shortening improves the keeping quality

Table 18.2   Amounts of Ingredients Relative to Flour in Yeast Breads

Ingredient	Percentage of the Weight of Flour (range)
Flour (all-purpose)	100
Fat	2–6
Liquid	60–65
Sugar	2–6
Salt	1.5–2
Yeast	1–6

Based on Lowe, B. *Experimental Cookery*, 4th ed.; Wiley: New York, 1955.

of bread as it is spread throughout the mixture and coats the gluten and starch. Emulsifying agents may be used at levels up to 20 percent of the weight of the fat as an aid in dispersing the fat on the gluten strands and starch during mixing. Mono- and diglycerides and lecithin are effective for this role in bread.

The amount of liquid in proportion to flour that is optimum varies with the individual flour, with flours made from soft wheat requiring less liquid than those from hard wheats. The elasticity, extensibility, and strength of bread doughs increase with increasing liquid up to a point, after which these qualities decline. In a classic study, Bailey and LeVesconte in 1924 found this maximum liquid content to be 64 percent, but this value may vary in the range 60 to 65 percent depending on the flour used.

Whole milk often is the liquid used in making yeast breads. Although milk is more than 87 percent water, its content of fat, protein, and lactose adds pleasing textural qualities to the bread. However, the milk used in making bread dough should be scalded to at least 92°C (198°F) for a minute, or it can be held at a slightly lower temperature for a longer time. Failure to heat the milk sufficiently results in a sticky dough and a baked product low in volume and rather coarse in texture. Apparently this brief heating denatures some of the protein, possibly one in the serum protein fraction, that is responsible for the negative effect that unscalded milk has on yeast breads. Bakers who add dry milk solids experience similar problems unless the milk has been heat processed adequately prior to drying. It is imperative that scalded milk be cooled to a temperature that is safe for the yeast before being combined with the yeast.

The content of sugar in yeast breads is variable, but may be as high as 16 percent in some sweet bread recipes. When the level of sugar is between 3 and 6 percent of the weight of the flour, fermentation is optimum, and the volume is at a maximum. Below or above this percentage, volume decreases. Sucrose, fructose, glucose, and invert sugar are fermented at about the same rate, but maltose and lactose are not fermented as well by yeast.

Inclusion of between 1.5 and 2 percent salt in a yeast dough reduces the rate of fermentation appropriately, allowing time for development of flavor in the dough and strengthening of the gluten. Too much salt, because of its osmotic effect, impairs the yeast fermentation process and slows carbon dioxide production. The result is a compact, firm bread. If salt is not added, fermentation proceeds too rapidly. This produces a bread that is coarse.

The form of the yeast dictates the temperature that should be used to disperse and hydrate the yeast in water prior to its addition to the other ingredients. Compressed yeast cakes are rather heat sensitive, and the temperature of the hydrating water should not exceed 37°C, which is body temperature. When active dry yeast is manufactured, the outer membrane enclosing the contents of the yeast cell is altered and becomes rather permeable, which facilitates loss of the components within the cells unless the temperature of rehydration is controlled carefully. The water should be between 40 and 46°C (105 and 115°F) if the permeability of the cell wall is to be controlled and prevent the loss of **glutathione,** the sulfhydryl-containing compound thought to be responsible for the very sticky nature of yeast doughs made with active dry yeast that has been rehydrated below 40°C. Temperatures above 46°C are likely to kill the yeast, which will cause either very slow fermentation or no fermentation, depending on the severity of the temperature insult. Quick-rise active dry yeast requires the same temperature controls as active dry yeast.

Glutathione
Peptide (γ-glutamylcysteinylglycine) that occurs in yeast cells and apparently is capable of passing through the cell walls of active dry yeast that has been hydrated below 40°C, causing stickiness in the yeast dough:

Dynamics in Mixing and Kneading

Mixing is done to distribute ingredients as uniformly as possible into the dough and to permit incorporation of an adequate amount of flour in relation to the level of liquid in the mixture. This liquid combines with flour to begin to hydrate damaged starch granules and also to lubricate gliadin and glutenin in preparation for developing the gluten complex needed for optimal texture and volume in the finished product. Glutenin (the elongated and quite fibrous protein in wheat flour) molecules appear to join to each other (Shewry et al., 1984), by forming disulfide (—S–S—) linkages. These polymerized units of glutenin are called **concatenations.** However, too much mixing causes some of the polymers of glutenin to dissociate, which reduces elasticity and results in a less desirable texture in the baked bread. Mixing brings glutenin concatenations (Schofield, 1986) not only into contact with each other, but also into contact with gliadin, the sticky, fluid protein. These two components then become intermeshed (Ewart, 1979) to form a continuous network, the gluten complex. Starch granules then become imbedded in this matrix as kneading progresses (Figure 18.3). Although it is possible for machine kneading to eventually physically break up part of the matrix, kneading by hand is not vigorous enough to cause this problem.

Bread doughs are usually made using the **straight-dough method** when prepared in homes and restaurants. This method requires scalding the milk and temperature control during hydration of the yeast and preparation of the dough. All of the ingredients are combined prior to the fermentation and proofing when the straight dough method is used. Considerable kneading is required to develop the gluten adequately for optimum texture when making bread by this method. A strong mixer with a dough hook or a food processor can be used satisfactorily if the baker does not wish to knead the dough extensively and vigorously by hand.

Concatenation
A linking together; nonspecific description of the association of glutenin molecules by disulfide linkages.

Straight-dough Method
Method of mixing yeast breads in which all of the ingredients are added, mixed, and kneaded prior to fermentation and proofing.

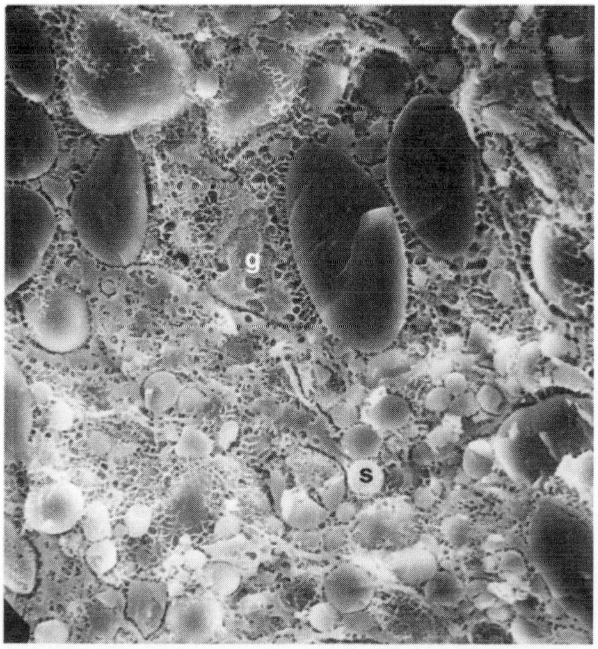

Figure 18.3 Starch granules (s) embedded in developing gluten matrix (g) (SEM 1,200X). (Courtesy of Dr. T. P. Freeman and *Food Technology 45* (3): 162–168. 1995. Copyright (c) by Institute of Food Technologists.)

Sponge Method
Method of mixing yeast breads in which the yeast, liquid, and part of the flour are mixed and fermented to make a sponge before the rest of the ingredients are added; used commercially with strong flours.

Commercial bakeries often use the **sponge method** to prepare breads. This mixing method begins with the mixing of liquid, yeast, and part of the flour (as well as possibly part of the sugar). This mixture is then allowed to ferment until it becomes quite spongy. Then the remaining ingredients are mixed in. The proofing time for breads made by the sponge method is somewhat shortened because of the fermentation that occurs when the initial mixture is developing its spongy character as the yeast produces carbon dioxide. Strong flours (e.g., bread flour) are necessary for successful use of the sponge method. The flavor of breads made with the sponge method is a bit more yeast-like than is true for those made by the straight-dough method.

Actions in Baking

Remarkable changes occur in the dough during baking as a result of the impact of the very hot oven (204–218°C). The initial phase of baking effects a rather dramatic increase in volume, the result of increased production of carbon dioxide because of the acceleration of yeast growth. This rather abrupt expansion is designated as *oven spring* and is also caused by the expansion of the existing carbon dioxide in the dough. The volume increase from this phenomenon is appreciable; the final volume represents an increase of as much as 80 percent beyond the volume of the shaped dough when it was placed in the oven. If the oven temperature is significantly above 218°C, the final volume will be reduced because the crust denatures before the gases in the dough have had sufficient time to achieve their maximum leavening. Too cool an oven temperature allows time for too much expansion. The product has the potential for having a very porous texture or for being quite compact as a result of gluten strands being stretched so far before the protein structure is rigid that the gluten strands collapse, and much of the leavening is lost.

Oven Spring
An increase in volume of yeast breads during the early part of baking resulting from the expansion of carbon dioxide and the increased production of carbon dioxide stimulated by the oven heat; the volume increase is usually about 80 percent.

In the early part of baking, the oven heat causes the dough to become softer, making it easier for the leavening gases to stretch the gluten. This softening is due in part to increased amylase activity in converting some starch molecules to dextrins. There is some shifting of water from gluten to starch when the baking dough temperature rises above 60°C and gelatinization is initiated (Figure 18.4 a,b,c). Gelatinized starch contributes significantly to the structure of the baked bread. Another effect of the heat during baking is killing of the yeast at about 60°C. This prevents additional generation of carbon dioxide. Amylase also is inactivated, which halts the degradation of starch to dextrins.

Crust browning, an aesthetically important change during baking, is largely the result of the Maillard or carbonyl-amine reaction. Milk in the formula enhances browning because lactose is available for the reaction, whereas water does not provide this added sugar. Browning is hastened once the surface of the baking bread becomes comparatively dry by evaporation because the dry surface increases in temperature much more than it would if still moist. In fact, the crust temperature may approach 150°C, which accelerates the carbonyl-amine browning.

Flour Options

Although breads have been made with flours from various cereals for centuries, new impetus was given to the use of flour alternatives in bread making about 20 years ago, and the present concern over fitness and fiber has extended the variety still more. Fiber from a variety of sources may be added to bread. Triticale bran is

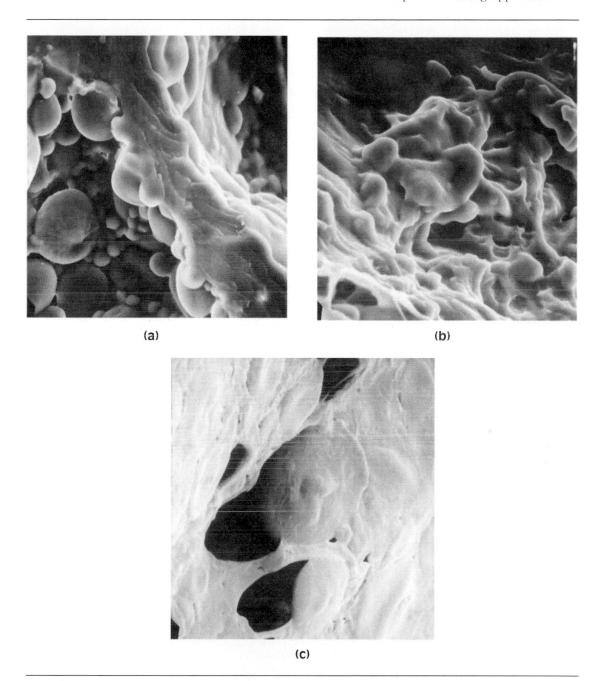

(a)

(b)

(c)

Figure 18.4 (a) Intact and gelatinized starch in the inner crust layer of bread (SEM 1,200X); (b) partially gelatinized starch granules in the center of a loaf of bread (SEM 120X); (c) gelatinized starch and thin strands separating air spaces in a loaf of bread (SEM 1,200X). (Courtesy of Dr. T. P. Freeman and *Food Technology 45* (3): 162–168, 1995. Copyright (c) Institute of Food Technologists.)

but one of the possibilities. Its use was studied by Lorenz (1976). Finely ground triticale bran can be added to a maximum level of 10 percent of the wheat flour and still receive sensory scores comparable to those of bread made without the bran; furthermore, even a level of 15 percent bran was satisfactory. The bran in the baked product was effective in retaining moisture longer and thus keeping the crumb softer. Bran of a coarser texture has a greater effect on texture than does a fine grind; its roughness can be detected on the tongue, and it also interferes somewhat with gluten development because of its cutting action during mixing. Wheat bran and microcrystalline celluloses can be used at a level of 7 percent (Pomeranz et al., 1977; see Figures 18.5 and 18.6).

Use of triticale flour in bread making also has been studied by Lorenz (1974). The quality of bread made entirely with triticale flour is better than that of bread made entirely with rye flour, but is not satisfactory. If sodium stearoyl-2-lactylate is added as a dough conditioner and mixing is reduced, the quality of triticale bread is improved. A shorter fermentation period also is helpful in enhancing the quality of bread made with triticale flour.

Soy flour is another product of nutritional interest in bread making. This flour may be either full-fat or defatted. If sodium stearoyl-2-lactylate is added to full-fat soy flour; as much as 24 percent soy flour can be used with acceptable results. In fact, the water-binding capability of the soy flour improves the softness of the

Figure 18.5 Interior view of whole wheat bread (1) and whole wheat bread supplemented with 7.5% of the following fibers; (2) flax hulls; (3) pea hulls; (4) coarse wheat bran; (5) sunflower hulls (coarse); and (6) cellulose. Flax was weak, darkest, reddest, and smallest; pea hulls produced a light color; cellulose was similar to whole wheat, according to judges. (Courtesy of A. M. Cadden, F. W. Sosulski, and J. P. Olson. University of Alberta. Reprinted from *Journal of Food Science*. 1983. Vol. 48: 1151. Copyright (c) by Institute of Food Technologists.)

Figure 18.6 Wheat bread containing 0% (a), 4% (b), and 8% (c) peanut hull flour. Even at 8% peanut hull flour, the bread was judged to be acceptable. Note the decreasing volume and the darkening of the bread as the percentage of wheat flour is reduced. (Courtesy of J. L. Collins, S. M. Kalantari, and A. R. Post. University of Tennessee. Reprinted from *Journal of Food Science.* 1982. Vol. 47: 1899. Copyright (c) by Institute of Food Technologists.)

crumb during storage compared with bread made using entirely wheat flour. One of the limiting factors in substitution with soy flour is the distinctive flavor, often described as beany, that can be detected at levels above 24 percent. **Sucroglycerides** are useful in offsetting the impact of soy flour in bread. Even with the use of dough conditioners, mixing time and fermentation time need to be shortened when soy flour is part of the formula. The remarkable ability of soy to absorb liquid also alters the amount of liquid required in relation to the flour.

Sucroglycerides
Sucrose esters (sucrose and glycerides or free fatty acids) used as a dough conditioner with soy flour.

Staling

Bread begins to undergo deteriorative changes commencing with removal from the oven. One of the first changes is thought to be retrogradation (increasing crystallinity caused by crosslinkage of molecules) of amylose released from starch granules during gelantization in the oven. The rather crystalline and firm character of the crumb that develops as bread is stored for a day or more may be the result of retrogradation within the starch granules and probably involves changes in the physical configuration of amylopectin (perhaps some folding of the branches and cross-linking of molecules). This retrogradation is reversible on reheating of the bread, but recurs when the warmed bread cools once again (Figure 18.7).

Moisture levels also are involved in the staling process. There is a reversal in the location of water; some of the water that migrated to starch from gluten during baking returns to the gluten proteins. Water also migrates from the center of the loaf toward the crust, causing the crust to gradually increase in leatheriness, while remaining rather soft. This migration occurs even when evaporation from the crust is prevented.

Storage temperature has an effect on staling. Refrigerator storage accelerates firming of the crumb compared with storage at a warm room temperature, the firmness after a day at 8°C being about the same as that after 6 days at 30°C. The advantage of refrigerator storage is only the inhibition of mold growth in breads made without preservatives. Freezer storage is effective in inhibiting the firming of the crumb.

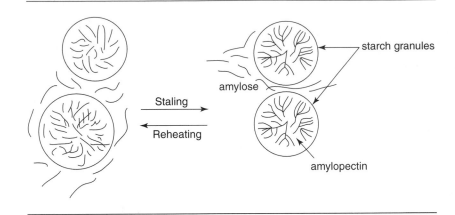

Figure 18.7 Diagram of possible changes during staling and reheating of bread.

Foam Cake
Cake featuring a large quantity of foam (usually egg white), which results in a light, airy batter and a baked cake with a some-what coarse texture with moderately large cells; angel, sponge, and chiffon cakes.

Angel Cake
Foam cake containing an egg white foam, sugar, and cake flour.

Sponge Cake
Foam cake containing an egg yolk foam, an egg white foam, sugar, and cake flour.

Chiffon Cake
Foam cake that includes oil and egg yolk as liquid in-gredients, an egg white foam, baking powder, sugar, and cake flour.

FOAM CAKES

Three subcategories of **foam cakes,** each with unique characteristics, are familiar in the United States. The simplest of these is angel or angel food cake. The others are sponge and chiffon cakes. The differences between these cakes result from in-gredient variations, as pointed out in Table 18.3. **Angel cake** basically is simply an egg white foam to which sugar and cake flour are added. **Sponge cake** contains two foams—an egg yolk foam and an egg white foam. Some liquid, sugar, and flour are other key ingredients. **Chiffon cakes** are the most complex of the foam cakes, for they contain oil and baking powder in addition to the ingredients in sponge cake. Angel cakes are white, whereas sponge cakes are yellow because of the egg yolk foam. Both of these foam cakes are leavened by air and steam only; thus the volume of the egg foams is of great consequence in determining the size and uniformity of the cells and the final cake volume. All of the foam cakes are quite delicate structurally when removed from the oven; therefore, they must be in-verted (suspended) during cooling to stretch the cells while the cell walls become cool and more rigid. Angel and sponge cakes are fairly tender; sponge cakes are a

Table 18.3 Comparison of Ingredients in Foam and Shortened Cakes

Ingredient	Foam Cakes			Shortened cakes	
	Angel	**Sponge**	**Chiffon**	**Layer**	**Pound**
Cake flour	1 c	1 c	1 c	1 c	1 c
Liquid	None	5 tbsp water	$5\frac{1}{3}$ tbsp water	8 tbsp milk	5 tbsp milk
Eggs	12 whites as foam	4 yolks, 4 whites as 2 foams	2 yolks; 4 whites as foam	1 whole beaten	2 whole, beaten
Fat	None	None	$3\frac{1}{3}$ tbsp oil	4 tbsp shortening	$8\frac{1}{2}$ tbsp butter
Sugar	12 tbsp	8 tbsp	11 tbsp	8 tbsp	9 tbsp
Baking powder	None	None	$1\frac{1}{4}$ tsp	1 tsp	None

little less tender than angel cakes because of the slight toughening provided by the yolks. Chiffon cakes are more tender than the other foam cakes because of the oil, which is very effective in tenderizing chiffon cakes.

Angel Cake

The basic ingredients in an angel cake are simply cake flour, sugar, egg white, and cream of tartar, and yet considerable variation in quality can result under varying conditions. When all-purpose flour is substituted for cake flour, the volume is smaller, the texture is more compact, and the cake may be less tender than a cake made with cake flour. This latter difficulty can be overcome by increasing the sugar a bit (see Figures 18.8 to 18.10).

Cream of tartar is important because of its action in stabilizing the egg white foam and in effecting a small reduction in the pH of the cake batter [between pH 5.2 and 6.0, according to Ash and Colmey (1973)]. As discussed in Chapter 15, adding cream of tartar at the foamy stage of beating egg whites delays foam formation and stabilizes the resulting foam. The smaller air cells that develop in a foam to which cream of tartar has been added are of merit in making an angel cake with a moderate cell size rather than the coarse texture that results when cream of tartar is omitted. The acidity of cream of tartar bleaches the flavonoid (anthoxanthin) pigments in flour, thus enhancing the whiteness desired in angel cake and avoiding the yellowish tint that is evident when the pH of the batter is higher. Cream of tar-

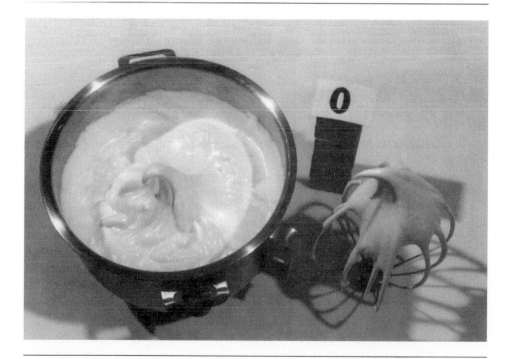

Figure 18.8   Typical peak formed by using sucrose in whipping an egg white foam (specific gravity = 0.193). (Courtesy of P. E. Coleman and C. A. Z. Harbers. Kansas State University. Reprinted from *Journal of Food Science*. 1983. Vol. 48: 452. Copyright (c) by Institute of Food Technologists.)

Figure 18.9 Typical peak formed by using all HFCS (high fructose corn syrup) in whipping an egg white foam (specific gravity = 0.183). (Courtesy of P. E. Coleman and C. A. Z. Harbers. Kansas State University. Reprinted from *Journal of Food Science*. 1983. Vol. 48: 452. Copyright (c) by Institute of Food Technologists.)

tar also exerts a tenderizing effect on angel cake, probably because of the improved stability of the foam and volume of the cake.

Sugar also helps to stabilize the foam and promote a finer texture in angel cakes. The levels of the ingredients in an angel cake influence the final cake. The larger the amount of flour relative to egg white, the less tender and drier the resulting angel cake. Lowe (1955) recommended the weight of flour be between 0.2 and 0.4 gram for each gram of egg white. Sugar usually is recommended at a level of one gram of sugar for one gram of egg white, although the level of sugar can be raised to a maximum of 1.25 grams if the cake is prepared at an altitude no higher than 1,000 feet and the maximum amount of flour is used to offset the tenderizing influence of the extra sugar. Too much sugar results in a somewhat crisp crust, with crystals of sugar giving a crystalline, rather shiny appearance to the crust (see Figure 18.11).

Volume is an important attribute of angel cakes. The quality and temperature of the egg whites are key factors determining the foam volume and, consequently, the cake volume achieved. Fresh eggs (Chapter 16) produce angel cakes of larger volume than older eggs. The reason for this difference has not been identified with certainty, although the likely factors are the rise in pH as an egg ages and the reduced amount of thick white and increased amount of thin white. Whites warmed to room temperature (21°C or 70°F) yield angel cake of maximum volume.

Oven temperature also influences the volume of angel cakes made with fresh egg whites. Volume is greatest when the cakes are baked at 218°C (425°F). At even

Figure 18.10 Angel cakes ranging from 0 to 100 percent HFCS (high fructose corn syrup) in combination with sucrose ranging from 100 to 0 percent. At 25% HFCS the cake was still satisfactory, but increasing levels caused browner crust, yellower crumb, firmer texture, and decreased sweetness. The beating time for the foams was decreased with higher levels of HFCS. (Courtesy of P. E. Coleman and C. A. Z. Harbers. Kansas State University. Reprinted from *Journal of Food Science*. 1983. Vol. 48: 452. Copyright (c) by Institute of Food Technologists.)

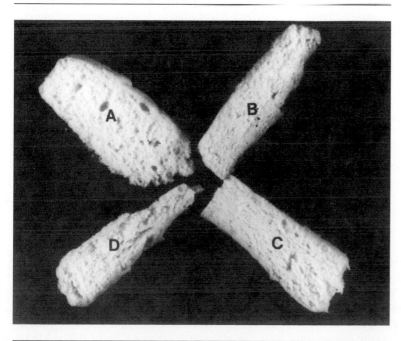

Figure 18.11 Cross-sectional view of model angel food cakes formulated with (A) liquid egg white, (B) Spherosil-QMA ion-exchange treated whey protein concentrate (63% protein, 20% lactose) replacing egg white, (C) 1:1 liquid egg white and reconstituted Spherosil-QMA whey protein concentrate, and (D) ultrafiltration whey protein concentrate. (Courtesy of C. V. Morr. Clemson University. Reprinted from *Journal of Food Science*. 1986. Vol. 51(4): 919. Copyright (c) by Institute of Food Technologists.)

higher temperatures, the volume is reduced, as is palatability. Between 177°C (350°F) and 281°C (425°F) volume increases consistently as temperature of the oven increases. However, the opposite effect is noted in angel cakes made using a commercial mix; an oven temperature of 177–191°C (350–375°F) yields better volume and palatability scores than are obtained at 204–218°C (400–425°F). Preheated ovens produce angel cakes of larger volumes than are reached by baking from a cold start.

The extent of beating of the egg white foam is of utmost importance in determining the volume of the foam and the angel cake into which the foam is incorporated. Underbeating of the whites causes a cake with a smaller volume than would be possible if the whites had been beaten more. This is due to the reduced amount of air introduced into the foam and the somewhat lower stability of the rather fluid foam, the result of limited denaturation of the egg white proteins during the brief period of beating. If the amount of beating is optimal so that the peaks just bend over (see Figure 18.8), the foam will have good stability, yet will retain the extensibility of the egg white proteins needed to stretch to a maximum during baking. Beating the egg whites to this point gives maximum volume in the baked cake, but it does not give the greatest volume possible during beating. However, it is the volume in the final product that is of greatest importance.

The various proteins that comprise egg white have somewhat different foaming properties and stability when beaten. When the various proteins were separated and beaten, the globulins foamed the best and also gave the largest volume when used to make angel cake (Johnson and Zabik, 1981). Ovalbumin also foamed very well and resulted in an angel cake that was somewhat smaller than the cake made with the globulin foam, but larger than one made with egg white (natural mixture of all white proteins). Angel cakes made with foams of lysozyme, ovomucoid, ovomucin, or conalbumin were smaller than the one made with the egg white mixture of proteins. However, a combination of lysozyme and ovomucin produced a larger angel cake than was obtained using either of these proteins separately.

If the whites are beaten until the peaks stand up straight, the volume of the foam will be greater than if they are beaten until the peaks bend over, but the stiff peak stage has reduced ability to stretch during baking because of the large amount of denaturation that has occurred in the egg white proteins by this stage of beating. Egg whites beaten to the stiff peak stage and beyond not only have reduced extensibility, but they also are difficult to fold with other ingredients. Their rather brittle nature at this stage causes many of the cells to break during the prolonged mixing needed to eliminate pieces of the egg white, and considerable air is lost from the foam, air that would have contributed to leavening during baking.

The level of sugar relative to flour influences volume, both because of the ability of the sugar to stabilize the egg white foam and because of the elevation of coagulation temperature of the egg white and gluten proteins as the level of sugar is increased. However, there must be a balance between these two ingredients, for too much sugar in relation to flour will elevate the coagulation temperature of the proteins to the point where some of the gluten strands break, and the cake begins to sag. The ratio of sugar to flour ordinarily should not exceed 3:1; a ratio of 2.5:1 is adequate, but will give a smaller volume than the higher level of sugar.

Use of all-purpose rather than cake flour reduces the volume and tenderness of angel cakes. The recommended amount of cake flour per gram of egg white is 0.2 to 0.4 gram, with the smaller amount promoting moistness and tenderness

(Lowe, 1955). The weight of sugar should not exceed the weight of the whites unless the flour is increased to the upper end of this range.

Sponge Cake

Angel and sponge cakes have many similarities, but the use of an egg yolk foam in addition to the white foam in sponge cakes adds unique aspects to sponge cakes. Sponge cakes contain both a very viscous egg yolk foam and a white foam.

Proper preparation of the egg yolk foam is a vital step in producing a high-quality sponge cake, and this foam requires considerably more beating than is required for the whites. Optimal results are obtained when the eggs are at room temperature or above. The specific gravity of the foam prepared from eggs that are at refrigerator temperature (1.7°C) will never be as low as can be achieved if the eggs are warmer when beating is initiated. The desired stage of beating an egg yolk foam is reached about twice as fast when the eggs are at 27°C (80°F) as at 4.4°C (40°F). Because a considerable amount of beating with an electric mixer is required to reach the appropriate foam stage for the yolks, there is a definite advantage in removing the eggs from the refrigerator well in advance of using them for beating the yolk foam.

The important steps to achieving quality in a sponge cake are the beating of the egg yolk foam and the subsequent beating of this foam after the addition of sugar and liquid until the mixture forms a very light foam. By extensive beating at this point, the yolk foam becomes sufficiently viscous to remain suspended in the white foam when they are folded together. The yolk foam also entraps a valuable quantity of air to aid in achieving a good volume and thin cell walls, a necessity for a tender sponge cake. After preparation of the egg yolk foam, the cake flour is folded into the yolks. Then the white foam is beaten until the peaks just bend over, at which point the yolk mixture is folded gently into the whites and transferred to a tube pan for baking, just as is done for angel cakes. The weak structure of sponge and other foam cakes makes it necessary to cool them in an inverted position so that the rather spongy cell walls are extended to their maximum. This enables the structure to become firm, with the cell walls being stretched as thin as possible.

Chiffon Cake

In some ways, chiffon cakes are hybrids between foam cakes and shortened cakes, for they do contain baking powder and fat (but in the form of a fluid oil). These ingredients promote tenderness and volume, yet the texture of the baked chiffon cake is neither as fine in cell size as shortened cakes nor as large as angel and sponge cakes.

The factors influencing the quality of angel cakes also are applicable to the quality of chiffon cakes. Much of the quality, particularly volume and tenderness, is influenced greatly by the quality of the egg white foam prepared in making a chiffon cake.

One of the important differences between chiffon cakes and the other two types of foam cake is the extent to which the egg whites are beaten. In both angel and sponge cakes, the tips of the whites should just bend over, but the peaks in a chiffon cake foam should stand up straight, yet not be dry or brittle. This extended beating is needed because the yolk mixture that is to be folded into it is extremely fluid and requires a great deal of folding before it can be dispersed uniformly and held within the white foam. Unless the white is beaten sufficiently and the yolk mixture is suspended throughout the whites, the yolks will drain to the bottom of the pan and form a rubbery layer.

SHORTENED CAKES

Ingredients

Shortened cakes are complex mixtures, and many variations are possible. Cake flour (bleached) is the flour of choice to produce a tender cake with a fine crumb. The smaller amount of protein and the more tender nature of this protein in comparison with the proteins in all-purpose flour are compatible with the qualities desired in a shortened cake (see Figure 18.12). Sugar, as discussed in Chapter 17, performs several critical roles in shortened cakes. Of particular interest is its role in influencing the volume of shortened cakes (see Figure 18.13). Because of its role in delaying gluten formation during mixing, the amount of mixing must be increased when the sugar level is increased. By increasing the mixing, the strength of the structure is enhanced, which helps to prevent the structure from falling.

Lowe (1955) suggested the following guidelines for preparation of shortened cakes in large quantities:[1]

1. The weight of the fat should not be over one half the weight of the sugar.
2. The weight of the fat should not exceed the weight of the eggs.
3. The weight of the sugar should not exceed the weight of the flour.[2]
4. The weight of the liquid (milk plus eggs, not weight of dried milk or eggs) should equal the weight of the flour.

Subsequently, Lawson (1970) recommended a significant departure from the third of Lowe's recommendations. Lawson recommended that the weight of the sugar be greater than the weight of the flour; the ratio is usually 115 parts sugar to 100 parts flour by weight, but is sometimes as high as 140: 100. An additional recommendation was that the combined weight of the liquid ingredients should at least equal the weight of the sugar or exceed it.

The color of chocolate cake depends on the color of the cocoa or chocolate used as well as on certain other variables. The color of cocoa and chocolate is influenced by the variety of the cacao beans from which they are produced, the extent of roasting of the beans, the addition of alkali, and oxidation. As would be anticipated, the deeper the roast, the darker is the color of the resulting chocolate or cocoa. On the basis of processing, natural-processed cocoas and chocolates range between pH 5.1 and 6.2, but Dutch-processed products range between pH 6.0 and 7.8.

Phlobaphene
Derivative of a polyphenol in cacao that is formed in the presence of oxygen and is responsible for the reddish color sometimes noted in cocoa and chocolate.

Oxidation of cacao polyphenol to form a **phlobaphene** is another factor determining the color of cocoa and chocolate. The phlobaphene is responsible for the reddish color seen in cocoa and chocolate to varying degrees, depending on the extent of oxidation. The presence of oxygen also influences the shelf life of cocoa and chocolate because of the potential for oxidative rancidity of the fat in these products.

---

[1]Lowe, B. *Experimental Cookery*. 4th ed. Wiley: New York, 1955, p. 489.
[2]If chocolate or cocoa is used, this weight is added to that of the flour.

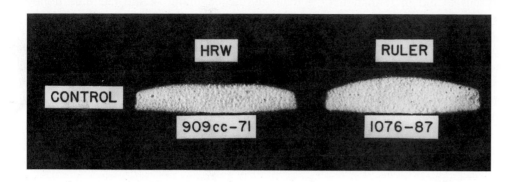

Figure 18.12   Cakes from chlorinated (bleached) hard red winter or all-purpose (HRW) and soft red winter wheat or cake (Ruler) flours. (Courtesy of J. R. Donelson, W. T. Yamazaki, and L. T. Kissell. The American Association of Cereal Chemists, Inc. 1984. *Cereal Chem. 61*(2): 88.)

The pH of chocolate or cocoa-containing cakes differs as a result of the cocoa or chocolate as well as the presence of leavening ingredients. For a desirable flavor, the pH of the batter should be no higher than pH 7.9 (Lowe, 1955). Chocolate-containing cakes range in color from a definite brown at a pH between 6.0 and 7.0 to mahogany between pH 7.0 and 7.5 and increasing redness above pH 7.5.

Sometimes honey is used as the sweetening agent in shortened cakes. Actually, the use of honey influences more than simply the sweetness of the cake because of its liquid content and acidity. Because honey is a liquid, it does not provide

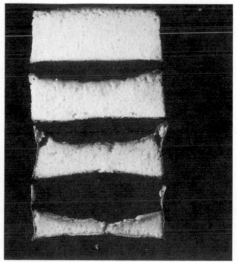

Figure 18.13   Cross section of cakes containing 0–240% sugar (flour basis): (Left, top to bottom) 9%; 40%; 80%; Right, top to bottom, 120%; 160%; 200%, 240%.) (Courtesy of M. Mizukoshi. The American Association of Cereal Chemists, Inc. 1985. *Cereal Chem. 62*(4): 242.)

crystals to aid in formation of a foam during creaming of the fat; thus honey-containing cakes tend to be a bit coarser than those made with only granular sugar. On the basis of sweetness, a cup of honey provides essentially the same sweetening as is provided by a cup of sugar. To compensate for the liquid that is added by honey, one fourth cup of liquid should be deleted from the recipe for each cup of honey used. The acidity is quite variable in different honeys; between $\frac{1}{12}$ and $\frac{1}{2}$ teaspoon of soda may be needed to neutralize a cup of honey, but the batter is permitted to remain more acidic in most cases.

Honey promotes rapid browning because of the abundance of reducing sugars it adds to the batter. Reducing sugars are very susceptible to carbonyl-amine browning reactions. The high fructose content of honey is noteworthy in its effect on browning.

Methods of Mixing

Conventional Method.   The large number of ingredients in cakes makes it possible to make cakes by a tremendous number of methods. However, the method used most frequently because of its excellent effect on both texture and keeping quality is the **conventional method.** The dry ingredients, with the exception of the sugar, are sifted together and set aside until needed. The fat and sugar are then creamed together in a mixing bowl, either by hand or with an electric mixer, to produce a light, fluffy foam. This foam is possible because the physical manipulation causes the sharp sugar crystals to dig into the soft fat and create small pockets of air, which then serve as the cells where steam and carbon dioxide can collect and expand during baking. A maximum volume of this creamed mixture can be achieved by having the fat at an optimum temperature and beating at a medium speed on an electric mixer. The optimum temperature for creaming butter is 25°C (77°F) (Lowe, 1955). Creaming should stop before the appearance of the fat foam changes toward a frothy or runny consistency.

Eggs are added to the creamed fat–sugar foam and creaming is continued to establish a water-in-fat emulsion superimposed on the sugar–fat foam. Ideally, the air bubbles are uniform, small, and surrounded by fat. This type of dispersion results in a shortened cake with the desired fine and uniform texture, plus a velvety crumb. Insufficient creaming at this point leads to a coarse and uneven texture with thick cell walls.

Usually the sifted mixture of flour and other dry ingredients is divided into thirds; the first third is added to the egg–fat–sugar mixture and mixed at a low setting on an electric mixer or beaten by hand with a wooden spoon. Then the first half of the liquid is added, and mixing is done to blend the ingredients. The second third of the dry ingredients is mixed in, followed by the last half of the liquid ingredients. Mixing follows this final addition of liquid ingredients before the last third of dry ingredients is added and beaten in. The amount of beating that is needed during these alternating additions varies, depending on the ratio of ingredients in the formula. Rich batters that are high in fat and sugar require more mixing than do leaner formulas. In any event, cakes must be mixed more than muffins if sufficient gluten is to be developed to provide the necessary structure.

Modified Conventional Method.   In the **modified conventional method,** creaming is done in the same fashion as for the conventional method. At this point, the yolks are added, but the whites are saved for addition as a foam after the dry

Conventional Method
Traditional method for making cakes; fat and sugar are creamed together, eggs are beaten in thoroughly, and the sifted dry ingredients then are stirred in (a third at a time) alternately with the liquid (half at a time).

Modified Conventional Method
Method of making cakes similar to the conventional method except that the whites are added as a foam at the end of mixing.

ingredients and the liquids have been added and mixing has been completed. The whites are beaten to a foam in which the peaks just bend over, and this foam is folded gently and efficiently into the batter just prior to baking. The modified conventional method produces a cake very similar to that made by the conventional method, although the egg white foam has the potential to produce a cake of very slightly larger volume.

Conventional Sponge Method.   Sometimes the whole egg or the egg white is not added until the rest of the ingredients (except part of the sugar) have been mixed to form the batter. At this point, a meringue of either whole egg or egg white is made with the sugar that was withheld. This meringue is then folded into the batter, and the cake is baked promptly.

This method (also called the conventional meringue method) avoids dissolving some of the sugar crystals that would otherwise be dissolved when the egg is added immediately after creaming. If sugar crystals dissolve in the fat–sugar foam, the volume of the resulting cake is reduced because of loss of air from the foam. For this reason, the **conventional sponge method** is a desirable method for obtaining maximum volume in shortened cakes. The amount of sugar used in making the meringue should not exceed the equivalent of two tablespoons of sugar per egg white.

Muffin Method.   The **muffin method** for making shortened cakes is the same as for making muffins. In other words, the liquid ingredients are mixed together in one bowl, and the dry ingredients are mixed in a second bowl. Then the liquid ingredients are poured into the dry ingredients and mixed to the desired end point. Appreciably more mixing is required than is done for muffins because of the delayed development of gluten resulting from the comparatively high ratios of fat and sugar to flour. The fat must either be oil or melted fat if this method is to be used.

The muffin method produces a batter that lacks the air that is incorporated when fat and sugar are creamed together. As a result, the volume of cakes made by the muffin method is not optimal. In addition, cakes made by the muffin method are rather coarse in texture and may not be as tender. This more open texture causes them to stale more rapidly than cakes in which the fat and sugar have been creamed.

Pastry-Blend Method.   Cakes can be made by creaming the flour and fat together, rather than creaming the sugar and fat. As gluten does not develop during this creaming period, creaming can be done until the fat has been dispersed extensively and considerable air has been incorporated into the foam. The baking powder and salt are dispersed in the sugar before being added with the liquid and stirred into the foam mixture. This method produces an excellent shortened cake even when ingredient ratios may vary rather widely.

Single-Stage Method.   The **single-stage method** is a rapid method of mixing in which all of the ingredients, with the possible exception of part of the liquid and the egg, are placed in a bowl and mixed together vigorously to disperse all of the ingredients and develop the gluten. Then the egg and any remaining liquid are added and the total batter is beaten. Fats must be comparatively soft, which usually means at least at room temperature, if this method is used. Shortenings containing mono- and diglycerides are important when this mixing method is used because these emulsifiers help to trap air in the mixture and promote a finer texture. Even

Conventional Sponge Method
Method of making cakes in which part of the sugar and all of the egg are withheld to make a sugar-stabilized meringue that is folded into the cake batter as the final step in preparation.

Muffin Method
Method in which the liquid ingredients (including oil or melted fat) are combined, the dry ingredients are sifted together, and then the two mixtures are stirred together until blended sufficiently to develop the necessary gluten; results in a cake with coarse texture and limited keeping qualities.

Pastry-Blend Method
Method in which the flour and fat are creamed (first step); sugar, baking powder, salt, and half the liquid are added (second step); and the last half of the liquid and the egg are combined (third step).

Single-Stage Method
Method in which all of the ingredients except the egg and half the liquid are added and beaten before the egg and the last of the liquid are beaten in.

then, the single-stage (sometimes called the quick-mix) method is very likely to produce a cake with a somewhat coarse texture and limited keeping qualities.

Baking

Cakes undergo remarkable changes during baking. Oven temperatures cause expansion of the air and carbon dioxide already in the batter and generate steam from the liquid. The heat also generates additional carbon dioxide production and expansion. Pressures from these leavening agents expand the cells and hold them in their stretched, thin state while the proteins are denaturing and coagulating and the starch is gelatinizing. In addition, some moisture is evaporated. This truly is an extremely dynamic state, one that is sufficiently fragile at a critical point for quality to be altered greatly under detrimental conditions. An appropriate amount of pressure must be maintained in the cells until the structure of cell walls is set by permanent changes in proteins (coagulation) and carbohydrates (gelatinization).

The depth of batter in baking pans influences final outcome. Shallow pans enable the heat to penetrate to the center of the batter more quickly, resulting in a cake of optimal volume. The surface is flatter and lighter in color than is produced when the batter is baked in a deeper pan. A cake baked in a deep pan also has a greater tendency to crack in the center than does one baked in a shallow pan. Regardless of the depth of the pan, sufficient batter should be used to almost fill the pan when baking is completed. This usually means filling the pans about half full

Figure 18.14 Too small a baking pan (top) results in batter running over the edge and cracking on top. Proper pan size (center) permits maximum volume and uniform browning. Too large a pan causes poor browning because hot air cannot circulate easily over the surface. (Courtesy of General Mills.)

with the batter. Trimbo and Miller (1973) found that tunnels were more likely to develop in cakes baked in 8- inch than in 9-inch cake pans (see Figure 18.14).

Oven temperature has an influence on the quality of shortened cakes. At too low a temperature, the volume is poor because some of the cells collapse while others become quite large with rather thick walls. As the temperature increases, the volume improves and so does the texture. However, if the oven temperature is too high, the crust sets while the interior is still fluid. The pressure generated within the fluid mass presses against the crust, causing it either to begin to hump or even to peak, depending on the temperature. A higher temperature can be used for a cake that is high in fat and sugar because these ingredients elevate the temperature at which the proteins in the crust coagulate. This allows a little more time for the crust to remain somewhat flexible and accommodate the pressures produced within the batter. Charley (1982) recommends an oven temperature of at least 185°C (365°F) for shortened cakes and suggests that some cakes are better when baked at 190°C (375°F). Regardless of baking temperature, preheating of the oven is recommended (see Figures 18.15 and 18.16).

Even the material of which the baking pans are made influences the quality of shortened cakes. Heat penetration is best (Peart et al., 1980) if the baking pan is dark and/or dull so that the heat is absorbed efficiently to promote rapid heating of the batter. However, this rapid heating causes the sides of the cake to set quickly before the interior has had time to generate much of its potential gas. Humping and cracking because of this lack of uniform heating within the batter can be a problem despite the fact that the total volume is increased. Shiny pans absorb heat more slowly because they reflect the heat so that there is time for the heat to spread into the interior of the cake before the sides of the cake are set. This leads to a cake that has a gently rounded or flat surface rather than one that is humped,

Figure 18.15   Too low a baking temperature causes a coarse-textured, heavy cake with poor volume and a pitted surface. (Courtesy of General Mills.)

Figure 18.16 Cake baked at too high a temperature is cracked and humped because the structure sets at the edges while gas continues to expand the uncoagulated central portion. (Courtesy of General Mills.)

and browning is more delicate and uniform as a consequence of the slower rate of baking. However, volume is reduced a little, and the cells are a bit coarser and their walls a little thicker.

Causes of Variations

Cakes are very sensitive to variations in formulation and baking conditions (Table 18.4). The results of these variations range from pleasing to disastrous. For example, alterations in pH as a consequence of variations in the acidity of the liquid can alter flavor, the color of both the crumb and the crust, cell size, and volume. Substitution of buttermilk for sweet (regular) milk reduces the pH, which tends to promote a light color and a fine grain. However, the taste may be detectably sour, and the volume may be slightly smaller. Sour milk gives similar results. If soda is added to neutralize the buttermilk or sour milk, the potential exists for an excess of soda. The higher pH promotes excessive browning of the crust, a yellowing of the interior crumb, a coarser texture (both larger cells and thicker walls), and possibly a slightly soapy flavor; these problems far outweigh the possibility of a small increase in volume. For optimum browning and optimum volume, the pH of the batter should be a bit acidic (about 6.3).

Alterations in the amount of sugar in a cake recipe can cause wide variations in the characteristics of cakes. As the content of sugar is increased, the volume of the cake increases (because of the longer time required to reach the elevated coagulation temperature of gluten) up to the point where the volume is so great and the gluten so weak that the gluten strands snap and the cake falls in the center. The exact amount of sugar required for the cake to fall is influenced by the amount

Table 18.4   *Some Causes of Variations in Shortened Cakes*

Variation	Possible Cause
Yellowing	Alkaline batter (excess soda)
Fallen center	Excess sugar Excess fat Inadequate mixing Excess baking powder Too low a temperature during baking Opening of oven door too early in baking
Tough, dry crumb	Too much flour Too much egg Too little fat Too little sugar Too much mixing Overbaking
Dark crust	Alkaline reaction (excess soda) Fructose (promotes rapid browning) Honey (fructose in it promotes rapid browning) Improper placement in oven (too near top or bottom) Overbaking Too much sugar
Gummy, crystalline appearance	Too much sugar
Coarse texture	Too much baking powder Too much sugar Too low a temperature during baking Inadequate mixing
Poor volume	Too little baking powder Too low a temperature during baking Improper level of sugar Improper level of fat
Humped	Too much flour Too much mixing Too deep a pan Too hot an oven Too little sugar Too little fat Too little liquid

of egg and shortening. Egg adds protein to help strengthen the cake when a large amount of sugar is included in the formula. Added fat increases the aeration of the batter to help increase viscosity of the batter, but it may weaken the structure, especially if mixing is inadequate. Liquid also usually is increased with increased sugar because of the need for additional liquid to dissolve the sugar and to compensate for the liquid that is adsorbed by the added sugar. To offset the effect on volume of the increased sugar, the level of baking powder may need to be reduced.

Table 18.5   Suggested alterations in cake formulas prepared at altitudes of 3,000 or more feet[a]

Ingredient	Altitude		
	3000 feet	5000 feet	7,000 feet
Baking powder	$-\frac{1}{8}$ tsp/tsp	$-\frac{1}{4}$ tsp/tsp	$-\frac{1}{3}$ tsp/tsp
Sugar	-1 tbsp/cup	$-2\text{–}3$ tbsp/cup	-3 tbsp/cup
Fat	-1 tbsp/cup	$-1\frac{1}{2}$ tbsp/cup	-2 tbsp/cup
Liquid	$+1$ tbsp/cup	$+3$ tbsp/cup	$+5$ tbsp/cup

[a]Increase mixing.

Altitude Adjustments

At high altitudes, the reduction in atmospheric pressure requires adjustments of cake formulas to avoid the collapse of the structure. Strengthening of gluten by a modest increase in mixing may be helpful in producing shortened cakes with an acceptable texture at elevations above 2,500 feet. This effort provides increased resistance to the pressure generated in the cells to offset the decreased resistance provided the lower atmospheric pressure at low mountain elevations. However, at 3,000 feet and above, more aggressive steps need to be taken, and the formulations need to be adjusted (Table 18.5).

The problem in adjusting cake formulas for higher elevations lies in providing an appropriate balance between the internal pressure generated in the cells and the opposing, rather low atmospheric pressure. Internal pressure can be reduced by reducing the amount of baking powder in the formula; a reduction of one-eighth is recommended at 3,000 feet and one-fourth at 5,000 feet. At 7,200 feet, Mc-Crittick (1923) suggested a reduction of one-third. Although the research on these modifications was done more than half a century ago, the physical principles underlying the recommendations are still true today. Sugar also needs to be decreased, probably at the rate of one tablespoon per cup of sugar between 3,000 and 5,000 feet and three tablespoons per cup of sugar between 5,000 and 7,000 feet. Another alteration that helps strengthen the cell walls is reduction of the fat by between one and two tablespoons per cup of fat in the original recipe.

The lower temperature at which water boils at these high elevations results in the evaporation of more liquid than normal from baking cakes. To compensate for this increased evaporation, the liquid can be increased by a tablespoon per cup of liquid at 3,000 feet and at each 1,000-foot gain in elevation, so that at 6,000 feet an extra four tablespoons (one-fourth cup) of liquid need to be added for each cup of liquid in the original recipe. The modifications made in cake formulas for high-altitude baking are based on the research of Barmore (1936, 1939) and Peterson (1930) at Colorado State University and McCrittick (1923) more than five decades ago.

PASTRY

Ingredients

Pastry, whether it is in the form of pie crust or puff pastry, is a very simple baked product that contains few ingredients, yet requires some skill for successful results. Pie crust is made with fat, flour, salt, and water—the same ingredients used for preparing puff pastry, the multilayered pastry in such products as napoleons. The difference between these two forms of pastry is the fat (Chapter 12). The fat differs in kind, amount, and method of incorporation into the dough. The fat usually selected for making puff pastry is butter, and it is used in a flour-to-fat ratio (on a volume basis) of 2:1, that is, twice as much flour as fat, which is a very rich dough. Pastry for pies usually is made with shortening, but sometimes oil, lard, or butter is selected. Although the ratio of flour to pure fat may vary from one pie dough recipe to another, a volume ratio commonly used is 3:1 (three times as much flour as fat). Skilled workers can make a satisfactory pastry with the leaner ratio of 4:1.

Fats are measured by volume when pastry is prepared in the home, but even when the same volume is measured carefully there is some difference in the amount of fat used in the recipe because of the physical differences between fats. For example, lard and shortening are both fats that contain only fat, but a cup of lard contains more fat than a cup of shortening because of the aeration of the shortening during its manufacturing. This difference is of greater academic interest than practical significance, because either fat can be measured very satisfactorily by volume to obtain excellent results. However, a cup of butter or of margarine cannot be used interchangeably with a cup of lard or shortening in making pastry because butter contains just over 80 percent fat and about 16 percent water, differences that require adjustments in the recipe if butter is to be used in making pastry. Oil flows readily when added to the pastry mixture, which makes it possible to use a 4:1 ratio (the leanest of the flour-to-fat ratios) when making an oil-containing pastry.

The fat to be used in making a pastry influences the character of the baked product. A yellow-hued fat such as a yellow-tinted shortening, butter, or margarine gives a somewhat golden color to the baked crust, which subtly suggests richness. Any flavor unique to the fat is imparted to the pastries. For instance, the distinctive flavor of lard can be detected in pastry even when the lard is very fresh. Similarly, butter or butter-flavored shortening or margarine adds flavor to a pastry. The texture and tenderness of pastries are influenced by the physical properties of the fat selected. Shortening and lard favor the production of a flaky and tender crust, whereas oil produces a very tender crust even when the flour-to-oil ratio is only 4:1. However, oil-containing crust ordinarily has a **mealy,** rather than a **flaky** texture. Unless the ingredient proportions are altered, butter and margarine produce rather tough pastries because they contain extra water and too little fat.

Mealy
Fine, granular.

Flaky
Consisting of numerous thin layers.

Causes of Variations

Pie crust varies in tenderness as a result of several possible variations. As noted earlier, oil has a greater ability to coat flour and prevent water from hydrating the protein to enhance gluten development than does any other form of fat. Therefore, the use of oil definitely enhances tenderness. Among the solid fats, those containing only fat have a greater shortening or tenderizing effect than those containing some water, that is, butter and margarine. Soft fats spread more readily than hard fats and are more effective tenderizing agents. Therefore, the warmer the temperature of a solid fat, the more effective it will be as a tenderizing agent in pastry. The smaller the particles of fat (in other words, the more cutting in that is done with the fat), the greater is the tenderizing effect on the pastry.

The time elapsed between addition of water to the dough and baking of the crust influences the tenderness of pastry. When dough is mixed and then allowed to stand before being rolled, the gluten has an opportunity to hydrate to a greater extent, and the pastry is less tender than if the dough is rolled immediately and baked.

The level of fat has a very important effect on tenderness, with high levels creating a more tender pastry than low levels of fat. Conversely, the higher the water content, the tougher the pastry because of the increased development of gluten. Pastry flour produces a more tender pastry than does all-purpose flour; an increased level of either type of flour causes the pastry to be less tender.

Flakiness in pastry is the result of the interspersion of regions of flour in which the fat has coated the proteins and blocked their hydration with other regions in which the proteins are hydrated so that the gluten develops readily during mixing. This condition is created when fat is cut into particles that are coated with flour. The finer the particles of fat are cut, the more the flour is coated with the fat and the greater is the restriction on gluten development. This means that flakiness is enhanced by limiting the cutting in of fat, a restriction that is contrary to the promotion of tenderness.

All-purpose flour results in a pastry more flaky than one made with pastry flour. This difference is due to the stronger character of the gluten in all-purpose flour. Apparently the tenacious nature of the hard-wheat gluten is effective in retaining steam fairly efficiently in pastry so that sufficient pressure is created by the steam during baking to separate the layers and develop the desired flaky texture.

It should be noted that oil ordinarily produces a mealy texture rather than a flaky one. However, with a considerable amount of mixing of the ingredients, enough air can be incorporated and sufficient gluten can be developed to produce some flakiness. This technique reduces tenderness, for the greater the mixing after the liquid has been added, the less tender the product.

Puff Pastry

Puff pastry is prepared to only a limited extent in American menus, but it is a very interesting pastry because of the unique way in which it is prepared. Only a portion of the fat is used in the first step, the preparation of a stiff dough. This dough is chilled thoroughly before being rolled out to a thickness of about a quarter of an inch. This chilling period increases hydration of the gluten, which helps to explain the distinctly tough nature of puff pastry despite the very high fat content. Half of this rectangle is spread with the rest of the fat. The dough is then folded to cover the butter and then this smaller rectangle is folded into thirds before being chilled again. When chilled, the dough is once again rolled to the size of the original rectangle and folded in the same fashion as described before, but no more butter is added. This process is repeated at least three times. With each folding and rolling, more layers are imprinted in the dough. Finally, the dough is baked, at which time the intense oven heat generates the necessary steam from the water in the butter and in the dough to force apart the layers. This flakiness causes a significant increase in the volume of the baked puff pastry, thus explaining its name.

SUMMARY

Quick breads include a wide variety of types and ingredients, but flour, liquid, and salt are common to all of them. The type of flour, liquid, and fat used can be altered to add variety; addition of fat, egg, sugar, and ingredients for flavor or texture heightens the array of quick breads. These breads are made by the biscuit method, the muffin method, or the conventional method.

Yeast breads rely on the use of wheat flour with a strong gluten because of the stretching required during the fermentation and baking of the dough. Fat is an optional ingredient, but often is included to promote tenderness and softness. The liquid may be water or milk. If milk is used, it should be scalded to at least 92°C for 1 minute and cooled prior to contacting the yeast. Sugar content varies considerably, although some usually is included to facilitate yeast fermentation. Doughs with more than 6 percent sugar are chosen for some sweet breads, but fermentation time is extended by the high levels. Salt slows fermentation, helping to produce a bread with desirable cell size. The level of yeast in the formula determines the length of time required for fermentation and proofing.

Baking at 204–218°C results in excellent volume and a pleasingly browned crust unless the sugar content is high, which necessitates a somewhat lower temperature. Oven spring occurs as the result of increased carbon dioxide production in the early part of baking and the expansion of existing gases at the hot oven temperature. Gluten stretches, the water shifts toward the starch to gelatinize some of the starch, amylases convert some starch to dextrins, and then yeast is killed, enzymes are inactivated, and the protein structure sets as the starch becomes more rigid as a result of gelatinization during baking. The carbonyl-amine reaction on the crust as the crust dries in the oven accounts for much of the browning.

Substitution of a portion of the wheat flour with triticale, rye, or soy flours and addition of some bran are ways of adding variety to wheat breads. Addition of sodium stearoyl-2-lactylate to triticale or soy flour improves the quality of bread baked from these flours. Sucroglycerides are other additives effective in enhancing the usefulness of soy flour in breads.

Staling of breads is accompanied by retrogradation of free amylose immediately after baking and by subsequent retrogradation of amylose and amylopectin in the gelatinized granules. Moisture migrates from starch to gluten and also from the interior to the surface of the bread. At refrigerator temperatures, the crumb becomes excessively firm within a day, but staling is much slower at warm room temperatures and is delayed considerably by freezing.

Foam cakes, so called because of their dependence on an egg foam for volume, include angel, sponge, and chiffon cakes. Angel cakes are made with an egg white foam. Sponge cakes contain both a yolk foam and a white foam. Chiffon cakes use liquid yolks and a white foam; they also include baking powder as a leavening agent and oil for tenderizing the cake. Shortened cakes, categorized as layer or pound cakes, contain a comparatively high amount of fat. A foam may be included in a shortened cake, but it is not the primary source of leavening. Layer cakes are leavened with baking powder as the source of carbon dioxide. Pound cakes traditionally are rather compact, because they are leavened only by the air creamed into them and by some steam generated during baking.

The ratios of ingredients in shortened cakes are critical to the quality of the baked cake. In proper proportions, shortened cakes can be made with a fine, velvety texture and a good volume. Too much sugar, fat, liquid, egg, or baking powder can have serious consequences, which are described in detail in this chapter. The methods of mixing also influence the characteristics of shortened cakes. Cakes of high quality can be produced using the conventional method, conventional sponge method, modified conventional method, and pastry-blend method. The muffin method and single-stage method create shortened cakes with a rather coarse texture and a tendency to stale readily. The conditions of baking also influence cake quality, with shallow pans and a baking temperature of 185°C generally giving good results. The effects of varying the level of the different ingredients and using natural-processed and Dutch-processed chocolate or cocoa are discussed in this chapter. Formulas for shortened cakes baked at altitudes of 3,000 feet or higher need to be adjusted by reducing baking powder, sugar, and fat and increasing the amount of liquid. More mixing also is needed.

Tenderness and flakiness are contradictory goals in making pie crust. Tenderness is enhanced by using oil, soft fats, or fat cut into very small pieces. Minimal mixing also increases tenderness. Flakiness is promoted by leaving the fat in coarse particles, which block water from some of the gluten and thus create areas where pressure from the steam evolved during baking forces apart layers or flaky areas of the dough.

Puff pastry is a very flaky pastry with slightly tough layers. The layering is created by spreading a large portion of butter on the dough and folding, chilling, and then rerolling the dough, a process that is repeated several times. This creates many thin layers of dough, which then are separated readily by steam during baking.

STUDY QUESTIONS

1. Describe the changes that occur in muffin batter and the baked muffins as a result of stirring 10 strokes, 25 strokes, and 200 strokes and explain why these changes happen.

2. Explain the reasons for the steps used in making biscuits by the biscuit method.

3. Describe the changes that occur during the baking of bread and during staling.

4. Carefully describe the desirable characteristics of angel cakes, sponge cakes, and chiffon cakes. What causes the differences between these three foam cakes?

5. Identify the factors that influence volume of an angel cake and discuss the effect of each factor.

6. What changes need to be made when honey is substituted for part of the granulated sugar in a shortened cake? Why is each change necessary?

7. Outline the steps in preparing shortened cakes by the conventional, pastry-blend, and single-stage methods. What are the advantages and disadvantages of each method.

8. Cite the factors that can cause a shortened cake to fall and explain why each factor has this result.

9. What roles are performed by each of the ingredients in pastry?

10. What factors influence tenderness of pastry? Explain the effect of each.

11. What factors influence flakiness of pastry? Explain the effect of each.

BIBLIOGRAPHY

Ash, D. J. and Colmey, J. C. 1973. "Role of pH in cake baking." *Baker's Digest 47* (1): 36.

Bailey, C. H. and LeVesconte, A. M. 1924. "Physical tests of flour quality with the Chopin extensimeter." *Cereal Chem. 1:* 38.

Barmore, M. A. 1936. *Influence of Various Factors, Including Altitude, in Production of Angel Food Cake.* Tech. Bull. 15; Colorado Agricultural Experimental Station: Fort Collins, CO.

Barmore, M. A. 1939. "Altitude vs. baking powder, using tentative A. A. C. C. cake formula." *Cereal Chem. 16:* 145.

Bean, M. M., et al. 1978. "Wheat-starch gelatinization in sugar solutions. 2. Fructose, glucose, and sucrose. Cake performance." *Cereal Chem. 55:* 945.

Berglund, P. T. and Hertsguard, D. M. 1986. "Use of vegetable oils at reduced levels in cake, pie crust, cookies, and muffins." *J. Food Sci. 51:* 640.

Bietz, J. A., et al. 1973. "Glutenin. Strength protein of wheat flour." *Baker's Digest 47* (1): 26.

Biltcliffe, D. O. 1972. "Active dried baker's yeast. II. Factors involved in fermentation of flour." *J. Food Technol. 7:* 63.

Birnbaum, H. 1978. "Surfactants and shortening in cake making." *Baker's Digest 52* (1): 28.

Boyle, P. J. and Hebeda, R. E. 1990. "Antistaling enzyme for baked goods." *Food Technol. 44* (6): 129.

Bowman, F., et al. 1973. "Rationale for baking wheat-, gluten-, egg- and milk-free products." *Baker's Digest 47* (2): 15.

Briant, A. M. and Willman, A. R. 1956. "Whole-egg sponge cake." *J. Home Econ. 48:* 420.

Bullock, L. M., Handel, A. P., Segall, S., and Wasserman, P. A. 1992. "Replacement of simple sugars in cookie dough." *Food Technol. 46* (1): 82.

Carroll, L. E. 1990. "Stabilizer systems reduce texture problems in multicomponent foods and bakery products." *Food Technol. 44* (4): 94.

Charley, H. 1982. *Food Science.* 2nd ed. Wiley: New York.

Colburn, J. T. and Pankey, G. R. 1964. "Margarines, roll-ins, and puff pastry shortenings." *Baker's Digest 38* (2): 66.

Cole, M. S. 1973. "Overview of modern dough conditions," *Baker's Digest 47* (12): 21.

d'Appolonia, B. L. 1972. "Effect of bread ingredients on starch gelatinization properties as measured by the amylograph." *Cereal Chem. 49:* 532.

d'Appolonia, B. L. and Gilles, K. A. 1971. "Effect of various starches in baking." *Cereal Chem. 48:* 625.

Derby, R. I., et al. 1975. "Visual observation of wheat-starch gelatinization in limited water systems." *Cereal Chem. 52:* 702.

Dyar, E. and Cassel, E. 1948. *Mile-High Cakes.* Tech. Bull. 404A: Colorado Agricultural Experimental Station: Fort Collins, CO.

Elgidaily, D. A., et al. 1969. "Baking temperature and quality of angel cakes." *J. Am. Dietet. Assoc. 54:* 401.

Ewart, J. A. D. 1979. "Glutenin structure." *J. Sci. Food Agric. 30:* 482.

Fellenz, D. C. and Moppett, F. K. 1991. "Browning agent enhances visual appeal of microwaved foods." *Food Technol. 45* (6): 111.

Freeman, T. P. and Shelton, D. R. 1991. "Microstructure of wheat starch from kernel to bread." *Food Technol. 45* (3): 162.

Haber, T., et al. 1976. "Rheological properties, amino acid composition and bread quality of hard red winter wheat, rye and triticale." *Baker's Digest 50* (3): 24.

He, H. and Hoseney, R. C. 1992. "Effect of quantity of wheat flour protein on bread loaf volume." *Cereal Chem. 69* (1): 17.

Herz, K. O. 1965. "Staling of bread—a review." *Food Technol. 19:* 1828.

Hoseney, R. E., et al. 1970. "Functional (breadmaking) and biochemical properties of wheat flour components. VI. Gliadin-lipid-glutenin interaction in wheat gluten." *Cereal Chem. 47:* 135.

Hoseney, R. C., et al. 1971. "Functional (breadmaking) and biochemical properties of wheat flour components. VIII. Starch." *Cereal Chem. 48:* 191.

Hosomi, K., Nishio, K., and Matsumoto, H. 1992. "Studies on frozen dough baking. I. Effects of egg yolk and sugar ester." *Cereal Chem. 69* (1): 89.

Howard, N. B. 1972. "Role of some essential ingredients in formation of layer cake structure." *Baker's Digest 46* (5): 28.

Howard, N. B., et al. 1968. "Function of starch granule in formation of layer cake structure." *Cereal Chem. 45:* 329.

Johnson, T. M. and Zabik, M. E. 1981. "Egg albumen protein interactions in an angel food cake system." *J. Food Sci. 46:* 1231.

Kamat, V. B., et al. 1973. "Contribution of egg yolk lipoproteins to cake structure." *J. Sci Food Agr. 24:* 77.

Kim, S. K. and d'Applonia, B. L. 1977. "Role of wheat flour constituents in bread staling." *Baker's Digest 51* (1): 38.

Knightly, W. H. 1973. "Evolution of softeners and conditioners used in baked foods." *Baker's Digest 47* (10): 64.

Knightly, W. H. 1977. "Staling of bread." *Baker's Digest 51* (10): 52.

Lawson, H. W. 1970. "Functions and applications of ingredients for cakes." *Baker's Digest 44* (Dec): 36.

Lindahl, L. and Eliasson, A. C. 1992. "Comparison of some rheological properties of durum and wheat flour doughs." *Cereal Chem. 69* (1): 30.

Lorenz, K. 1974. "Triticale—promising new cereal grain for baking industry?" *Baker's Digest 48* (3): 24.

Lorenz, K. 1976. "Triticale bran in fiber breads." *Baker's Digest 50* (6): 27.

Lowe, B. 1955. *Experimental Cookery.* 4th ed. Wiley: New York.

Magoffin, C. D. and Hoseney, R. C. 1974. "Review of fermentation." *Baker's Digest 48* (12): 22.

Martin, M. L., et al. 1991. "A mechanism of bread firming. I. Role of starch swelling." *Cereal Chem. 68:* 498.

Marston, P. E. and Wannan, T. L. 1976. "Bread baking—transformation from dough to bread." *Baker's Digest 50* (4): 24.

McCrittick, E. J. 1923. "Cake baking at high altitudes." *J. Home Econ. 15:* 538.

Miller, D., et al. 1957. "Effect of pH on cake volume and crumb browning." *Cereal Chem. 34:* 179.

Miller, E. L. and Vail, G. E. 1943. "Angel food cake from fresh and frozen egg whites." *Cereal Chem. 20:* 528.

Morrison, W. R. 1976. "Lipids in flour, dough, and bread." *Baker's Digest 50* (4): 29.

Peart, V., et al. 1980. "Optimizing oven radiant energy use." *Home Econ. Res. J. 8:* 242.

Peterson, M. W. 1930. *Baking Flour Mixtures at High Altitude.* Tech. Bull. 365; Colorado Agricultural Experimental Station: Fort Collins, CO.

Pomeranz, Y. 1966. "Soy flour in breadmaking—review of its chemical composition, nutritional value and functional properties." *Baker's Digest 40* (3): 44.

Pomeranz, Y. 1968. "Relation between chemical composition and bread-making potentialities of wheat flour." *Adv. Food Res. 16:* 335.

Pomeranz, Y., et al. 1969. "Improving breadmaking properties with glycolipids. I. Improving soy products with sucroesters." *Cereal Chem. 46:* 503.

Pomeranz, Y., et al. 1977. "Fiber in breadmaking—effects on functional properties." *Cereal Chem. 54:* 25.

Schofield, J. D. 1986. "Flour proteins: Structure and functionality in baked products." In *Chemistry and Physics of Baking.* Blanshard, J. M. V., Frazier, P. J., and Gailliard, T. eds. Royal Society of Chemistry: London, England, 117.

Shewry, P. R., Field, J. M., Faulks, A. J., Parmar, S., Miflin, B. J., Dietler, M. D., Lew, F. J. L., and Kasarda, D. D. 1984. "Purification and N-terminal amino acid sequence analysis of high molecular weight gluten polypeptides of wheat." *Biochem. Biophys. Acta* 788: 23.

Tieckelmann, R. E. and Steele, R. E. 1991. "Higher assay grade of calcium peroxide improves properties of dough." *Food Technol. 45* (1): 106.

Trimbo, H. B. and Miller, B. S. 1973. "Development of tunnels in cakes." *Baker's Digest 47* (5): 24.

Tsen, C. C. and Hoover, W. J. 1973. "High-protein bread from wheat flour fortified with full-fat soy flour." *Cereal Chem. 50:* 7.

Vollmar, A. and Meuser, F. 1992. "Influence of starter cultures consisting of lactic acid bacteria and yeasts on the performance of a continuous sourdough fermenter." *Cereal Chem. 69* (1): 20.

Volpe, T. and Meres, C. 1976. "Use of high fructose syrups in white layer cake." *Baker's Digest 50* (2): 38.

Volpe, T. and Zabik, M. E. 1975. "Whey protein contributing to loaf volume depression." *Cereal Chem. 52:* 188.

Yasunaga, T., et al. 1968. "Gelatinization of starch during bread-baking." *Cereal Chem. 45:* 269.

Zobel, H. F. 1973. "Review of bread staling." *Baker's Digest 47* (5): 52.

6

Food Supply Perspectives

CHAPTER 19

Food Safety: Concerns and Controls

DEFINING THE PROBLEM

The word "food" conjures up different images for all of us, but probably most are very pleasurable. However, the truth of the matter is that food presents a curious paradox. We all must eat food to live, but sometimes food actually can cause deaths. This latter negative aspect of food cannot be ignored, despite its very distasteful nature. The good news is that food safety can be assured if it is handled correctly from the farm to the dinner table. Education regarding food safety and constant vigilance throughout the entire sequence by all those involved in production, marketing, preparation, and service of food are needed to bring safe food to diners.

Considerable safeguards are in place by virtue of laws and inspections, but outbreaks of foodborne illnesses occur each year and are reported to the Centers for Disease Control and Prevention in Atlanta, Georgia. Doubtless, far more individual episodes of foodborne illness occur, but they are not diagnosed by physicians or reported. These illnesses may be the result of errors anywhere in the sequence from the farm to the table. The problems may occur in the commercial arena, but the handling of food in homes can often be the source. Foodborne illnesses stemming from errors in handling food commercially grab news headlines, e.g., the outbreak of hepatitis A resulting from use of frozen strawberries in school lunches in Michigan in 1997 (apparently resulting from illegal use of imported fruit that had been harvested in fields that lacked toilets for the pickers). Foodborne illnesses that result from poor practices at home ordinarily are not publicized, and little has been done in the past to reduce risks in the home. However, attention toward improving food handling practices in homes is increasing as a result of findings such as those from consumer surveys (Lewis, 1998) that show many unsafe food practices in the majority of households interviewed.

MICROBIOLOGICAL HAZARDS

Various kinds of microorganisms can cause foodborne illnesses. These include many different bacteria, viruses, molds, yeasts, protozoa, and algae (Figure 19.1). Some of the more common causes of foodborne illnesses are certain bacteria. Bacterial infections from food and also selected other types of microorganisms causing illnesses in humans are highlighted in this chapter.

Procaryotic
Cellular organism without a distinct nucleus.

Spore
Specialized structure of bacteria capable of retaining viability under extremely adverse conditions.

Enterobacteriaceae
Bacteria that can go through the stomach and be viable in the intestines, reproducing there to cause illness.

Aerobic
Requiring oxygen for survival and growth.

Anaerobic
Requiring an oxygen-free environment for survival and growth.

Cryophilic
Optimal reproduction and survival below 15°C.

Mesophilic
Optimal reproduction and survival between 15 and 45°C.

Thermophilic
Optimal reproduction and survival between 45 and 95°C.

Bacteria

Bacteria are extremely tiny, single organisms measuring an average of between 1 to 3 μm and weighing only about 1×10^{-12} g. Their ability to reproduce by binary fission to achieve very large populations in a very short time (attributable to generation time sometimes as brief as 20 minutes) can result in dangerous levels of bacteria in some foods before they are consumed. They are very abundant in nature and are simple **procaryotic** organisms that survive under extremely harsh conditions by forming **spores** (a structure that is very difficult to kill, even with the use of high heat, abrasion, dehydration, chemicals, or freezing). These qualities (rapid reproduction and spore formation) help explain why it is so important to eliminate or at least minimize bacterial contamination initially and to maintain high levels of sanitation and temperature control outside the favorable range for reproduction when working with food.

The conditions influencing the viability of ***Enterobacteriaceae*** and their reproductive rates include the requirements for oxygen and temperature. Bacteria that require oxygen are classified as **aerobic;** those that fail to grow if oxygen is present are classed as **anaerobic.** Bacteria thriving below 15°C are said to be **cryophilic,** while those preferring temperatures between 15 and 45°C are **mesophilic,** and those living at 45 to 95°C are **thermophilic.** These criteria dictate the handling recommendations to minimize bacterial risks in certain foods.

Bacterial infections of different types are all too familiar to consumers and public health workers because of their frequency and sometimes serious health consequences or even death. Among the bacterial agents causing foodborne illnesses are

Bacteria	Virus	Fungi	Microalgae	Parasites	Protozoa
Clostridium botulinum	HAV	Aspergillus flavus	Gonyaulax catanella	Trichinella spiralis	Giardia lamblia
Staphylococcus aureus					
Clostridium perfringens				Ascaris lumbricoides	Entamoeba histolytica
Salmonella enteritidis					
Salmonella typhi					Cestodes
Escherichia coli					
Campylobacter jejuni					Flukes
Listeria monocytogenes					
Shigella boydii					
Vibrio cholerae					
Morganella morganii					

Figure 19.1 Classification of some disease-causing microorganisms.

various strains of *Salmonella, Shigella, Campylobacter, Listeria, Clostridium, Vibrio,* and *Eschericia coli.* The illnesses associated with these bacteria are caused by the toxins they produce (chemical compounds produced by microorganisms capable of causing illnesses in the host who ingests them). Bacterial toxins are classified as **exotoxins** or as **endotoxins.** Exotoxins are formed as waste products when bacteria thrive and multiply. They attack specific parts of the body and trigger the production of antibodies in the host. This makes it possible to produce immunity against such exotoxin-producing bacteria as ***Clostridium botulinum.*** Endotoxins are actually part of the cell wall of some bacteria, but they are released into the host by enzymes following ingestion of the bacteria. The actions of endotoxins are quite diverse and impact various physiological actions. *Salmonella typhi* bacteria produce endotoxins, as do several other bacteria that are considered in this chapter.

Clostridium botulinum.   The exotoxin produced by *C. botulinum* is highly lethal, often causing death unless antitoxin is administered very promptly to the infected person. The scenario for botulism to occur begins with the fact that *C. botulinum* is quite widespread in soils and casts spores into the soil and water. The development of toxin occurs if the spores are in an anaerobic and non acidic environment for an extended period of time, as is the case in canned vegetables and meat that have not been heat processed adequately. Pressure canning is required when processing canned vegetables and meats to ensure that any spores of *C. botulinum* that might be present have been killed. The bacteria are killed at lower temperatures than the spores, which are so heat resistant that they must be heated under pressure (at least 15 pounds of pressure, a temperature of 115°C) for an extended period that is determined by the size of the containers being processed. Commercial canning operations are monitored and almost always produce foods free of viable *C. botulinum* spores. The **botulism** cases that occur usually are the result of improperly processed home-canned vegetables or other low-acid products. Home-canned vegetables and meats should be boiled actively for at least 15 minutes before they are even tasted to assure safety.

Staphylococcus aureus.   Staphylococcal infections are the result of contact with toxins produced by ***Staphylococcus aureus.*** Among its 10 different toxins is an exotoxin that is responsible for more cases of foodborne illness than are caused by any other bacteria. The symptoms include vomiting, diarrhea, nausea, weakness, headache, and fuzzy vision; some of these may be apparent within 2 hours of ingestion of the toxin and disappear within 12 hours, a short, albeit seemingly endless time for patients in the grip of truly violent symptoms.

The problem in preventing infection of this type is to be sure nobody with boils or other possible Staph infections comes in contact with food being prepared and/or served to others. Active bacteria that are introduced into the food can grow and produce the enterotoxin, which is the actual agent causing the illness. The other precaution is to be sure that prepared foods (dishes containing vegetables, meat, fish, poultry, milk, and fruits) are either served promptly or kept chilled below 4°C (40°F). This prevents active growth of the bacteria, thus blocking production of the illness-triggering enterotoxin.

Heat treatment of food that has been infected with *Staphylococcus aureus* and handled so that the bacteria grow and produce enterotoxin will kill the bacteria. However, the enterotoxin that has formed prior to killing the bacteria is not altered even by temperatures of 100°C for 10 minutes, by refrigeration for weeks, or by

Exotoxin
Poison formed as waste when certain bacteria thrive and multiply.

Endotoxin
Poison in cell walls of certain bacteria.

Clostridium botulinum
Anaerobic, spore-forming bacteria that can produce a highly poisonous toxin capable of killing people.

Botulism
Potentially fatal food poisoning resulting from ingesting even a minuscule amount of toxin produced by *Clostridium botulinum.*

Staphylococcus aureus
Bacteria capable of producing an enterotoxin as it grows, which can lead to foodborne illness.

drying. The only protection against this type of infection is to avoid the original contamination.

Clostridium perfringens.   *Clostridium perfringens* is classified as an anaerobic, spore-forming type of bacteria. The toxin formed by **C. perfringens** during growth and spore formation is stored in the spore's coat. The toxin may be released into the food that is infected with the bacteria, or it may be released in the intestines of the person eating the food. Whether the toxin is already in the food or is released into the diner's intestines is not important. In either case, the unlucky person will experience such discomforts as mild diarrhea, headache, nausea, and stomach pain, all of which will usually be gone in between 12 and 24 hours. These problems are uncomfortable, but far less distressing than those caused by *Staphylococcus aureus*. Nevertheless, avoidance of the toxin clearly is to be preferred. Meat-containing dishes that have been cooked should be served immediately or else refrigerated very promptly to avoid growth of *C. perfringens*. Such foods are attractive to this microorganism because they provide the desired anaerobic circumstance; room temperatures promote rapid growth of *C. perfringens* if any are present.

Salmonella enteritidis.   *Salmonella enteritidis* has been recognized during the last quarter of the 20th century as a cause of illness that can be transmitted through ingestion of raw or undercooked eggs even if sanitary handling conditions prevailed. The problem has been traced to intact eggs containing *S. enteritidis* in the yolk. Infection of the egg occurs in the egg during its formation and before the shell is deposited. Occurrence of these contaminated eggs is rare (estimated to be about 1 in 10,000 eggs in the supermarket), but steps are taken in egg-laying operations to attempt to reduce this figure still more by maintaining extremely sanitary conditions and combating infections in their flocks. Consumers need to be sure to either use pasteurized egg products or to cook eggs to a temperature of at least 71°C (160°F) before eating them or incorporating them into products that will not be heated. Refrigeration of eggs at all times during storage and avoidance of room temperatures except when actually preparing products containing eggs are measures that are effective in retarding bacterial growth. Hot dishes made with eggs need to be served promptly or held at a temperature of 60°C (140°F) or warmer to greatly retard growth of any *S. enteritidis* that might be viable.

The symptoms of **Salmonella enteritidis** infection include fever, chills, diarrhea, vomiting, abdominal pains, and headache. These usually are apparent between 12 and 36 hours. Deaths have occurred each year from this type of Salmonella infection, most commonly among the frail elderly in nursing homes. This type of salmonella infection is responsible for more than half of the reported bacterial outbreaks in the United States.

Salmonella typhi.   A particularly virulent type of salmonella is **Salmonella typhi,** which causes typhoid fever. Like other salmonella infections, onset occurs as early as 10 hours after ingestion, but the symptoms are more severe than other types of **salmonellosis.** Prompt medical attention with antibiotic therapy can overcome the infection in about 2 to 3 weeks, but death can result without treatment. Fortunately, *S. typhi* infections do not occur commonly in the United States, and public health officials track any occurrence to contain potential outbreaks.

C. perfringens
Clostridium perfringens is an anaerobic, spore-forming bacteria that can produce a toxin capable of causing a mild foodborne illness.

Salmonella enteritidis
Type of salmonella sometimes found in the yolks of unbroken eggs; capable of causing salmonellosis (a foodborne illness).

Salmonella typhi
Type of salmonella causing typhoid fever.

Salmonellosis
General name for illness caused by salmonella, regardless of the specific species.

Other species of **salmonella** also are capable of causing foodborne infections, although they are not nearly as virulent as *S. typhi.* Nevertheless, any salmonella infection can be extremely unpleasant and is to be avoided. Salmonella are ubiquitous in the environment, which makes sanitation measures to avoid fecal contamination of water and food essential to reduce the possibility of consuming contaminated products. Thorough handwashing with hot water and soap must be a strong habit for all food handlers, and this measure also is needed for all cutting boards and other surfaces coming in contact with food. The other essential is temperature control, with time at temperatures between 4°C (40°F) and 60°C (140°F) being kept to an absolute minimum.

Escherichia coli.   One of the more highly publicized bacteria causing foodborne illness is ***Escherichia coli,*** commonly referred to as *E. coli.* This **coliform** occurs in a great many different **serotypes** (very closely related organisms having a common set of antigens or toxins capable of stimulating production of antibodies). The particular serotype that popped into the news in the early 1990s was *E. coli* 0157:H7. This specific *E. coli* has been found as the causative agent in numerous outbreaks of foodborne illness, the sources being traced to a range of foods including undercooked ground beef, unpasteurized milk, low-acid apple cider, mayonnaise, unchlorinated water, poultry, and uncooked fruits and vegetables.

The presence of *E. coli* in food or water can be traced to fecal contamination at some point around the farm or on through the sequence involved in moving food and water through the marketing and preparation steps that precede consumption. Fecal waste can contaminate food any time workers with unclean hands and/or fingernails handle any kind of food or utensil that comes in contact with food. Unsanitary slaughter and food processing plants also afford unfortunate opportunities for contamination of food with *E. coli* (as well as other pathogenic microorganisms).

Ideally, *E. coli* will not be introduced into food and water, but sometimes people and such other vectors as flies and cockroaches do cause contamination. Actually, the wise thing to do when handling food is to assume that *E. coli* or other bacteria are present. Fresh produce should be washed thoroughly in chlorinated water. Storage of protein-rich foods (meats, poultry, fish, milk and milk products, and eggs) should be at temperatures below 4°C (40°F) or above 60°C (140°F).

Illnesses caused by ingestion of viable *E. coli* and the presence of its toxins include what is sometimes dubbed "turista" or "Montezuma's revenge" by travelers and watery diarrhea. In some cases, blood and some flecks of mucus are expelled in the stool. Vomiting, nausea, and a low fever also may be present. Meningitis can also be caused by *E. coli.*

Campylobacter jejuni.   Although several strains of *Campylobacter* are known, the one responsible for many of the cases of **campylobacteriosis** is ***Campylobacter jejuni.*** The most likely sources of this type of bacterial contamination are raw milk, undercooked or raw meats or poultry, and contaminated water. Development of symptoms can occur between 2 and 10 days following ingestion; symptoms start with a fever, muscle pains, and headache, with stomach discomfort, nausea, and diarrhea following. Even though campylobacteriosis is usually less dangerous than some other infections caused by contaminated food, it still is quite uncomfortable and should be avoided. Adequate heating of meats (71°C or 160°F)

Salmonella
Genus name for several species of gram-negative bacteria that can cause gastrointestinal illnesses, including typhoid fever.

Escherichia coli
Type of coliform bacterium with many different serotypes, some of which produce toxins that cause foodborne illnesses.

Coliform
Colonic bacterium.

Serotypes
Very closely related organisms, such as *E. coli,* having a common set of antigens.

Campylobacteriosis
Foodborne illness caused by toxin from *Campylobacter jejuni* (or other toxin-producing strains).

Campylobacter jejuni
Common strain of Campylobacter that can cause campylobacteriosis.

and poultry (82°C or 180°F) and use of only pasteurized milk and chlorinated water are useful measures in avoiding *Campylobacter jejuni.*

Listeria monocytogenes
Type of bacteria sometimes found in meats, meat products, unpasteurized milk, and sometimes other foods; toxin causes listeriosis.

Listeriosis
Foodborne illness caused by *Listeria.*

Listeria monocytogenes.   Foodborne illnesses associated with the presence of viable **Listeria monocytogenes** were not diagnosed until the 1980s, although the microorganism had been identified in farm animals early in the 20th century. The illness is **listeriosis,** a condition that can develop within a few hours following consumption or may require as long as 6 weeks before truly serious symptoms are evident. In some cases death occurs, but fatigue, fever, nausea, vomiting, and diarrhea are the early symptoms and may be the only problems.

The obvious way of avoiding the hazards of *L. monocytogenes* is to prevent contamination of foods, particularly of meats, meat products, and milk, including soft cheeses. The bacteria are destroyed by heating meats to 71°C (160°F), poultry to 82°C (180°F), and by pasteurizing milk. As is true for promoting storage of food safety, room temperature should be avoided, with refrigeration being helpful in slowing bacterial growth and holding temperatures above 60°C (140°F) actually destroying *Listeria.* Unfortunately, cold merely slows multiplication; even commercial freezing at −18°C (0°F) does stop *L. monocytogenes* from multiplying, but does not kill them.

Bacilary Dysentery
Foodborne illness characterized by very severe diarrhea and electrolyte loss, accompanied by intense abdominal cramps and a high fever and capable of ending in death.

Shigella boydii
Type of Shigella most likely to cause the foodborne illness designated as bacilary dysentery.

Vibrio cholerae
Bacteria carried by fecal contamination to food and causing cholera when ingested.

Cholera
Foodborne illness especially problematic in tropical areas around the world; caused by *V. cholerae.*

Shigella.   One type of dysentery, **bacilary dysentery,** is caused by ingestion of Shigella; the most common cause is ***Shigella boydii.*** The condition requires between 1 and 5 days to develop until fairly sudden abdominal pains and extreme diarrhea and an accompanying high fever become evident. The extreme loss of fluids includes electrolytes, which can quickly lead to shock and even death unless fluids and electrolytes are aggressively and quickly replaced. Infection from Shigella usually is transmitted from person to person via the route of fecal contamination of food and/or water.

Vibrio cholerae.   Water that is heavily contaminated with human fecal matter unfortunately is a favored site for ***Vibrio cholerae*** bacteria to flourish and ultimately infect humans via either food and/or water. India has been plagued by this microorganism and the resulting illness, **cholera,** but it is not the only region where cholera occurs. Southeast Asia, the northern area of Africa, and South America also combat this illness. Very severe diarrhea, as well as nausea and vomiting abruptly announce the presence of cholera. If antibiotics, glucose, electrolytes, and adequate water to replace the lost fluids are administered promptly, the prognosis for recovery is excellent; without timely and appropriate treatment, the death rate can range as high as 75 percent. The key to overcoming the threat of cholera in very hot countries where it poses health risks is to improve sanitation so that water and food sources are not exposed to *Vibrio cholerae* by workers who fail to follow sound sanitary practices to avoid fecal contamination.

Scombrotoxin Poisoning
Allergic-type response to ingestion of high levels of histamine, saurine, and other metabolites produced by action of *Morganella morganii* on tuna and related fish.

Morganella morganii
Bacteria producing scombrotoxin from histidine on the surface of tuna and related fish.

Morganella Morganii.   **Scombrotoxin poisoning** is caused by ingestion of fish having an elevated level, as much as 50 to 100 milligrams of histamine per 100 grams of tuna, mahi-mahi, or bluefish. Actually, histamine is produced from histidine on the surface of these fish by ***Morganella morganii,*** a type of bacteria. Allergic responses to the histamine, saurine, and other metabolites may include a rash, and gastrointestinal upset. The problems occur about an hour after eating and are usually gone in about half a day. Control of this possible problem is simply to keep these types of fish refrigerated to keep formation of histamine to a minimum; cooking has no effect.

Viruses

Viruses are macromolecules that can sometimes be taken into humans via water and/or food. The harm caused by viruses in the body occurs when a viral macromolecule is engulfed by a cell in the host and then eventually interacts with DNA in the cell to form viral genes capable of altering or even killing the host cell. Hepatitis A and poliomyelitis are viral infections that can sometimes be traced to contaminated water or food.

Hepatitis A.   **Hepatitis A** is caused by hepatitis A virus **(HAV).** This type of hepatitis virus is sometimes present in situations where fecal contamination of food and/or water has occurred. Tracing the source of the HAV infection may be quite difficult because the incubation period lasts from 2 to 4 weeks from ingestion until symptoms are noted. Among the symptoms are an enlarged liver and jaundice, which are caused by the virus' focus in the liver; abdominal pain, loss of appetite, and nausea also are evident. Recovery in 8 to 12 weeks is usual, although a few people may die if the illness is not treated. Inadequately cooked shellfish (mussels, clams, oysters, and shrimp) are the most likely food sources of HAV contamination. Prevention and control of possible hepatitis A outbreaks requires careful control of sanitation and an uncontaminated water supply.

Fungi

Fungi are found throughout the world; certain species of fungi are significant in some foods—sometimes providing benefits, and occasionally causing spoilage and toxins that can cause human illness and even death. In terms of food safety, the fungi of importance to consider are molds that produce **mycotoxins.**

Aspergillus flavus.   **Aspergillus flavus** is a microfungi that can thrive in various cereals, peanuts, and some other crops that are stored under damp, warm conditions. Under such conditions *A. flavus* can produce **aflatoxin,** a mycotoxin that can cause humans to develop **aflatoxicosis.** The progress of this condition proceeds from nausea and vomiting to the central nervous system, which is evidenced by convulsions, coma, and death. Prevention of aflatoxin in the food supply is based on avoiding formation of visible mold in stored grains and other field crops. If mold is detected, the moldy product needs to be removed from the food supply. Vigilance in searching for any mold is essential to protect consumers from aflatoxin in any of the aforementioned crops and also in milk.

Microalgae

Some microalgae are capable of causing **paralytic shellfish poisoning,** a condition characterized by tingling sensations and then numbness and finally paralysis of the tongue, lips, and mouth. Subsequent symptoms are vomiting and diarrhea, with difficulty breathing, cardiac arrest, and loss of consciousness preceding death if the level of toxin ingested is high. The route to an episode of paralytic shellfish poisoning begins when such dinoflagellates or microalgae as **Gonyaulax catanella**

Virus
Chemical macromolecule capable of being engulfed by a body cell and eventually altering or killing the host cell.

Hepatitis A
Foodborne illness characterized by inflammation of the liver; caused by hepatitis A virus.
HAV
Hepatitis A virus, the cause of a foodborne illness that attacks liver cells.

Fungus
Lower plant that is parasitic, saprophytic, and lacking in chlorophyll (e.g., molds, mildew, mushrooms).
Mycotoxin
Toxic substance produced by a fungus.
Aspergillus flavus
Mold (microfungi) capable of forming aflatoxin, the toxin that causes aflatoxicosis.
Aflatoxin
Toxin produced by *Aspergillus flavus,* which can cause aflatoxicosis.
Aflatoxicosis
Foodborne illness caused by ingestion of aflatoxin produced by *A. flavus.*
Paralytic Shellfish Poisoning
Often fatal, paralytic condition caused by ingesting shellfish containing high levels of toxin in their flesh, the result of red tide feeding.
Gonyaulax catanella
Type of microalgae capable of producing paralytic shellfish poison.

Red Tide
Visible evidence of unusually large populations of dinoflagellates (microalgae) capable of causing paralytic shellfish poisoning.

reproduce in such unusually large numbers that a so-called **"red tide"** can be seen in the sea during the day and a phosphorescent glow is discernible at night. These dinoflagellates produce a toxin descriptively named "paralytic shellfish poison." This toxin is ingested when shellfish eat the microalgae, and the toxin is concentrated in their tissues. During periods when red tide occurs, shellfish gorge on the huge population of *Gonyaulax catanella* and other dinoflagellates. The toxin causes no symptoms in the shellfish, but the high concentrations in their flesh are capable of causing paralytic shellfish poisoning in humans eating the shellfish. For this reason, it is imperative that shellfish not be harvested or consumed at times when the phenomenon of red tide is occurring.

Parasites

Parasite
An organism living in or on a host organism.

Parasites differ from other agents causing foodborne illnesses because these organisms have to be ingested by humans or other suitable hosts for them to proceed through their life cycles. The sources of parasites that may invade humans are contaminated food and water. Usually, the symptoms associated with ingestion of viable parasites are most evident at times of growth or reproduction of the parasites.

Nematode
Roundworms that are parasitic; type of parasite.

Trichinella spiralis
Parasite sometimes found in pork or wild game.

Trichinosis
Illness caused by eating meat containing viable *Trichinella spiralis.*

Ascaris lumbricoides
Type of parasitic roundworm that may be present in some seafood and cause illness leading to possible pneumonia if food is not heated enough to kill it.

Protozoa
Parasitic single-celled complex microorganism or simple animal; some cause illnesses in humans when fecal contamination of water or food occurs and live organisms are ingested.

Giardia lamblia
Type of protozoa that causes giardiasis in humans when they are alive at the time of ingestion.

Giardiasis
Parasitic illness caused by *Giardia lamblia,* a type of protozoa, and characterized by diarrhea.

Nematodes.   Of the four types of parasites that have been identified in patients in the United States (nematodes, protozoa, cestodes or tapeworms, and trematodes or flukes), the most common are **nematodes** (also referred to as roundworms) and protozoa. Adequate cooking of food that is infected with roundworms eliminates the risk for humans even if they happen to ingest infected food. ***Trichinella spiralis*** is a roundworm occasionally found in pork from pigs that have been fed uncooked garbage. This is the reason for recommending that all pork be cooked to an internal temperature of 77°C (170°F). This also is the temperature recommended for cooking wild game because of the possible presence of *Trichinella spiralis.* The illness resulting from ingestion of viable *Trichinella spiralis* is **trichinosis,** a condition that damages the intestinal lining, reducing absorption and triggering muscle pain when larvae invade them.

Ascaris lumbricoides is another roundworm or nematode. The dietary source for humans is contaminated seafood. The practice of eating raw or undercooked seafood is not recommended because of the possibility of ingesting viable roundworms such as *Ascaris lumbricoides* along with delectable morsels. Detection of roundworms in fish is difficult, which means that prudence requires killing any that might be viable in seafood. If fish is cooked until it flakes, this parasite will be killed. Ingesting live *Ascaris lumbricoides* not only leads to damage to the intestinal lining, but also may make its host susceptible to developing pneumonia because of possible damage in the lung and its capillaries.

Protozoa.   Only a few **protozoa** (single-celled complex microorganism or simple animal) are likely to cause foodborne illnesses in people. Two that may be ingested from contaminated food or water are *Giardia lamblia* and *Entamoeba histolytica,* both of which can cause serious diarrhea. The ingestion of viable ***Giardia lamblia*** is a particular problem in regions where fecal contamination caused by poor sewage management and general lack of personal sanitation are found. **Giardiasis** severity is determined by the number of viable protozoa present, with symptoms ranging from vague stomachache, some tenderness in the abdomen, and mild diarrhea to a severe diarrhea. *G. lamblia* can be eliminated by repeated doses of quinacrine hydrochloride.

Entamoeba histolytica causes **amebic dysentery,** which means a malfunctioning caused by an ameba (or amoeba). The presence of *Entamoeba histolytica* is a particular problem in the very hot regions near the equator, especially in areas where fecal contamination of water and food due to faulty sewage treatment and general lack of good sanitation are the norm. The long delay between ingestion of *E. histolytica* and appearance of symptoms (between 10 days and up to 4 months) complicates the identification of the actual source of contamination. Some people have mild symptoms of flatulence and diarrhea or constipation, while others have severe abdominal pains, fever, chills, and diarrhea that includes some mucus and blood. Very severe cases result in ulceration of the intestine, which often leads to peritonitis, hepatitis, and even involvement of the brain, any of which may cause death unless treated with an effective medication, such as chloroquine.

Cestodes (Tapeworms).   Tapeworms or **cestodes** are yet another type of parasite, some of which use humans as their hosts. *Taenia solium* is the name of the tapeworm sometimes found in pigs and which can be transmitted into humans via infected, undercooked pork. In beef and a variety of wild game (e.g., deer, buffalo, and antelope), *Taenia saginata* and *Taeniarhynchus saginatus* are examples of tapeworms that might be present. If they are present in meat that is eaten without being heated sufficiently, their eggs will develop within the host and thrive to produce tapeworms as long as 3 meters. This remarkable growth is possible because the head of the worm attaches to the intestinal lining and obtains the nutrients it needs from the host. The usual type of tapeworm from fish is *Dibothriocephalus latus,* which is found in fish from the Great Lakes, Scandinavia, and Russia. This tapeworm can reach lengths of as much as 12 meters. Prevention of this problem hinges on very sanitary handling of uncooked fish from areas of possible infestation and then thorough cooking of the fish before even tasting it to assure that no larvae are still viable.

Flukes.   Trematodes (flukes) are a class of flatworm capable of invading certain tissues of human hosts. The life cycle of various flukes may involve invasion of snails and then a period in fish before ultimately arriving in a human host. Generally the cycle involves an opportunity for fecal contamination in water, such as might occur in a rice paddy or small stream passing through an area exposed to human or animal waste. Even plants grown in such water (water chestnuts, for example) may harbor flukes which then can be ingested by humans. *Opisthorchis sinensis,* also called the Chinese liver fluke, can cause serious health problems and even death when many of them invade the liver as they mature following ingestion of contaminated raw or inadequately cooked fish. *Fasciola hepatica* is another example of a liver fluke that can be found in many parts of the world. *Fasciolopsis buski* is yet another fluke that can invade humans; in this case the effects are in the small intestine. Control of snails and avoidance of uncooked water plants in addition to sanitary management of human and animal waste, are measures important in avoiding this intestinal fluke.

Southeast Asia not only is faced with the possibility of Chinese liver flukes, but also with a lung fluke called *Paragonimus westermanni.* The problem arises from the common practice in this region of eating raw crabs, crayfish, and shellfish. Un-

---

Entamoeba histolytica
Type of protozoa that can cause amebic dysentery in humans.

Amebic Dysentery
Protozoa infection characterized by diarrhea of varying severity (sometimes containing mucus and blood) and sometimes more severe symptoms.

Cestodes
Parasitic tapeworms, some of which use humans as hosts; possible food sources are various meats and fish that have been undercooked or eaten raw.

Flukes
Flatworms (parasites) that can invade the liver, small intestine, or lungs.

cooked juice from infected crabs and crayfish must also be avoided. In contrast to many of the other flukes that may be only an inch or 2 long, *P. westermanni* may grow as long as 4 inches. This lung invasion leads to coughing, chest and throat discomfort, and flecks of blood in the sputum. The coughing forces the flukes into other tissues, and the situation becomes critical when the brain and central nervous system become involved.

CONTROLLING FOOD SAFETY

Since food has the potential for becoming unsafe to eat all along the way from the farm to the table, control of contaminants, including microorganisms, is a complex matter. Governmental agencies, the food industry (both manufacturers and food service), and consumers need to work together. In other words, food safety is achieved only when consumers obtain food that is safe and then continue to maintain adequate standards to assure safety at the time of consumption. Any errors in handling along the route can result in food-borne illnesses, some of which can be fatal.

Throughout production, marketing, and in the home, food must be treated with respect to assure that it is safe to eat. This dictates a need to assure a sanitary environment at all times, including clean floors, counters, sinks, utensils, and dishes. Tasting spoons must not be used more than one time! Even more important is the cleanliness of the food handler: hands and fingernails must be washed thoroughly with soap and hot water before handling food and any time when one has used the bathroom, sneezed, or touched either face or hair. Hair should be covered, and clothes need to be clean. Obviously, food handlers need to be in good health and not carriers of illnesses.

Temperature control also is vital to the quality and safety of many foods. Foods from animal sources are particularly susceptible to spoilage because they provide an ideal environment for many microorganisms to thrive. Particular attention needs to be given to assuring that meat, fish, poultry, and dairy products are kept at temperatures below 4°C (40°F) or above 60°C (140°F). Microorganisms grow much more slowly when they are either below or above this danger zone between 4°C and 60°C (40°F and 140°F).

Federal Regulators

Authority to regulate the food supply and to provide correct information on food handling to consumers is spread across three departments at the federal level: U.S. Department of Health and Human Services, U.S. Department of Agriculture, and U.S. Department of Commerce. In some cases, such as in the development of the Food Guide Pyramid, departments and/or agencies have worked together relatively effectively. In many other cases, they have worked either in isolation or even against each other. Despite internal problems, the nation's food supply clearly is generally safe. It is the occasional episode that soars into the headlines. Nevertheless, there is need not only for continued vigilance, but for avoidance of possible problems through proactive measures.

The Food and Drug Administration in the Department of Health and Human Services has especially heavy responsibilities for a safe food supply. Labeling requirements for the majority of foods, regulation of food additives, and inspection of many food plants are under the jurisdiction of the Food and Drug Administration. Programs focusing on consumer education about food safety also are found in their domain. The Centers for Disease Control is another powerful agency in the Department of Health and Human Services.

The National Marine Fisheries Service is housed in the Department of Commerce. Inspection and safety of seafood and freshwater fish are the responsibility of this agency.

Inspection of meat and poultry are the domain of the Food Safety and Inspection Service (FSIS) of the Department of Agriculture (USDA). In the same department are other agencies, including the Agricultural Marketing Service and the Agricultural Research Service.

Although microorganisms and their control are a primary interest of these agencies, their attention extends to other areas that impact the food supply. For example, pesticide and chemical residues and environmental contaminants need to be monitored and eliminated or significantly reduced if problems exist. New products in the marketplace often mean new uses of approved additives or petitions to use new substances in formulating and packaging foods. Indeed, the area of packaging is extremely dynamic and represents the potential for significant modifications in the food supply. Developments in biotechnology and also in food processing are other areas requiring surveillance.

This plethora of agencies seems somewhat overwhelming if you are wanting to obtain specific information. Table 19.1 is a guide to contacting some of the agencies.

Federal and Industrial Cooperative Efforts

Much of the current focus on safety in the food supply chain is on a program often referred to simply as HACCP. This acronym translates to the **Hazard Analysis and Critical Control Point system.** Although publicity has only recently been given to HACCP, the system actually was developed in the 1960s through the joint efforts of The Pillsbury Co., the National Aeronautics and Space Administration, and the U.S. Army Natick Research and Development Laboratories. The principles of HACCP have evolved over time to 7 principles. They are:

1. Conduct Hazard Analysis and Risk Assessment.
2. Determine Critical Control Points (CCP).
3. Establish specifications for each CCP.
4. Monitor each CCP.

Hazard Analysis and Critical Control Point System (HACCP)
System for analyzing, monitoring, and controlling food production.

Table 19.1   Some Sources of Food Safety Information

Agency	Phone

Consumer Nutrition Hotline
   National Center for Nutrition and Dietetics:
   American Dietetic Assoc.
	(800) 366-1655

Food Safety and Inspection Service	(202) 720-9113
Retail Food Protection Branch (FDA)	(202) 205-8140
Meat and Poultry Hot Line (FSIS)	(800) 535-4555
Seafood Hot Line (FDA)	(800) 332-4010
National Live Stock and Meat Board	(312) 467-5520

5. Establish corrective action to be taken if a deviation occurs at a CCP.
6. Establish a recordkeeping system.
7. Establish verification procedures.

This system is being implemented in many food and food service companies throughout the nation. For each company, it is necessary to do a very detailed assessment and then to identify the points where control is critical. Workable plans for maintaining high quality food products from start to finish are essential to making HACCP work. The entire workforce in a food company needs to be aware of its HACCP system and to be conscientious about conformance with the plan as it impacts the responsibilities of individual employees. Continual vigilance is needed to assure that HACCP is working effectively within each company employing this system.

HACCP also is being used by federal agencies involved in monitoring the food supply. The Food Safety and Inspection Service and the Food and Drug Administration are basing inspection plans on the principles of HACCP. Although development and implementation of regulations are underway, use of HACCP by federal agencies is still in an evolutionary phase. However, HACCP does seem to be a foundation on which future inspection will be based.

International Food Safety Control Efforts

ISO 9000
Overall document of standards for food quality, established by ISO.

International Organization of Standardization (ISO)
International federation of standards boards from 91 participating countries.

In today's global economy, food safety is an international issue, which has led to the establishment of **ISO 9000** quality standards. These standards are under the **International Organization of Standardization (ISO),** which is based in Geneva, Switzerland, and is a federation of the standards boards of 91 countries. The European Community (EC) has given considerable impetus toward developing and using standards for food that is to pass between and into other countries. The United States is gradually moving into involvement with ISO 9000 quality standards, a move that doubtless will grow stronger in future years.

Actually, ISO 9000 quality standards are not a single document, but actually 5 standards: ISO 9000, ISO 9001, ISO 9002, ISO 9003, and ISO 9004. ISO 9000 provides an overview of the rest of the documents in the series to direct users to the pertinent one(s) for specific users. Companies that do product development and manufacturing of products use ISO 9001. Companies doing only manufacturing use IOS 9002; companies supplying commodities use ISO 9003. ISO 9004 deals with quality management and quality system elements. Registration is done by a registering organization in each of the participating countries, which means that registration can mean very different quality in some countries versus others. The standards that are easiest for a company to meet are in ISO 9003, but this registration is only valid for commodity suppliers. The most comprehensive and the most stringent standards are those in ISO 9001.

SOME COMMERCIAL APPROACHES TO EXTEND SHELF LIFE

Use of Antimicrobial Agents

Spoilage of foods has concerned people for centuries, and such familiar additives as sugar, salt, vinegar, and smoke from various woods were used long ago and still are used to extend shelf life and reduce food losses due to spoilage. However, the palette of additives (particularly acids) has been expanded greatly by food scientists. Commercial food products often contain not only vinegar, but many other organic acids and their derivatives. Particularly prominent are benzoic and sorbic acids and their related compounds. Citric acid also is used in numerous products. Carbon dioxide, ethylene, and propylene oxide are examples of gases that can be used to extend shelf life. These are but a few of the additives that may be used in various foods to help to maintain food quality during the marketing process. Many others are identified in Chapter 21.

Another approach to food safety is the use of antimicrobial rinses for poultry during processing. This is one means of reducing the microbial contamination prior to marketing.

Energy

Dunn et al. (1995) described pulsed light treatment of food as "intense flashes of broad-spectrum 'white' light to kill microorganisms." The pulsed light, which is about 20,000 times the intensity of sunlight, uses long wavelengths that do not cause ionization of the small molecules that may be in a food. Tests have shown pulsed light treatment to be an effective means of killing such dangerous microorganisms as *E. coli* 0157:H7 and *Listeria monocytogenes*. Bread treated with pulsed light was found to still be free of mold after 11 days of storage at room temperature. Pulsed light treatment of shrimp resulted in shrimp that were still edible after 7 days of refrigerated storage. FDA approval for pulsed light treatment currently is being requested, the request having been initiated in 1994.

Irradiation is another means of helping to extend the shelf life of foods (see Chapter 6) by killing microorganisms. Exposure to gamma rays is approved by the FDA at different dosages for various types of foodstuffs. Wheat and spices can be irradiated to eliminate insect problems. Potatoes and fresh fruits will retain their fresh and desirable qualities in the market for significantly longer times than they do without irradiation. *Salmonella, Campylobacter, Listeria,* and other bacteria can be destroyed in poultry and meats. However, it is important to recognize that irradiation only kills microorganisms that were present at the time of treatment; contamination that occurs subsequently can mean that poultry or meats may be carrying viable microorganisms at the time of purchase and preparation. Refrigerated storage still is required.

Foods that have been irradiated must be identified with the international logo that was first used in the Netherlands (Figure 19.2). The FDA has required that irradiated foods be labeled since 1966. Internationally, the Committee on the Wholesomeness of Irradiated Food has been studying food irradiation issues for more than 15 years and has deemed that irradiation of any food up to a level of 10 kilo-

Figure 19.2   Logo used internationally and required in the United States to indicate that food has been irradiated.

Table 19.2   Foods Approved for Irradiation in the U.S.[a]

Food	Dosage (kGy)	Approved Use
Spices, dry vegetable seasoning	30	Decontaminate, control insects and microorganisms
Dry or dehydrated enzyme preparations	10	Control insects and microorganisms
Beef, lamb, pork	4.5 fresh 7 frozen	Control spoilage and disease-causing microorganisms
Poultry	3	Control disease-causing microorganisms
All foods	1	Control insects
Fresh foods	1	Delay maturation
Wheat, wheat flour	0.2–0.5	Control insect infestation
White potatoes	0.05–0.15	Sprout inhibition

[a]Adapted from Henkel, J. 1998. Irradiation: safe measure for safer food. *FDA Consumer 32* (3): 16.

Grays produces no toxicological hazard. This level is far greater than the 3 kilo-Grays the FDA has approved for irradiating poultry. Almost 40 nations now utilize irradiation as a means of helping to make the food supply safer and/or of good quality. This technology has found very limited use in the United States to date, largely because of some emotional campaigning on the part of certain consumer activists.

The increasing focus on the potential hazards associated with ground meats and poultry as well as some other foods identified as sources in outbreaks of foodborne illnesses has been altering public perceptions regarding safeguarding the food we eat. This shift in the late 1990s is helping to modify consumer attitudes toward the irradiation of food. Table 19.2 presents a list of the foods approved for irradiation by 1998. Others doubtless will be approved fairly quickly. However, approval does not mean that such foods will swiftly appear in the markets as irradiated products. The demonstrated safety of irradiated foods (Chapter 6) and the potential savings because of extended shelf life are two compelling reasons to promote the entry of more irradiated foods into the marketplace fairly soon.

SUMMARY

Foodborne illnesses are a fact of life—and sometimes death! The causes are varied and include bacteria and their toxins, viruses, molds, algae, and parasites. Among the bacteria responsible for foodborne illnesses are *Clostridium botulinum, Staphylococcus aureus, Clostridium perfringens, Salmonella enteritidis, Salmonella typhi, Escherichia coli, Campylobacter jejuni, Listeria monocytogenes, Shigella boydii, Vibrio cholerae,* and *Morganella morganii.* Hepatitis A virus (HAV) is a virus carried in food and capable of causing hepatitis A. The aflatoxin formed by *Aspergillus flavus* (a microfungi or mold) can cause serious illness and even death when ingested. The microalgae such as *Gonyaulax catanella* causing "red tide" produce toxins that are concentrated in shellfish, causing paralytic shellfish poisoning if humans eat the shellfish. Parasites include nematodes such as *Trichinella spiralis,* protozoa (e.g., *Giardia lamblia* and *Entamoeba histolytica*), cestodes or tapeworms (e.g., *Taenia saginata*), and flukes or flatworms. Control of foodborne illnesses focuses on temperature controls to avoid the danger zone between 4 and 60°C (40 and 140°F) and careful sanitation at all times (from growing the food and continuing throughout marketing and preparation) to be sure that neither water nor food is contaminated with fecal material or other possible hazards.

The Food and Drug Administration in the Department of Health and Human Services, the Department of Agriculture, and the National Marine Fisheries Service in the Department of Commerce all have significant roles in assuring that the nation's food supply is safe when it reaches consumers. Food safety information is provided to consumers and to industry by these groups as well as by various food companies and organizations.

Hazard Analysis and Critical Control Points (HACCP) is the system being implemented by the government and by many food companies to help assure food safety and quality.

The International Organization of Standardization has developed ISO 9000–ISO 9004 quality standards to help assure a high quality and safe food supply internationally.

Various commercial approaches to help extend the shelf life of fresh food have been developed. Antimicrobial agents in food rinses or as additives are one technique. Gases in packaging also afford longer shelf life for some products. Pulsed light treatment kills some microorganisms to add some time to normal shelf life of selected products. Irradiation is an even more powerful approach to the use of energy to extend shelf life. Gamma rays can be used to kill microorganisms and insect infestations in various food products.

STUDY QUESTIONS

1. Have you ever had a foodborne illness? Carefully describe the symptoms you had. If possible, try to identify the food that caused the problem and explain what circumstances caused the microorganisms to be at dangerous levels. What microorganism do you think caused your illness?

2. What are some important control points in your laboratory work to help avoid foodborne illnesses stemming from your food products in the laboratory?

3. Identify a question that you have about a food. Decide what agency might be able to answer your question. Call the appropriate agency and obtain the answer. State your question, identify the agency you called, describe the way in which your call was handled, and state the answer.

4. What steps would you follow in finding information to answer a question on food safety that a consumer asks you?

5. Why is ISO 9000 important to you?

BIBLIOGRAPHY

Anonymous. 1995. *Salmonella and Egg Safety*. American Egg Board. Park Ridge, IL.

Anonymous. 1998. "Confronting a crisis." *Best Practices 2* (3): 6.

Beard, T. D., III. 1991. "HACCP and the home: need for consumer education." *Food Technol.* *45* (6): 123.

Bernard, D. T. and Scott, V. N. 1999. "*Listeria monocytogenes* in meats: New strategies are needed." *Food Technol.* *53* (3): 124.

Blumenthal, D. 1990. "From the chicken to the egg." *FDA Consumer 24* (4): 24.

Boisseau, P. 1994. "Irradiation and the food industry in France." *Food Technol.* *48* (5): 138.

Bruhn, C. and Wood, O. B. 1996. Position of the American Dietetic Association: Food irradiation. *J. Am. Diet. Assoc. 96* (1): 69.

Bushway, R. J. and Fan, T. S. 1995. "Detection of pesticide and drug residues in food by immunoassay." *Food Technol.* *49* (2): 108.

Cassens, R. G. 1995. "Use of sodium nitrite in cured meats today." *Food Technol.* *49* (7): 72.

Cody, M. I. and Keith, M. 1991. *Food Safety for Professionals.* American Dietetic Assoc.: Chicago, IL.

Crawford, L. M. 1998. President's Council on Food Safety. *Food Technol.* *52* (10): 124.

Daniels, R. W. 1991. "Applying HAACP to new generation refrigerated foods at retail and beyond." *Food Technol.* *45* (6): 122.

Dunn, J., Ott, T., and Clark, W. 1995. "Pulse-light treatment of food and packaging. *Food Technol.* *49* (9): 95.

Durant, D. 1999. Listeria: public health strategies. *Food Safety Educator 4* (1): 1.

Food Safety Education and Communication Staff. 1997. Campylobacter. Backgrounder. U.S.D.A. Food Safety and Inspection Service. Washington, D.C.

Giese, J. 1994. "Antimicrobials: assuring food safety." *Food Technol.* *48* (6): 102.

Gillespie, H. 1998. "'Ounce of prevention' is curing U.S. food ills." *Today's Chemist at Work 7* (2): 79.

Golomski, W. A. 1994. "ISO 9000—the global perspective." *Food Technol.* *48* (12): 57.

Grijspaardt-Vink, C. 1994. "Still many misconceptions concerning food safety." *Food Technol.* *48* (1): 39.

Hall, R. L. 1992. "Toxicological burdens and the shifting burden of toxicology." *Food Technol.* *46* (3): 109.

Henkel, J. 1998. "Irradiation: Safe measure for safer food." *FDA Consumer 32* (3): 12.

Henkel, J. 1999. Five faces of hepatitis. *FDA Consumer 33* (2): 26.

Hollingsworth, P. 1993. "Food fright." *Food Technol.* *47* (10): 63.

Hoover, D. G. 1997. "Minimally processed fruits and vegetables: reducing microbial loss by nonthermal physical treatments." *Food Technol.* *51* (6): 66.

Jackson, G. J., et al. 1997. "*Clyclospora*—still another new foodborne pathogen." *Food Technol.* *51* (1): 120.

Kalish, F. 1991. "Extending HACCP concept to product distribution." *Food Technol.* *45* (6): 119.

Kurtzwell, P. 1998. "Safer eggs: Laying the groundwork." *FDA Consumer 32* (5): 10.

Lewis, C. 1998. "Critical controls for juice safety." *FDA Consumer 32* (5): 16.

Loaharanu, P. 1994. "Cost/benefit aspects of food irradiation." *Food Technol.* *48* (1): 104.

Loaharanu, P. 1994. "Status and prospects of food irradiation." *Food Technol.* *48* (5): 124.

Mermelstein, N. H. 1993. "Controlling *E. coli* 0157:H7 in meat." *Food Technol.* *47* (4): 90.

Nettleton, J. A. 1994. "Of food safety, pineapple, and HACCP." *Food Technol.* *48* (5): 27.

Newsome, R. 1994. "Microbiological food safety issue raises questions." *Food Technol.* *48* (1): 31.

Pallett, A. J. M. 1994. "ISO 9000—the company's viewpoint." *Food Technol. 48* (12): 60.

Park, D. L. 1993. "Controlling aflatoxin in food and feed." *Food Technol. 47* (10): 92.

Parmley, M. A. 1993. "*E. coli* 0157:H7—asking researchers about their latest findings." *Food News for Consumers Summer Supplement:* 3.

Pinner, R. W., et al. 1992. "Role of foods in Listeriosis: microbiologic and epidemiologic investigation." *J. Am. Med. Assoc.* April 14.

Pohlman, A. J., Woods, O. B., and Mason, A. C. 1994. "Influences of audiovisuals and food samples on consumer acceptance of food irradiation." *Food Technol. 48* (12): 46.

Pszczola, D. 1993. "Irradiated poultry makes U.S. debut in Midwest and Florida markets." *Food Technol. 47* (11): 89.

Pszczola, D. R. 1997. "20 ways to market the concept of food irradiation." *Food Technol. 51* (2): 40.

Smith, M. A. 1998. "Minimizing microbial hazards for fresh produce." *Food Technol. 52* (12): 140.

Sperber, W. H. 1991. "Modern HACCP system." *Food Technol. 45* (6): 116.

Stevenson, M. H. 1994. "Identification of irradiated foods." *Food Technol. 48* (5): 141.

Surak, J. G. 1992. "ISO 9000 standards: establishing a foundation for quality." *Food Technol. 46* (11): 74.

Thayer, D. W. 1994. "Wholesomeness of irradiated foods." *Food Technol. 48* (5): 132.

Thayer, D. W., et al. 1996. *Issue Paper: Radiation Pasteurization of Food.* Council for Agricultural Science and Technology. Ames, IA.

Vela, G. R. 1997. *Applied Food Microbiology.* Star Publishing. Belmont, CA.

Wolf, I. 1992. "Critical issues in food safety, 1991–2000." *Food Technol. 46* (1): 64.

CHAPTER 20

Food Preservation

The dynamic nature of food during storage and the need for a food supply throughout the year require careful management so that the food available for consumption is safe to eat. Emphasis in food preservation is on safety, for this is the ultimate concern. Certainly quality is important, but this facet of preserved foods is secondary to safety. Unsafe foods engender health risks ranging from simple gastrointestinal upset to death. A brief review of microorganisms of concern is presented in Chapter 19.

METHODS OF PRESERVATION (COMMERCIAL AND HOME)

Several techniques are available for either retarding growth of microorganisms or actually killing the bacteria, yeast, and molds that may be present in food to be preserved. Canning sterilizes food by heating it to a high enough temperature to kill all of the microorganisms and to seal that environment against subsequent invasion by microorganisms during storage. Pasteurization is a more moderate heat treatment that kills harmful microorganisms, but does not permit long-term storage because viable microorganisms remain and cause spoilage.

Freezing kills some microorganisms and slows the growth of others, yet frozen foods have finite storage periods because of enzymatic and microorganism actions. This method of preservation is particularly popular in the home and commercially today.

Drying dehydrates microorganisms, as well as the food containing them. At moisture levels below 13 percent, food can be stored at room temperature for extended periods. Salting is a method of preservation that sometimes is used to preserve fish and meats. The heavy concentration of salt draws moisture out of the microorganisms by osmotic pressure, killing the microorganisms and making the food safe when stored at room temperature. Addition of sugar to fruits (jams and jellies) is a related technique for preservation, for sugar similarly creates unfavorable osmotic pressure to kill the microorganisms. Pickling, which is associated with low pH because acid is used, also provides a hostile environment for microorganisms; this preservation technique usually is combined with heat treatment (canning) to ensure absolute safety.

Freezing

Most foods can be held satisfactorily in short-term storage either at room temperature or in the refrigerator. Foods that are to be stored for more than a few days before they are to be eaten often require special treatment to control the microorganisms with which they may be contaminated. The treatments commonly available commercially and in the home are freezing, canning, and drying. Two other methods—freeze-drying and irradiation—are used to a limited extent commercially today; irradiation shows some likelihood of increasing in importance in the future (Chapter 19).

Freezing is a popular method of preserving many foods because of its relative convenience and the quality of many foods after freezing. Freezing and frozen storage are effective in permitting safe food storage with only limited quality loss for up to 6 months or even 12 months with somewhat more deteriorative changes in quality than in safety. Freezing retards growth of microorganisms, killing some and slowing reproduction of others; the extent of control depends on the temperature maintained during frozen storage. The textural characteristics of frozen foods may be altered. In some cases, such as strawberries, the changes are quite detrimental; in other products, such as bread, little difference is noted.

Ayres et al. (1980) classify frozen foods into four classes: perishable raw foods (meats, poultry, fish, fruits and fruit juices, a few vegetables, and fluid eggs), perishable heated or cooked foods (blanched vegetables, TV dinners, pies, cooked deboned meats, and some baked items), semiperishable foods (breads, partially baked breads, unheated dough products, cheese, butter), and nonperishable foods (nuts). Preparation for freezing differs with the class.

Perishable raw foods require very limited preparation for freezing. For fruits and a few vegetables (red and green peppers and onions), the main action is washing, after which they can be frozen satisfactorily without heat treatment. Washing reduces the microbiological count prior to freezing. Grape juice needs to be pasteurized at 60°C (140°F) to kill yeasts and molds that enter the juice when it is extracted from the whole grapes, which have these microorganisms on their skins. Very rigid sanitation measures are necessary in the commercial production of frozen orange juice to avoid formation of diacetyl and organic acids by the variety of microorganisms (*Lactobacillus, Leuconostoc, Achromobacter, Enterobacter,* and *Xanthomonas*) that can flourish in the equipment in which the juice is processed.

Most vegetables are blanched before being frozen to halt the detrimental action of lipoxidase, peroxidases, and catalase. The heat of blanching also is effective in killing many of the microorganisms that are present even after washing. Blanching also sets chlorophyll so that the bright green color seen in blanching is retained in the frozen vegetable. Greens that are being blanched must be dispersed vigorously to ensure that heat penetrates the greens; clumped greens would impede heat distribution. Unfortunately, bacterial recontamination occurs very quickly after blanching when vegetables are frozen commercially. Very rapid cooling in large quantities of cold water in an air-conditioned facility helps to keep the temperature low enough to retard bacterial growth while the vegetables are packaged and frozen. The net result of commercial efforts in processing frozen vegetables has been a great reduction in bacterial counts, and frozen vegetables are not likely causes of foodborne illnesses. Vegetables frozen in the home are processed in such small quantities and frozen so promptly that they do not present a hazard.

Most bacteria are killed by freezing, and some of those that survive die after frozen storage. However, some freeze-resistant bacteria remain viable even though their reproduction is retarded greatly. As many as 60 percent of the bacteria in a food are killed by freezing, and still more are killed during storage. Even so, there is good reason to maintain excellent standards of sanitation when preparing any food for freezing.

Although most vegetables are blanched in boiling, salted water to retain chlorophyll and halt enzymatic action (Hudson et al., 1974), fruits usually are not blanched in preparation for freezing because of the change in flavor and soft texture engendered by the blanching process. Enzymatic browning does present problems in such fruits as peaches and apples during frozen storage. To halt this action, ascorbic acid (sometimes mixed with citric acid) or a coating of sugar or a sugar syrup may be used to prevent oxidation and browning. Dry sugar causes fruits to become limp because it creates unfavorable osmotic pressure that draws juice from the fruit, collapsing many of the cells. A sugar syrup, because of its somewhat lower concentration of sugar, is less detrimental to texture. The texture of frozen strawberries can be improved if the berries are frozen whole and then coated with a 60 percent sugar solution (Hudson et al., 1975). The comparatively delicate structure of fruits is ruptured by ice crystals that form during freezing, and the juice tends to drain out, leaving a rather flabby texture. This textural problem is reduced if frozen fruits are served while they still have a few ice crystals in them to add textural interest.

Meats, poultry, and fish frequently are frozen, but they do not require treatment prior to packaging and freezing. The effect of freezing on tenderness of meats has been studied extensively, and the results are contradictory (Kemp et al., 1976; Lind et al., 1971; Bannister et al., 1971; Smith et al., 1969), in some cases indicating increased tenderness, and in other instances decreased tenderness, after freezing (see Figure 20.1).

Flavor changes are influenced appreciably by the type of fat; ground beef flavor was shown by Baldwin et al. (1972) to decrease in 6 weeks, whereas Bannister et al. (1971) noted comparable loss of quality in pork chops after only 1 to 4 weeks of frozen storage. Fats that are higher in unsaturated fatty acids undergo oxidative rancidity more rapidly during frozen storage than do fats with more saturated fatty acids, which explains the difference noted by the Baldwin and Bannister groups. This is also demonstrated by the comparatively rapid development of rancidity in fish compared with poultry. The heme pigments in red meats promote the onset of rancidity in red meats, particularly in ground meats (Fennema, 1975). The spices used in making sausage and some other highly seasoned ground meat products delay the development of rancidity during frozen storage, whereas sodium chloride promotes rancidity.

Color and drip loss caused by textural changes also are noted. The darkening that sometimes is seen in frozen poultry near the bone is caused by damage to the marrow as a result of freezing and consequent release of some of the hemoglobin. The drip loss from frozen meats during thawing and cooking can result in weight

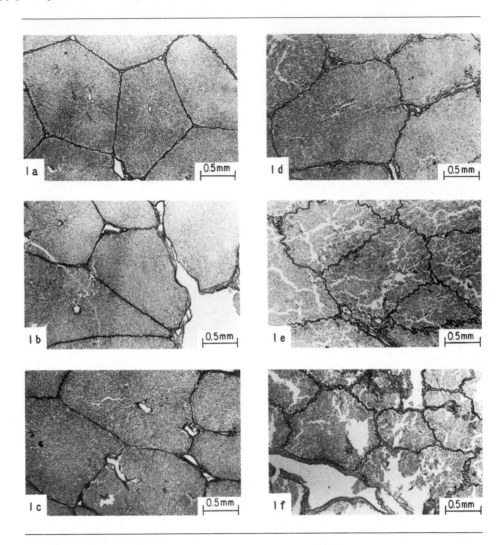

Figure 20.1 Photomicrographs of silver carbonate-stained pork liver sections: (a) 3-hr postmortem; (b) refrigerated for 4 days; (c) refrigerated for 6 days; (d) after 1 freeze-thaw cycle; (3) after 6 freeze-thaw cycles. (Courtesy of E. D. Strange, et al. Reprinted from *Journal of Food Science*. 1985. Vol. 50: 1484. Copyright (c) by Institute of Food Technologists.)

loss and reduced juiciness. This undesirable effect of freezing can be minimized by very rapid freezing so that there is less growth of large ice crystals and hence reduced damage to the cells in the tissues. The amount of drip loss increases gradually as frozen storage is extended, because of the dynamic changes in the size of ice crystals—as small crystals thaw, larger crystals grow and puncture the cell walls.

Many other products also can be frozen either in the home or commercially. Sugar or salt must be added to whole eggs and egg yolks to avoid the gummy, lumpy character evident when these products are frozen without additives. The whites freeze satisfactorily without additives. Some baked products are of higher quality if they are frozen after baking than if they are frozen prior to baking.

Breads and quick breads in particular are of better quality when frozen after baking, although yeast dough can be frozen, then shaped and baked after thawing. However, pies are better if they are baked after (placed into a preheated oven directly from the freezer) rather than before frozen storage, because the bottom crust is less soggy. Starch-thickened fillings in iced cakes retrograde during frozen storage, but the baked cakes themselves freeze well. Equally good results can be obtained if the batter of shortened cakes is frozen and thawed completely before baking.

Certain foods present unique problems when frozen. Salad dressings and other emulsions tend to break when frozen, giving a rather curdled appearance and a watery consistency to foods containing them. This phenomenon makes it unwise to freeze sandwich fillings or other mixtures containing mayonnaise or other emulsified salad dressings unless the dressing is made with an oil that does not crystallize and cause the emulsion to break at the temperatures involved in freezing and in frozen storage. Safflower oil has a lower crystallization temperature than the other oils commonly used in salad dressings, and does not even crystallize at −7°C (19°F). It can be winterized to a temperature of −12°C (10°F), two degrees below the temperature often used for freezing and frozen storage; however, safflower oil cannot be winterized at −18°C (0°F) because of the limited amount of fluid oil remaining. Peanut oil actually solidifies at a slightly higher temperature than safflower oil, but it can be used satisfactorily if emulsifying agents are added. These ingredients make it possible to create a salad dressing with little tendency to crystallize and break the emulsion during frozen storage. This unique behavior of peanut oil is thought to be due to the gelatinous properties of the oil at freezer temperatures.

Meringues are susceptible to considerable loss of quality during frozen storage. The quality of soft meringues is optimized by a sugar content of at least 46 percent by weight, the amount ordinarily included in their preparation (Cimino et al., 1967). These workers also tested baked and unbaked soufflés; they found that frozen baked soufflés were greater in volume than soufflés baked after frozen storage. Adequate flour in the soufflé (about 8 percent) helped to minimize loss of volume during frozen storage.

Starch-thickened mixtures have a strong tendency to curdle during frozen storage as a result of retrogradation of the starch. If the product can be heated and stirred before serving, as can be done with a cream soup, this is not a serious problem, but it is a definite disadvantage in a chicken pot pie or other item that cannot be stirred. The problem has been traced to the amylose fraction of starch, which explains why waxy starches (Chapter 9) are preferable when preparing starch-thickened mixtures for freezing. Of the waxy starches, waxy rice starch is preferred because it can be stored longer than any other waxy starch before retrogradation is noted. Unfortunately, waxy rice starch produces a gel texture similar to the stringy quality characteristic of tapioca starch mixtures. Although the pure waxy rice starch has this textural defect, waxy rice flour is effective in delaying retrogradation in frozen storage while also promoting a texture similar to that of wheat flour-thickened items.

The superior storage characteristics of waxy rice starch relative to other waxy starches are attributed to the very extensive amount of branching of the amylopectin constituting this starch and to the very small particle size. Waxy rice flour has a larger particle size than waxy rice starch, and the frozen and thawed sauces made with waxy rice flour will separate when they have been held in frozen storage at −12°C (10°F) for only 2 months. Surprisingly, the finer particles of the waxy rice starch appear to be responsible for the ability of sauces made with them to be stored for a year or more at −18°C (0°F) without separating on thawing.

Some interesting changes occur in products as they freeze. Freezing does not occur uniformly throughout complex food mixtures. Instead, freezing begins at the edges and proceeds inward toward the center as the mixture chills. Water freezes first, but it actually is **supercooled** to about −8°C (17°F) before crystals start to form. Then the **latent heat of crystallization** causes the temperature to rise to 0°C (32°F), where it remains until all of the free water is frozen. At that point, the temperature can be brought well below 0°C. As water freezes, salts, sugars, proteins, and other components of the food system become more concentrated in the remaining water. The increased concentration of salts and/or sugars lowers the freezing temperature of the remaining solution. The cycle of freezing of water and consequent reduction in freezing temperature of the unfrozen solution continues until all of the water is frozen or until the freezing point drops below the temperature of the environment in which the food is being frozen. This means that such items as frozen orange juice concentrate have a very low freezing temperature and often have a mushy interior, with considerable unfrozen water. The increase in lactose concentration that occurs as ice cream freezes explains why lactose sometimes crystallizes, giving a gritty, granular texture to ice creams lacking stabilizing agents.

In the home, foods are frozen at a slow rate unless only a small amount of food is frozen at one time. The thinner the package of food, the faster the food freezes. Careful attention to these two parameters will enhance the quality. Commercially, much larger quantities must be handled. Creative developments in the frozen food industry have helped to speed freezing. **Sharp freezing,** the practice of freezing in still air, used to be the method for freezing foods commercially. This method is quite slow compared with the fast freezing methods currently in use. Today, sharp freezing has been modified. Now **air-blast freezers** force frigid (−30 to −45°C, −22 to −49°F, respectively) air to circulate at a high velocity in the chamber or tunnel where the food is being frozen (Potter, 1986). The result is a great acceleration in the rate of freezing and much finer ice crystals in the frozen food.

In addition to **freezing in air,** commercial freezing operations may be based on indirect-contact freezing techniques or immersion freezing (Potter, 1986). Indirect contact freezing is often done by placing flat packages of the food on metal shelves that are maintained at the desired freezing temperature by refrigerant circulating through the shelves. In a very fast **indirect-contact method** for liquid, the liquid is forced through a chilled tube and the frozen crystals are constantly removed (scraped off the walls) as they freeze. This intimate contact causes freezing to occur almost immediately.

In immersion freezing either the food itself or packages of food are immersed directly in a refrigerant. Two media may be used—low-freezing-point liquids and **cryogenic liquids.** A 21 percent sodium chloride solution can be used as the immersion liquid, because it remains fluid at −18°C (0°F); however, the food must be packaged to protect it from the extreme saltiness. Other media in which packaged foods can be frozen are glycerol and water, propylene glycol, and, rarely, a 62 percent sugar solution. The cryogenic liquids are liquid nitrogen, which has a boiling point of −196°C (−321°F), and liquid carbon dioxide, which boils at −79°C (−110°F). Liquid nitrogen frequently is used despite its high cost, because it freezes foods at a very rapid rate, resulting in high quality because of small ice crystals. Their fluidity makes it possible for these cryogenic liquids to chill oddly shaped foods very quickly. These liquids vaporize while the food is being frozen and do not remain

---

Supercooling
Reduction of the temperature of water below freezing until crystallization begins, after which the temperature rises to 0°C because of the latent heat of crystallization.

Latent Heat of Crystallization
Heat released during transition from the liquid state (higher energy) to the frozen state (lower energy).

Sharp Freezing
Freezing in still air at a temperature between −23 and −30°C (−9 and −22°F); an outmoded method because of the large ice crystals formed.

Blast-Freezing
Freezing in air-blast freezers with frigid (−30 to −45°C) air circulating at a high velocity; causes rapid freezing and small ice crystals.

Freezing in Air
Freezing of food in an extremely cold environment with still air or blasts of air.

Indirect-Contact Freezing
Freezing accomplished by placing packages of food in contact with cold shelves or by passing liquids through a chilled tube.

Cryogenic Liquids
Substances that are liquid (not solids) at extremely cold temperatures.

part of the frozen food. Plate freezers usually can freeze a flat package of food about 1.3 centimeters thick in an hour and reach a temperature of −18°C (0°F) or less, whereas cryogenic liquids can freeze a comparable amount in only a very few minutes.

The final temperature that needs to be reached for successful freezing and then maintained during frozen storage is −18°C (0°F) or below. At this temperature, deteriorative changes do occur, but it represents a satisfactory compromise between quality and cost. Although maintenance of a temperature of −30°C (−22°F) is considerably more costly, the quality remains high for a longer period at this colder temperature than at −18°C (0°F). Temperatures at which frozen foods are stored actually may rise above the recommended level of −18°C, but the storage life decreases with storage at higher temperatures (Table 20.1).

Canning

Canning is the preservation of food by heat, a method that requires careful control of both time and temperature. When food is canned properly, pathogenic microorganisms and their spores are destroyed although some safe microorganisms may still be viable in the sealed container. Canned foods can be stored at room temperature for at least 2 years and still be safe to eat if they have been processed so that they are *commercially sterile,* the term used to designate that sterilization has killed all microorganisms that are toxic or that form toxins. Unfortunately, some deterioration in flavor, texture, and nutritive content does occur in such long-term storage.

The rate at which bacteria and bacterial spores are destroyed by heat is termed the *logarithmic order of death,* because approximately the same percentage is killed each minute that the food is held at a given temperature. In other words, if the temperature is so hot that 95 percent are killed in the first minute of heating, 95 percent of the remaining viable microorganisms will be killed the next minute, and so on throughout the processing period. This explains why careful timing is so im-

Commercially Sterile
Food that has been heat processed enough to kill all pathogenic microorganisms and spores.

Logarithmic Order of Death
Percentage of bacteria and bacterial spores killed per minute at a constant temperature.

Table 20.1 Approximate Storage Life of Frozen Foods at Three Different Temperatures

Food	Approximate Storage Life (months)		
	−18°C (0°F)	−12°C(10°F)	−6.7°C (20°F)
Orange juice (heated)	27	10	4
Peaches	12	<2	6 days
Strawberries	12	2.4	10 days
Cauliflower	12	2.4	10 days
Green beans	11–12	3	1
Peas	11–12	3	1
Spinach	6–7	3	21 days
Raw chicken	27	$15\frac{1}{2}$	<8
Fried chicken	<3	<1	<18 days
Turkey pies	>30	$9\frac{1}{2}$	$2\frac{1}{2}$
Beef (raw)	13–14	5	<2
Pork (raw)	10	<4	$<1\frac{1}{2}$
Lean fish (raw)	3	$<2\frac{1}{4}$	$<1\frac{1}{2}$
Fat fish (raw)	2	$1\frac{1}{2}$	24 days

From U.S. Department of Agriculture.

portant in canning. A deficiency of even a minute of processing time can make a critical difference in the number of pathogens in a food. It also underlines the importance of beginning with food that has been cleaned carefully so that the original pathogen count is low.

Temperature is another key factor in determining the death rate of microorganisms. The higher the temperature, the more quickly microorganisms die. This is true despite the fact that some microorganisms are much more heat resistant than others, and spores are very resistant. **Thermal death time curves** (Pflug and Esselen, 1979) can be plotted by careful research to determine the rate at which a specific microorganism is destroyed at different temperatures. These thermal death time curves show clearly that the time for heat processing at a high temperature is much shorter than that at a lower temperature.

By processing under pressure to control the processing temperature, the time required to achieve commercial sterility is reasonable; that is, not as many hours are required as would be at atmospheric pressure. This is why pressure canning is the method selected for safe canning of vegetables, meats, and other low-acid foods that have the potential for contamination by *Clostridium botulinum* and its very heat-resistant spores.

Thermal death time curves are used to determine the processing times and temperatures that are used in the food industry and in home canning. These times are calculated to include a margin of safety because of the possibility of variability in the populations and the types of microorganisms that need to be killed during processing. As *C. botulinum* is quite sensitive to acid, foods with a pH below 4.5 can be processed at a lower temperature or for a shorter period to achieve commercial sterility.

Heating must be adequate at all points in the food, a task complicated by the fact that heat is transferred throughout the food in the can by both conduction and convection and at rates determined by the nature of the food being processed. Convection is more rapid than is conduction. Foods that are rather fluid can be heated comparatively easily throughout because of the convection currents that develop and circulate throughout the material, but solid foods are heated primarily by conduction. The rate of heating by conduction is influenced by the shape and composition of the food. In both types of heating, there will be a **cold point** in the can, and this point is the critical point where the time and temperature required for safe processing should be determined.

Commercial canners have available many choices, both in packaging and in equipment for processing. For example, cans may be processed in a retort without movement or they may be agitated to promote conduction within the can during processing. Actually, canning does not even have to be done in cans; retort pouches are being used for many so-called canned foods because of advantages in processing time and other economies. These are but a few of the innovations in industry (see Figure 20.2).

In the home, the choice generally is dictated by the food being processed. Vegetables (Figure 20.3), meat, fish, and poultry must be canned with a pressure canner to ensure that a sufficiently high temperature is reached and maintained to kill *C. botulinum* spores. The pH of the food being canned dictates whether or not pressure canning is necessary. Foods with a pH of 4.5 or lower (fruits [Figure 20.4] and pickles) are classified as high-acid foods and can be canned in a water bath canner because they are sufficiently acidic to prevent growth of *C. botulinum* dur-

Thermal Death Time Curve
Comparison of the rate of death of pathogenic microorganisms over a range of processing temperatures.

Cold Point
Coldest area of food in a can being heat-processed.

Figure 20.2   A pressure canner is needed to achieve the extremely high temperatures needed to process vegetables and meats safely. (Courtesy of Plycon Press.)

ing storage. Those above pH 4.5 must be processed in a pressure canner to achieve the temperatures needed to prevent survival of spores of *C. botulinum,* which can flourish in low-acid foods if processing is inadequate. The approximate pH values of many foods that are canned are shown in Figure 20.5).

In recent years, there has been concern regarding the suitability of water bath canning for tomatoes. Some varieties, such as Ace, Rutgers, and Beefsteak, may have pH values well above the level that can be processed safely in a water bath. Additional problems occur when other ingredients are added to tomatoes to make such items as stewed tomatoes with green pepper and onion. These added vegetables raise the pH of the mixture and frequently necessitate pressure canning. For home water bath canning of tomatoes, the addition of 30 ml (2 tablespoons) bottled lemon juice per quart (or $\frac{1}{2}$ teaspoon citric acid/quart or 3 tablespoons 5% vinegar/quart) is sufficient to ensure a low enough pH for safety.

Food to be canned is cleaned and trimmed to eliminate bones or other inedible portions. Sometimes spinach or other bulky foods may be cooked briefly to shrink the volume and then placed in the canning jars while hot, a technique termed *hot pack.* However, most foods are cold packed into jars. In both hot and cold pack, liquid is added until there is approximately $\frac{1}{2}$ to 1 inch of headspace remaining at the top of the jar. A sugar syrup usually is used with fruits because it reduces osmotic pressure and helps to retain the desired slightly firm texture. Then the jars are sealed according to the directions for the specific type of closure, placed in either a water bath canner (fruits) or a pressure canner (low-acid foods)

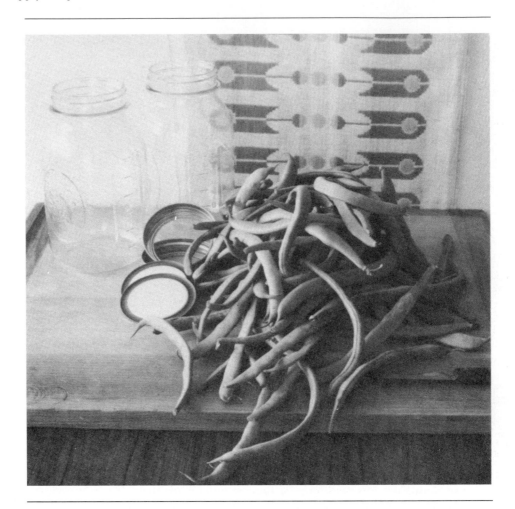

Figure 20.3 Green beans, because of their comparatively high pH (pH > 5), require processing in a pressure canner to avoid the risk of production of toxin from *C. botulinum* spores, a risk that can cause often-fatal botulism. (Courtesy of Plycon Press.)

Water Bath Canning
Heat processing of food in containers immersed in water at atmospheric pressure.

Sulfide Spoilage
Canned food contaminated with hydrogen sulfide produced by viable *Clostridium nigrificans.*

Clostridium nigrificans
Bacteria capable of producing hydrogen sulfide in canned foods to cause sulfide spoilage.

and processed at the correct time and temperature. A seal develops as the jars cool undisturbed and the gas in the headspace contracts. This seal is essential in preventing the entry of additional microorganisms during storage.

Water bath canning is done by immersing the jars and their holding rack in water that is heated to and maintained at boiling throughout the processing period. The time required for processing is determined by the size of the jar, the type of fruit, and the elevation. At higher elevations, the processing time needs to be increased because the water bath boils at a lower temperature than at sea level. Table 20.2 indicates the alteration in time needed to adjust for the effect of altitude in water bath canning (see Figure 20.6).

Sulfide spoilage is revealed by the distinctive aroma of hydrogen sulfide in canned foods in which viable ***Clostridium nigrificans*** bacteria are present. If spoilage proceeds long enough, sufficient hydrogen sulfide gas is generated to

Figure 20.4   Peaches, whether canned in the sauce or pickled in vinegar, are sufficiently acidic (pH < 4) to be canned safely in a water bath canner. (Courtesy of Plycon Press.)

bulge the top of the can, but even before bulging occurs the food is inedible because of the hydrogen sulfide.

Failure to process adequately or to achieve a tight seal in canning allows microorganisms to grow within the jars or cans. Four types of spoilage are likely to occur if contaminated food is not commercially sterile when canned. **Flat-sour spoilage** can occur if *Bacillus coagulans* is viable in the container. Lactic acid is formed from sugar by this anaerobic bacillus if it is viable in the sealed jar. This results in increased acidity without the production of any gas to signal spoilage by a bulging lid.

Hydrogen swells is a condition seen only in home-canned foods processed in metal cans that have become contaminated with **thermophilic anaerobes.** A bulging can likely is caused by this problem, but it is not a common occurrence.

Botulism is by far the most dangerous of the common forms of spoilage occurring in canned foods. This disease is the result of the presence of a paralyzing exo-

Flat-Sour Spoilage
Increased acidity caused by viable *Bacillus coagulans* digesting sugar without producing gas.

Bacillus coagulans
Anaerobic bacillus that digests sugar to lactic acid in canned foods, causing flat-sour spoilage.

Hydrogen Swells
Spoilage of food and bulging of cans caused by anaerobic, thermophilic microorganisms that produce hydrogen during storage.

Anaerobic
Capable of surviving and reproducing without oxygen.

Thermophilic
Capable of withstanding very high processing temperatures.

Figure 20.5 Average pH of selected foods. (Courtesy of Plycon Press.)

pH	Food
2.5	
	Plums
	Gooseberries
	Prunes
	Dill pickles, rhubarb, apricots
3.0	Apples, blackberries
	Sour cherries, strawberries
	Peaches
	Sauerkraut, raspberries
	Blueberries
	Sweet cherries
	Pears
4.0	
	Tomatoes
	Pimiento (dry roasted)
	Okra
5.0	Pumpkins, carrots
	Pimiento (lye peeled)
	Turnips, cabbage
	Parsnips, beets, string beans, green peppers
	Sweet potatoes, baked beans (tomato sauce)
	Spinach
	Asparagus, cauliflower
	Baked beans (plain sauce)
	Red kidney beans
	Lima beans
	Succotash, meats, poultry
6.0	
	Peas
	Corn, hominy, salmon
	White fish
	Shrimp, wet pack
7.0	Lye hominy
8.0	

Table 20.2 Increase in Processing Time for Water Bath Canning at Selected Altitudes

Altitude (feet)	Increase in Time (minutes)	
	Processed ≤ 20 minutes at Sea Level	Processed > 20 minutes at Sea Level
1000	1	2
2000	2	4
3000	3	6
4000	4	8
5000	5	10
6000	6	12
7000	7	14
8000	8	16
9000	9	18

From McWilliams, M. and Paine, H. *Modern Food Preservation,* Plycon Press: Redondo Beach, CA, 1977; p. 59.

Figure 20.6   Water bath canning is satisfactory for high-acid foods, such as fruits and pickles. (Courtesy of Plycon Press.)

toxin produced by viable spores of *C. botulinum* during storage. Three types—A, B, and E—are found most commonly, but two others also have been observed—C and F. Contamination leading to Type A and B botulism is generally from soil, and these two types are the most resistant to heat. Occasionally fish may be contaminated with Type E because of contaminated waters, but its limited resistance to heat makes its destruction complete when proper controls are exercised during commercial canning operations. Home canning of fish requires pressure canning and careful control of both pressure and time to prevent this potential source of food poisoning.

Clostridium botulinum
Anaerobic bacteria that form spores capable of producing a toxin that frequently is fatal to humans.

Dehydration

Drying, the original method of food preservation, has been practiced for at least 3,000 years. Even today the practice is followed by some consumers, and the food industry uses dehydration rather extensively. Commercial methods include drum drying, spray drying, vacuum shelf drying, vacuum belt drying, atmospheric belt drying, freeze-drying, rotary drying, cabinet drying, and tunnel drying. Obviously, these processes are far more sophisticated than the original, simple sun drying that still persists today. In the home, foods are dried in the sun, in the oven, or in a dehydrator.

Drying is an effective means of food preservation if the moisture level of the dried food is sufficiently low to kill harmful microorganisms. Bacteria generally do not survive at moisture levels below 16 percent (Table 20.3), whereas yeasts require a moisture level of about 20 percent or higher for survival. Molds can survive

Table 20.3 Minimum Moisture Levels Required to Maintain Selected Viable Microorganisms

Type of Microorganism	Minimum Moisture Level for Survival (%)
Molds	13
Bacteria	16
Yeasts	20

unless the moisture level is as low as 13 percent, and thus are the most likely source of spoilage in dried foods. The foods must be dried sufficiently to drop below 13 percent moisture level and then stored in airtight packaging to prevent resorption of some moisture.

To achieve the very low moisture level needed for storage without spoilage by molds, foods must be dried quite thoroughly. This requires mild heating and evaporation. The process is most efficient and effective if the food to be dried is in thin pieces with exposed surfaces; this increases the surface area from which moisture can be removed. As the water in the food changes in state from liquid to water vapor, heat is absorbed—the **heat of vaporization**—and the surface is cooled. Mild heat, even that from direct sunlight, adds energy to the system to help maintain a sufficiently high temperature and energy level in the food, enabling evaporation to continue.

Evaporation is enhanced when relative humidity is low, air temperature is warm, and air is circulating above the food. Water can be removed from food quite efficiently when these conditions are met. When relative humidity is low and the air temperature is warm, the air is capable of holding considerably more water, and water from the food evaporates readily to increase the saturation of the air. Warm temperatures are also needed to provide the energy needed for the heat of vaporization. Currents of air passing over the food aid in removing the evaporating water from the food, which helps to maintain a comparatively low humidity directly above the food. These conditions are met very effectively by the practice of spreading thin slices of food on a clean towel in direct sunlight in the desert, but they can also be satisfied by the machinery designed for commercial drying described earlier.

Food should be as sterile as is practical prior to drying. For vegetables, this means a thorough scrubbing and usually blanching. Blanching is important not only for sanitizing, but also for inactivating enzymes that can cause deterioration during storage. Fruits are washed, but usually are not blanched. Meats are wiped clean. Usually foods are sliced between 3 and 6 millimeters ($\frac{1}{8}$ and $\frac{1}{4}$ inch) thick. Grapes and plums often are dried whole; the many holes that are poked in their skins allow evaporation to occur and result in raisins and prunes, respectively.

Color changes during drying can present problems in some foods. Apricots and peaches brown rather unattractively unless they have been subjected to sulfuring or blanching prior to drying. **Sulfuring** is accomplished by exposing the cut fruit to smoke from burning sulfur flowers. This treatment produces the rather bright orange usually seen in apricots that have been dried commercially. Blanching minimizes the color change of drying, but is not totally effective in retaining the original orange color of these fruits. Blanching does aid in maintaining an acceptable color in vegetables that are being dried. Apples and bananas are examples of fruits that retain their color better during drying if they are dipped in an acidic fruit juice or a solution of ascorbic acid as soon as the cut surfaces are exposed to air. This minimizes browning.

Heat of Vaporization
Heat energy absorbed by water as it changes state from a liquid to water vapor.

Sulfuring
Exposure of cut fruits to the smoke fumes created by burning sulfur flowers to retain a bright color during drying.

During drying, browning sometimes occurs as a result of the Maillard reaction, particularly during the period when the moisture level drops from 20 to 15 percent. The ease of reaction between aldehydes and amino groups increases during drying because as the moisture decreases, the solids increase in concentration. Browning caused by caramelization of sugars also occurs sometimes when fruits reach very low moisture levels after being dried at too high a temperature.

Proteins may become partially denatured during drying because of the high concentrations of salts resulting from the reduced moisture and the heat. Some sugar and salts are lost from damaged cells during drying. Starch and gums may lose some of their ability to absorb moisture during rehydration. The combination of these changes often limits the ease of rehydration of dried foods. Fortunately, simmering in water is quite effective in promoting rehydration and is also a wise technique to avoid growth of microorganisms, which can be a hazard when food is rehydrated for an extended period at room temperature.

Food slices that are dried simply on a clean cloth in a sunny spot must be taken indoors as the temperature drops in late afternoon and then returned to the sun each morning until dried sufficiently. The biggest hazards in sun drying are birds and other pests. The drying food must be protected from such possible sources of contamination.

Oven drying eliminates the environmental hazards posed by sun drying. Good air circulation is needed beneath as well as above the food. A screen or cheesecloth fastened across the oven racks can be used effectively to hold the food being dried. The lowest oven setting, usually 60°C (140°F), is used to minimize browning and achieve drying at a reasonable rate. The oven door can be left ajar to maintain good air flow over the food.

Dehydrators vary in their design, but they are usually quite simple devices with a source of moderate heat and a fan to promote air circulation and removal of moisture. Trays of screens framed with metal are spaced above each other in the dehydrator to permit the drying of a considerable amount of food at one time.

The exact duration of drying varies with the thickness of the food, the type of food, and the drying conditions. Dehydrators and oven drying provide more rapid dehydration than usually is accomplished by sun drying. In most cases this equipment can dry foods to the desired moisture level of about 10 percent in a matter of a few hours, whereas sun drying may take several days, depending on weather conditions. As soon as the desired level of drying has been reached, the food needs to be packaged in airtight containers to prevent additional contamination by microorganisms and to block the rehydration possible at moisture levels above 13 percent, which can lead to spoilage by mold growth.

Preserving with Sugar

Jams and jellies represent yet another way of preserving food. The high concentration of sugar establishes unfavorable osmotic pressure which, in combination with the boiling period during preparation, effectively kills microorganisms. Jams and jellies are pectin gels containing fruit pieces (jams) and fruit juice to which sugar and pectin are added at levels enabling a pectin gel to form on cooling. Frequently, acid also is added to enhance gel formation (see Figure 20.7).

Each ingredient in jelly plays a crucial role in forming the desired gel. Pectin is a complex carbohydrate polymer of galacturonic acid (an organic acid derivative of galactose). As noted in Chapter 10, pectin is only one of the pectic substances, but

Figure 20.7   Sugar is an effective preserving agent because of the osmotic pressure it creates, a pressure that is fatal to microorganisms. (Salt can be used as a preservative, too, because of its effect on osmotic pressure; health concerns limit the use of salt as a preservative.)

Protopectin
Nonmethylated polymers of galacturonic acid incapable of forming a gel; the first pectic substance to be formed in a fruit.

Pectinic Acid or Pectin
Methylated polymers of galacturonic acid formed from protopectin as fruit becomes barely ripe; capable of forming a gel.

Pectic Acid
Shorter derivative of pectinic acid formed as fruit becomes overripe; incapable of forming a gel.

it is the key substance in the formation of the gel structure needed in jams and jellies. In underripe fruit, protopectin is the pectic substance. As fruit ripens, **protopectin** gradually is methylated by esterification of methanol with the acid radical on the sixth (external to the ring) carbon atom. This methylation converts protopectin to **pectin or pectinic acid;** these compounds are capable of crosslinking under optimal conditions to form a pectin gel in which the pectin or pectinic acid molecules form the continuous network or solid phase in which the liquid juice is trapped. Hydrogen bonding between these long, rather fibrous molecules locks the molecules into a seemingly semi-rigid structure that is capable of trapping water to form a spreadable gel. The pectin in overripe fruit undergoes chemical changes, resulting in shorter chains that do not provide an opportunity for sufficient crosslinkage between molecules and hence gel formation.

Sugar is an essential ingredient in pectin gel formation. Its role appears to be that of binding some of the water to the pectin network so that free water does not flow or move out of the gel. The concentration of sugar needs to be between 60 and 65 percent in the finished gel to achieve the desired firmness without too much free water. This rather high concentration is achieved by using a liberal amount of sugar in the initial recipe and then boiling off the liquid until the proper concentration is achieved.

If the amount of sugar added to the mixture is decreased, longer boiling will be required to concentrate the sugar appropriately. This will also concentrate the pectin and cause the resulting jelly to be rather rubbery. In addition, the prolonged cooking darkens the color of the jam or jelly. Addition of too much sugar will dilute the pectin and cause the product to be rather soft or even fluid. In addition to its role in gel formation, sugar at its recommended concentration (60 to 65 percent) is very effective in killing microorganisms. This role of sugar must be remembered in making low-calorie jams and jellies, because the preserving action of sugar will not be available if its concentration is reduced.

For optimal pectin gel formation, the pH of the mixture must be below pH 3.5 (Kertesz, 1951) and preferably about 3.3. As the pH is modified toward the optimum pH for a particular type of jelly, the jelly increases in firmness. Acid may need to be added to the jelly mixture as an ingredient. Citric acid or lemon juice frequently is the ingredient of choice for modifying pH. Addition of the acid to the jelly prior to boiling has the advantage of hydrolyzing some of the sucrose to produce invert sugar, which reduces the likelihood of crystal formation in the jelly during storage. Unfortunately, the pectin in the mixture is hydrolyzed somewhat at the same time, which reduces its gel-forming capability. However, if the mixture is boiled at a moderate rate, acid can be added prior to boiling without having an appreciable negative impact on the resulting jelly.

The pectin content of fruits is quite variable, being determined both by the type of fruit and by ripeness. When jellies and jams are made at home, the usual practice is to add a commercial pectin to ensure that adequate pectin is present to form a gel. Commercial pectins, available in either liquid or powdered form, are prepared by extraction either from the albedo (white portion of the skin) of citrus fruits or from apple cores and skins. The granular pectin products have a longer shelf life than the liquids. Low-methoxyl pectins are also available for preparation of low-calorie jams and jellies. Interestingly, these pectins are able to gel without addition of sugar to the mixture, which explains why the resulting products using low-methoxyl pectins are low in calories. Bonding, in the form of ionic bonding, is achieved between molecules of this special pectin by an added divalent ion (usually calcium) when the ion crosslinks to carboxyl groups on two molecules of pectin, as shown:

Low Methoxyl Pectin

Preparation of jams and jellies requires washing and preliminary preparation of the fruit, including sorting and cutting. In commercial operations, the level of the pectin in the fruit is determined by measuring the viscosity of the extracted fruit juice. A jelmeter is the device commonly used for this measurement. It is similar to a pipette. If the juice is allowed to drain through the pipette, the relative flow properties can be determined and the amount of sugar needed can be calculated. The more viscous the juice, the greater is the amount of sugar that must be added to achieve the desired gel.

In the home, the length of time the mixture should be boiled is determined with a cooking thermometer or by the sheeting-off test. Usually boiling is continued until the temperature is between 104 and 105°C (219–221°F), which indicates a sugar concentration of about 65 percent at sea level. At higher elevations, the thermometer should read between 4 and 5°C above the temperature of boiling water at that elevation. The sheeting-off test is a visual method in which a spoonful of jelly is allowed to flow slowly from the edge of a large spoon. When it is sufficiently viscous to separate into two streams, the sugar concentration is approximately correct.

Special Commercial Methods

Freeze-Drying
Preservation of food by first freezing and then dehydrating the product.

Freeze-Drying.   **Freeze-drying** is a commercial technique that is a variation of dehydration. The difference is that the food is frozen, and then the water is sublimated from the frozen food. This procedure results in dried foods that have a volume comparable to the original food and a porous texture because of the loss of water from the food. Storage is comparable to that of other dried foods, that is, airtight packaging and storage at room temperature. **Sublimation** is accomplished by having the food in a frozen state at a temperature of 0°C or lower and then placing it in a vacuum chamber at a pressure of 4.7 millimeters of mercury or less. The low temperature keeps the water in its frozen state as ice, and the low atmospheric pressure enables frozen water molecules to escape quickly as water vapor to dehydrate the food.

Sublimation
Transition from the frozen state directly to the gaseous state without liquefaction.

Strawberries and other fruits and vegetables are well suited to freeze-drying. This process is effective in retaining much of the original flavor of the food and in maintaining individual pieces that are light, rather than extremely compact. These characteristics make freeze-dried fruits useful ingredients in dry breakfast cereal products. However, the comparatively high energy costs for freeze-drying have limited the use of this form of food preservation.

Irradiation.   Radiant energy can be used commercially to preserve food. Gamma rays radiated from ^{60}Co (cobalt-60) and beta particles produced by special electronic machines are the sources of energy used for preserving food by irradiation (see Chapter 6). The goal of irradiation is to kill the microorganisms and inactivate the enzymes without altering the food. Changes in the food itself are minimized if the food being irradiated is in a vacuum or in an inert gas and if ascorbic acid or another scavenger of the free radicals formed by irradiation is present.

Varying doses of irradiation energy are needed in different foods to achieve the desired end results. Desrosier and Rosenstock (1960) found that a dosage of 7,500 rads halted sprouting of potatoes enough that they could be stored for at least 2 years. Insects in flour can be killed by 50,000 rads. Berries subjected to 150,000 rads keep for at least 3 weeks. Meats sealed in a semipermeable film and stored at 0°C can be held at least 2 months after irradiation with 1,000,000 rads. Because of its great resistance, *Clostridium botulinum* is used to determine the level of irradiation needed to achieve death of bacteria and safety of food. Pork may be irradiated to eliminate this potential hazard. Enzymes usually are even more resistant to change than are microorganisms, so the need to inactivate specific enzymes can also determine the amount of irradiation necessary.

The greater the amount of irradiation, the greater is the cost for preserving food in this way. Cost and public resistance to consumption of irradiated foods because of perceived potential hazards are limiting the use of irradiation in commercial food preservation (see Chapter 19). Although spices have been approved for irradiation by the Food and Drug Administration, even these rather costly food ingredients rarely are available in markets at the present time in an irradiated form. However, they are used in some processed foods.

SUMMARY

Spoilage by growth of molds, bacteria, and yeasts limits the time that food can be stored and still be safe and palatable. The environmental conditions optimal for reproduction vary with the type of microorganism. Foods can be preserved by altering them so that they no longer serve as a suitable host for the microorganisms. Alterations in moisture level, pH, temperature, and solute concentration are ways of preserving foods. In addition to the economic losses represented by spoiled food, health hazards may develop while foods are stored unless they are preserved effectively. Salmonellosis, streptococcal infection, staphylococcal poisoning, and botulism are some of the illnesses that can result from eating contaminated foods.

Freezing protects foods by reducing the rate at which viable microorganisms reproduce by holding the foods below the freezing point of water. Blanching is done prior to freezing vegetables to inactivate enzymes and thus retard deteriorative changes during storage. Browning in sensitive fruits can be avoided by coating them with sugar, a sugar syrup, lemon or other acidic juice, or a solution of ascorbic acid. Specific foods, such as egg yolks, salad dressings, and starch-thickened mixtures, require use of ingredients selected to overcome textural problems that would otherwise occur during frozen storage. Freezing should be done at a very rapid rate to create numerous small ice crystals, thus minimizing the damage done to cell walls. Commercial techniques are more effective at accomplishing rapid freezing than are those available in the home.

Canning is somewhat laborious, but this rigorous heat treatment and sealing in air-tight containers enable canned foods to be stored at room temperature for a very long time. Time and temperature of processing must be controlled very carefully to ensure that spores of *Clostridium botulinum* or other microorganisms that may be present are killed. Low-acid foods such as vegetables and meats must be processed in pressure canners to reach a high enough temperature. High-acid foods (pH 4.5 or lower) can be processed safely in a water bath canner. Inadequate processing can result in flat-sour spoilage, sulfide spoilage, hydrogen swells, and botulism, as well as other less common problems.

Drying preserves food by reducing the moisture level below 13 percent (usually to 10 percent or slightly less), a level at which microorganisms, even molds, are killed. Cleanliness of food to be dried should be stressed. In the home, foods may be dried in the sun, in the oven, or in a dehydrator. Vegetables should be blanched before being dried to inactivate enzymes and reduce the changes in color and flavor that develop during drying. Sulfuring protects the color of apricots and peaches during drying. Browning in apples and bananas can be blocked somewhat by coating the slices with acidic fruit juice or a solution of ascorbic acid before drying.

Sugar at high concentrations (60 percent or more) has a preserving action on foods because of the unfavorable osmotic pressure created by this solute at these levels. Pectin gels often are prepared using fruit juices, sugar, added pectin, and sometimes added acid. The pH must be below 3.5 and preferably should be about 3.3 to form a gel of satisfactory strength. Sugar binds much of the water within the gel structure. Pectin forms the solid network by hydrogen-bonding between long, fibrous molecules. Acid helps to keep enough water away from the pectin molecules for the necessary hydrogen bonds to form. Low-methoxyl pectin can crosslink when calcium is present, forming a structure sufficiently strong to eliminate the need for sugar to hold the water in the gel. This makes it possible to prepare low-calorie jams and jellies, but a preservative is necessary because the level of sugar is inadequate to prevent growth of microorganisms.

Freeze-drying differs from other methods of drying in that the food is frozen to convert water into ice crystals. The ice then is sublimated to water vapor by placing the frozen food in a partial vacuum for dehydration. The result is a porous dried food with good shelf life when stored in an airtight package.

Gamma rays from ^{60}Co and beta particles generated by machines are used to irradiate food. This method of preservation is quite costly, but it is very effective in preventing deteriorative changes for prolonged periods. Irradiation is authorized to a very limited extent by the Food and Drug Administration at the present time, because of the need for additional research to determine safe conditions for treating many foods by this method.

STUDY QUESTIONS

1. What conditions generally favor the growth of (a) yeasts, (b) molds, (c) bacteria?

2. What changes occur during the blanching of vegetables in preparation for freezing?

3. What changes may occur in meats, poultry, and fish during frozen storage?

4. What is likely to occur when mayonnaise is frozen? Explain why this may happen and how it probably can be prevented.

5. What starch product is best for use in starch-thickened products that are to be frozen? Explain what happens when most starches are used and why this starch is a good choice.

6. What precautions need to be taken when foods are being canned? Why are these precautions necessary?

7. Why is pressure canning used for canning vegetables and meats?

8. Why are fruits canned in a water bath canner, but not in a pressure canner?

9. Describe the drying of (a) onions and (b) apricots at home.

10. What differences would be expected between two apple jellies made with (a) a comparatively low level of sugar and (b) the optimum amount of sugar? Explain why these differences develop.

BIBLIOGRAPHY

Anonymous, 1982. "Food irradiation: ready for a comeback." *Food Eng. 54* (4): 71.

Ayres, J. C., et al. 1980. *Microbiology of Foods.* Freeman: San Francisco.

Baldwin, R. and Ellis, R. F. 1985. "Unique bi-level conveyor moves products through gamma radiation stages." *Food Process. 46* (4): 82.

Baldwin, R. E., et al. 1972. "Palatability of ground beef home frozen and stored in selected wraps." *Home Econ. Res. J. 1:* 119.

Bannister, M. A., et al. 1971. "Effects of cryogenic and three home freezing methods on selected characteristics of pork loin chops." *J. Food Sci. 36:* 951.

Black, S. A. and Smit, C. J. B. 1972. "Effect of demethylation procedures on quality of low-ester pectins used in dessert gels." *J. Food Sci. 37:* 730.

Blumenthal, D. 1990. "Food irradiation—toxic to bacteria, safe for humans." *FDA Consumer 24* (9): 11.

Brown, M. S. 1976. "Effects of freezing on fruit and vegetable structure." *Food Technol. 30* (5): 106.

Cimino, S. L., et al. 1967. "Stability of souffles and meringues subjected to frozen storage." *Food Technol. 21:* 97.

Cohen, B. L. 1980. "Cancer risk from low-level radiation." *Health Phys. 39:* 659.

Desrosier, N. W. and Desrosier, J. N. 1977. *Technology of Food Preservation.* 4th ed. AVI Publishing: Westport, CT.

Desrosier, N. W. and Rosenstock, H. M. 1960. *Radiation Technology in Food, Agriculture and Biology.* AVI Publishing: Westport, CT.

Desrosier, N. W. and Tressler, D. K. 1977. *Fundamentals of Food Freezing.* AVI Publishing: Westport, CT.

Elias, P. S. and Cohen, A. J. 1983. *Recent Advances in Food Irradiation.* Elsevier: New York.

Fennema, O. R. 1975. "Freezing preservation." In *Principles of Food Science.* Karel, M., et al., ed. Dekker: New York, p. 85.

Fennema, O. R. 1975. *Principles of Food Science.* Dekker: New York.

Fields, M. L., et al. 1977. "Microbiological analysis of home-canned tomatoes and green beans." *J. Food Sci. 42:* 931.

Hudson, M. A., et al. 1974. "Quality of home frozen vegetables. I. Effects of blanching and/or cooling in various solutions on organoleptic assessments and Vitamin C content." *J. Food Technol. 9:* 95.

Hudson, M. A. et al. 1975. "Home frozen strawberries. I. Influences of freezing medium, fanning, syrup temperature, soaking time, storage time and temperature, and rates of freezing and thawing on sensory assessments." *J. Food Technol. 10:* 681.

Jay, J. M. 1978. *Modern Food Microbiology.* 2nd ed. Van Nostrand: New York.

Josephson, E. S. and Peterson, M. S. 1982. *Preservation of Food by Ionizing Radiation.* CRC Press: Boca Raton, FL.

Kemp, J. D., et al. 1976. "Chemical, palatability, and cooking characteristics of normal and low quality pork loins as affected by freezer storage." *J. Food Sci. 41:* 1.

Kertesz, Z. 1951. *Pectic Substances.* Interscience: New York.

Lind, M. L. et al. 1971. "Freezing and thawing rates of lamb chops: effects on palatability and related characteristics." *J. Food Sci. 36:* 629.

Lopez, A. 1981. *Complete Course in Canning.* 11th ed. The Canning Trade: Baltimore.

McWilliams, M. and Paine, H. 1977. *Modern Food Preservation.* Plycon: Redondo Beach, CA.

Mellor, J. D. 1978. *Freeze Drying*. Academic Press: New York.

Palmer, H. H. 1968. "Sauces and gravies; thickened desserts and fillings; whipped toppings; salad dressings and souffles." In *Freezing Preservation of Foods*. Tressler, D. K., et al., eds. AVI Publishing: Westport, CT, p. 231.

Pflug, I. J. and Esselen, W. B. 1979. "Heat sterilization of canned food," In *Fundamentals of Food Canning Technology*. Jackson, J. M., and Shinn, B. M., eds. AVI Publishing: Westport, CT, p. 15.

Potter, N. N. 1986. *Food Science*. 4th ed. AVI Publishing: Westport, CT.

Schoch, T. J. 1968. "Effects of freezing and cold-storage on pasted starches." In *Freezing Preservation of Foods*. Tressler, D. K., et al., eds. AVI Publishing: Westport, CT, p. 247.

Smith, G. C., et al. 1969. "Considerations for beef tenderness evaluations." *J. Food Sci. 34:* 612.

Tressler, D. K., et al. eds. 1968. *Freezing Preservation of Foods*. AVI Publishing: Westport, CT.

Yaciuk, G. 1982. *Food Drying*. UNIPUB: New York.

CHAPTER 21

Food Additives

OVERVIEW

Food additives have been a source of considerable controversy in this nation and throughout other industrial nations. They constitute such a debatable topic that even their definition is the subject of argument. The dictionary states that food additives are substances added in relatively small amounts to impart or improve desirable qualities or suppress undesirable ones. Other groups have defined food additives, including the Food Protection Committee of the National Academy of Sciences–National Research Council and the U.S. Food and Drug Administration.

The Food Protection Committee considers an additive to be "a substance or a mixture of substances other than a basic foodstuff, which is present in a food as a result of any aspect of production, processing, storage, or packaging. The term does not include chance contaminants" (Food Protection Committee, 1981). This definition clearly indicates that accidental additives or contaminants are not considered to be additives even though they may be there because of environmental circumstances. This definition is helpful and clear, but it does not have legal implications.

The definition used by the Food and Drug Administration is the definition bearing legal impact in this country. Therefore, its somewhat tortured language was developed to eliminate as many ambiguities and questions as possible. According to the FDA, a food additive is "any substance, the intended use of which results or may reasonably be expected to result, directly or indirectly, in its becoming a component of or otherwise affecting the characteristics of any food (including any substance intended for use in producing, manufacturing, packing, processing, preparing, treating, transporting or holding a food; and including any source of radiation intended for any such use), if such substance is not generally recognized, among experts qualified by scientific training and experience to evaluate its safety, as having been adequately shown through scientific procedures (or, in the case of substances used in food prior to January 1, 1958, through either scientific procedures or experience based on common use in food) to be safe under the conditions of its intended use." This definition is included in the Food Additives Amendment to the Federal Food, Drug, and Cosmetic Act of 1938; the amendment was passed in 1958 and is still in effect. The final parenthetic clause established the concept for creating a list of additives "generally recognized as safe," a list usually referred to simply as the **GRAS list.** In essence, any substance that a manufacturer wants to market to the food industry as an additive has to be proven safe for human consumption by scientific experiments or else has to be on the GRAS list.

The cost of the testing to obtain clearance for a new additive is great, and considerable money has been spent since 1958 to conduct federally funded tests on the additives that were identified on the GRAS list. The motivation for testing is to ensure safety from health risks in the nation's food supply. The motivation for using the additives is to enhance the quality of the foods being consumed.

GRAS List
Additives "generally recognized as safe" because of their common and safe use prior to January 1, 1958.

RATIONALE

Consumers reading ingredient labels on the many processed and prepared foods in the market today seem to develop a wide range of emotions ranging from embarrassment at not being able to pronounce the tongue-twisting chemical names to utter panic about the perceived hazards of the "unnatural chemical feast" that greets them at the store. Of course, the option still exists that practically all menu items could be prepared from basic ingredients at home, which would reduce the intake of additives significantly. Some people opt for this basic approach to solve their food problems, sometimes because of health concerns and sometimes for the pleasure of creating exactly the foods they desire. However, many people buy convenience foods and other processed food items to save time, to improve food quality, to save energy, or for a host of other reasons. The fact is that foods containing a wide array of additives are now consumed on a regular basis by most of the American public.

Food that reaches the typical American table today has not been rushed from the field to the table. Frequently it has been shipped many miles, sometimes even from other countries. Convenience items ranging from packaged mixes to fully prepared meals that need only to be reheated are assembled and packaged in factories quite remote from the consumer's table, and they pass through many hands en route to that table. Such foods are subjected to far more stresses than are foods that are served as soon as they are prepared in the home, and yet the quality of the convenience items needs to be competitive with food prepared in the home. The only way to ensure suitable quality at the consumer's table is through the use of additives to overcome the problems engendered by the long and complex supply route that convenience foods must traverse. The ready acceptance and strong market for these items support food manufacturers in their commitment to using additives to bring the world of food to the consumer.

Although communication between manufacturer and consumer would appear to be direct, there actually is a very prominent, though less visible, voice in the matter of food additives, and that voice is the U.S. Food and Drug Administration. The FDA has the power of law behind its voice. Much of the power of the FDA in relation to additives is contained within the Food Additives Amendment of 1958, although the original strength was provided by the Food, Drug, and Cosmetic Act of 1938. The 1958 legislation was of particular importance because it shifted the burden of proof for safety of additives from the federal government to the manufacturers of new additives proposed for use. Proof of safety requires animal feeding tests for an extended period, occasionally as long as 7 years. People also are used in a portion of the testing, although human testing is quite limited and is not done in the early phase. These tests usually are contracted to testing services by the manufacturer.

The 1958 legislation contained a highly controversial clause, the Delaney clause. This rather emotionally charged legislation requires that additives that produce cancer when consumed at any level by animals or by people cannot be added to foods. An additive that has been prominent in the challenge to the enforcement of the Delaney clause is saccharin, which the FDA moved to ban in 1972. Cyclamates had been banned in 1969 under the Delaney clause, leaving only saccharin as a nonnutritive sweetener. The fact that saccharin had been used by large numbers of people over many years without any evidence of a carcinogenic effect made the banning of saccharin seem to be an overly zealous and perhaps even totally unnecessary action, and the objections to this proposed action were both loud and numerous. The results of this controversy have been continuous extensions of permission to use saccharin in foods and preliminary efforts to find a way to introduce logic into the Delaney clause rather than require automatic banning of a substance when there is only limited evidence of possible carcinogenicity, and that evidence is in laboratory animals administered at totally unrealistic levels of the substance.

The concept of "risk versus benefit" has evolved from the additives controversy. A useful illustration is provided by the flurry over the use of nitrates and nitrites in curing meats. Concern stemmed from evidence that nitrites can combine with amines to form nitrosamines during intensive heating (as in frying bacon to the very crisp stage) and in the intestines when nitrites are eaten. Nitrosamines are of concern because they are quite potent carcinogens. That would seem to be justification for enforcing the Delaney clause and prohibiting the use of nitrites and nitrates in cured meats. However, this is the risk side of the equation. On the benefit side is the protection provided by nitrites and nitrates against the risk of botulism from these meats; botulism is a real and very lethal risk without these additives. Consequently, nitrates and nitrites presently still are permitted in cured meats, but the level used has been reduced somewhat. If an effective replacement can be found, nitrates and nitrites likely will be banned from the food supply. Nevertheless, this controversy illustrates the application of the concept of "risk versus benefit" despite the fact that such action actually violates the Delaney clause.

The Color Additive Amendments of 1960 are superimposed on the other legislation affecting the use of additives in the food industry. This legislation covers the use of all substances used to color food, whether they are additives extracted from other foods or synthetic compounds. This has been an area of considerable interest because some colors that had been used extensively were banned under this legislation when they were found to be carcinogenic as defined under the Delaney clause. The Color Additive Amendments of 1960 formed the basis for banning FD&C Red No. 2 and No. 4, as well as carbon black.

The Miller Pesticide Amendment of 1954 is the legislation regulating the use of agricultural pesticides and their residues in the food supply. The Environmental Protection Agency has authority to establish the amounts of residues that are allowable. Enforcement is under the Food and Drug Administration. A recent illustration of the effectiveness of this legislation was the banning of ethylene dibromide, a pesticide that was being used extensively in stored grains and citrus fruits to prevent losses from insects during storage.

A book of particular interest to the food industry regarding additives is the *Food Chemicals Codex*. This guide states the standards for purity, clearly indicating the methods of analysis and the allowable levels of trace contaminants. This work was developed by the Food Protection Committee of the National Academy of Sciences–National Research Council and is updated regularly to maintain currency with the present state of the art in the arena of food additives.

Consumers are aided in knowing what they are eating by the legal requirement for ingredient labeling on all food packages. All ingredients contained in a food, including all additives, are identified in descending order by weight. Such labeling is mandatory.

Additives are used for a variety of reasons, some of which are listed here:

1. To enhance nutritive value
2. To improve flavor
3. To improve color
4. To extend shelf life
5. To improve texture
6. To control pH
7. For leavening
8. For bleaching and maturing
9. To ease manufacturing problems

All of these reasons have economic implications because of the improved sales potential for highly palatable and/or nutritionally enhanced foods and because of modifications that make production and processing easier. Today's health-conscious consumers continue to maintain a high level of interest in the nutritive value of the foods they are eating and may be attracted to products to which specific nutrients have been added. Addition of thiamine, riboflavin, niacin, and iron to breads and cereal products and of iodine to salt has been sanctioned for many years to enrich the intake of nutrients noted to be inadequate in the diets of a large proportion of the population. More recently, nutrients have been added to a wide array of foods to meet consumer interest and demand for fortified foods.

Pleasure is a vital reason why people eat, and pleasure can be increased if the sensory qualities of a food are enhanced. This compelling rationale explains the motivation for adding ingredients that affect flavor, color, and texture. Additives that have particular appeal to the senses have dominated a considerable amount of research money because of the large economic potential for food products that are able to gain broad consumer acceptance and carve a niche in the highly competitive food industry.

Additives can be crucial to development of food products with a satisfactory shelf life. Foods with molds or other microbiological contamination not only are offensive to the consumer who has purchased them, but they may also eliminate that consumer as a customer. Food manufacturers cannot afford this loss of market. In addition, harmful food products have the potential for lawsuits, which can be very damaging to the company that is the object of the complaint. Additives that interfere with growth of microorganisms can be essential to avoiding such problems. Other ingredients help extend shelf life by aiding in retention of moisture.

Manufacturers may use additives to avoid or at least alleviate production problems resulting from behavioral properties of a food during its production. For example, the foaming that develops in the preparation of dried beans or in milk is but one illustration of problems faced in processing large quantities of food. Numerous other reasons for the inclusion of additives can be found throughout the food industry.

The use of additives is sanctioned by the Food and Drug Administration only if the additive:

1. Performs a useful function,
2. Does not deceive the customer by obscuring use of low-quality ingredients or poor manufacturing,
3. Does not reduce nutritive value substantially,
4. Does not merely accomplish the same result that improved manufacturing techniques could provide,
5. Can be measured in the product by a recognized method of analysis.

INTENTIONAL ADDITIVES

Functions

Additives in foods can be divided into accidental and intentional additives. The accidental additives that sometimes occur in foods are the result of some unintentional incident, perhaps a hair, oil from a machine, or another contaminant that was not intended to be a part of the product, yet is there. Careful monitoring of production from the initial ingredients to the packaged product is essential to elimination of such problems. There is no intent that these should be a part of the food.

Intentional additives, however, represent quite a different type of additive; these are added to the food deliberately and at intended levels. According to the five criteria to be met by additives, capricious use of additives in food manufacturing is not allowed by the Food and Drug Administration. Unnecessary use of additives is not favored by the food industry either because of the added cost.

Various food additives were classified in the *Federal Register* [**1974,** 39(185), 34175] according to their technical functions in foods:

1. Anticaking agents, free-flow agents
2. Antimicrobial agents
3. Antioxidants
4. Colors, coloring adjuncts (color stabilizers, color fixatives, colorretentive agents, etc.)
5. Curing, pickling agents
6. Dough strengtheners
7. Drying agents

8. Emulsifiers, emulsifier salts

9. Enzymes

10. Firming agents

11. Flavor enhancers

12. Flavoring agents, adjuvants (enhancers)

13. Flour-treating agents (including bleaching and maturing agents)

14. Formulation aids (carriers, binders, fillers, plasticizers, film formers, tabletting aids, etc.)

15. Fumigants

16. Humectants, moisture-retention agents, antidusting agents

17. Leavening agents

18. Lubricants, release agents

19. Nonnutritive sweeteners

20. Nutrient supplements

21. Nutritive sweeteners

22. Oxidizing and reducing agents

23. pH control agents (including buffers, acids, alkalies, and neutralizing agents)

24. Processing aids (clarifying agents, clouding agents, catalysts, flocculents, filter aids, etc.)

25. Propellants, aerating agents, gases

26. Sequestrants

27. Solvents, vehicles

28. Stabilizers, thickeners (suspending and bodying agents, setting agents, gelling agents, bulking agents, etc.)

29. Surface-active agents (other than emulsifiers, including solubilizing agents, dispersants, detergents, wetting agents, rehydration enhancers, whipping agents, foaming agents, and defoaming agents)

30. Surface-finishing agents (including glazes, polishes, waxes, and protective coatings)

31. Synergists

32. Texturizers

Short Dictionary of Additives

An exhaustive list of food additives is impractical because it would include more than 2,000 entries. Therefore, this list identifies and describes briefly the role of some of the more commonly used food additives:

Acacia gum   stabilizer, thickener, surface finishing

Acetanisole   flavoring (nutty)

Acetic acid   acidulant, antimicrobial agent (bacteria and yeast)

Acetone peroxide   flour bleaching and maturing, solvent, oxidizing

Acetophenone   flavoring (fruity)

Adipic acid   pH control

Agar agar   thickener

Alanine   nutrient enrichment (amino acid)

Alcohol   solvent

Alginates   water binding, thickener

Allyl disulfde   flavoring (garlic, onion)

Aluminum phosphate   anticaking

Aluminum sodium sulfate   buffer

Aluminum stearate   defoaming

Aluminum sulfate   firming

Ammonium alginate   stabilizer, thickener, texturizer

Ammonium stearate   defoaming

Ammonium sulfate   buffer, dough conditioner

Amylase   enzyme, digests starch

Amyl propionate   flavoring (fruity)

Annatto   food coloring, used in cheese

Arabic, gum   (acacia gum) stabilizer, thickener, surface finishing

Arabinogalactose   stabilizer, thickener, texturizer

Arginine   nutrient enrichment (amino acid)

Ascorbic acid   antioxidant, prevents enzymatic browning in fruits

Aspartic acid   nutrient enrichment (amino acid)

Azodicarbonamide   flour bleaching and maturing

Baking powder   leavening

Baking soda   texturizer, pH modification, leavening with acid

Beeswax   surface finishing

Bentonite   adsorbs protein

Benzoic acid   antimicrobial agent (yeast and bacteria)

Benzoyl acetate   flavoring (fruity)

Benzoyl isoeugenol   flavoring (spicy)

Benzoyl peroxide   flour bleaching and maturing, oxidizing

Bisulfite salts   antioxidants

Black pepper   flavoring

Butyl paraben   preservative

Butyl stearate   defoaming

BHA (butylated hydroxyanisole)   antioxidant

BHT (butylated hydroxytoluene)   antioxidant

Calcium alginate   stabilizing, thickening

Calcium bromate   maturing, bleaching

Calcium carbonate   acidity control, leavening

Calcium chloride   firming agent

Calcium citrate   buffer, chelator

Calcium disodium EDTA   chelator (see EDTA)

Calcium gluconate   buffer, chelator

Calcium lactate   preservative

Calcium lactobionate   foaming

Calcium peroxide   oxidizing

Calcium propionate   preservative

Calcium pyrophosphate   buffer

Calcium silicate   anticaking

Calcium sorbate   preservative

Calcium stearate   anticaking

Calcium stearoyl-2-lactylate   emulsifier

Calcium sulfate   processing aid

Canthaxanthin   coloring

Caramel   coloring

Carbon dioxide   effervescent

Carnauba wax   surface finishing

Carob bean gum   stabilizer, thickener, texturizer

Carotenes   coloring

Carrageenan   thickener, stabilizer, emulsifier

Cellulose   stabilizer, thickener, texturizer

Cholic acid   emulsifier

Citric acid   acidifying agent, synergist, chelator, preservative, antioxidant

Citrus Red No. 2   coloring

Cobalt sulfate   source of cobalt and sulfur in diet

Cochineal   beverage color

Cornstarch   anticaking, thickener

Corn syrup   formulation aid, texturizer, sweetener

Cupric chloride   copper source

Cyclamates   presently banned in the United States; nonnutritive sweetener

Decanoic acid   defoaming

Desoxycholic acid   emulsifier

Dextrin   stabilizer

Dextrose   formulation aid, sweetener (glucose)

Dicalcium phosphate   acidity control, leavening, anticaking

Diglycerides   emulsifiers

Dimagnesium phosphate   anticaking

Dimethyl polysiloxane   defoaming

Dioctyl sodium sulfosuccinate   emulsifier

Disodium EDTA   chelator

Disodium guanylate   flavor potentiator

Disodium inosinate   flavor potentiator

Disodium phosphate   emulsifier

EDTA (ethylenediaminetetracetate)   sequestrant, antioxidant

Ethyl caproate   artificial fruit flavoring

Ethyl pelargonate   alcoholic beverage flavoring

Ethyl phenylacetate   honey flavoring

Ethyl vanillin   chocolate and vanilla flavoring

Ethylene oxide   antimicrobial agent

Eugenol   defoaming

Fatty acids   emulsifiers

FD & C Blue No. 1   coloring

FD & C Green No. 2   green coloring in mint jelly

FD & C Red No. 3   red coloring in baked goods

FD & C Yellow No. 5   yellow coloring

Ferrous gluconate   nutrient enrichment, iron source

Ferrous sulfate   nutrient enrichment, iron source

Fructose   sweetener, monosaccharide

Fumaric acid   acidity control

Furcelleran   texturizer

Gelatin   thickener

Gibberellic acid   fermentation aid

Glucose oxidase   oxygen scavenger

Glycerine   solvent, texturizer, humectant

Glycerol mono- and *diesters*   emulsifiers

Glycerol monostearate   dough conditioner

Glycocholic acid   emulsifier

Guar gum   thickener

Gum ghatti   stabilizer, thickener, texturizer

Gum guaiac   antioxidant

Heptylparaben   preservative

Honey   sweetener, texturizer

Hydrochloric acid   acidulant

Hydrogen peroxide   bleaching, antimicrobial agent, oxidizing

Hydrolyzed vegetable protein   stabilizer, thickener

Invert sugar   sweetener

Iodate, potassium   nutrient enrichment, iodine source

Iron oxide   coloring

Karaya gum   stabilizer, thickener, texturizer

Lactylic acid esters of fatty acids   surface active agents, emulsifiers

Larch gum   stabilizer, thickener, texturizer

Lauric acid   defoaming

Lecithin   emulsifier (from corn and soybeans)

Lipase   dairy flavor developer

Locust bean gum   also called carob bean; dough conditioner

Magnesium carbonate   anticaking

Magnesium silicate   anticaking

Magnesium stearate   formulation aid, anticaking

Magnesium sulfate   nutrient enrichment, magnesium source

Manganese citrate   nutrient enrichment, manganese source

Mannitol   formulation aid, sweetener, anticaking, stabilizer, thickener, texturizer

Methyl bromide   kills undesirable organisms

Methyl cellulose   bulking

Methyl glucoside   coconut oil ester; clouding and crystallization inhibitor

Methylparaben   preservative

Mineral oil   defoaming

Modified food starch   stabilizer, thickener, texturizer

Monocalcium phosphate   leavening, dough conditioner

Monoglycerides   emulsifiers

Monosodium glutamate (MSG)   flavor enhancer

Mustard   flavoring

Nickel sulfate   nutrient enrichment, nickel source

Nicotinamide   nutrient enrichment, niacin

Nitrates   antimicrobial action; effective against spores of *Clostridium botulinum*

Nitrites   antimicrobial action; effective against spores of *Clostridium botulinum*

Oleic acid   defoaming

Oxystearin   clouding and crystallization inhibitor, defoaming

Palmitic acid   defoaming

Papain   proteolytic enzyme from papaya; meat tenderizer

Pectin   stabilizer, thickener, texturizer

Pectinase   clarifies beverages

Peroxidase   enzyme used to destroy glucose in dried egg white

Petroleum waxes   defoaming

Phosphates   acidity control

Phosphoric acid   chelator, acidity control

Phostoxin   fumigant

Polysorbate 60, 65, and *80*   emulsifiers

Polyvinyl pyrrolidine   surface finishing

Potassium acid citrate   buffer

Potassium alginate   stabilizer, thickener, texturizer

Potassium bromide flour bleaching and maturing, dough conditioner, fermentation aid

Potassium citrate chelator

Potassium gibberellate fermentation aid

Potassium iodide nutrient enrichment, potassium source

Potassium phosphate chelator, emulsifier

Potassium polymetaphosphate emulsifier

Potassium propionate preservative

Potassium pyrophosphate emulsifier

Propylene glycol formulation aid, humectant, solvent

Propylene glycol monostearate humectant

Propylene oxide antimicrobial agent

Propyl gallate antioxidant

Propylparaben preservative

Red Dye No. 40 color

Rennet enzyme; clots milk

Resins insoluble materials used to remove ions from water, juices, and other liquids; forms are acrylate–acrylamide, sulfonated copolymers of styrene, sulfonated anthracite coal

Rice wax surface finishing

Saccharin nonnutritive sweetener

Saffron coloring

Shellac wax surface finishing

Silica aerogel anticaking

Silicon dioxide defoaming, anticaking

Sodium acetate acidity control

Sodium acid phosphate leavening

Sodium acid pyrophosphate buffer, chelator

Sodium alginate stabilizer, thickener, texturizer

Sodium aluminum citrate anticaking

Sodium aluminum phosphate leavening, emulsifier in cheese

Sodium aluminum silicate anticaking

Sodium aluminum sulfate leavening

Sodium benzoate preservative

Sodium bicarbonate texturizer, pH influence, cleaning

Sodium calcium alginate texturizer, stabilizer, thickener

Sodium carbonate acidity control, leavening

Sodium carboxymethylcellulose bulking

Sodium caseinate formulation aid

Sodium chloride flavor enhancer

Sodium citrate   acidity control

Sodium diacetate   chelator

Sodium erythorbate   curing agent, preservative

Sodium gluconate   chelator

Sodium hexametaphosphate   chelator

Sodium hydroxide   pH control

Sodium lauryl sulfate   surfactant

Sodium metaphosphate   sequestrant, curing, emulsifier

Sodium nitrate   curing, prevents formation of toxin from *Clostridium botulinum* spores

Sodium nitrite   curing, prevents formation of toxin from *Clostridium botulinum* spores

Sodium potassium tartrate   buffer, chelator

Sodium propionate   preservative

Sodium silicoaluminate   anticaking

Sodium sorbate   preservative

Sodium stearyl fumarate   maturing, bleaching, conditioning

Sodium thiosulfate   chelator

Sodium tripolyphosphate   curing, humectant, chelator

Sorbic acid   mold and yeast inhibitor

Sorbitan monooleate   emulsifier

Sorbitan monopalmitate   emulsifier

Sorbitan tristearate   emulsifier

Sorbitol   chelator, humectant, sweetener

Starch   thickener, moisture retention, bulking

Stearic acid   defoaming

Sucrose   flavoring, preservative

Sugar   flavoring, preservative

Sulfites   general antimicrobial agent

Sulfur dioxide   preservative

Sulfuric acid   acidity control

Tagetes   coloring (Aztec marigold), in chicken feed only

Tannic acid   complexes protein

Tartaric acid   chelator, acidity control

Tertiary butyl hydroquinone (TBHQ)   antioxidant

Thiamin hydrochloride   nutrient enrichment, thiamin

Thiodopropionic acid   decomposes hydroperoxide

Thiosulfate   reducing agent

Titanium dioxide   coloring

α-Tocopherol   reducing agent, nutrient enrichment, vitamin E

Tragacanth gum   stabilizer, thickener, texturizer

Triacetin   solvent

Tricalcium phosphate   synergist, anticaking

Tricalcium silicate   anticaking

Trimethyl citrate   solvent

Turmeric   flavoring, coloring

Ultramarine   blue color, animal feed only

Xanthan gum   body, bulking

Yeasts   leavening

Yellow Dye No. 5   coloring

Yellow prussiate of soda   anticaking

Manufacturing Applications

Selection of specific food additives for incorporation into commercial food products is based on the characteristics of the food requiring modification and the suitability of a particular additive, in terms of both its effectiveness in the food item and its cost compared with possible alternatives. As alternative additives frequently exist for a particular application (Table 21.1), considerable research usually is done by food technologists to determine the most appropriate additives and the levels to use in formulating new products.

Safety

The safety of additives in the food supply is a question of personal and social significance, yet one that is proving to be difficult to document. The protocol for testing the toxicity of an additive includes acute tests, prolonged tests, and chronic, long-term or extended tests.

- *Acute tests:* Single massive dose administered to two species, at least one being a nonrodent. This dosage level is lethal to half of the test animals. Survivors are studied for 7 days.

- *Prolonged tests:* Three different doses administered daily to two species for a minimum of 3 months. The control group and the three test groups usually have at least 10 males and 10 females each. Weekly physical examinations are conducted throughout the test period, which is followed by complete autopsies and histologic study of organs.

- *Chronic tests:* Same testing as for prolonged tests, but the time frame is at least a year and often at least $1\frac{1}{2}$ years and the number of animals tested is three or four times greater. Some additives are tested for possible effects on reproduction and may include a three-generation study.

Selection of animals for testing is difficult. Rodents have many more intestinal bacteria than humans, thus modifying the products available for absorption and creating differences in the potential risks to the subjects. Additional differences are found in the ways in which various species metabolize substances.

Table 21.1 Functional Needs and Some Possible Additives to Meet Manufacturing Requirements for Food Products

Functional Need	Some Possible Additives to Meet Need
Enhance nutritive value	Potassium iodide, ferrous gluconate and other iron salts, calcium salts, vitamins, amino acids
Improve flavor	Acetanisole, acetophenone, allyl disulfide, amyl propionate, benzoyl acetate, benzoyl isoeugenol, corn syrup, dextrose and other sweeteners, disodium guanylate and inosinate
Improve color	Annatto, canthaxanthin, caramel, carotenes, citrus red No. 2, cochineal, turmeric; FD&C blue No. 1, green No. 2, red Nos. 3 and 40, yellow No. 5; saffron
Extend shelf life	Ascorbic acid, bisulfite salts, BHA, BHT, butyl paraben, calcium lactate, sorbic acid, calcium propionate and sorbate, citric acid, EDTA, gum guaiac, heptyl parabens
Improve texture	Gums (acacia or arabic, carob bean, carrageenan, guar, ghatti, karaya, tragacanth, xanthan), agar, alginates, aluminum phosphate, aluminum and ammonium sulfates, ammonium and calcium alginates, calcium chloride, calcium salts (stearate, silicate, stearoyl-2-lactylate), cellulose, cholic acid, cornstarch, dextrin, diglycerides, disodium phosphate, lecithin, modified food starch, polysorbates, silicon dioxide
Control pH	Acetic acid, adipic acid, baking soda, benzoic acid, calcium salts (carbonate, citrate, gluconate, pyrophosphate), citric acid, dicalcium phosphate, hydrochloric acid, phosphates, phosphoric acid, potassium acid citrate
Leaven	Baking powder, baking soda, calcium carbonates, yeasts, glucono-delta-lactone
Bleach and mature	Azodicarbonamide, benzoyl peroxide, calcium bromate, glycerol monostearate, hydrogen peroxide, potassium bromide
Ease manufacturing problems	Aluminum phosphate and stearate, butyl stearate, calcium salts (lactobionate, silicate, stearate, sulfate), decanoic acid, dimagnesium phosphate, dimethyl polysiloxane, dioctyl sodium sulfosuccinate, magnesium carbonate, oleic acid

Table 21.2 Some Natural Toxicants in Food

Compound	Food Source	Characteristics
Unidentified	Fava beans	Hemolysis, vomiting, dizziness, prostration
Aflatoxin	Moldy peanuts with *Aspergillus flavus* contamination	Liver damage, chronic consumption may lead to cancer
Ergot	Moldy rye	Severe muscle contraction, serious to fatal involvement of nervous system
Antitrypsin	Legumes	Blocks protein digestion, inactivated by heat
Goitrogen	Cabbage	Blocks thyroxine synthesis
Phytin	Cereals	Restricts utilization of calcium and iron
Solanine	Sunburned potato	Vomiting and diarrhea
Oxalic acid	Spinach, rhubarb	Binds calcium
Caffeine	Coffee, tea	Possible teratogen and carcinogen
Benzopyrene	Charbroiled meat	Carcinogen
Nitrates and nitrites	Some vegetables	Potential carcinogen
Gossypol	Cottonseed	Toxic to animals
Cyanogens (amygdalin)	Almonds, peach and apricot pits	Headache, heart palpitations, weakness, can be fatal
Pressor amines (histamine, tyramine)	Camembert cheese, bananas	Elevated blood pressure resulting from constriction of blood vessels

Clearly it is important to ascertain the safety of substances that are deliberately added to the food supply and to ban the use of those found to be unsafe. Unfortunately, nature incorporates some hazardous substances into some foods, too. Some of these natural toxicants are identified in Table 21.2.

SUMMARY

Food additives are important constituents of processed and convenience foods in the United States. Regulation of the commercial use of additives is under the U.S. Food and Drug Administration. The Food Additives Amendment to the Federal Food, Drug, and Cosmetic Act of 1938, passed in 1958, requires that the safety of all additives other than those on the GRAS list be demonstrated by the additive manufacturer and approved by the FDA prior to inclusion in foods being prepared for sale.

Additives are used to improve nutritive value, flavor, color, and texture, to reduce losses during marketing, and to ease manufacturing problems that occur in quantity production. Accidental additives must be avoided by careful control of manufacturing. Intentional additives must serve a useful purpose without being harmful to health. More than 2,000 additives are available for inclusion in foods and serve in improving processed and convenience foods in many ways. This chapter includes a selected list of the more common additives and their reasons for use. The safety of these additives is tested in acute, prolonged, and chronic tests.

STUDY QUESTIONS

1. What legislation determines the use of additives in foods (include all legislative actions that apply)?

2. What are the pros and cons of the use of additives?

3. What is the Delaney clause and how does it conflict with the concept of "risk versus benefit"?

4. What conditions must be met by an additive before it is used in a food?

5. Identify five specific additives that might be used for each of the following functions: color enhancement, flavor enhancement, thickening, pH control.

BIBLIOGRAPHY

Ayres, J. C. and Kirschman, J. C. 1981. *Impact of Toxicology on Food Processing*. AVI Publishing: Westport, CT.

Dziezak, J. D. 1990. "Acidulants: ingredients that do more than meet the acid test." *Food Technol. 44* (1): 75.

Fennema, O. R. 1985. *Principles of Food Science*. 2nd ed. Dekker: New York.

Food and Drug Administration. 1980. *Food and Drug Administration Acts*. U.S. Department of Health and Human Services Pub. No. (FDA) 80–1051; Washington, DC.

Food Protection Committee. 1973. *Toxicants Occurring Naturally in Foods*. 2nd ed. National Academy of Sciences–National Research Council: Washington, DC.

Food Protection Committee. 1981. *Food Chemicals Codex*. 3rd ed. National Academy of Sciences–National Research Council: Washington, DC.

Furia, T. E. 1973. *Handbook of Food Additives*. CRC Press: Boca Raton, FL., Vol. 1.

Furia, T. E. 1982. *Handbook of Food Additives*. CRC Press: Boca Raton, FL., Vol. 2.

Kimbrell, E. F. 1982. "Codex Alimentarius food standards and their relevance to U.S. standards." *Food Technol. 36* (6): 93.

Potter, N. N. 1986. *Food Science*. 4th ed. AVI Publishing: Westport, CT.

Pszczola, D. E. 1990. "Food irradiation: Countering the tactics and claims of opponents." *Food Technol. 44* (6): 92.

Schultz, H. W. 1981. *Food Law Handbook*. AVI Publishing: Westport, CT.

Taylor, R. J. 1980. *Food Additives*. Wiley: New York.

Glossary

A band Total portion of the sarcomere in which thick and thin myofilaments overlap; includes the H band.

Acidophilus milk Fermented milk product (usually whole milk) to which *Lactobacillus acidophilus* is added to digest the lactose.

Acrolein A highly irritating and volatile aldehyde formed when glycerol is heated to the point where two molecules of water split from it.

Actin Myofibrillar protein existing primarily in two forms (F and G).

Actinidin Proteolytic enzyme in kiwi fruit.

Active dry yeast Granular form of dried *Saccharomyces cerevisiae* (8 percent moisture); storage is at room temperature and rehydration at 40°–46°C.

Actomyosin Protein complex of actin and myosin that forms to effect contraction of the sarcomere.

Aflatoxin Carcinogenic mycotoxin produced by *Aspergillus flavus* and *Aspergillus parasiticus*.

Aging (maturing) of flour Chemical process to modify the sulfhydryl groups in flour to disulfide linkages, usually utilizing a chlorine-containing compound.

Albumen White of an egg; consists of three layers.

Albumen index Grading measurement of albumen to determine quality on the basis of the amount of thick white.

Alliin Odorless precursor in garlic that ultimately is converted to diallyl disulfide.

Alliinase Enzyme in garlic responsible for catalyzing the conversion of alliin to diallyl thiosulfinate, the precursor of diallyl disulfide.

Allium Genus that includes onions, chives, garlic, and leeks; unique for its sulfur-containing flavor compounds.

α crystals Extremely fine and unstable fat crystals.

α-amylase Amylose-digesting enzyme contained in abundance in egg yolk and to a lesser extent in egg white.

Amphoteric Capable of functioning as either an acid or a base, depending on the pH of the medium in which the compound is found.

Amylograph Device designed to control temperature of a starch paste and to measure its viscosity.

Amylopectin Branched fraction of starch consisting primarily of glucose units linked with 1,4-α-glucosidic linkages, but interrupted occasionally with a 1,6-α-linkage.

Amylose Straight-chain, slightly soluble starch fraction consisting of glucose units joined by 1,4-α-glucosidic linkages.

Anthocyanidin Anthocyanin-type pigment that lacks a sugar in its structure.

Anthocyanin Flavonoid pigment in which the oxygen in the central ring is charged positively.

Anthoxanthin Flavonoid pigment in which the oxygen in the central ring does not carry an electrical charge.

Aspartame Very sweet, low-calorie methylated dipeptide (phenylalanine and aspartic acid) used as a sweetener.

Aspergillus flavus Mold capable of making aflatoxin in stored nuts, grains, and legumes.

Aspergillus parasiticus Mold capable of making aflatoxin in stored nuts, grains, and legumes.

509

Bacillus coagulans Anaerobic bacillus that digests sugar to lactic acid in canned foods to cause flat-sour spoilage.

Benzoyl peroxide Food additive used for bleaching the xanthophylls in refined flours.

β crystals Extremely coarse and, therefore, undesirable fat crystals.

Betacyanins Group of betalains responsible for the reddish-purple color of beets; not an anthocyanin, but behaving colorwise in the same fashion.

Betalains Two groups of pigments that contribute the anthocyanin-like color to beets, but differ chemically from the anthocyanins.

β′ crystals Very fine and reasonably stable fat crystals.

Beta ray Radiant energy that is very slightly longer than gamma rays and that can penetrate food, but not aluminum.

Birefringence Refraction of light in two slightly different directions.

Bloom gelometer Modification of a penetrometer designed especially for measuring the tenderness of gels.

Botulism Frequently fatal food poisoning caused by ingesting toxin produced by spores of *Clostridium botulinum*.

Bound water Water that is bound to other substances and no longer exhibits the flow properties and solvent capability commonly associated with water.

Bran Outer layers (fibrous and very high in cellulose) encasing the interior endosperm and germ of cereal grains.

Bromelain Proteolytic enzyme in pineapple.

Caramelization Fragmentation of monosaccharide into a variety of compounds, including organic acids, aldehydes, and ketones, as a result of extremely intense heat.

Carotenes Group of carotenoids containing only hydrogen and carbon in a polymer of isoprene.

Carotenoids Class of pigments contributing red, orange, or yellow color as a result of the resonance provided by the isoprene polymers.

Casein Collective name for milk proteins precipitated at pH 4.6.

Catechins Flavonoid pigments that are a subgroup of the flavonols.

Cathepsins Group of proteolytic enzymes that can catalyze hydrolytic reactions leading to the passing of rigor mortis.

Cellulose Complex carbohydrate composed of glucose units joined together by 1,4-β-glucosidic linkages.

Chalazae Thick, ropelike extensions of the chalaziferous layer that aid in centering the yolk in the egg.

Chlorophyll a Blue-green, more abundant form of chlorophyll; the chlorophyll form in which the *R* group is a methyl group.

Chlorophyll b Yellowish-green form of chlorophyll in which the *R* group is an aldehyde group.

Chlorophyllase Plant enzyme that splits off the phytyl group to form chlorophyllide from chlorophyll.

Chlorophyllide Chlorophyll molecule minus the phytyl group; water-soluble derivative of chlorophyll responsible for the light green tint of water in which green vegetables have been cooked.

Chlorophyllin Abnormally green pigment formed when the methyl and phytyl groups are removed from chlorophyll in an alkaline medium.

Chloroplast Type of plastid containing chlorophyll.

Chromoplast Type of plastid containing carotenoids.

Circumvallate papillae Large, obvious protuberances always containing taste buds and distinguished easily because they form a "V" near the back of the tongue.

Cis configuration The hydrogen is attached to the carbon atoms on either end of the double bond from the same direction, causing a lower melting point than its trans counterpart.

Climacteric Maximum respiratory rate just prior to the full ripening of many fleshy fruits.

Clostridium botulinum Anaerobic bacteria that form spores capable of producing a toxin that frequently is fatal to humans.

Clostridium nigrificans Bacteria capable of producing hydrogen sulfide in canned foods to cause sulfide spoilage.

Collagen Fibrous protein composed of three strands of tropocollagen.

Collenchyma tissue Aggregates of elongated collenchyma cells providing supportive structure to various plant foods, notably vegetables.

Colloidal dispersion Two-phase system in which the particles in the dispersed phase are between 0.001 and 1 micron in diameter.

Color-difference meter An objective machine, such as the Hunter color-difference meter or Gardner color-difference meter; capable of measuring color difference between samples utilizing the C.I.E. or Munsell color systems.

Compressed yeast *Saccharomyces cerevisiae* in a cornstarch-containing cake with a moisture level of 72 percent; requires refrigerated storage; dispersion is best at 32–38°C.

Compressimeter Objective equipment that measures the force required to compress a food sample a predetermined amount.

Conalbumin Protein in egg albumen capable of complexing with iron and copper ions to form red and yellow colors, respectively.

Consistometer A device for measuring spread or flow of semisolid foods in a specified length of time.

Crosslinked starch Starch produced under alkaline conditions, usually in combination with acetic or succinic anhydride; notable as a thickener and stabilizing agent with good ability to exhibit minimal retrogradation.

Cruciferae Family that includes Brussels sprouts, cabbage, rutabagas, turnips, cauliflower, kale, and mustard; contains sulfur-containing flavor compounds that differ from those found in *Allium* vegetables.

Cyclodextrins (α, β, γ CD) Cyclic compounds containing 6 to 8 glucose units derived from starch by bacterial enzymes (cyclodextrin glucosyl transferases).

Denaturation Relaxation of the tertiary structure to the secondary structure, accompanied by decreasing solubility of a protein.

Denatured globin hemichrome A gray-brown pigment formed when myoglobin is heated.

Dermal system Outer protective covering on fruits and vegetables, as well as other parts of plants.

Dextrinization Hydrolytic breakdown of starch effected by intense, dry heat and producing dextrins.

Dextrins Polysaccharides composed entirely of glucose units linked together and distinguishable from starch by a shorter chain length.

Diallyl disulfide Key flavor aromatic compound from garlic.

Diet margarines Spreads made from plant oils that have been partially hydrogenated and then blended with more than twice as much water as is used in stick margarines.

Difference testing Sensory testing designed to determine whether detectable differences exist between products.

Docosahexanoic acid (DHA) Omega-3 fatty acid containing 22 carbon atoms and 6 double bonds.

Duo-trio test Difference test in which two samples are judged against a control to determine which of the two samples is different from the control.

Dutch-processed cocoa and chocolate Cocoa and chocolate produced from cacao with an alkaline treatment to produce a pH of 6.0 to 7.8 and a more soluble, darker-colored product than the natural product.

Eicosapentanoic acid (EPA) Omega-3 fatty acid with 20 carbon atoms and 5 double bonds.

Elastin Yellow connective tissue occurring in limited amounts intramuscularly and in somewhat greater concentrations in deposits outside the muscles.

Emulsifying agent Compound containing both polar and nonpolar groups so that it is drawn to the interface between the two phases of an emulsion to coat the surface of the droplets.

Endomysium Very delicate connective tissue found between fibers.

Endosperm Large inner portion of cereal grains composed largely of starch and some protein.

Endothermic reaction Reaction in which heat is absorbed without an increase in temperature of the reactants.

Enolization Reversible reaction between an alkene and a ketone.

Epiderm Layer of cells providing a continuous outer covering for fruits and vegetables.

Epimysium Connective tissue surrounding an entire muscle (many bundles of bundles of fibers).

Farinograph Objective testing equipment that measures the resistance of stirring rods moving through a batter or dough and records results.

Fiber Bundle of myofibrils and sarcoplasm encased in the sarcolemma.

Ficin Proteolytic enzyme in figs

Flat-sour spoilage Increased acidity caused when viable *Bacillus coagulans* digest sugar without producing gas in canned foods.

Flavonoids Group of chemically related pigments usually containing two phenyl groups and an intermediate five- or six-membered ring connecting the two phenyl rings.

Flavor Blend of taste and smell perceptions noted when food is in the mouth.

Flavor potentiator Compound that enhances the flavor of other compounds without adding its own unique flavor.

Flavor profile panel Thoroughly trained panel that works as a team to describe flavor of a sample specifically in words.

Free radical Unstable compound containing an unpaired electron.

Freeze-thaw stability Ability of a starch-thickened product to be frozen and thawed without developing a gritty, crystalline texture.

Fungiform papillae Mushroomlike protuberances often containing taste buds and located on the sides and tip of the tongue.

Gamma ray Radiant energy of very short wavelength and capable of penetrating food, but not lead.

Gel Colloidal dispersion of a liquid dispersed in a solid.

Gelatinization Swelling of starch granules and loss of some amylose when starch is heated in water to thicken various food products.

Gelation Process of forming a gel.

Germ (embryo) Small portion of cereal grain containing fat and a small amount of protein, as well as thiamine, riboflavin, and other B vitamins.

Gliadin   Wheat gluten protein fraction that is soluble in alcohol, compact and elliptical in shape, sticky, and fluid.

Glutathione   Peptide in yeast cells that causes stickiness in dough if the dried yeast is hydrated below 40°C.

Gluten flour   Specialty wheat flour made by adding vital wheat gluten to increase the protein level to about 41 percent.

Glutenin   Alcohol-insoluble protein fraction of wheat gluten that is characterized by its fibrous, elongated shape and elastic quality.

Glycerol   Polyhydric alcohol containing three carbon atoms, each of which is joined to a hydroxyl group.

Glycogen   Complex carbohydrate that serves as the storage form of carbohydrate in animals.

Glycolipid   Molecule with a sugar moiety and a lipid portion.

GRAS list   Additives "generally recognized as safe" for use in foods because of long use with no evidence of carcinogenicity.

Ground substance   Undifferentiated matrix of plasma proteins and glycoproteins in which fibrous molecules of collagen and/or elastin are bound.

Gums   Complex carbohydrates of plant origin, usually containing galactose and at least one other sugar or sugar derivative, but excluding glucose.

Gustatory cells   Elongated cells in taste buds from which a cilia-like hair extends into the pore of the taste bud.

H band   Region in the center of a sarcomere where only thick myofilaments of myosin occur.

Heat of fusion   Heat released when a liquid is transformed into a solid (80 calories per gram of water); also called heat of solidification.

Heat of vaporization   The heat energy absorbed in the conversion of water into steam (540 calories per gram of water).

Hedonic ratings   Measures of the degree of pleasure provided by specific characteristics of various food samples.

Hemicelluloses   Carbohydrate polymers composed of various sugars and uronic acids; structural feature of plant cell walls.

Hemoglobin   Very large, iron-containing compound consisting of heme and four polypeptide polymers; contributes to meat color.

High-fructose corn syrup   An especially sweet corn syrup made using isomerase to convert some glucose to fructose.

Hilum   Innermost layer or the nucleus of a starch granule.

Homogenization   Mechanical process in which milk is forced through tiny apertures under 2,000 to 2,500 psi, breaking up the fat globules into smaller units that do not separate from the milk.

Hydrogenation   Addition of hydrogen to an unsaturated fatty acid in the presence of a catalyst to reduce the unsaturation of the molecule and raise the melting point.

Hydrogen swells   Spoilage of food and bulging of cans caused by anaerobic, thermophilic microorganisms that produce hydrogen during storage.

Hydrolysis   Splitting of a molecule by the uptake of a molecule of water.

Hydrolytic rancidity   Lipolysis (hydrolysis) of lipids to free fatty acids and glycerol, often catalyzed by lipases.

Hygroscopicity   Ability to attract and hold water that is characteristic of sugars to varying degrees.

I band   Light region on either side of the Z line in a sarcomere, consisting of non-overlapping myofilaments of actin.

Index to volume   Indirect means of comparing volume by measuring the circumference of a cross section of the product.

Ink blot   In food research, an impression made on paper by first pressing a cross section of the sample onto an ink pad.

Interesterification   Treatment of a fat, usually lard, with sodium methoxide or another agent to split fatty acids from glycerol and then to reorganize them on glycerol to form different fat molecules with less tendency to form coarse crystals.

Intermediate crystals   Slightly coarse fat crystals that form when β′ crystals melt and recrystallize.

Intraesterification   Catalyzed reaction in which the fatty acids split from glycerol and rejoin in a different configuration, but with the same fatty acids being retained in the molecule.

Inulin   Complex carbohydrate that is a polymer of fructose.

Inversion   Formation of invert sugar by either boiling a sugar solution (especially with acid added) or adding an enzyme (invertase) to the cool candy.

Invertase   Enzyme that catalyzes the breakdown of sucrose to invert sugar (fructose and glucose).

Invert sugar   Sugar formed by hydrolysis of sucrose; an equal mixture of fructose and glucose.

Irradiation   Preservation of food by exposure to beta and gamma rays.

Isoelectric point   The pH at which a protein molecule has lost its electrical charge and is most susceptible to denaturation and precipitation.

Jelmeter   Pipette-like viscometer designed to measure the adequacy of the pectin content of fruit juices used to make jams and jellies.

Lactase   Enzyme that catalyzes the breakdown of lactose to equal amounts of glucose and galactose.

Lactobacillus sanfrancisco Bacterium used to produce lactic acid in some bread doughs.

Latent heat of crystallization Heat released when the transition is made from the liquid state (higher energy) to the solid state (lower energy).

Lecithin Egg yolk phospholipid that is a very effective emulsifying agent.

Leucoanthocyanins Flavonoid pigments that are a subgroup of the flavanols and are often termed *procyanidins*.

Leucoplast Plastid in the cytoplasm of plant cells; site of starch storage as granules.

Lignin Structural component of some plant foods that is removed to avoid a woody quality in the prepared food.

Line-spread test Measurement of flow of a viscous liquid or semisolid food as the spread of a certain amount of sample in a given time at 90° intervals on a template of concentric rings.

Linoleic acid Fatty acid (18 carbons) containing two double bonds.

Linolenic acid Fatty acid (18 carbons) containing three double bonds.

Lipase Enzyme that catalyzes the hydrolysis of fat to release free fatty acids from glycerol.

Lipovitellin High-density lipoprotein in granules in egg yolk.

Low-methoxyl pectinic acids (low-methoxyl pectins) Galacturonic acid polymers in which only between an eighth and a fourth of the acid radicals have been esterified with methanol; pectic substance found in fruit that is just beginning to ripen.

Lysozyme Albumen protein with an isoelectric point of pH 10.7; notable for its ability to hydrolyze a polysaccharide in the cell wall of some bacteria to protect against contamination by these bacteria.

Magnetron tube Tube in a microwave oven that generates microwaves at a frequency of 915 or 2450 megahertz.

Maillard reaction Nonenzymatic browning that occurs when protein and a sugar are heated or stored together for some time.

Marbling Small fatty deposits within muscles of meat.

Masticometer Machine that measures comparative tenderness of meat and other foods by simulating chewing action.

Megahertz Measure of frequency defined as one million cycles per second.

Mellorine Imitation ice cream in which the milk fat has been removed and replaced by a different fat.

Metmyoglobin Brownish-red form of myoglobin formed when the ferrous iron is oxidized to the ferric form and water is complexed to the oxidized iron.

Micelle Casein aggregate that is comparatively stable and remains colloidally dispersed unless a change, such as a shift toward the isoelectric point or the use of rennin, destabilizes and precipitates casein.

Microwave Comparatively short (1–100 centimeters) electromagnetic wave.

Middle lamella Region between adjacent cells that cements the cells together, composed mostly of pectic substances.

Millimicron Billionth of a meter.

Molasses Sweetener produced as a by-product of the refining of sucrose from sugarcane.

Monosaccharide Carbohydrate containing only one saccharide unit.

Monosodium glutamate Flavor potentiator; sodium salt of glutamic acid.

Munsell system System of identifying colors on the basis of hue, value, and chroma, using a numerical scale.

Mycotoxin Poisonous substance produced by some molds.

Myofibril Linear bundle of several myofilaments that contains a number of sarcomeres.

Myofilament Simplest level of organization in muscle; classified as thick or thin.

Myoglobin Purplish-red pigment consisting of heme-containing ferrous iron and a polypeptide polymer (globin).

Myosin Principal myofibrillar protein.

Naive panel Sensory evaluation panel that has not been trained specifically regarding the product evaluation being undertaken in the study.

Natural-processed cocoa and chocolate Cocoa and chocolate produced from cacao without the addition of alkali.

Number of chews Subjective test in which a judge chews similar bites of food to the same endpoint and records the actual number of chews required to reach that point for each sample.

Objective evaluation Measurement of physical properties of a food by the use of mechanical devices.

Oleic acid Monounsaturated 18-carbon fatty acid.

Olfactory epithelium Yellow, mucus-coated area in the nose containing basal cells, supporting cells, and perikarya.

Olfactory receptors Nasal organs capable of detecting aromas.

Oligosaccharide Carbohydrate consisting of three to ten monosaccharides joined by the elimination of water.

Omega-3 fatty acid Polyunsaturated fatty acid with the first double bond occurring on the third carbon from the methyl end of the molecule.

Oryzanols   Class of sterols in rice bran oil with antioxidant properties.

Ovalbumin   By far the most abundant protein in egg albumin; readily denatured by heat.

Oven spring   An increase in the volume (usually about 80 percent) of yeast breads during the early part of baking caused by expansion of carbon dioxide and increased production of carbon dioxide in the hot oven.

Overrun   Increase in volume (expressed as percent) that occurs when ice cream is frozen with agitation.

Ovomucin   Rather fibrous protein abundant in thick white; contributes to the viscous texture of the thick white.

Oxidative rancidity   Development of off flavors and odors in fats as a result of the uptake of oxygen and the formation of peroxides, hydroperoxides, and numerous other compounds.

Oxidized starches   Thin-boiling starches produced by alkaline (sodium hypochlorite) treatment, but forming only soft gels.

Oxymyoglobin   Cherry red form of myoglobin formed by the addition of two oxygen atoms.

Paired comparison   Difference test in which a specific characteristic is to be evaluated in two samples, and the sample with the greater level of that characteristic is to be identified.

Papain   Proteolytic enzyme from papaya.

Parenchyma cells   Predominant type of cell in the fleshy part of fruits and vegetables.

Parevine   Imitation ice cream in which both the milk fat and the milk solids have been replaced by nondairy ingredients.

Pasteurization   Heat treatment of milk adequate to kill microorganisms that can cause illness in people.

Pearl tapioca   Large pellets of partially gelatinized tapioca that are dried, resulting in a product needing a long soaking period before use.

Pectic acid   The smallest of the pectic substances and one lacking methyl esters; occurs in overripe fruits and vegetables; incapable of gelling.

Pectic substances   Group of complex carbohydrates in fruits; polymers of galacturonic acid linked by 1,4-α-glycosidic linkages with varying degrees of methylation.

Pectinic acid or pectin   Methylated polymers of galacturonic acid formed from protopectin as fruit becomes barely ripe; capable of forming a gel.

Penetrometer   Machine that measures tenderness by determining the distance a cone or other device penetrates a food during a defined period and using only gravitational force.

Peptization   Acid hydrolysis of some of the peptide linkages in a protein to yield peptides.

Percent sag   [(Depth in container − depth on plate)/ depth in container] × 100.

Periderm   Layer of corklike cells protecting vegetable tissues underground.

Perikarya   Bodies of olfactory cells in the olfactory epithelium from which dendrites extend to the olfactory vesicles.

Perimysium   Connective tissue surrounding a bundle of several fibers.

Pheophorbide   Chlorophyll derivative in which the magnesium and phytyl group have been removed; an olive-drab pigment.

Pheophytins a and b   Compounds formed from chlorophyll a and b in which the magnesium ion is replaced by hydrogen, altering the color to greenish gray for pheophytin a and olive green for pheophytin b.

Phlobaphene   Derivative of a polyphenol in cacao, which is formed in the presence of oxygen and is responsible for the reddish color in cocoa and chocolate.

Phloem   Portion of the vascular system that transports aqueous solutions.

Phosvitin   Small protein in yolk granules that binds iron in yolk.

Phytol   Alcohol component of chlorophyll responsible for the hydrophobic nature of chlorophyll.

Planimeter   Engineering tool designed to measure distance as its pointer is traced around a pattern.

Plasmalemma   Thin membrane between the cell wall and the interior of the cell.

Plastids   Organelles in the cytoplasm that contain pigments or starch.

Polygalacturonase   Pectic enzyme promoting degradation of pectic substances in avocados, pears, tomatoes, and pineapple.

Polyphenoloxidases   Group of enzymes capable of oxidizing flavonoid compounds to cause browning or other discoloration after harvest.

Polysaccharide   Carbohydrate containing many saccharide units joined with the elimination of a molecule of water at each point of linkage.

Preference testing   Sensory testing designed to provide information on selected characteristics and to indicate preference or acceptability of products.

Press fluids   Juices formed from meat or other food under pressure.

Processed cheese   Cheese product made by heating natural cheeses with an emulsifier and then cooling in a brick form.

Profiling   Very detailed word description (usually of flavor) developed by a highly trained panel against which subsequent production is evaluated to maintain quality of production.

Proline   Imino acid prominent in gliadin and collagen with a cyclic ring structure that restricts protein shape.

Propenylsulfenic acid Compound in onions that causes eye irritation and tears.

Protopectin Non-methylated polymers of galacturonic acid incapable of forming a gel; first pectic substance to be formed in a fruit.

Quick breads Breads leavened with a leavening agent other than yeast, ordinarily either with steam or carbon dioxide generated from reaction of an acid and an alkali.

Quick-rise active dry yeast Special form of *Saccharomyces cerevisiae* available as the active dry yeast and capable of producing carbon dioxide so rapidly that fermentation is cut approximately in half.

Rad Ionizing energy equal to 10^{-5} joule per gram of absorbing material.

Rank order Preference test in which all samples are ranked in order of intensity of a specific characteristic.

Rennet Unpurified extract from the fourth stomach of unweaned calves, which contains rennin, an enzyme causing milk curds to form.

Rennin Enzyme from the lining of calves' stomachs that eliminates the protective function of κ-casein in mi cells and results in formation of a curd.

Reticulin A type of connective tissue protein associated with a fatty acid.

Retrogradation Gradual increase of crystalline aggregates in starch gels during storage that results from breaking of hydrogen bonds between amylose molecules and slow rearrangement into a more orderly configuration and establishment of new hydrogen bonds.

Reversion Development of an off-flavor (beany or fishy) in soybean, rapeseed, or various fish oils as a result of a reaction involving only very minor amounts of oxygen.

Rheological properties Characteristics of flow and deformation of fats and other substances with flow properties.

Rotating dull knife tenderometer Objective testing device that measures relative tenderness of meat by determining the depth of penetration effected by a rotating dull knife.

Saccharomyces cerevisiae Yeast (single-celled plant) used in baking.

Saccharomyces exigus Yeast used to produce carbon dioxide in acidic bread doughs.

Saccharomyces inusitatus Yeast used to produce carbon dioxide in acidic bread doughs.

Sarcolemma Thin, transparent membrane surrounding the bundle of myofibrils that constitute a fiber.

Sarcomere Portion of a myofibril consisting of the area between two Z lines.

Sarcoplasm Jelly-like protein surrounding the myofibrils in muscle fibers.

SAS-phosphate baking powder Leavening containing sodium aluminum sulfate and monocalcium phosphate; double-acting baking powder.

Saturated fatty acids Organic acids containing all of the hydrogen they could possibly hold.

Sclereid Type of sclerenchyma cell that gives the somewhat gritty texture to pears and certain other fruits.

Sclerenchyma cells Unique supportive cells with a chewy, fibrous character.

Sensory evaluation A synonym for subjective evaluation; measurements determined by using the senses of sight, smell, taste, and sometimes touch.

Shear press Objective testing machine that measures compressibility, extrusion, and shear of food samples.

Shortometer Device designed to measure the tenderness of fairly tender, crisp foods.

Sinigrin Potassium myronate, an isothiocyanate glucoside in cabbage that is broken down to highly pungent allyl isothiocyanate.

Sodium stearoyl-2-lactylate Dough conditioner of particular merit in improving baking quality of triticale and soy flours.

Soft meringue Egg white foam containing about 30 milliliters of sugar per egg white; often used as topping on cream pies.

Sol Colloidal dispersion in which a solid is the dispersed phase and a liquid is the continuous phase.

Sorghum Syrup sweetener produced by boiling the juice of grain sorghum.

Specific gravity Ratio of the density of a food (or other substance) to that of water.

Starch Complex carbohydrate consisting of two fractions—amylose and amylopectin—both of which are polymers of glucose joined together by the elimination of water.

Starch granule Concentric layers of amylose and amylopectin molecules formed in the leucoplasts and held together by hydrogen bonding.

Stearic acid Saturated 18-carbon fatty acid.

Subjective evaluation Evaluation by a panel of individuals using a scoring system based on various characteristics that can be judged with the senses.

Sublimation Transition from the frozen state directly to the gaseous state without liquefaction.

Subthreshold level Concentration of a taste compound at a level that is not detectable, but can influence other taste perceptions.

Sucroglycerides Sucrose esters (sucrose and glycerides or free fatty acids) used as dough conditioners with soy flour.

Sulfide spoilage Canned food contaminated with hydrogen sulfide produced by viable *Clostridium nigrificans.*

Sulfuring   Exposure of cut fruits to the smoke fumes created by burning sulfur flowers to retain a bright color during drying.

Supercooling   Reduction of the temperature of water below freezing until crystallization begins, after which the temperature rises to 0°C because of the latent heat of crystallization.

Supersaturated solution   True solution containing more solute than theoretically can be dissolved at that temperature; a situation created by cooling a heated saturated solution very carefully.

Surface tension   Attraction between molecules at the surface of a liquid.

Suspensoid   Colloidal dispersion of a gas dispersed in a solid.

Syneresis   Weeping or drainage of liquid from a gel.

Tapioca   Root starch derived from cassava, a tropical plant.

Taste buds   Tight clusters of gustatory and supportive cells encircling a pore, usually in the upper surface of the tongue; organ capable of detecting sweet, sour, salt, and/or butter.

Tempering   Removal of heat resulting from crystallization of fats and maintenance of a selected temperature to promote the formation of stable, desirable crystals.

Texturometer   Simulation device used to measure such physical textural properties as hardness, cohesiveness, and crushability of foods.

Thearubigens   Dark orange-yellow compounds formed when polyphenoloxidases oxidize epigallocatechin gallate and epigallocatechin to theaflavin gallate and theaflavin for ultimate oxidation to thearubigens in oolong and black teas.

Thick myofilament   Thicker, longer myofilament; composed of myosin molecules joined together to form a screwlike filament.

Thin-boiling starch   An acid-hydrolyzed starch containing many debranched amylopectin molecules; useful for making gum drops and other products where the hot mixture must flow and then cool to form a firm gel.

Thin myofilament   Thin filament formed by the helical twisting of two strands of polymerized actin.

Threshold level   Concentration of a taste compound at a barely detectable level.

Tocotrienols   Sterols related to vitamin E and valued as antioxidants.

Tofu   Soybean curd.

Tofutti   Frozen dessert of sweetened, flavored tofu.

Torsion balance   Very sensitive laboratory balance, to within 0.02 gram, particularly useful for weighing very small quantities or quantities greater than 2 kilograms.

Trained panel   Sensory evaluation panel that has been thoroughly trained regarding the use of the scorecard and the evaluation of various characteristics.

Trans configuration   The hydrogen is attached to the carbon atoms on either end of the double bond from opposite directions, causing a higher melting point than its cis counterpart.

Triangle test   Difference test in which three samples (two of which are the same) are presented, and the odd sample is to be identified.

Triglyceride   Simple fat containing three fatty acids esterified to glycerol; the most common form of simple fat.

Trip balance   Balance with two pans, the one on the left being used to hold the food and the one on the right being used to hold the weights needed to counterbalance the left pan.

Triticale   Hybrid grain produced by crossing wheat and rye.

Tropocollagen   Fibrous protein consisting of three strands twisted together and containing large amounts of glycine, proline, and hydroxyproline.

Tropomyosin   Least abundant of the three principal myofibrillar proteins.

TVP (or TSP)   Textured vegetable (soy) protein made of fibers of soy protein.

UHT pasteurization   Extreme pasteurization (138°C for at least two seconds) that kills all microorganisms and makes possible the storage of milk in a closed, sterile container at room temperature.

Universal testing machine   Multipurpose, complex machine capable of measuring various textural properties of food samples.

Vacuole   Portion of the cell containing most of the water, flavoring components, nutrients, and flavonoid pigments.

Vapor pressure   Pressure exerted as molecules of a liquid attempt to escape and become a vapor.

Vascular system   System in plants that transports water and other essential compounds; composed of xylem and phloem.

Viscometer   Objective testing device for measuring viscosity of liquids that flow on the basis of rotational resistance or capillary action.

Vital wheat gluten   Dried crude gluten.

Vitelline membrane   Sac enclosing the yolk.

Volumeter   Machine for measuring volume of baked products; consists of a reservoir for storing the seeds, a transparent column for measuring volume, and a lower compartment in which the sample is placed.

Warner-Bratzler shear   Objective testing device for measuring the force required to shear a sample of meat or other food with measurable tensile strength.

Water bath canning   Heat processing of food in containers immersed in water at atmospheric pressure.

Water-binding capacity   Amount of water held by muscle protein as bound water; cookery reduces capacity.

Waxy starch Starch containing only amylopectin, the result of genetic research and breeding for this composition.

Whey Liquid that drains from the curd of clotted milk; contains lactose, proteins, water soluble vitamins, and some minerals.

Winterizing Refining step in which oils are chilled carefully to precipitate and remove fractions with high melting points that would interfere with the pourability of salad dressings or other products containing the oils.

Xanthophylls Group of carotenoids containing some oxygen, as well as hydrogen and carbon, in a polymer of isoprene.

Xylan A hemicellulose that is composed of xylose and some glucuronic acid that contributes structure to plant cell walls.

Xylem The water transport system in plants; the tubular cells that move water.

Yeasts Single-celled fungi that reproduce by budding, are active at room temperature, and die at moisture levels below 20 percent.

Yogurt Clabbered milk product resulting from controlled fermentation by *Streptococcus thermophilus, Placamo-bacterium yogbourti,* and *Lactobacillus bulgaricus* or other lactose-fermenting microorganisms.

Yolk index Measure of egg quality based on the ratio of yolk height to yolk width.

Z lines Region in a myofibril where the thin myofilaments of actin adjoin, creating a dark line that defines the end of a sarcomere.

Index